THE BOOK OF
PROVERBS AND WISDOM

THE BOOK OF PROVERBS AND WISDOM
A Reference Manual

Curt "CT" Tomlin

ELM HILL

A Division of
HarperCollins Christian Publishing

www.elmhillbooks.com

The Book of Proverbs and Wisdom

A Reference Manual

Published in Nashville, Tennessee, by Elm Hill, an imprint of Thomas Nelson. Elm Hill and Thomas Nelson are registered trademarks of HarperCollins Christian Publishing, Inc.

Elm Hill titles may be purchased in bulk for educational, business, fund-raising, or sales promotional use. For information, please e-mail SpecialMarkets@ ThomasNelson.com.

Library of Congress Cataloging-in-Publication Data

Library of Congress Control Number: 2019951142

ISBN 978-1-400327393 (Paperback)
ISBN 978-1-400327409 (Hardbound)
ISBN 978-1-400327416 (eBook)

**All books proceeds will be channeled to assist "The Least of These"
(Matthews 25:40):**

The author is a strong and solid believer in what Jesus Christ stated in Matthew 25:40, in part, "*In as much as you did it to the least of these My brethren, you did it to Me.*" Accordingly, and as a 100% affirmation of this verse, *ALL PROCEEDS* from the sales of this book, *The Book of Proverbs and Wisdom: A Reference Manual*, will be equally distributed to the following three IRS 501(c)(3) charitable organizations:

(A) **Rescue Missions Ministries, Inc.**
   dba **Durham Rescue Mission**
   (Homes For The Homeless Project Fund)
   1201 East Main Street
   Durham, NC 27701 / P.O. Box 11858, Durham, NC 27703
   EIN/TID#58–1482590

(B) **The Foundation**
   dba **Friends of Mukhanyo**
   P.O.Box 51385
   Durham, NC 27717
   EIN/TID# 56–2194734

(C) **Beautiful Gate Outreach Center, Inc.**
   604 North Walnut Street
   Wilmington, DE 19801
   EIN/TID#: 51–040723

Author's Personal Thank You and Acknowledgements

Typist and Word Processors:
Sheri Ackerman Chase,*
Sheri Betts,
David Solomon, and
Jennifer Wigle.

Chapter Narratives:
Rev. Dr. Tammara Combs,*
Beverly Brown Tomlin, and
Jennifer Wigle.

Chapter Reviewers:
Larry Andrews,
Renee Beaman,
Rev. Silvester Beaman,
Sheri Betts,
Keith Brown,
Coach Steven Hale,*
Kelly Gordon,
Shirley Hamilton,
Wilhelmenia Jordan,
Justin Lacey,
Gale Mills,
Eddie O'Brien,
Tayo Okusanya,
Ed Retting,
Brad Taylor,
Carolyn Tomlin,
Crystal Tomlin Casey, and
Paul Williams.

Author's Deepest Appreciation

Heartfelt "Thank You," "Thank You," and "Thank You" to each of the names listed below, for going over and beyond the call of duty regarding assistance provided on *The Book of Proverbs and Wisdom: A Reference Manual.*

A) **Coach Steven Hale:**   Words are NOT enough for me to express, my deepest and most sincere "THANK YOU," appreciation, and gratitude for ALL the Coaching and assistance provided to me by Coach Steve, for the better part of three plus years on this project! Without Coach Steve's ongoing coaching, support, and mentoring, I can safely and honestly state that I would NOT have been able to see this project through to the end. I LOVE YOU, Brother Steve, and no matter what I do again in this next season of my life, I know that it was Father God who placed you in my life in 1987 as MBA interns at American Express Company in NYC. That friendship has spawn these many years, and without hesitation or hiccup along the way that most friendships have to go through. THANK YOU, my beloved Brother and Coach, and may Father God continue to Bless you and your family!

B) **Sister Sheri Ackerman Chase:**   My dear Sister Sheri walked with me during the first two to two and a half years serving as my Word Processing expert, as I would complete each semiannual spiritual retreat with a new handwritten addendum for the Book, and graciously partnered with me during those first initial years. Her dedication to excellence, as well as her willingness to work on this project "free of charge," speaks volumes regarding Sister Sheri's character, resolve, and willingness to "*wash the feet*" of this poor laborer in the mission field, serving the Lord Jesus in bringing a different type of reference manual to the table for others to review and learn from. THANK YOU again, Sister Sheri, and may Father God continue to Bless you and your family!

C) **Rev. Dr. Tammara Combs**:   As mentioned in the "Preface" section of this reference manual, it was Sister Tammara who brought forward the idea of developing and writing "Chapter Narratives" for each Chapter Theme based on or highlighting my life experiences with said "Chapter Narratives" or having myself describe what said "Chapter Narrative" meant for a respective Chapter Theme. As previously mentioned, this author went "kicking and screaming" through the thought process and actual writing of said "Chapter Narratives"! But once I had written the final one, I saw the wisdom and merits of why Sister Tammara stepped out on the ledge and practiced Proverbs 27:6—"***Faithful are the wounds of a friend, But the kisses of an enemy are deceitful.***" Thus, while I did not see the merits when Sister Tammara first offered this suggestion to me, it was not until ***The Book of Proverbs and Wisdom: A Reference Manual*** was completed that I say the full merits of her wisdom! To God be the Glory!

TABLE OF CONTENTS

COMMENTARY

A Letter from a Friend

CT,

I spent a good part of yesterday reading just Chapter 13. It hit me in many ways. One of blessings and one of regret. I know that may sound strange. Let me explain. I was blessed by the chapter of "**Correction, Discipline and Reproofs**" as it pointed out how important Correction and Discipline is. It left me with a yearning that I wanted this to be part of my life when I was raising my kids who are now practically grown up as they are fifteen and twenty-two. They are great kids, however, I feel I did not discipline them or correct them the way I should or could have and there are some consequences. I feel I have not taught them that discipline is good. Proverbs *15:*31*: "***The ear that hears the rebukes of life* Will abide among the *wise*.**" Proverbs *15:*32*: "**He who disdains *instruction* despises his own soul, But he who *heeds rebuke* gets understanding.**" I think we all are taught to dislike rebuke or even hate it. I know I do. If we only had the spirit to listen to what others are trying to tell us, that is for our own good, as they are not trying to put us down in any way. Proverbs *27:*17*: "***As iron sharpens iron, So a man sharpens the countenance of his friend.***" What is a friend if you will not let him be honest to you about you. Who invites that?

I feel I missed a lot of God's wisdom you have presented to my face that could have changed me in meaningful ways had I marinated on it and in it many years ago, the way you have helped me do so now. I am too proud and hardheaded to hear and receive correction or rebuke the way I should, and I have taught this same arrogance to my children. I hope this book will become part of the lives of those who need the wisdom—that would be all of us—that just the Book of Proverbs 13 has been able to give to me. And I have just begun this part of my journey through your writings. **I accept the correction.** I have, by the way, read all of Proverbs many times. I have made notes throughout its teachings. My mother taught me to read a Proverb a day. I read a book called ***How to Ruin Your Life By 30*** by Steve Farbar that zeroed in on his truth and life lessons in Proverbs. The last chapter Steve Farber says is the most important chapter in his book instructs us to read Proverbs and apply it to our lives **or we will fail in life**. That is strong. I gave this to each of our scouts and we read it together. That truth didn't even stick then like it now has with your book of wisdom. For me, that should be the title of your book, "The Book of Wisdom." Hopefully for others, like for me, and I think most of us in the American culture, can wake up to what God's Word is telling us about correction and discipline, and early enough in their kids' and families' lives to make the difference God intended for these words to make.

I know it is never too late, but I am so blessed by it now that I must look back as I look forward and say, "Wow, I wish I had this in my tool box from the beginning." If each of us only had the inspiration to study it the way you have. But we, in our lives, are called to do different things. You, my friend, have done this for me, leading me to the wisdom of our Lord and Savior, and you have put it in my face. This was the right chapter for me to begin on as I am struggling with this very issue. Ask my wife! He has inspired you to inspire me. I will use this book for my life's journey and inspiration to become a better person, a better father, a better husband, keeping myself bathed in the gospel. **THANK YOU** for being with me in this journey. You will never know how much this first chapter has meant to me. It will save lives. It will enrich all who read it. God is great. He has the map for our lives, as you say, the GPS. Only if we would each take the time to recognize that it really is all there. Your book vividly points that out and will be the beginning of many who will then journey through all of what God has in store for each of us.

Thank you and Blessings. May others be blessed through this book.

Keith

Pastor Reflections

"CT Tomlin has devoted an enormous amount of time and energy to help readers of the Book of Proverbs unpack its myriad themes and spiritual maxims into a practical resource for personal edification and for teaching in small group studies. It is a reference guide that chronicles God's Word through the lens of themes and topics that provide insights for personal growth and spiritual formation. In addition, the opening narratives of each chapter presents an open door of discovery for the reader from the author's personal experiences that he shares in the writing of his work.

The Book of Proverbs and Wisdom: A Reference Manual is worth reading for academic scholars and biblical students!"

The Rev. Carey G. Anderson, D. Min.
First AME Church
Seattle, WA

"*The Book of Proverbs and Wisdom: A Reference Manual* contains 915 verses, each of which is very relevant to various aspects of pursuing a godly lifestyle. Living a godly lifestyle includes a plethora of choices that one needs to make in a variety of categories and/or circumstances. "The purpose of the Book of Proverbs is 'to teach people wisdom and discipline, and to help them understand wise sayings. Through these Proverbs, people will receive instruction in discipline, good conduct, and doing what is right, just, and fair. These Proverbs will make the simpleminded clever. They will give knowledge and purpose to young people. Let those who are wise listen to these Proverbs and become even wiser. And let those who understand receive guidance by exploring the depth of meaning in these Proverbs, parables, wise sayings, and riddles.'" (Proverbs 1:1–6 NLT).

"*The Book of Proverbs and Wisdom: A Reference Manual* allows one who is dealing with a set of circumstances in life to quickly find help or direction as seen through the eyes of King Solomon, Agur, and King

Lemuel under the inspiration of the Holy Spirit. Curt Tomlin has identified most every conceivable area of life that one may encounter and arranged them in chapters. For example, if you are dealing with financial issues in your life, Chapter 24 addresses: "Financial Resources, Gain, Provisions, Profitability, and Money." Within Chapter 24, you will find all of the scriptures in the Book of Proverbs regarding financial matters. What could have taken hours of research and reading to find these references in Proverbs can now be done in minutes.

"I recommend this book for anyone who is seeking the Lord's direction in matters that deal with life and the pursuit of godliness as seen through the eyes of King Solomon."

Rev. Dr. Phillip E. Davis Sr.
Senior Pastor Covenant Faith Ministry
Holly Springs, NC
Author, *5 Minutes with Jesus*
www.facebook.com/christianoutfitters

A Servants Bio

Curt "CT" Tomlin serves as a skilled financial management coach to numerous individuals and not for profit organizations. CT has over thirty years of leadership experience in the Corporate/Business Fortune 500 sectors. CT was a senior finance executive, having held Vice President and Corporate Controller positions with two Fortune 500 companies. CT worked in executive positions in international businesses, including being based in Brussels, Belgium. CT has also served as a professional coach and mentor to senior executives and professional associates within numerous Fortune 500 companies. For over twelve years, CT was an active Executive Leadership Council (ELC) board member, including serving as the ELC Chairperson in 2008 and 2009.

Born and raised in Pasadena, California, CT earned his Bachelor of Science degree in Finance and Accounting from the University of Southern California, where he was a member of the Beta Alpha Si academic society. He also earned an MBA in Finance and General Management from Harvard Business School, where he was a leader in the African American Business Students Union. Currently residing Chapel Hill, North Carolina, CT enjoys financial coaching, reading, traveling, and spending time with his two adult daughters, Crystal and Sydney and granddaughter, Kennedy.

Most importantly, CT is a Servant and an Ambassador of the Lord, and has followed the Lord's call to fulfill the Lord's work in any way CT can. CT is extremely blessed and honored to bring forward his first written work, *The Book of Proverbs and Wisdom: A Reference Manual*, for your spiritual insight, edification, and knowledge transfer of Father God's truths and spiritual wisdom and knowledge. TO GOD BE THE GLORY!

Preface

First of all, during 2012 or early 2013, during one of my semiannual spiritual retreats, I felt the Holy Spirit speak into my heart regarding one of my favorite books in the Bible, that being the _Book of Proverbs_! My walking papers or instructions that I received from the Holy Spirit, was to write an "**illuminated**," _The Book of Proverbs and Wisdom: A Reference Manual_, whereby every Book of Proverbs verse would be positioned and contained in one or more Chapter Theme(s). Accordingly, each Chapter Theme(s) characterizes and reflects the various Proverbs verses listed and/or contained in the biblical _Book of Proverbs_. Thus, every Proverbs verse(s), phrase, and/or series of Proverbs verses has been positioned into one or more of the seventy chapters contained in _The Book of Proverbs and Wisdom: A Reference Manual_. Additionally, as it is more often the case, that a specific Proverbs verse might be listed within multiple Chapter Themes! For example, one of my all-time favorite Proverbs verse is Proverbs 1:7, which states, "_**The fear of the LORD is the beginning of knowledge, But fools despise wisdom and instruction.**_" Accordingly, you will find this Proverbs verse listed in six different Chapter Themes, namely: (a) "**Fear of the LORD**"; (b) "**Knowledge**"; (c) "**Fools/Foolishness**"; (d) "**Hate/Despise**"; (e) "**Wisdom**"; and (f) "**Instruction**" based on the "keyword(s)" listed above. Additionally, I have used the **New King James Version (NKJV)** of the Bible, including this versions citations, punctuations, fonts, and appropriateness for inclusion for said Chapter Themes.

Secondly as stated above, I have included and/or assigned each Proverbs verse to a specific Chapter Theme based on such keyword(s), phrase(s), and/or overall Theme or tenor of such Proverbs verse. For example: (1) Where there is a **direct, one-on-one** *tie in* to a Chapter Theme from a Proverbs verse, then such keyword has been "**Bolded, Underscored**, and *Italicized*." As an example, (1) "***Fear of the LORD***" currently represented in **Chapter 23, page 245**; (2) If a key word, phrase, and/or theme or tenor of a Proverbs verse has, what I might call, a "One Degree of Separation from such Chapter Theme," then such Proverbs verse has been "*Italicized*" and "Underscored," (i.e. "*Fear of the LORD*"); (3) And if such Proverbs verse, in my opinion, has "Two Degrees of Separation from such Chapter Theme," then such Proverbs verse has been "*Italicized*" or Underscored only (i.e. "*Fear of the LORD*") or (i.e. "Fear of the LORD").

Accordingly, what I have attempted to do for this, *The Book of Proverbs and Wisdom: A Reference Manual*, is assign a Proverbs verse to one or more Chapter Theme(s) based on: (1) A specific direct word or collection of words from such Proverbs verse or verses (i.e. "***Fear of the LORD***"); and/or (2) "One Degree of Separation" of a keyword or phrase to such Chapter Theme; and/or (3) "Two Degrees of Separation" of a keyword or phrase to such Chapter Theme. Proverbs verse guideline notations for (1) and/or (2) should be fairly concise and crystal clear. Where one may have some degree of hesitation, might be in "Category Three" classifications, and if so, I would strongly encourage one to mediate on such Proverbs verse(s) to see if there does exist a "Two Degrees of Separation" to the Chapter Theme. And if it does not in your opinion, then I am requesting that one refer to one's own spiritual illumination for such phrase and/or word(s) and move onward.

Thirdly, *The Book of Proverbs and Wisdom: A Reference Manual* contains my personal "author's notations" that I have assigned to most of *The Book of Proverbs and Wisdom: A Reference Manual* verses, such that the following author's notations are specified: Thus for example, for many biblical Proverbs verses, I have assigned **One** (*), **Two** (**), or **Three** (***)

notation for that Proverbs verse, and such a rating, from my perspective, represents how that Proverbs verse *spoke to my heart* (i.e. "Good*,*" "*Better**,*" or "*Best****") . And you will note that *ALL* category Three (***) Proverbs verse notations have been "**Bolded**" where such Proverbs verse appears within *The Book of Proverbs and Wisdom: A Reference Manual*! For example, Proverbs 1:7—"*The fear of the LORD is the beginning of knowledge, But fools despise wisdom and instruction*"—appears in the already mentioned Chapter Themes in a "**bold**" fashion.

Fourthly, *another unique characteristic* of *The Book of Proverbs and Wisdom: A Reference Manual* is this: On numerous occasions within a particular Chapter Theme, I have included surrounding Proverbs verse(s) within such specific Chapter Theme verse notation, such that, in my opinion, including such ancillary Proverbs verses, helps to "*illuminate*" such Proverbs verse(s) for that particular Proverbs Theme. Thus, "one size" or one Proverb verse may not fully provide the spiritual wisdom, knowledge, discernment, and/or instructional message that such Proverbs verse might say on a stand-alone basis.

From my perspective, a great illustrative example of the above reference characteristics of *The Book of Proverbs and Wisdom: A Reference Manual*, I would refer one to Chapter 61, "**Righteousness, Upright, Right, and Just**," beginning on page **661** to page **676**.

Finally, one truly unique characteristic that has been incorporated into the body of *The Book of Proverbs and Wisdom: A Reference Manual* is the inclusion of what is being characterized as a "**Chapter Narrative,**" which precedes each Chapter Theme and represents either the author's personalized reflection of how the upcoming Chapter Theme has impacted the author's life, or it reflects the author's interpretation of how that Chapter Theme has spoken to the author for inclusion into *The Book of Proverbs and Wisdom: A Reference Manual*.

The author would like to personally extend a heartfelt "*THANK YOU*" to Rev. Dr. Tammara Combs, who strongly suggested that the author include a "*Chapter Narrative*" component into this reference manual. Initially, the author went "*kicking and screaming*" in my aversion regarding including a "*Chapter Narrative*" within this reference manual. But, as is usually the case, "the proof is in the pudding, so to speak," and the author found that each "*Chapter Narrative*" added to each Chapter Theme contained in *The Book of Proverbs and Wisdom: A Reference Manual*, and it is my hope and prayer that each reader will find some degree of insightful and illuminating wisdom from one or more of these "*Chapter Narratives*"!

In conclusion, after nearly six years of intense writing, rewriting, editing, and re-editing, I am blessed to bring forward *The Book of Proverbs and Wisdom: A Reference Manual* for your spiritual insight, edification, and knowledge transfer of God's Word, spiritual truths, and spiritual wisdom that have been written by Father God for all of mankind in the Bible's thirty-one Chapters that comprise the *Book of Proverbs*, and are summarized and illuminated within this *Book of Proverbs and Wisdom: A Reference Manual*'s seventy chapters!

Enjoy and may God's Blessings enrich your study, journey, and illumination contained within *The Book of Proverbs and Wisdom: A Reference Manual*! To God be the GLORY!

TABLE REFERENCE FOR NOMENCLATURE USED THROUGHOUT THE BOOK

IDENTIFICATION	MEANING
*	Strong impact to the author
**	Stronger impact to the author
***	Strongest impact to the author
Bold + *Italic* + <u>Underlined</u>	***<u>A direct tie to the Chapter Theme</u>***
Italic + <u>Underlined</u>	*<u>One degree of separation to the Chapter Theme</u>*
Italic **or** <u>Underlined</u>	*Two degrees of separation to the Chapter Theme*

CHAPTER 1

ABILITY, AGILITY, MIGHTY, STRENGTH, STRONG

Modestly and humbly speaking, most people who know me would, more likely than not, rate me in the above average to excellent quartile as it pertains to *Ability*, *Agility*, and *Strength*. Frankly, I would be hard-pressed to disagree with such assessments. So where does one's *Ability*, *Agility*, and *Strength* come from? For some, it is periodic exercise, which could involve hitting the heavy weights. Yes, while I don't do a lot of core exercises, or stretching at the fitness center as I used to and/or should, I can still move the heavy weights a time or two!

But to truly address this question, I believe that all one needs to do is assess how truthfully one can respond to at least four key Proverbs verses that are highlighted in this Chapter Theme in Proverbs, namely, Proverbs 8:14: "*Counsel is mine, and sound wisdom, I am understanding, I have strength*"; Proverbs 14:26: "*In the fear of the Lord there is strong confidence, and His children will have a place of refuge*"; Proverbs 18:10: "*The name of the Lord is a strong tower, The righteous run to it and are safe*"; and finally, my foundational Proverbs verse for this Chapter Theme is Proverbs 24:5 and 6: "*A wise man is strong, Yes, a man of knowledge* *increases **strength**; For by wise counsel you will wage your own war, And in a multiple of counselors there is safety"*.

Not much to add after that in my humble opinion!

To God be the GLORY!

(Guidance for the Young)

Proverbs 3:7*–8*

Do not be wise in your own eyes; Fear the LORD and depart from evil. It will be health to your flesh, And **strength** to your bones.

(The Crafty Harlot)

Proverbs 7:24–27

(24) Now therefore, listen to me, my children; Pay attention to the words of my mouth:

(25) Do not let your heart turn aside to her ways, Do not stray into her paths;

(26) For she has cast down many wounded, And all who were slain by her were **strong** men.

(27) Her house is the way to hell, Descending to the chambers of death.

(The Excellence of Wisdom)

Proverbs 8:12–14

(12) "I, wisdom, dwell with prudence, And find out knowledge and discretion.

(13) The fear of the LORD is to hate evil; Pride and arrogance and the evil way And the perverse mouth I hate.

(14) Counsel is mine, and sound wisdom; I am understanding, I have **strength**.

(Wise Sayings of Solomon)

Proverbs 10:15
The rich man's wealth is his ***strong city***; The destruction of the poor is their poverty.

Proverbs *10:*29*
The way of the LORD is *strength* for the upright, But destruction will come to the workers of iniquity.

Proverbs 14:4*
Where no oxen are, the trough is clean; But much *increase* comes by the ***strength*** of an ox.

Proverbs 14:26*
In the fear of the LORD there is ***strong*** confidence, And His children will have a place of refuge.

Proverbs 16:*32*
He who is *slow to anger* is better than the ***mighty***, And he who *rules his spirit* than he who *takes a city*.

Proverbs 18:*10*
The name of the LORD is a ***strong tower***; The righteous run to it and are safe.

Proverbs 18:11
The rich man's wealth is his ***strong city***, And like a high wall in his own esteem.

Proverbs 18:19
A brother offended is harder to win than a ***strong city***, And contentions are like the bars of a castle.

Proverbs 20:1
Wine is a mocker, ***Strong drink*** is a brawler, And whoever is led astray by it is not wise.

Proverbs 20:29*
The glory of young men is their **_strength_**, And the splendor of old men is their gray head.

Proverbs 21:14
A gift in secret pacifies anger, And a bribe behind the back, **_strong_** wrath.

Proverbs 21:22*
A wise man _scales_ the city of the **_mighty_**, And brings _down the trusted_ **_stronghold_**.

(Sayings of the Wise)

Proverbs *24:*5*–*6*
A wise man is _strong_, Yes, a man of knowledge increases _strength_; _For by wise counsel you will wage your own war_, And in a multitude of counselors there is safety.

Proverbs *24:*10*
If you faint in the day of adversity, Your _strength_ is small.

(Further Wise Sayings of Solomon)

Proverbs 25:28
Whoever has no rule over his own spirit Is like a city broken down, without walls.

Proverbs 29:4
The king establishes the land by justice, But he who receives bribes over-throws it.

(The Wisdom of Agur)

Proverbs 30:24*–28*
(24) There are four things which are little on the earth, But they are exceedingly wise;

(25) The ants are a people not **strong**, *Yet they prepare their food in the summer*;

(26) The rock badgers are a *feeble* folk, *Yet they make their homes in the crags*;

(27) The locusts have no king, *Yet they all advance in ranks*;

(28) The spider *skillfully grasps with its hands*, And it is in kings' palaces.

Proverbs 30:29–31

(29) There are three things which are majestic in pace, Yes, four which are stately in walk:

(30) A lion, which is **mighty** among beasts And does not turn away from any;

(31) A greyhound, A male goat also, And a king whose troops are with him.

(*The Words King Lemuel's Mother Taught Him*)

Proverbs 31:1–9

(1) The words of King Lemuel, the utterance which his mother taught him:

(2) What, my son? And what, son of my womb? And what, son of my vows?

(3) Do not give your **strength** to women, Nor your ways to that which destroys kings.

(4) It is not for kings, O Lemuel, It is not for kings to drink wine, Nor for princes intoxicating drink;

(5) Lest they drink and forget the law, And pervert the justice of all the afflicted.

(6) Give **strong** drink to him who is perishing, And wine to those who are bitter of heart.

(7) Let him drink and forget his poverty, And remember his misery no more.

(8) Open your mouth for the speechless, In the cause of all who are appointed to die.

(9) Open your mouth, judge righteously, And plead the cause of the poor and needy.

(The Virtuous Wife)

Proverbs *31:*16*–*18* and 24*–27*

(16)* *She <u>considers</u> a field and <u>buys</u> it; From her profits she <u>plants</u> a vineyard.*

(17)* *She <u>girds</u> herself with <u>strength</u>, And <u>strengthens</u> her arms.*

(18)* *She <u>perceives</u> that her merchandise is good,* **And her lamp does not go out by night.**

(24) She <u>makes</u> linen garments and <u>sells</u> them, And <u>supplies</u> sashes for the merchants.

(25)* *<u>Strength</u> and honor are her clothing; She shall rejoice in time to come.*

(26)* ***She opens her mouth with wisdom, And on her tongue is the law of kindness.***

(27) She <u>watches</u> over the ways of her household, And does not eat the bread of idleness.

CHAPTER 2

ABOMINATION TO
THE LORD/ABOMINATION

I struggled for the better part of one week crafting my thoughts on this Chapter Narrative on the Theme "***Abomination to the Lord***." With direction from the Holy Spirit, I was led to address this Theme from three different perspectives, i.e. (a) Definitional; (b) the Proverbs verses summarization of this specific Theme; and (c) Father God's attitude on sin as read in His Holy Word.

(A)   From a definitional perspective, the word "***Abomination***" is generally defined as follows:

- Anything greatly disliked or abhorred;
- Intense aversion to something or loathing/detestation;
- A vile, shameful or detestable action, condition, habit, etc.

A few examples that highlight the definition might include: (a) The Lord regarded lying with ***Abomination***; or (b) Spitting in public is an ***Abomination***.

The Proverbs verses that are mentioned in Chapter 6, that speak to this Chapter Theme of "***Abomination to the Lord***" are contained in thirty (30) Scripture verses that I have attempted to categorized, are as follows:

TOPIC:	NUMBER OF PROVERB VERSES:
Wicked/Wickedness	11
Lying Lips	4
Dishonest Scales/Weights and Measures	3
Evil	2
Perverse	2
Pride	2
Unjust	2
Dislike/Abhorred	1
Murder	1
Perverse Heart	1
Scoffer/Laziness	1

As an example, one only needs to read, meditate, study, and reference Proverbs 6:16–19, which states the following:

- 6:16: *These six things the LORD hates, Yes, seven are an* ***abomination*** *to Him:*
- 6:17: *A* **proud** *look, A* **lying** *tongue, Hands that* **shed innocent blood***,*
- 6:18: *A heart that devises* **wicked** *plans, Feet that are swift in running to* **evil***,*
- 6:19: *A* **false witness** *who speaks* **lies***, And one who sows* **discord** *among brethren.*

(B)   And finally, it is abundantly clear from all sixty-six (66) Chapters of the Bible, i.e. from Genesis to Revelations, God's Word states unequivocally that **Father God Hates All Sin**! It amazes me to hear and read, whether from Christians and nonbelievers alike, how many try to compartmentalize sin/sins by "shades of gray." For example, how often does one hear how **"telling one little white lie"** is not anywhere as bad as **"murder"**?

Suffice it to say, and we know it to be a biblical and spiritual truth, that "**SIN**" is "**SIN,**" and that Father God makes no demarcation between types of sin. Thus, at the end of the day, we know that "*for all have sinned and fall short of the glory of God,*" (Romans 3:23); Thus, recognizing the fact that "**Father God Hates All Sin**"! But for those who are "in Christ," one can rest in God's grace, mercy, forgiveness, and love, believing and resting in the biblical and spiritual truth contained in Romans 8:1, which gracefully states, "*There is therefore no condemnation to those who are in Christ Jesus, who do not walk according to the flesh, but according to the Spirit*"! Accordingly, at the end of the day, one can rest in 100% assurance that "*if Christ is in you, the body is dead because of sin, but the Spirit is life because of righteousness*"! And to that I say, graciously and meekly, "Thank You, Jesus; Thank You, Jesus; and Thank You, Jesus!"

To God be the GLORY, Forever, and Forever. Amen!

(Guidance for the Young)

Proverbs *3:31–35

(31)   Do not envy the oppressor, And choose none of his ways;

(32)* For the perverse person is an ***abomination to the LORD***, But His secret counsel is with the upright.

(33)   The ***curse of the LORD*** is on the house of the wicked, But He blesses the home of the just.

(34)* **Surely He scorns the scornful, But gives grace to the humble.**

(35)   The *wise* shall inherit glory, But shame shall be the legacy of fools.

(The Wicked Man)

Proverbs 6:16–19

(16) These six things the **_LORD hates_**, Yes, seven are an **_abomination to Him_**;

(17) A proud look, A lying tongue, Hands that shed innocent blood,

(18) A heart that devises wicked plans, Feet that are swift in running to evil,

(19) A false witness who speaks lies, And one who sows discord among brethren.

(The Excellence of Wisdom)

Proverbs *8:*6*–9

(6)* **Listen, for I (*wisdom*) will speak of excellent things, And from the opening of my lips will come right things;**

(7)* **For my mouth will speak truth; Wickedness is an _abomination to my lips_.**

(8)* All the words of my mouth are with righteousness; Nothing crooked or perverse is in them.

(9) They are plain to him who understands, And right to those who find knowledge.

(Wise Sayings of Solomon)

Proverbs 11:1

Dishonest scales are an **_abomination to the LORD_**, But a just weight is His delight.

Proverbs 11:20

Those who are of a perverse heart are an **_abomination to the LORD_**, But the blameless in their ways are His delight.

Proverbs *12:*22*

Lying lips are an *abomination to the LORD*, But those who deal truthfully are His delight.

Proverbs 13:19

A desire accomplished is sweet to the soul, But it is an *abomination* to *fools* to depart from evil.

Proverbs *14:*31*

He who *oppresses* the poor *reproaches his Maker*, But he who honors Him has mercy on the needy.

Proverbs 15:8

The sacrifice of the wicked is an *abomination to the LORD*, But the prayer of the upright is His delight.

Proverbs 15:*9*

The way of the wicked is an *abomination to the LORD*, But He loves him who follows righteousness.

Proverbs 15:26

The thoughts of the wicked are an *abomination to the LORD*, But the words of the pure are pleasant.

Proverbs 16:5

Everyone proud in heart is an *abomination to the LORD*; Though they join forces, none will go unpunished.

Proverbs 16:12

It is an *abomination* for kings to commit wickedness, For a throne is established by righteousness.

Proverbs 17:*15*

He who justifies the wicked, and he who condemns the just, Both of them alike are an *abomination to the LORD*.

Proverbs 20:10
Diverse weights and diverse measures, They are both alike, an _**abomination to the LORD.**_

Proverbs 20:23
Diverse weights are an _**abomination to the LORD**_, And dishonest scales are not good.

Proverbs 21:27*
The sacrifice of the wicked is an _**abomination**_; How much more when he brings it with wicked intent!

Proverbs 22:14
The mouth of an immoral woman is a deep pit; He who is _**abhorred by the LORD**_ will fall there.

(Sayings of the Wise)

Proverbs 24:8*–9*
He who plots to do evil Will be called a schemer. The devising of foolishness is sin, And the scoffer is an _**abomination**_ to men.

Proverbs *24:*17*–*18*
Do not rejoice when your enemy falls, And do not let your heart be glad when he stumbles; _**Lest the LORD see it, and it displease Him, And He turn away His wrath from him**_.

(Further Sayings of the Wise)

Proverbs 26:24*–26
(24)* He who hates, disguises it with his lips, And lays up deceit within himself;

(25) When he speaks kindly, do not believe him, For there are _seven_ _**abominations in his heart**_;

(26) Though his hatred is covered by deceit, His wickedness will be revealed before the assembly.

Proverbs 28:9
One who turns away his ear from hearing the law, Even his prayer is an ***abomination***.

Proverbs 29:27*
An unjust man is an ***abomination*** to the righteous, And he who is upright in the way is an ***abomination*** to the wicked.

CHAPTER 3

ABUNDANCE, BLESSINGS, FAVOR, PROSPERITY, GOODWILL

What a privilege, honor, and *Blessing* to have been selected by the Holy Spirit to author and pen this version of what I like to call, or am calling, *The Book of Proverbs and Wisdom: A Reference Manual*. As I look back over the nearly six years of on again, pause, start again process that drafting what I now graciously and affectionately call "The Manual," I consider myself extremely *Favored*, *Blessed*, *Abounding* in His *Abundance*, Grace, Mercy, *Goodwill*, and *Prosperity* to name a few superlatives that adequately describe my first authorship, marathon, and journey into the biblical pages of *The Book of Proverbs and Wisdom: A Reference Manual*!

When I exchange a personal greeting with someone, most individuals ask the question, "How are you doing?" And my standard and/or typical reply, and I mean this in ALL sincerity, is the following statement, "I am *Blessed*, Highly *Favored*, Forgiven, and Mightily Loved!" And as for this early on Chapter Narrative, I will focus on the first foundational pillar in this personal greeting, that being "*BLESSED*"!

First of all, when one thinks about being "*BLESSED*" and "Forgiven," one need look no further than Christ Jesus, nailed to Calvary's Cross;

Dying the sin death that I should be paying for upon my death; His death that I can never begin to repay upon my death; as well as paying for my sin penalty of death; and finally, Christ Jesus, by His gracious gift of Forgiveness; One— more specifically, I, myself—can never begin to repay Christ Jesus for this gift of salvation and eternal life!

Secondly, when I think of being "***Blessed***" in this life, as I do my very best to walk a life journey that brings praise, glory, and honor to Father God, I cannot lose sight of the "***Blessedness***" that Jesus spoke about at the beginning of the Sermon on the Mount (Matthew 5:3-12). Specifically, within "*The Beatitudes*," Jesus called out and/or broadly stated nine "***Blessed***" life conditions and/or situations that most everyone has personally experienced at one point or another in one's lifetime. Unlike most people, when they experience poverty, death, and/or persecution for righteousness sake (Matthew 5:3, 4, and 10), to name just three, Jesus emphatically declares and states that each of these life encountered situations, that these are indeed "***Blessings***," "*For theirs is the kingdom of heaven*," "*For they shall be comforted*," and "*For theirs is the kingdom of heaven*," respectively.

The Greek translation of "***Blessed***" means "happy, blissful", or, literally, "to be enlarged." From my perspective, in ***The Beatitudes***, Jesus uses the word "***Blessed***" to refer to more than just a sense of happiness. Instead, it appears to me that "***Blessed***" refers to a spiritual state of well-being and ***Prosperity***, which will lead to, according to Matthew 5:12, "*Rejoice and be exceedingly glad, for great is your reward in heaven....*"

Accordingly, at the end of the day, I personally challenge anyone not to feel "***Blessed***, Highly ***Favored***, Forgiven, and Mightily Loved!"

(The Value of Wisdom)

Proverbs *2:*20*–22

(20)* ***So you may walk in the way of goodness***, **And keep *to* the paths of righteousness**.

16

(21)* For the upright will dwell in the land, And the blameless will remain in it;

(22) But the wicked will be cut off from the earth, And the unfaithful will be uprooted from it.

(Guidance for the Young)

Proverbs *3:*3*–4*
Let not mercy and truth forsake you; Bind them around your neck, Write them on the tablet of your heart, *And* so find *favor* and high esteem In the sight of God and man.

Proverbs *3:*9*–*10*
Honor **the LORD with your *possessions*,** *And with the first fruits of all your increase; So your barns will be filled with plenty, And your vats will overflow with new wine.*

Proverbs *3:*27*–*28*
Do not withhold good from those to whom it is due, When it is in the power of your hand to do so. **Do not say to your neighbor, "Go, and come back, And tomorrow I will give it,"** *When you have it with you.*

Proverbs 3:33*
The curse of the LORD is on the house of the wicked, But He *blesses* the home of the just.

(Security in Wisdom)

Proverbs *4:*18*–19
But the path of the just is like the shining sun, That shines even brighter unto the perfect day. The way of the wicked is like darkness: They do not know what makes them stumble.

(The Peril of Adultery)

Proverbs *5:*15*–20

(15)* **Drink water from your own cistern, And running water from your own well.**

(16) Should your fountains be dispersed abroad, Streams of water in the streets?

(17) Let them be only your own, And not for strangers with you.

(18)* **Let your fountain be _blessed_, And rejoice with the wife of your youth.**

(19)* As a loving deer and a graceful doe, **Let her breasts satisfy you at all times; And always be enraptured with her love.**

(20) For why should you, my son, be enraptured by an immoral woman, And be embraced in the arms of a seductress?

(The Excellence of Wisdom)

Proverbs *8:*32*–36

(32)* **"Now therefore, listen to me, my children, For _blessed_ are those who keep my ways.**

(33)* **Hear instruction and be wise, And do not distain it.**

(34)* _**Blessed**_ is the man who listens to me, Watching daily at my gates, Waiting at the posts of my doors.

(35)* _**For whoever finds me finds life, And obtains favor from the LORD**_;

(36) But he who sins against me wrongs his own soul; All those who hate me love death."

(Wise Sayings of Solomon)

Proverbs 10:*6*–7

**Blessings** are on the head of the righteous, But violence covers the mouth of the wicked. The memory of the righteous is _**blessed**_, But the name of the wicked will rot.

Proverbs *10:*22*
The *blessing* of the LORD makes one rich, And He adds no sorrow with it.

Proverbs 11:11
By the ***blessing*** of the upright the city is *exalted*, But it is overthrown by the mouth of the wicked.

Proverbs 11:18*
The wicked man does deceptive work, *But he who sows righteousness will have a sure **reward**.*

Proverbs *11:*24*
There is one who scatters, yet <u>increases more</u>; And there is one who withholds more than is right, But it leads to poverty.

Proverbs *11:*25*
The *generous* soul *will be made rich, And he who waters will also be <u>watered himself</u>.*

Proverbs 11:26
The people will curse him who withholds grain, But ***<u>blessing</u>*** will be on the head of him who sells it.

Proverbs 11:*27*
He who earnestly seeks good finds ***<u>favor</u>***, But trouble will come to him who seeks evil.

Proverbs 12:2*
A good man obtains ***<u>favor</u>*** from the LORD, But a man of wicked intentions He will condemn.

Proverbs 12:12
The wicked covet the catch of evil men, *But the root of the righteous <u>yields fruit</u>.*

Proverbs 12:14*

A man will be <u>satisfied</u> with the good by the fruit of his mouth, And the recompense of a man's hands will be rendered to him.

Proverbs 13:*7*

There is one who makes himself rich, yet has nothing; *And one who makes himself poor, yet has <u>great riches</u>.*

Proverbs 13:11*

Wealth *gained* by dishonesty will be diminished, *But he who gathers by labor <u>will increase</u>.*

Proverbs 13:*13*

He who despises the word will be destroyed, *But he who fears the commandment <u>will be rewarded</u>.*

Proverbs 13:15*

Good understanding *gains <u>favor</u>*, But the way of the unfaithful is hard.

Proverbs 13:21*

Evil pursues sinners, *But to the righteous, <u>good shall be repaid</u>.*

Proverbs *13:*22*

***<u>A good man leaves an inheritance to his children's children</u>*, But the wealth of the sinner is stored up for the righteous.**

Proverbs 14:4*

Where no oxen are, the trough is clean; But much *increase* comes by the strength of an ox.

Proverbs 14:*9*

Fools mock at sin, But among the upright there is ***<u>favor</u>***.

Proverbs 14:11*

The house of the wicked will be overthrown, *But the tent of the upright will <u>flourish</u>.*

Proverbs 14:23
*In all labor there is **profit**,* But idle chatter leads only to poverty.

Proverbs 14:35
The king's ***favor*** is toward a wise servant, But his wrath is against him who causes shame.

Proverbs 15:3
The eyes of the LORD are in every place, *Keeping watch on the evil and the good.*

Proverbs 16:15
In the light of the king's face is life, And his ***favor*** is like a cloud of the latter rain.

Proverbs 16:*20*
He who heeds the word wisely <u>will find good</u>, And whoever trusts in the LORD, <u>happy is he</u>.

Proverbs 17:2
A wise servant will rule over a son who causes shame, *And will share an inheritance among the brothers.*

Proverbs 17:8
A present is a precious stone in the eyes of its possessor; Whenever he turns, he ***prospers***.

Proverbs 18:5*
It is not good to show *partiality* to the wicked, Or to overthrow the righteous in judgment.

Proverbs *18:*22*
He who finds a wife finds a good thing, And obtains <u>favor</u> from the LORD.

Proverbs 19:6
Many entreat the *favor* of the nobility, And every man is a friend to the *one who gives gifts.*

Proverbs 19:12
The king's wrath is like the roaring of a lion, But his *favor* is like dew on the grass.

Proverbs *19:*17*
He who has pity on the poor lends to the LORD, *And He will pay back what he has given.*

Proverbs 19:23*
The fear of the LORD leads to life, And he who has it will abide in satisfaction; *He will not be visited with evil.*

Proverbs 20:7*
The righteous man walks in his integrity; His children are **blessed** after him.

Proverbs *20:*21*
An inheritance gained hastily at the beginning Will not be *blessed* **at the end.**

Proverbs *21:*5*
The plans of the diligent lead surely to plenty, **But those of everyone who is hasty, surely to poverty.**

Proverbs 21:10
The soul of the wicked desires evil; His neighbor finds no *favor* in his eyes.

Proverbs *21:*13*
Whoever *shuts his ears* **to the cry of the poor** *Will also cry himself and not be heard.*

Proverbs 21:20*
There is desirable pleasure, *And oil in the dwelling of the wise*, But a foolish man squanders it.

Proverbs *21:*21*
He who follows righteousness and mercy Finds life, righteousness and honor.

Proverbs 21:31*
The horse is prepared for the day of battle, *But deliverance is of the LORD.*

Proverbs 22:*1*
A good name is to be chosen rather than great riches, Loving **_favor_** rather than silver and gold.

Proverbs *22:*4*
By humility and the fear of the LORD Are riches and honor and life.

Proverbs *22:*9*
He who has a generous eye will be _blessed_, For he gives of his bread to the poor.

Proverbs 23:17–18
Do not let your heart envy sinners, But be zealous for the fear of the LORD all the day; *For surely there is a hereafter, And your hope will not be cut off.*

Proverbs *24:13–*14*
My son, eat honey because it is good, And the honeycomb which is sweet to your taste; *So shall the knowledge of wisdom be to your soul; If you have found it, there is a prospect, And your hope will not be cut off.*

(Further Sayings of the Wise)

Proverbs *24:*23*–*25*
(23)* **These things also belong to the wise: It is not good to show _partiality_ in judgment.**

(24) He who says to the wicked, "You are righteous," Him the people will curse; Nations will abhor him.

(25)* **But those who rebuke the wicked will have delight, And a good _blessing_ will come upon them.**

(Further Wise Sayings of Solomon)

Proverbs *25:*21*–*22*

If your enemy is hungry, give him bread to eat; And if he is thirsty, give him water to drink; For so you will heap coals of fire on his head, _And the LORD will reward you_.

Proverbs 27:14

He who **_blesses_** his friend with a loud voice, rising early in the morning, It will be counted a curse to him.

Proverbs 27:18

Whoever keeps the fig tree will eat its fruit; So he who waits on his master will be honored.

Proverbs 28:10

Whoever causes the upright to go astray in an evil way, He himself will fall into his own pit; _But the blameless will inherit good._

Proverbs *28:*13*

He who covers his sins will not prosper, _But whoever confesses and forsakes them will have mercy_.

Proverbs 28:14*

Happy is the man who is always reverent, But he who hardens his heart will fall into calamity.

Proverbs 28:19

He who tills his land will have plenty of bread, But he who follows frivolity will have poverty enough!

Proverbs 28:20
*A faithful man will abound with **blessings**,* But he who hastens to be rich will not go unpunished.

Proverbs *28:*23*
He who rebukes a man will find more *favor* afterward Than he who flatters with the tongue.

Proverbs 28:*25*
He who is of a proud heart stirs up strife, But he who trusts in the LORD will be ***prospered.***

Proverbs *28:*27*
He who gives to the poor will not lack, **But he who hides his eyes will have many curses.**

Proverbs 29:10
The bloodthirsty hate the blameless, *But the upright seek his well-being.*

Proverbs 29:18*
Where there is no revelation, the people cast off restraint; *But **happy** is he who keeps the law.*

Proverbs 29:23*
A man's pride will bring him low, *But the humble in spirit will retain honor.*

Proverbs 29:26
Many seek the ruler's ***favor***, But justice for man comes from the LORD.

(The Virtuous Wife)

Proverbs *31:*10*–*12* and *28*–31
(10)* **Who can find a virtuous wife? For her worth is far above rubies.**
(11)* **The heart of her husband safely trusts her;** *So he will have no lack of gain.*
(12)* *She does him good and not evil All the days of her life.*

(28)* **Her children rise up and call her _blessed_; Her husband also, and he praises her:**

(29) "Many daughters have done well, But you excel them all."

(30)* **_Charm_ is deceitful and beauty is passing, But a woman who fears the LORD, she shall be praised.**

(31) Give her of the fruit of her hands, And let her own works praise her in the gates.

CHAPTER 4

ADULTERY, LUST, SEXUAL IMMORALITY, INFIDELITY, SEXUAL UNFAITHFULNESS

Sexual Immorality is Against *God's* Law!

G od's Word is "Crystal Clear" in that ***Adultery***, ***Lust***, and ***Sexual Immorality*** are **ALL** Sins and/or Sinful Behaviors that are against the will of Father God. Whether one examines, studies, and/or marinates on God's Word in the Old Testament (i.e. Deuteronomy 5:18, Exodus 20:14, and Proverbs 5), or the numerous commandments and biblical truths detailed in the New Testament (i.e. Matthew 5:27–28, Matthew 18:9, Mark 10:11–12, Luke 16:18, Romans 7: 2–3, 1 Corinthians 6:9, or Hebrews 13:4, just to name a few), ***Adultery***, ***Lust***, and ***Sexual Immorality*** are sins that have in the past and continue to challenge and plague our current societal norms, practices, lifestyles, and families, as they are forbidden and not in accordance with God's Word, as well as are not His will and purpose for one's life!

Without boring the reader with a detailed accounting of my lifelong failures and personal challenges in this area, I can unfortunately say that

I have spent my entire adult life falling short of God's Word and will for my life in these specific areas. As I periodically reflect and personally analyze as well as publicly share my challenges and testimonies in these areas, especially in recognizing how these past failures in my human flesh and personal *Sexual* desires played an active part in the failure of my past marriages, as well as still providing current and ongoing personal *Sexual* challenges and temptations, I am comforted in knowing and believing that because of Father God's overwhelming grace, mercy, forgiveness, and love, my past, present, and future challenges and sins have been and will continue to be *"washed under the blood of Jesus Christ"*! With that said, I would be less than candid, if I did not share with you, that there are many moments in my life that I wish I had been stronger in my faith with Father God; that I had been stronger in my walk with Christ, as well as wishing that I had been stronger in listening to and being more obedient to the directions of the Holy Spirit; as well as better understanding, comprehending, and needless to say, applying Father God's Word decades ago regarding the subjects of ***Adultery***, ***Lust***, ***Sexual Immorality***, ***Unfaithfulness***, and ***Infidelity***, for if I had been, then maybe, just maybe, I might not have practiced and lived out a habitual pattern of ***Adultery***, ***Lust***, **and** *Sexual **Immorality*** in my cumulative thirty-five years of marriage with three different wives. Then maybe, a few of life's negative consequences might not have become a permanent record of my earthly walk in these areas!

As one delves into the fundamental DNA of ***Adultery***, ***Lust***, and ***Sexual Immorality***, I would content that *sexuality* lies at the core of these three flesh-based sins. In fact, I would content that *sexuality* lies at the center of one's spiritual life! It has been said that a healthy *sexuality* is the single most powerful vehicle there is, in that it can lead one to selflessness and joy. In contrast, an **unhealthy *Sexuality*** helps constellate selfishness and unhappiness, and does little or nothing else. One can be happy, joyous, godly, and more righteous in this life if one adopts a healthy *sexuality*.

"One of the fundamental tasks of spirituality, therefore, is to help one to understand and channel one's sexuality correctly. This, however,

is not an easy task. Sexuality is such a powerful fire that it is not always easy to channel it in life-giving ways. It can be very powerful, and it is one of the most powerful forces on earth; thereby, making it a force not just for formidable love, life and blessings, but it also plays a contributing factor for the worst hate, death and destruction imaginable. It has been said that sex is responsible for most of the ecstasies that occur on earth, but it also is responsible for various types of murders and suicides. Sexuality is one of the most powerful of fires, the best of all fires, the most dangerous of all fires, and the fire which, ultimately, lies at the base of everything, including one's spiritual life." (**Ronald Rolheiser 1999**).

In looking back at my past, I would also say that, while my soul was "*void*" of Father God's Word regarding **_Adultery_**, **_Lust_**, and **_Sexual Immorality_**, I also lacked a sound definition of *sexuality* and *sex*. The word "*sex*" has a Latin root that literally means "to cut off," "to sever," "to amputate," and/or "to disconnect from the whole." To be "*sexed*," therefore, literally means to be cut off, to be severed from, and/or to be amputated from the whole.

It is important to know the difference between having **sex** and having **sexuality**:

1. **Sex** is the energy inside oneself that works incessantly against being alone.
2. **Sexuality** is not simply about finding a lover or even finding a friend. It is more about overcoming separateness by giving life and blessing it.

Thus, while I was growing up into adulthood and even thereafter, I was misguided in believing that one needed to be engaged in "*sex*" whether single or married, and in my case, having a strong desire to be engaged with "**sex** outside of marriage" that I became completely lost in the allure of **_Adultery_**, **_Lust_**, and **_Sexual Immorality_**. But today, as I have gained a greater sense of maturity, I have come to better understand that **_Sexuality_** is about giving oneself over to community, friendship, family, service, creativity, humor, delight, marriage, as well as service and obedience to Father God, so that one can bring a Christian life into the world with a key focus of righteousness, love, and obedience to Father God and all that He has created!

Finally, in closing, one needs to remember Father God's Words contained in Hebrews 13:4: "*Marriage is honorable among all, and the bed undefiled; but the **fornicators** and **adulterers** God will judge.*"

(*The Value of Wisdom*)

Proverbs *2:16–22

(16) To deliver you from the ***immoral woman***, From the ***seductress*** who flatters with ***her*** words,

(17) Who forsakes the companion of ***her*** youth, And forgets the covenant of ***her*** God.

(18) For ***her*** house leads down to death, And ***her*** paths to the dead;

(19) None who go to ***her*** return, Nor do they regain the paths of life—

(20)* **So you may walk in the way of goodness, And keep to the paths of righteousness.**

(21)* **For the upright will dwell in the land, And the blameless will remain in it;**

(22) But the wicked will be cut off from the earth, And the ***unfaithful*** will be uprooted from it.

(*The Peril of Adultery*)

Proverbs *5:1–6; 7–14, and *15*–*23*

(1) My son, pay attention to my wisdom; Lend your ear to my understanding.

(2) That you may preserve discretion, And your lips may keep knowledge.

(3) For the lips of an ***immoral woman*** drip honey, And ***her*** mouth is smoother than oil;

(4) But in the end **_she_** is bitter as wormwood, Sharp as a two-edged sword.

(5) **_Her_** feet go down to death, **_Her_** steps lay hold of hell.

(6) Lest you ponder **_her_** path of life—**_her_** ways are unstable; You do not know them.

(7) Therefore hear me now, my children, And do not depart from the words of my mouth.

(8) Remove your way far from **_her_**, And do not go near the door of **_her_** house,

(9) Lest you give your honor to others, And your years to the cruel one;

(10) Lest aliens be filled with your wealth, And your labors go to the house of a foreigner;

(11) And you mourn at last, When your flesh and your body are consumed,

(12) And say: "How I have hated instruction, And my heart despised correction!

(13) I have not obeyed the voice of my teachers, Nor inclined my ear to those who instructed me!

(14) I was on the verge of total ruin, In the midst of the assembly and congregation."

(15)* **Drink water from your own cistern, And running water from your own well.**

(16) Should your fountains be dispersed abroad, streams of water in the streets?

(17) Let them be only your own, *And not for strangers with you.*

(18)* **Let your fountain be blessed, And rejoice with the <u>wife</u> of your youth.**

(19)* As a loving deer and a graceful doe, **Let her breasts satisfy you at all times; And always be enraptured with her love.**

(20) For why should you, my son, be enraptured by an **_immoral woman_**, And be embraced in the arms of a **_seductress_**?

(21)* **For the ways of *man* are before the eyes of the LORD, And He ponders all *his* paths.**

(22)* ***His* own iniquities entrap the wicked *man*, And *he* is caught in the cords of *his* sin.**

(23)* ***He* shall die for lack of instruction, And in the greatness of *his* folly *he* shall go astray.**

(Beware of Adultery)

Proverbs *6:20*–29* and *32*–35

(20)* My son, keep your father's command, And do not forsake the law of your mother.

(21) Bind them continually upon your heart; Tie them around your neck.

(22) *When you roam*, they will lead you; When you sleep, they will keep you; And when you awake, they will speak with you.

(23)* **For the commandment is a lamp, And the law a light; Reproofs of instruction are the way of life,**

(24)* To keep you from the ***evil woman***, *From the flattering tongue of a **seductress**.*

(25) Do not ***lust*** after ***her*** beauty in your heart, Nor let ***her*** ***allure*** you with ***her*** eyelids.

(26) For by means of a ***harlot***, *A man is reduced to a crust of bread*; And an ***adulteress*** will ***prey*** upon his precious life.

(27) Can a man take *fire* to his bosom, And his *clothes not be burned*?

(28) Can one *walk on hot coals*, And his *feet not be seared*?

(29)* *So is he who goes in to his **neighbor's wife**; Whoever **touches her** shall not be innocent.*

(32)* **Whoever commits *adultery* with a woman lacks understanding; He who does so destroys his own soul.**

(33)* **Wounds and dishonor he will get, And his reproach will not be wiped away.**

(34) *For jealousy is a husband's fury; Therefore he will not spare in the day of vengeance.*

(35) *He will accept no recompense, Nor will he be appeased though you give many gifts.*

Proverbs *7:*1*–5*

(1)* **My son, keep my words, And treasure my commands within you.**

(2)* **Keep my commands and live, And my law as the apple of your eye.**

(3)* Bind them on your fingers; Write them on the tablet of your heart.

(4)* **Say to wisdom, "You are my sister," And call understanding your nearest kin,**

(5)* *That they may keep you from the* **immortal woman**, *From the* **seductress** *who flatters with* **her words**.

(The Crafty Harlot)

Proverbs 7:6–9, 10–20, 21–23, and 24–27

(6) For at the window of my house I looked through my lattice,

(7) And saw among the simple, I perceived among the youths, A young man devoid of understanding,

(8) Passing along the street near **her** corner;

(9) And he took the path to **her** house In the twilight, in the evening, In the black and dark night.

(10) And there a **woman** met him, With the attire of a **harlot**, and a *crafty* heart.

(11) **She** was loud and rebellious, **Her** feet would not stay at home.

(12) At times **she** was outside, at times in the open square, *Lurking* at every corner.

(13) So **she** caught him and *kissed* him; With an impudent face **she** said to him:

(14) *"I have peace offerings with* **me***; Today I have paid* **my** *vows.*

(15) *So I came out to meet you, Diligently to seek your face. And I have found you.*

(16) *I have spread __my__ bed with tapestry, Colored coverings of Egyptian linen.*

(17) *I have perfumed __my__ bed With myrrh, aloes, and cinnamon.*

(18) **__Come, let us take our fill of love until morning; Let us delight ourselves with love__**.

(19) *For __my__ husband is not at home; He has gone on a long journey;*

(20) *He has taken a bag of money with him, And will come home on the appointed day."*

(21) With __her__ *enticing speech* __she__ caused him to yield, With __her__ *flattering* lips __she seduced__ him.

(22) Immediately he went after __her__, as an ox goes to the slaughter, Or as a fool to the correction of the stocks,

(23) Till an arrow struck his liver. As a bird hastens to the snare, He did not know it *would cost his life.*

(24) Now therefore, listen to me, my children; Pay attention to the words of my mouth:

(25) Do not let your heart turn aside to __her__ ways, Do not stray into __her__ paths;

(26) For __she__ has *cast down many wounded*, And all who were *slain* by __her__ were strong men

(27) *__Her__ house is the way to hell, Descending to the chambers of death.*

(The Way of Folly)

Proverbs 9:13–18

(13) A **__foolish woman__** is clamorous; __She__ is simple, and knows nothing.

(14) For __she__ sits at the door of __her__ house, On a seat by the highest places of the city,

(15) To *call* to those who pass by, Who go straight on their way:

(16) "*Whoever is simple, let him turn in here*"; And as for him who lacks understanding, __she__ says to him,

(17)* "**_Stolen water is sweet, And bread eaten in secret is pleasant_**."

(18) But he does not know that the dead are there, That **_her_** guests are in the depths of hell.

(Wise Sayings of Solomon)

Proverbs 11:6

The righteousness of the upright will deliver them, But the **_unfaithful_** will be caught by their **_lust_**.

Proverbs 20:16

Take the garment of one who is surety for a stranger, And hold it as a pledge when it is for a **_seductress_**.

Proverbs 22:14

The mouth of an **_immoral woman_** _is a deep pit_; He who is abhorred by the LORD will fall there.

Proverbs 23:26–28

(26) My son, give me your heart, And let your eyes observe my ways.

(27) For a **_harlot_** is a deep pit, And a **_seductress_** is a narrow well.

(28) **_She_** also lies in wait as for a victim, And increases the **_unfaithful_** among men.

Proverbs 27:13

Take the garment of him who is surety for a stranger, And hold it in pledge when he is surety for a **_seductress_**.

Proverbs *29:*3*

Whoever loves wisdom makes his father rejoice, But a _companion_ of _harlots_ wastes his wealth.

(The Wisdom of Agur)

Proverbs 30:20

This is the way of an **_adulterous woman_**: **_She_** eats and wipes **_her_** mouth, And says, "*I* have done no wickedness."

(The Words of King Lemuel's Mother)

Proverbs 31:1–3

(1) The words of King Lemuel, the utterance which his mother taught him:

(2) What, my son? And what, son of my womb? And what, son of my vows?

(3) **_Do not give your strength to women_**, Nor your ways to that which destroys kings.

CHAPTER 5

ADVERSITY, CALAMITY, CONTENTION, HARM, QUARREL, STRIFE, TROUBLE

*A**dversity*** and ***Strife*** in a person's life is as certain as death and taxes! In fact, Jesus had His share of ***Adversity*** and ***Trouble*** during His three-year missionary journeys while on earth, leading His perfect life as the Son of God; but His ***Adversity*** and ***Troubles*** were not self-inflicted like most of ours yesterday, today, and tomorrow. Jesus proclaimed that we would always have ***Adversity***, ***Trouble***, and *Tribulation* (John 14:27, John 16:33), but as He also said that "*He has overcome the world*" (John 16:33 and 1 John 5:4).

One of the challenges of ***Adversity*** and ***Trouble*** is the fact that it comes in the form of a two-edged sword. What I mean by that is that there are many shades of ***Trouble***, which comes into an individual's life, especially from the actions of others. While such ***Troubles*** can be short- or long-lived, minimal and/or costly, one can take solace in biblical verses like Proverbs 12:21, which states, "*No grave **trouble** will overtake the righteous, But the wicked shall be filled with evil.*"

Now, the other side of that two-edged, ***Trouble***-filled sword is the pain that one endures because of one's poor decision making choices. Exercising poor judgment and/or one's inability to listen to the Holy Spirit's direction, thereby believing that one knows better and/or that one might overstate one's depth of wisdom on a particular item; thereby allowing pride and overconfidence to set in, which can make one wonder out loud, "What in the heck was I thinking, and/or who was I trying to impress?" I don't know about you, but the consequences of self-inflicted **_Trouble_** is, more often than not, much more painful, deep, and long-lived than other forms of **_Trouble_**!

At the end of the day, whichever road that **_Trouble_** arrives from (i.e. whether from external sources and/or circumstances, or from self-inflicted wounds such as poor judgment and/or poor decision making), I must not allow Satan to turn me away from the lane of righteousness to the highway of evil and/or wickedness. I must always repent and seek forgiveness from Almighty God, being prayerful and hopeful that Romans 8:28 will play itself out in this circumstance—"_And we know that all things work together for the good to those who love God, to those who are called according to His purpose._"

(The Call of Wisdom)

Proverbs *1:*20*–27 and 28–*33*

(20)* **Wisdom calls aloud outside; She raises her voice in the open squares.**

(21) She cries out in the chief concourses, At the openings of the gates in the city She speaks her words:

(22) "How long, you simple ones, will you love simplicity? For scorners delight in their scorning, And fools hate knowledge.

(23) Turn at my rebuke; Surely I will pour out my spirit on you; I will make my words known to you.

(24) Because I have called and you refused, I have stretched out my hand and no one regarded,

(25) Because you disdained all my counsel, And would have none of my rebuke,

(26) I also will laugh at your **_calamity_**; I will mock when your terror comes,

(27) *When your terror comes like a storm, And your destruction comes like a whirlwind, When distress and anguish come upon you.*

(28) Then they will call on me, but I will not answer; They will seek me diligently, but they will not find me.

(29) Because they hated knowledge And did not choose the fear of the LORD,

(30) They would have none of my counsel And despised my every rebuke.

(31) *Therefore they shall eat the fruit of their own way, And be filled to the full with their own fancies.*

(32) *For the turning away of the simple will slay them, And the complacency of fools will destroy them;*

(33)* **But whoever listens to me will dwell safely, And will be secure, without fear of evil."**

(Guidance for the Young)

Proverbs 3:25–26*
Do not be afraid of sudden terror, Nor of **_trouble_** from the wicked when it comes; For the LORD will be your confidence, And will keep your foot from being caught.

Proverbs 3:30
Do not strive with a man without cause, If he has done you no **_harm_**.

(Security in Wisdom)

Proverbs *4:*10*–*13* and *14*–17

(10)* **Hear, my son, and receive my sayings, And the years of your life will be many.**

(11)* **I have taught you in the way of wisdom; I have led you in right paths.**

(12)* **When you *walk*, your *steps* will not be hindered, And when you *run*, you will not *stumble*.**

(13)* **Take firm hold of instruction, do not let her go; Keep her, for she is your life.**

(14)* ***Do not enter the path of the wicked, And do not walk in the way of evil.***

(15) Avoid it, do not travel on it; Turn away from it and pass on.

(16) *For they do not sleep unless they have done evil; And their sleep is taken away unless they make someone fall.*

(17) For they eat the bread of wickedness, And drink the wine of violence.

(The Wicked Man)

Proverbs 6:12–15 and 16–19

(12) A worthless person, a wicked man, Walks with a perverse mouth;

(13) He winks with his eyes, He shuffles his feet, He points with his fingers;

(14) *Perversity is in his heart, He devises evil continually, He sows discord.*

(15) *Therefore his **calamity** shall come suddenly; Suddenly he shall be broken without remedy.*

(16) These six things the LORD hates, Yes, seven are an abomination to Him:

(17) A proud look, A lying tongue, *Hands that shed innocent blood,*

(18) *A heart that devises wicked plans, Feet that are swift in running to evil,*

(19) *A false witness who speaks lies, And one who <u>sows</u> <u>discord</u> among brethren.*

Proverbs *6:*32*–35*

(32)* **Whoever commits adultery with a woman lacks understanding; He who does so *destroys* his own soul.**

(33)* ***Wounds and dishonor he will get, And his reproach will not be wiped away.***

(34) For jealousy is a husband's fury; Therefore he will not spare in the *day of vengeance.*

(35)* He will accept no recompense, Nor will he be appeased though you give many gifts.

(The Way of Wisdom)

Proverbs *9:7–12

(7) "He who corrects a scoffer gets shame for himself, And he who rebukes a wicked man only ***harms*** himself.

(8)* **Do not correct a scoffer, lest he hate you; Rebuke a wise man, and he will love you.**

(9)* **Give instruction to a wise man, and he will be still wiser; Teach a just man, and he will increase in learning.**

(10)* **The fear of the LORD is the beginning of wisdom, And the knowledge of the Holy One is understanding.**

(11) For by me your days will be multiplied, And years of life will be added to you.

(12) If you are wise, you are wise for yourself, And if you scoff, you will bear it alone."

(Wise Sayings of Solomon)

Proverbs 10:10

He who winks with the eye causes ***trouble,*** But a prating fool will *fall.*

Proverbs *10:*12*
Hatred stirs up _strife_, But love covers all sins.

Proverbs 11:8
The righteous is delivered from **_trouble_,** And it comes to the wicked instead.

Proverbs 11:15*
He who is surety for a stranger will _suffer_, But one who hates being surety is secure.

Proverbs 11:17
The merciful man does good for his own soul, But he who is cruel **_troubles_** his own flesh.

Proverbs 11:23
The desire of the righteous is only good, But the expectation of the wicked is _wrath_.

Proverbs 11:*27*
He who earnestly seeks good finds favor, But **_trouble_** will come to him who seeks evil.

Proverbs *11:*29*
He who _troubles_ his own house will inherit the wind, And the fool will be servant to the wise of heart.

Proverbs 12:13*
The wicked is ensnared by the transgression of his lips, But the righteous will come through **_trouble_.**

Proverbs 12:21*
No grave **_trouble_** will overtake the righteous, But the wicked shall be filled with evil.

Proverbs 13:6*
Righteousness guards him whose way is blameless, *But wickedness* <u>*overthrows the sinner*</u>.

Proverbs *13:*10*
By pride comes nothing but <u>**strife**</u>, **But with the well-advised is wisdom.**

Proverbs 13:13*
He who despises the word will be *destroyed*, But he who fears the commandment will be rewarded.

Proverbs 13:15
Good understanding gains favor, But the way of the unfaithful is *hard*.

Proverbs 13:17
A wicked messenger falls into <u>***trouble***</u>, But a faithful ambassador brings health.

Proverbs 13:21*
Evil pursues sinners, But to the righteous, good shall be repaid.

Proverbs 15:*1*
A soft answer turns away wrath, But a harsh word stirs up anger.

Proverbs *15:*6*
In the house of the righteous there is much treasure, But in the revenue of the wicked is <u>**trouble**</u>.

Proverbs *15:*16*
Better is a little with fear of the LORD, Than great treasure with <u>**trouble**</u>.

Proverbs 15:18
A *wrathful* man stirs up <u>***strife***</u>, But he who is *slow to anger* allays <u>***contention***</u>.

Proverbs 15:*27*
He who is greedy for gain <u>***troubles***</u> his own house, But he who hates bribes will live.

Proverbs 16:5

Everyone proud in heart is an abomination to the LORD; Though they join forces, none will go *unpunished*.

Proverbs *16:*18*

Pride goes before destruction, And a haughty spirit before a <u>fall</u>.

Proverbs 16:28

A perverse man sows ***strife***, And a whisperer separates the best of friends.

Proverbs 16:29

A *violent* man entices his neighbor, *And leads him in a way that is not good.*

Proverbs 17:1

Better is a dry morsel with quietness, Than a house full of feasting with ***strife***.

Proverbs 17:5*

He who mocks the poor reproaches his Maker; He who is glad at ***calamity*** will not go *unpunished*.

Proverbs 17:*9*

He who covers a transgression seeks love, *But he who repeats a matter separates friends.*

Proverbs 17:11

An evil man seeks only *rebellion*; Therefore a cruel messenger will be sent against him.

Proverbs 17:*14*

The beginning of ***strife*** is like releasing water; Therefore stop ***contention*** before a ***quarrel*** starts.

Proverbs *17:*17*

A friend loves at all times, And a brother is born for *adversity*.

Proverbs 17:19*
He who loves transgression loves *strife*, And he who exalts his gate seeks *destruction*.

Proverbs 18:6
A fool's lips enter into *contention*, And his mouth calls for blows.

Proverbs *18:*12*
Before *destruction* the heart of a man is haughty, And before honor is humility.

Proverbs 18:18
Casting lots causes *contentions* to cease, And keeps the mighty apart.

Proverbs 18:19
A brother offended is harder to win than a strong city, And *contentions* are like the bars of a castle.

Proverbs 19:5*
A false witness will not go *unpunished*, And he who speaks lies will not escape.

Proverbs 19:9*
A false witness will not go *unpunished*, And he who speaks lies shall *perish*.

Proverbs 19:*13*
A foolish son is the ruin of his father, And the *contentions* of a wife are a continual dripping.

Proverbs 19:19*
A man of great *wrath* will suffer *punishment*; For if you rescue him, you will have to do it again.

Proverbs 19:29
Judgments are prepared for scoffers, And *beatings* for the backs of fools.

Proverbs 20:3
It is honorable for a man to stop striving, Since any fool can start a **quarrel**.

Proverbs 20:17
Bread gained by deceit is sweet to a man, But afterward his mouth will be filled with *gravel*.

Proverbs 20:26
A wise king sifts out the wicked, *And brings the threshing wheel over them.*

Proverbs 20:30
Blows that hurt cleanse away evil, *As do stripes the inner depths of the heart.*

Proverbs 21:6
Getting treasures by a lying tongue Is the fleeting fantasy of those who seek death.

Proverbs 21:7
The violence of the wicked will *destroy* them, Because they refuse to do justice.

Proverbs *21:*9*
Better to dwell in a corner of a housetop, Than in a house shared with a _contentious_ woman.

Proverbs 21:*11*
When the scoffer is *punished*, the simple is made wise; But when the wise is instructed, he receives knowledge.

Proverbs 21:12*
The righteous God wisely considers the house of the wicked, *Overthrowing* the wicked for their wickedness.

Proverbs 21:15*
It is a joy for the just to do justice, But *destruction* will come to the workers of iniquity.

Proverbs *21:*19*
Better to dwell in the wilderness, Than with a _contentious_ and _angry_ woman.

Proverbs 21:*23*
Whoever guards his mouth and tongue Keeps his soul from **_troubles_**.

Proverbs 22:3*
A prudent man foresees evil and hides himself, But the simple pass on and are _punished_.

Proverbs 22:5
Thorns and snares are in the way of the perverse; He who guards his soul will be far from them.

Proverbs 22:*10*
Cast out the scoffer, and **_contention_** will leave; Yes, **_strife_** and reproach will cease.

Proverbs 22:14
The _mouth_ of an _immoral woman_ is a _deep pit_; He who is abhorred by the LORD _will fall there._

Proverbs 22:16*
He who oppresses the poor to increase his riches, And he who gives to the rich, will surely come to poverty.

(Sayings of the Wise)

Proverbs *22:*22*-*23*
Do not rob the poor because he is poor, Nor oppress the afflicted at the gate; For the LORD will plead their cause, _And_ plunder _the soul of those who_ plunder _them._

Proverbs 23:26–28
(26) My son, give me your heart, And let your eyes observe my ways.

(27) *For a harlot is a <u>deep pit</u>, And a seductress is a <u>narrow well</u>.*

(28) She also lies in wait as for a victim, And increases the unfaithful among men.

Proverbs 23:29–30

Who has woe? Who has *sorrow*? Who has **contentions**? Who has complaints? Who has wounds without cause? Who has redness of eyes? Those who linger long at the wine, Those who go in search of mixed wine.

Proverbs 24:1–2

Do not be envious of evil men, Nor desire to be with them; For their heart devises violence, And their lips talk of **troublemaking**.

Proverbs *24:*10*

If you faint in the day of *adversity*, Your strength is small.

Proverbs 24:11–12*

Deliver those who are drawn toward death, And hold back those stumbling to the slaughter. If you say, "Surely we did not know this," Does not He who weighs the hearts consider it? He who keeps your soul, does He not know it? *And will He not render to each man according to his deeds?*

Proverbs *24:*15–*16*

Do not lie in wait, O wicked man, against the dwelling of the righteous; Do not <u>plunder</u> his resting place; **For a righteous man may *fall* seven times And rise again, But the wicked shall *fall* by *calamity*.**

Proverbs *24:*17*–*18*

Do not rejoice when your enemy *falls*, And do not let your heart be glad when he *stumbles*; Lest the LORD see it, and it displease Him, And He turn away His *wrath* from him.

Proverbs 24:21–22

My son, fear the LORD and the king; Do not associate with those given to change; For their **calamity** will rise suddenly, And who knows the *ruin* those two can bring?

(Further Wise Sayings of Solomon)

Proverbs 25:8–10

(8) *Do not go hastily to court; For what will you do in the end, When your neighbor has put you to shame?*

(9) Debate your case with your neighbor, And do not disclose the secret to another;

(10) Lest he who hears it expose your shame, And your reputation be ruined.

Proverbs 25:19

Confidence in an unfaithful man in time of **_trouble_** *Is like a bad tooth and a foot out of joint.*

Proverbs 25:20

Like one who takes away a garment in cold weather, And like vinegar on soda, *Is one who sings songs to a heavy heart.*

Proverbs *25:*24*

It is better to dwell in a corner of a housetop, Then in a house shared with a _contentious_ woman.

Proverbs 26:2

Like a flitting sparrow, like a flying swallow, *So a _curse_ without cause shall not alight.*

Proverbs 26: 6

He who sends a message by the hand of a fool *Cuts off his own feet and drinks violence.*

Proverbs 26:*17*

*He who passes by and _meddles_ in a **quarrel** not his own Is like one who takes a dog by the ears.*

Proverbs 26:20*–21*

Where there is no wood, the fire goes out; And where there is no tale-bearer, **_strife_** ceases. As charcoal is to burning coals, and wood to fire, So is a **_contentious_** man to kindle **_strife_**.

Proverbs 26:27
Whoever <u>digs a pit</u> will <u>fall</u> into it, And he who <u>rolls a stone</u> will have it <u>roll back on him</u>.

Proverbs 26:28*
A lying tongue hates those who are crushed by it, And a *flattering mouth* works *<u>ruin</u>*.

Proverbs 27:4
Wrath is cruel and anger a torrent, But who is able to stand before jealousy?

Proverbs 27:10
Do not forsake your own friend or your father's friend, Nor go to your brother's house in the day of your **<u>calamity</u>**; Better is a neighbor nearby than a brother far away.

Proverbs 27:12*
A prudent man foresees evil and hides himself; The simple pass on and are *punished*.

Proverbs 27:15*–16
*A <u>continual dripping</u> on a very rainy day And a **<u>contentious</u>** woman are alike*; Whoever restrains her restrains the wind, And grasps oil with his right hand.

Proverbs 28:3
A poor man who oppresses the poor Is like a driving rain which leaves no food.

Proverbs 28:4
Those who forsake the law praise the wicked, But such as keep the law **<u>contend</u>** with them.

Proverbs 28:10
Whoever causes the upright to go astray in an evil way, He himself will <u>*fall*</u> *into his own pit*; But the blameless will inherit good.

Proverbs 28:12
When the righteous rejoice, there is great glory; *But when the wicked arise, men hide themselves.*

Proverbs 28:14*
Happy is the man who is always reverent, But he who hardens his heart will *fall* into **calamity**.

Proverbs 28:17
A man burdened with bloodshed will flee into a pit; Let no one help him.

Proverbs 28:18*
Whoever walks blamelessly will be saved, *But he who is perverse in his ways will suddenly fall.*

Proverbs 28:22
A man with an evil eye hastens after riches, And does not consider that poverty will come upon him.

Proverbs 28:*25*
He who is of a proud heart stirs up **strife**, But he who trusts in the LORD will be prospered.

Proverbs *28:*27*
He who gives to the poor will not lack, *But he who hides his eyes will have many curses.*

Proverbs 29:1*
He who is often rebuked, and hardens his neck, Will suddenly be destroyed, and that without remedy.

Proverbs 29:4
The king establishes the land by justice, *But he who receives bribes overthrows it.*

Proverbs 29:9
If a wise man **contends** with a foolish man, *Whether the fool rages or laughs, there is no peace.*

Proverbs 29:16

When the wicked are multiplied, transgression increases; But the righteous will see their *fall*.

Proverbs 29:22

An angry man stirs up **strife**, And a furious man abounds in *transgression*.

Proverbs 29:23*

A man's pride will bring him low, But the humble in spirit will retain honor.

(The Wisdom of Agur)

Proverbs 30:32–33

If you have been foolish in exalting yourself, Or if you have devised evil, put your hand on your mouth. For as the churning of milk produces butter, And wringing the nose produces blood, So the *forcing of wrath* produces **strife**.

(The Words of King Lemuel's Mother)

Proverbs 31:1–3 and 4–5

(1)   The words of King Lemuel, the utterance which his mother taught him:

(2)   What, my son? And what, son of my womb? And what, son of my vows?

(3)   *Do not give your strength to women, Nor your ways to that which destroys kings.*

(4)   It is not for kings, O Lemuel, It is not for kings to drink wine, Nor for princes intoxicating drink;

(5)   *Lest they drink and forget the law, And pervert the justice of all the afflicted.*

CHAPTER 6

ANGER, WRATH, VIOLENCE, TEMPER, OPPRESSOR, CRUEL

I am positive that I can affirm that every human being who has ever walked the face of this earth has experienced, displayed, and/or expressed some sort of *Anger, Temper*, physical outburst, or maybe even some form of *Wrath*! And it's not uncommon to find people who will attempt to justify such sentiments by stating that even Jesus Christ became and/or exhibited *Anger* or *frustration* on several occasions (Matthew 21:12–13, Mark 11:15–17, and Luke 19:45–46).

While Jesus's *Anger* was what one calls "**righteous indignation**," that doesn't excuse anyone, especially those who are followers of Christ Jesus, to exhibit any form of *Anger, Wrath,* and/or *Temper* outburst, which sometimes leads to cruelty, oppression, and worst of all, *Violence*.

Sometimes, I wish that I had the secret formula or the secret sauce that I could use and share with others, such that myself and others around me could raise one's temperament, such that my (one's) pressure point for *Anger* might be controlled in all present and future circumstances. I personally believe that an individual who expresses *Anger* must seek ways to control it and/or learn to mellow out, or as I like to say to myself, to "take a chill pill" so that such *Anger* does not ruin relationships, hurt people's feelings, or impacts another person in any way, shape, form, or fashion. Given the fact that most of us, no matter what "front" one portrays to the outside world, are all sensitive beings; Accordingly, **_Anger_** hurts either oneself or others, whether it be for the moment or for a lifetime.

And of course, one must always remember Jesus's discourse on the Sermon on the Mount, where He addressed and spoke quite succinctly regarding **_"Anger"_** in Matthew 5:21–26, whereby in verse 22, Jesus says in part, "_But I say to you that whoever is **angry** with his brother without a cause, shall be in danger of the judgment...._" Thus, all of us can and should practice better **_Anger_** management lessons, such that the frequency and intensity of one's **_Temper_** remains on a level that Jesus would be proud of!

(Guidance for the Young)

Proverbs 3:31–32*
Do not envy the **_oppressor_**, And choose none of his ways; For the perverse person is an abomination to the LORD, But His secret counsel is with the upright.

(Security in Wisdom)

Proverbs *4:*14*–17
(14)* **Do not enter the path of the wicked, And do not walk in the way of evil.**
(15)   Avoid it, do not travel on it; Turn away from it and pass on.
(16)   For they do not sleep unless they have done evil; And their sleep is taken away unless they make someone fall.
(17)   For they eat the bread of _wickedness_, And drink the wine of **_violence_**.

(The Folly of Indolence)

Proverbs 6:16–19
(16)   These six things the LORD hates, Yes, seven are an abomination to Him;

(17) A proud look, A lying tongue, *Hands that shed innocent blood,*

(18) *A heart that devises wicked plans,* Feet that are swift in running to evil,

(19) A false witness who speaks lies, *And one who sows discord among brethren.*

(Beware of Adultery)

Proverbs *6:*32*–35

(32)* **Whoever commits adultery with a woman lacks understanding; He who does so destroys his own soul.**

(33)* **Wounds and dishonor he will get, And his reproach will not be wiped away.**

(34) For jealousy is a husband's *fury*; Therefore he will not spare in the day of *vengeance*.

(35) He will accept no recompense, Nor will he be appeased though you give many gifts.

(Wise Sayings of Solomon)

Proverbs 10:*6*

Blessings are on the head of the righteous, But *violence* covers the mouth of the *wicked*.

Proverbs 10:11*

The mouth of the righteous is a well of life, But *violence* covers the mouth of the *wicked*.

Proverbs 11:*4*

Riches do not profit in the day of **wrath**, But righteousness delivers from death.

Proverbs 11:23*

The desire of the righteous is only good, But the expectation of the wicked is **wrath**.

Proverbs 11:26
The people will *curse* him who withholds grain, But blessing will be on the head of him who sells it.

Proverbs 12:16
A fool's **wrath** is known at once, But a prudent man covers shame.

Proverbs 13:2
A man shall eat well by the fruit of his mouth, But the soul of the unfaithful feeds on **violence**.

Proverbs 14:16*
A wise man fears and departs from evil, But a fool *rages* and is self-confident.

Proverbs 14:17
A **quick-tempered** man acts foolishly, And a man of *wicked* intentions is hated.

Proverbs *14:*29*
He who is slow to *wrath* has great understanding, But he who is impulsive exalts folly.

Proverbs *14:*31*
He who *oppresses* the poor *reproaches* his Maker, But he who honors Him has mercy on the needy.

Proverbs 14:35
The king's favor is toward a wise servant, But his **wrath** is against him who causes shame.

Proverbs 15:*1*
A soft answer turns away **wrath**, But a *harsh* word stirs up **anger**.

Proverbs 15:18
A **wrathful** man stirs up *strife*, But he who is slow to **anger** allays *contention*.

Proverbs 16:14

As messengers of death is the kings **_wrath_**, But a wise man will appease it.

Proverbs 16:29-30

A **_violent_** man entices his neighbor, And leads him in a way that is not good. He winks his eye to devise perverse things; He purses his lips and brings about evil.

Proverbs 16:*32*

He who is slow to **_anger_** is better than the mighty, And he who rules his spirit than he who takes a city.

Proverbs 17:1

Better is a dry morsel with quietness, _Than a house full of feasting with strife._

Proverbs 17:11

An evil man seeks only _rebellion_; Therefore a _cruel_ messenger will be sent against him.

Proverbs 17:*14*

The beginning of _strife_ is like releasing water; Therefore stop _contention_ before a _quarrel_ starts.

Proverbs 17:26

Also, to punish the righteous is not good, Nor to _strike_ princes for their uprightness.

Proverbs 18:23

The poor man uses entreaties, But the rich answers _roughly_.

Proverbs 19:3

The foolishness of a man twists his way, And his heart _frets_ against the LORD.

Proverbs 19:*11*
The discretion of a man makes him slow to **anger**, And his glory is to overlook a transgression.

Proverbs 19:12*
The king's **wrath** is like the roaring of a lion, But his favor is like dew on the grass.

Proverbs 19:*13*
A foolish son is the ruin of his father, And the *contentions* of a wife are a *continual dripping*.

Proverbs 19:19*
A man of great **wrath** will suffer punishment; For if you rescue him, you will have to do it again.

Proverbs 20:2
The **wrath** of a king is like the roaring of a lion; Whoever provokes him to **anger** sins against his own life.

Proverbs 20:3
It is honorable for a man to stop striving, Since any fool can start a *quarrel*.

Proverbs 20:30
Blows that hurt cleanse away evil, As do stripes the inner depths of the heart.

Proverbs 21: 7
The **violence** of the wicked will destroy them, Because they refuse to do justice.

Proverbs *21:*9*
Better to dwell in a corner of a housetop, Than in a house shared with a *contentious* woman.

Proverbs 21:14
A gift in secret pacifies **anger**, And a bribe behind the back, strong **wrath**.

Proverbs *21:*19*

Better to dwell in the wilderness, Than with a _contentious_ and _angry_ woman.

Proverbs 21:24

A proud and haughty man—"Scoffer" is his name; He acts with _arrogant_ pride.

Proverbs 22:8*

He who sows iniquity will reap sorrow, And the rod of his **_anger_** will fail.

Proverbs 22:16*

He who **_oppresses_** the poor to increase his riches, And he who gives to the rich, will surely come to poverty.

(Sayings of the Wise)

Proverbs *22:*22*–*23*

Do not rob the poor because he is poor, Nor _oppress_ the afflicted at the gate; For the LORD will plead their cause, And plunder the soul of those who plunder them.

Proverbs 22:24–25

Make no friendship with an **_angry_** man, And with a _furious_ man do not go, Lest you learn his ways And set a snare for your soul.

Proverbs 24:1–2

Do not be envious of evil men, Nor desire to be with them; For their heart devises **_violence_**, And their lips talk of _troublemaking_.

Proverbs *24:*17*–*18*

Do not rejoice when your enemy falls, And do not let your heart be glad when he stumbles; Lest the LORD see it, and it displease Him, And He turn away His _wrath_ from him.

Proverbs 24:19–20

Do not *fret* because of evildoers, Nor be envious of the *wicked*; For there will be no prospect for the evil man; The lamp of the *wicked* will be put out.

(Further Sayings of the Wise)

Proverbs *24:*28*–*29*

Do not be a witness against your neighbor without cause, For would you deceive with your lips? *Do not say, "I will do to him just as he has done to me; I will render to the man according to his work."*

(Further Wise Sayings of Solomon)

Proverbs 25:23*

The north wind brings forth rain, And a *backbiting* tongue an **angry** countenance.

Proverbs *25:*24*

It is better to dwell in a corner of a housetop, Than in a house shared with a *contentious* woman.

Proverbs 26:2

Like a flitting sparrow, like a flying swallow, So a *curse* without cause shall not alight.

Proverbs 26:6

He who sends a message by the hand of a fool Cuts off his own feet and drinks **violence**.

Proverbs 26:*17*

He who passes by and meddles in a *quarrel* not his own Is like one who takes a dog by the ears.

Proverbs 26:18–19

Like a madman who throws firebrands, arrows, and death, Is the man who deceives his neighbor, And says, "I was only joking!"

Proverbs 26:20*–21*

Where there is no wood, the fire goes out; And where there is no talebearer, strife ceases. As charcoal is to burning coals, and wood to fire, So is a contentious man to kindle strife.

Proverbs 26:24*–26*

(24)* *He who hates, disguises it with his lips, And lays up deceit within himself;*

(25) When he speaks kindly, do not believe him, For there are seven abominations in his heart;

(26)* *Though his hatred is covered by deceit, His wickedness will be revealed before the assembly.*

Proverbs 26:28*

A lying tongue hates those who are crushed by it, And a flattering mouth works ruin.

Proverbs 27:3

A stone is heavy and sand is weighty, But a fool's **_wrath_** is heavier than both of them.

Proverbs 27:4

Wrath is cruel and **_anger_** a torrent, But who is able to stand before jealousy?

Proverbs 27:*15*–16

A continual dripping on a very rainy day And a *contentious* woman are alike; Whoever restrains her restrains the wind, And grasps oil with his right hand.

Proverbs 27:20*

Hell and Destruction are never full; So the eyes of man are never satisfied.

Proverbs 28:3

A poor man who **_oppresses_** the poor Is like a driving rain which leaves no food.

Proverbs 28:8
One who increases his possessions by usury and _extortion_ Gathers it for him who will pity the poor.

Proverbs 28:15
Like a roaring lion and a charging bear Is a wicked ruler over poor people.

Proverbs 28:16
A ruler who lacks understanding is a great **_oppressor_**, But he who hates covetousness will prolong his days.

Proverbs 28:17
A man burdened with _bloodshed_ will flee into a pit; Let no one help him.

Proverbs 29:8*
Scoffers set a city aflame, But wise men turns away **_wrath_**.

Proverbs 29:9
If a wise man contends with a foolish man, Whether the fool _rages_ or laughs, there is no peace.

Proverbs 29:10
The bloodthirsty hate the blameless, But the upright seek his well-being.

Proverbs 29:11*
_A fool _vents_ all his feelings_, But wise a man holds them back.

Proverbs 29:13
The poor man and the **_oppressor_** have this in common: The LORD gives light to the eyes of both.

Proverbs 29:22
An **_angry_** man stirs up _strife_, And a _furious_ man abounds in transgression.

(The Wisdom of Agur)

Proverbs 30:11–14

(11) There is a generation that _curses_ its father, And does not bless its mother.

(12) There is a generation that is pure in its own eyes, Yet is not washed from its filthiness.

(13) There is a generation—oh, how lofty are their eyes! And their eyelids are lifted up.

(14) *There is a generation whose _teeth are like swords_, And _whose fangs are like knives_, To _devour_ the poor from off the earth, And the needy from among men.*

Proverbs 30:32–33

If you have been foolish in exalting yourself, Or if you have devised evil, put your hand on your mouth. For as the churning of milk produces butter, And wringing the nose produces blood, So the forcing of **wrath** produces *strife*.

CHAPTER 7

ANXIETY, DEPRESSION, GRIEF, BITTERNESS, SORROW

The Bible clearly states that Christians are not to subscribe to the acronym that I affectionately call "*SAW*" and coach about during my one-on-one financial coaching sessions with individuals and couples at the Durham Rescue Mission as part of the biannual Dave Ramsey's Financial Peace University (FPU) sessions; Whereby Christian Concern (C2) ≠ *SAW*, for which the *SAW* acronym represents **S** = *Stress,* **A** = *Anxiety,* and **W** = *Worry.*

Take for example, *Stress* and *Worry*! Again, from Jesus's teaching on the Sermon on the Mount, one finds clear, concise, and unambiguous scriptural teaching in Matthew 6:25–34, whereby Jesus strongly encourages Christians to bring all of life's needs, challenges, and Christian concerns to Father God in prayer, rather than *Worrying* about them and shouldering them during one's Christian walk. Jesus admonishes Christians to avoid all sentiments of *Stress* and/or *Worry* regarding one's physical needs like clothing and food. Jesus reassures Christians that our Heavenly Father will satisfy all our needs, whatever they might be. His guaranteed promise is best reflected in Matthew 6:30, which states: "*Now if God so clothes the grass of the field, which today is, and tomorrow is thrown into the oven, will He not much more clothe you, O you of little faith.*"

And in the area of being **_Anxious_** or exhibiting **_Anxiety_**, Paul unequivocally states in one of my favorite biblical principles contained in Philippians 4:6 and 7: "*Be **anxious** for nothing, but in everything by prayer and supplication, with thanksgiving, let your requests be made known to God; and the peace of God, which surpasses all understanding, will guard your hearts and minds through Christ Jesus.*"

Thus, in closing, I am reminded of four equally and powerful biblical principles and Scripture verses that, from my perspective, address and eliminate all real or imagined elements of "**_SAW_**," namely:

1. 1 Peter 5:7: "*casting all your care upon Him, for He cares for you*";
2. Proverbs 12:25: "***anxiety** in the heart of man causes **depression**, But a good word makes it glad*";
3. Matthew 11:28–30: "*Come to Me all you who labor and are heavy laden, and I will give you rest. Take My yoke upon you and learn from Me, for I am gentle and lowly in heart, and you will find rest for your souls. For My yoke is easy and My burden is light*"; and,
4. Matthew 6:33: "*But seek first the kingdom of God and His Righteousness, and all these things shall be added to you.*"

To God be the GLORY!

(The Peril of Adultery)

Proverbs 5:1–6

(1) My son, pay attention to my wisdom; Lend your ear to my understanding.

(2) That you may preserve discretion, And your lips may keep knowledge.

(3) For the lips of an immoral woman drip honey, And her mouth is smoother than oil;

(4) But in the end she is ***bitter*** as wormwood, Sharp as a two-edged sword.

(5) Her feet go down to death, Her steps lay hold of hell.

(6) Lest you ponder her path of life—her ways are unstable; You do not know them.

(Wise Sayings of Solomon)

Proverbs 10:1*

A wise son makes a glad father, But a foolish son is the ***grief*** of his mother.

Proverbs *10:*22*

The blessing of the LORD makes one rich, And He adds no *sorrow* with it.

Proverbs 12:25*

Anxiety in the heart of man causes ***depression***, But a good word makes it glad.

Proverbs 14:10

The heart knows its own ***bitterness***, And a stranger does not share its joy.

Proverbs 14:13

Even in laughter the heart may ***sorrow***, And the end of mirth may be ***grief***.

Proverbs 14:30

A sound heart is life to the body, *But envy is **rottenness** to the bones*.

Proverbs 15:13

A merry heart makes a cheerful countenance, But by ***sorrow*** of the heart the spirit is broken.

Proverbs 17:21

He who begets a scoffer does so to his ***sorrow***, And the father of a fool has no joy.

Proverbs 17:*25*

A foolish son is a *grief* to his father, And ***bitterness*** to her who bore him.

Proverbs 19:3

The foolishness of a man twists his way, And his heart *frets* against the LORD.

Proverbs 19:19*

A man of great wrath will *suffer punishment*; For if you rescue him, you will have to do it again.

Proverbs 20:17

Bread gained by deceit is sweet to a man, *But afterward his mouth will be filled with gravel.*

Proverbs 21:15*

It is a joy for the just to do justice, *But destruction will come to the workers of iniquity.*

Proverbs 22:8*

He who sows iniquity will reap ***sorrow***, And the rod of his anger will fail.

(Use of Wine)

Proverbs 23:29–35

(29) Who has *woe*? Who has ***sorrow***? Who has *contentions*? Who has *complaints*? Who has *wounds without cause*? Who has redness of eyes?

(30) Those who linger long at the wine, Those who go in search of mixed wine.

(31) Do not look on the wine when it is red, When it sparkles in the cup, When it swirls around smoothly;

(32) At the last it *bites* like a serpent, And *stings* like a viper.

(33) Your eyes will see strange things, And your heart will utter perverse things.

(34)   Yes, you will be like one who lies down in the midst of the sea, Or like one who lies at the top of the mast, saying:

(35)   *"They have struck me, but I was not hurt; They have beaten me, but I did not feel it.* When shall I awake, that I may seek another drink?"

Proverbs 24:19–20

Do not *fret* because of evildoers, Nor be envious of the wicked; For there will be no prospect for the evil man; The lamp of the wicked will be put out.

Proverbs 25:19

Confidence in an unfaithful man in time of trouble Is like a *bad tooth* and a *foot out of joint.*

Proverbs 25:20

Like one who takes away a garment in cold weather, And like vinegar on soda, Is one who sings songs to a heavy heart.

Proverbs 27:7

A satisfied soul loathes the honeycomb, But to a hungry soul every **bitter** thing is sweet.

Proverbs 27:15*–16

A continual dripping on a very rainy day And a contentious woman are alike; Whoever restrains her restrains the wind, And grasps oil with his right hand.

Proverbs 29:2

When the righteous are in authority, the people rejoice; *But when a wicked man rules, the people groan.*

(The Words King Lemuel's Mother Taught Him)

Proverbs 31:1–3 and 4–9

(1)   The words of King Lemuel, the utterance which his mother taught him:

(2) What, my son? And what, son of my womb? And what, son of my vows?

(3) Do not give your strength to women, Nor your ways to that which destroys kings.

(4) It is not for kings, O Lemuel, It is not for kings to drink wine, Nor for princes intoxicating drink;

(5) Lest they drink and forget the law, And pervert the justice of all the afflicted.

(6) Give strong drink to him who is perishing, And wine to those who are ***bitter*** of heart.

(7) Let him drink and forget his poverty, And remember his misery no more.

(8) Open your mouth for the speechless, In the cause of all who are appointed to die.

(9) Open your mouth, judge righteously, And plead the cause of the poor and needy.

CHAPTER 8

ATONEMENT, FORGIVENESS, REPENTANCE

W hy oh why is it so difficult for individuals to **_Forgive_** one another, especially those who are "in Christ"? One would think—given how Father God **_Forgives_** His earthly children when they come to Him with remorse, deep repentance, and sorrow—that His Word is very, very clear; Whereby He will **_Forgive_** His children. But when it comes to our individual capabilities to practice such universal **_Forgiveness_**, we have so much trouble **_Forgiving_** others irrespective of how deeply one's hurt may be that has been caused by someone else, especially those we know and love so deeply.

Father God, through Jesus Christ and especially throughout the Gospels and the New Testament, admonishes one and all to practice the Godly and biblical principle and truth of **_Forgiveness_**! Whom among us has not been convicted of sin, yet we come so intuitively as well as instinctively to the throne of prayer, knowing what Father God's Word says in biblical passages like 1 John 1:9, which states: "_If we confess our sins, He is faithful and just to **forgive** us our sins and to cleanse us from all unrighteousness._" Or how about Ephesians 1:7, which states: "_In Him we have redemption through His blood, the **forgiveness** of sins, according to the_ *riches of His grace.*" Or Colossians 1:14, which states: "*in whom we have redemption through His blood, the forgiveness of sins.*" And, of course, there are numerous others whereby Father God's Words are explicitly clear about His ongoing and consistent will to **Forgive** and forget one's sins and transgressions!

Given Father God's loving, kind, and **Forgiving** spirit and nature, it's amazing how God's children, especially those who are of the household of faith, frequently have trouble practicing and living out what Jesus so unequivocally spoke about in the "*Parable of the Unforgiving Servant*" in Matthew 18:21–35 regarding one's ongoing spiritual requirement to practice without hesitation the biblical standard of constant **Forgiveness**! From verses 21 and 22, Jesus reminds Peter of the following: "*Then Peter came to Him and said, 'Lord, how often shall my brother sin against me, and I forgive him? Up to seven times?' Then Jesus said to him, 'I do not say to you, up to seven times, but up to seventy times seven*'"!

Why is it so very difficult and challenging for God's people to wholeheartedly practice the biblical principle of **Forgiveness**, especially when Father God's Word is so, so clear and indisputable of the importance of practicing a lifetime of **Forgiveness**? Maybe it's because Father God's people are equally challenged on the flip side of **Forgiveness**, and that being the biblical principle of "*Love.*" It seems quite natural to me that as Father God's people have challenges in "*Loving*" like Father God "*Loves*" us, then one would be equally challenged in exhibiting and practicing the ongoing biblical principle of **Forgiveness**!

I can share a real-life situation regarding **Forgiveness**, or should I more accurately say, a lack thereof. One of my close friends, or as I like to call them, one of my "Inner circle of friends," has failed in the past several years to **Forgive** me for something that I do not even know, as to this very day, what I did wrong! During the past several years, I have reached out to him during his birthday, Christmas, as well as written overtures on my part via email, voicemails, cards, etc., but to this day, he has failed to explain to me what I have done that has him angry with me, yet alone, his constant failure to **Forgive** me even though I have offered up numerous apologies while seeking his ***Forgiveness*** for whatever personal offense that I might have unknowingly committed against him and/or his family. What makes this lack of ***Forgiveness*** so very painful is the fact that this friendship goes back to the late 1970s, when I personally recruited him from USC to join the then Big Eight public accounting firm of Arthur Andersen & Co. I have been there through career challenges, relationship challenges, parents homegoings, child-rearing, and public support of professional endeavors, marriages, as well as his serving as the "Godfather" of my eldest daughter. I have tried, for the life of me, over these past few years to understand why he has failed to accept my apologies, but more importantly, why he has failed to practice Father God's principle of ongoing ***Forgiveness***. While I keep praying, seeking, and hoping that our relationship might be restored, I can firmly state that I continue to ***Forgive*** him for his failure and/or reluctance to practice and/or extend the biblical principle of ***Forgiveness*** toward me.

As I continue to study, meditate, and marinate on the biblical concept and importance of ***Forgiveness***, I am also reminded of Jesus's closing Words in the aforementioned parable, in verse 35 of Matthew 18, which states with a promise the following: *"So my Heavenly Father also will do to you if each of you, from his heart, does not **forgive** his brother his trespasses."* Thus, it behooves one and all, just as God's Word is very clear, to "<u>Love</u>" one another; we are equally commanded to ***Forgive*** one another just like our Heavenly Father "<u>Loves</u>" and ***Forgives*** each one of us!

(Guidance for the Young)

Proverbs *3:*27*-*28*
Do not withhold good from those to whom it is due, When it is in the power of your hand to do so. Do not say to your neighbor, "Go, and come back, And tomorrow I will give it," *When you have it with you.*

(Wise Sayings of Solomon)

Proverbs *16:*6*

In mercy and truth _Atonement_ is provided for iniquity; And by the fear of the LORD one departs from evil.

Proverbs *17:*9*

He who covers a transgression seeks love, **But he who repeats a matter separates friends.**

Proverbs 19:*11*

The discretion of a man makes him slow to anger, And his glory is to <u>overlook a transgression</u>.

Proverbs 20:9

Who can say, *"I have made my heart clean, <u>I am pure from my sin</u>"*?

Proverbs 20:22

Do not say, *"I will recompense evil";* <u>*Wait for the LORD, and He will save you*</u>.

Proverbs 22:5

Thorns and snares are in the way of the perverse; *He who guards his soul will be far from them.*

Proverbs 23:17*–18

Do not let your heart envy sinners, *But be zealous for the fear of the LORD all the day; For surely there is a hereafter, And your hope will not be cut off.*

Proverbs 24:11–12

Deliver *those who are drawn toward death, And hold back those stumbling to the slaughter.* If you say, "Surely we did not know this," *Does not He who weighs the hearts consider it? He who keeps your soul, does He not know it? And will He not render to each man according to his deeds?*

(Further Sayings of the Wise)

Proverbs *24:*28*–29*

Do not be a witness against your neighbor without cause, **For would you deceive with your lips?** Do not say, *"I will do to him just as he has done to me; I will render to the man according to his work."*

(Further Wise Sayings of Solomon)

Proverbs 25:8–10

(8) *Do not go hastily to court*; For what will you do in the end, When your neighbor has put you to shame?

(9) *Debate your case with your neighbor, And do not disclose the secret to another;*

(10) Lest he who hears it expose your shame, And your reputation be ruined.

Proverbs *25:*21*–*22*

If your enemy is hungry, give him bread to eat; And if he is thirsty, give him water to drink; For so you will heap coals of fire on his head, And the LORD will reward you.

Proverbs *28:*13*

He who covers his sins will not prosper, *But whoever <u>confesses</u> and <u>forsakes</u> them will have mercy.*

Proverbs 28:18*

Whoever walks blamelessly will be <u>saved</u>, But he who is perverse in his ways will suddenly fall.

Proverbs 29:13*

The poor man and the oppressor have this in common: *The LORD <u>gives light</u> to the eyes of both.*

Proverbs 29:26

Many seek the ruler's favor, *But <u>justice for man</u> comes from the LORD.*

CHAPTER 9

BORROWING, INDEBTEDNESS, LENDING, PLEDGE, SURETY

This is a tough Chapter Theme for me to write about personally because **_Debt_** and **_Borrowing_** **money** are foreign concepts for me, except for the typical home mortgage, which I have been blessed not to have given that, when I sold my stupid egocentric much-too-large home in 2005, Father God knocked some biblical and common sense into my head and instructed me to pay "all cash" for my much-downsized last North Carolina home. And the other primary **_Debt_** challenge for most people is their **car loan**. Upon my return in March 1999 from my three-year expat assignment in Brussels, Belgium, the Holy Spirit instructed me to pay "all cash" for a new 1999 Jeep Grand Cherokee Limited edition. Father God has super blessed me to still be driving that Jeep some twenty-plus years later. I affectionately call my Jeep my "donkey." I call my Jeep my donkey because when Jesus rode into Jerusalem on Palm Sunday, He rode in on a "donkey". And if a tired old donkey was good enough for the King of Kings and Lord of Lords, then this humble servant is blessed to ride around in a vintage twenty-plus-year old "donkey"!

But let me address this Chapter Theme's topic of "**_Borrowing_** and **_Indebtedness_**" from the lenses of most of my financial mentees' perspective. Without a doubt, most—if not all—of my financial mentees' struggle with "***Borrowing*** and ***Indebtedness***," whether it be (1) a **mortgage/excessive mortgage**; (2) one or more **car loans**; (3) **credit card debts/obligations**; and /or (4) from the perspective of millenials and/or parents of millenials—**student loan obligations**.

It's safe to assume that we all know people who are struggling with one or more of the above categories of ***Indebtedness***. What causes individuals to become "***a servant to the lender***" (Proverbs 22:7) are varied and numerous. But with that said, here are a few symptoms from my experience as a financial coach, and this short list is not by any degree all inclusive. But here are a few observations:

(1) Living beyond one's means (i.e., trying to keep up with the Jones's);

(2) Worshiping "Things or Stuff";

(3) Not devising and working from a periodic budget and/or financial plan;

(4) Not having an adequate "Emergency fund" of three to six months' expenses;

(5) Not believing that "Headwinds" are a constant fact of life;

(6) Not having an "Accountability Partner" to hold one accountable for being a responsible money manager; and last but definitely not least,

(7) Loving money more than Loving Father God!

While the above list is not all inclusive, it does capture some of the life expenses and experiences that I have observed regarding individuals and money. Needless to say, I could go on and on regarding this seductive topic, but suffice it to say, in closing, that from my perspective, this teachable moment and biblical principle illuminating from Proverbs 22:7 continues to stand the test of time in that: "*The rich rules over the poor, And the **borrower** is servant to the **lender**!*"

Thus, in conclusion, and as the world famous financial coach Dave Ramsey would say, "Buyer Beware"!

(Guidance for the Young)

Proverbs *3:*27*–28*
Do not withhold good from those to whom it is due, When it is in the power of your hand to do so. Do not say to your neighbor, "Go, and come back, And tomorrow I will give it," When you have it with you.

(The Folly of Suretyship)

Proverbs 6:1–5
(1) My son, if you become **surety** for your friend, If you have shaken hands in **pledge** for a stranger,
(2) You are *snared* by the words of your mouth; You are taken by the words of your mouth.
(3) So do this, my son, and *deliver yourself*; For you have come into the hand of your friend: *Go and humble yourself*; *Plead with your friend.*
(4) *Give no sleep to your eyes, Nor slumber to your eyelids.*
(5) *Deliver yourself like a gazelle from the hand of the hunter, And like a bird from the hand of the fowler.*

(Wise Sayings of Solomon

Proverbs 11:15*
He who is a **surety** for a stranger will suffer, But one who hates being **surety** is secure.

Proverbs 17:18
A man devoid of understanding shakes hands in a **pledge**, And becomes **surety** for his friend.

Proverbs *19:*17*

He who has pity on the poor _lends to the LORD_**, And** _He will pay back_ **what he has** _given_**.**

Proverbs 20:16

Take the garment of one who is **_surety_** for a stranger, And hold it as a **_pledge_** when it is for a seductress.

Proverbs *22:*7*

The rich rules over the poor, And the _borrower_ _is servant to the_ _lender__._

(Sayings of the Wise)

Proverbs 22:26*–27*

Do not be one of those who shakes hands in a **_pledge_**, One of those who is **_surety_** for **_debts_**; _If you have nothing with which to pay_, Why should he take away your bed from under you?

(Further Wise Sayings of Solomon)

Proverbs 27:13

Take the garment of him who is **_surety_** for a stranger, And hold it in **_pledge_** when he is **_surety_** for a seductress.

Proverbs 28:8

One who increases his possessions by _usury_ and _extortion_ Gathers it for him who will pity the poor.

CHAPTER 10

BRIBES, GIFTS

This Chapter Narrative will be very short in nature because, as to the best of my knowledge and recall, I have never entertained a "*Bribe*" either by giving or receiving one. Additionally, to the best of my knowledge and recall, I have never participated in giving and/or receiving any type of "**special *Gift***" to influence the outcome of a specific situation or personal favor. From my perspective, and not to pass judgment, as "*all have sinned and fallen short of the glory of God*" (Romans 3:23), but I am hard-pressed to understand the "why" in such behavioral practices that are so prevalent in today's society.

The following two Proverbs verses are among several that admonish one and all not to entertain, engage, and/or knowingly participate in any type of "*Bribes*" and/or "**special *Gifts*.**" Proverbs 15:27: "*He who is greedy for gain troubles his own house, But he who hates **bribes** will live.*" Proverbs 21:14: "*A **gift** in secret pacifies anger, And a **bribe** behind the back, strong wrath.*"

One question that quite naturally might arise in any person's life who knowingly or inadvertently has knowledge of or becomes aware of a "*Bribe*" or "**special *Gift***" is what should that person do? And before I reply as to what I would do in such a situation, please let me "take off all of my self-righteous attire" and state the following: From my perspective, any form or type of "**_Bribe_**" or "**special _Gift_**" made to influence a person for a specific or desired outcome is tantamount to stealing, lying, and/or cheating. Such behavioral traits challenge me personally as I try, more times than not, to "_treat people the way that I would like to be treated_" (Matthew 7:12). Better yet, I will ask myself the following—"WWJD" (i.e. "What Would Jesus Do). And that, my friend, and my Lord and Savior, should lead me to do what's right and not who's right!

(Beware of Adultery)

Proverbs *6:*32*–35
(32)* **Whoever commits adultery with a woman lacks understanding; He who does so destroys his own soul.**
(33)* **Wounds and dishonor he will get, And his reproach will not be wiped away.**
(34) For jealousy is a husband's fury; Therefore he will not spare in the day of vengeance.
(35) He will accept no recompense, Nor will he be appeased though you give many **_gifts_**.

(Wise Sayings of Solomon)

Proverbs 15:*27*
He who is greedy for gain troubles his own house, But he who hates **_bribes_** will live.

Proverbs 17:8
A **_present_** is a precious stone in the eyes of its possessor; Wherever he turns, he _prospers_.

Proverbs 17:23
A wicked man accepts a **_bribe_** behind the back To pervert the ways of justice.

Proverbs 18:16
A man's **_gift_** _makes room for him_, And brings him before great men.

Proverbs 19:6*
Many entreat the favor of the nobility, And every man is a friend to one who gives **_gifts_**.

Proverbs 21:14
A **_gift_** in secret pacifies anger, And a **_bribe_** behind the back, strong wrath.

Proverbs 21:27
The _sacrifice_ of the wicked is an abomination; _How much more when he brings it with wicked intent!_

Proverbs 22:16*
He who oppresses the poor to increase his riches, _And he who gives to the rich_, will surely come to poverty.

(Sayings of the Wise)

Proverbs 23:1–3
(1)   When you sit down to eat with a ruler, _Consider carefully what is before you;_
(2)   And put a knife to your throat _If you are a man given to appetite._
(3)   _Do not desire his delicacies, For they are deceptive food._

(Further Wise Sayings of Solomon)

Proverbs 25:14
Whoever falsely boasts of giving Is like clouds and wind without rain.

Proverbs 28:8
One who increases his possessions by _usury_ and _extortion_ Gathers it for him who will pity the poor.

Proverbs 28:21

To show partiality is not good, *Because for a* <u>*piece of bread*</u> *a man will transgress.*

Proverbs 29:4

The king establishes the land by justice, But he who receives **_bribes_** overthrows it.

CHAPTER 11

CHARACTER, REPUTATION

As one reviews this Chapter Theme entitled "*Character/Reputation*," one will note that, unlike most if not all the other Chapter Themes contained in this reference manual, one will generally note that the Chapter Theme is embedded with that Chapter's Proverbs verses. However, for this Chapter, one will be hard-pressed to find such a direct correlation within this Chapter's Proverbs verses. Instead, one will glean from this Chapter's Proverbs verses that the themes of "*Character/Reputation*" is clearly evident from each Proverbs verses. For example, Proverbs 22:1 states the following: "A **good name** *is to be chosen rather than great riches, Loving favor rather than silver and gold.*" Clearly called out in this Proverbs verse is how "a **good name**" signifies one with a good **Reputation**, which is a derivative or fruit of one who possesses good **Character**!

Proverbs 22:1 serves as an excellent proxy for defining "*Character/Reputation*," which is generally defined as one possessing strong moral fiber (i.e., individuals who are rooted with the personal values of integrity and ethics). An individual's **Character** is not a "one size fits all" definition; instead, one's **Character** is generally comprised of the sum of various components, including but not limited to one's actions, choices, desires, disposition, intentions, thoughts, and moral values, to name a few.

Take for example, the Old Testament noble **Character** role models, such as Ruth, Daniel, Job, Joseph, and King David. Yes, even King David who had several moral failures during his reign as Israel's King, namely adultery, murder, and pride. But Father God still found great favor with King David, as Father God has referenced and said, "*I have found David, the son of Jesse, a man after My own heart, who will do all My will!*" (Acts 13:22).

Thus, one must acknowledge and recognize that "*for all have sinned and fall short of the glory of God, being justified freely by His grace through the redemption that is in Christ Jesus*" (Romans 3:23–24). However, one must never lose sight that one's **Character** can and will assist one in navigating the numerous challenges and storms that one faces in life, including assisting one to overcome the challenges of sin (i.e. Proverbs 10:9a), which states:, "*He who walks with integrity walks securely.*"

Finally, Scripture unequivocally states that: "*For Whom He foreknew, He also predestined to be conformed to the image of His Son, that He might be the firstborn among many brethren*" (Romans 8:29). Accordingly, it is Father God's stated purpose to develop Christlike **Character** within those who are "in Christ." Such **Character** manifests itself from numerous venues and portals, such as:

1. The work of the Holy Spirit as part of an individual's sanctification process;
2. Turning away from one's sin nature by "*walking in the Spirit*" (Galatians 5:16); thereby adopting, embracing, and living out all nine elements of "*the fruit of the Spirit*," namely, "*love, joy, peace, longsuffering, kindness, goodness, faithfulness, gentleness and self-control*" (Galatians 5:22 and 23);
3. "*...glory in tribulations, knowing that tribulations produces perseverance, and perseverance **character**; and **character**, hope*" (Romans 5:3 and 4); and finally,
4. "*...add to your faith virtue, to virtue knowledge, to knowledge self-control, to self-control perseverance, to perseverance godliness, to*

godliness brotherly kindness, and to brotherly kindness love"
(2 Peter 1:5–7).

(The Value of Wisdom)

Proverbs *2:1*–*9* and *10*–*11*

(1)* My son, if you receive my words, And treasure my commands within you,

(2)* **So that you incline your ear to wisdom, And apply your heart to understanding;**

(3)* Yes, if you cry out for discernment, And lift up your voice for **understanding,**

(4) If you seek her as silver, And search for her as for hidden treasures;

(5)* **Then you will understand the fear of the LORD, And find the knowledge of God.**

(6)* **For the LORD gives wisdom; From His mouth come knowledge and understanding;**

(7)* **He stores up** *sound wisdom* **for the** *upright*; **He is a shield to those who** *walk uprightly*;

(8)* **He guards the paths of justice, And preserves the way of His saints.**

(9)* **Then you will understand righteousness and justice, Equity and every good path.**

(10)* **When wisdom enters your heart, And knowledge is pleasant to your soul,**

(11)* **Discretion will preserve you; Understanding will keep you,**

(Guidance for the Young)

Proverbs *3:*3*–4*

Let not mercy and truth forsake you; Bind them around your neck, Write them on the tablet of your heart, And so find *favor* and *high esteem* In the sight of God and man.

(Security in Wisdom)

Proverbs *4:*20*–*27*

(20)* **My son, give attention to my words; Incline your ear to my sayings.**

(21)* **Do not let them depart from your eyes; Keep them in the midst of your heart;**

(22)* **For they are life to those who find them, And health to all their flesh.**

(23)* ***Keep your heart with all diligence, For out of it spring the issues of life.***

(24)* **Put away from you a deceitful mouth, And put perverse lips far from you.**

(25) Let your eyes look straight ahead, And your eyelids look right before you.

(26)* **Ponder the path of your feet, And let all your ways be established.**

(27)* **Do not turn to the right or the left; Remove your foot from evil.**

(The Excellence of Wisdom)

Proverbs *8:12*–21*

(12)* *"I, wisdom, dwell with prudence, And find out knowledge and discretion.*

(13) *The fear of the LORD is to hate evil; Pride and arrogance and the evil way And the perverse mouth I hate.*

(14) *Counsel is mine, and sound wisdom; I am understanding, I have strength.*

(15) *By me kings reign, And rulers decree justice.*

(16) *By me princes rule, and nobles, All the judges of the earth.*

(17)* ***I love those who love me, And those who seek me diligently will find me.***

(18) *Riches and honor are with me, Enduring riches and righteousness.*

(19) *My fruit is better than gold, yes, than fine gold, And my revenue than choice silver.*

(20)* *I traverse the way of righteousness, In the midst of the paths of justice,*
(21)* *That I may cause those who love me to inherit wealth, That I may fill their treasuries.*

(Wise Sayings of Solomon)

Proverbs 10:*6*

Blessings are on the head of the righteous, But violence covers the mouth of the wicked.

Proverbs 10:7

The memory of the righteous is blessed, But the name of the wicked will rot.

Proverbs 10:9*

He who walks with integrity walks securely, But he who perverts his ways will become known.

Proverbs 10:19*

In the multitude of words sin is not lacking, *But he who restrains his lips is wise.*

Proverbs *10:*20*

The tongue of the righteous is choice silver; The heart of the wicked is worth little.

Proverbs *10:*21*

The lips of the righteous feed many, But fools die for lack of wisdom.

Proverbs 10:28

The hope of the righteous will be gladness, But the expectation of the wicked will perish.

Proverbs 11:3

The integrity of the upright will guide them, But the perversity of the unfaithful will destroy them.

Proverbs 11:10
When it goes well with the righteous, the city rejoices; And when the wicked perish, there is jubilation.

Proverbs 11:20
Those who are of a perverse heart are an abomination to the LORD, *But the blameless in their ways are His delight.*

Proverbs 12:3
A man is not established by wickedness, *But the root of the righteous cannot be moved.*

Proverbs 12:5*
The thoughts of the righteous are right, But the counsels of the wicked are deceitful.

Proverbs 12:7*
The wicked are overthrown and are no more, *But the house of the righteous will stand.*

Proverbs 12:12*
The wicked covet the catch of the evil men, *But the root of the righteous yields fruit.*

Proverbs 13:17
A wicked messenger falls into trouble, *But a faithful ambassador brings health.*

Proverbs *13:*22*
A good man leaves an inheritance to his children's children, But the wealth of the sinner is stored up for the righteous.

Proverbs 14:35
The king's favor is toward a wise servant, But his wrath is against him who causes shame.

Proverbs 16:10
Divination is on the lips of the king; His mouth must not transgress in judgment.

Proverbs 17:*3*
The refining pot is for silver and the furnace for gold, *But the LORD tests the hearts.*

Proverbs 20:7*
The righteous man walks in his integrity; His children are blessed after him.

Proverbs 20:8
A king who sits on the throne of judgment Scatters all evil with his eyes.

Proverbs 20:11*
Even a child is known by his deeds, Whether what he does is pure and right.

Proverbs 20:28
Mercy and truth preserve the king, And by lovingkindness he upholds his throne.

Proverbs 22:*1*
A good name is to be chosen rather than great riches, Loving favor rather than silver and gold.

Proverbs *22:*6*
Train up a child in the way he should go, And when he is old he will not depart from it.

(Sayings of the Wise)

Proverbs 22:29*
Do you see a man who excels in his work? He will stand before kings; He will not stand before unknown men.

Proverbs *24:*10*

If you faint in the day of adversity, Your strength is small.

(Further Wise Sayings of Solomon)

Proverbs 25:2

It is the glory of God to conceal a matter, *But the glory of kings is to search out a matter.*

Proverbs 25:5

Take away the wicked from before the king, *And his throne will be established in righteousness.*

Proverbs 25:8–10

(8) Do not go hastily to court; For what will you do in the end, When your neighbor has put you to shame?

(9) Debate your case with your neighbor, And do not disclose the secret to another;

(10) Lest he who hears it expose your shame, And your **reputation** be ruined.

Proverbs *27:*19*

As in water face reflects face, *So a man's heart reveals the man.*

Proverbs 27:21

The refining pot is for silver and the furnace for gold, ***And a man is valued by what others say of him.***

Proverbs 28:1*

The wicked flee when no one purses, *But the righteous are bold as a lion.*

Proverbs 28:2

Because of the transgression of a land, many are its princes; *But by a man of understanding and knowledge Right will be prolonged.*

Proverbs 28:11*

The rich man is wise in his own eyes, *But the poor who has understanding searches him out.*

Proverbs 28:20

A faithful man will abound with blessings, But he who hastens to be rich will not go unpunished.

Proverbs 29:14

The king who judges the poor with truth, His throne will be established forever.

(The Virtuous Wife)

Proverbs *31:*10*–*12*

(10)* **Who can find a _virtuous wife_? For her worth is far above rubies.**

(11)* **The heart of her husband safely trusts her; So he will have no lack of gain.**

(12)* ***She does him good and not evil All the days of her life.***

CHAPTER 12

CONDEMNATION, DAMNATION, DESTRUCTION, OVERTHROW

As I read, reread, and meditated on the various Proverbs verses contained in this Chapter Theme, one major takeaway that I've gleaned is Father God Does Not Like Ugly! And what I mean by "ugly" jumps off the page as one reads, studies, and meditates each keyword in a Proverbs verse for this Chapter Theme! Take for example, Proverbs 10:29: "*The way of the Lord is strength for the upright, But, **destruction** will come to the workers of iniquity.*" So, if God's Word is truth, and it is, why would anyone ever try and pursue iniquity on another person, given the fact that the consequences of such action(s) will lead to **Destruction**? Take a closer look at the second part of this verse: "*But, **destruction** will come to the workers of iniquity*"! There is no maybe contained in this verse, but a definite "will"! Why, in heavens name, would I run that risk and try and put Father God to such a test? It's a losing proposition, plain and simple!

Let's ponder another verse, Proverbs 13:20: "*He who walks with wise men will be wise, But the companion of fools will be **destroyed**.*" So, let me attempt to break this verse into its two segments:

(a) When one "*walks with wise men*," one, not may, not could, but "*will be wise*"! What an awesome promise that Father God will give one who chooses/elects to hang around wise people.

(b) However, if one chooses or elects to hang around with "fools," then God's Word states unambiguously that one, not may, not could, but "will" be **Destroyed**!

Given that Father God gives us free will and free choice, which one do you choose? Would your choice be wisdom and the way of the Lord? Or would you choose the path of the ill-advised that leads to **Condemnation**, **Damnation**, **Destruction**, and/or being **Overthrown**? From my perspective, this is an easy choice: "Father God Does Not Like Ugly, so let this poor man from Pasadena, CA., choose–'Wisdom!'"

(The Call of Wisdom)

Proverbs *1:*20*–33

(20)* **Wisdom calls aloud outside; She raises her voice in the open squares**.

(21) She cries out in the chief concourses, At the openings of the gates in the city She speaks her words:

(22) "How long, you simple ones, will you love simplicity? For scorners delight in their scorning, And fools hate knowledge.

(23) Turn at my rebuke; Surely I will pour out my spirit on you; I will make my words known to you.

(24) Because I have called and you refused, I have stretched out my hand and no one regarded,

(25) Because you disdained all my counsel, And would have none of my rebuke,

(26) I also will laugh at your *calamity*; I will mock when your *terror* comes,

(27) *When your terror comes like a storm, And your **destruction** comes like a whirlwind, When distress and anguish come upon you.*

(28) "Then they will call on me, but I will not answer; They will seek me diligently, but they will not find me.

(29) Because they hated knowledge And did not choose the fear of the LORD,

(30) They would have none of my counsel And despised my every rebuke.

(31) *Therefore they shall eat the fruit of their own way, And be filled to the full with their own fancies.*

(32) *For the turning away of the simple will slay them, And the complacency of fools will **destroy** them;*

(33) But whoever listens to me will dwell safely, And will be secure, without fear of evil."

(The Value of Wisdom)

Proverbs *2:*20*–22

(20)* **So you may walk in the way of goodness, And keep to the paths of righteousness.**

(21)* **For the upright will dwell in the land, And the blameless will remain in it;**

(22) But the wicked will be *cut off* from the earth, And the unfaithful will be *uprooted* from it.

(The Peril of Adultery)

Proverbs *5:*21*–*23*

(21)* **For the ways of man are before the eyes of the LORD, And He ponders all his paths.**

(22)* **His own iniquities *entrap* the wicked man, And he is *caught* in the *cords* of his sin.**

(23)* **He shall *die* for lack of instruction, And in the greatness of his folly he shall *go astray*.**

(The Wicked Man)

Proverbs 6:12–15

(12) A *worthless* person, a wicked man, Walks with a perverse mouth;

(13) He winks with his eyes, He shuffles his feet, He points with his fingers;

(14) Perversity is in his heart, He devises evil continually, He sows discord.

(15) Therefore his *calamity* shall come suddenly; Suddenly he shall be *broken* without remedy.

(Beware of Adultery)

Proverbs *6:*32*–35

(32)* **Whoever commits adultery with a woman lacks understanding; He who does so *destroys* his own soul.**

(33)* ***Wounds* and dishonor he will get, And his reproach will not be wiped away.**

(34) For jealousy is a husband's fury; Therefore he will not spare in the day of *vengeance.*

(35) He will accept no recompense, Nor will he be appeased though you give many gifts.

(The Way of Folly)

Proverbs 9:13–18*

(13) A foolish woman is clamorous; She is simple, and knows nothing.

(14) For she sits at the door of her house, On a seat by the highest places of the city,

(15) To call to those who pass by, Who go straight on their way:

(16) "Whoever is simple, let him turn in here"; And as for him who lacks understanding, she says to him,

(17) "Stolen water is sweet, And bread eaten in secret is pleasant."

(18)* But he does not know that the *dead* are there, That her guests are in the **_depths of hell_**.

(Wise Sayings of Solomon)

Proverbs 10:14*
Wise people store up knowledge, But the mouth of the foolish is near **_destruction_**.

Proverbs 10:15
The rich man's wealth is his strong city; The **_destruction_** of the poor is their poverty.

Proverbs *10:*29*
The way of the LORD is strength for the upright, But _destruction_ will come to the workers of iniquity.

Proverbs 11:3
The integrity of the upright will guide them, But the perversity of the unfaithful will **_destroy_** them.

Proverbs 11:4
Riches do not profit in the day of wrath, But righteousness delivers from *death*.

Proverbs 11:*9*
The hypocrite with his mouth **_destroys_** his neighbor, But through knowledge the righteous will be delivered.

Proverbs 11:11
By the blessing of the upright the city is exalted, But it is **_overthrown_** by the mouth of the wicked.

Proverbs 12:2*
A good man obtains favor from the LORD, But a man of wicked intentions He will **_condemn_**.

Proverbs 12:7*

The wicked are **_overthrown_** and are no more, But the house of the righteous will stand.

Proverbs 12:8*

A man will be commended according to his wisdom, But he who is of a perverse heart will be *despised*.

Proverbs 13:*3*

He who guards his mouth preserves his life, But he who opens wide his lips shall have **_destruction_**.

Proverbs 13:*6*

Righteousness guards him whose way is blameless, But wickedness **_overthrows_** the sinner.

Proverbs 13:*13*

He who despises the word will be **_destroyed_**, But he who fears the commandment will be rewarded.

Proverbs 13:17

A wicked messenger *falls into trouble*, But a faithful ambassador brings health.

Proverbs *13:*20*

He who walks with wise men will be wise, But the companion of fools will be _destroyed_.

Proverbs 14:11*

The house of the wicked will be **_overthrown_**, But the tent of the upright will flourish.

Proverbs 15:11

Hell and **_Destruction_** are before the LORD; So how much more the hearts of the sons of men.

Proverbs 22:14

The mouth of an immoral woman is a *deep pit*; He who is abhorred by the LORD *will fall there.*

(Sayings of the Wise)

Proverbs *22:*22*–*23*

Do not rob the poor because he is poor, Nor oppress the afflicted at the gate; For the LORD will plead their cause, And <u>plunder</u> the soul of those who <u>plunder</u> them.

Proverbs *23:*13*–*14*

Do not withhold correction from a child, For if you beat him with a rod, he will not *die*. You shall beat him with a rod, And deliver his soul from *hell*.

Proverbs 24:11–12

Deliver those who are drawn toward *death*, And hold back those stumbling to the *slaughter*. If you say, "Surely we did not know this," Does not He who weighs the hearts consider it? He who keeps your soul, does He not know it? *And will He not render to each man according to his deeds?*

Proverbs *24:15–*16*

Do not lie in wait, O wicked man, against the dwelling of the righteous; Do not *plunder* his resting place; **For a righteous man may *fall* seven times And rise again, *But the wicked shall fall by calamity.***

Proverbs *24:*17*–*18*

Do not rejoice when your enemy *falls*, And do not let your heart be glad when he *stumbles*; Lest the LORD see it, and it displease Him, And He turn away His *wrath* from him.

Proverbs 24:19–20

Do not fret because of evildoers, Nor be envious of the wicked; For there will be no prospect for the evil man; *The lamp of the wicked will be put out.*

(Further Wise Sayings of Solomon)

Proverbs 25:8–10

(8) Do not go hastily to court; For what will you do in the end, When your neighbor has put you to shame?

(9) Debate your case with your neighbor, And do not disclose the secret to another;

(10) Lest he who hears it expose your shame, And your reputation be *ruined.*

Proverbs 26:28*

A lying tongue hates those who are crushed by it, And a flattering mouth works *ruin.*

Proverbs 27:12*

A prudent man foresees evil and hides himself; The simple pass on and are *punished.*

Proverbs 27:20*

Hell and **Destruction** are never full; So the eyes of man are never satisfied.

Proverbs 28:10

Whoever causes the upright to go astray in an evil way, He himself will *fall into his own pit*; But the blameless will inherit good.

Proverbs 28:14*

Happy is the man who is always reverent, But he who hardens his heart will *fall* into *calamity.*

Proverbs 28:17

A man burdened with bloodshed will flee into a pit; Let no one help him.

Proverbs 28:18*

Whoever walks blamelessly will be saved, But he who is perverse in his ways will suddenly *fall.*

Proverbs *28:*27*

He who gives to the poor will not lack, But he who hides his eyes will have many <u>curses</u>.

Proverbs 29:1*

He who is often rebuked, and hardens his neck, Will suddenly be ***<u>destroyed</u>,*** and that without remedy.

Proverbs 29:4

The king establishes the land by justice, But he who receives bribes ***<u>over-throws</u>*** it.

Proverbs 29:16

When the wicked are multiplied, transgression increases; But the righteous will see their *<u>fall</u>*.

(The Wisdom of Agur)

Proverbs 30:17

The eye that mocks his father, And scorns obedience to his mother, *The ravens of the valley will <u>pick it out</u>, And the young eagles will <u>eat it</u>.*

CHAPTER 13

CORRECTION, DISCIPLINE, REPROOF, INSTRUCTION, LEARNING

A s I was meditating on the combined Chapter Theme's Narrative for **_Correction_**, **_Discipline_**, **_Reproof_**, **_Instruction_**, **and** **_Learning_**, the difficulty of separating these five Theme's into separate and independent Chapters became more challenging, in that **_Correction_** and **_Discipline_** are, in essence, one and the same; in that **_Correction_** has, at its root, the principle of **_Discipline_**. Such that whether one plants the seed of **_Correction_**, followed by the watering of **_Discipline_**, what spawns from that is the tree of **_Instruction and Learning_**. As **_Instruction_** takes hold and broadens itself in the DNA of an individual, then hopefully and prayerfully, a more righteous and Christlike attitude and approach to life will (might) emerge.

As one will note in this "teachable moments" Chapter, the verses from Proverbs in these five areas of individual growth and development are, from my perspective, rather specific, directional, as well as instructional. Accordingly, I will only make specific reference to a few Proverbs verses on these combined Themes. While, at the same time, I believe that there is directional and significant value in briefly mentioning both Old and New Testament Scriptures that highlights on these combined Themes, namely:

- Job 5:17 and 18: "*Behold, happy is the man whom God **corrects**; Therefore do not despise the **chastening** of the Almighty. For He bruises, but He binds up; He wounds, but His hands make whole*";
- Psalms 94:12 and 13: "*Blessed is the man whom You **instruct**, O Lord, And **teach** out of Your Law, That You may give him rest from the days of adversity, Until the pit is dug for the wicked*";
- 1 Corinthians 11:32: "*But when we are judged, we are **chastened** by the Lord, that we may not be condemned with the world*";
- Hebrews 12:5–11: (5) "*And you have forgotten the exhortation which speaks to you as to sons: "My son, do not despise the **chastening** of the LORD, Nor be discouraged when you are rebuked by Him. (6) For whom the LORD loves He **chastens**, And scourges every son whom He receives.(7) If you endure **chastening**, God deals with you as with sons; for what son is there whom a father does not **chasten**? (8) But if you are without **chastening**, of which all have become partakers, then you are illegitimate and not sons. (9) Furthermore, we have had human fathers who **corrected** us and we paid them respect. Shall we not much more readily be in subjection to the Father of spirits and live? (10) For they indeed for a few days **chastened** us as seemed best to them, but He for our profit, that we may be partakers of His holiness. (11) Now no **chastening** seems to be joyful for the present, but painful; nevertheless, afterward it yields the peaceful fruit of righteousness to those who have been **trained** by it.*"
- Psalms 50:17: "*Seeing you hate **instruction** And cast My words behind you?*"
- Ephesians 6:4: "*And you, fathers, do not provoke your children to wrath, but bring them up in the **training** and admonition of the Lord*";

- 1 Timothy 4:7: "*But reject profane and old wives' fables, and exercise yourself toward godliness*";
- 2 Timothy 1:7: "*For God has not given us a spirit of fear, but of power and of love and of a sound mind*";
- Revelation 3:19: "*As many as I love, I rebuke and* **chasten**, *Therefore, be zealous and repent.*"

Needless to say, the specific Proverbs for this Chapter Narrative are much too numerous to highlight, but suffice it to say, here are a few of my favorites:

- Proverbs 3:11: "*My son, do not despise the* **chastening** *of the LORD*";
- Proverbs 3:12: "*For whom the LORD loves he* **corrects**, *Just as a father the son in whom he delights*";
- Proverbs 6:23: "*For the commandment is a lamp, And the law a light;* **Reproofs** *of* **instruction** *are the way of life*";
- Proverbs 13:1: "*A wise son heeds his father's* **instruction**, *But a scoffer does not listen to rebuke*";
- Proverbs 15:5: "*A fool despises his father's* **instruction**, *But he who receives* **correction** *is prudent*";
- Proverbs 15:32: "*He who disdains* **instruction** *despises his own soul, But he who heeds rebuke gets understanding*";
- Proverbs 19:18: "***Chasten*** *your son while there is hope; And do not set your heart on his destruction*";
- Proverbs 19:27: "*Cease listening to* **instruction**, *my son, And you will stray from the words of knowledge*"; And,
- Proverbs 23:12: "*Apply your heart to* **instruction**, *And your ears to words of knowledge.*"

I have heard it said that "God's ***Discipline*** moves you away from the ugliness of sin and toward the beauty of Holiness" (Lessin 2010).

Accordingly, at the end of the day, one who embraces and understands the importance of Father God's *__Correction__*, *__Discipline__*, and *__Instruction__* in one's life has a much greater appreciation and insight regarding the how and why:

a) God uses *__Correction__*/*__Discipline__*/*__Instruction__* to encourage us, not to discourage us;

b) God uses *__Correction__*/*__Discipline__*/*__Instruction__* as a means to show us His love for us;

c) God uses *__Correction__*/*__Discipline__*/*__Instruction__* to confirm that we are His heir apparent, equal with His Son, Christ Jesus;

d) God uses *__Correction__*/*__Discipline__*/*__Instruction__* to better reveal His love for us by not allowing anything to neglect or interfere with His glory nor supplant all that is good for us;

e) God uses *__Correction__*/*__Discipline__*/*__Instruction__* to proactively move us away from the ugliness of sin and toward the beauty of His Holiness and righteousness;

f) God uses *__Correction__*/*__Discipline__*/*__Instruction__* as tools for His eternal purpose; and

g) God uses *__Correction__*/*__Discipline__*/*__Instruction__* as safeguards or guardrails to bring us back to the pathway of righteousness and peace!

Now, the final question is: Are you ready to embrace *__Correction__*/*__Discipline__*/*__Instruction__* as a proactive measure to become more Christlike? And my answer is a resounding "Yes!"

(Guidance to the Young)

Proverbs *3:*11*–*12*

My son, do not despise the *__chastening of the LORD__*, Nor detest His *__correction__*; For whom the LORD loves He *__corrects__*, Just as a father the son in whom he delights.

(The Peril of Adultery)

Proverbs 5:7–14

(7)   Therefore hear me now, my children, And do not depart from the words of my mouth.

(8)   Remove your way far from her, And do not go near the door of her house,

(9)   Lest you give your honor to others, And your years to the cruel one;

(10) Lest aliens be filled with your wealth, And your labors go to the house of a foreigner;

(11) And you mourn at last, When your flesh and your body are consumed,

(12) And say: "How I have hated *instruction*, And my heart despised ***correction***!

(13) I have not obeyed the voice of my teachers, Nor inclined my ear to those who *instructed* me!

(14) I was on the verge of total ruin, In the midst of the assembly and congregation."

(Beware of Adultery)

Proverbs *6:20*–29*

(20)* My son, keep your father's command, And do not forsake the law of your mother.

(21) Bind them continually upon your heart; Tie them around your neck.

(22) When you roam, they will lead you; When you sleep, they will keep you; And when you awake, they will speak with you.

(23)* **For the commandment is a lamp, And the law a light; *Reproofs* of *instruction* are the way of life,**

(24) To keep you from the evil woman, From the flattering tongue of a seductress.

(25) Do not lust after her beauty in your heart, Nor let her allure you with her eyelids.

(26) For by means of a harlot, A man is reduced to a crust of bread; And an adulteress will prey upon his precious life.

(27) Can a man take fire to *his* bosom, And *his* clothes not be burned?

(28) Can one walk on hot coals, And *his* feet not be seared?

(29)* So is *he* who goes in to *his* neighbor's wife; Whoever touches her shall not be innocent.

(The Crafty Harlot)

Proverbs 7:21–23 and 24–27

(21) With her enticing speech she caused him to yield, With her flattering lips she seduced him.

(22) Immediately he went after her, as an ox to the slaughter, Or as a fool to the **correction** of the stocks,

(23) Till an arrow struck his liver. And as a bird hastens to the snare, He did not know it would cost his life.

(24) Now therefore, listen to me, my children; Pay attention to the words of my mouth:

(25) Do not let your heart turn aside to her ways, Do not stray into her paths;

(26) For she has cast down many wounded, And all who were slain by her were strong men.

(27) *Her house is the way to hell, Descending to the chambers of death.*

(The Way of Wisdom)

Proverbs *9:7–12

(7) "He who corrects a scoffer gets shame for himself, And he who rebukes a wicked man only harms himself.

(8)* Do not **correct** a scoffer, lest he hate you; **Rebuke** a wise man, and he will love you.

(9)* **Give *instruction* to a wise man, and he will be still wiser; *Teach* a just man, and he will increase in *learning*.**

(10)* **The fear of the LORD is the beginning of wisdom, And the knowledge of the Holy One is understanding.**

(11) For by me your days will be multiplied, And years of life will be added to you.

(12) If you are wise, you are wise for yourself, And if you scoff, you will bear it alone."

(Wise Sayings of Solomon)

Proverbs 10:13*

Wisdom is found on the lips of him who has understanding, But a *rod* is for the back of him who is devoid of understanding.

Proverbs 10:*17*

He who keeps *instruction* is in the way of life, But he who refuses ***correction*** goes astray.

Proverbs *12:*1*

Whoever loves *instruction* loves knowledge, But he who hates *correction* is stupid.

Proverbs 12:2*

A good man obtains favor from the LORD, But a man of wicked intentions He will *condemn*.

Proverbs *13:*1*

A wise son *heeds* his father's *instruction*, But a scoffer does not *listen* to *rebuke*.

Proverbs 13:8*

The ransom of a man's life is his riches, But the poor does not *hear* ***rebuke***.

Proverbs *13:*18*

Poverty and shame will come to him who disdains *correction*, But he who regards a *rebuke* will be honored.

Proverbs *13:*24*
He who spares his rod hates his son, But he who loves him <u>disciplines</u> him promptly.

Proverbs *15:*5*
A fool despises his father's *instruction*, But he who receives *correction* is prudent.

Proverbs 15:10*
Harsh ***discipline*** is for him who forsakes the way, And he who hates <u>***correction***</u> will die.

Proverbs 15:*12*
A scoffer does not love one who <u>***corrects***</u> him, Nor will he go to the *wise*.

Proverbs *15:*31*
The ear that hears the <u>rebukes of life</u> Will abide among the wise.

Proverbs *15:*32*
He who disdains *instruction* despises his own soul, But he who <u>*heeds rebuke*</u> gets understanding.

Proverbs *15:*33*
The fear of the LORD is the *instruction of wisdom,* And before honor is *humility*.

Proverbs 16:22*
Understanding is a wellspring of life to him who has it, But the <u>***correction***</u> of fools is folly.

Proverbs 17:*10*
<u>***Rebuke***</u> is more effective for a wise man Than a hundred blows on a fool.

Proverbs 17:26
Also, to <u>*punish*</u> the righteous is not good, Nor to *strike* princes for their uprightness.

Proverbs 18:3
When the wicked comes, contempt comes also; And with dishonor comes *reproach.*

Proverbs 19:5*
A false witness will not go *unpunished,* And he who speaks lies will not escape.

Proverbs 19:18
Chasten your son while there is hope, And do not set your heart on his destruction.

Proverbs 19:19*
A man of great wrath will suffer *punishment*; For if you rescue him, you will have to do it again.

Proverbs *19:*25*
Strike a scoffer, and the simple will become wary; *Rebuke* one who has understanding, and he will discern knowledge.

Proverbs 19:29
Judgments are prepared for scoffers, And *beatings* for the backs of fools.

Proverbs 20:11*
Even a child is known by his deeds, Whether what he does is pure and right.

Proverbs 20:26
A wise king sifts out the wicked, *And brings the threshing wheel over them.*

Proverbs 20:30
Blows that hurt cleanse away evil, *As do stripes the inner depths of the heart.*

Proverbs 21:1
The king's heart is in the hand of the LORD, Like the rivers of water; *He turns it wherever He wishes.*

Proverbs 21:*11*
When the scoffer is *punished*, the simple is made wise; But when the *wise* is *instructed*, he receives knowledge.

Proverbs *22:*6*
Train up a child in the way he should go, And when he is old, he will not depart from it.

Proverbs *22:*15*
Foolishness is bound up in the heart of a child; The *rod* of *correction* will drive it far from him.

(Sayings of the Wise)

Proverbs *23:*13*–*14*
Do not withhold *correction* from a child, For if you *beat* him with a *rod*, he will not die. You shall *beat* him with a *rod*, And deliver his soul from hell.

(Further Sayings of the Wise)

Proverbs *24:*23*-*25*
(23)* **These things also belong to the wise: It is not good to show partiality in judgment.**
(24)* **He who says to the wicked, "You are righteous," Him the people will curse; Nations will abhor him.**
(25)* **But those who *rebuke* the wicked will have delight, And a good blessing will come upon them.**

(Further Wise Sayings of Solomon)

Proverbs 25:12
Like an earring of gold and an ornament of fine gold Is a *wise **rebuker*** to an obedient ear.

Proverbs 25:28*
Whoever has <u>no rule</u> over his own spirit Is like a city broken down, without walls.

Proverbs 26:3
A *whip* for the horse, A *bridle* for the donkey, And a <u>*rod*</u> for the fool's back.

Proverbs 27:5*
Open **<u>rebuke</u>** is better Than love carefully concealed.

Proverbs *27:*6*
Faithful are <u>the wounds</u> of a friend, But the kisses of an enemy are deceitful.

Proverbs 27:11
My son, be wise and make my heart glad, That I may answer him who *reproaches* me.

Proverbs 27:12*
A prudent man foresees evil and hides himself; The simple pass on and are *punished*.

Proverbs *27:*17*
As iron sharpens iron, So a man sharpens the countenance of his friend.

Proverbs 28:10
Whoever causes the upright to go astray in an evil way, He himself will fall into his own *pit*; But the blameless will inherit good.

Proverbs 28:17
A man burdened with bloodshed will flee into a <u>pit</u>; Let no one help him.

Proverbs *28:*23*
He who <u>rebukes a man</u> will find more favor afterward Than he who flatters with the tongue.

Proverbs 29:1*

*He who is often **rebuked**, and hardens his neck,* Will suddenly be destroyed, and that without remedy.

Proverbs *29:*15*

The rod and rebuke give wisdom, But a child left to himself brings shame to his mother.

Proverbs *29:*17*

Correct your son, and he will give you rest: Yes, he will give delight to your soul.

Proverbs 29:19

A servant will not be **corrected** by mere words; For though he understands, he will not respond.

(The Wisdom of Agur)

Proverbs *30:*5*–6

Every word of God is pure; He is a shield to those who put their trust in Him. Do not add to His words, Lest He **rebuke** you, and you be found a liar.

CHAPTER 14

COVETOUSNESS, ENVY, GREED, JEALOUSY, SELFISHNESS

During my meditation on how best to summarize this Chapter Narrative's Theme's with no less than five slightly different but similar Themes (i.e. *Covetousness*, *Envy*, *Greed*, *Jealousy*, and *Selfishness*), I was led by the Holy Spirit to speak to and reference the two Themes of *Envy* and *Jealousy* that are, in fact, mirror images of one another. Additionally, while *Envy* and *Jealousy* are generally not character traits that describe who I am, but I did experience a momentary hint of *Envy* the night before I drafted this Chapter Narrative, as I will briefly speak to that episode below.

To better understand the negative character flaw that *Envy* represents, it might be helpful to define the term. The Greek translation for "*Envy*" means to "burn with zeal," which, stated another way, means "to be heated or to boil over with anger, hatred, or jealousy." *Envy* has also been defined as a feeling of displeasure produced by observing or hearing of the advantage or prosperity of others.

Examine, if you will, the following Proverbs verses, namely:

- Proverbs 3:31: "*Do not **envy** the oppressor, And choose none of his ways*";
- Proverbs 14:30: "*A sound heart is life to the body, But **envy** is rottenness to the bones*"; and
- Proverbs 23:17: "*Do not let your heart **envy** sinners, But be zealous for the fear of the Lord all the day*";

which, on balance, challenges one to forgo craving what someone else might have and/or possess, rather than embracing and being grateful and blessed for any and all that Father God has graciously given or provided one with.

In examining **_Envy_**, one only has to refer to Matthew 27:18, whereby the religious leaders were so consumed with **_Envy_** and **_Jealousy_** that they handed over our Lord and Savior, Jesus Christ, to Pilate so that He would be crucified! And my momentary hint of **_Envy_**/**_Jealousy_** occurred on March 30, 2016, as I was reviewing the Executive Leadership Council (ELC), 2016 Q1 "ELC Members on the Move Section" of the Media Newsletter, I thought of where I might be today, as it relates to potentially being a SVP and CFO of a Corporate 500 company, had I stayed in Corporate America and not resigned back in February 2008 to pursue the calling that the Holy Spirit had placed on my heart—that being to pursue a full-time position, working for the Lord, which I am exceedingly thankful that I yielded to His calling and repositioning of my Life for Christ!

At the end of the day, God's Word directs one and all not to be **_Envious_** and/or **_Jealous_** of others, but we are called to love all, just as Father God has loved us and directed us to have "*love for one another*" (John 13:34–35; 1 John 2:10; 1 John 3:10 and 18; 1 John 4:7, 8, 11, 12, 16, 18, 19–21; 1 Peter 2:17). Father God's love is true love, which rejoices when others are blessed and surrounded by the essence of love. Love has no room for **_Envy_** or **_Jealousy_** (1 Corinthians 13:4), nor does love seek to benefit itself, but is content with what it has since love desires to meet the needs of each and every loved one!

To God be the GLORY!

(Shun Evil Counsel)

Proverbs *1:8–*19*

(8) My son, hear the instruction of your father, And do not forsake the law of your mother;

(9) For they will be a graceful ornament on your head, And chains about your neck.

(10) My son, if sinners entice you, Do not consent.

(11) If they say, "Come with us, Let us lie in wait to shed blood; Let us lurk secretly for the innocent without cause;

(12) Let us swallow them alive like Sheol, And whole, like those who go down to the Pit;

(13) We shall find all kinds of precious possessions, We shall fill our houses with spoil;

(14) Cast in your lot among us, Let us all have one purse"—

(15) My son, do not walk in the way with them, Keep your *foot* from their path;

(16) For their feet run to evil, And they make haste to shed blood.

(17) Surely, in vain the net is spread In the sight of any bird;

(18) But they lie in wait for their own blood, They lurk secretly for their own lives.

(19)* **So are the ways of everyone who is _greedy_ for gain; It takes away the life of its owners.**

(Guidance for the Young)

Proverbs *3:*27*–28*

Do not withhold good from those to whom it is due, When it is in the power of your hand to do so. Do not say to your neighbor, "Go, and come back, And tomorrow I will give it," When you have it with you.

Proverbs 3:31–32*

Do not _envy_ the oppressor, And choose none of his ways; For the perverse person is an abomination to the LORD, But His secret counsel is with the upright.

(Beware of Adultery)

Proverbs *6:*32*–35

(32)* **Whoever commits adultery with a woman lacks understanding; He who does so destroys his own soul.**

(33)* **Wounds and dishonor he will get, And his reproach will not be wiped away.**

(34) For *jealousy* is a husband's fury; Therefore he will not spare in the day of vengeance.

(35) He will accept no recompense, Nor will he be appeased though you give many gifts.

(Wise Sayings of Solomon)

Proverbs *11:*24*–26

(24)* **There is one who scatters, yet increases more;** *And there is one who* withholds *more than is right*, **But it leads to poverty.**

(25)* **The generous soul will be made rich, And he who waters will also be watered himself.**

(26) *The people will curse him who* withholds *grain*, But blessing will be on the head of him who sells it.

Proverbs 12:9

Better is the one who is slighted but has a servant, *Than he who honors himself but lacks bread.*

Proverbs 12:12*

The wicked *covet* the catch of evil men, But the root of the righteous yields fruit.

Proverbs *13:*7*

There is one who makes himself rich, yet has nothing; **And one who makes himself poor, yet has great riches.**

Proverbs 14:30
A sound heart is life to the body, But *envy* is rottenness to the bones.

Proverbs 15:*27*
He who is *greedy* for gain troubles his own house, But he who hates bribes will live.

Proverbs 18:16
A man's gift makes room for him, And brings him before great men.

Proverbs 19:4
Wealth makes many friends, But the poor is separated from his friend.

Proverbs 21:6
Getting treasures by a lying tongue Is the fleeting fantasy of those who seek death.

Proverbs *21:*13*
Whoever shuts his ears to the cry of the poor Will also cry himself and not be heard.

Proverbs 21:17*
He who loves pleasure will be a poor man; He who loves wine and oil will not be rich.

Proverbs *21:25*-*26*
The *desire* of the lazy man kills him, For his hands refuse to labor. He *covets greedily* all day long, **But the righteous gives and does not spare.**

Proverbs *22:*7*
The rich rules over the poor, And the borrower is servant to the lender.

Proverbs 22:16*
He who oppresses the poor to <u>*increase his riches,*</u> *And he who gives to the rich, will surely come to poverty.*

(Sayings of the Wise)

Proverbs *22:*22*–*23*

Do not *rob* the poor because he is poor, Nor *oppress* the afflicted at the gate; For the LORD will plead their cause, And plunder the soul of those who plunder them.

Proverbs 22:28

Do not remove the ancient landmark Which your fathers have set.

Proverbs 23:1–3

(1)   When you sit down to eat with a ruler, Consider carefully what is before you;

(2)   *And put a knife to your throat If you are a man given to appetite.*

(3)   *Do not desire his delicacies*, For they are deceptive food.

Proverbs *23:*4*–*5*

***Do not overwork to be rich*; Because of your own understanding, cease! *Will you set your eyes on that which is not?* For riches certainly make themselves wings; They fly away like an eagle toward heaven.**

Proverbs 23:6–8

(6)   Do not eat the bread of a miser, *Nor desire his delicacies*;

(7)   *For as he thinks in his heart, so is he.* "Eat and drink!" he says to you, But his heart is not with you.

(8)   The morsel you have eaten, you will vomit up, And waste your pleasant words.

Proverbs 23:10–11

Do not remove the ancient landmark, Nor enter the fields of the fatherless; For their Redeemer is mighty; He will plead their cause against you.

Proverbs 23:17*–18*

Do not let your heart **_envy_** sinners, But be zealous for the fear of the LORD all the day; For surely there is a hereafter, And your hope will not be cut off.

Proverbs 24:1–2

Do not be **envious** of evil men, Nor *desire* to be with them; For their heart devises violence, And their lips talk of troublemaking.

Proverbs 24:19–20

Do not fret because of evildoers, Nor be **envious** of the wicked; For there will be no prospect for the evil man; The lamp of the wicked will be put out.

(Further Wise Sayings of Solomon)

Proverbs 27:4

Wrath is cruel and anger a torrent, But who is able to stand before **jealousy**?

Proverbs 27:20*

Hell and Destruction are never full; *So the eyes of man are never satisfied.*

Proverbs 28:3

A poor man who oppresses the poor Is like a driving rain which leaves no food.

Proverbs 28:8

One who increases his possessions by usury and extortion Gathers it for him who will pity the poor.

Proverbs 28:16

A ruler who lacks understanding is a great oppressor, But he who hates **covetousness** will prolong his days.

Proverbs 28:20

A faithful man will abound with blessings, *But he who hastens to be rich will not go unpunished.*

Proverbs 28:21

To show partiality is not good, <u>*Because for a piece of bread*</u> *a man will transgress.*

Proverbs 28:22

A man with an evil eye <u>*hastens after riches*</u>, And does not consider that poverty will come upon him.

Proverbs *28:*27*

He who gives to the poor will not lack, ***But he who*** <u>***hides his eyes***</u> ***will have many curses***.

Proverbs 29:7*

The righteous considers the cause of the poor, *But the wicked does not understand such knowledge.*

Proverbs 29:10

The bloodthirsty hate the blameless, But the upright seek his well-being.

CHAPTER 15

DEATH, HELL, PERISH, PLUNDER

*D**eath*** is generally defined as "separation from the living." There are several types of ***Death's*** known to man (i.e. physical and spiritual). A physical ***Death*** is the separation of the soul from the body. Spiritual ***Death***, on the other hand, and which is of greater significance, is generally defined as the separation of the soul from Father God. In Genesis 2:17, Father God tells Adam that in the day he eats of the forbidden fruit that he will "*surely die.*" And as we know, Adam does indeed fall, but his physical ***Death*** does not occur immediately; Father God must have had another type of ***Death*** in mind or plan (i.e. spiritual ***Death***). This separation from Father God is exactly what one observes in reading Genesis 3:8. When Adam and Eve hear the voice of the Lord, they "*hid themselves from the presence of the Lord God.*" The fellowship with our Heavenly Father had been broken. Accordingly, they became spiritually ***Dead***, and as we know, opened up the rest of humanity to sin and the corresponding spiritual ***Death***, resulting from sin.

When Jesus was hanging on the cross, Jesus paid the price for those "in Christ" by dying the spiritual ***Death*** that we should have borne yesterday, today, or tomorrow. Even though Jesus is God, He still had to suffer the agony of a temporary separation from our Heavenly Father, resulting from the sin of the world that Jesus Christ carried and bore on the cross for the sin debt that was ours to bear! After three hours of supernatural darkness, Jesus cried out, "*My God, My God, why have you forsaken Me?*" (Mark 15:33–34). This **spiritual separation** from our Heavenly Father was the direct result of Jesus Christ, our Lord and Savior, taking our sins upon Himself as the propitiation for our sins. Sin is the exact opposite of Father God, in that God, our Heavenly Father, had to turn away from His own Son for that period of time. When one mediates and marinates on both the supreme sacrifices that Jesus Christ made on our behalf for sin, as well as the total separation that both our Heavenly Father and Jesus Christ endured on our behalf, it should encourage and embolden one and all in the ways of righteousness, and forsake sin at all cost!

At the end of the day, a person without Jesus Christ is spiritually **_Dead_**! Paul describes it as "*being alienated from the life of God*" (Ephesians 4:18). One might equate being separated from life as the equivalent of being **_Dead_**! The natural men or women, like Adam and Eve, hiding in the garden were and/or are equally isolated from Father God. When one is born again, the spiritual **_Death_** is altered and reversed. Before salvation, we were all spiritually **_Dead_** in our sins, but our Lord Jesus Christ has given us new life; a life born in Christ Jesus, freed from the penalties of sin, and has provided the free gift of salvation that only comes from one's belief in Christ Jesus, so that we can inherit and partake of eternal life. "*And you He made alive, who were **dead** in trespasses and sins,*" (Ephesians 2:1). "*And you, being **dead** in your trespasses and the uncircumcision of your flesh, He has made alive together with Him, having forgiven you all trespasses,*" (Colossians 2:13).

As an illustration, recall the story of Lazarus being raised from the **_Dead_** by Jesus Christ in John 11. The physically dead Lazarus could do nothing for himself as he lay **_Dead_** in the tomb after four days. He was unresponsive to all earthly stimuli, oblivious to all existing life around him, beyond all help and/or hope from human cries of assistance, except for the help of his close friend, Jesus Christ, who is the "*resurrection and the life*" (John 11:25). At the direct call from Jesus Christ, Lazarus was filled with new life, and he responded accordingly. In a similar way, we were spiritually **Dead**, unable to save ourselves, powerless to perceive the life of Father God until Jesus called us to Himself, and we answered the call by believing in Him as our Lord and Savior! He "awoken" us "*not by works of righteousness which we have done, but according to His mercy He saved us, through the washing of regeneration and renewing of the Holy Spirit*" (Titus 3:5).

Finally, the Book of Revelation speaks of a "second **Death**," which is a final (and eternal) separation from Father God. Only those who have never experienced new life "in Christ" will partake of the second **Death** (Revelation 2:11; 20:6, 14; and 21:8).

(Partial reference and source—2002–2015, Got Questions Ministries.)

(Shun Evil Counsel)

Proverbs *1:8*–*19*

(8)* My son, hear the instruction of your father, And do not forsake the law of your mother;

(9) For they will be a graceful ornament on your head, And chains about your neck.

(10) My son, if sinners entice you, Do not consent.

(11) If they say, "Come with us, *Let us lie in wait to shed blood*; Let us lurk secretly for the innocent without cause;

(12) *Let us swallow them alive like Sheol, And whole, like those who go down to the Pit;*

(13) We shall find all kinds of precious possessions, We shall fill our houses with spoil;

(14) Cast in your lot among us, Let us all have one purse"—

(15) My son, do not walk in the way with them, Keep your foot from their path;

(16) For their feet run to evil, *And they make haste to shed blood.*

(17) Surely, in vain the net is spread In the sight of any bird;

(18) *But they lie in wait for their own blood, They lurk secretly for their own lives.*

(19)* **So are the ways of everyone who is greedy for gain;** *It takes away the life of its owners*.

(The Value of Wisdom)

Proverbs 2:10*–22*

(10)* When wisdom enters your heart, And knowledge is pleasant to your soul,

(11)* Discretion will preserve you; Understanding will keep you,

(12)* To deliver you from the way of evil, From the man who speaks perverse things,

(13) From those who leave the paths of uprightness To walk in the ways of darkness;

(14) Who rejoice in doing evil, And delight in the perversity of the wicked;

(15) Whose ways are crooked, And who are devious in their paths;

(16) To deliver you from the immoral woman, From the seductress who flatters with her words,

(17) Who forsakes the companion of her youth, And forgets the covenant of her God.

(18) For her house leads down to **death**, And her paths to the **dead**;

(19) None who go to her return, Nor do they regain the paths of life—

(20)* **So you may walk in the way of goodness, And keep to the paths of righteousness.**

(21)* **For the upright will dwell in the land, And the blameless will remain in it;**

(22)* *But the wicked will be* <u>cut off</u> *from the earth, And the unfaithful will be* <u>uprooted</u> *from it*.

(The Peril of Adultery)

Proverbs *5:1–6 and *21*–*23*

(1) My son, pay attention to my wisdom; Lend your ear to my understanding,

(2)   That you may preserve discretion, And your lips may keep knowledge.

(3)   For the lips of an immoral woman drip honey, And her mouth is smoother than oil;

(4)   But in the end she is bitter as wormwood, Sharp as a two-edged sword.

(5)   Her feet go down to **_death_**, Her steps lay hold of **_hell_**.

(6)   Lest you ponder her path of life—Her ways are unstable: You do not know them.

(21)* **For the ways of man are before the eyes of the LORD, And He ponders all his paths.**

(22)* **His own iniquities entrap the wicked man, And he is caught in the cords of his _sin_.**

(23)* **He shall _die_ for lack of instruction, And in the greatness of his folly he shall go _astray_.**

(Beware of Adultery)

Proverbs *6:20*–29* and *32*–35

(20)* My son, keep your father's command, And do not forsake the law of your mother.

(21)   Bind them continually upon your heart; Tie them around your neck.

(22)   When you roam, they will lead you; When you sleep, they will keep you; And when you awake, they will speak with you.

(23)* **For the commandment is a lamp, And the law a light; Reproofs of instruction are the way of life,**

(24)* To keep you from the evil woman, From the flattering tongue of a seductress.

(25)   Do not lust after her beauty in your heart, Nor let her allure you with her eyelids.

(26)   For by means of a harlot _A man is reduced to a crust of bread; And an adulteress will prey upon his precious life._

(27) Can a man take *fire* to his bosom, And his *clothes not be burned?*

(28) Can one *walk on hot coals,* And his *feet not be seared?*

(29)* *So is he who goes in to his neighbor's wife; Whoever touches her shall not be innocent.*

(32)* **Whoever commits _adultery_ with a woman lacks understanding; He who does so _destroys his own_ _soul_.**

(33)* **Wounds and dishonor he will get, And his reproach will not be wiped away.**

(34) For jealousy is a husband's fury; *Therefore he will not spare in the day of vengeance.*

(35) *He will accept no recompense,* Nor will he be appeased though you give many gifts.

(The Crafty Harlot)

Proverbs 7:21–23 and 24–27

(21) With her enticing speech she caused him to yield, With her flattering lips she seduced him.

(22) Immediately he went after her, *as an ox goes to the _slaughter,_* Or as a fool to the correction of the stocks,

(23) Till an arrow struck his liver. As a bird hastens to the snare, *He did not know it would **cost his life**.*

(24) Now therefore, listen to me, my children; Pay attention to the words of my mouth:

(25) Do not let your heart turn aside to her ways, Do not stray into her paths;

(26) For she has cast down many wounded, And all who were **_slain_** by her were strong men.

(27) Her house is the way to **_hell_**, Descending to the chamber of **_death_**.

(The Excellence of Wisdom)

Proverbs *8:*32*–36*

(32)* **"Now therefore, listen to me (wisdom), my children, For blessed are those who keep my (wisdom) ways,**

(33)* **Hear instruction and be wise, And do not disdain it.**

(34)* Blessed is the man who listens to me (wisdom), Watching daily at my gates, Waiting at the posts of my doors.

(35)* **For whoever finds me finds life, And obtains favor from the LORD;**

(36)* But he who sins against me *wrongs his own soul*; All those who hate me love **_death_**."

(The Way of Folly)

Proverbs 9:13–18

(13) A foolish woman is clamorous; She is simple, and knows nothing.

(14) For she sits at the door of her house, On a seat by the highest places of the city,

(15) To call to those who pass by, Who go straight on their way:

(16) "Whoever is simple, let him turn in here"; And as for him who lacks understanding, she says to him,

(17) "Stolen water is sweet, And bread eaten in secret is pleasant."

(18) But he does not know that the **_dead_** are there, That her guests are in the depths of **_hell._**

(Wise Sayings of Solomon)

Proverbs 10:2*

Treasures of wickedness profit nothing, But righteousness delivers from **_death_**.

Proverbs 10:3*

The LORD will not allow the righteous <u>soul to famish</u>, But He <u>cast away the desire of the wicked</u>.

Proverbs *10:*21*

The lips of the righteous feed many, But fools _die_ for lack of wisdom.

Proverbs 10:27–*29*

(27) The fear of the LORD prolongs days, _But the years of the wicked will be shortened._

(28) The hope of the righteous will be gladness, But the expectation of the wicked will **perish**.

(29)* The way of the LORD is strength for the upright, _But destruction will come to the workers of iniquity._

Proverbs 11:*4*

Riches do not profit in the day of wrath, But righteousness delivers from **death**.

Proverbs 11:7

When a wicked man **_dies_**, his expectation will **perish**, And the hope of the unjust **perishes**.

Proverbs 11:10

When it goes well with the righteous, the city rejoices; And when the wicked **perish**, there is jubilation.

Proverbs 11:19*

As righteousness leads to life, So he who pursues evil pursues it to his own **_death_**.

Proverbs 12:28*

In the way of righteousness is life, And in its pathway there is no **_death_**.

Proverbs 13:*3*

He who guards his mouth preserves his life, But he who opens wide his lips shall have _destruction._

Proverbs 13:9
The light of the righteous rejoices, But the lamp of the wicked will be *put out*.

Proverbs 13:*13*
He who despises the word will be *destroyed*, But he who fears the commandment will be rewarded.

Proverbs 13:14
The law of the wise is a fountain of life, To turn one away from the snares of *death*.

Proverbs *13:*20*
He who walks with wise men will be wise, But the companion of fools will be *destroyed*.

Proverbs *14:*12*
There is a way that seems right to a man, But its end is the way of *death*.

Proverbs 14:27*
The fear of the LORD is a fountain of life, To turn one away from the snares of *death*.

Proverbs 14:32
The wicked is banished in his wickedness, But the righteous has a refuge in his *death*.

Proverbs 15:10*
Harsh *discipline* is for him who forsakes the way, And he who hates *correction* will *die*.

Proverbs 15:11
Hell and *Destruction* are before the LORD; So how much more the hearts of the sons of men.

Proverbs 15:24*
The way of life winds upward for the wise, That he may turn away from *hell* below.

Proverbs *15:*32*
He who disdains instruction *despises his own soul*, But he who heeds rebuke gets understanding.

Proverbs 16:4
The LORD has made all for Himself, Yes, even the wicked for the day of *doom*.

Proverbs 16:14
As messengers of *death* is the king's wrath, But a wise man will appease it.

Proverbs *16:*18*
Pride goes before *destruction*, And a haughty spirit before a *fall*.

Proverbs *16:*25*
There is a way that seems right to a man, But its end is the way of *death*.

Proverbs 18:21
Death and life are in the power of the tongue, And those who love it will eat its fruit.

Proverbs 19:*9*
A false witness will not go unpunished, And he who speaks lies shall *perish*.

Proverbs 19:16*
He who keeps the commandment keeps his soul, But he who is careless of his ways will *die*.

Proverbs 20:2
The wrath of a king is like the roaring of a lion; Whoever provokes him to anger *sins against his own life*.

Proverbs 20:20
Whoever curses his father or his mother, *His lamp will be <u>put out in deep darkness</u>.*

Proverbs 21:6
Getting treasures by a lying tongue Is the fleeting fantasy of those who seek **death**.

Proverbs 21:7
The violence of the wicked will <u>destroy</u> them, Because they refuse to do justice.

Proverbs 21:12*
The righteous God wisely considers the *house* of the wicked, <u>*Overthrowing*</u> the wicked for their wickedness.

Proverbs 21:*15*
It is a joy for the just to do justice, But <u>*destruction*</u> will come to the workers of iniquity.

Proverbs 21:*16*
A man who wanders from the way of understanding Will rest in the assembly of the **_dead_**.

Proverbs 21:25*–*26*
The desire of the lazy man **_kills_** *him,* For his hands refuse to labor. He covets greedily all day long, **But the righteous gives and does not spare.**

Proverbs 21:28
A false witness shall **_perish_**, But the man who hears him will speak endlessly.

Proverbs 22:3*
A prudent man foresees evil and hides himself, But the simple pass on and are <u>*punished*</u>.

Proverbs 22:13

The lazy man says, "There is a lion outside! I shall be *slain* in the streets!"

Proverbs 22:14

The mouth of an immoral woman is a *deep pit*; He who is abhorred by the LORD *will fall there*.

(Sayings of the Wise)

Proverbs *22:*22*–*23*

Do not rob the poor because he is poor, Nor oppress the afflicted at the gate; For the LORD will plead their cause, And *plunder* the soul of those who *plunder* them.

Proverbs *23:*13*–*14*

Do not withhold correction from a child, For if you beat him with a rod, he will not *die*. You shall beat him with a rod, And deliver his soul from *hell*.

Proverbs 24:11–12

Deliver those who are drawn toward ***death***, And hold back those stumbling to the *slaughter*. If you say, "Surely we did not know this," Does not He who weighs the hearts consider it? He who keeps your soul, does He not know it? *And will He not render to each man according to his deeds?*

Proverbs *24:15–*16*

Do not lie in wait, O wicked man, against the dwelling of the righteous; Do not *plunder* his resting place; **For a righteous man may <u>fall</u> seven times And rise again, But the wicked shall <u>fall</u> by calamity.**

Proverbs *24:*17*–*18*

Do not rejoice when your enemy <u>falls</u>, And do not let your heart be glad when he <u>stumbles</u>; Lest the LORD see it, and it displease Him, And He turn away His *wrath* from him.

Proverbs 24:19–20
Do not fret because of evildoers, Nor be envious of the wicked; For there will be no prospect for the evil man; The *lamp* of the wicked will be *put out*.

(Further Wise Sayings of Solomon)

Proverbs 26:18–19
Like a madman who throws firebrands, arrows, and **death**, Is the man who deceives his neighbor, And says, "I was only joking!"

Proverbs 27:20*
Hell and *Destruction* are never full; So the eyes of man are never satisfied.

Proverbs 28:10
Whoever causes the upright to go astray in an evil way, He himself will *fall* into his own *pit*; But the blameless will inherit good.

Proverbs 28:18*
Whoever walks blamelessly will be saved, But he who is perverse in his ways will suddenly *fall*.

Proverbs 28:28
When the wicked arise, men hide themselves; But when they **perish**, the righteous increase.

Proverbs 29:1*
He who is often rebuked, and hardens his neck, Will suddenly be *destroyed*, and that without remedy.

(The Wisdom of Agur)
(Prayer of Devotion)

Proverbs 30:7-9*
(7) Two things I request of You (Deprive me not before I **die**):
(8) Remove falsehood and lies far from me; Give me neither poverty nor riches – Feed me with the food allotted to me;

(9)*   Lest I be full and deny You, And say, "Who is the LORD?" Or lest I be poor and steal, And profane the name of my God.

Proverbs 30:15–16

The leech has two daughters—Give and Give! There are three things that are never satisfied, Four never say, "Enough!": The **_grave_**, The barren womb, The earth that is not satisfied with water—And the fire never says, "Enough!"

Proverbs 30:17

The eye that mocks his father, And scorns obedience to his mother, _The ravens of the valley will pick it out, And the young eagles will eat_.

(The Words of King Lemuel's Mother)

Proverbs 31:4–9

(4)   It is not for kings, O Lemuel, It is not for kings to drink wine, Nor for princes intoxicating drink;

(5)   Lest they drink and forget the law, And pervert the justice of all the afflicted.

(6)   Give strong drink to him who is **_perishing_**, And wine to those who are bitter of heart.

(7)   Let him drink and forget his poverty, And remember his misery no more.

(8)   Open your mouth for the speechless, In the cause of all who are appointed to **_die_**.

(9)   Open your mouth, judge righteously, And plead the cause of the poor and needy.

CHAPTER 16

DECEIT, DECEPTION, LIES, LYING, SLANDER, TALEBEARER (GOSSIPER)

W e all have heard the statement, "It was just a little white _**Lie**_." Or how about this one, "I just fudged a little bit, no one will be the wiser!"

My response to either or both of the above statements is an emphatic, "Really!" May I suggest that one needs to look no further than to Father God's Word on the subject of "_**Dishonesty**_," "_**Falsehood**_," and "_**Lying**_," specifically Exodus 20:16: "_You shall not **bear false witness** against your neighbor_"; or Matthew 12:36: "_But I say to you that for every idle word men may speak, they will give account of it in the day of judgment_"; and Matthew 12:37: "_For by your words you will be justified, and by your words you will be condemned._"

If one could summarize Father God's Word from the above biblical scriptures, it's clear that "_**bearing false witness**_" by leaving something out of a story, telling a "**half-truth**," **twisting the facts, and/or inventing/ creating a** _falsehood_ is nothing but _Deception_ to the first order, which, from my perspective, is not in accordance with Father God's Word or His will for His people. While _**Deception**_ in the form of "_**Dishonesty**_," "_**Falsehood**_," and/or outright "_**Lying**_" is and can be a way of normal, everyday life for secular people, and unfortunately, sometimes for those of us who are "in Christ." But with that said, Father God's people must not give in to any lapses of the "truth" by engaging in any form of "**Dishonesty**," "**Falsehood**," and/or outright "**Lying**" and not letting it become a normal part of one's DNA!

(Security in Wisdom)

Proverbs *4:*20*–*27*

(20)* **My son, give attention to my words; Incline your ear to my sayings.**

(21)* **Do not let them depart from your eyes; Keep them in the midst of your heart;**

(22)* **For they are life to those who find them, And health to all their flesh.**

(23)* **Keep your heart with all diligence, For out of it spring the issues of life.**

(24)* **Put away from you a _deceitful_ mouth, And put _perverse lips_ far from you.**

(25) Let your eyes look straight ahead, And your eyelids look right before you.

(26)* **Ponder the path of your feet, And let all your ways be established.**

(27)* **Do not turn to the right or the left; Remove your foot from evil.**

(The Wicked Man)

Proverbs 6:12–15 and 16–19

(12) A worthless person, a wicked man, Walks with a _perverse_ _mouth_;

(13) He winks with his eyes, He shuffles his feet, He points with his fingers;

(14) _Perversity_ is in his heart, He devises evil continually, He sows discord.

(15) Therefore his calamity shall come suddenly; Suddenly he shall be broken without remedy.

(16) These six things the LORD hates, Yes, seven are an abomination to Him:

(17) A proud look, A *lying* tongue, Hands that shed innocent blood,

(18) A heart that devises wicked plans, Feet that are swift in running to evil,

(19) A *false witness* who speaks **lies,** And one who sows discord among brethren.

(The Way of Folly)

Proverbs 9:13–18

(13) A *foolish* woman is clamorous; She is *simple*, and knows nothing.

(14) For she sits at the door of her house, On a seat by the highest places of the city,

(15) *To call to those who pass by*, Who go straight on their way:

(16) *"Whoever is simple, let him turn in here"*; And as for him who lacks understanding, she says to him,

(17) *"Stolen water is sweet, And bread eaten in secret is pleasant."*

(18) *But he does not know that the dead are there, That her guests are in the depths of hell.*

(Wise Sayings of Solomon)

Proverbs 10:10

He who *winks with the eye* causes trouble, But a prating fool will fall.

Proverbs 10:18

Whoever hides hatred has **lying lips,** And whoever spreads **slander** is a fool.

Proverbs 10:19

In the multitude of words sin is not lacking, But he who *restrains his lips* is wise.

Proverbs 11:13
A **_talebearer_** (**_gossiper_**) reveals secrets, But he who is of a faithful spirit conceals a matter.

Proverbs 11:18*
The wicked man does **_deceptive_** work, But he who sows righteousness will have a sure reward.

Proverbs 12:5*
The thoughts of the righteous are right, But the counsels of the wicked are **_deceitful_**.

Proverbs 12:*17*
He who speaks truth declares righteousness, But a _false witness_, **_deceit_**.

Proverbs 12:*19*
The truthful lip shall be established forever, But a **_lying_** _tongue_ is but for a moment.

Proverbs 12:20*
Deceit is in the heart of those who devise evil, But counselors of peace have joy.

Proverbs *12:*22*
Lying lips are an abomination to the LORD, But those who deal truthfully are His delight.

Proverbs 13:5
A righteous man hates **_lying_**, But a wicked man is loathsome and comes to shame.

Proverbs 13:*11*
Wealth gained by _dishonesty_ will be diminished, But he who gathers by labor will increase.

Proverbs 14:5
A faithful witness does not **_lie_**, But a _false witness_ will utter **_lies_**.

Proverbs 14:*8*
The wisdom of the prudent is to understand his way, But the folly of fools is *deceit*.

Proverbs 14:25
A true witness delivers souls, But a *deceitful witness* speaks *lies*.

Proverbs 15:27*
He who is *greedy* for gain troubles his own house, But he who hates *bribes* will live.

Proverbs 16:27–30
(27) *An ungodly man digs up evil,* And it is on *his lips* like a burning fire.

(28) A *perverse* man sows strife, And a *whisperer* separates the best of friends.

(29) A violent man *entices his neighbor,* And leads him in a way that is not good.

(30) He winks his eye to devise *perverse* things; He purses *his lips* and brings about evil.

Proverbs 17:4
An evildoer gives heed to *false lips*; A *liar* listens eagerly to a *spiteful tongue*.

Proverbs 17:7
Excellent speech is not becoming to a fool, Much less *lying lips* to a prince.

Proverbs 17:20
He who has a *deceitful* heart finds no good, And he who has a *perverse tongue* falls into evil.

Proverbs 17:23
A wicked man accepts a *bribe* behind the back To *pervert* the ways of justice.

Proverbs 18:8*
The words of a *talebearer* (*gossiper*) are like tasty trifles, And they go down into the inmost body.

Proverbs *19:*1*
Better is the poor who walks in his integrity Than one who is *perverse* in *his lips,* and is a fool.

Proverbs 19:5*
A *false witness* will not go unpunished, And he who speaks **lies** will not escape.

Proverbs 19:*9*
A *false witness* will not go unpunished, And he who speaks **lies** shall perish.

Proverbs 19:*22*
What is desired in a man is kindness, And a poor man is better than a **liar.**

Proverbs 19:28
A *disreputable witness* scorns justice, And the mouth of the wicked devours iniquity.

Proverbs 20:10
Diverse weights and *diverse* measures, They are both alike, an abomination to the LORD.

Proverbs 20:14
"*It is good for nothing,*" *cries the buyer;* But when he has gone his way, then he boasts.

Proverbs 20:17
Bread gained by **deceit** is sweet to a man, But afterward his mouth will be filled with gravel.

Proverbs 20:19
He who goes about as a **talebearer** (**gossiper**) reveals secrets; Therefore do not associate with one who *flatters* with *his lips.*

Proverbs 20:23
Diverse weights are an abomination to the Lord, And *dishonest* scales are not good.

Proverbs 20:25

It is a _snare_ for a man to devote rashly _something as holy_, And afterward to reconsider his vows.

Proverbs 21:6

Getting treasures by a **_lying tongue_** Is the fleeting fantasy of those who seek death.

Proverbs 21:14

A _gift in secret_ pacifies anger, And a _bribe_ behind the back, strong wrath.

Proverbs 21:27

The sacrifice of the wicked is an abomination; How much more when he brings it with wicked _intent_!

Proverbs 21:28

A _false witness_ shall perish, But the man who hears him will speak endlessly.

Proverbs 22:13

The lazy man says, "_There is a lion outside! I shall be slain in the streets!_"

Proverbs 22:14

The mouth of an immoral woman is a deep pit; He who is abhorred by the LORD will fall there.

(Sayings of the Wise)

Proverbs 22:28

Do not remove the ancient landmark Which your fathers have set.

Proverbs 23:1–3

(1) When you sit down to eat with a ruler, Consider carefully what is before you;

(2) And put a knife to your throat If you are a man given to appetite.

(3) Do not desire his delicacies, For they are **_deceptive_** food.

Proverbs 23:10–11

Do not remove the ancient landmark, Nor enter the fields of the fatherless; For their Redeemer is mighty: He will plead their cause against you.

Proverbs 23:26–28

(26)   My son, give me your heart, And let your eyes observe my ways.

(27)   *For a harlot is a deep pit, And a seductress is a narrow well.*

(28)   *She also **lies** in wait as for a victim, And increases the unfaithful among men.*

(Further Sayings of the Wise)

Proverbs *24:*23*–*25* and *28*–*29*

(23)* **These things also belong to the wise: *It is not good to show partiality in judgment.***

(24)* **He who says to the wicked, "*You are righteous*," Him the people will curse; Nations will abhor him.**

(25)* **But those who rebuke the wicked will have delight, And a good blessing will come upon them.**

(28)* ***Do not be a witness against your neighbor without cause, For would you <u>deceive</u> with your <u>lips</u>?***

(29)* ***<u>Do not say</u>, "I will do to him just as he has done to me; I will render to the man according to his work."***

(Further Sayings of the Wise)

Proverbs 25:8–10

(8)   Do not go hastily to court; For what will you do in the end, When your neighbor has put you to shame?

(9)   Debate your case with your neighbor, *And do not <u>disclose</u> the secret to another;*

(10)   Lest he who hears it expose your shame, And your reputation be ruined.

Proverbs 25:14
Whoever falsely boasts of giving Is like clouds and wind without rain.

Proverbs 25:*18*
A man who bears false witness against his neighbor Is like a club, a sword and a sharp arrow.

Proverbs 25:20
Like one who takes away a garment in cold weather, And like vinegar on soda, *Is one who sings songs to a heavy heart.*

Proverbs 26:12*
Do you see a man wise in his own eyes? There is more hope for a fool than for him.

Proverbs 26:13–16*
(13) The lazy man *says, "There is a lion in the road! A fierce lion in the streets!"*
(14) As a door turns on its hinges, So does the lazy man on his bed.
(15) The lazy man buries his hand in the bowl; It wearies him to bring it back to his mouth.
(16)* *The lazy man is wiser in his own eyes* Than seven men who can answer sensibly.

Proverbs 26:18–19
Like a madman who throws firebrands, arrows, and death, *Is the man who deceives his neighbor, And says, "I was only joking!"*

Proverbs 26:20*–21
Where there is no wood, the fire goes out; And where there is no ***talebearer* (*gossiper*)**, strife ceases. As charcoal is to burning coals, and wood to fire, So is a contentious man to kindle strife.

Proverbs 26:22
The words of a ***talebearer* (*gossiper*)** are like tasty trifles, And they go down into the inmost body.

Proverbs 26:23

Fervent lips with a wicked heart Are like earthenware covered with silver dross.

Proverbs 26:24*–26

(24)* He who hates, *disguises it with his lips*, And lays up **deceit** within himself;

(25) When he *speaks kindly*, *do not believe him*, For there are seven abominations in his heart;

(26) Though his hatred is covered by **deceit**, His wickedness will be revealed before the assembly.

Proverbs 26:28*

A **lying** *tongue* hates those who are crushed by it, And a *flattering mouth* works ruin.

Proverbs 27:5*

Open rebuke is better Than *love carefully concealed*.

Proverbs *27:*6*

Faithful are the wounds of a friend, But the kisses of an enemy are *deceitful*.

Proverbs *28:*6*

Better is the poor who walks in his integrity Than one *perverse* in his ways, though he be rich.

Proverbs 28:8

One who increases his possessions by *usury* and *extortion* Gathers it for him who will pity the poor.

Proverbs 28:18*

Whoever walks blamelessly will be saved, But he who is *perverse* in his ways will suddenly fall.

Proverbs *28:*23*

He who rebukes a man will find more favor afterward Than he who _flatters_ with the _tongue_.

Proverbs 28:24

Whoever robs his father or his mother, And says, "_It is no transgression,_" The same is companion to a destroyer.

Proverbs 29:4

The king establishes the land by justice, But he who receives _bribes_ overthrows it.

Proverbs 29:5

A man who _flatters_ his neighbor Spreads a net for his feet.

Proverbs 29:12

If a ruler pays attention to **_lies_**, All his servants become wicked.

Proverbs 29:24

Whoever is a partner with a thief hates his own life; He swears to tell the truth, _but reveals nothing._

(The Wisdom of Agur)

Proverbs *30:*5*–6

Every word of God is pure; He is a shield to those who put their trust in Him. Do not add to His words, Lest He rebuke you, and you be found a **_liar_**.

(Prayer of Devotion)

Proverbs 30:7*-9*

(7)* Two things I request of You (Deprive me not before I die):

(8)* Remove **_falsehood_** and **_lies_** far from me; Give me neither poverty nor riches—Feed me with the food allotted to me;

(9)* Lest I be full and deny You, And say, "Who is the LORD?" Or lest I be poor and steal, And _profane_ the name of my God.

<u>Proverbs 30:10</u>

Do not *malign* a servant to his master, Lest he curse you, and you be found guilty.

<u>*(The Virtuous Wife)*</u>

<u>Proverbs *31:*30*–31</u>

Charm is <u>*deceitful*</u> and beauty is passing, But a woman who fears the LORD, she shall be praised. Give her of the fruit of her hands, And let her own works praise her in the gates.

CHAPTER 17

DILIGENCE, DILIGENT, LABOR(S), WORK(S), HARDWORKING, INDUSTRIOUS

W ith your permission, I would like to turn this mirror of intro-
spection and deep study regarding this Chapter Narrative of
Diligence, **_Hard Work_**, **_Labors_** into the practice of being **_Industrious_**.
Such introspective look begins with my mother who has had her share
of life issues, was positioned to raise three sons by herself without any
public assistance, and without ANY financial assistance from my earthly
father (which did not become fully transparent to me until my early fif-
ties). As the eldest son, I have no recall of ever living with two parents in
the home (maybe this is a contributing factor to my failed marriages).
What I do remember was my first "**chore**," which, to the best of my recall,
was periodically attempting to wash the family dishes when I was approximately four or five years old. This was my first taste of the concept of
"**_Work_**." And to my pleasant surprise, my mother began the process of
homeschooling and teaching the biblical principal clearly admonished in
Proverbs 22:6: "**_Train up a child in the way he should go, And, when he
is old, he will not depart from it._**"

Additionally, in looking back on my early childhood life through college, I remember my mother **_Working_** two and often three jobs on a daily basis. She did this to ensure that our family of four had the basics of life that included housing, clothing, and food. As I travel down memory lane, I am reminded of the Book of Proverbs' sub-theme of "_The Folly of Indolence_" found in Proverbs 6:6–11, which lays out the importance of **_Working_** and **supplying the needs** for one's family. I have always found verse 6 extremely illustrative by what it states and promises: "_Go to the ant, you sluggard! Consider her ways and be wise_"! From my perspective, truer words were never more important than passing on the importance of **_Work_** and wisdom!

Needless to say, this Chapter Theme is extremely rich in content and salient words of wisdom. Take, for example, Proverbs 10:4: "_He who has a slack hand becomes poor, But the hand of the **diligent** makes rich._" Or Proverbs 10:16: "_The **labor** of the righteous leads to life, The wages of the wicked to sin._" And for the planner, Proverbs 21:5: "_The plans of the **diligent** leads surely to plenty, But, those of everyone who is hasty, surely to poverty._" And there are several other verses that capture these Chapter Theme's, (i.e. Proverbs 14:23; 16:3; 21:25—26, 23:4—5, and 24:27)!

But the Proverbs verses that, from my perspective, fully capture and resonated with me on these Chapter Theme's are contained within the Chapter sub-theme of "_**The Virtuous Wife**_" (i.e. Proverbs 31:10 –22 and 24–31)! I would strongly encourage one and all to read, study, meditate, and marinate on these Proverbs verses to fully encapsulate the true essence of these Chapter Theme's!

To God be the GLORY!

(The Call of Wisdom)

Proverbs *1:*20*–27 and 28–33*

(20)* **_Wisdom_ calls aloud outside; _She_ raises her voice in the open squares.**

(21) *She* cries out in the chief concourses, At the openings of the gates in the city *She* speaks her words:

(22) "How long, you simple ones, will you love simplicity? For scorners delight in their scorning, And fools hate knowledge.

(23) Turn at *my* rebuke; Surely *I* will pour out *my* spirit on you; *I* will make *my* words known to you.

(24) Because *I* have called and you refused, *I* have stretched out *my* hand and no one regarded,

(25) Because you disdained all *my* counsel, And would have none of *my* rebuke,

(26) *I* also will laugh at your calamity; *I* will mock when your terror comes,

(27) When your terror comes like a storm, And your destruction comes like a whirlwind, When distress and anguish come upon you.

(28) "Then they will call on *me*, but *I* will not answer; They will seek *me* **diligently**, but they will not find *me*.

(29) Because they hated knowledge And did not choose the fear of the LORD,

(30) They would have none of *my* counsel And despised *my* every rebuke.

(31) Therefore they shall eat the fruit of their own way, And be filled to the full with their own fancies.

(32) For the turning away of the simple will slay them, And the complacency of fools will destroy them;

(33)* But whoever *listens to me* will dwell safely, And will be secure, without fear of evil."

(Security in Wisdom)

Proverbs *4:*20*–*27*

(20)* **My son, give attention to my words; Incline your ear to my sayings.**

(21)* **Do not let them depart from your eyes; Keep them in the midst of your heart;**

(22)* **For they are life to those who find them, And health to all their flesh.**

(23)* **Keep your heart with all _diligence_, For out of it spring the issues of life.**

(24)* **Put away from you a deceitful mouth, And put perverse lips far from you.**

(25) Let your eyes look straight ahead, And your eyelids look right before you.

(26)* **Ponder the path of your feet, And let all your ways be established.**

(27)* **Do not turn to the right or the left; Remove your foot from evil.**

(The Peril of Adultery)

Proverbs 5:7–14

(7) Therefore hear me now, my children, And do not depart from the words of my mouth.

(8) Remove your way far from her, And do not go near the door of her house,

(9) Lest you give your honor to others, And your years to the cruel one;

(10) Lest aliens be filled with your wealth, And your _labors_ go to the house of a foreigner;

(11) And you mourn at last, When your flesh and your body are consumed,

(12) And say: "How I have hated instruction, And my heart despised correction!

(13) I have not obeyed the voice of my teachers, Nor inclined my ear to those who instructed me!

(14) I was on the verge of total ruin, In the midst of the assembly and congregation."

(The Folly of Indolence)

Proverbs 6:6–11

(6)   *Go to the ant*, you sluggard! <u>*Consider **her ways** and be wise.*</u>

(7)   Which, having no captain, Overseer or ruler,

(8)   ***Provides her supplies*** *in the summer,* <u>*And **gathers her food** in the harvest.*</u>

(9)   How long will you slumber, O sluggard? When will you rise from your sleep?

(10) A little sleep, a little slumber, A little folding of the hands to sleep—

(11) So shall your poverty come on you like a prowler, And your need like an armed man.

(The Crafty Harlot)

Proverbs 7:10–20

(10) And there a woman met him, With the attire of a harlot, and a crafty heart.

(11) She was loud and rebellious, Her feet would not stay at home.

(12) At times she was outside, at times in the open square, Lurking at every corner.

(13) So she caught him and kissed him; With an impudent face she said to him:

(14) "I have peace offerings with me; Today I have paid my vows.

(15) So I came out to meet you, ***Diligently*** to seek your face. And I have found you.

(16) I have spread my bed with tapestry, Colored coverings of Egyptian linen.

(17) I have perfumed my bed With myrrh, aloes, and cinnamon.

(18) Come, let us take our fill of love until morning; Let us delight ourselves with love.

(19) For my husband is not at home; He has gone on a long journey;

(20) He has taken a bag of money with him, And will come home on the appointed day."

(The Excellence of Wisdom)

Proverbs *8:*12*–21

(12)* **"I, wisdom, dwell with prudence, And find out knowledge and discretion.**

(13) The fear of the LORD is to hate evil; Pride and arrogance and the evil way And the perverse mouth, I (Wisdom) hate.

(14)* Counsel is mine, and sound wisdom; I (Wisdom) am understanding, I (Wisdom) have strength.

(15) By me (wisdom) kings reign, And rulers decree justice.

(16) By me (wisdom) princes rule, and nobles, All the judges of the earth.

(17)* **I (Wisdom) love those who love me (wisdom), And those who seek me (wisdom) _diligently_ will find me (wisdom).**

(18) Riches and honor are with me (wisdom), Enduring riches and righteousness.

(19)* My (Wisdom) fruit is better than gold, yes, than fine gold, Any my (wisdom) revenue than choice silver.

(20) I (Wisdom) traverse the way of righteousness, In the midst of the paths of justice,

(21) That I (Wisdom) may cause those who love me (wisdom) to inherit wealth, That I (Wisdom) may fill their treasures.

(Wise Sayings of Solomon)

Proverbs 10:4*

He who has a slack hand becomes poor, But the hand of the **_diligent_** makes rich.

Proverbs 10:5*

He who **_gathers_** _in summer_ is a wise son; He who sleeps in harvest is a son who causes shame.

Proverbs 10:16
The **_labor_** of the righteous leads to life, The wages of the wicked to sin.

Proverbs 11:18
The wicked man does deceptive **_work_**, But he who sows righteousness will have a sure reward.

Proverbs 12:11
He who _tills his land_ will be satisfied with bread, But he who follows frivolity is devoid of understanding.

Proverbs 12:14
A man will be satisfied with good by the fruit of his mouth, And the _recompense of a man's hands_ will be rendered to him.

Proverbs 12:24
The hand of the **_diligent_** will rule, But the lazy man will be put to _forced_ **_labor_**.

Proverbs 12:27
The lazy man does not roast what he took in hunting, But **_diligence_** is man's precious possession.

Proverbs 13:4*
The soul of a lazy man desires, and has nothing; But the soul of the **_diligent_** shall be made rich.

Proverbs 13:*11*
Wealth gained by dishonesty will be diminished, But he who **_gathers_** by **_labor_** will increase.

Proverbs 14:*4*
Where no oxen are, the trough is clean; But _much increase comes by the strength of an ox._

Proverbs *14:*23*
In all _labor_ there is profit, But _idle_ chatter leads only to poverty.

Proverbs 14:35

The king's favor is toward a *wise servant*, But his wrath is against him who causes shame.

Proverbs *16:*3*

Commit your *works* to the LORD, And your thoughts will be established.

Proverbs 16:26

The person who ***labors***, ***labors*** for himself, For his hungry mouth drives him on.

Proverbs 17:2

A *wise servant* will rule over a son who causes shame, And will share an inheritance among the brothers.

Proverbs 18:9

He who is slothful in his ***work*** Is a brother to him who is a great destroyer.

Proverbs 20:*4*

The lazy man will not *plow* because of winter; He will beg during harvest and have nothing.

Proverbs 20:*13*

Do not love sleep, lest you come to poverty; *Open your eyes, and you will be satisfied with bread.*

Proverbs *21:*5*

The plans of the *diligent* lead surely to plenty, But those of everyone who is hasty, surely to poverty.

Proverbs 21:8*

The way of a guilty man is perverse; But as for the pure, his ***work*** is right.

Proverbs 21:22

A wise man scales the city of the mighty, And brings down the trusted stronghold.

Proverbs *21:25*-*26*

The desire of the lazy man kills him, For his hands refuse to **_labor_**. He covets greedily all day long, **But the righteous gives and does not spare**.

Proverbs *22:*6*

Train up a child in the way he should go, And when he is old he will not depart from it.

Proverbs 22:13*

The lazy man says, "There is a lion outside! I shall be slain in the streets!"

(Sayings of the Wise)

Proverbs 22:29*

Do you see a man who _excels_ in his **_work_**? He will stand before kings; He will not stand before unknown men.

Proverbs *23:*4*–*5*

Do not _overwork_ to be rich; Because of your own understanding, cease! Will you set your eyes on that which is not? For riches certainly make themselves wings; They fly away like an eagle toward heaven.

Proverbs 23:17*–18

Do not let your heart envy sinners, But be _zealous_ for the fear of the LORD all the day; For surely there is a hereafter, And your hope will not be cut off.

(Further Sayings of the Wise)

Proverbs *24:*27*

Prepare your outside **work**, Make it fit for yourself in the field; And afterward _build your house_.

Proverbs *24:*28*–*29*

Do not be a witness against your neighbor without cause, For would

you deceive with your lips? Do not say, "I will do to him just as he has done to me; I will render to the man according to his *work*."

(Further Wise Sayings of Solomon)

Proverbs 25:13
Like the cold of snow in time of harvest Is a faithful messenger to those who send him, For he refreshes the soul of his masters.

Proverbs 26:28*
A lying tongue hates those who are crushed by it, And a flattering mouth **works** ruin.

Proverbs 27:18
Whoever keeps the fig tree will eat its fruit; So he who *waits on his master will be honored.*

Proverbs 27:23–27
(23) Be **diligent** to know the state of your flocks, And *attend* to your herds;

(24) For riches are not forever, Nor does a crown endure to all generations.

(25) *When the hay is removed, and the tender grass shows itself, And the herbs of the mountains are* **gathered** *in,*

(26) The lambs will provide your clothing, And the goats the price of a field;

(27) You shall have enough goats' milk for your food, For the food of your household, And the nourishment of your maidservants.

Proverbs 28:19
He who tills his land will have plenty of bread, But he who follows frivolity will have poverty enough!

(The Wisdom of Agur)

Proverbs 30:24*–28*

(24)* There are four things which are little on the earth, But they are exceedingly wise:

(25)* The ants are a people not strong, *Yet they <u>prepare</u> their food in the summer*;

(26)* The rock badgers are a feeble folk, *Yet they <u>make</u> their homes in the crags*;

(27)* The locusts have no king, *Yet they <u>all advance in ranks</u>*;

(28)* The spider <u>*skillfully grasps with its hands*</u>, And it is in kings' palaces.

(The Virtuous Wife)

Proverbs *31:*10*–22* and 24*–31*

(10)* **Who can find a <u>*virtuous wife*</u>? For <u>*her worth*</u> is *far above rubies*.**

(11)* **The heart of <u>*her*</u> husband safely *trusts <u>her</u>*; So he will *have no lack of gain*.**

(12)* **<u>*She*</u> does *him good* and not evil All the *days* of <u>*her*</u> life.**

(13) **<u>*She*</u> seeks wool and flax, *And <u>willingly works</u>* with <u>*her*</u> hands.**

(14) **<u>*She*</u> is like the merchant ships, *<u>She brings her</u>* food from *afar*.**

(15) **<u>*She*</u> also *rises* while it is yet night, And <u>*provides*</u> food for <u>*her*</u> household, And a portion for <u>*her*</u> maidservants.**

(16)* **<u>*She*</u> considers a field and *buys it*; From <u>*her*</u> profits <u>she</u> plants a vineyard.**

(17)* **<u>*She*</u> girds <u>*herself*</u> with *strength*, And *strengthens <u>her</u>* arms.**

(18) **<u>*She*</u> perceives that <u>*her*</u> merchandise is good, And <u>*her*</u> lamp does not go out by night.**

(19) **<u>*She*</u> stretches out <u>*her*</u> hands to the distaff, And <u>*her*</u> hand holds the spindle.**

(20)* **<u>*She*</u> extends <u>*her*</u> hand to the *poor*, Yes, <u>she</u> reaches out <u>*her*</u> hands to the *needy*.**

(21) **<u>*She*</u> is not afraid of snow for <u>*her*</u> household, For all <u>*her*</u> household is clothed with scarlet.**

(22)* **_She makes_** tapestry for **_herself; Her_** clothing is fine linen and purple.

(24)* **_She makes_** linen garments and *sells* them, And **_supplies_** sashes for the merchants.

(25)* **_Strength_** and **_honor_** are **_her_** clothing; **_She_** shall rejoice in time to come.

(26)* **_She_** opens **_her mouth_** with **_wisdom_**, And on **_her tongue_** is the law of **_kindness_**.

(27) **_She_** watches over the *ways* of **_her_** household, *And does not eat the bread of idleness.*

(28) **_Her_** *children* rise up and call **_her_** *blessed*; **_Her_** *husband* also, and he *praises* **_her_**;

(29) "Many daughters have done well, But **_you excel_** them all."

(30)* **Charm is deceitful and beauty is passing,** *But a woman who fears the LORD, **she shall be praised**.*

(31) Give **_her_** of the fruit of **_her_** hands, And let **_her_** own **_works_** praise **_her_** in the gates.

CHAPTER 18

DIRECTION, LEAD(S), PATH, WALK, WAY, SEND

When I think of the various descriptors of this Chapter Theme, I generally focus on the subtheme of the "*Way*"; And as a Christian, one is generally led to one of the foundational biblical verses regarding salvation, that being John 14:6: "*Jesus answered, 'I am the way, the truth, and the life. No one comes to the Father except through Me.'*" Jesus clearly and unambiguously distinguished Himself as "*the only Way.*" The definition of "*Way*" is generally defined as a ***Path*** or route. Jesus then, on the last night before His crucifixion, was instructing His disciples, as He continues to do through His Word today, that there is no other ***Path*** to heaven, no other ***Way*** to the Father except through Him!

I'm reminded of when I accepted Jesus Christ as my Lord and Savior some time during my teens, whereby Romans 10:9–10 still stands out to me as I came to acknowledge and accept that the "*Way*" became illuminated in a crystal clear fashion: "*that if you confess with your mouth the Lord Jesus and believe in your heart that God has raised Him from the dead, you will be saved. For with the heart one believes unto righteousness, and with the mouth confession is made unto salvation.*" To God be the Glory!

I wonder how many times have I <u>failed</u> to acknowledge Father God by <u>failing</u> to do what His Word instructs one to do in ALL of life's situations? In these Chapter Narrative's, I have already shared my two deepest failures and regrets during my Christian ***Walk***. They were my failed marriages and my adulterous affairs. Father God knows as well as I know, how going off the Christian ***Path*** while being forgiven by Father God, more likely than not, altered the ***Path***, ***Direction***, and ***Way*** of my life. While I am a strong believer in Romans 8:28—"*And we know that all things work together for good to those who love God, to those who are called according to His purpose*"— I cannot help but to ask myself and/or challenge myself to think about the trajectory or ***Path*** my Life might have taken had those two major life/sin failures not occurred. Needless to say, this reflective sentimental state is a waste of time, energy, and thought! But let me leave you with one of the cornerstone Proverbs verses that appropriately addresses, reflects, and speaks to these Chapter's Narrative Theme's, that being Proverbs 3:5–6: "***Trust in the Lord with all your heart And lean not on your own understanding; In all your ways acknowledge Him, And He shall direct your paths***"!

(Shun Evil Counsel)

Proverbs *1:15–*19*

(15) My son, do not ***walk*** in the ***way*** with them, Keep your foot from their ***path***;

(16) For their feet run to evil, And they make haste to shed blood.

(17) Surely, in vain the net is spread In the sight of any bird;

(18) But they lie in wait for their own blood, They lurk secretly for their own lives.

(19)* **So are the *ways* of everyone who is greedy for gain; It takes away the life of its owners.**

(The Call of Wisdom)

Proverbs 1:28–33*

(28) "Then they will call on me, but I (Wisdom) will not answer; They will seek me diligently, but they will not find me.

(29)* Because they hated knowledge And did not choose the fear of the LORD,

(30) They would have none of my counsel And despised my every rebuke.

(31) Therefore they shall eat the fruit of their own _way_, And be filled to the full with their own fancies.

(32) For the turning away of the simple will slay them, And the complacency of fools will destroy them;

(33)* But whoever listens to me (wisdom) will dwell safely, And will be secure, without fear of evil."

(The Value of Wisdom)

Proverbs *2:1*–*9* and 10*–22*

(1)* My son, if you receive my words, And treasure my commands within you,

(2)* **So that you incline your ear to wisdom, And apply your heart to understanding;**

(3)* Yes, if you cry out for discernment, And lift up your voice for understanding,

(4)* If you seek her as silver, And search for her as for hidden treasures;

(5)* **Then you will understand the fear of the LORD, And find the knowledge of God.**

(6)* **For the LORD gives wisdom; From His mouth come knowledge and understanding;**

(7)* **He (Wisdom) stores up sound wisdom for the upright; He is a shield to those who _walk_ uprightly:**

(8)* **He guards the _paths_ of justice, And preserves the _way_ of His saints.**

(9)* **Then you will understand righteousness and justice, Equity and every good _path_.**

(10)* When wisdom enters your heart, And knowledge is pleasant to your soul,

(11)* Discretion will preserve you; Understanding will keep you,

(12)* To deliver you from the _**way**_ of evil, From the man who speaks perverse things,

(13) From those who leave the _**paths**_ of uprightness To _**walk**_ in the _**ways**_ of darkness;

(14) Who rejoice in doing evil, And delight in the perversity of the wicked;

(15) Whose _**ways**_ are crooked, And who are devious in their _**paths**_:

(16) To deliver you from the immoral woman, From the seductress who flatters with her words,

(17) Who forsakes the companion of her youth, And forgets the covenant of her God.

(18) For her house _**leads**_ down to death, And her _**paths**_ to the dead;

(19) None who go to her return, Nor do they regain the _**paths**_ of life—

(20)* **So you may _walk_ in the _way_ of goodness, And keep to the _paths_ of righteousness.**

(21)* **For the upright will dwell in the land, And the blameless will remain in it;**

(22)* But the wicked will be cut off from the earth, And the unfaithful will be uprooted from it.

(Guidance for the Young)

Proverbs *3:*5*–*6*

Trust in the LORD with all your heart, And lean not on your own understanding; In all your _ways_, acknowledge Him, And He shall _direct_ your _paths_.

Proverbs *3:*13*–18*

(13)* **Happy is the man who finds wisdom, And the man who gains understanding;**

(14) For her (wisdom) proceeds are better than the profits of silver, And her gain than fine gold.

(15) She (*Wisdom)* is more precious than rubies, And all the things you may desire cannot compare with her.

(16) Length of days is in her right hand, In her left hand riches and honor.

(17)* Her *ways* are *ways* of pleasantness, And all her *paths* are peace.

(18)* She is a tree of life to those who take hold of her, And happy are all who retain her.

Proverbs *3:*21*–26

(21)* My son, let them not depart from your eyes—**Keep sound wisdom and discretion;**

(22) So they (wisdom and discretion) will be life to your soul And grace to your neck.

(23)* Then you will *walk* safely in your *way*, And your foot will not stumble.

(24)* When you lie down, you will not be afraid; Yes, you will lie down and your sleep will be sweet.

(25) Do not be afraid of sudden terror, Nor of trouble from the wicked when it comes;

(26)* For the LORD will be your confidence, And will keep your foot from being caught.

Proverbs 3:31-32*

Do not envy the oppressor, And choose none of his *ways*; For the perverse person is an abomination to the LORD, But His secret counsel is with the upright.

(Security in Wisdom)

Proverbs *4:*10*–*13*, 14*–16, 17, 18, 19, and 20*–*27*

(10)* **Hear, my son, and receive my sayings, And the years of your life will be many.**

(11)* **I have taught you in the _way_ of wisdom; I have led you in right _paths_.**

(12)* **When you _walk_, your _steps_ will not be hindered, And when you _run_, you will not stumble.**

(13)* **Take firm hold of instruction, do not let her go; Keep her, for she is your life.**

(14)* **Do not enter the _path_ of the wicked, And do not _walk_ in the _way_ of evil.**

(15) Avoid _it_, do not travel on _it;_ Turn away from _it_ and pass on.

(16) For they do not sleep unless they have done evil; And their sleep is taken away unless they make someone fall.

(17) For they eat the bread of wickedness, And drink the wine of violence.

(18)* **But the _path_ of the just is like the shining sun, That shines ever brighter unto the perfect day.**

(19) The _way_ of the wicked is like darkness; They do not know what makes them stumble.

(20)* **My son, give attention to my words; Incline your ear to my sayings.**

(21)* **Do not let them depart from your eyes; Keep them in the midst of your heart;**

(22)* **For they are life to those who find them, And health to all their flesh.**

(23)* **Keep your heart with all diligence, For out of it spring the issues of life.**

(24)* **Put away from you a deceitful mouth, And put perverse lips far from you.**

(25) Let your eyes look straight ahead, And your eyelids look right before you.

(26)* **Ponder the _path_ of your feet, And let all your _ways_ be established.**

(27)* **Do not turn to the right or the left; Remove your foot from evil.**

(The Peril of Adultery)

Proverbs *5:1*–6

(1)* My son, pay attention to my wisdom; Lend your ear to my understanding,

(2)* That you may preserve discretion, And your lips may keep knowledge.

(3) For the lips of an immoral woman drip honey, And her mouth is smoother than oil;

(4) But in the end she is bitter as *wormwood*, Sharp as a two-edged sword.

(5) Her feet go down to death, Her steps lay hold of hell.

(6) Lest you ponder her ***path*** of life—Her ***ways*** are unstable; You do not know them.

Proverbs *5:7–14

(7) Therefore hear me now, my children, And do not depart from the words of my mouth.

(8) Remove your ***way*** far from her, And do not go near the door of her house,

(9) Lest you give your honor to others, And your years to the cruel one;

(10) Lest aliens be filled with your wealth, And your labors go to the house of a foreigner;

(11) And you mourn at last, When your flesh and your body are consumed,

(12) And say: "How I have hated instruction, And my heart despised correction!

(13) I have not obeyed the voice of my teachers, Nor inclined my ear to those who instructed me!

(14) I was on the verge of total ruin, In the midst of the assembly and congregation."

Proverbs *5:*21*–*23*

(21)* **For the _ways_ of man are before the eyes of the LORD, And He ponders all his _paths_.**

(22)* **His own iniquities entrap the wicked man, And he is caught in the cords of his sin.**

(23)* **He shall die for lack of instruction, And in the greatness of his folly he shall go _astray_.**

(The Folly of Indolence)

Proverbs 6:6–11*

(6) Go to the ant, you sluggard! Consider her _ways_ and be wise,

(7) Which, having no captain, Overseer or ruler,

(8) Provides her supplies in the summer, And gathers her food in the harvest.

(9) How long will you slumber, O sluggard? When will you rise from your sleep?

(10) A little sleep, a little slumber, A little folding of the hands to sleep—

(11)* So shall your poverty come on you like a prowler, And your need like an armed man.

(The Wicked Man)

Proverbs 6:12–19

(12) A worthless person, a wicked man, _Walks_ with a perverse mouth;

(13) He winks with his eyes, He shuffles his feet, _He points with his fingers_;

(14) Perversity is in his heart, He devises evil continually, He sows discord.

(15) Therefore his calamity shall come suddenly; Suddenly he shall be broken without remedy.

(16) These six things the LORD hates, Yes, seven are an abomination to Him;

(17) A proud look, A lying tongue, Hands that shed innocent blood,

(18) A heart that devises wicked plans, _Feet that are swift in running to evil,_

(19) A false witness who speaks lies, And one who sows discord among brethren.

(Beware of Adultery)

Proverbs *6:20*–29*

(20)* My son, keep your father's command, And do not forsake the _law_ of your mother.

(21)* Bind them continually upon your heart; Tie them around your neck.

(22)* When you _roam_, they will **_lead_** you; When you sleep, they will keep you; And when you awake, they will speak with you.

(23)* **For the _commandment_ is a _lamp_, And the _law_ a _light_; Reproofs of instruction are the _way_ of life,**

(24) To keep you from the evil woman, From the flattering tongue of a seductress.

(25) Do not lust after her beauty in your heart, Nor let her allure you with her eyelids.

(26) For by means of a harlot A man is reduced to a crust of bread; And an adulteress will prey upon his precious life.

(27) Can a man take fire to his bosom, And his clothes not be burned?

(28) Can one **_walk_** on hot coals, And his feet not be seared?

(29)* So is he who goes in to his neighbor's wife; Whoever touches her shall not be innocent.

(The Crafty Harlot)

Proverbs 7:6–9 and 24–27*

(6) For at the window of my house I looked through my lattice,

(7) And saw among the simple, I perceived among the youths, A young man devoid of understanding,

(8) Passing along the street near her corner; And he took the **_path_** to her house

(9) In the twilight, in the evening, In the black and dark night.

(24) Now therefore, listen to me, my children; Pay attention to the words of my mouth:

(25)* Do not let your heart turn aside to her **_ways_**, Do not *stray* into her **_paths_**;

(26) For she has cast down many wounded, And all who were slain by her were strong men.

(27)* Her house is the **_way_** to hell, *Descending to the chambers of death.*

(The Excellence of Wisdom)

Proverbs *8:*1*–5*, 12*–14*, 20–22, and 32*–36*

(1)* **Does not wisdom cry out, And understanding lift up her voice?**

(2) She (wisdom) takes her stand on the top of the high hill, Beside the **_way_**, where the **_paths_** meet.

(3) She (wisdom) cries out by the gates, at the entry of the city, At the entrance of the doors:

(4) "To you, O men, I call, And my voice is to the sons of men.

(5)* O you simple ones, understand prudence, And you fools, be of an understanding heart.

(12)* "I, wisdom, dwell with prudence, And find out knowledge and discretion.

(13)* The fear of the LORD is to hate evil: Pride and arrogance and the evil **_way_** And the perverse mouth I hate.

(14)* Counsel is mine, and sound wisdom; I am understanding, I have strength.

(20) I (Wisdom) traverse the **_way_** of righteousness, In the midst of the **_paths_** of justice,

(21) That I may cause those who love me to inherit wealth, That I may fill their treasures.

(22) "The LORD possessed me at the beginning of His **_way_**, Before His works of old.

(32)* "Now therefore, listen to me, my children, For blessed are those who keep my **_ways_**.

(33)* **Hear instruction and be wise, And do not disdain it.**

(34)* **Blessed is the man who listens to me, Watching daily at my gates, Waiting at the posts of my doors.**

(35)* **For whoever finds me finds life, And obtains favor from the LORD;**

(36)* But he who sins against me wrongs his own soul; All those who hate me love death."

(The Way of Wisdom)

Proverbs *9:4–*6*

(4) "Whoever is simple, let him turn in here!" As for him who lacks understanding, she (wisdom) says to him,

(5) "Come, eat of my bread And drink of the wine I have mixed.

(6)* **Forsake foolishness and live, And go the _way_ of understanding.**

(The Way of Folly)

Proverbs 9:13–18

(13) A foolish woman is clamorous; She is simple, and knows nothing.

(14) For she sits at the door of her house, On a seat by the highest places of the city,

(15) *To call to those who <u>pass</u> by, Who go straight on their <u>*way*</u>:*

(16) "Whoever is simple, *let him turn in here*"; And as for him who lacks understanding, she says to him,

(17) "Stolen water is sweet, And bread eaten in secret is pleasant."

(18) But he does not know that the dead are there, *That her guests are in the depths of hell.*

(Wise Sayings of Solomon)

Proverbs 10:9*
He who **<u>walks</u>** with integrity **<u>walks</u>** securely, But he who perverts his **<u>*ways*</u>** will become known.

Proverbs 10:16
The labor of the righteous **leads** to life, The wages of the wicked to sin.

Proverbs 10:*17*
He who keeps instruction is in the **way** of life, But he who refuses correction goes *astray.*

Proverbs 10:26
As vinegar to the teeth and smoke to the eyes, So is the lazy man to those who **send** him.

Proverbs *10:*29*
The <u>way</u> of the LORD is strength for the upright, But destruction will come to the workers of iniquity.

Proverbs 11:3
The integrity of the upright will <u>*guide*</u> them, But the perversity of the unfaithful will destroy them.

Proverbs 11:5*
The righteousness of the blameless will **<u>*direct*</u>** his **<u>*way*</u>** aright, But the wicked will fall by his own wickedness.

Proverbs 11:19
As righteousness *leads* to life, So he who *pursues* evil *pursues* it to his own death.

Proverbs 11:20*
Those who are of a perverse heart are an abomination to the LORD, But the blameless in their *ways* are His delight.

Proverbs *11:*24*–*25*
There is one who scatters, yet increases more; And there is one who withholds more than is right, But it *leads* to poverty. The generous soul will be made rich, And he who waters will also be watered himself.

Proverbs *12:*15*
The *way* of a fool is right in his own eyes, But he who heeds counsel is wise.

Proverbs 12:*26*
The righteous should choose his friends carefully, For the *way* of the wicked *leads* them *astray.*

Proverbs 12:28*
In the *way* of righteousness is life, And in its *pathway* there is no death.

Proverbs 13:6*
Righteousness guards him whose *way* is blameless, But wickedness overthrows the sinner.

Proverbs 13:15*
Good understanding gains favor, But the *way* of the unfaithful is hard.

Proverbs *13:*20*
He who *walks* with wise men will be wise, But the companion of fools will be destroyed.

Proverbs *13:*24*

He who spares his rod hates his son, But he who loves him disciplines him promptly.

Proverbs 14:2

He who **walks** in his uprightness fears the LORD, But he who is perverse in his **ways** despises Him.

Proverbs 14:*8*

The wisdom of the prudent is to understand his **way**, But the folly of fools is deceit.

Proverbs *14:*12*

There is a _way_ that seems right to a man, But its end is the _way_ of death.

Proverbs 14:14*

The backslider in heart will be filled with his own **ways**, But a good man will be satisfied from above.

Proverbs 14:*15*

The simple believes every word, But the prudent considers well his *steps*.

Proverbs 14:*22*

Do they not go *astray* who devise evil? But mercy and truth belong to those who devise good.

Proverbs *14:*23*

In all labor there is profit, But idle chatter _leads_ only to poverty.

Proverbs 15:*9*

The **way** of the wicked is an abomination to the LORD, But He loves him who *follows* righteousness.

Proverbs 15:10*

Harsh discipline is for him who forsakes the **way**, And he who hates correction will die.

Proverbs 15:19*
The *way* of the lazy man is like a hedge of thorns, But the **way** of the upright is a *highway*.

Proverbs 15:21*
Folly is joy to him who is destitute of discernment, But a man of understanding **walks** uprightly.

Proverbs 15:24*
The *way* of life winds upward for the wise, That he may *turn away* from hell below.

Proverbs 15:29*
The LORD is *far* from the wicked, But He hears the prayer of the righteous.

Proverbs 16:*2*
All the **ways** of a man are pure in his own eyes, But the LORD weighs the spirits.

Proverbs 16:6*
In mercy and truth Atonement is provided for iniquity; And by the fear of the LORD one *departs from evil.*

Proverbs 16:7
When a man's **ways** please the LORD, He makes even his enemies to be at peace with him.

Proverbs *16:*9*
A man's heart plans his *way*, But the LORD *directs* his *steps*.

Proverbs *16:*17*
The *highway* of the upright is to *depart* from evil; He who keeps his *way* preserves his soul.

Proverbs *16:*25*
There is a *way* that seems right to man, But its end is the *way* of death.

Proverbs 16:26

The person who labors, labors for himself, For his hungry mouth *drives* him on.

Proverbs 16:29

A violent man entices his neighbor, And **leads** him in a **way** that is not good.

Proverbs *16:*31*

The silver-haired head is a crown of glory, If it is found in the _way_ of righteousness.

Proverbs 17:23

A wicked man accepts a bribe behind the back To pervert the **ways** of justice.

Proverbs *19:*1*

Better is the poor who _walks_ in his integrity Than one who is perverse in his lips, and is a fool.

Proverbs 19:3

The foolishness of a man twists his **way**, And his heart frets against the LORD.

Proverbs 19:7

All the brothers of the poor hate him; How much more do his friends *go far from him*! He may pursue them with words, yet they abandon him.

Proverbs 19:16*

He who keeps the commandment keeps his soul, But he who is careless of his **ways** will die.

Proverbs *19:*23*

The fear of the LORD _leads_ to life, And he who has it will abide in satisfaction; He will not be visited with evil.

Proverbs *19:*27*
Cease listening to instruction, my son, And you will *stray* from the words of knowledge.

Proverbs 20:1
Wine is a mocker, Strong drink is a brawler, And whoever is _led astray_ by it is not wise.

Proverbs 20:7*
The righteous man **_walks_** in his integrity; His children are blessed after him.

Proverbs 20:11*
Even a child is known by his *deeds*, Whether what he does is pure and right.

Proverbs 20:14
"It is good for nothing," cries the buyer; But when he has gone his **_way_**, then he boasts.

Proverbs *20:*24*
A man's *steps* are of the LORD; How then can a man understand his own _way_?

Proverbs 20:27*
The *spirit* of a man is the *lamp* of the LORD, Searching all the inner depths of his heart.

Proverbs *21:*2*
Every _way_ of a man is right in his own eyes, But the LORD weighs the hearts.

Proverbs *21:*5*
The plans of the diligent _lead_ surely to plenty, But those of everyone who is hasty, surely to poverty.

Proverbs 21:8*

The **_way_** of a guilty man is perverse; But as for the pure, his work is right.

Proverbs 21:*16*

A man who _wanders_ from the **_way_** of understanding Will rest in the assembly of the dead.

Proverbs *21:*21*

He who _follows_ righteousness and mercy, Finds life, righteousness and honor.

Proverbs 21:29

A wicked man hardens his face, But as for the upright, he establishes his **_way_**.

Proverbs 22:5

Thorns and snares are in the **_way_** of the perverse; He who guards his soul will be far from them.

Proverbs *22:*6*

Train up a child in the **way** he should go, And when he is old he will not depart from it.

(Sayings of the Wise)

Proverbs *22:*17*–21* and 24–25

(17)* **Incline your ear and hear the words of the wise, And apply your heart to my knowledge.**

(18)* For it is a pleasant thing if you keep them within you; Let them all be fixed upon your lips.

(19)* So that your trust may be in the LORD; I have instructed you today, even you.

(20)* Have I not written to you excellent things Of counsels and knowledge.

(21)* That I may make you know the certainty of the words of truth, That you may answer words of truth To those who **_send_** to you?

(24) Make no friendship with an angry man, And with a furious man do not go,

(25) Lest you learn his **_ways_** And set a snare for your soul.

Proverbs 23:19*

Hear, my son, and be wise; And *guide* your heart in the **_way._**

Proverbs 23:26–28

(26) My son, give me your heart, And let your eyes observe my **_ways._**

(27) For a harlot is a deep pit, And a seductress is a narrow well.

(28) She also lies in wait as for a victim, And increases the unfaithful among men.

(Further Wise Sayings of Solomon)

Proverbs 25:13

Like the cold of snow in time of harvest Is a faithful messenger to those who **_send_** him, For he refreshes the soul of his masters.

Proverbs 26:6

He who **_sends_** a message by the hand of a fool Cuts off his own feet and drinks violence.

Proverbs 27:8

Like a bird that *wanders* from its nest Is a man who *wanders* from his place.

Proverbs *28:*6*

Better is the poor who _walks_ in his integrity, Than one perverse in his _ways_, though he be rich.

Proverbs 28:10

Whoever causes the upright to go *astray* in an evil **way**, He himself will fall into his own pit; But the blameless will inherit good.

Proverbs 28:18*

Whoever **walks** blamelessly will be saved, But he who is perverse in his **ways** will suddenly fall.

Proverbs 28:26*

He who trusts in his own heart is a fool, But whoever **walks** wisely will be delivered.

Proverbs 29:27*

An unjust man is an abomination to the righteous, And he who is upright in the **way** is an abomination to the wicked.

(The Wisdom of Agur)

Proverbs 30:18–19

There are three things which are too wonderful for me, Yes, four which I do not understand: The **way** of an eagle in the air, The **way** of a serpent on a rock, The **way** of a ship in the midst of the sea, And the **way** of a man with a virgin.

Proverbs 30:20

This is the **way** of an adulterous woman: She eats and wipes her mouth, And says, "I have done no wickedness."

Proverbs 30:29–31

(29)   There are three things which are majestic in pace, Yes, four which are stately in **walk**:

(30)   A lion, which is mighty among beasts And does not turn away from any;

(31)   A greyhound, A male goat also, And a king whose troops are with him.

(The Words of King Lemuel)

Proverbs 31:1–3

(1)　The words of King Lemuel, the utterance which his mother taught him: What, my son?

(2)　And what, son of my womb? And what, son of my vows?

(3)　Do not give your strength to women, Nor your ***ways*** to that which destroys kings.

(The Virtuous Wife)

Proverbs *31:24–27*

(24)　She makes linen garments and sells them, And supplies sashes for the merchants.

(25)* **Strength and honor are her clothing: She shall rejoice in time to come.**

(26)* **She opens her mouth with wisdom, And on her tongue is the law of kindness.**

(27)* She watches over the ***ways*** of her household, And does not eat the bread of idleness.

CHAPTER 19

DISCERNMENT, DISCRETION, WISE COUNSEL

I t never ceases to amaze me how some people think they know all that they need to know about a particular subject matter and make decisions based on their limited knowledge of events, facts, and/or circumstances. How often does human pride get in the way of making sound judgments and/or decision making by thinking that one can make critical decisions in a vacuum, by oneself, without any thought or awareness of **bouncing an idea or upcoming potential decision off another person(s)**? Or how often have we heard from leaders, young and old alike, that being a leader requires a high level of critical thinking and decision-making abilities, resulting in making decisions without the advice and/or perspective of others?

So as one reflects on the realities of the above questions for this Chapter Narrative regarding the topic of "***Discernment/Discretion/ Wise Counsel***;" One can quickly see how the knowledge of the following foundational Proverbs verse has significant application for this Chapter. Specifically, Proverbs 11:14 states: "*Where there is **no counsel**, the people fall; But in the **multitude of counselors**, there is safety*"! It goes without saying that a good and effective leader needs and embraces the ***Counsel***, learnings, experiences, knowledge, and wisdom of _**Wise Counselors**_. One person's or individual's perspective and understanding can be severely limited since such individual may not have all the pertinent facts of each and every situation, and/or may be blinded by personal, cultural or environmental bias, emotions, or wrong impressions.

Therefore, to be an effective decision maker and wise leader, irrespective of the circumstances or venue, one must and absolutely should seek the experience, knowledge, and guidance of _**Wise Counsel**_ from others, as well as being open and willing to **listen to such advice**. Upon receiving such **advice and** _**Counsel**_, and after considering and evaluating all the relevant facts, then one is better prepared and positioned to make more effective, prudent, and sound decisions.

For most of my personal and professional life, I have been blessed to have and, more times than not, to draw upon the experience, knowledge, understanding, and wisdom of a cadre of personal advisors, or "**kitchen cabinet**" as I like to call them, who are individuals who have served as my personal "**board of directors**," and were/are willing to listen, **advise, and pour into me all forms of wisdom and guidance, even when such advice and** _**Counsel**_ **was/is difficult to hear, receive, and process**.

To highlight the importance of having a "**kitchen cabinet**," Proverbs 15:22 states: "_without **counsel**, plans go awry, But, in the **multitude of counselors**, they are established._" For most people, we generally operate from a position of pride as well as tunnel vision, whereby one is locked into a singular way of thinking. Accordingly, one is more likely than not to miss the most appropriate road to travel down, simply because of closed-mindedness to new options, thoughts, and/or alternative ways to achieve the desired outcome. **Everyone needs the assistance of those who can enlarge one's vision or aperture while broadening one's perspective and insight on life and life circumstances**.

Accordingly, everyone should seek to secure and engage a "**kitchen cabinet**," whereby one can obtain the **advice and** _**Wise Counsel**_ of those who know us and who possess a treasure chest of experience, knowledge, understanding, and wisdom. Once obtained, one's challenge is to be receptive to new ideas; be willing to assess, evaluate, and weigh their suggestions carefully and judiciously, thereby allowing one's plans and decisions to be more ***Discerning***, as well as better positioned for success.

(The Beginning of Knowledge)

Proverbs *1:1–6*

(1) The Proverbs of Solomon the son of David, king of Israel:

(2)* **To know *wisdom* and *instruction*, To perceive the *words of understanding*,**

(3)* **To receive the *instruction* of *wisdom*, Justice, judgment, and equity;**

(4)* To give *prudence* to the simple, To the young man *knowledge* and ***discretion*—**

(5)* **A *wise* man will *hear and increase learning*, And a man of *understanding* will attain *wise counsel*,**

(6)* To understand a proverb and an enigma, The *words* of the ***wise*** and their riddles.

(The Call of Wisdom)

Proverbs *1:*20*–27 and 28–33*

(20)* ***Wisdom*** **calls aloud outside; *She* raises *her* voice in the open squares.**

(21) ***She*** cries out in the chief concourses, At the openings of the gates in the city ***She*** speaks ***her*** words:

(22) "How long, you simple ones, will you love simplicity? For scorners delight in their scorning, And fools hate knowledge.

(23) Turn at ***my*** rebuke; Surely ***I*** will pour out ***my*** spirit on you; ***I*** will make ***my*** words known to you.

(24) Because ***I*** have called and you refused, ***I*** have stretched out ***my*** hand and no one regarded,

(25) *Because you disdained all **my counsel**, And would have none of **my** rebuke,*

(26) *I* also will laugh at your calamity; *I* will mock when your terror comes,

(27) When your terror comes like a storm, And your destruction comes like a whirlwind, When distress and anguish come upon you.

(28) "Then they will call on *me*, but *I* will not answer; They will seek *me* diligently, but they will not find *me*.

(29) Because they hated knowledge And did not choose the fear of the LORD,

(30) *They would have none of **my counsel** And despised **my** every rebuke.*

(31) Therefore they shall eat the fruit of their own way, And be filled to the full with their own fancies.

(32) For the turning away of the simple will slay them, And the complacency of fools will destroy them;

(33)* *But whoever **listens to me** will dwell safely, And will be secure, without fear of evil."*

(The Value of Wisdom)

Proverbs *2:1*–9* and *10*–22

(1)* My son, if you *receive my words*, And treasure *my commands* within you,

(2)* **So that you incline your ear to *wisdom*, And apply your heart to understanding;**

(3)* *Yes, if you cry out for **discernment**, And lift up your voice for understanding,*

(4)* *If you seek **her (wisdom)** as silver, And search for **her** as for hidden treasures;*

(5)* ***Then you will understand the fear of the LORD, And find the knowledge of God.***

(6)* ***For the LORD gives wisdom; From His mouth come knowledge and understanding;***

(7)* *He stores up sound <u>wisdom</u> for the upright; <u>He</u> is a shield to those who walk uprightly;*

(8)* *<u>He</u> guards the paths of justice, And preserves the way of <u>His</u> saints.*

(9)* *Then you will understand righteousness and justice, Equity and every good path.*

(10)* *When <u>wisdom</u> enters your heart, And knowledge is pleasant to your soul,*

(11)* *<u>Discretion</u> will preserve you; Understanding will keep you,*

(12) To deliver you from the way of evil, From the man who speaks perverse things,

(13) From those who leave the paths of uprightness To walk in the ways of darkness;

(14) Who rejoice in doing evil, And delight in the perversity of the wicked;

(15) Whose ways are crooked, And who are devious in their paths;

(16) To deliver you from the immoral woman, From the seductress who flatters with her words,

(17) Who forsakes the companion of her youth, And forgets the covenant of her God.

(18) For her house leads down to death, And her paths to the dead;

(19) None who go to her return, Nor do they regain the paths of life—

(20)* *So you may walk in the way of goodness, And keep to the paths of righteousness.*

(21)* *For the upright will dwell in the land, And the blameless will remain in it;*

(22) *But the wicked will be cut off from the earth, And the unfaithful will be uprooted from it.*

(Guidance for the Young)

Proverbs 3:7*–8*

*Do not be **wise** in your own eyes; Fear the LORD and depart from evil. It will be health to your flesh, And strength to your bones.*

Proverbs *3:*21*–26

(21)* My son, let them not depart from your eyes—**Keep sound *wisdom* and *discretion*;**

(22) *So they will be life to your soul And grace to your neck.*

(23) *Then you will walk safely in your way, And your foot will not stumble.*

(24) *When you lie down, you will not be afraid; Yes, you will lie down and your sleep will be sweet.*

(25) *Do not be afraid of sudden terror, Nor of trouble from the wicked when it comes;*

(26) *For the LORD will be your confidence, And will keep your foot from being caught.*

Proverbs 3:31–32*

(31) *Do not envy the oppressor, And choose none of his ways;*

(32)* For the perverse person is an abomination to the LORD, But *His* secret *counsel* is with the upright.

(Security in Wisdom)

Proverbs *4:1*–*13*

(1)* Hear, my children, the *instruction of a father*, And give *attention to know understanding;*

(2) *For I give you good doctrine Do not forsake the law.*

(3) When *I* was my father's son, Tender and the only one in the sight of my mother,

(4) ***He also taught me, and said to me; "Let your heart retain my words; Keep my commands, and live.***

(5)* *Get <u>wisdom</u>! Get <u>understanding</u>! Do not forget, <u>nor turn away</u>* <u>*from the words of my mouth.*</u>

(6)* *Do not forsake <u>her</u> (<u>Wisdom</u>), and <u>she</u> will preserve you; Love <u>her</u>, and <u>she</u> will keep you.*

(7)* <u>**Wisdom**</u> **is the principal thing; Therefore get <u>wisdom</u> And in all your getting, get <u>understanding</u>.**

(8) *Exalt <u>her</u> (<u>Wisdom</u>), and <u>she</u> will promote you; <u>She</u> will bring you honor, when you embrace <u>her</u>.*

(9) *<u>She</u> will place on your head an ornament of grace; A crown of glory <u>she</u> will deliver to you.*

(10)* **Hear, <u>my</u> son, and <u>receive my sayings</u>, And the years of your life will be many.**

(11)* **<u>I</u> have taught you in the way of <u>wisdom</u>; <u>I</u> have led you in the right paths;**

(12)* **When you walk, your steps will not be hindered, And when you run, you will not stumble.**

(13)* <u>***Take firm hold of instruction***</u>**, do not let go; Keep <u>her</u>, for <u>she</u> is your life.**

Proverbs *4:*14*–17

(14)* ***Do not enter the path of the wicked, And do not walk in the way of evil.***

(15) *Avoid it, do not travel on it; Turn away from it and pass on.*

(16) For they do not sleep unless they have done evil; And their sleep is taken away unless they make someone fall.

(17) For they eat the bread of wickedness, And drink the wine of violence.

Proverbs *4:*18*–*27*

(18)* **But the path of the just is like the shining sun, That shines ever brighter unto the perfect day.**

(19) The way of the wicked is like darkness; They do not know what makes them stumble.

(20)* <u>***My*** son, ***give attention to my words***; ***Incline your ear to my sayings***</u>.

(21)* *Do not let them depart from your eyes; Keep them in the midst of your heart;*

(22)* *For they are life to those who find them, And health to all their flesh.*

(23)* *Keep your heart with all diligence, For out of it spring the issues of life.*

(24)* *Put away from you a deceitful mouth, And put perverse lips far from you.*

(25) *Let your eyes look straight ahead, And your eyelids look right before you.*

(26)* *Ponder the path of your feet, And let all your ways be established.*

(27)* *Do not turn to the right or the left; Remove your foot from evil.*

(The Peril of Adultery)

Proverbs 5:1–6

(1) *My* son, pay attention to *my wisdom*; Lend your ear to *my* understanding,

(2) That you may preserve **discretion**, And your lips may keep knowledge.

(3) For the lips of an immoral woman drip honey, And her mouth is smoother than oil;

(4) But in the end she is bitter as wormwood, Sharp as a two-edged sword.

(5) Her feet go down to death, Her steps lay hold of hell.

(6) Lest you ponder her path of life—Her ways are unstable; You do not know them.

(The Excellence of Wisdom)

Proverbs *8:6*–14*, 17*–21, 32*–36*

(6)* *Listen, for **I** (**wisdom**) speak of excellent things, And from the opening of my lips will come right things;*

(7)* *For my mouth will speak truth; Wickedness is an abomination to my lips.*

(8)* *All the words of my mouth are with righteousness; Nothing crooked or perverse is in them.*

(9) *They are all plain to him who understands, And right to those who find knowledge.*

(10)* *Receive **my instruction**, and not silver, And **knowledge** rather than choice gold;*

(11)* *For wisdom is better than rubies, And all the things one may desire cannot be compared with her.*

(12) *"**I**, **wisdom**, dwell with pruden*ce, *And find out knowledge and **discretion**.*

(13) *The fear of the LORD is to hate evil; Pride and arrogance and the evil way And the perverse mouth **I** hate.*

(14)* ***Counsel** is **mine**, and sound **wisdom**; I am **understanding**, I have strength.*

(17)* ***I** (**wisdom**) love those who love me, And those who seek me diligently will find me.*

(18) *Riches and honor are with **me**, Enduring riches and righteousness.*

(19) ***My** fruit is better than gold, yes, than fine gold, And **my** revenue than choice silver.*

(20) *I traverse the way of righteousness, In the midst of the paths of justice,*

(21) *That **I** may cause those who love me to inherit wealth, That **I** may fill their treasuries.*

(32)* *"Now therefore, **listen to me**, **my** children, For blessed are those who keep **my** ways.*

(33)* ***Hear instruction** and be **wise**, And do not disdain it.*

(34)* *Blessed is the man who **listens** to me, Watch daily at **my** gates, Waiting at the posts of **my** doors.*

(35)* *For whoever finds me finds life, And obtains favor from the LORD;*

(36)* *But he who sins against **me** wrongs his own soul; All those who hate* *me love death."*

(The Way of Wisdom)

Proverbs *9:7–12*

(7) *He who corrects a scoffer gets shame for himself, And he who rebukes a wicked man only harms himself.*

(8)* **Do not correct a scoffer, lest he hate you; Rebuke a <u>wise</u> man, and he will love you.**

(9)* **<u>Give instruction to a wise man, and he will be still wiser; Teach a just man, and he will increase in learning</u>.**

(10)* **<u>"The fear of the LORD is the beginning of wisdom, And the knowledge of the Holy One is understanding</u>.**

(11) *For by **me** your days will be multiplied, And years of life will be added to you.*

(12)* *If you are <u>wise</u>, you are <u>wise</u> for yourself, And if you scoff, you will bear it alone."*

(Wise Sayings of Solomon)

Proverbs 10:1

A **<u>wise</u>** son makes a glad father, But a foolish son is the grief of his mother.

Proverbs 10:5

He who gathers in summer is a **<u>wise</u>** son; He who sleeps in harvest is a son who causes shame.

Proverbs 10:8

The **<u>wise</u>** in heart will **<u>receive commands</u>**, But a prating fool will fall.

Proverbs 10:*14*

<u>Wise</u> people store up <u>knowledge</u>, But the mouth of the foolish is near destruction.

Proverbs 10:19
*In the multitude of words sin is not lacking, But he who restrains his lips is **wise**.*

Proverbs 11:14*
Where there is no **counsel**, the people fall; But in the multitude of **counselors** there is safety.

Proverbs 11:22
As a ring of gold in a swine's snout, So is a lovely woman who lacks **discretion**.

Proverbs 11:27*
He who earnestly seeks good finds favor, But trouble will come to him who seeks evil.

Proverbs *11:*29*
He who troubles his own house will inherit the wind, And the fool will be servant to the *wise* of heart.

Proverbs *11:*30*
The fruit of the righteous is a tree of life, And he who wins souls is *wise*.

Proverbs 12:5*
The thoughts of the righteous are right, But the **counsels** of the wicked are deceitful.

Proverbs *12:*15*
The way of a fool is right in his own eyes, But he who heeds *counsel* is *wise*.

Proverbs 12:*18*
*There is one who speaks like the piercings of a sword, But the tongue of the **wise** promotes health.*

Proverbs 12:20*

Deceit is in the heart of those who devise evil, But **_counselors_** of peace have joy.

Proverbs *13:*1*

A _wise_ son _heeds his father's instruction_, But a scoffer does not listen to rebuke.

Proverbs *13:*10*

By pride comes nothing but strife, But with the _well-advised_ is _wisdom_.

Proverbs 13:14

The law of the **wise** is a fountain of life, To turn one away from the snares of death.

Proverbs *13:*20*

He who walks with _wise_ men will be _wise_, But the companion of fools will be destroyed.

Proverbs *13:*22*

A good man leaves an inheritance to his children's children, But the wealth of the sinner is stored up for the righteous.

Proverbs 14:1

The **wise** woman builds her house, But the foolish pulls it down with her hands.

Proverbs *14:*12*

There is a way that seems right to a man, But its end is the way of death.

Proverbs 14:14*

The backslider in heart will be filled with his own ways, _But a good man will be satisfied from above._

Proverbs 14:16*

A **wise** man fears and departs from evil, But a fools rages and is self-confident.

Proverbs 14:24
*The crown of the **wise** is their riches, But a deceitful witness speaks lies.*

Proverbs 14:28
In a <u>multitude of people</u> is a king's honor, But in the lack of people is the downfall of a prince.

Proverbs *15:*5*
A fool despises his <u>father's instruction</u>, But he who receives correction is prudent.

Proverbs *15:*14*
<u>The heart of him who has understanding seeks knowledge, But the mouth of fools feeds on foolishness</u>.

Proverbs 15:20*
*A **wise** son makes a father glad, But a foolish man despises his mother.*

Proverbs 15:21*
Folly is joy to him who is destitute of ***discernment**, <u>But a man of understanding walks uprightly</u>.*

Proverbs *15:*22*
Without <u>counsel</u>, plans go awry, But in the multitude of <u>counselors</u>, they are established.

Proverbs 15:24*
*The way of life winds upward for the **wise**, That he may turn away from hell below.*

Proverbs *15:*31*
The ear that hears the rebukes of life Will abide among the <u>wise</u>.

Proverbs *16:*20*
He who heeds the word *wisely* will find good, And whoever trusts in the LORD, happy is he.

Proverbs 16:21

The **wise** in heart will be called prudent, And sweetness of the lips increases learning.

Proverbs 16:23

The heart of the **wise** teaches his mouth, And adds learning to his lips.

Proverbs 17:28

Even a fool is counted **wise** when he holds his peace; When he shuts his lips, he is considered perceptive.

Proverbs 18:1

A man who isolates himself seeks his own desire; He rages against all **wise** judgment.

Proverbs 19:*11*

The ***discretion*** of a man makes him slow to anger, And his glory is to overlook a transgression.

Proverbs 19:18

Chasten your son while there is hope, And do not set your heart on his destruction.

Proverbs *19:*20*

Listen to *counsel* and receive *instruction*, That you may be *wise* in your latter days.

Proverbs *19:*21*

There are many plans in a man's heart, Nevertheless the *LORD's* *counsel*—that will stand.

Proverbs *19:*25*

Strike a scoffer, and the simple will become wary; **Rebuke one who has understanding, and he will *discern* *knowledge*.**

Proverbs *19:*27*
Cease listening to instruction, my son, And you will stray from the words of knowledge.

Proverbs 20:1
*Wine is a mocker, Strong drink is a brawler, And whoever is led astray by it is not **wise**.*

Proverbs 20:5
Counsel in the heart of man is like deep water, *But a man of understanding will draw it out.*

Proverbs 20:18*
Plans are established by **counsel**; By **wise counsel** wage war.

Proverbs 20:29*
The glory of young men is their strength, And the splendor of old men is their gray head.

Proverbs *21:*2*
Every way of a man is right in his own eyes, But the LORD weighs the hearts.

Proverbs *21:*9*
Better to dwell in a corner of a housetop, Than in a house shared with a contentious woman.

Proverbs 21:11*
*When the scoffer is punished, the simple is made **wise**; But when the **wise** is instructed, he receives knowledge.*

Proverbs 21:22
*A **wise** man scales the city of the mighty, And brings down the trusted stronghold.*

Proverbs 21:30*
There is no *wisdom* or *understanding* Or **counsel** against the *LORD*.

Proverbs 22:3*

A prudent man foresees evil and hides himself, But the simple pass on and are punished.

Proverbs 22:5

Thorns and snares are in the way of the perverse; He who guards his soul will be far from them.

Proverbs *22:*6*

Train up a child in the way he should go, And when he is old he will not depart from it.

Proverbs *22:*7*

The rich rules over the poor, And the borrower is servant to the lender.

(Sayings of the Wise)

Proverbs *22:*17*–21*, *22*–*23*, 24–27

(17)* *Incline your ear and hear the words of the wise, And apply your heart to my knowledge;*

(18)* *For it is a pleasant thing if you keep them within you; Let them all be fixed upon your lips,*

(19)* *So that your trust may be in the LORD; I have instructed you today, even you.*

(20)* *Have I not written to you excellent things Of counsels and knowledge,*

(21)* *That I may make you know the certainty of the words of truth, That you may answer words of truth To those who send to you?*

(22)* **Do not rob the poor because he is poor, Nor oppress the afflicted at the gate;**

(23)* **For the LORD will plead their cause, And plunder the soul of those who plunder them.**

(24) *Make no friendship with an angry man, And with a furious man do not go,*

(25) Lest you learn his ways And set a snare for your soul.

(26) *Do not be one of those who shakes hands in a pledge, One of those who is surety for debts;*

(27) If you have nothing with which to pay, Why should he take away your bed from under you?

Proverbs *23:*4*–*5*

Do not overwork to be rich; Because of your own understanding, cease! Will you set your eyes on that which is not? For riches certainly make themselves wings; They fly away like an eagle toward heaven.

Proverbs 23:9*

*Do not speak in the hearing of a fool, For he will despise the **wisdom** of your words.*

Proverbs *23:*12*

Apply your heart to instruction, And your ears to words of knowledge.

Proverbs *23:*13*–*14*

Do not withhold correction from a child, For if you beat him with a rod, he will not die. **You shall beat him with a rod, And deliver his soul from hell.**

Proverbs *23:*15*–*16*

My son, if your heart is wise, My heart will rejoice—indeed, I myself, Yes, my inmost being will rejoice When your lips speak right things.

Proverbs 23:17–18

Do not let your heart envy sinners, But be zealous for the fear of the LORD all the day; For surely there is a hereafter, And your hope will not be cut off.

Proverbs 23:19*–21

(19)* *Hear, my son, and be **wise**: And guide your heart in the way.*

(20) *Do not mix with winebibbers, Or with gluttonous eaters of meat;*

(21)   *For the drunkard and the glutton will come to poverty, And drowsiness will clothe a man with rags.*

Proverbs 23:*22*

Listen *to your father who begot you, And do not despise your mother when she is old.*

Proverbs *23:*23*

Buy the truth, and do not sell it, Also wisdom and instruction and understanding.

Proverbs 23:26–28

(26)   *My son, give me your heart, And let your eyes observe my ways.*

(27)   *For a harlot is a deep pit, And a seductress is a narrow well.*

(28)   *She also lies in wait as for a victim, And increases the unfaithful among men.*

Proverbs 24:1–2

Do not be envious of evil men, Nor desire to be with them; For their heart devises violence, And their lips talk of troublemaking.

Proverbs 24:3*–4*

Through **wisdom** *a house is built, And by* understanding *it is established; By* knowledge *the rooms are filled With all precious and pleasant riches.*

Proverbs *24:*5*–*6*

A **wise** man is strong, Yes, a man of **knowledge** increases strength; *For by* wise counsel *you will wage your own war, And in a multitude of* counselors *there is safety.*

Proverbs 24:7

Wisdom *is too lofty for a fool; He does not open his mouth in the gate.*

Proverbs *24:*17*–*18*

Do not rejoice when your enemy falls, And do not let your heart be glad

when he stumbles; Lest the LORD see it, and it displease Him, And He turn away His wrath from him.

Proverbs 24:21–22

My son, fear the LORD and the king; Do not associate with those given to change; For their calamity will rise suddenly, And who knows the ruin those two can bring?

(Further Sayings of the Wise)

Proverbs *24:*23*–*25*

(23)* **These things also belong to the <u>wise</u>:** *<u>It is not good to show partiality in judgment.</u>*

(24) He who says to the wicked, "You are righteous," Him the people will curse; Nations will abhor him.

(25)* *But those who rebuke the wicked will have delight, And a good blessing will come upon them.*

Proverbs *24:*26*

<u>He who gives a right answer kisses the lips.</u>

Proverbs *24:*27*

<u>Prepare your outside work, Make it fit for yourself in the field; And afterward build your house.</u>

Proverbs *24:*28*–*29*

<u>Do not be a witness against your neighbor without cause, For would you deceive with your lips? Do not say, "I will do to him just as he has done to me; I will render to the man according to his works."</u>

(Further Wise Sayings of Solomon)

Proverbs 25:6–12

(6) *Do not exalt yourself in the presence of the king, And do not stand in the place of the great;*

(7) *For it is better that he say to you, "Come up here," Than that you should be put lower in the presence of the prince, Whom your eyes have seen.*

(8) *Do not go hastily to court; For what will you do in the end, When your neighbor has put you to shame?*

(9) *Debate your case with your neighbor, And do not disclose the secret to another;*

(10) *Lest he who hears it exposes your shame, And your reputation be ruined.*

(11) *A word fitly spoken is like apples of gold In settings of silver.*

(12) *Like an earring of gold and an ornament of fine gold Is a **wise** rebuke to an obedient ear.*

Proverbs 25:14

Whoever falsely boasts of giving Is like clouds and wind without rain.

Proverbs 25:17

Seldom set foot in your neighbor's house, Lest he become weary of you and hate you.

Proverbs 25:*18*

A man who bears false witness against his neighbor Is like a club, a sword, and a sharp arrow.

Proverbs 25:19

Confidence in an unfaithful man in time of trouble Is like a bad tooth and a foot out of joint.

Proverbs *25:*21*–*22*

If your enemy is hungry, give him bread to eat; And if he is thirsty, give him water to drink; For so you will heap coals of fire on his head, And the LORD will reward you.

Proverbs *25:*24*

It is better to dwell in a corner of a housetop, Than in a house shared with a contentious woman.

Proverbs 25:26*

A righteous man who falters before the wicked Is like a murky spring and a polluted well.

Proverbs 25:28

Whoever has no rule over his own spirit Is like a city broken down, without walls.

Proverbs 26:4*–9

(4)* *Do not answer a fool according to his folly, Lest you also be like him.*

(5)* *Answer a fool according to his folly, Lest he be **wise** in his own eyes.*

(6) *He who sends a message by the hand of a fool Cuts off his own feet and drinks violence.*

(7)* *Like the legs of a lame that hang limp, Is a proverb in the mouth of fools.*

(8)* *Like one who binds a stone in a sling Is he who gives honor to a fool.*

(9) *Like a thorn that goes into the hand of a drunkard Is a proverb in the mouth of fools.*

Proverbs *26:*11*

As a dog returns to his own vomit, So a fool repeats his folly.

Proverbs *26:*12*

Do you see a man _wise_ in his own eyes? There is more hope for a fool than for him.

Proverbs *26:*16*

The lazy man is _wiser_ in his own eyes Than seven men who can answer sensibly.

Proverbs 26:*17*

He who passes by and meddles in a quarrel not his own Is like one who takes a dog by the ears.

Proverbs 26:18–19

Like a madman who throws firebrands, arrows, and death, Is the man who deceives his neighbor, And says, "I was only joking!"

Proverbs 26:20*–22

(20)* *Where there is no wood, the fire goes out; And where there is no tale-bearer, strife ceases.*

(21) *As charcoal is to burning coals, and wood to fire, So is a contentious man to kindle strife.*

(22) *The words of a talebearer are like tasty trifles, And they go down into the inmost body.*

Proverbs 26:23

Fervent lips with a wicked heart Are like earthenware covered with silver dross.

Proverbs 26:24*–26

(24)* *He who hates, disguises it with his lips, And lays up deceit within himself;*

(25) *When he speaks kindly, do not believe him, For there are seven abominations in his heart;*

(26) *Though his hatred is covered by deceit, His wickedness will be revealed before the assembly.*

Proverbs 26:27*

Whoever digs a pit will fall into it, And he who rolls a stone will have it roll back on him.

Proverbs 26:28*

A lying tongue hates those who are crushed by it, And a flattering mouth works ruin.

Proverbs 27:5*

Open rebuke is better Than love carefully concealed.

Proverbs *27:*6*

Faithful are the wounds of a friend, But the kisses of an enemy are deceitful.

Proverbs 27:*9*

Ointment and perfume delight the heart, And the sweetness of a man's friend gives delight by hearty **counsel**.

Proverbs 27:10

Do not forsake your own friend or your father's friend, Nor go to your brother's house in the day of your calamity; Better is a neighbor nearby than a brother far away.

Proverbs 27:11

*My son, be **wise** and make my heart glad, That I may answer him who reproaches me.*

Proverbs 27:12*

A prudent man foresees evil and hides himself; The simple pass on and are punished.

Proverbs *27:*17*

As iron sharpens iron, So a man sharpens the countenance of his friend.

Proverbs 28:7*

Whoever keeps the law is a ***discerning*** son, But a companion of gluttons shames his father.

Proverbs *28:*23*

He who rebukes a man will find more favor afterward Than he who flatters with the tongue.

Proverbs 28:26*

He who trusts in his own heart is a fool, *But whoever walks **wisely** will be delivered.*

Proverbs 29:8*

Scoffers set a city aflame, *But **wise** men turn away wrath.*

Proverbs 29:23*

A man's pride will bring him low, But the humble in spirit will retain honor.

(The Words of King Lemuel's Mother)

Proverbs 31:1–3, 4–7, and 8--9

(1) The words of King Lemuel, the utterance which his mother taught him:

(2) What my son? And what, son of my womb? And what, son of my vows?

(3) *Do not give your strength to women, Nor your ways to that which destroys kings.*

(4) *It is not for kings, O Lemuel, It is not for kings to drink wine, Nor for princes intoxicating drink;*

(5) Lest they drink and forget the law, And pervert the justice of all the afflicted.

(6) *Give strong drink to him who is perishing, And wine to those who are bitter of heart.*

(7) Let him drink and forget his poverty, And remember his misery no more.

(8) *Open your mouth for the speechless, In the cause of all who are appointed to die.*

(9) *Open your mouth, judge righteously, And plead the cause of the poor and needy.*

CHAPTER 20

DISHONEST, DISHONESTY, FALSE, FALSE WITNESS

We all have heard the statement, "It was just a little white _Lie._" Or how about this one: "I just fudged a little bit, no one will be the wiser!"

And my response to either or both of the above statements is an emphatic, "Really!" May I suggest that one needs to look no further than to Father God's Word on the subject of "**_Dishonesty_**," "**_Falsehood_**," and "**_Lying_**," specifically, Exodus 20:16: "_You shall not bear **false witness** against your neighbor_"; or Matthew 12:36: "_But I say to you that for every idle word men may speak, they will give account of it in the day of judgment_"; and Matthew 12:37: "_For by your words you will be justified, and by your words you will be condemned._"

If one could summarize Father God's Word from the above biblical Scriptures, it's clear that "**bearing _False Witness_**," by leaving something out of a story, telling a "half-truth," twisting the facts, and/or inventing/creating a **_Falsehood_** is nothing but **deception** to the first order, which, from my perspective, is not in accordance with Father God's Word or His will for His people. **Deception** in the form of "**_Dishonesty_**," "**_Falsehood_**," and/or outright "**_Lying_**" is and can be a way of normal, everyday life for secular people, and unfortunately, sometimes for those of us who are "in Christ." But with that said, Father God's people must not give in to any **lapses of the "truth"** by engaging in any form of **"_Dishonesty_,"** **"_Falsehood_,"** and/or outright **"_Lying_"** and letting it become a normal part of one's DNA!

(Security in Wisdom)

Proverbs *4:*20*–*27*

(20)* **My son, give attention to my words; Incline your ear to my sayings.**

(21)* **Do not let them depart from your eyes; Keep them in the midst of your heart;**

(22)* **For they are life to those who find them, And health to all their flesh.**

(23)* **Keep your heart with all diligence, For out of it spring the issues of life.**

(24)* **Put away from you a _deceitful mouth_, And put _perverse lips_ far from you.**

(25) Let your eyes look straight ahead, And your eyelids look right before you.

(26)* **Ponder the path of your feet, And let all your ways be established.**

(27)* **Do not turn to the right or the left; Remove your foot from evil.**

(The Wicked Man)

Proverbs 6:16–19

(16) These six things the _LORD hates_, Yes, seven are an _abomination to Him_;

(17) A proud look, A _**lying tongue**_, Hands that shed innocent blood,

(18) A heart that devises wicked plans, Feet that are swift in running to evil,

(19) A _**false witness**_ who _**speaks lies**_, And one who sows discord among brethren.

(Wise Sayings of Solomon)

Proverbs 10:18

Whoever has hatred has *lying lips*, And whoever spreads *slander* is a fool.

Proverbs 11:1

Dishonest scales are an abomination to the LORD, But a just weight is His delight.

Proverbs 11:3

The integrity of the upright will guide them, But the *perversity* of the *unfaithful* will destroy them.

Proverbs 12:17*

He who speaks truth, declares righteousness, But a *false witness*, *deceit*.

Proverbs 12:19*

The truthful lip shall be established forever, But a *lying tongue* is but for a moment.

Proverbs *12:*22*

Lying lips are an abomination to the LORD, But those who deal truthfully are His delight.

Proverbs 13:5

A righteous man hates *lying*, But a wicked man is loathsome and comes to shame.

Proverbs 13:*11*

Wealth gained by *dishonesty* will be diminished, But he who gathers by labor will increase.

Proverbs 14:5*

A faithful witness does not *lie*, But a *false witness* will utter *lies*.

Proverbs 14:25

A true witness delivers souls, But a *deceitful witness* speaks *lies*.

Proverbs 15:*27*

He who is *greedy* for gain troubles his own house, But he who hates _bribes_ will live.

Proverbs 16:10

Divination is on the lips of the king; His _mouth_ must not _transgress_ in judgment.

Proverbs 16:28

A **_perverse man_** sows *strife*, And a _whisperer_ separates the best of friends.

Proverbs 17:4

An evildoer gives heed to **_false lips_**, A **_liar_** listens eagerly to a *spiteful tongue*.

Proverbs 17:7

Excellent speech is not becoming to a fool, Much less **_lying lips_** to a prince.

Proverbs 17:8

A _present_ is a precious stone in the eyes of its possessor; Wherever he turns, he prospers.

Proverbs 17:23

A wicked man accepts a _bribe_ behind the back To **_pervert_** the ways of justice.

Proverbs 18:8*

The words of a *talebearer (gossiper)* are like tasty trifles, And they go down into the inmost body.

Proverbs 18:16

A man's *gift* makes room for him, And brings him before great men.

Proverbs *19:*1*

Better is the poor who walks in his integrity, Than one who is _perverse_ in his _lips_, and is a fool.

Proverbs 19:5*
A *false witness* will not go unpunished, And he who *speaks lies* shall not escape.

Proverbs 19:*9*
A *false witness* will not go unpunished, And he who *speaks lies* shall perish.

Proverbs 19:*22*
What is desired in a man is kindness, And a poor man is better than a *liar*.

Proverbs 19:28
A *disreputable witness* scorns justice, And the *mouth* of the *wicked* devours *iniquity*.

Proverbs 20:10
Diverse weights and *diverse* measures, They are both alike, an abomination to the LORD.

Proverbs 20:14
"It is good for nothing," cries the buyer; But when he has gone his way, *then he boasts*.

Proverbs 20:17
Bread gained by *deceit* is sweet to a man, But afterward his mouth will be filled with gravel

Proverbs 20:19
He who goes about as a *talebearer (gossiper)* reveals secrets; Therefore do not associate with one who *flatters* with his *lips*.

Proverbs 20:23
Diverse weights are an abomination to the LORD, And *dishonest* scales are not good.

Proverbs 20:25

It is a _snare_ for a man to _devote rashly_, something as holy, And afterward to _reconsider_ his vows.

Proverbs 21:6

Getting treasures by a **_lying tongue_** Is the fleeting fantasy of those who seek death.

Proverbs 21:14

A gift in secret pacifies anger, And a _bribe_ behind the back, strong wrath.

Proverbs 21:27*

The _sacrifice_ of the _wicked_ is an abomination; How much more when he brings it with _wicked intent_.

Proverbs 21:28

A **_false witness_** shall perish, But the man who hears him will speak endlessly.

(Sayings of the Wise)

Proverbs 22:28

Do not remove the ancient landmark Which your fathers have set.

Proverbs 23:6–8

(6)   Do not eat the bread of a _miser_, Nor desire his delicacies;

(7)   _For as he thinks in his heart, so is he._ "Eat and drink!" he says to you, _But his heart is not with you._

(8)   The morsel you have eaten, you will vomit up, And waste your pleasant words.

Proverbs 23:10–11

Do not remove the ancient landmark, Nor enter the fields of the fatherless; For their Redeemer is mighty; He will plead their cause against you.

(Further Sayings of the Wise)

Proverbs *24:*23*–*25*

(23)* *These things also belong to the wise*: **It is not good to show** *partiality* **in** *judgment*.

(24)* *He who says to the wicked, "You are righteous,"* **Him the people will curse; Nations will abhor him.**

(25)* **But those who rebuke the wicked will have delight, And a good blessing will come upon them.**

Proverbs *24:*28*–*29*

Do not be a witness against your neighbor without cause, For would you *deceive* **with your** *lips*? *Do not say,* **"I will do to him just as he has done to me; I will render to the man according to his work."**

(Further Wise Sayings of Solomon)

Proverbs 25:14

Whoever *falsely* boasts of giving Is like clouds and wind without rain.

Proverbs 25:*18*

A man who bears *false witness* against his neighbor Is like a club, a sword, and a sharp arrow.

Proverbs 26:20*–21

Where there is no wood, the fire goes out; And where there is no *talebearer*, strife ceases. As charcoal is to burning coals, and wood to fire, So is a contentious man to kindle strife.

Proverbs 26:23

Fervent lips with a *wicked heart* Are like earthenware covered with silver dross.

Proverbs 26:24*–26

(24)* He who *hates, disguises* it with his *lips*, And lays up ***deceit*** within himself;

(25) When he *speaks kindly*, *do not believe* him, For there are seven *abominations* in his heart;

(26) Though his *hatred* is covered by ***deceit***, His wickedness will be *revealed* before the assembly.

Proverbs 26:28*

A ***lying tongue*** hates those who are crusted by it, And a *flattering mouth* works ruin.

Proverbs 28:8

One who increases his possessions by *usury* and *extortion* Gathers it for him who will pity the poor.

Proverbs 28:21

To show *partiality* is not good, Because for a piece of bread a man will *transgress*.

Proverbs *28:*23*

He who rebukes a man will find more favor afterward Than he who *flatters* with the *tongue*.

Proverbs 29:5

A man who *flatters* his neighbor Spreads a net for his feet.

Proverbs 29:12

If a ruler pays attention to ***lies***, All his servants become *wicked*.

Proverbs 29:24

Whoever is a partner with a thief hates his own life; He *swears* to tell the *truth*, but *reveals nothing*.

(The Wisdom of Agur)

Proverbs *30:*5*–6

Every word of God is pure: He is a shield to those who put their trust

in Him. *Do not add to His words*, Lest He rebuke you, and you be found a <u>*liar*</u>.

<u>Proverbs 30:10</u>

Do not <u>*malign*</u> a servant to his master, Lest he curse you, and you be found guilty.

CHAPTER 21

EVIL, INIQUITY, PERVERSE, PERVERSITY

Instead of providing my narrow definition for this Chapter Theme's Narrative, I have researched two Christian authorities, namely GotQuestions.org and In Touch Ministries, for their definition of the term *Evil*. GotQuestions.org defines "*Evil*" as: "What is morally wrong, sinful or wicked." *Evil* is the result of bad actions stemming from a bad character. Biblically, *Evil* is anything that contracts the Holy nature of God (Psalm 51:4). **Evil** behavior can be thought of as falling into two categories: *Evil* committed against other people (i.e. murder, theft, adultery—Okay, with this last behavioral definition, which includes "adultery," then I have committed "*Evil*"). And *Evil* committed against God (i.e. unbelief, idolatry, and blasphemy). From the disobedience in the Garden of Eden (Genesis 2:9) to the wickedness of Babylon the Great (Revelation 18:2), the Bible speaks of the existence of *Evil*!

From a recent sermon outtake that I heard by the Rev. Dr. Charles F. Stanley of In Touch Ministries in August 2017, Dr. Stanley defines "*EVIL*" in what I will categorize in its more simplest terms—that being "*EVIL*" means: "Any immorality and/or disobedience of God's Word"! Dr. Stanley further stated that "God hates '*Evil*' and '*Evil*' by its very nature is corrupting and disrupting"!

Accordingly, as I have reflected on these Chapter Theme's of *Evil*, *Perversity*, and *Iniquity*, it is accurate and fair to state without conjecture, as unfortunately mentioned in Romans 3:23, that ALL human beings, whether Christian or not, have all "*sinned*" in some way or in some fashion, within the purview of *Evil*, *Perversity*, or *Iniquity*! How often have we heard someone say, "It was just a little white lie!" But as we all know all too well, "sin is sin," and by equal definition, "*Evil*" is "*Evil*," whether large or small, whether murder or adultery!

Thus, in conclusion, as one recites the model prayer that Jesus taught His disciples as well as all believers in Matthew 6:5–14, and as I recited the Lord's Prayer today during my daily devotional period, specifically verses 9–13, I marinated on verse 13, which states: "*And do not lead us into temptation, But, deliver us from the 'evil' one. For Yours is the kingdom, And the power and the glory forever, Amen*".

When I originally drafted my opening paragraph for these Chapter Theme's of *Evil*, *Perversity*, and *Iniquity*, I originally stated that from my narrative perspective, or one's aspect of one's human and/or Christian walk of life, that these Chapter Themes were totally foreign to me. But as I wrapped my head, ears, arms, and faith around the definition of "*Evil*" above, then I have had to admit and confess that I, too, have indeed committed "*Evil*."

So, it seems quite natural that one must/should define the term "*Evil*" such that as one's journey down the Christian life via one's daily walk with Christ, that one can call out "*Evil*" for what it is and why one must reframe from any type of "*Evil*" like any sin, at any cost!

(Shun Evil Counsel)

Proverbs 1:15–16

My son, do not walk in the way with them, Keep your foot from their path; For their feet run to *evil*, And they make haste to shed blood.

(The Call of Wisdom)

Proverbs 1:33
But whoever listens to me will dwell safely, And will be secure, without fear of *evil*.

(The Value of Wisdom)

Proverbs *2:*10*–15
(10)* **When wisdom enters your heart, And knowledge is pleasant to your soul,**
(11)* **Discretion will preserve you; Understanding will keep you,**
(12) To deliver you from the way of *evil*, From the man who speaks *perverse* things,
(13) From those who leave the paths of uprightness To walk in the ways of darkness;
(14) Who rejoice in doing *evil*, And delight in the *perversity* of the *wicked*;
(15) Whose ways are *crooked*, And who are *devious* in their paths;

(Guidance for the Young)

Proverbs 3:7*–8*
Do not be wise in your own eyes; Fear the LORD and depart from *evil*. It will be health to your flesh, And strength to your bones.

Proverbs *3:29–*34*
(29) Do not devise *evil* against your neighbor, For he dwells by you for safety's sake.
(30) Do not strive with a man without cause, If he has done you no harm.
(31) Do not envy the *oppressor*, And choose none of his ways;
(32)* For the *perverse* person is an abomination to the LORD, But His secret counsel is with the upright.

(33) The curse of the LORD is on the house of the *wicked*, But He blesses the home of the just.

(34)* **Surely He *scorns* the *scornful*, But gives grace to the humble.**

(Security in Wisdom)

Proverbs *4:*10*–*13*, *14*–17, *18*–19, and *20*–*27*

(10)* **Hear, my son, and receive my sayings, And the years of your life will be many.**

(11)* **I have taught you in the way of wisdom; I have led you in the right paths;**

(12)* **When you walk, your steps will not be hindered, And when you run, you will not stumble.**

(13)* **Take firm hold of instruction, do not let go; Keep her (Wisdom) for she is your life.**

(14)* **Do not enter the path of the *wicked*, And do not walk in the way of *evil*.**

(15) Avoid it, do not travel on it; Turn away from it and pass on.

(16) For they do not sleep unless they have done *evil*; And their sleep is taken away unless they make someone fall.

(17) For they eat the bread of *wickedness*, And drink the wine of violence.

(18)* **But the path of the just is like the shining sun, That shines ever brighter unto the perfect day.**

(19) The way of the *wicked* is like darkness; They do not know what makes them stumble.

(20)* **My son, give attention to my words; Incline your ear to my sayings.**

(21)* **Do not let them depart from your eyes; Keep them in the midst of your heart;**

(22)* **For they are life to those who find them, And health to all their flesh.**

(23)* **Keep your heart with all diligence, For out of it spring the issues of life.**

(24)* **Put away from you a *deceitful* mouth, And put *perverse* lips far from you.**

(25) Let your eyes look straight ahead, And your eyelids look right before you.

(26)* **Ponder the path of your feet, And let all your ways be established.**

(27)* **Do not turn to the right or the left; Remove your foot from *evil*.**

(The Peril of Adultery)

Proverbs *5:*21*–*23*

(21)* **For the ways of man are before the eyes of the LORD, And He ponders all his paths.**

(22)* **His own *iniquities* entrap the *wicked* man, And he is caught in the cords of his sin.**

(23)* **He shall die for lack of instruction, And in the greatness of his folly he shall go astray.**

(The Wicked Man)

Proverbs *6:12*–15 and 16–19*

(12)* A worthless person, a *wicked* man, Walks with a ***perverse*** mouth;

(13) He winks with his eyes, He shuffles his feet, He points with his fingers;

(14) ***Perversity*** is in his heart, He *devises **evil*** continually, He sows *discord*.

(15) Therefore his calamity shall come suddenly; Suddenly he shall be broken without remedy.

(16) These six +things the LORD hates, Yes, seven are an abomination to Him;

(17)   A proud look, A lying tongue, Hands that shed innocent blood,

(18)* A heart that *devises wicked* plans, Feet that are swift in running to *evil*,

(19)* A false witness who speaks lies, And one who sows *discord* among brethren.

(Beware of Adultery)

Proverbs *6:*23*–25

(23)* **For the commandment is a lamp, And the law a light; Reproofs of instruction are the way of life,**

(24)   To keep you from the *evil* woman, From the flattering tongue of a seductress.

(25)   Do not lust after her beauty in your heart, Nor let her allure you with her eyelids.

(The Excellence of Wisdom)

Proverbs *8:*6*–9*

(6)*   **Listen, for I (wisdom) will speak of excellent things; And from the opening of my lips will come right things;**

(7)*   **For my mouth will speak truth; *Wickedness* is an abomination to my lips.**

(8)*   All the words of my mouth are with righteousness; Nothing *crooked* or *perverse* is in them.

(9)*   They are all plain to him who understands, And right to those who find knowledge.

Proverbs*8:12–13

"I, wisdom, dwell with prudence, And find out knowledge and discretion. The fear of the LORD is to hate *evil*; Pride and arrogance and the *evil* way And the *perverse* mouth I hate.

(Wise Sayings of Solomon)

Proverbs 10:9*

He who walks with integrity walks securely, But he who ***perverts*** his ways will become known.

Proverbs 10:23*

To do ***evil*** is like sport to a fool, But a man of understanding has wisdom.

Proverbs *10:*29*

The way of the LORD is strength for the upright, But destruction will come to the workers of *iniquity*.

Proverbs 10:30*

The righteous will never be removed, But the *wicked* will not inhabit the earth.

Proverbs 10:*31*

The mouth of the righteous brings forth wisdom, But the ***perverse*** tongue will be cut out.

Proverbs 10:32*

The lips of the righteous know what is acceptable, But the mouth of the *wicked* what is ***perverse***.

Proverbs 11:3

The integrity of the upright will guide them, But the ***perversity*** of the *unfaithful* will destroy them

Proverbs 11:6*

The righteousness of the upright will deliver them, But the *unfaithful* will be caught by their lust.

Proverbs 11:9

The *hypocrite* with his mouth destroys his neighbor, But through knowledge the righteous will be delivered.

Proverbs 11:16
A gracious woman retains honor, But *ruthless* men retain riches.

Proverbs 11:17
The merciful man does good for his own soul, But he who is *cruel* troubles his own flesh.

Proverbs 11:19*
As righteousness leads to life, So he who pursues **_evil_** pursues it to his own death.

Proverbs 11:20
Those who are of a **_perverse_** heart are an abomination to the LORD, But the blameless in their ways are His delight.

Proverbs 11:*27*
He who earnestly seeks good finds favor, But trouble will come to him who seeks **_evil_**.

Proverbs 11:31
If the righteous will be recompensed on the earth, How much more the *ungodly* and the *sinner*?

Proverbs 12:8*
A man will be commended according to his wisdom, But he who is of a **_perverse_** heart will be despised.

Proverbs 12:12*
The **_wicked_** covet the catch of **_evil_** men, But the root of the righteous yields fruit.

Proverbs 12:20*
Deceit is in the heart of those who *devise* **_evil_**, But counselors of peace have joy.

Proverbs 12:21*

No grave trouble will overtake the righteous, But the _wicked_ shall be filled with **_evil_**.

Proverbs 13:2

A man shall eat well by the fruit of his mouth, But the soul of the _unfaithful_ feeds on violence.

Proverbs 13:19

A desire accomplished is sweet to the soul, But it is an abomination to fools to depart from **_evil_**.

Proverbs 13:21*

Evil pursues _sinners_, But to the righteous, good shall be repaid.

Proverbs 14:2

He who walks in his uprightness fears the LORD, But he who is **_perverse_** in his ways despises Him.

Proverbs 14:*16*

A wise man fears and departs from **_evil_**, But a fool rages and is self-confident.

Proverbs 14:19*

The **_evil_** will bow before the good, And the _wicked_ at the gates of the righteous.

Proverbs 14:*22*

Do they not go astray who devise **_evil_**? But mercy and truth belong to those who devise good.

Proverbs 15:3*

The eyes of the LORD are in every place, Keeping watch on the **_evil_** and the good.

Proverbs 15:4

A wholesome tongue is a tree of life, But **_perverseness_** in it breaks the spirit.

Proverbs 15:15*

All the days of the afflicted are _evil_, But he who is of a merry heart has a continual feast.

Proverbs *15:*28*

The heart of the righteous studies how to answer, But the mouth of the _wicked_ pours forth _evil_.

Proverbs *16:*6*

In mercy and truth Atonement is provided for _iniquity_; And by the fear of the LORD one departs from _evil_.

Proverbs 16:10

Divination is on the lips of the king; His mouth must not _transgress_ in judgment.

Proverbs *16:*17*

The highway of the upright is to depart from _evil_; He who keeps his way preserves his soul.

Proverbs 16:27–30

(27) An _ungodly_ man digs up **_evil_**, And it is on his lips like a burning fire.

(28) A **_perverse_** man sows strife, And a whisperer separates the best of friends.

(29) A _violent_ man entices his neighbor, And leads him in a way that is not good.

(30) He winks his eye to _devise_ **_perverse_** things; He purses his lips and brings about **_evil_**.

Proverbs 17:4

An **_evildoer_** gives heed to false lips; A liar listens eagerly to a spiteful tongue.

Proverbs 17:11
An ***evil*** man seeks only *rebellion*; Therefore a *cruel* messenger will be sent against him.

Proverbs 17:*13*
Whoever rewards ***evil*** for good, ***Evil*** will not depart from his house.

Proverbs 17:20
He who has a *deceitful* heart finds no good, And he who has a ***perverse*** tongue falls into ***evil***.

Proverbs 17:23
A *wicked* man accepts a bribe behind the back To ***pervert*** the ways of justice.

Proverbs *19:*1*
Better is the poor who walks in his integrity Than one who is *perverse* in his lips, and is a fool.

Proverbs 19:19*
A man of great *wrath* will suffer punishment; For if you rescue him, you will have to do it again.

Proverbs *19:*23*
The fear of the LORD leads to life, And he who has it will abide in satisfaction; He will not be visited with *evil*.

Proverbs 19:26
He who *mistreats* his father and chases away his mother Is a son who causes shame and brings reproach.

Proverbs 19:28
A disreputable witness scorns justice, And the mouth of the *wicked* devours ***iniquity***.

Proverbs 20:8
A king who sits on the throne of judgment Scatters all ***evil*** with his eyes.

Proverbs 20:10
Diverse weights and diverse measures, They are both alike, an abomination to the LORD.

Proverbs 20:11
Even a child is known by his <u>deeds</u>, Whether what he does is pure and right.

Proverbs 20:22
Do not say, "I will recompense *<u>evil</u>*"; Wait for the LORD, and He will save you.

Proverbs 20:23
Diverse weights are an abomination to the LORD, And dishonest scales are not good.

Proverbs 20:30
Blows that hurt cleanse away *<u>evil</u>*, As do stripes the inner depths of the heart.

Proverbs 21:8*
The way of a guilty man is *<u>perverse</u>*; But as for the pure, his work is right.

Proverbs *21:*9*
Better to dwell in a corner of a housetop, Than in a house shared with a *<u>contentious</u>* woman.

Proverbs 21:10
The soul of the *<u>wicked</u>* desires *<u>evil</u>*; His neighbor finds no favor in his eyes.

Proverbs 21:*15*
It is a joy for the just to do justice, But destruction will come to the workers of ***iniquity***.

Proverbs 21:18
The *<u>wicked</u>* shall be a ransom for the righteous, And the *unfaithful* for the upright.

Proverbs 22:*3*

A prudent man foresees *evil* and hides himself, But the simple pass on and are punished.

Proverbs 22:5

Thorns and snares are in the way of the ***perverse***; He who guards his soul will be far from them.

Proverbs 22: 8*

He who sows ***iniquity*** will reap sorrow, And the rod of his anger will fail.

(Sayings of the Wise)

Proverbs 23:6–8

(6)   Do not eat the bread of a *miser*, Nor desire his delicacies;

(7)   *For as he thinks in his heart, so is he.* "Eat and drink!" he says to you, But his heart is not with you.

(8)   The morsel you have eaten, you will vomit up, And waste your pleasant words.

Proverbs 23:31–33

(31)   Do not look on the wine when it is red, When it sparkles in the cup, When it swirls around smoothly;

(32)   At the last it bites like a serpent, And stings like a viper.

(33)   Your eyes will see strange things, And your heart will utter ***perverse*** things.

Proverbs 24:1–2

Do not be envious of ***evil*** men, Nor desire to be with them; For their heart *devises violence*, And their lips talk of *troublemaking*.

Proverbs 24:8*–9*

He who plots to do ***evil*** Will be called a schemer. *The devising of foolishness is sin,* And the scoffer is an *abomination* to men.

Proverbs 24:19–20
Do not fret because of *evildoers*, Nor be envious of the *wicked*; For there will be no prospect for the *evil* man; The lamp of the *wicked* will be put out.

(Further Sayings of the Wise)

Proverbs *24:*28*–*29*
Do not be a witness against your neighbor without cause, For would you *deceive* with your lips? Do not say, "*I will do to him just as he has done to me; I will render to the man according to his work*."

(Further Sayings of Solomon)

Proverbs 25:20
Like one who takes away a garment in cold weather, And like vinegar on soda, *Is one who sings songs to a heavy heart.*

Proverbs *25:*21*–*22*
If you enemy is hungry, give him bread to eat; And if he is thirsty, give him water to drink; For so you will heap coals of fire on his head, And the LORD will reward you.

Proverbs *25:*24*
It is better to dwell in a corner of a housetop, Than in a house shared with a *contentious* woman.

Proverbs 26:18–19
Like a madman who throws firebrands, arrows, and death, Is the man who deceives his neighbor, And says, "I was only joking!"

Proverbs 26:27*
Whoever digs a pit will fall into it, And he who rolls a stone will have it roll back on him.

Proverbs 26:28*

A lying tongue hates those who are crushed by it, And a flattering mouth works ruin.

Proverbs 27:12*

A prudent man foresees *evil* and hides himself; The simple pass on and are punished.

Proverbs 28:2

Because of the *transgression* of a land, many are its princes; But by a man of understanding and knowledge Right will be prolonged.

Proverbs 28:5*

Evil men do not understand justice, But those who seek the LORD understand all

Proverbs *28:*6*

Better is the poor who walks in his integrity Than one *perverse* in his ways, though he be rich.

Proverbs 28:10

Whoever causes the upright to go astray in an *evil* way, He himself will fall into his own pit; But the blameless will inherit good.

Proverbs 28:14*

Happy is the man who is always reverent, *But he who hardens his heart will fall into calamity.*

Proverbs 28:17

A man burdened with *bloodshed* will flee into a pit; Let no one help him.

Proverbs 28:18*

Whoever walks blamelessly will be saved, But he who is *perverse* in his ways will suddenly fall.

Proverbs 28:22

A man with an **evil** eye hastens after riches, And does not consider that poverty will come upon him.

Proverbs 29:6

By *transgression* an **evil** man is snared, But the righteous sings and rejoices.

Proverbs 29:10

The *bloodthirsty* hate the blameless, But the upright seek his well-being.

Proverbs 29:13

The poor man and the *oppressor* have this in common: The LORD gives light to the eyes of both.

Proverbs 29:22

An angry man stirs up strife, And a furious man abounds in transgression.

Proverbs 29:27*

An *unjust* man is an *abomination* to the righteous, And he who is upright in the way is an *abomination* to the *wicked*.

(The Wisdom of Agur)

Proverbs 30:12

There is a generation that is pure in its own eyes, Yet is not washed from its *filthiness*.

Proverbs 30:32–33

If you have been foolish in exalting yourself, Or if you have devised **evil**, put your hand on your mouth. For as the churning of milk produces butter, And wringing the nose produces blood, So the forcing of *wrath* produces strife.

(The Virtuous Wife)

Proverbs *31:*10*–*12*

(10)* **Who can find a virtuous wife? For her worth is far above rubies.**

(11)* **The heart of her husband safely trusts her; So he will have no lack of gain.**

(12)* **She does him good and not *evil* All the days of her life.**

CHAPTER 22

FAITHFUL, FAITHFULNESS, FAITH, BLAMELESS

From my perspective, three significant Proverbs verses found in this Chapter Theme include the following:

20:6: "*Most men will proclaim each his own goodness, But who can find a **faithful** man*"?

27:6: "***Faithful** are the wounds of a friend, But the kisses of an enemy are deceitful*"; and,

28:20: "*A **faithful** man will abound with blessings, But he who hastens to be rich will not go unpunished.*"

The common word represented in these three verses is the Chapter Theme title of "**_Faithful_**.". But to better understand what "**_Faithful_**" truly represents, it seems to me that one should fully understand the root word of "**_Faith_**."

So, what is "**_Faith_**"? Father God's Word in Hebrews 11:1 states the universally accepted definition of **_Faith_** to mean: "*Now **faith** is the substance of things hoped for, the evidence of things not seen.*"

Hebrews 11 continues to detail out those past "*Heroes of **Faith***" who kept their eyes on the promises of Father God, and endured to the end of their respective lives believing that Father God's promises would be realized either in this life or in eternity.

We, too, must live with the same degree of obedience to Christ, as our heritage and legacy forefathers did. To live effectively, one must keep one's eyes on Jesus, and to recognize that: "*without **faith**, it is impossible to please Him, for he who comes to God must believe that He is, and that He is a rewarder of those who diligently seek Him*" (Hebrews 11:6).

When one faces hardships and discouragement, it is sometimes easy to lose sight of the big picture. But one is never alone as we have the indwelling of the Holy Spirit to guide and encourage us. We have Father God's Word of encouragement which states: "*So I will be with you. I will not leave you nor forsake you*" (Joshua 1:5).

It has been said that **_Faith_** is the cornerstone for confidence and certainty. As a former football running back, let me utilize a football analogy to better explain this **_Faith_** derivative. On a football field, one has two goal posts respectively named confidence and certainty. As I receive the "kickoff of life" somewhere in the end zone of confidence, I must trust in Father God's character that He is who He says He is, and will be my primary blocker in this life as I meander through this life, dodging life's potholes, life's challenges, life's ensuing attacks from Satan and the dark side.

I must constantly believe in the promises of Father God as I continue to navigate running through the football field of life, knowing and believing that as I jump over and/or straight arm one or more final defenders, whether that be fear, doubt, uncertainty, etc., that as I approach and eventually cross the goal line of this earthly life, that I will transition into eternal life having crossed over the goal line of certainty, whereby: "*we are confident, yes, well pleased rather to be absent from the body and to be present with the Lord*" (2 Corinthians 5:8).

This requires that one keeps at least one's eye—preferable two—on the prize of eternal life with Christ Jesus and Father God! Always remember that one is called to: "*run with endurance, the race that is set before* *us, looking unto Jesus, the author and finisher of our **faith**, who for the joy that was set before Him endured the cross, despising the shame, and has sat down at the right hand of the throne of God*" (Hebrews 12:1–2).

Now, that's a touchdown that I look forward to scoring, AS NO ONE gets into Heaven and eternal life except by **_Faith_** in the saving work of the Lord Jesus Christ on one's behalf.

To God be the GLORY!

(The Value of Wisdom)

Proverbs *2:*20*–22*

(20)* **So you may walk in the way of goodness, And keep to the paths of righteousness.**

(21)* **For the *upright* will dwell in the land, And the _blameless_ will remain in it;**

(22)* But the wicked will be cut off from the earth, And the unfaithful will be uprooted from it.

(Guidance for the Young)

Proverbs *3:*3*–4*

Let not mercy and truth forsake you; **Bind them around your neck, Write them on the tablet of your heart**, And so find favor and high esteem in the sight of God and man.

(Wise Sayings of Solomon)

Proverbs 11:5

The righteousness of the **_blameless_** will direct his way aright, But the wicked will fall by his own wickedness.

Proverbs 11:13

A talebearer reveals secrets, But he who is of a **_faithful_** spirit conceals a matter.

Proverbs 11:20

Those who are of a perverse heart are an abomination to the LORD, But the **_blameless_** in their ways are His delight.

Proverbs 13:*6*

Righteousness guards him whose way is **_blameless_**, But wickedness over-throws the sinner.

Proverbs 13:17

A wicked messenger falls into trouble, But a **_faithful_** ambassador brings health.

Proverbs 14:5*

A **_faithful_** witness does not lie, But a false witness will utter lies.

Proverbs 14:30

A sound heart is life to the body, But envy is rottenness to the bones.

Proverbs *15:*16*

Better is a little with the fear of the LORD, Than great treasure with trouble.

Proverbs 20:6*

Most men will proclaim each his own goodness, But who can find a **_faithful_** man?

Proverbs 21:22

A wise man scales the city of the mighty, And brings down the trusted stronghold.

(Sayings of the Wise)

Proverbs *22:*17*–*21*

(17)* **Incline your ear and hear the words of the wise, And apply your heart to my knowledge;**

(18)* For it is a pleasing thing if you keep them within you; Let them all
     be fixed upon your lips,

(19)* *So that your trust may be in the LORD*; I have instructed you today,
     even you.

(20)* Have I not written to you excellent things Of counsels and
     knowledge,

(21)* **That I may make you know the certainty of the words of truth,**
     That you may answer words of truth To those who send to you?

Proverbs 22:28

Do not remove the *ancient landmark* Which your *fathers* have *set.*

Proverbs 23:10–11

Do not remove the *ancient landmark*, Nor enter the fields of the fatherless; For their Redeemer is mighty; He will plead their cause against you.

(Further Wise Sayings of Solomon)

Proverbs 25:13

Like the cold of snow in time of harvest Is a ***faithful*** messenger to those who send him, For he refreshes the soul of his masters.

Proverbs *27:*6*

Faithful **are the wounds of a friend, But the kisses of an enemy are deceitful.**

Proverbs 27:9*

Ointment and perfume delight the heart, *And the sweetness of a man's friend gives delight by hearty counsel.*

Proverbs 27:10

Do not forsake your own friend or your father's friend, Nor go to your brother's house in the day of your calamity; Better is a neighbor nearby than a brother far away.

Proverbs 28:4

Those who forsake the law praise the wicked, But such as _keep the law_ contend with them.

Proverbs 28:10

Whoever causes the upright to go astray in an evil way, He himself will fall into his own pit; But the **_blameless_** will inherit good.

Proverbs 28:18*

Whoever walks **_blamelessly_** will be saved, But he who is perverse in his ways will suddenly fall.

Proverbs 28:20

A **_faithful_** man will abound with blessings, But he who hastens to be rich will not go unpunished.

Proverbs *28:*23*

He who rebukes a man will find more favor afterward Than he who flatters with the tongue.

Proverbs 28:28

When the wicked arise, men hide themselves; But when they perish, _the righteous increase_.

Proverbs 29:10

The bloodthirsty hate the **_blameless_**, But the _upright_ seek his well-being.

Proverbs 29:23

A man's pride will bring him low, _But the humble in spirit will retain honor_.

CHAPTER 23

FEAR OF THE LORD, REVERENCE FOR GOD

T he first Proverbs verse that speaks specifically to the topic "***Fear of the Lord***" and serves as the foundational biblical principle and truth toward gaining knowledge, wisdom, and instruction is Proverb 1:7, which states unequivocally that: "***The fear of the Lord is the beginning of knowledge, But fools despise wisdom and instruction.***" From my perspective, "***Fear of the Lord***," in its most basic, simplest, definitional, and biblical principle and truth centers on ***Reverencing, praising,*** and ***honoring*** God as our Heavenly Father and Jesus Christ as our Lord and Savior. One could state, from an earthly, human, or natural perspective that the created creature should, by the natural order of things, honor such a creator; but from a spiritual perspective, the created creature, being mankind, owes a debt of ***Reverence***, respect, glory, honor, and **praise to our Heavenly Father**, and as well to **His only begotten Son** who was crucified on Calvary's cross to bear the penalty and pay the sin debt that was mankind's to bear.

Accordingly, "***The Fear of the Lord***" is the beginning or initial step or component towards gaining and developing knowledge. Thus, as mankind desires and pursues the initial phase of gaining wisdom, the foundational place to begin, from my perspective, is for mankind to pursue daily ***Reverencing of God***, His Word, the Lord Jesus Christ, as well as embracing the indwelling presence of the Holy Spirit. Trusting in and obeying the Trinity positions one for gaining knowledge, wisdom, and instruction, while at the same time positions one to rise above foolishness, as well as foregoing temptations and the worldly and sinful nature that are ever present during one's daily walk with Father God.

Finally, it's extremely important to embrace the concept of ***Fear*** as it relates to ***Reverence*** and *honor* in and for the ***Godhead***, but mankind must not let *earthly fear* gain any presence or preference in man's daily walk with Father God. One must replace any *earthly fear* with an overwhelming dose of faith, trust, obedience, and **confidence in God**, His Word, and Christ Jesus, as Psalm 23:4 reminds us: "*Yea, though I walk through the valley of the shadow of death, I will **fear** no evil; For You are with me; Your rod and Your staff, they comfort me*"!

(The Beginning of Knowledge)

Proverbs *1:*7*
The *fear of the LORD* is the beginning of knowledge, But fools despise wisdom and instruction.

(The Call of Wisdom)

Proverbs 1:27–33*
(27) When your terror comes like a storm, And your destruction comes like a whirlwind, When distress and anguish come upon you.
(28) "Then they will call on me (*wisdom*), but I (*wisdom*) will not answer; They will seek me (*wisdom*) diligently, but they will not find me (*wisdom*).
(29)* Because they hated knowledge And did not choose the ***fear of the LORD***,
(30) They would have none of my (*wisdom*) counsel And despised my (*wisdom*) every rebuke.

(31) Therefore they shall eat the fruit of their own way, And be filled to the full with their own fancies.

(32) For the turning away of the simple will slay them, And the complacency of fools will destroy them;

(33)* But whoever listens to me (wisdom) will dwell safely, And will be secure, without fear of evil."

(The Value of Wisdom)

Proverbs *2:1*–*9*

(1)* My son, if you receive my words, And treasure my commands within you,

(2)* **So that you incline your ear to wisdom, And apply your heart to understanding;**

(3)* Yes, if you cry out for discernment, And lift up your voice for understanding,

(4)* If you seek her (*wisdom*) as silver, And search for her (*wisdom*) as for hidden treasures;

(5)* **Then you will understand the *fear of the LORD*, And find the knowledge of God.**

(6)* **For *the LORD* gives wisdom; From *His* mouth come knowledge and understanding;**

(7)* ***He* stores up sound wisdom for the upright; *He* is a shield to those who walk uprightly;**

(8)* ***He* guards the paths of justice, And preserves the way of *His* saints.**

(9)* **Then you will understand righteousness and justice, Equity and every good path.**

(Guidance for the Young)

Proverbs *3:*5* and *6*

Trust in the LORD with all your heart, And lean not on your own understanding; In all your ways acknowledge *Him*, and *He* shall direct your paths.

Proverbs 3:7*–8*

Do not be wise in your own eyes; *Fear the LORD* and depart from evil. It will be health to your flesh, And strength to your bones.

Proverbs *3:*9*–*10*

Honor the LORD with your possessions, And with the first fruits of all your increase; So your barns will be filled with plenty, And your vats will overflow with new wine.

(The Wicked Man)

Proverbs 6:16–19

(16) These six things *the LORD* hates, Yes, seven are an abomination to *Him*:

(17) A proud look, A lying tongue, Hands that shed innocent blood,

(18) A heart that devises wicked plans, Feet that are swift in running to evil,

(19) A false witness who speaks lies, And one who sows discord among brethren.

(The Excellence of Wisdom)

Proverbs *8:13*

The *fear of the LORD* is to hate evil; Pride and arrogance and the evil way And the perverse mouth I hate.

(The Way of Wisdom)

Proverbs *9:*10*–12

(10)* "The *fear of the LORD* is the beginning of wisdom, And the knowledge of the *Holy One* is understanding.

(11) For by me your days will be multiplied, And years of life will be added to you.

(12) If you are wise, you are wise for yourself, And if you scoff, you bear it alone."

(Wise Sayings of Solomon)

Proverbs 10:27
The fear of the LORD prolongs days, But the years of the wicked will be shortened.

Proverbs 13:*13*
He who *despises the word* will be destroyed, But he who *fears the commandment* will be rewarded.

Proverbs 14:2
He who walks in his uprightness *fears the LORD*, But he who is perverse in his ways despises *Him*.

Proverbs 14:16*
A wise man *fears* and departs from evil, But a fool rages and is self-confident.

Proverbs 14:26*
In the *fear of the LORD* there is strong confidence, And *His* children will have a place of refuge.

Proverbs 14:27*
The *fear of the LORD* is a fountain of life, To turn one away from the snares of death.

Proverbs *15:*16*
Better is a little with the *fear of the LORD*, Than great treasure with trouble.

Proverbs *15:*33*
The *fear of the LORD* is the instruction of wisdom, And before honor is humility.

Proverbs *16:*6*
In mercy and truth Atonement is provided for iniquity; And by the *fear of the LORD* one departs from evil.

Proverbs 19:*23*
The *fear of the LORD* leads to life, And he who has it will abide in satisfaction; He will not be visited with evil.

Proverbs *22:*4*
By humility and the *fear of the LORD* Are riches and honor and life.

(Sayings of the Wise)

Proverbs *22:*17*–21*
(17)* **Incline your ear and hear the words of the wise, And apply your heart to my knowledge;**

(18)* For it is a pleasant thing if you keep them within you; Let them all be fixed upon your lips.

(19)* So that your **trust may be in the LORD**; I have instructed you today, even you.

(20)* Have I not written to you excellent things Of counsels and knowledge.

(21)* That I may make you know the certainty of the words of truth, That you may answer words of truth too.

Proverbs 23:17*–18*
Do not let your heart envy sinners, But be zealous for the *fear of the LORD* all the day; For surely there is a hereafter, And your hope will not be cut off.

Proverbs 24:21–22

My son, **_fear the LORD_** and the king; Do not associate with those given to change; For their calamity will rise suddenly, And who knows the ruin those two can bring?

(Further Wise Sayings of Solomon)

Proverbs 28:14

Happy is the man who is always **_reverent_**, But he who hardens his heart will fall into calamity.

Proverbs 29:18*

Where there is no *revelation*, the people cast off restraint; But happy is he who keeps the law.

Proverbs 29:25*

The *fear* of man brings a snare, But whoever **_trusts in the LORD_** shall be safe.

(The Virtuous Wife)

Proverbs *31:29–31

(29)   "Many daughters have done well, But you excel them all."

(30)* **Charm is deceitful and beauty is passing, But a woman who _fears the LORD_, she shall be praised.**

(31)   Give her of the fruit of her hands, And let her own works praise her in the gates.

CHAPTER 24

FINANCIAL RESOURCES, GAIN, PROVISIONS, PROFITABILITY, MONEY

I believe there are at least three fundamental/foundational principles regarding *Financial Money Management* that lead to **Financial Wisdom** and **Financial Peace**. These three **Financial Wisdom** principles include the following:

(A) Father God is the **Owner** of "**All**" things, as revealed in His words from Genesis 1, as well as Psalms 24:1. While we are required to be faithful and trusted Stewards/Trustees of "**All**" of His provided *Resources*, whether they be **Time**, **Talent**, **Treasury**, and **Tent** (i.e. Self). These are what I like to affectionately call the **4 T's**, adapted from the "*Parable of the Talents*" in Matthew 25:14–30.

(B) The Acquisition of Father **God's** *Possessions* requires the fundamental execution of the following work/life principles:

1) Understanding the importance of Hard work;

2) Understanding the Concept of Needs, Wants, and Desires;

3) Understanding the importance of Diligence and Fruitfulness vs. Waste and Bad Choices (Proverbs 19:15);

4) Understanding the importance that Laziness and Idleness, which can lead one to hunger and/or poverty (Proverbs 6:6–11); and

5) Understanding the importance that Strategic and Minimum Utilization of Debt (Proverbs 22:7) can result in Godly Peace, as well as enhanced *__Financial__* **Security**.

(C) And finally, embracing and supporting the appropriate Allocation and Utilization of Father **God's** *__Resources__* that can enhance Kingdom Building initiatives, as well as supporting the needs of Father God's Kingdom, for example, **Honoring the Lord with His allocated portion of First Fruits and earthly *Possessions*** by:

1) **Giving of First Fruits** for His Church and other Kingdom building activities;

2) Providing adequate *__Provisions__* and *__Resources__* for one's family;

3) Providing adequate *__Provisions__* and *__Resources__* for the needy, widows, orphans, and disadvantaged;

4) Understanding the importance of Planning, Prioritization, and **Living Below One's Means**; and finally,

5) Minimizing the impact that Desire(s) can have on one's **asset allocation** and *__Wealth__* *__Accumulation__* strategies, as well as remembering the fact that if a "donkey" was good enough for Jesus to ride into Jerusalem on Passover Sunday, for the King of kings and Lord of lords, then all of us must ask the question—as I like to humbly refer to my twenty-plus-year-old Jeep Grand Cherokee Limited that I purchased new in 1999 as my "donkey"—by kindly and humbly remembering that if a "donkey" was good enough for Jesus, then my twenty-plus-year-old Jeep is still good enough for me!

(Shun Evil Counsel)

Proverbs *1:*19*

So are the ways of everyone who is *greedy for gain*; It takes away the life of its owners.

(Guidance for the Young)

Proverbs *3:*9*–*10*

Honor the LORD with your *possessions*, And with the *first fruits* of all your *increase*; So your *barns* will be *filled* with *plenty*, And your *vats* will *overflow* with *new wine*.

Proverbs *3:*13*–18

(13)* **Happy is the man who finds wisdom, And the man who *gains* understanding;**

(14) For her (wisdom) *proceeds* are *better* than the *profits* of *silver*, And her *gain* than fine *gold*.

(15) She (wisdom) is more ***precious*** than ***rubies***, And all the things you may desire cannot compare with her.

(16) Length of days is in her right hand, In her left hand *riches* and honor.

(17)* Her (wisdom) ways are ways of pleasantness, And all her paths are peace,

(18) She (wisdom) is a tree of life to those who take hold of her, And happy are all who retain her.

Proverbs *3:*27*–*28*

Do not withhold *good* from those to whom it is due, When it is in the power of your hand to do so. Do not say to your neighbor, "Go, and come back, And tomorrow I will give it," *When you have it with you*.

(The Excellence of Wisdom)

Proverbs *8:*17*–21

(17)* **I (wisdom) love those who love me, And those who seek diligently will find me.**

(18)   *Riches* and honor are with me, Enduring *riches* and righteousness.

(19)   My *fruit* (wisdom) is *better* than **gold**, yes, than fine **gold**, And my *revenue* than choice **silver**.

(20)   I traverse the way of righteousness, In the midst of the paths of justice,

(21)   That I may cause those who love me to *inherit wealth*, That I may fill their *treasuries*.

(Wise Sayings of Solomon)

Proverbs 10:2*-3*

Treasures of wickedness **profit** nothing, But righteousness delivers from death. The LORD will not allow the righteous soul to famish, But He casts away the desire of the wicked.

Proverbs *10:*22*

The ***blessing of the LORD*** **makes one** *rich*, **And He adds no sorrow with it.**

Proverbs 11:1

Dishonest scales are an abomination to the LORD, But a *just weight* is His delight.

Proverbs 11:*4*

Riches do not **profit** in the day of wrath, But righteousness delivers from death.

Proverbs 11:15*

He who is *surety* for a stranger will suffer, But one who hates being *surety* is *secure*.

Proverbs *11:*24*
There is one who scatters, yet *increases more*; **And *there is one who with-holds more than is right*, But it leads to poverty.**

Proverbs *11:*25*
The *generous* soul will be made *rich*, And *he who *waters* will also be *watered* himself.

Proverbs 11:28
He who trusts in his *riches* will fall, But the righteous will ***flourish*** like foliage.

Proverbs 12:9
Better is the one who is slighted but has a servant, Than he who honors himself but *lacks* **bread**.

Proverbs 12:11
He who tills his land will be satisfied with **bread**, But he who follows frivolity is devoid of understanding.

Proverbs *13:*7*
There is one who makes himself *rich*, yet has *nothing*; And one who makes himself poor, yet has *great riches*.

Proverbs 13:*11*
Wealth **gained** by dishonesty will be *diminished*, But he who *gathers by labor* will **increase**.

Proverbs 13:15*
Good understanding ***gains*** favor, But the way of the unfaithful is hard.

Proverbs *13:*22*
A good man leaves an *inheritance* to his children's children, But the *wealth* of the sinner is *stored up* for the righteous.

Proverbs *14:*23*
In all labor there is ***profit***, But idle chatter leads only to poverty.

Proverbs 14:24
The *crown* of the wise is their *riches*, But the foolishness of fools is folly.

Proverbs *15:*6*
In the house of the righteous there is much _treasure_, But in the _revenue_ of the wicked is trouble.

Proverbs *15:*16*
Better **is a _little_ with the fear of the LORD, Than _great treasure_ with trouble.**

Proverbs 15:17
Better is a **_dinner of herbs_** where love is, Than a **_fatted calf_** with hatred.

Proverbs 15:*27*
He who is *greedy* for **_gain_** troubles his **_own house_**, But he who hates bribes will live.

Proverbs *16:*8*
Better **is a _little_ with righteousness, Than _vast revenues_ without justice.**

Proverbs 16:*16*
How much *better* to get *wisdom* than **_gold_**! And to get *understanding* is to be chosen rather than **_silver_**.

Proverbs *16:*19*
Better **to be of a humble spirit with the lowly, Than to _divide the spoil_ with the proud.**

Proverbs 17:8
A *present* is a **_precious stone_** in the eyes of its possessor; Wherever he turns, he **_prospers_**.

Proverbs 18:10*
The name of the LORD is a strong tower; The righteous run to it and are safe.

Proverbs 18:11
The _rich_ man's _wealth_ is his **strong city**, And like a _high wall_ in his own esteem.

Proverbs *19:*1*
Better is the poor who walks in his integrity Than one who is _perverse in his lips, and is a fool._

Proverbs 19:10
Luxury is not fitting for a fool, Much less for a servant to rule over princes.

Proverbs 19:*14*
Houses and _riches_ are an _inheritance_ from fathers, But a prudent wife is from the LORD.

Proverbs *19:*17*
He who has pity on the poor _lends to the LORD_, And _He will pay back_ what he has _given_.

Proverbs 20:*4*
The lazy man will not plow because of winter; _He will beg during harvest and **have nothing**._

Proverbs 20:10
Diverse weights and diverse measures, They are both alike, an abomination to the LORD.

Proverbs 20:14
"It is good for nothing," cries the buyer; But when he has gone his way, then he boasts.

Proverbs 20:*15*
There is **gold** and a _multitude of **rubies**_, But the _lips of knowledge_ are a **_precious jewel_**.

Proverbs 20:16

*Take the **garment** of one who is surety for a stranger,* And hold it as a pledge when it is for a seductress.

Proverbs 20:17

Bread gained by deceit is sweet to a man, But afterward his mouth will be filled with gravel.

Proverbs *20:*21*

An *inheritance gained* hastily at the beginning Will not be blessed at the end.

Proverbs 20:23

Diverse weights are an abomination to the LORD, And dishonest scales are not good.

Proverbs 20:25

It is a snare for a man to *devote rashly something as holy,* And afterward to *reconsider his vows.*

Proverbs *21:*5*

The *plans of the diligent lead surely* to *plenty,* But those of everyone who is hasty, surely to poverty.

Proverbs 21:6

Getting *treasures* by a lying tongue Is the fleeting fantasy of those who seek death.

Proverbs *21:*13*

Whoever shuts his ears to the cry of the poor Will also cry himself and not be heard.

Proverbs 21:*17*

He who loves *pleasure* will be a poor man; He who loves ***wine and oil*** will not be *rich.*

Proverbs 21:*20*
There is *desirable treasure*, And **oil** in the **dwelling** of the *wise*, But a foolish man squanders it.

Proverbs *21:25–*26*
The desire of the lazy man kills him, For his hands refuse to labor. He covets greedily all day long, **But the righteous gives and does not *spare*.**

Proverbs 22:*1*
A *good name* is to be chosen rather than *great riches*, *Loving favor* rather than ***silver and gold***.

Proverbs 22:2
The *rich* and the poor have this in common, *The LORD is the maker of them all.*

Proverbs *22:*4*
By humility and the fear of the LORD Are *riches* and *honor* and *life*.

Proverbs *22:*7*
The *rich* rules over the poor, And the borrower is servant to the lender.

Proverbs *22:*9*
He who has a *generous eye* will be *blessed*, For he *gives* of his *bread* to the poor.

Proverbs 22:16*
He who oppresses the poor to ***increase*** his *riches*, And he who *gives* to the *rich*, will surely come to poverty.

(Sayings of the Wise)

Proverbs *22:*22*–*23*
Do not *rob* the poor because he is poor, Nor *oppress* the afflicted at the gate; For the LORD will plead their cause, And plunder the soul of those who plunder them.

Proverbs 22:26*–27*

Do not be one of those who *shakes hands in a pledge*, One of those who is *surety* for *debts*; *If you have **nothing** with which **pay**, Why should he take away your <u>bed</u> from under you?*

Proverbs *23:*4*–*5*

Do not overwork to be <u>rich</u>; Because of your own understanding, cease! Will you set your eyes on that which is not? For <u>riches</u> certainly make themselves wings; *They fly away like an eagle toward heaven.*

Proverbs 23:6–8

(6) Do not eat the ***bread*** of a miser, Nor desire his ***delicacies***;

(7) For as he thinks in his heart, so is he. "Eat and drink!" he says to you, But his heart is not with you.

(8) The *morsel* you have eaten, you will vomit up, And waste your pleasant words.

Proverbs 23:19*–21*

(19)* Hear, my son, and be wise; And guide your heart in the way.

(20) Do not mix with winebibbers, Or with gluttonous eaters of *meat*;

(21)* For the drunkard and the glutton will come to poverty, *And drowsiness will <u>clothe</u> a man with **rags**.*

Proverbs 24:3*-4*

*Through wisdom a **house** <u>is built</u>, And by understanding <u>it is established</u>; By knowledge the <u>rooms are filled</u> With all **precious** and <u>pleasant riches</u>.*

(Further Sayings of the Wise)

Proverbs 24:30–34

(30) I went by the ***field*** of the lazy man, And by the ***vineyard*** of the man devoid of understanding;

(31) And there it was, all overgrown with thorns; ***Its*** surface was covered with nettles; ***Its stone wall*** was broken down.

(32) When I saw *it*, I considered *it* well; I looked on *it* and received instruction:

(33) A little sleep, a little slumber, A little folding of the hands to rest;

(34) So shall your poverty come like a prowler, And your need like an armed man.

(Further Wise Sayings of Solomon)

Proverbs 27:13
Take the **garment** of him who is *surety* for a stranger, And hold *it* in pledge when he is *surety* for a seductress.

Proverbs 27:20*
Hell and Destruction are never full; *So the eyes of man are never satisfied.*

Proverbs 28:3
A poor man who oppresses the poor *Is like a driving rain which leaves no **food**.*

Proverbs *28:*6*
Better is the poor who walks in his integrity Than one perverse in his ways, though he be *rich*.

Proverbs 28:8
One who **increases** his **possessions** by *usury* and *extortion* Gathers *it* for him who will pity the poor.

Proverbs *28:*13*
He who covers his sins will not *prosper*, But whoever confesses and forsakes them will have mercy.

Proverbs 28:19
*He who tills his **land** will have **plenty of bread**,* But he who follows frivolity will have poverty enough!

Proverbs 28:20

A faithful man will *abound with blessings*, But he who hastens to be *rich* will not go unpunished.

Proverbs 28:21

To show partiality is not good, Because for a piece of **bread** a man will transgress.

Proverbs 28:22

A man with an evil eye *hastens after riches*, And does not consider that poverty will come upon him.

Proverbs 28:*25*

He who is of a proud heart stirs up strife, But he who **trusts in the LORD** will be *prospered*.

Proverbs *29:*3*

Whoever loves wisdom makes his father rejoice, But a companion of harlots *wastes* his *wealth*.

(Prayer of Devotion)

Proverbs 30:7*–9*

(7)* Two things I request of You (Deprive me not before I die):

(8)* Remove falsehood and lies far from me; Give me neither poverty nor *riches*—*Feed me with the food allotted to me*;

(9)* Lest I be full and deny You, And say, "Who is the LORD?" Or lest I be poor and steal, And profane the name of my God.

(The Virtuous Wife)

Proverbs *31:*10*–*12* and *16*–*18*

(10)* **Who can find a virtuous wife? For her *worth* is far above *rubies*.**

(11)* **The heart of her husband safely trusts her; So he will have *no lack of gain*.**

(12)* She does him good and not evil, All the days of her life.

(16)* She considers a _field_ and _buys it_; From her _profits_ she _plants a vineyard_.

(17)* She girds herself with strength, And strengthens her arms.

(18)* She perceives that her _merchandise_ is good, And her lamp does not go out by night.

CHAPTER 25

FLATTERY

While there are not a lot of Proverbs verses directly or indirectly mentioning this Chapter Theme on the topic of "*Flattery*," the few verses that do reference and highlight this Chapter Theme generally use and/or highlight this Theme in an unfavorable manner, specifically surrounding adultery, lust, and/or sexual immorality. For example, Proverbs 2:16 and 17 states the following: "*To deliver you from the immoral woman, From the seductress who **flatters** with her words. Who forsakes the companion of her youth, And forgets the covenant of her God.*" Or Proverbs 6:23–25, which states: "*For the commandment is a lamp, And the law a light; Reproofs of instruction are the way of life. To keep you from the evil woman, From the **flattering** tongue of a seductress. Do not lust after her beauty in your heart, Nor let her allure you with her eyelids.*"

In looking back at my own personal challenges surrounding adultery, lust, and sexual immorality, as previously highlighted in Chapter 4, one could easily attempt to deflect one's own personal culpability by referencing another poignant Proverbs verse on this specific subject matter by attempting to shift blame and/or personal responsibility to the other two women in my specific cases by highlighting Proverbs 7:21, which states: "*With her enticing speech she caused him to yield, With her **flattering** lips she seduced him.*"

But the ultimate and primary guilty party rested and resided within my sinful nature, and no degree of ***Flattery*** and/or sweet talk pushed me over the top into violating Father God's commandment regarding adultery, lust, and sexual immorality. My pride, arrogance, sinful nature, and personal desires for self-pleasure placed me outside the will of Father God, Father God's truth, as well as His Word! Thus, while "***Flattery***" might have been the so-called "icing on the cake" associated with my prior slippery slope into adultery, the primary guilty factor was that I allowed my heart to periodically yield to my sinful nature that occasionally overpowered my Christian desire to be totally obedient and submissive to Father God's will and purpose for my life!

(The Value of Wisdom)

Proverbs *2:*10*–22*

(10)* **When wisdom enters your heart, And knowledge is pleasant to your soul,**

(11)* **Discretion will preserve you; Understanding will keep you,**

(12)* To deliver you from the way of evil, From the man who speaks perverse things,

(13) From those who leave the paths of uprightness To walk in the ways of darkness;

(14) Who rejoice in doing evil, And delight in the perversity of the wicked;

(15) Whose ways are crooked, And who are devious in their paths;

(16) To deliver you from the immoral woman, From the seductress who *flatters* with her *words*,

(17) Who forsakes the companion of her youth, And forgets the covenant of her God.

(18) For her house leads down to death, And her paths to the dead;

(19) None who go to her return, Nor do they regain the paths of life—

(20)* **So you may walk in the way of goodness, And keep to the paths of righteousness.**

(21)* **For the upright will dwell in the land, And the blameless will remain in it;**

(22)* But the wicked will be cut off from the earth, And the unfaithful will be uprooted from it.

(The Peril of Adultery)

Proverbs 5:1–6

(1) My son, pay attention to my wisdom; Lend your ear to my understanding,

(2) That you may preserve discretion, And your *lips* may keep knowledge.

(3) *For the lips of an immoral woman drip honey, And her mouth is smoother than oil;*

(4) But in the end she is bitter as wormwood, sharp as a two-edged sword.

(5) Her feet go down to death, Her steps lay hold of hell.

(6) Lest you ponder her path of life—Her ways are unstable, You do not know them.

(Beware of Adultery)

Proverbs *6:*23*–29

(23)* **For the commandment is a lamp, And the law a light; Reproofs of instruction are the way of life,**

(24) To keep you from the evil women, From the *flattering tongue* of a seductress.

(25) Do not lust after her beauty in your heart, *Nor let her allure you with her eyelids.*

(26) For by means of a harlot A man is reduced to a crust of bread; And an adulteress will prey upon his precious life.

(27) Can a man take fire to his bosom, And his clothes not be burned?

(28) Can one walk on hot coals, And his feet not be seared?

(29) So is he who goes in to his neighbor's wife, Whoever touches her shall not be innocent.

Proverbs *7:*1*–5*

(1)* **My son, keep my words, And treasure my commands within you**.

(2)* **Keep my commands and live, And my law as the apple of your eye**.

(3)* Bind them on your fingers; Write them on the tablet of your heart.

(4)* **Say to wisdom, "You are my sister," And call understanding your nearest kin**,

(5)* That they may keep you from the immoral woman, From the seductress who *flatters* with her *words*.

(The Crafty Harlot)

Proverbs 7:21–23

(21) *With her enticing speech she caused him to yield, With her **flattering lips** she seduced him.*

(22) Immediately he went after her, as an ox goes to the slaughter, Or as a fool to the correction of the stocks,

(23) Till an arrow struck his liver, As a bird hastens to the snare, He did not know it would cost his life.

(Wise Sayings of Solomon)

Proverbs 17:8

A *present* is a precious stone in the eyes of its possessor; Wherever he turns, he prospers.

Proverbs 20:19

He who goes about as a *talebearer (gossiper)* reveals secrets; Therefore do not associate with one who *flatters* with his *lips*.

(Further Wise Sayings of Solomon)

Proverbs 26:28*

A *lying tongue* hates those who are crushed by it, And a ***flattering*** *mouth* works ruin.

Proverbs 27:14

He who *blesses* his friend with a *loud voice*, rising early in the morning, It will be counted a curse to him.

Proverbs *28:*23*

He who rebukes a man will find more favor afterward Than he who *flatters* with the *tongue*.

Proverbs 29:5

A man who ***flatters*** his neighbor Spreads a net for his feet.

CHAPTER 26

FOOLS, FOOLISHNESS, FOLLY, SIMPLE, SIMPLICITY, STUPID

The Bible has a lot to say about this Chapter Theme's subcategories, especially *Fools* and *Foolishness*. And when I say a lot, I truly mean a lot. No other Chapter Theme has more Proverbs verses detailed and/or listed on a subject matter than the Themes of **Wise** and **Wisdom**, which are captured and reflected in Chapter 70 of *The Book of Proverbs and Wisdom: A Reference Manual*, which are reflected and listed in the final Chapter of this book.

Accordingly, I am only highlighting just five Proverbs verses that are contained in these Chapter Themes, as examples of the various Proverbs verses that signify these Chapter Themes; They include:

- 9:6: "Forsake *foolishness* and live, And go in the way of understanding";
- 10:21: "The lips of the righteous feed many, But *fools* die for lack of wisdom";
- 12:15: "The way of a *fool* is right in his own eyes, But he who heeds counsel is wise";

- 14:29: "*He who is slow to wrath has great understanding, But he who is impulsive exalts **folly***";

  And the last Proverbs verse, from my experience and personal perspective, clearly highlights most of the "***Fools***" and/or "***Foolish***" behavior that I have come across in my life, namely:

- 15:14: "*The heart of him who has understanding seeks knowledge, But the mouth of **fool's** feeds on **foolishness**.*"

I strongly believe, that every person on earth has one or more personal testimonies regarding theses Chapter Theme's, and as the old saying goes, "you know it when you see it;" Thus, I will not share a bucket full of personal experiences in dealing with this Chapter Theme's subtitles. But with that said, I thought it might be beneficial to attempt to briefly define "***Foolishness***" and provide biblical examples of such.

Foolishness is generally defined as the result of a person misusing the intelligence Father God has given such person. A ***Fool*** generally utilizes his or her reasoning skills to make inappropriate, ill-advised, and/or wrong decisions. From a biblical perspective, it has been said that one of the most basic examples of ***Foolishness*** called out in the Bible is denying Father God's existence and/or saying "no" to Father God (Psalm 14:1). Several behavior traits that the Bible associates with ***Folly*** are a **short fuse/quick temper** (Proverbs 19:1) and **disobedience to parents** (Proverbs 15:5).

As I have studied and meditated on most of the Proverbs listed in this Chapter Theme, what strikes me most of all is that when wisdom, knowledge, and understanding are prevalent, evident, and consistently applied in an individual's behavioral repertoire, and/or consistent with an individual's spiritual walk as they live out in the real world, Father God's words, biblical principles, and/or directions from the indwelling Holy Spirit that ***Foolishness***, ***Folly***, and ***Stupidity***, generally speaking, are less of an issue with that individual. And from my life experiences, that is always, a Good Thing!

(The Beginning of Knowledge)

Proverbs *1:1–4*

(1)　The Proverbs of Solomon the son of David, king of Israel:

(2)*　**To know wisdom and instruction, To perceive the words of understanding,**

(3)*　**To receive the instruction of wisdom, Justice, judgment, and equity;**

(4)*　To give prudence to the *simple*, To the young man knowledge and discretion-

Proverbs *1:*7*

The fear of the LORD is the beginning of knowledge, But fools despise wisdom and instruction.

(The Call of Wisdom)

Proverbs *1:*20*–27 and 28–33*

(20)*　**Wisdom calls aloud outside; She raises her voice in the open squares.**

(21)　She cries out in the chief concourses, At the openings of the gates in the city She speaks her words:

(22)*　"How long, you *simple* ones, will you love *simplicity*? For scorners delight in their scorning, And *fools* hate knowledge.

(23)　Turn at my rebuke; Surely I will pour out my spirit on you; I will make my words known to you.

(24)　Because I have called and you refused, I have stretched out my hand and no one regarded,

(25)　Because you disdained all my counsel, And would have none of my rebuke,

(26)　I also will laugh at your calamity; I will mock when your terror comes,

(27)　When your terror comes like a storm, And your destruction comes like a whirlwind, When distress and anguish come upon you.

(28) "Then they will call on me, but I will not answer; They will seek me diligently, but they will not find me.

(29)* Because they hated knowledge And did not choose the fear of the LORD,

(30) They would have none of my counsel And despised my every rebuke.

(31) Therefore they shall eat the fruit of their own way, And be filled to the full with their own fancies.

(32) For the turning away of the *simple* will slay them, And the complacency of *fools* will destroy them;

(33)* But whoever listens to me will dwell safely, And will be secure, without fear of evil."

(Guidance for the Young)

Proverbs 3:35*

The wise shall inherit glory, But shame shall be the legacy of *fools*.

(The Peril of Adultery)

Proverbs *5:*21*–*23*

(21)* **For the ways of man are before the eyes of the LORD, And He ponders all his paths.**

(22)* **His own iniquities entrap the wicked man, And he is caught in the cords of his sin.**

(23)* **He shall die for lack of instruction, And in the greatness of his *folly* he shall go astray.**

(The Crafty Harlot)

Proverbs 7:6–9

(6) For at the window of my house I looked through my lattice,

(7) And say among the *simple*, I perceived among the youths, A young man devoid of understanding,

(8) Passing along the street near her corner; And he took the path to her house

(9) In the twilight, in the evening, In the black and dark light.

Proverbs 7:21–23

(21) With her enticing speech she caused him to yield, With her flattering lips she seduced him.

(22) Immediately he went after her, as an ox goes to the slaughter, Or as a ***fool*** to the correction of the stocks,

(23) Till an arrow struck his liver. As a bird hastens to the snare, He did not know it would cost his life.

(The Excellence of Wisdom)

Proverbs *8:*1*–5*

(1)* **Does not wisdom cry out, And understanding lift up her voice?**

(2) She takes her stand on the top of the high hill, Beside the way, where the paths meet.

(3) She cries out by the gates, at the entry of the city, At the entrance of the doors:

(4) "To you, O men, I call, And my voice is the sons of men.

(5)* O you ***simple*** ones, understand prudence, And you ***fools***, be of an understanding heart."

(The Way of Wisdom)

Proverbs *9:1–*6*

(1) Wisdom has built her house, She has hewn out her seven pillars;

(2) She has slaughtered her meat, She has mixed her wine, She has also furnished her table.

(3) She has sent out her maidens, She cries out from the highest places of the city,

(4) "Whoever is ***simple***, let him turn in here!" As for him who lacks understanding, she (wisdom) says to him,

(5) "Come, eat of my bread And drink of the wine I (wisdom) have mixed.

(6)* **Forsake _foolishness_ and live, And go in the way of understanding.**

(The Way of Folly)

Proverbs 9:13–18

(13) A **_foolish_** woman is clamorous; She is **_simple_**, and knows nothing.

(14) For she sits at the door of her house, On a seat by the highest places of the city,

(15) To call to those who pass by, Who go straight on their way:

(16) "_Whoever is **simple**, let him turn in here_"; _And as for him who lacks understanding, she says to him,_

(17) "_Stolen water is sweet, And bread eaten in secret is pleasant._"

(18) But he does not know that the dead are there, That her guests are in the depths of hell.

(Wise Sayings of Solomon)

Proverbs 10:1

The Proverbs of Solomon: A wise son makes a glad father, But a **_foolish_** son is the grief of his mother.

Proverbs 10:8

The wise in heart will receive commands, But a prating **_fool_** will fall.

Proverbs 10:10

He who winks with the eye causes trouble, But a prating **_fool_** will fall.

Proverbs 10:14*

Wise people store up knowledge, But the mouth of the **_foolish_** is near destruction.

Proverbs 10:18
Whoever hides hatred has lying lips, And whoever spreads slander is a _fool_.

Proverbs *10:*21*
The lips of the righteous feed many, But _fools_ die for lack of wisdom.

Proverbs 10:23*
To do evil is like sport to a _fool_, But a man of understanding has wisdom.

Proverbs *11:*29*
He who troubles his own house will inherit the wind, And the _fool_ will be servant to the wise of heart.

Proverbs *12:*1*
Whoever loves instruction loves knowledge, But he who hates correction is _stupid_.

Proverbs 12:11
He who tills his land will be satisfied with bread, But he who follows _frivolity_ is devoid of understanding.

Proverbs *12:*15*
The way of a _fool_ is right in his own eyes, But he who heeds counsel is wise.

Proverbs 12:16
A _fool's_ wrath is known at once, But a prudent man covers shame.

Proverbs 12:23*
A prudent man conceals knowledge, But the heart of _fools_ proclaims _foolishness_.

Proverbs 13:16*
Every prudent man acts with knowledge, But a _fool_ lays open his _folly_.

Proverbs 13:19

A desire accomplished is sweet to the soul, But it is an abomination to **_fools_** to depart from evil.

Proverbs *13:*20*

He who walks with wise men will be wise, But the companion of _fools_ will be destroyed.

Proverbs 14:1

The wise woman builds her house, But the **_foolish_** pulls it down with her hands.

Proverbs 14:3

In the mouth of a **_fool_** is a rod of pride, But the lips of the wise will preserve them.

Proverbs 14:7

Go from the presence of a **_foolish_** man, When you do not perceive in him the lips of knowledge.

Proverbs 14:*8*

The wisdom of the prudent is to understand his way, But the **_folly_** of **_fools_** is deceit.

Proverbs 14:*9*

Fools mock at sin, But among the upright there is favor.

Proverbs 14:*15*–19

(15)* The **_simple_** believes every word, But the prudent considers well his steps.

(16)* A wise man fears and departs from evil, But a **_fool_** rages and is self-confident.

(17) A quick-tempered man acts **_foolishly_**, And a man of wicked intentions is hated.

(18)* The **_simple_** inherit folly, But the prudent are crowned with knowledge.

(19) The evil will bow before the good, And the wicked at the gates of the righteous.

Proverbs 14:24*

The crown of the wise is their riches, But the *foolishness of fools is folly*.

Proverbs *14:*29*

He who is slow to wrath has great understanding, But he who is impulsive exalts *folly*.

Proverbs *14:*33*

Wisdom rests in the heart of him who has understanding, But what is in the heart of *fools* is made known.

Proverbs 15:*2*

The tongue of the wise uses knowledge rightly, But the mouth of *fools* pours forth *foolishness.*

Proverbs *15:*5*

A *fool* despises his father's instruction, But he who receives correction is prudent.

Proverbs 15:*7*

The lips of the wise disperse knowledge, But the heart of the *fool* does not do so.

Proverbs *15:*14*

The heart of him who has understanding seeks knowledge, But the mouth of *fools* feeds on *foolishness.*

Proverbs *15:*20*

A wise son makes a father glad, But a *foolish* man despises his mother.

Proverbs 15:21*

Folly is joy to him who is destitute of discernment, But a man of understanding walks uprightly.

Proverbs 16:22*

Understanding is a wellspring of life to him who has it. But the correction of _**fools**_ is _**folly**_.

Proverbs 17:7

Excellent speech is not becoming to a _**fool**_, Much less lying lips to a prince.

Proverbs 17:*10*

Rebuke is more effective for a wise man Than a hundred blows on a _**fool**_.

Proverbs 17:12*

Let a man meet a bear robbed of her cubs, Rather than a _**fool**_ in his _**folly**_.

Proverbs 17:16

Why is there in the hand of a _**fool**_ the purchase price of wisdom, Since he has no heart for it?

Proverbs 17:21

He who begets a scoffer does so to his sorrow, And the father of a _**fool**_ has no joy.

Proverbs *17:*24*

Wisdom is in the sight of him who has understanding, But the eyes of a _fool_ are on the ends of the earth.

Proverbs 17:*25*

A _**foolish**_ son is a grief to his father, And bitterness to her who bore him.

Proverbs 17:28

Even a _**fool**_ is counted wise when he holds his peace; When he shuts his lips, he is considered perceptive.

Proverbs 18:2

A _**fool**_ has no delight in understanding, But in expressing his own heart.

Proverbs 18:6

A _**fool's**_ lips enter into contention, And his mouth calls for blows.

Proverbs 18:7
A _fool's_ mouth is his destruction, And his lips are the snare of his soul.

Proverbs 18:*13*
He who answers a matter before he hears it, It is _folly_ and shame to him.

Proverbs *19:*1*
Better is the poor who walks in his integrity Than one who is perverse in his lips, and is a _fool_.

Proverbs 19:3
The _foolishness_ of a man twists his way, And his heart frets against the LORD.

Proverbs 19:10
Luxury is not fitting for a _fool_, Much less for a servant to rule over princes.

Proverbs 19:*13*
A _foolish_ son is the ruin of his father, And the contentions of a wife are a continual dripping.

Proverbs *19:*25*
Strike a scoffer, and the _simple_ will become wary; Rebuke one who has understanding, and he will discern knowledge.

Proverbs 19:29
Judgments are prepared for scoffers, And beatings for the backs of _fools_.

Proverbs 20:3
It is honorable for a man to stop striving, Since any _fool_ can start a quarrel.

Proverbs 21:*11*
When the scoffer is punished, the _simple_ is made wise; But when the wise is instructed, he receives knowledge.

Proverbs 21:*20*

There is desirable treasure, And oil in the dwelling of the wise, But a **_foolish_** man squanders it.

Proverbs 22:*3*

A prudent man foresees evil and hides himself, But the **_simple_** pass on and are punished.

Proverbs 22:13

The _lazy_ man says, "There is a lion outside! I shall be slain in the streets!"

Proverbs *22:*15*

Foolishness is bound up in the heart of a child; The rod of correction will drive it far from him.

(Sayings of the Wise)

Proverbs 23:9*

Do not speak in the hearing of a **_fool_**, For he will despise the wisdom of your words.

(The Foolishness of Wine/Drunkenness)

Proverbs 23:29–35

(29) Who has woe? Who has sorrow? Who has contentions? Who has complaints? Who has wounds without cause? Who has redness of eyes?

(30) _Those who linger long at the wine, Those who go in search of mixed wine._

(31) Do not look on the wine when it is red, When it sparkles in the cup, When it swirls around smoothly;

(32) _At the last it bites like a serpent, And stings like a viper._

(33) _Your eyes will see strange things, And your heart will utter perverse things._

(34) *Yes, you will be like one who lies down in the midst of the sea, Or like one who lies at the top of the mast, saying:*

(35) *They have struck me, but I will not hurt; They have beaten me, but I did not feel it. When shall I awake, that I may seek another drink?*

Proverbs 24:7
Wisdom is too lofty for a ***fool***; He does not open his mouth in the gate.

Proverbs 24:8*–9*
He who plots to do evil Will be called a schemer. The devising of ***foolishness*** is sin, And the scoffer is an abomination to men.

(Further Wise Sayings of Solomon)

Proverbs 26:1
As snow in summer and rain in harvest, So honor is not fitting for a ***fool***.

Proverbs *26:3*–*12*
(3)* A whip for the horse, A bridle for the donkey, And a rod for the ***fool's*** back.

(4)* Do not answer a ***fool*** according to his ***folly***, Lest you also be like him.

(5)* Answer a ***fool*** according to his ***folly***, Lest he be wise in his own eyes.

(6)* He who sends a message by the hand of a ***fool*** Cuts off his own feet and drinks violence.

(7)* Like the legs of a lame that hang limp Is a proverb in the mouth of ***fools***.

(8)* Like one who binds a stone in a sling Is he who gives honor to a ***fool***.

(9)* Like a thorn that goes into the hand of a drunkard Is a proverb in the mouth of ***fools***.

(10) The great God who formed everything Gives the ***fool*** his hire and the transgressor his wages.

(11)* *As a dog returns to his own vomit, So a **fool** repeats his folly.*

(12)* **Do you see a man wise in his own eyes? There is more hope for a *fool* than for him.**

Proverbs 26:18–19
Like a *madman* who throws firebrands, arrows, and death, *Is the man who deceives his neighbor, And says, "I was only joking!"*

Proverbs 27:3
A stone is heavy and sand is weighty, But a ***fool's*** wrath is heavier than both of them.

Proverbs 27:12*
A prudent man foresees evil and hides himself; The **simple** pass on and are punished.

Proverbs 27:22*
Though you grind a ***fool*** in a mortar with a pestle along with crushed grain, Yet his ***foolishness*** will not depart from him.

Proverbs 28:19
He who tills his land will have plenty of bread, But he who follows ***frivolity*** will have poverty enough!

Proverbs 28:26*
He who trusts in his own heart is a ***fool***, But whoever walks wisely will be delivered.

Proverbs 29:9*
If a wise man contends with a ***foolish*** man, Whether the ***fool*** rages or laughs, there is no peace.

Proverbs 29:11*
A ***fool*** vents all his feelings, But a wise man holds them back.

Proverbs 29:20*
Do you see a man hasty in his words? There is more hope for a ***fool*** than for him.

(The Wisdom of Agur)

Proverbs 30:2–3

Surely I am more ***stupid*** than any man, And do not have the under-standing of a man. I neither learned wisdom Nor have knowledge of the Holy One.

Proverbs 30:21–23

(21) For three things the earth is perturbed, Yes, for four it cannot bear up:

(22) For a servant when he reigns, A ***fool*** when he is filled with food,

(23) A hateful woman when she is married, And a maidservant who suc-ceeds her mistress.

Proverbs 30:32*–33*

If you have been ***foolish*** in exalting yourself, Or if you have devised evil, put your hand on your mouth. For as the churning of milk produces but-ter, And wringing of the nose produces blood, So the forcing of wrath produces strife.

CHAPTER 27

GENTLE, GENTLENESS, KINDNESS, GOODWILL

During the narrative discussion on the biblical principle of Mercy, I referenced that one cannot legitimately discuss Mercy without acknowledging its siblings of ***Gentleness***/***Kindness*** and ***Goodwill***. I would call your attention to the following Scripture verses from Micah 6:8, which states: "*He has shown you, O man, what is **good**; And what does the Lord require of you, But to do justly, To love mercy, And to walk humbly with your God*"; Romans 12:20 and 21, which states: "*Therefore, 'if your enemy is hungry, feed him; If he is thirsty, give him a drink; For in doing so you will heap coals of fire on his head.'*" "*Do not be overcome by evil, but overcome evil with **good**.*" And finally, Proverbs 3:3, which states: "*Let not (**kindness**)/mercy and truth forsake you; Bind them around your neck, Write them on the tablet of your heart.*"

So, the question du jour is, "Am/Are, I/We doing enough to exhibit ***Kindness***, ***Gentleness***, and ***Goodness*** on a frequent and consistent basis in one's everyday walk?" If one were absolutely truthful in answering this practical question, one's response would more than likely be "No!" If one is absolutely honest within oneself, one could rightly state that we are a "work in progress"! But is that good enough for Father God? My response would be a definite and emphatic "NO," as Father God's Word clearly instructs one to write the life application principles of **_Gentleness/_** **_Kindness_** on one's heart (Remember the "_Fruits of the Spirit_" contained in Galatians 5:22–23). Are these life application principles difficult to incorporate into one's daily walk? Absolutely NOT; as Father God's Word in Philippians 4:13 states unequivocally that: "_I/(one) can do all things through Christ who strengthens me._"

Thus, my challenge, and I would rightfully surmise your challenge also, is to allow, the blood from the heart of Jesus, to seep into one's DNA, thereby allowing the righteousness of **_Gentleness/Kindness_** and **_Goodwill_** to be more proactively and matter-of-factly becoming the norm, rather than the exception as one lives out one's life for Christ.

(Guidance for the Young)

Proverbs *3:*27*–*28*
Do not withhold good from those to whom it is due, When it is in the **_power of your hand to do so_**. **Do not say to your neighbor, "Go, and come back, And tomorrow I will give it," _When you have it with you_.**

(Wise Sayings of Solomon)

Proverbs 11:16
A _gracious_ woman retains honor, But ruthless men retain riches.

Proverbs 11:17
The _merciful_ man does _good_ for his own soul, But he who is cruel troubles his own flesh.

Proverbs 12:14
A man will be satisfied with good by the fruit of his mouth, And the recompense of a man's hands will be rendered to him.

Proverbs 15:1*
A _soft answer_ turns away wrath, But a harsh word stirs up anger.

Proverbs 15:26
The thoughts of the wicked are an abomination to the LORD, But the words of the pure are *pleasant*.

Proverbs 19:*22*
What is desired is a man's **_kindness_**, And a poor man is better than a liar.

Proverbs 20:28
Mercy and truth preserve the king, And by loving **_kindness_** he upholds his thrown.

Proverbs 21:13*
Whoever shuts his ears to *the cry of the poor* Will also cry himself and not be heard.

(Further Wise Sayings of Solomon)

Proverbs 25:15
By long *forbearance* a ruler is persuaded, And a **_gentle_** tongue breaks a bone.

Proverbs *25:*21*–*22*
*If your enemy is hungry, **give him bread to eat**; And if he is thirsty, give him water to drink; For so you will heap coals of fire on his head, **And the LORD will reward you**.*

Proverbs 26:24–26
(24) He who hates, disguises it with his lips, And lays up deceit within himself;
(25) When he speaks **_kindly_**, do not believe him, For there are seven abominations in his heart;
(26) Though his hatred is covered by deceit, His wickedness will be revealed before the assembly.

Proverbs 28:27

He who gives to the poor will not lack, But he who hides his eyes will have many curses.

(The Virtuous Wife)

Proverbs *31:19–*20* and *26*

(19) She stretches out her hand to the distaff, And her lamp does not go out by night.

(20)* ***She extends her hand to the poor, Yes, she reaches out her hands to the needy.***

(26)* **She opens her mouth with wisdom, And on her tongue is the law of *kindness*.**

CHAPTER 28

GIVING, GENEROSITY, CARING, AND SHARING

W hat is *__Giving__*? What is *__Sharing__*? And what is *__Generosity__*? Rightly or wrongly, each one of us has our own definition of what the appropriate answer(s) are or is or should be in response to *__Giving__*, *__Sharing__*, and *__Generosity__*. More compelling than what one might think and how one might live out the concepts of *__Giving__*, *__Sharing__*, and *__Generosity__*, the biblical scriptures are numerous, descriptive, and to some degree, absolute in justifying the biblical importance of *__Giving__*, *__Sharing__*, and *__Generosity__*. Accordingly, below are a few of my personal favorites (all NKJV) with my really, really favorites **boldly** highlighted:

- Exodus 35:21: "*Then everyone came whose heart was stirred, and everyone whose spirit was willing, and they brought the LORD's offering for the work of the tabernacle of meeting, for all its service, and for the holy garments.*"
- **Proverbs 3:9 and 10: "*Honor the Lord with your possessions, And with the first fruits of all your increase; So your barns will be filled with plenty, And your vats will overflow with new wine.*"**

- Malachi 3:8 and 10: "*Will a man rob God? Yet you have robbed Me! But you say, 'In what way have we robbed You?' In your* **tithes** *and* **offerings.** "*Bring all the* **tithes** *into the storehouse, That there may be food in My house, And try Me now in this,*" *Says the LORD of hosts,* "*If I will not open for you the windows of heaven, And* **pour out** *for you such blessing, That there will not be room enough to receive it.*"
- Matthew 10:8: "*Freely you have received,* **freely give.**"
- **Luke 6:38**: "***Give, and it will be given to you: good measure, pressed down, shaken together, and running over will be put into your bosom. For with the same measure that you use, it will be measured back to you.***"
- **Mark 12:43 and 44/Luke 21:3–4**: "***Assuredly, I say to you that this poor widow has put in more than all those who have given to the treasury; for they all put in out of their abundance, but she out of her poverty put in all that she had, her whole livelihood.***"
- Acts 4:34 and 35: "*Nor was there anyone among them who lacked; for all who were possessors of lands or houses sold them, and brought the proceeds of the things that were sold, and laid them at the apostle's feet; and they* **distributed** *to each as anyone had need.*"
- **Acts 20:35**: "*I have shown you in every way, by laboring like this, that you must* **support the weak.**" And remember the words of the Lord Jesus, when He said: **'It is more blessed to give than to receive.'**"
- **2 Corinthians 8:8–15** (namely verses 8, 9, 12, and 15): (8) "*I speak not by commandment, but I am testing the sincerity of your love by the diligence of others.*" **(9)** "***For you know the grace of our Lord Jesus Christ, that though He was rich, yet for your sakes He became poor, that you through His poverty might become rich.***" (12) "*For if there is a willing mind, it is accepted according to what one has, and not according to what he does not*

have"; **(15)** "*...He who gathered much had nothing left over, and he who gathered little had no lack.*"

- **2 Corinthians 9:6–11: (6)** "*But this I say: He who sows sparingly will also reap sparingly, and he who sows bountifully will also reap bountifully*"; **(7)** "*So let each one give as he purposes in his 'heart', not grudgingly or of necessity; for 'God Loves a Cheerful Giver*'"; (8) "*And God is able to make all grace abound toward you, that you, always having all sufficiency in all things, may have an abundance for every good work*"; (9) *As it is written: "He has dispersed abroad, He has given to the poor; His righteousness endures forever."* **(10)** "*Now may He who supplies seed to the sower, and bread for food, supply and multiply the seed you have sown and increase the fruits of your righteousness,*" (11) "*while you are enriched in everything for all liberality, which causes thanksgiving through us to God*"; and

- **Hebrews 7:7:** "*Now beyond all contradiction **the lessor is blessed by the better.**"*

Finally, I have come to know, operate, and see the immediate and near-term benefits from living out these biblical principles of ***Giving, Sharing,*** and ***Generosity*** for most of my entire life. In fact, I have come to know and appreciate "*the manifestation of the Spirit*" (1 Corinthians 12:7), as I have attempted to be obedient, as well as operate from a spirit of strength in living out one of my "*spiritual gifts*" of "*being a **Giver**"* as called out in Romans 12:8: "***he who gives, with liberality.***" Accordingly, one might summarize the above referenced biblical scriptures regarding "***Giving, Sharing,*** and ***Generosity***" by their essential biblical principles and truth as follows:

1. One's willingness to "***Give*** cheerfully" is more important than the amount that one ***Gives***;
2. ***Give*** **freely** and watch how Father God can, and often does, provide blessings to both the ***Giver*** and the **gift** recipient;

3. One should strive to fulfill one's financial commitments;

4. *Giving*, in response to what I call the **4 T's** (i.e. Time, Talent, Treasury, and/or Tent—i.e. "Self," Matthew 25:14–30), to one in need might someday be reciprocated as, or when, we might be in need of something one day;

5. One should *Give* as a response to Christ and <u>not</u> for anything that one might receive from *Giving*;

6. Faithfulness freely *Gives* not for gain, but to honor the Lord in the fulfillment of good deeds and good works;

7. One should *Give* as much as one is able and/or being called to *Give*;

8. One should *Give* in proportion to what Father God has placed on one's <u>heart</u> to *Give*;

9. Wise *Givers, Give* prayerfully and responsibly, but not to the exclusion of the Spirit's leading;

   a. <u>Sacrificial</u> *Giving* must be <u>responsible</u>;

   b. Father God *Gives* to each of us, so that we can *Give* and should be a <u>blessing</u> to others; and last but definitely not least;

   c. WE CAN NOT BEAT FATHER GOD'S *GIVING*, especially given the fact that Father God has *Given* each one of us salvation, grace, mercy, forgiveness, joy, love, and eternal life through the Life and Resurrection of Jesus Christ our Lord!

And lastly, remember what Jesus said about the importance of *Giving*: "*...Freely you have received, freely give*" (Matthew 10:8).

(The Beginning of Knowledge)

<u>Proverbs *1:1–4*</u>

(1) The Proverbs of Solomon the son of David, king of Israel:

(2)* **To know *wisdom* and instruction, To perceive the words of understanding,**

(3)* **To receive the instruction of *wisdom*, Justice, judgment, and equity;**

(4)* To ***give*** prudence to the simple, To the young man knowledge and discretion—

(Guidance for the Young)

Proverbs *3:*9*–*10*

Honor the LORD with *your possessions*, And with the *first fruits* of all your *increase*; So your barns will be *filled* with *plenty*, And your vats will *overflow* with new wine.

Proverbs *3:*27*–*28*

Do not withhold good from those to *whom it is due*, When it is in the *power of your hand* to do so. Do not say to your neighbor, "Go, and come back, *And tomorrow I will give it*," *When you have it with you*.

Proverbs *3:*34*

Surely He scorns the scornful, But *gives* grace to the humble.

(Security in Wisdom)

Proverbs *4:*20*–*27*

(20)* **My son, *give* attention to my words; Incline your ear to my sayings.**

(21)* **Do not let them depart from your eyes; Keep them in the midst of your heart;**

(22)* **For they are life to those who find them, And health to all their flesh.**

(23)* **Keep your heart with all diligence, For out of it spring the issues of life.**

(24)* **Put away from you a deceitful mouth, And put perverse lips far from you.**

(25) Let your eyes look straight ahead, And your eyelids look right before you.

(26)* **Ponder the path of your feet, And let all your ways be established.**
(27)* **Do not turn to the right or the left; Remove your foot from evil.**

(The Peril of Adultery)

Proverbs 5:7–14

(7) Therefore *hear* me now, my children, And do not depart from the words of my mouth.

(8) Remove your way far from her, And do not go near the door of her house,

(9) Lest you **give** your honor to others, And your years to the cruel one;

(10) Lest aliens be filled with your wealth, And your labors go to the house of a foreigner;

(11) And you mourn at last, When your flesh and your body are consumed,

(12) And say: "How I have hated *instruction*, And my heart despised correction!

(13) I have not obeyed the voice of my teachers, Nor inclined my ear to those who *instructed* me!

(14) I was on the verge of total ruin, In the midst of the assembly and congregation."

(Balance Generosity with Good Stewardship)

Proverbs 6:1–5

(1) My son, if you become *surety* for your friend, If you have shaken hands in *pledge* for a stranger,

(2) You are *snared* by the words of your mouth; You are taken by the words of your mouth.

(3) So do this, my son, and deliver yourself; For you have come into the hand of your friend; Go and humble yourself; Plead with your friend.

(4) **Give** no sleep to your eyes, Nor slumber to your eyelids.

(5) *Deliver* yourself like a gazelle from the hand of the hunter, And like a bird from the hand of the fowler.

(Beware of Adultery)

Proverbs *6:30–35
(30) People do not despise a thief If he steals to satisfy himself when he is starving.
(31) Yet when he is found, he must *restore* sevenfold; *He may have to **give** up all the substance of his house.*
(32)* **Whoever commits adultery with a woman lacks understanding; He who does so destroys his own soul.**
(33)* **Wounds and dishonor he will get, And his reproach will not be wiped away.**
(34) For jealousy is a husband's fury; Therefore he will not spare in the day of vengeance.
(35) He will accept no recompense, Nor will he be appeased though you ***give*** many *gifts*.

(The Way of Wisdom)

Proverbs *9:7–12
(7) "He who corrects a scoffer gets shame for himself, And he who rebukes a wicked man only harms himself.
(8)* Do not correct a scoffer, lest he hate you: **Rebuke a wise man, and he will love you.**
(9)* ***Give*** **instruction to a wise man, and he will be still wiser;** *Teach* **a just man, and he will increase in learning.**
(10)* **The fear of the LORD is the beginning of wisdom, And the knowledge of the Holy One is understanding.**
(11) For by me your days will be multiplied, And years of life will be added to you.
(12) If you are wise, you are wise for yourself, And if you scoff, you will bear it alone."

(Wise Sayings of Solomon)

Proverbs *11:*24*–*25*
There is one who <u>scatters</u>, yet <u>increases more</u>; And there is one who withholds more than is right, But it leads to poverty. The *generous* soul will be made rich, And *he who waters* will also be <u>watered himself</u>.

Proverbs 11:26
The people will curse him who withholds grain, But *blessing will be on the head of him who sells it*.

Proverbs 12:14
A man will be satisfied with *good* by the fruit of his mouth, And the <u>recompense</u> of a *man's hands* will be <u>rendered</u> to him.

Proverbs 12:*26*
The righteous should choose his friends <u>carefully</u>, For the way of the wicked leads them astray.

Proverbs *13:*7*
There is one who makes himself rich, yet has nothing; *And <u>one who makes himself poor, yet has great riches</u>.*

Proverbs *13:*22*
A good man <u>leaves an inheritance</u> to his children's children, But the wealth of the sinner is stored up for the righteous.

Proverbs 14:10
The heart knows its own bitterness, And a stranger does not <u>*share*</u> its joy.

Proverbs 14:21*
He who despises his neighbor sins; But he who has <u>mercy on the poor</u>, happy is he.

Proverbs *14:*31*
He who oppresses the poor reproaches his Maker, *But he who <u>honors Him</u> has <u>mercy on the needy</u>.*

Proverbs *15:*16*

***Better is a little* with the fear of the LORD, Than great treasure with trouble.**

Proverbs 15:*27*

He who is greedy for **_gain_** troubles his own house, But he who hates bribes will live.

Proverbs *16:*8*

***Better is a little* with righteousness, Than vast revenues without justice.**

Proverbs 17:2

A wise servant will rule over a son who causes shame, And will **_share_** an *inheritance* among the brothers.

Proverbs 17:8

A *present* (bribe) is a precious stone in the eyes of it possessor: Wherever he turns, he prospers.

Proverbs 17:23

A wicked man accepts a *bribe* (*gift)* behind the back To pervert the ways of justice.

Proverbs 18:16

A man's *gift* (*bribe*) makes room for him, And brings him before great men.

Proverbs 19:6

Many *entreat* the *favor of the nobility*, And every man is a friend to one who **gives *gifts*.**

Proverbs *19:*14*

Houses and riches are _an inheritance_ from fathers, But a prudent wife is from the LORD.

Proverbs *19:*17*

He who has _pity on the poor lends to the LORD_, And He will _pay back_ what he has _given_.

Proverbs 20:*21*

An *inheritance* *gained* hastily at the beginning Will not be blessed at the end.

Proverbs 20:25

It is a snare for a man to *devote* rashly *something as holy*, And afterward to *reconsider his vows*.

Proverbs 21:*3*

To do righteousness and justice, Is more *acceptable* to the LORD than *sacrifice*.

Proverbs *21:*9*

Better to dwell in a corner of a housetop, Than in a house *shared* with a contentious woman.

Proverbs 21:*13*

Whoever *shuts his ears* to the *cry of the poor* Will also *cry himself* and *not be heard*.

Proverbs 21:14

A *gift* (*bribe*) in secret pacifies anger, And a *bribe* (*gift*) behind the back, strong wrath.

Proverbs *21:25*–*26*

The desire of the lazy man kills him, For his hands refuse to labor. He covets greedily all day long, **But *the righteous gives* and does not *spare*.**

Proverbs*22:*9*

He who has a *generous eye* will be *blessed*, For he *gives* up his bread to the poor.

Proverbs 22:16*

He who oppresses the poor to increase his riches, And he who ***gives*** to the rich, will surely come to poverty.

(Sayings of the Wise)

Proverbs *22:*22*–*23*
Do not rob the poor because he is poor, Nor oppress the afflicted at the gate; For the LORD will _plead their cause_, And plunder the soul of those who plunder them.

Proverbs 22:26*–27
Do not be one of those who *shakes hands* in a _pledge_, One of those who is *surety* for *debts*; If you have *nothing with which to pay*, Why should he take away your bed from under you?

Proverbs 23:1–3
(1) When you sit down to eat with a ruler, Consider _carefully_ what is before you;
(2) And put a knife to your throat If you are a man *given* to appetite.
(3) Do not desire his delicacies, For they are deceptive food.

Proverbs 23:6–8
(6) Do not *eat the bread* of a miser, Nor *desire* his delicacies;
(7) For as he thinks in his heart, so is he. "Eat and drink!" he says to you, But his heart is not with you.
(8) *The morsel you have eaten*, you will vomit up, And waste your pleasant words.

(Further Wise Sayings of Solomon)

Proverbs 25:14
Whoever *falsely* boasts of **giving** Is like clouds and wind without rain.

Proverbs *25:*21*–*22*
If your enemy is hungry, _give him bread to eat_; And if he is thirsty, _give him water to drink_; For so you will heap coals of fire on his head, *And the LORD will _reward you_*.

Proverbs *25:*24*

It is better to dwell in a corner of a housetop, Than in a house _shared_ with a contentious woman.

Proverbs 27:5*

Open rebuke is better Than love _carefully_ concealed.

Proverbs 27:*9*

Ointment and perfume delight the heart, And the sweetness of a man's friend **gives** delight by hearty counsel.

Proverbs 27:13

Take the garment of him who is _surety for a stranger_, And hold it in _pledge_ when he is _surety for a seductress_.

Proverbs *27:*17*

As iron sharpens iron, So a _man sharpens the countenance of his friend_.

Proverbs 27:18

Whoever keeps the fig tree will eat its fruit; So he who _waits_ on his master will be honored.

Proverbs 28:8

One who _increases his possessions_ by _usury_ and _extortion_ Gathers it for him who will _pity the poor_.

Proverbs *28:*27*

He who gives to the poor will not lack, **But he who hides his eyes will have many curses.**

Proverbs 29:4

The king establishes the land by justice, But he who receives _bribes (gifts)_ overthrows it.

Proverbs 29:7*

The righteous considers the _cause of the poor_, But the wicked does not understand such knowledge.

Proverbs 29:13*

The poor man and the oppressor have this in common: The LORD *__gives__* light to the eyes of both.

Proverbs *29:*15*

The rod and rebuke __give__ wisdom, **But a child left to himself brings shame to his mother.**

Proverbs *29:*17*

Correct your son, and he will *__give__* you rest; Yes, he will *__give__* delight to your soul.

(The Wisdom of Agur / Prayer of Devotion)

Proverbs 30:7*–9*

(7)* Two things I request of You (Deprive me not before I die):

(8)* Remove falsehood and lies far from me; *__Give__ me neither poverty nor riches—__Feed me__ with the food allotted to me;*

(9)* Lest I be full and deny You, And say, "Who is the LORD?" Or lest I be poor and steal, And profane the name of my God.

(The Virtuous Wife)

Proverbs *31:*20*

She extends her hand to the poor, Yes, she reaches out her hands to the __needy.__

CHAPTER 29

GLAD, HAPPY, JOY, REJOICE, DELIGHT

As one thinks about the subthemes contained within this Chapter Theme's Narrative, one would objectively have to state that each and every human alive, over a certain age of course, could provide at least one testimony related to and reflective of one or more of these Chapter Theme's. As I draft this Chapter Theme Narrative, I am sitting outside a Paris laundromat, washing twelve days of clothes, having spent the past thirteen days in Europe with visits in Bruges, Belgium for five nights, seven nights in London, England, and now having arrived last night in Paris, the "City of Lights," for a fifteen-night vacation.

Thus, as I personally reflect on the "*Joy*" that I have experienced, having traveled to Paris for vacation on an annual basis since 2003, I get excited, "*Joyous*," and I "*Rejoice*" in the blessings that Father God has given to me, especially given my start in life and the absence of any meaningful travel prior to the spring semester of my senior year at the University of Southern California (USC).

To better understand, these feelings of "*Gladness*," "*Joyousness*," and "*Delight*" of being in Paris in August 2017 for the fourteenth time since 2003, one must understand my primary and adolescent life, as it relates to the pleasurable experiences of travel. I grew up "*PO*"—not "*poor*," because my mother and two other brothers could not afford the "*O*" and the "*R*" of being "*poor*." The extent of my early years of any so called travel was visiting my grandparents in Yuma, Arizona; taking the trains from Pasadena, California to Yuma primarily because my maternal grandfather was a "porter" for Amtrak, a US-based train and transport company. My other noteworthy travel experience was shortly after my high school graduation in 1971. Myself and six other high school friends of mine drove two VW Bugs, roundtrip from Pasadena, California to San Francisco, California. From that summer of 1971, prior to starting my freshman year of college, I enjoyed a five-night trip to San Francisco, whereby I fell in love with the "City by the Bay." And since approximately twenty-four or twenty-five years of age, I have visited San Francisco at least annually, except for 1998 when I was living and working in Brussels, Belgium, and I could not justify a business trip out to the West Coast in general, and San Francisco specifically!

Now, back to my senior year at USC, as a double major in Accounting and Finance, I had interviewed with seven out of the then "Big 8" national public accounting firms; Whereby I received a permanent job offer from six of the Big 8 CPA firms. But to cover my bases, I decided to interview with one Fortune 500 company, and that was General Telephone & Electronics Corporation (GTE), then based in Stanford, Connecticut. I was successful during the on-campus interview and was extended an offer to fly back to GTE's corporate headquarters to complete the last leg of the Financial Management job opportunity. So, on Thursday—April 24, 1975—at the age of twenty-two years, I was blessed to experience my "*first*" airplane ride, which was a nonstop transcontinental, wide body flight on United Airlines between Los Angeles (LAX) to New York City (JFK) with only "sixty" people on board. You talk about "**_Rejoicing_**," while at the same time being **_Glad_**, **_Joyous_**, and **_Delighted_** with such a blessing! And by the way, I returned home with a full-time employment job offer from GTE!

So here I am, on August 17, 2017, at a laundromat in Paris, "City of

Lights," "*Rejoicing*," "*Glad*," "*Delighted*," and "*Joyous*" that Father God has blessed me one more time with this amazing "*Joyous*" opportunity and moment!

To God be the GLORY!

(The Call of Wisdom)

Proverbs *1:*20*–27

(20)* **Wisdom calls aloud outside; She raises her voice in the open squares.**

(21) She cries out in the chief concourses, At the openings of the gates in the city She speaks her words:

(22) "How long, you simple ones, will you love simplicity? For scorners *delight* in their scorning, And fools hate knowledge.

(23) Turn at my rebuke; Surely I will pour out my spirit on you; I will make my words known to you.

(24) Because I have called and you refused, I have stretched out my hand and no one regarded,

(25) Because you disdained all my counsel, And would have none of my rebuke,

(26) I also will laugh at your calamity; I will mock when your terror comes,

(27) When your terror comes like a storm, And your destruction comes like a whirlwind, When distress and anguish come upon you.

(The Value of Wisdom)

Proverbs *2:*10*–22*

(10)* **When wisdom enters your heart, And knowledge is pleasant to your soul,**

(11)* **Discretion will preserve you; Understanding will keep you,**

(12)* To deliver you from the way of evil, From the man who speaks perverse things,

(13)　From those who leave the paths of uprightness To walk in the ways of darkness;

(14)　Who **_rejoice_** in doing evil, And **_delight_** in the perversity of the wicked;

(15)　Whose ways are crooked, And who are devious in their paths;

(16)　To deliver you from the immoral woman, From the seductress who flatters with her words,

(17)　Who forsakes the companion of her youth, And forgets the covenant of her God.

(18)　For her house leads down to death, And her paths to the dead;

(19)　None who go to her return, Nor do they regain the paths of life—

(20)* **So you may walk in the way of goodness, And keep to the paths of righteousness.**

(21)* **For the upright will dwell in the land, And the blameless will remain in it;**

(22)* But the wicked will be cut off from the earth, And the unfaithful will be uprooted from it.

(Guidance for the Young)

Proverbs *3:*11*–*12* and *13*–18

(11)* **My son, do not despise the chastening of the LORD, Nor detest His correction;**

(12)* **For whom the LORD loves He corrects, Just as a father the son in whom he _delights_.**

(13)* **_Happy_ is the man who finds wisdom, And the man who gains understanding;**

(14)　For her proceeds are better than the profits of silver, And her gain than fine gold.

(15)　She is more precious than rubies, And all the things you may desire cannot compare with her.

(16) Length of days is in her right hand, In her left hand riches and honor.

(17)* Her ways are ways of pleasantness, And all her paths are peace.

(18) She is a tree of life to those who take hold of her, And **happy** are all who retain her.

(The Peril of Adultery)

Proverbs *5:*15*–20

(15)* **Drink water from your own cistern, And running water from your own well.**

(16) Should your fountains be dispersed abroad, Streams of water in the streets?

(17) Let them be only your own, And not for strangers with you.

(18) Let your fountain be blessed, And **rejoice** with the *wife* of your youth.

(19) As a loving deer and a graceful doe, Let her breasts satisfy you at all times; And always be **enraptured** with her love.

(20) For why should you, my son, be **enraptured** by an immoral woman, And be embraced in the arms of a seductress?

(The Crafty Harlot)

Proverbs 7:10–20

(10) And there a woman met him, With the attire of a harlot, and a crafty heart.

(11) She was loud and rebellious, Her feet would not stay at home.

(12) At times she was outside, at times in the open square, Lurking at every corner.

(13) So she caught him and kissed him; With an impudent face she said to him:

(14) "I have peace offerings with me; Today I have paid my vows.

(15) So I came out to meet you, Diligently to seek your face. And I have found you.

(16) I have spread my bed with tapestry, Colored coverings of Egyptian linen.

(17) I have perfumed my bed With myrrh, aloes, and cinnamon.

(18) Come, let us take our fill of love until morning; Let us *delight* ourselves with love.

(19) For my husband is not at home; He has gone on a long journey;

(20) He has taken a bag of money with him, And will come home on the appointed day."

(The Excellence of Wisdom)

Proverbs *8:22–31 and *32*–36*

(22) "The LORD possessed me (wisdom) at the beginning of His way, Before His works of old.

(23) I (wisdom) have been established from everlasting, From the beginning, before there was ever an earth.

(24) When there were no depths I (wisdom) was brought forth, When there were no fountains abounding with water.

(25) Before the mountains were settled, Before the hills, I (wisdom) was brought forth;

(26) While as yet He had not made the earth or the fields, Or the primal dust of the world.

(27) When He prepared the heavens, I (wisdom) was there, When He drew a circle on the face of the deep,

(28) When He established the clouds above, When He strengthened the fountains of the deep,

(29) When He assigned to the sea its limit, So that the waters would not transgress His command, When He marked out the foundations of the earth,

(30) Then I (wisdom) was beside Him as a master craftsman; And I (wisdom) was daily His *delight*, *Rejoicing* always before Him.

(31) *Rejoicing* in His inhabited world, And my (wisdom) *delight* was the sons of men.

(32)* "Now therefore, listen to me, my children, For blessed are those who keep my ways,

(33)* Hear instruction and be wise, And do not distain it.

(34)* Blessed is the man who listens to me, Watching daily at my gates, Waiting at the posts of my doors.

(35)* For whoever finds me finds life, And obtains *favor* from the LORD;

(36)* But he who sins against me wrongs his own soul; All those who hate me love death."

(Wise Sayings of Solomon)

Proverbs 10:1*
A wise son makes a **_glad_** father, But a foolish son is the grief of his mother.

Proverbs 10:28
The hope of the righteous will be **_gladness_**, But the expectation of the wicked will perish.

Proverbs 11:1
Dishonest scales are an abomination to the LORD, But a just weight is **_His delight_**.

Proverbs 11:10–11
When it goes well with the righteous, the city **_rejoices_**; And when the wicked perish, there is *jubilation*. By the blessing of the upright the city is *exalted*, But it is overthrown by the mouth of the wicked.

Proverbs 11:20
Those who are of a perverse heart are an abomination to the LORD, But the blameless in their ways are **_His delight_**.

Proverbs 12:4*
An *excellent wife* is the *crown* of her husband, But she who causes shame is like rottenness in his bones.

Proverbs 12:14

A man will be *satisfied with good* by the fruit of his mouth, And the recompense of a man's hands will be rendered to him.

Proverbs 12:20*

Deceit is in the heart of those who devise evil, But counselors of peace have *joy*.

Proverbs *12:*22*

Lying lips are an abomination to the LORD, But those who deal truthfully are *His delight*.

Proverbs 12:25*

Anxiety in the heart of man causes depression, But a *good word* makes it *glad*.

Proverbs 13:9

The light of the righteous *rejoices*, But the lamp of the wicked will be put out.

Proverbs 13:19

A *desire accomplished* is sweet to the soul, But it is an abomination to fools to depart from evil.

Proverbs 14:10

The heart knows its own bitterness, And a stranger does not share its *joy*.

Proverbs 14:13

Even in *laughter* the heart may sorrow, And the end of mirth may be grief.

Proverbs 14:14*

A backslider in heart will be filled with his own ways, But a *good man* will be *satisfied from above*.

Proverbs 14:*21*

He who despises his neighbor sins; But he who has *mercy on the poor*, *happy* is he.

Proverbs 15:8

The sacrifice of the wicked is an abomination to the LORD, But the prayer of the upright is ***His delight.***

Proverbs 15:13

A *merry* heart makes a *cheerful countenance*, But by sorrow of the heart the spirit is broken.

Proverbs 15:15

All the days of the afflicted are evil, But he who has a *merry* heart has a *continual feast.*

Proverbs 15:*20*

A wise son makes a father ***glad***, But a foolish man despises his mother.

Proverbs 15:21*

Folly is ***joy*** to him who is destitute of discernment, But a man of understanding walks uprightly.

Proverbs 15:23*

A man has ***joy*** by the answer of his mouth, And a word spoken in due season, *how good it is*!

Proverbs 15:30

The light of the eyes ***rejoices*** the heart, And a *good report* makes the bones healthy.

Proverbs 16:13*

Righteous lips are the ***delight*** of kings, And they love him who speaks what is right.

Proverbs *16:*20*

He who *heeds the word wisely*, will find *good*, And whoever *trusts in the* LORD, *happy* is he.

Proverbs 17:5*
He who mocks the poor reproaches his Maker; He who is **glad** at calamity will not go unpunished.

Proverbs 17:21
He who begets a scoffer does so to his sorrow, And the father of a fool has no **joy**.

Proverbs 17:22*
A _merry_ heart does _good_, like medicine, But a broken spirit dries the bones.

Proverbs 18:2
A fool has no **delight** in understanding, But in expressing his own heart.

Proverbs 19:10
Luxury is not fitting for a fool, Much less for a servant to rule over princes.

Proverbs *19:*23*
The _fear of the LORD_ leads to _life_, And he who has it will _abide_ in _satisfaction_, He will not be visited with evil.

Proverbs 21:6
Getting treasures by a lying tongue Is the _fleeting fantasy_ of those who seek death.

Proverbs *21:*9*
Better to _dwell_ in a corner of a housetop, Than in a house shared with a contentious woman.

Proverbs 21:*15*
It is a **joy** for the just to do justice, But destruction will come to the workers of iniquity.

Proverbs 21:17*
He who loves _pleasure_ will be a poor man; He who loves wines and oil will not be rich.

Proverbs *21:*19*

Better to *dwell* in the wilderness, Than with a contentious and angry woman.

Proverbs 21:20*

There is *desirable* treasure, And oil in the dwelling of the wise. But a foolish man squanders it.

(Sayings of the Wise)

Proverbs *23:*15*–*16*

My son, if your heart is wise, My heart will *rejoice*—indeed, I myself; Yes, my inmost being will *rejoice* When your lips speak right things.

Proverbs 23:17–18

Do not let your heart envy sinners, But be zealous for the fear of the LORD all the day; For surely there is a hereafter, And your *hope* will not be cut off.

Proverbs 23:24–25

The father of the righteous will greatly *rejoice,* And he who begets a wise child will *delight* in him. Let your father and your mother be *glad,* And let her who bore you *rejoice*.

Proverbs *24:13–*14*

My son, eat honey (wisdom) because it is good, And the honeycomb (wisdom) which is sweet to your taste; **So shall the knowledge of wisdom be to your soul; If you have found it, there is a *prospect*, And your hope will not be cut off.**

Proverbs *24:*17*–*18*

Do not *rejoice* when your enemy falls, And do not let your heart be *glad* when he stumbles; Lest the LORD see it, and it displease Him, And He turn away His wrath from him.

(Further Sayings of the Wise)

Proverbs *24:*23*–*25*

(23)* These things also belong to the wise: It is not good to show partiality in judgment.

(24)* He who says to the wicked, "You are righteous," Him the people will curse; Nations will abhor him.

(25)* But those who rebuke the wicked will have *delight*, And a *good blessing* will come upon them.

(Further Wise Sayings of Solomon)

Proverbs 25:25

As cold water to a weary soul, So is *good news* from a far country.

Proverbs 27:*9*

Ointment and perfume **_delight_** the heart, And the sweetness of a man's friend gives **_delight_** by hearty counsel.

Proverbs 27:11

My son, be wise, and make my heart **_glad_**, That I may answer him who reproaches me.

Proverbs 28:12

When the righteous **_rejoice_**, there is great glory; But when the wicked arise, men hide themselves.

Proverbs 28:14*

Happy is the man who is always reverent, But he who hardens his heart will fall into calamity.

Proverbs 29:2

When the righteous are in authority, the people **_rejoice_**; But when a wicked man rules, the people groan.

Proverbs *29:*3*
Whoever loves wisdom makes his father <u>rejoice</u>, **But a companion of harlots wastes his wealth.**

Proverbs 29:6*
By transgression an evil man is snared, But the righteous sings and *<u>rejoices</u>.*

Proverbs 29:10
The bloodthirsty hate the blameless, But the upright seek his *<u>well-being</u>.*

Proverbs *29:*17*
Correct your son, and he will give you rest; Yes, he will give *<u>delight</u>* to your soul.

Proverbs 29:18*
Where there is no revelation, the people cast off restraint; But *<u>**happy**</u>* is he who keeps the law.

Proverbs 29:23*
A man's pride will bring him low, But the humble in spirit will retain *honor.*

<u>(The Virtuous Wife)</u>

Proverbs *31:*25*–27
(25)* **Strength and *honor* are her clothing; She shall *<u>rejoice</u>* in time to come.**
(26)* **She opens her mouth with wisdom, And on her tongue is the law of *kindness*.**
(27) She watches over the ways of her household, And does not eat the bread of idleness.

CHAPTER 30

GLORY, HONOR, PRAISE, HOLINESS

*"**Holy, holy, holy** is the LORD of hosts: The whole earth is full of His **glory!**"*

(ISAIAH 6:3)

What an awesome experience to live in and personally feel the *Glory* of our Father God in one's life, as well as share His *Honor*, *Holiness*, and *Praise* whenever and wherever one can!

It has been said that Father God's *Glory*, *Honor*, *Praise*, and *Holiness*, imminent from the reverence and fear of the Lord that resides in one's heart. Could it also be that Father God's *Glory* and *Holiness*, appropriately restrains one from cavalier attitudes and actions toward the things of Father God? Could it also be Father God's *Glory*, *Honor*, and *Holiness*, that might prevent one from becoming careless toward Father God in one's walk, speech, attitude, humor, and relationship with our Lord? My response would be an emphatic, "Yes!" "Yes!" and "Heavenly Yes!" In fact, in my humble opinion, as one mediates and marinates about the *Glory* of Father God, one cannot help but desire to *Praise*, *Honor*, and *Glorify* His *Holy* name, now and forever!

Father God's ***Glory*** and ***Holiness*** are forever spiritually linked. While Father God's ***Glory***, ***Honor***, ***Praise***, and ***Holiness*** should humble each and every one of us, one's individual and collective ***Praises*** and shouts of "***glory to God in the highest***" should resonate, excite, transform, and adorn one's lips as one shouts to our Heavenly Father, "***Holy, holy, holy is the LORD of hosts: The whole earth is full of His glory!***" (Isaiah 6:3)

Thus, as one lives out one's life attempting to bear much fruit for His Kingdom here on earth, our Father in Heaven is ***Glorified*** (John 15:8). What an awesome joy it is knowing that Father God is ***Glorified*** when people come into a right relationship with Him, and begin the daily process of bearing much fruit from one's walk with Christ, and in the fulfillment of serving and helping others, especially the "*least of these*" (Matthew 25:40).

Finally, what an awesome feeling to know that when Jesus was speaking with Father God, how ***Glorified*** Jesus was with us when He stated the following: "*And all Mine are Yours, and Yours are Mine, and I am 'glorified' in them*" (John 17:10). "*Therefore, whether you eat or drink, or whatever you do, do all to the 'glory' of God*" (1 Corinthians 10:31).

To God be the ***GLORY***, Now and Forever. Amen, Amen, and Amen!

(Guidance for the Young)

Proverbs *3:*9*–*10*

Honor the LORD **with your possessions, And with the first fruits of all your increase; So your barns will be filled with plenty, And your vats will overflow with new wine.**

Proverbs *3:*13*–18

(13)* **Happy is the man who finds wisdom, And the man who gains understanding;**

(14) **For her proceeds are better than the profits of silver, And her gain than fine gold.**

(15) **She is more precious than rubies, And all the things you may desire cannot compare with her.**

(16) Length of days is in her right hand, In her left hand riches and **_honor_**.

(17) Her ways are ways of pleasantness, And all her paths are peace.

(18) She is a tree of life to those who take hold of her, And happy are all who retain her.

Proverbs 3:35*

The wise shall inherit **_glory_**, But shame shall be the legacy of fools.

(Security in Wisdom)

Proverbs 4:*7*–9

(7)* **Wisdom is the principal thing; Therefore get wisdom. And in all your getting, get understanding**.

(8) Exalt her, and she will promote you; She will bring you **_honor_**, when you embrace her.

(9) She will place on your head an ornament of grace; A **_crown of glory_** she will deliver to you."

(The Peril of Adultery)

Proverbs 5:7–14

(7) Therefore hear me now, my children, And do not depart from the words of my mouth.

(8) Remove your way far from her, And do not go near the door of her house,

(9) Lest you give your **_honor_** to others, And your years to the cruel one;

(10) Lest aliens be filled with your wealth, And your labors go to the house of a foreigner;

(11) And you mourn at last, When your flesh and your body are consumed,

(12) And say: "How I have hated instruction, And my heart despised correction!

(13) I have not obeyed the voice of my teachers, Nor inclined my ear to those who instructed me!

(14) I was on the verge of total ruin, In the midst of the assembly and congregation."

(The Excellence of Wisdom)

Proverbs *8:12*–14* and *17*–21

(12)* "I, wisdom, dwell with prudence, And find out knowledge and discretion.

(13) The fear of the LORD is to hate evil; Pride and arrogance and the evil way And the perverse mouth I hate.

(14)* Counsel is mine, and sound wisdom; I am understanding, I have strength.

(17)* **I love those who love me, And those who seek me diligently will find me.**

(18) Riches and ***honor*** are with me, Enduring riches and righteousness.

(19)* My fruit is better than gold, yes, than fine gold, And my revenue than choice silver.

(20) I traverse the way of righteousness, In the midst of the paths of justice,

(21) That I may cause those who love me to inherit wealth, That I may fill their treasures.

(Wise Sayings of Solomon)

Proverbs 11:16

A gracious woman retains ***honor***, But ruthless men retain riches.

Proverbs 12:8*

A man will be *commended* according to his wisdom, But he who is of a perverse heart will be despised.

Proverbs 12:9

Better is the one who is slighted but has a servant, Than he who ***honors*** himself but lacks bread.

Proverbs *13:*18*
Poverty and shame will come to him who disdains correction, But he who regards a rebuke will be *honored*.

Proverbs 14:19
The evil will *bow* before the *good*, And the wicked at the *gates of the righteous*.

Proverbs 14:28
In a multitude of people is a *king's honor*, But in the lack of people is the downfall of a prince.

Proverbs *14:*31*
He who oppresses the poor reproaches his Maker, But he who *honors Him* has mercy on the needy.

Proverbs *15:*33*
The fear of the LORD is the instruction of wisdom, And before *honor* is humility.

Proverbs *16:*31*
A *silver-haired head* is a *crown of glory*, If it is found in the way of righteousness.

Proverbs 17:6*
*Children's children are the *crown of old men*, And the **glory** of children is their father.*

Proverbs *18:*12*
Before destruction the heart of a man is haughty, And before *honor* is humility.

Proverbs 19:*11*
The discretion of a man makes him slow to anger, And his **glory** is to overlook a transgression.

Proverbs 19:16
He who _keeps the commandment_ keeps the soul; But he who is careless of his ways will die.

Proverbs 20:3
It is **_honorable_** for a man to stop striving, Since any fool can start a quarrel.

Proverbs 20:29*
The **_glory_** of young men is their strength, And the _splendor of old men_ is their _gray head_.

Proverbs *21:*21*
He who follows righteousness and mercy, Finds life, righteousness and _honor_.

Proverbs *22:*4*
By humility and the fear of the LORD Are riches and _honor_ and life.

(Sayings of the Wise)

Proverbs 22:29*
Do you see a man who _excels_ in his work? _He will stand before kings_; He will not stand before unknown men.

(Further Wise Sayings of Solomon)

Proverbs 25:2
It is the **_glory of God_** to conceal a matter, But the **_glory of kings_** is to search out a matter.

Proverbs 25:6*–7*
Do not exalt yourself in the presence of the king, And _do not stand in the place of the great_; For it is better that he say to you, "_Come up here_," Than that you should be put lower in the presence of the prince, Whom your eyes have seen.

Proverbs 25:*27*

It is not good to eat much honey; So to *seek one's own* **glory** is not **glory**.

Proverbs 26:1

As snow in summer and rain in harvest, So **honor** is not fitting for a fool.

Proverbs 26:8*

Like one who binds a stone in a sling Is he who gives **honor** to a fool.

Proverbs 27:2*

Let another man **praise** *you*, and not your own mouth; *A stranger*, and not your own lips.

Proverbs 27:18

Whoever keeps the fig tree will eat its fruit; So he who waits on his master will be **honored**.

Proverbs 27:21

The refining pot is for silver and the furnace for gold, And a man is *valued by what others say of him*.

Proverbs 28:4

Those who forsake the law **praise** *the wicked*, But such as keep the law contend with them.

Proverbs 28:7

Whoever keeps the law is a discerning son, But a companion of gluttons shames his father.

Proverbs 28:12

When the righteous rejoice, there is great **glory**; But when the wicked arise, men hide themselves.

Proverbs *28:*23*

He who rebukes a man will find more favor afterward Than he who *flatters* with the tongue.

Proverbs 29:5

A man who *flatters* his neighbor Spreads a net for his feet.

Proverbs 29:12

If a ruler pays *attention to lies*, All his servants become wicked.

Proverbs 29:18*

Where there is no revelation, the people cast off restraint; But happy is he who *keeps the law*.

Proverbs 29:23*

A man's pride will bring him low, But the humble in spirit will retain **_honor_**.

(The Virtuous Wife)

Proverbs *31:*10*–*12*, *25*–*26*, *28*, 29–31*

(10)* **Who can find a _virtuous_ wife? For her worth is far above rubies.**

(11)* **The heart of her husband safely trusts her; So he will have no lack of gain.**

(12)* **She does him good and not evil All the days of her life.**

(25)* **Strength and _honor_ are her clothing; She shall rejoice in time to come.**

(26)* **She opens her mouth with wisdom, And on her tongue is the law of kindness.**

(28)* **Her children rise up and call her *blessed*; Her husband also, and he _praises_ her:**

(29) "Many daughters have done well, But you *excel* them all."

(30)* **Charm is deceitful and beauty is passing, But a woman who fears the LORD, she shall be _praised_.**

(31)* **Give her of the fruit of her hands, And let her own works _praise_ her in the gates.**

CHAPTER 31

GOOD, GOODNESS, PURE, WHOLESOME, BETTER

How many of us can recall from our early Sunday school days the phrase, "God is *Good*!" The simplicity of these three words does not reveal the essential breadth and depth of the remarkable attributes of Father God. That Father God is absolutely Holy and perfect, which by definition means that He alone is the standard bearer of all *righteousness*. Given the fact that the expression of Father God's *Goodness* is made evident through His actions, all that Father God does is just, *righteous*, and Holy. Accordingly, as Father God is Holy and *Good*, we are tasked to be Holy and *Good* (1 Peter 1:15 and 16).

It goes without saying then that Father God is and has been *Good* to us, especially to those who are believers. Father God's *Goodness* is ever present, far reaching, long lasting, and eternal. There is nothing bad that we can do that stains the character of our relationship with our Lord and Savior, Jesus Christ.

Father God's *Goodness* is expressed in a multitude of ways. For example, He is our Creator and we are His people. Every breath that one breathes is a gift given to us by Father God. As our loving Savior, He watches over us and provides for all our needs (Philippians 4:19). But without a doubt, the greatest gift and historical event in all of eternity past, eternity present, and eternity future has, is, and will be the resurrection of Jesus Christ!

Accordingly, from the cross of Jesus Christ, one draws comfort in knowing that Jesus Christ is **_Good_**; His wisdom is always **_Good_**; His answers to one's prayers are **_Good_**; His forgiveness is **_Good_** and everlasting; His grace is **_Good_** and abounds to all who seek Him; His gift of eternal life is **_Good_** and available to all who diligently seek Him for the forgiveness of sin, and acknowledge Jesus Christ as Lord and Savior of their life. And at the end of the day, Father God's **_Goodness_** is representative of all **_Pure_**, *righteous*, and **_wholesome Goodness_**.

Believing in Father God's **_Goodness_** is one of the pillars of one's faith. Additionally, as one walks in the pathway of Father God's **_Goodness_** and *righteousness* (Proverbs 2:20), we also have a responsibility to exhibit **_Goodness_** and *righteousness* to others. Receiving **_Goodness_** and grace from on high does require one to exhibit **_Goodness_**, grace, and *righteousness* to others. Galatians 6:9 and 10 clearly states the following mandate: (9) "*And let us not grow weary while doing **good**, for in due season we shall reap if we do not lose heart. (10) Therefore, as we have opportunity, let us do **good** to all, especially to those who are of the household of faith.*"

From my perspective, being **_Good_** and exhibiting **_Goodness_** must be a lifestyle and not conditional on how one is feeling. As a direct result of Father God's **_Goodness_**, grace, and *righteousness* in our respective lives, one must reciprocate to others this same degree of **_Goodness_**, grace, and *righteousness*. Doing **_Good_** involves yielding to the Holy Spirit and exhibiting the "*Fruits of the Spirit*," namely: "*love, joy, peace, patience, kindness, goodness, faithfulness, gentleness and self-control*" (Galatians 5:22 and 23).

Fittingly, as the "*Fruit of the Spirit*" dominates one's life, being **_Good_**, doing **_Good_**, and sharing **_Goodness_** and *righteousness* will become an inevitable result; Thereby becoming a lifestyle, as well as an essential characteristic of one's DNA. Therefore, while we might not be able to match Father God's degree of **_Good_**, **_Goodness_**, and **_Purity_** during this season of one's life, I am reminded of how Father God must feel when His children try to match Him—**_Good_** for **_Good_**, **_Goodness_** for **_Goodness_**, and **_Purity_** for **_Purity_**! Are you up to the challenge? I know that I am trying each and every day!

(The Value of Wisdom)

Proverbs *2:*6*–*9* and *20*–22

(6)* **For the LORD gives wisdom; From His mouth come knowledge and understanding;**

(7)* **He stores up sound wisdom for the upright; He is a shield to those who walk uprightly;**

(8)* **He guards the paths of justice, And preserves the way of His saints.**

(9)* **Then you will understand righteousness and justice, Equity and every _good_ path.**

(20)* **So you may walk in the way of _goodness_, And keep to the paths of righteousness.**

(21)* **For the upright will dwell in the land, And the _blameless_ will remain in it;**

(22) But the wicked will be cut off from the earth, And the unfaithful will be uprooted from it.

(Guidance for the Young)

Proverbs *3:*13*–18

(13)* **Happy is the man who finds wisdom, And the man who gains understanding;**

(14) For her proceeds are **_better_** than the profits of silver, And her gain than fine gold.

(15) She is more precious than rubies, And all the things you may desire cannot compare with her.

(16) Length of days is in her right hand, In her left hand riches and honor.

(17) Her ways are ways of pleasantness, And all her paths are peace.

(18) She is a tree of life to those who take hold of her, And happy are all who retain her.

Proverbs *3:*27*–*28*

Do not withhold _good_ from those to whom it is due, When it is in the power of your hand to do so. Do not say to your neighbor, "Go, and come back, And tomorrow I will give it," When you have it with you.

(Security in Wisdom)

Proverbs 4:1*–2*

Hear, my children, the instruction of a father, And give attention to know understanding; For I give you **_good_** doctrine: Do not forsake my law.

(The Excellence of Wisdom)

Proverbs *8:*6*–*11* and *17*–21*

(6)* **Listen, for I (wisdom) will speak of excellent things; And from the opening of my lips will come right things;**

(7)* **For my mouth will speak truth; Wickedness is an abomination to my lips.**

(8)* **All the words of my mouth are with righteousness; Nothing crooked or perverse is in them.**

(9)* They are all plain to him who understands, And right to those who find knowledge.

(10)* Receive my instruction, and not silver, And knowledge rather than choice gold;

(11)* **For wisdom is _better_ than rubies, And all the things one may desire cannot be compared with her.**

(17)* **I (wisdom) love those who love me, And those who seek me diligently will find me.**

(18) Riches and honor are with me, Enduring riches and righteousness.

(19)* My fruit is **better** than gold, yes, than fine gold, Any my revenue than choice silver.

(20) I (wisdom) traverse the way of righteousness, In the midst of the paths of justice,

(21)* That I may cause those who love me to inherit wealth, That I may fill their treasuries.

(Wise Sayings of Solomon)

Proverbs 11:17

The merciful man does **good** for his own soul, But he who is cruel troubles his own flesh.

Proverbs 11:23*

The desire of the righteous is only **good**, But the expectation of the wicked is wrath.

Proverbs 11:*27*

He who earnestly seeks **good** finds favor, But trouble will come to him who seeks evil.

Proverbs 12:2*

A **good** man obtains favor from the LORD, But a man of wicked intentions He will condemn.

Proverbs 12:9

Better is the one who is slighted but has a servant, Than he who honors himself but lacks bread.

Proverbs 12:14

A man will be satisfied with **good** by the fruit of his mouth, And the recompense of a man's hands will be rendered to him.

Proverbs 12:25*

Anxiety in the heart of a man causes depression, But a **good** word makes it glad.

Proverbs 13:15*

Good understanding gains favor, But the way of the unfaithful is hard.

Proverbs 13:17

A wicked messenger falls into trouble, But a faithful ambassador brings _health_.

Proverbs 13:21*

Evil pursues sinners, But to the righteous, **_good_** shall be repaid.

Proverbs *13:*22*

A _good_ man leaves an inheritance to his children's children, But the wealth of the sinner is stored up for the righteous.

Proverbs 14:14*

A backslider in heart will be filled with his own ways, _But a **good** man will be satisfied from above._

Proverbs 14:19

The evil will bow before the **_good_**, And the wicked at the gates of the righteous.

Proverbs 14:*22*

Do they not go astray who devise evil? But mercy and truth belong to those who devise **_good_**.

Proverbs 15:3*

The eyes of the LORD are in every place, Keeping watch on the evil and the **_good_**.

Proverbs 15:4

A **_wholesome_** tongue is a tree of life, But perverseness in it breaks the spirit.

Proverbs *15:*16*

Better is a little with the fear of the LORD, Than great treasure with trouble.

Proverbs 15:17
Better is a dinner of herbs where love is, Than a fatted calf with hatred.

Proverbs 15:23*
A man has joy by the answer of his mouth, And a word spoken in due season, how *good* it is!

Proverbs 15:26
The thoughts of the wicked are an abomination to the LORD, But the words of the *pure* are pleasant.

Proverbs 16:*2*
All the ways of a man are *pure* in his own eyes, But the LORD weighs the spirits.

Proverbs *16:*8*
Better is a little with righteousness, Than vast revenues without justice.

Proverbs 16:16*
How much *better* to get wisdom than gold! And to get understanding is to be chosen rather than silver.

Proverbs *16:*19*
Better to be of a humble spirit with the lowly, Than to divide the spoil with the proud.

Proverbs *16:*20*
He who heeds the word wisely will find *good*, And whoever trusts in the LORD, happy is he.

Proverbs 16:29–30
A violent man entices his neighbor, And leads him in a way that is not *good.* He winks his eye to devise perverse things; He purses his lips and brings about evil.

Proverbs 16:*32*

He who is slow to anger is **_better_** than the mighty, And he who rules his spirit than he who takes a city.

Proverbs 17:1

Better is a dry morsel with quietness, Than a house full of feasting with strife.

Proverbs 17:*13*

Whoever rewards evil for **_good_**, Evil will not depart from his house.

Proverbs 17:20

He who has a deceitful heart finds no **_good_**, And he who has a perverse tongue falls into evil.

Proverbs 17:*22*

A merry heart does **_good_**, like medicine, But a broken spirit dries the bones.

Proverbs 17:26

Also, to punish the righteous is not **_good_**, Nor to strike princes for their uprightness.

Proverbs 18:5*

It is not **_good_** to show partiality to the wicked, Or to overthrow the righteous in judgment.

Proverbs *18:*22*

He who finds a wife finds a _good_ thing, And obtains favor from the LORD.

Proverbs *19:*1*

Better is the poor who walks in his integrity Than one who is perverse in his lips, and is a fool.

Proverbs 19:*2*

Also it is not **good** for a soul to be without knowledge, And he sins who hastens with his feet.

Proverbs 19:*8*

He who gets wisdom loves his own soul; He who keeps understanding will find **good**.

Proverbs 19:*22*

What is desired in a man is kindness, And a poor man is **better** than a liar.

Proverbs 20:3

It is *honorable* for a man to stop striving, Since any fool can start a quarrel.

Proverbs 20:6*

Most men will proclaim each his own **goodness**, But who can find a faithful man?

Proverbs 20:9

Who can say, "I have made my heart *clean*, I am **pure** from my sin?"

Proverbs 20:11*

Even a child is known by his *deeds*, Whether what he does is **pure** and right.

Proverbs 20:23

Diverse weights are an abomination to the LORD, And dishonest scales are not **good**.

Proverbs 20:25

It is a snare for a man to devote rashly something as *holy*, And afterward to reconsider his vows.

Proverbs 21:8*

The way of a guilty man is perverse; But as for the **pure**, his work is right.

Proverbs *21:*9*

Better to dwell in a corner of a housetop, Than in a house shared with a contentious woman.

Proverbs *21:*19*

Better to dwell in the wilderness, Than with a contentious and angry woman.

Proverbs *21:*21*

He who follows righteousness and mercy, Finds life, righteousness, and *honor*.

Proverbs 22:*1*

A ***good*** name is to be chosen rather than great riches, Loving favor rather than silver and gold.

Proverbs 22:11

He who loves ***purity*** of heart And has grace on his lips, The king will be his friend.

(Sayings of the Wise)

Proverbs 22:28

Do not remove the ancient landmark Which your fathers have set.

Proverbs *24:13–*14*

My son, eat honey (wisdom) because it is ***good***, And the honeycomb (wisdom) which is sweet to your taste; **So shall the knowledge of wisdom be to your soul; If you have found it, there is a *prospect*, And your hope will not be cut off.**

(Further Sayings of the Wise)

Proverbs *24:*23*–*25*

(23)* *These things also belong to the wise*: **It is not *good* to show partiality in judgment.**

(24)   He who says to the wicked, "You are righteous," Him the people will curse; Nations will abhor him.

(25)* **But those who rebuke the wicked will have delight, And a _good blessing_ will come upon them.**

(Further Wise Sayings of Solomon)

Proverbs 25:6–7*
Do not exalt yourself in the presence of the king, And do not stand in the place of the great; For it is _**better**_ that he say to you, "Come up here," Than that you should be put lower in the presence of the prince, Whom your eyes have seen.

Proverbs *25:*21*–22*
If your enemy is hungry, give him bread to eat; And if he is thirsty, give him water to drink; For so you will heap coals of fire on his head, And the LORD will reward you.

Proverbs *25:*24*
It is _better_ to dwell in a corner of a housetop, Than in a house shared with a contentious woman.

Proverbs 25:25
As cold water to a weary soul, So is _**good**_ news from a far country.

Proverbs 25:*27*
It is not _**good**_ to eat much honey; So to seek one's own glory is not glory.

Proverbs 27:5*
Open rebuke is _**better**_ Than love carefully concealed.

Proverbs 27:10
Do not forsake your own friend or your father's friend, Nor go to your brother's house in the day of your calamity; _**Better**_ is a neighbor nearby than a brother far away.

Proverbs *28:*6*

Better is the poor who walks in his integrity Than one perverse in his ways, though he be rich.

Proverbs 28:10

Whoever causes the upright to go astray in an evil way, He himself will fall into his own pit; But the *blameless* will inherit **_good_**.

Proverbs 28:21

To show partiality is not **_good_**, Because for a piece of bread a man will transgress.

Proverbs 29:10*

The bloodthirsty hate the *blameless*, But the upright seek his *well-being*.

Proverbs 29:27*

An unjust man is an abomination to the *righteous*, And he who is *upright* in the way is an abomination to the wicked.

(The Wisdom of Agur)

Proverbs *30:*5*–6

Every word of God is _pure_; He is a shield to those who put their trust in Him. Do not add to His words, Lest He rebuke you, and you be found a liar.

Proverbs 30:12

There is a generation that is **_pure_** in its own eyes, Yet is not washed from its filthiness.

(The Virtuous Wife)

Proverbs *31:*10*–*12* and *16*–*18*

(10)* **Who can find a virtuous wife? For her worth is far above rubies.**
(11)* **The heart of her husband safely trusts her; So he will have no lack of gain.**

(12)* **She does him _good_ and not evil All the days of her life.**

(16)* **She considers a field and buys it; From her profits she plants a vineyard.**

(17)* She girds herself with strength, And strengthens her arms.

(18)* **She perceives that her merchandise is _good_, And her lamp does not go out by night.**

CHAPTER 32

GRACE, GRACIOUS, GRACEFUL

As I sit here on the seashores of Aruba, I am surrounded and reminded of Father God's magnificent creations. Daily, I am reminded of Father God's *Grace* in my life, as well as in the lives of all who believe in Father God as our Creator, and Jesus Christ as our Lord and Savior!

How frequently I have come to appreciate Father God's *Grace* in my life. When I marinate and meditate on Father God's Word, as well as accepting, believing, and praising Father God for His wonderful, everlasting and eternal *Grace*, Forgiveness, and overwhelming Love in my life, I cannot help but stop and praise Him for His *Grace* and Mercy in my life.

Accordingly, one might ask, "What is *Grace*?" I've heard *Grace* being defined as: (a) All the divine resources needed by Christians to live and serve Father God; (b) His undeserved Favor in one's life, whereby we are saved by *Grace* (Ephesians 2:8 and 9), whereby we should live by *Grace* (Colossians 2:6), and accordingly, we should trust completely in Christ, His power, and not try to live for Christ in one's strength alone.

But the clearest definition of Father God's *Grace*, from my perspective, rest in Father God's "*Throne of Grace*"! Just think, while we were still sinners, Father God sent His only begotten Son, Christ Jesus, to die for us (Romans 5:8). How often does one feel unworthy, hopeless, and helpless? Yet from His "*Throne of Grace*," Father God extends His awesome Mercy,

Forgiveness, and Love by taking away all of our sins yesterday, today, and forever! How great is His *Grace*! As Romans 5:20–21 states in part: "*...But where sin abounded, Grace abounded much more, so that as sin reigned in death, even so Grace might reign through righteousness to eternal life through Jesus Christ our Lord.*"

Just think and remember, that once we have "*confessed with our mouth that Jesus Christ is the Lord Jesus and believe in our hearts that God raised Him from the dead*" (Romans 10:9), that as believers in Christ Jesus, that as we cry out to Jesus Christ to save us because we know that we cannot save ourselves, that the eternal door of Heaven swings open and we are escorted into Father God's "*Throne Room of Grace*"; Whereby we will be "saved" by Father God's *Grace* for eternal life in the presence of God the Father and Jesus Christ our Lord. I tell you, it doesn't get any better than that! Praise God and Thank You, Father God, for your endless displays of Mercy and *Grace*.

(Shun Evil Counsel)

Proverbs 1:8–9
My son, hear the instruction of your father, And do not forsake the law of your mother; For they will be a ***graceful*** ornament on your head, And chains about your neck.

(Guidance for the Young)

Proverbs *3:19–20, *21*–24*, and *34*
(19) The LORD by wisdom founded the earth; By understanding He established the heavens;
(20) By His knowledge the depths were broken up, And clouds drop down the dew.

(21)* **My son, let them not depart from your eyes—Keep sound wisdom and discretion;**
(22) So they will be life to your soul And ***grace*** to your neck.

(23) Then you will walk safely in your way, And your foot will not stumble.

(24)* When you lie down, you will not be afraid; Yes, you will lie down and your sleep will be sweet.

(34)* **Surely He scorns the scornful, But gives _grace_ to the humble**.

(Security in Wisdom)

Proverbs *4:*7*–9

(7)* **Wisdom is the principal thing; Therefore get wisdom, And in all your getting, get understanding**.

(8) Exalt her, and she will promote you; She will bring you honor, when you embrace her.

(9) She will place on your head an ornament of **_grace_**; A crown of glory she will deliver to you.

(The Peril of Adultery)

Proverbs *5:*15*–20

(15)* **Drink water from your own cistern, And running water from your well**.

(16) Should your fountains be dispersed abroad, Streams of water in the streets?

(17) Let them be only your own, And not for strangers with you.

(18) Let your fountain be blessed, And rejoice with the wife of your youth.

(19) As a loving deer and a **_graceful_** doe, Let her breasts satisfy you at all times; And always be enraptured with her love.

(20) For why should you, my son, be enraptured by an immoral woman, And be embraced in the arms of a seductress?

(Wise Sayings of Solomon)

Proverbs 11:16

A **_gracious_** woman retains honor, But ruthless men retain riches.

Proverbs 22:11

He who loves purity of heart And has **_grace_** on his lips, The king will be his friend.

(Wise Sayings of the Wise)

Proverbs *24:*28*–*29*

Do not be a witness again your neighbor without cause, **For would you deceive with your lips?** _Do not say, "I will do to him just as he had done to me;_ **I will render to the man according to his work."**

(Further Wise Sayings of Solomon)

Proverbs *25:*21*–*22*

If your enemy is hungry, _give him bread to eat_; And if he is thirsty, _give him water to drink_; For so you will heap coals of fire on his head, And the LORD will reward you!

Proverbs *28:*13*

He who covers his sins will not prosper, But whoever _confesses_ and _forsakes_ them will have _mercy_.

CHAPTER 33

GUILT, GUILTY

As I write this Chapter Theme Narrative on the topic of **_Guilt_**, I find myself at the start of Holy Week. When I think about, marinate, and reflect on the Christian significance of Holy Week (i.e. Christ Jesus paying our "*sin debt in full*" through His death and resurrection on the Cross), I cannot fully grasp or absorb how Jesus Christ voluntarily bore the sins of mankind, which has resulted in those who have accepted Jesus Christ as their Lord and Savior, moving from a position of "**_Guilty_** to **_Not Guilty_**"! What an awesome, awesome blessing of sin forgiveness!

Generally speaking, it has been said that there are two types of "**_Guilt_**": biblical/spiritual and false **_Guilt_**. The former originates from a violation of biblical/spiritual law, whereby one has sinned and should repent of such sin in order to reestablish a right relationship with Father God. Given that those who are "in Christ" as it relates to one's sin debt have been justified by Christ's death on Calvary's Cross, they have been declared "**_Not Guilty_**." Accordingly, one should recognize and progress forward from a feeling of "**_Guilty_**" to the reality and state of being "**_Not Guilty_**"!

It's been said that the second type of "**_Guilt_**" results from feeling **_Guilty_** after confession of one's sin, which is not based in truth or supported by biblical principles. For example, 1 John 1:9 states: "*If we confess*

347

our sins, He is faithful and just to forgive us our sins and to cleanse us from all unrighteousness." Accordingly, those "in Christ" must recognize that our Heavenly Father has forgiven us; thus, there is no need to linger in ongoing shame. This is further highlighted by 1 John 3:9, which states: "*Whoever has been born of God does not sin, for His seed remains in him; and he cannot sin, because he has been born of God.*"

Individuals struggle with the idea of "*false **Guilt***" for many reasons, including but not limited to the following, namely: (a) Legalistic Teaching; (b) Self-Reproach; (c) Perfectionism; as well as (d) Low Self-Esteem. Symptoms that can result from a sense of "*false **Guilt***" include: Elements of never being able to measure up; Self-Condemnation; and of course, Remorse. In addition, Satan never misses any opportunity to make us feel a sense of "*false **Guilt***," shame, and/or potentially to paralyze one's Christian walk or testimony. For example, I personally have struggled mightily with ***Guilt*** and shame associated with my previous marital adulteries and lust. But I am extremely grateful for a former Bible study friend who appropriately and strongly spoke spiritual truth into my life several years ago, as he reassured me that Father God has forgiven me of those sins, as well as all my sins. Accordingly, Brother/Pastor Phil greatly assisted me to recognize and remember that Father God loves me, cares about me; that I am made in Father God's image, redeemed by Him, and "*predestined to be confirmed to the image of His Son*" (Romans 8:29). And to that, and for that, I say, "Free At Last, Free At Last! Thank God Almighty that I am FREE AT LAST!"

(Wise Sayings of Solomon)

Proverbs 14:19
The *evil* will *bow* before the good, And the *wicked* at the *gates* of the righteous.

Proverbs 14:30
A sound heart is life to the body, But envy is *rottenness* to the bones.

Proverbs 20:26

A wise king *sifts* out the *wicked*, And brings the *threshing wheel* over them.

Proverbs 21:8*

The way of a **guilty** man is perverse; But as for the pure, his work is right.

(Further Wise Sayings of Solomon)

Proverbs 27:12*

A prudent man foresees evil and hides himself; The simple pass on and are *punished*.

Proverbs 28:17

A man burdened with *bloodshed* will flee into a pit; Let no one help him.

Proverbs 28:18*

Whoever walks blamelessly will be saved, But he who is *perverse* in his ways will suddenly fall.

Proverbs 28:24

Whoever *robs* his father or his mother, And says, "It is no *transgression*," *The same is companion to a destroyer.*

Proverbs 29:6*

By *transgression* an evil man is *snared*, But the righteous sings and rejoices.

Proverbs 29:24

Whoever is a *partner* with a *thief* hates his own life; He swears to tell the truth, but reveals nothing.

Proverbs 29:26

Many seek the ruler's favor, *But justice for man comes from the LORD.*

(The Wisdom of Agur)

Proverbs 30:10

Do not malign a servant to his master, Lest he curse you, and you be found *guilty*.

(The Words of King Lemuel's Mother)

Proverbs 31:8

Open your mouth for the speechless, In the cause of all who are *appointed to die.*

CHAPTER 34

HATE, HATRED, DESPISE, DISDAIN

What is "*__Hatred__*"? According to Wikipedia, "*__Hatred__*" is a deep and emotional extreme dislike. It can be directed against individuals, groups, entities, objects, or ideas. *__Hatred__* is often associated with feelings of anger, disgust, and a disposition toward hostility.

Both the Old and New Testament deal with the concept and feelings of *__Hatred__*. Ecclesiastes 3:8 teaches that there is "*A time to love, And a time to hate*"; However, the Old Testament also contains condemnation of *__Hatred__*. For example: "*You shall not __hate__ your brother in your heart*" (Leviticus 19:17). And the New Testament emphasizes that evil intentions can be as serious as evil actions (2 Corinthians 6:8). Thus, John counted *__Hatred__* as serious as murder: "*Whosoever __hates__ his brother is a murderer, and you know that no murderer has eternal life abiding in him*" (1 John 3:15).

It is popularly assumed that one cannot "*__Hate__*" and "love" the same person at the same time. However, Psalm 139:22 says there is a kind of "**perfect *Hatred***" which is consistent with love, and is different from the "**cruel *Hatred***" shown by God's enemies. The Hebrew word describing David's "**perfect *Hatred***" means that it "brings a process to completion" (Harris 1980), in other words, goal oriented opposition. The ultimate opposition to those who oppose God would be to get them from destroying others. The New Testament describes a similar, if not the same, process: "*deliver such a one to Satan for the destruction of the flesh, that his spirit may be saved...*" (1 Corinthians 5:5).

Today's popular characterization of **good** *Hatred* is to "*Hate the sin, but love the sinner.*" Examples of this concept can be found in the Old Testament through David's actions. It is not recorded that David ever physically punished or fought anybody for merely *Hating* or denying Father God, but only for acts of aggression. He responded to evil proportionately. He defended himself and his nation from violence, but when people merely turned from Father God in their hearts without physical violence, he composed Psalms. Presumably, this was the kind of "*Hatred*" in David's mind when he and his son wrote the only five verses in the Old Testament that suggest Father God "*Hates*" not just the sin but the sinner (Psalm 5). The New Testament unambiguously aligns with the modern concept—it never says Father God or Jesus *Hates* any person, or that anyone else should (Luke 14:26).

Accordingly, in Revelations 2:15 and Revelations 2:6, Jesus *Hates* the "doctrines" and "deeds" of the Nicolaitans, but not the Nicolaitans themselves. While Jesus *Hates* sin (Matthew 5:44), He inspires us to love our enemies by pointing out that Father God equally blesses: "*the evil and the good*" (Matthew 5:45).

Finally, as Christians, Father God has given each one of us who are "in Christ" His instructions to march to the beat of a very different drummer when the secular world attempts to assault the very nature of who we are "in Christ" through "*Hatred*," persecutions, and sometimes death. Father God's Word requires that those who are "in Christ" to rise above any and all forms of "*Hatred*," and to exhibit the endless quality of "love"! Whom amongst us has not silently confessed and repented of any "*Hateful*" thoughts, attitudes, or even any wrongful actions that one might have committed toward those who are not of the faith, but when confronted by the Holy Spirit in our prayers, one comes to understand why love and not "*Hate*" is a foundational and fundamental tenet and principle of our Lord Jesus Christ! We, who are of and in the Body of Christ, must always, even when it hurts, look into the eyes of all who "**_Hate_**" or express "**_Hatred_**" in their actions/deeds, thoughts, and/or words, and universally and unequivocally state that "I forgive you and I love you!"

(The Beginning of Knowledge)

Proverbs *1:*7*
The fear of the LORD is the beginning of knowledge, But fools despise wisdom and instruction.

(The Call of Wisdom)

Proverbs *1:*20*–27 and 28–33*

(20)* **Wisdom calls aloud outside; She raises her voice in the open squares.**

(21) She cries out in the chief concourses, At the openings of the gates in the city She speaks her words:

(22) "How long, you simple ones, will you love simplicity? For scorners delight in their scorning, *And fools **hate** knowledge.*

(23) Turn at my rebuke; Surely I will pour out my spirit on you; I will make my words known to you.

(24) Because I have called and you refused, I have stretched out my hand and no one regarded,

(25) Because *you **disdained** all my counsel*, And would have none of my rebuke,

(26) I also will laugh at your calamity; I will mock when your terror comes,

(27) When your terror comes like a storm, And your destruction comes like a whirlwind, When distress and anguish come upon you.

(28) "Then they will call on me, but I will not answer; They will seek me diligently, but they will not find me.

(29) *Because they **hated** knowledge* And did not choose the fear of the LORD,

(30) They would have none of my counsel *And **despised** my every rebuke.*

(31) Therefore they shall eat the fruit of their own way, And be filled to the full with their own fancies.

(32) For the turning away of the simple will slay them, And the complacency of fools will destroy them;

(33)* But whoever listens to me will dwell safely, And will be secure, without fear of evil."

(Guidance for the Young)

Proverbs *3:*11*–*12*

My son, do not *despise* the chastening of the LORD, Nor detest His correction; For whom the LORD loves He corrects, Just as a father the son in whom he delights.

(The Peril of Adultery)

Proverbs 5:7–14

(7) Therefore hear me now, my children, And do not depart from the words of my mouth.

(8) Remove your way far from her, And do not go near the door of her house,

(9) Lest you give your honor to others, And your years to the cruel one;

(10) Lest aliens be filled with your wealth, And your labors go to the house of a foreigner;

(11) And you mourn at last, When your flesh and your body are consumed,

(12) And say: "How I have **hated** instruction, And my heart **despised** correction!

(13) I have not obeyed the voice of my teachers, Nor inclined my ear to those who instructed me!

(14) I was on the verge of total ruin, In the midst of the assembly and congregation."

(The Wicked Man)

Proverbs 6:*12*–15* and 16*–19

(12)* A worthless person, a wicked man, Walks with a perverse mouth;

(13) He winks with his eyes, He shuffles his feet, He points with his fingers;

(14) Perversity is in his heart, He devises evil continually, He sows *discord*.

(15)* Therefore his calamity shall come suddenly; Suddenly he shall be broken without remedy.

(16)* These six things the LORD ***hates***, Yes, seven are an abomination to Him:

(17) A proud look, A lying tongue, Hands that shed innocent blood,

(18) A heart that devises wicked plans, Feet that are swift in running to evil,

(19) A false witness who speaks lies, And one who sows discord among brethren.

(Beware of Adultery)

Proverbs 6:30–31

People do not ***despise*** a thief If he steals to satisfy himself when he is starving. Yet when he is found, he must restore sevenfold; He may have to give up all the substance of his house.

(The Excellence of Wisdom)

Proverbs*8:*12*–14*

(12)* "I, wisdom, dwell with prudence, And find out knowledge and discretion.

(13)* The fear of the LORD is to **_hate_** evil; Pride and arrogance and the evil way And the perverse mouth I **_hate_**.

(14)* Counsel is mine, and sound wisdom; I am understanding, I have strength.

Proverbs *8:*32*–36

(32)* **"Now therefore, listen to me, my children, For blessed are those who keep my ways.**

(33)* **Hear instruction and be wise, And do not _disdain_ it.**

(34)* Blessed is the man who listens to me, Watching daily at my gates, Waiting at the posts of my doors.

(35)* **For whoever finds me finds life, And obtains favor from the LORD;**

(36) But he who sins against me wrongs his own soul; All those who **_hate_** me love death."

(The Way of Wisdom)

Proverbs *9:7–12

(7) "He who corrects a scoffer gets shame for himself, And he who rebukes a wicked man only harms himself,

(8)* **Do not correct a scoffer, lest he _hate_ you; Rebuke a wise man, and he will love you.**

(9)* **Give instruction to a wise man, and he will be still wiser; Teach a just man, and he will increase in learning.**

(10)* **"The fear of the LORD is the beginning of wisdom, And the knowledge of the Holy One is understanding.**

(11) For by me your days will be multiplied, And years of life will be added to you.

(12) If you are wise, you are wise for yourself, And if you scoff, you will bear it alone."

(Wise Sayings of Solomon)

Proverbs *10:*12*

Hatred stirs up strife, But love covers all sins.

Proverbs 10:18
Whoever hides *hatred* has lying lips, And whoever spreads slander is a fool.

Proverbs *11:*12*
He who is devoid of wisdom *despises* his neighbor, But a man of understanding holds his peace.

Proverbs 11:15*
He who is surety for a stranger will suffer, But one who *hates* being surety is secure.

Proverbs *12:*1*
Whoever loves instruction loves knowledge, But he who *hates* correction is stupid.

Proverbs 12:8*
A man will be commended according to his wisdom, But he who is of a perverse heart will be *despised*.

Proverbs 13:5*
A righteous man *hates* lying, But a wicked man is loathsome and comes to shame.

Proverbs 13:*13*
He who *despises* the word will be destroyed, But he who fears the commandment will be rewarded.

Proverbs *13:*18*
Poverty and shame will come to him who *disdains correction*, But he who regards a rebuke will be honored.

Proverbs *13:*24*
He who spares his rod *hates* his son, But he who loves him *disciplines* him promptly.

Proverbs 14:2
He who walks in his uprightness fears the LORD, But he who is perverse in his ways *despises* Him.

Proverbs 14:17
A quick-tempered man acts foolishly, And a man of wicked intentions is ***hated***.

Proverbs 14:20
The poor man is ***hated*** even by his own neighbor, But the rich has many friends.

Proverbs 14:*21*
He who ***despises*** his neighbor sins; But he who has mercy on the poor, happy is he.

Proverbs *15:*5*
A fool *despises* his father's instruction, But he who receives correction is prudent.

Proverbs 15:10*
Harsh discipline is for him who forsakes the way, And he who ***hates*** correction will die.

Proverbs 15:17
Better is a dinner of herb where love is, Than a fatted calf with ***hatred***.

Proverbs 15:18
A *wrathful* man stirs up *strife*, But he who is slow to anger allays contention.

Proverbs 15:*20*
A wise son makes a father glad, But a foolish man ***despises*** his mother.

Proverbs 15:*27*
He who is greedy for gain troubles his own house, But he who ***hates*** bribes will live.

Proverbs *15:*32*
He who *disdains* instruction *despises* his own soul, But he who heeds rebuke gets understanding.

Proverbs 17:*14*
The beginning of *strife* is like releasing water; Therefore stop *contention* before a *quarrel* starts.

Proverbs 19:7
All the brothers of the poor **_hate_** him; How much more do his friends go far from him! He may pursue them with words, yet they abandon him.

Proverbs 21:7
The *violence* of the wicked will destroy them, Because they refuse to do justice.

Proverbs 22:14
The mouth of an immoral woman is a deep pit; He who is _abhorred_ by the LORD will fall there.

(Sayings of the Wise)

Proverbs 23:9*
Do not speak in the hearing of a fool, For he will **_despise_** the wisdom of your words.

Proverbs 23:22*
Listen to your father who begot you, And do not **_despise_** your mother when she is old.

(Further Sayings of the Wise)

Proverbs *24:*28*–*29*
Do not be a witness against your neighbor without cause, For would you deceive with your lips? *Do not say, "I will do to him just as he has done to me; I will render to the man according to his work."*

(Further Wise Sayings of Solomon)

Proverbs 25:17
Seldom set foot in your neighbor's house, Lest he become weary of you and **_hate_** you.

Proverbs 26:23–26

(23) Fervent lips with a wicked heart Are like earthenware covered with silver dross.

(24)* He who **_hates_**, disguises it with his lips, And lays up deceit within himself;

(25) When he speaks kindly, do not believe him, For there are seven abominations in his heart;

(26) Though his **_hatred_** is covered by deceit, His wickedness will be revealed before the assembly.

Proverbs 26:28*

A lying tongue **_hates_** those who are crushed by it, And a flattering mouth works ruin.

Proverbs 28:16

A ruler who lacks understanding is a great oppressor, But he who **_hates_** covetousness will prolong his days.

Proverbs 29:10

The bloodthirsty **_hate_** the blameless, But the upright seek his well-being.

Proverbs 29:24

Whoever is a partner with a thief **_hates_** his own life; He swears to tell the truth, but reveals nothing.

(The Wisdom of Agur)

Proverbs 30:21–23

(21) For three things the earth is perturbed, Yes, for four it cannot bear up:

(22) For a servant when he reigns, A fool when he is filled with food.

(23) A **_hateful_** woman when she is married, And a maidservant who succeeds her mistress.

CHAPTER 35

HEART

One of my favorite movies is *The Wizard of Oz*. Why one might ask. It's the fact that each of the four primary characters desires to achieve and/or receive "something" from "the Wizard": For Dorothy, it is a pathway "Home"; For the Scarecrow, he desires a "Brain"; For the Tin Man, he wants a "***Heart***"; And for the Lion, he desires a little bit of "Courage." And as the narrative exchange unfolds for the Tin Man and his request for a ***Heart***, and in amazing unison, the other three main characters say, "No ***Heart***," and the Tin Man says, "No ***Heart***."

As I reflect on the Tin Man's request for a "***Heart***," I began to think about the fact that while mankind has no so-called Wizard to seek out favors or request of certain inanimate and/or physical objects in one's life, how blessed we all are to have our Father God who stands ready, willing, and able to grant, provide, and/or bless each one of His believers if we/they: "*Delight yourself also in the LORD, And He shall give you the desires of your 'Heart'*" (Psalm 37:4).

From birth, Father God gives each person both a "Brain" as well as a "***Heart***." Additionally, Father God does provide and/or grants various degrees of "Courage" (Joshua 1:5–9). Most of all, Father God provides a pathway "Home" via the forgiveness of sins that comes through His Son, Jesus Christ, as the only way to His Heavenly Kingdom! Jesus Christ stated emphatically and succinctly in John 14:6: "*I am the way, the truth, and the life. No one comes to the Father except through me*"! Thus, as one desires eternal life, one has it all by one's faith and trust in Christ Jesus. And guess what, the way of the cross through Christ Jesus could be construed as one's "yellow brick road." Home toward Father God's Heavenly Kingdom!

I am strongly encouraging one and all to study the verses found in this Chapter Theme on *Heart*, as one will find encouragement and verses that challenge one's mind, direction, and purpose in life, and for one's *Heart*. Listed below are several of my favorite Proverbs verses, highlighting the Chapter Theme of "*Heart*":

- 2:2: "*So that you incline your ear to wisdom, And apply your heart to understanding*";
- 3:3: "*Let not mercy and truth forsake you; Bind them around your neck, Write them on the tablet of your heart*";
- 3:5 & 6: "*Trust in the LORD with all your heart, And lean not on your own understanding; In all your ways acknowledge Him, And He shall direct your paths*";
- 16:9: "*A man's heart plans his way, But the LORD directs his steps*";
- 20:27: "*The spirit of a man is the lamp of the LORD, Searching all the inner depths of his heart*";
- 21:2: "*Every way of a man is right in his own eyes, But the LORD weights the heart*"; and,
- 23:12: "*Apply your heart to instruction, And your ears to words of knowledge.*"

Accordingly, in the end of *The Wizard of Oz*, the Tin Man receives his much desired "*Heart*," and believers in Christ Jesus will receive the ultimate gift of "*eternal Life*"! And that, my friends, is something to be exceedingly glad in!

To God be the GLORY!

(The Value of Wisdom)

Proverbs *2:1*–*5* and *10*–15

(1)* My son, if you receive my words, And treasure my commands within you,

(2)* So that you incline your ear to wisdom, And apply your _heart_ to understanding;

(3) Yes, if you cry out for discernment, And lift up your voice for understanding,

(4) If you seek her as silver, And search for her as for hidden treasures;

(5)* Then you will understand the fear of the LORD, And find the knowledge of God.

(10)* When wisdom enters your _heart_, And knowledge is pleasant to your soul,

(11)* Discretion will preserve you; Understanding will keep you,

(12) To deliver you from the way of evil, From the man who speaks perverse things,

(13) From those who leave the paths of uprightness, To walk in the ways of darkness;

(14) Who rejoice in doing evil, And delight in the perversity of the wicked;

(15) Whose ways are crooked, And who are devious in their paths.

(Guidance for the Young)

Proverbs *3:1–2,*3*–4*, *5*–*6*, and 7*–8*

(1) My son, do not forget my law, But let your _heart_ keep my commands;

(2) For length of days and long life And peace they will add to you.

(3)* Let not mercy and truth forsake you; Bind them around your neck, Write them on the tablet of your _heart_,

(4)* And so find favor and high esteem In the sight of God and man.

(5)* **Trust in the LORD with all your _heart_, And lean not on your own understanding;**

(6)* **In all your ways acknowledge Him, And He shall direct your paths.**

(7)* Do not be wise in your own eyes; Fear the LORD and depart from evil.

(8)* _It will be health to your flesh, And strength to your bones._

(Security in Wisdom)

Proverbs *4:1*–9

(1)* Hear, my children, the instruction of a father, And give attention to know understanding;

(2)* For I give you good doctrine: Do not forsake my law.

(3) When I was my father's son, Tender and the only one in the sight of my mother,

(4)* **He also taught me, and said to me: "Let your _heart_ retain my words; Keep my commands, and live.**

(5)* **Get wisdom! Get understanding! Do not forget, nor turn away from the words of my mouth.**

(6)* **Do not forsake her (wisdom), and she will preserve you: Love her, and she will keep you.**

(7)* **Wisdom is the principal thing; Therefore get wisdom, And in all your getting, get understanding.**

(8) Exalt her, and she will promote you; She will bring you honor, when you embrace her.

(9) She will place on your head an ornament of grace; A crown of glory she will deliver to you."

Proverbs *4:*20*–*27*

(20)* **My son, give attention to my words; Incline your ear to my sayings.**

(21)* **Do not let them depart from your eyes; Keep them in the midst of your _heart_;**

(22)* **For they are life to those who find them, And health to all their flesh.**

(23)* **Keep your _heart_ with all diligence, For out of it spring the issues of life.**

(24)* **Put away from you a deceitful mouth, And put perverse lips far from you.**

(25) Let your eyes look straight ahead, And your eyelids look right before you.

(26)* **Ponder the path of your feet, And let all your ways be established.**

(27)* **Do not turn to the right or the left; Remove your foot from evil.**

(The Wicked Man)

Proverbs 6:12–15 and 16–19

(12) A worthless person, a wicked man, Walks with a perverse mouth;

(13) He winks with his eyes, He shuffles his feet, He points with his fingers;

(14) Perversity is in his **_heart_**, He devises evil continually, He sows discord.

(15) Therefore his calamity shall come suddenly; Suddenly he shall be broken without remedy.

(16) These six things the LORD hates, Yes, seven are an abomination to Him:

(17) A proud look, A lying tongue, Hands that shed innocent blood,

(18) A **_heart_** that devises wicked plans, Feet that are swift in running to evil,

(19) A false witness who speaks lies, And one who sows discord among brethren.

(Beware of Adultery)

Proverbs *7:1*–5*

(1)* My son, keep my words, And treasure my commands within you.

(2)* **Keep my commands and live, And my law as the apple of your eye.**

(3)* Bind them on your fingers; Write them on the tablet of your *heart*.

(4)* **Say to wisdom, "You are my sister," And call understanding your nearest kin,**

(5)* That they may keep you from the immortal woman, From the seductress who flatters with her words.

(The Crafty Harlot)

Proverbs 7:10–20 and 24–27

(10) And there a woman met him, With the attire of a harlot, and a *crafty heart*.

(11) She was loud and rebellious, Her feet would not stay at home.

(12) At times she was outside, at times in the open square, Lurking at every corner.

(13) So she caught him and kissed him; With an impudent face she said to him:

(14) "I have peace offerings with me; Today I have paid my vows.

(15) So I came out to meet you, Diligently to seek your face. And I have found you.

(16) I have spread my bed with tapestry, Colored coverings of Egyptian linen.

(17) I have perfumed my bed With myrrh, aloes, and cinnamon.

(18) Come, let us take our fill of love until morning; Let us delight ourselves with love.

(19) For my husband is not at home; He has gone on a long journey;

(20) He has taken a bag of money with him, And will come home on the appointed day."

(24) Now therefore, listen to me, my children; Pay attention to the words of my mouth:

(25) Do not let your **_heart_** turn aside to her ways, Do not stray into her paths;

(26) For she has cast down many wounded, And all who were slain by her were strong men.

(27) Her house is the way to hell, Descending to the chambers of death.

(Wise Sayings of Solomon)

Proverbs 10:8
The wise in **_heart_** will receive commands, But a prating fool will fall.

Proverbs *10:*20*
The tongue of the righteous is choice silver; The _heart_ of the wicked is worth little.

Proverbs 11:20
Those who are of a perverse **_heart_** are an abomination to the LORD, But the blameless in their ways are His delight.

Proverbs *11:*29*
He who troubles his own house will inherit the wind, And the fool will be servant to the wise of _heart_.

Proverbs 12:8*
A man will be commended according to his wisdom, But he who is of a perverse **_heart_** will be despised.

Proverbs 12:20*
Deceit is in the **_heart_** of those who devise evil, But counselors of peace have joy.

Proverbs 12:23*
A prudent man conceals knowledge, But the **_heart_** of fools proclaims foolishness.

Proverbs 12:25*

Anxiety in the **_heart_** of a man causes depression, But a good word makes it glad.

Proverbs *13:*12*

Hope deferred makes the _heart_ sick, But when the desire comes, it is a tree of life.

Proverbs 14:10

The **_heart_** knows its own bitterness, And a stranger does not share its joy.

Proverbs 14:13

Even in laughter the **_heart_** may sorrow, And the end of mirth may be grief.

Proverbs 14:14*

The backslider in **_heart_** will be filled with his own ways, But a good man will be satisfied from above.

Proverbs 14:30

A sound **_heart_** is life to the body, But envy is rottenness to the bones.

Proverbs *14:*33*

Wisdom rests in the _heart_ of him who has understanding, But what is in the _heart_ of fools is made known.

Proverbs 15:*7*

The lips of the wise disperse knowledge, But the **_heart_** of the fool does not do so.

Proverbs 15:11

Hell and Destruction are before the LORD; So how much more the **_hearts_** of the sons of men.

Proverbs 15:13

A _merry_ **_heart_** makes a cheerful countenance, But by sorrow of the **_heart_** the spirit is broken.

Proverbs *15:*14*
The _heart_ of him who has understanding seeks knowledge, But the mouth of fools feeds on foolishness.

Proverbs 15:*15*
All the days of the afflicted are evil, But he who is of a _merry_ **_heart_** has a continual feast.

Proverbs *15:*28*
The _heart_ of the righteous studies how to answer, But the mouth of the wicked pours forth evil.

Proverbs 15:30
The light of the eyes rejoices the **_heart_**, And a good report makes the bones healthy.

Proverbs *16:*1*
The preparations of the _heart_ belong to man, But the answer of the tongue is from the LORD.

Proverbs 16:2*
All the ways of a man are pure in his own _eyes_, But the LORD weighs the _spirits_.

Proverbs 16:5
Everyone proud in **_heart_** is an abomination to the LORD; Though they join forces, none will go unpunished.

Proverbs *16:*9*
A man's _heart_ plans his way, But the LORD directs his steps.

Proverbs 16:21*
The wise in **_heart_** will be called prudent, And sweetness of the lips increases learning.

Proverbs 16:23
The **_heart_** of the wise teaches his mouth, And adds learning to his lips.

Proverbs 17:*3*

The refining pot is for silver and the furnace for gold, But the LORD tests the **_hearts_**.

Proverbs 17:16

Why is there in the hand of a fool the purchase price of wisdom, Since he has no **_heart_** for it?

Proverbs 17:20

He who has a deceitful **_heart_** finds no good, And he who has a perverse tongue falls into evil.

Proverbs 17:*22*

A _merry_ **_heart_** does good, like medicine, But a broken _spirit_ dries the bones.

Proverbs 18:2

A fool has no delight in understanding, But in expressing his own **_heart_**.

Proverbs *18:*12*

Before destruction the _heart_ of man is haughty, And before honor is humility.

Proverbs *18:*15*

The _heart_ of the prudent acquires knowledge, And the ear of the wise seeks knowledge.

Proverbs 19:3

The foolishness of a man twists his way, And his **_heart_** frets against the LORD.

Proverbs 19:18

Chasten your son while there is hope, And do not set your **_heart_** on his destruction.

Proverbs *19:*21*
There are many plans in a man's _heart_, Nevertheless the LORD's counsel—that will stand.

Proverbs 20:5
Counsel in the **_heart_** of man is like deep water, But a man of understanding will draw it out.

Proverbs 20:9
Who can say, "I have made my **_heart_** clean, I am pure from sin"?

Proverbs 20:27*
The spirit of a man is the lamp of the LORD, Searching all the inner depths of his **_heart_**.

Proverbs 20:30
Blows that hurt cleanse away evil, As do stripes the inner depths of the **_heart_**.

Proverbs 21:1
The king's **_heart_** is in the hand of the LORD, Like the rivers of water; He turns it wherever He wishes.

Proverbs *21:*2*
Every way of a man is right in his own eyes, But the LORD weights the _hearts_.

Proverbs 21:4
A haughty look, a proud **_heart_**, And the plowing of the wicked are sin.

Proverbs 21:27*
The sacrifice of the wicked is an abomination; How much more when he brings it with wicked _intent_!

Proverbs 22:11
He who loves purity of **_heart_** And has grace on his lips, The king will be his friend.

Proverbs *22:*15*

Foolishness is bound up in the _heart_ of a child; The rod of correction will drive it far from him.

(Sayings of the Wise)

Proverbs *22:*17*–21*

(17)* **Incline your ear and hear the words of the wise, And apply your _heart_ to my knowledge;**

(18)* **For it is a pleasing thing if you keep them within you; Let them all be fixed upon your lips,**

(19)* **So that your trust may be in the LORD; I have instructed you today, even you.**

(20)* **Have I not written to you excellent things Of counsels and knowledge,**

(21)* **That I may make you know the certainty of the words of truth, That you may answer words of truth To those who send to you?**

Proverbs 23:6–8

(6)　Do not eat the bread of a miser, Nor desire his delicacies;

(7)　For as he thinks in his _heart_, so is he. "Eat and drink!" he says to you, But his _heart_ is not with you.

(8)　The morsel you have eaten, you will vomit up, And waste your pleasant words.

Proverbs *23:*12*

Apply your _heart_ to instruction, And your ears to words of knowledge.

Proverbs *23:*15*–*16*

My son, if your _heart_ is wise, My _heart_ will rejoice—indeed I myself; Yes, my inmost being will rejoice When your lips speak right things.

Proverbs 23:17*–18*

Do not let your _heart_ envy sinners, But be zealous for the fear of the

LORD all the day; For surely there is a hereafter, And your hope will not be cut off.

Proverbs 23:19*

Hear, my son, and be wise; And guide your **_heart_** in the way.

Proverbs 23:26–28

(26) My son, give me your **_heart_**, And let your eyes observe my ways.

(27) For a harlot is a deep pit, And a seductress is a narrow well.

(28) She also lies in wait as for a victim, And increases the unfaithful among men.

Proverbs 24:1–2

Do not be envious of evil men, Nor desire to be with them; For their **_heart_** devises violence, And their lips talk of troublemaking.

Proverbs 24:11–12

Deliver those who are drawn toward death, And hold back those stumbling to the slaughter. If you say, "Surely we did not know this," Does not He who weighs the **_hearts_** consider it? He who keeps your soul, does He not know it? And will He not render to each man according to his deeds?

Proverbs *24:*17*–*18*

Do not rejoice when your enemy falls, And do not let your _heart_ be glad when he stumbles; Lest the LORD see it, and it displease Him, And He turn away His wrath from him.

(Further Wise Sayings of Solomon)

Proverbs 25:3

As the heavens for height and the earth for depth, So the **_heart_** of kings is unsearchable.

Proverbs 25:20

Like one who takes away a garment in cold weather, And like vinegar on soda, Is one who sings songs to a heavy **_heart_**.

Proverbs 26:23

Fervent lips with a wicked *heart* Are like earthenware covered with a silver dross.

Proverbs 26:24*–26

(24)* He who hates, disguises it with his lips, And lays up deceit within himself;

(25) When he speaks kindly, do not believe him, For there are seven abominations in his *heart*;

(26) Though his hatred is covered by deceit, His wickedness will be revealed before the assembly.

Proverbs 27:*9*

Ointment and perfume delight the *heart*, And the sweetness of a man's friend gives delight by *hearty* counsel.

Proverbs 27:11

My son, be wise, and make my *heart* glad, That I may answer him who reproaches me.

Proverbs *27:*19*

As in water face reflects face, So a man's *heart* reveals the man.

Proverbs 28:14*

Happy is the man who is always reverent, But he who hardens his *heart* will fall into calamity.

Proverbs 28:*25*

He who is of a proud *heart* stirs up strife, But he who trusts in the LORD will be prospered.

Proverbs 28:26*

He who trusts in his own *heart* is a fool, But whoever walks wisely will be delivered.

(The Virtuous Wife)

Proverbs *31:*10*–*12*

(10)* **Who can find a virtuous wife? For her worth is far above rubies.**

(11)* **The *heart* of her husband safely trusts her; So he will have no lack of gain.**

(12)* **She does him good and not evil All the days of her life.**

CHAPTER 36

HONEST, HONESTY

W hy is the biblical principle and truth of "*Honesty*" such a difficult value and/or personal characteristic to adhere to, live out, and/ or practice on a daily basis? Why isn't "*Honesty*" a core principle, truth, and/or value that is built into one's personal DNA? Why is it popular in today's societal norms, as well as vernacular, to sometimes hear and/or say phrases like, "Let me be," "*Honest*," or "In all *Honesty*"? Aren't such statements an oxymoron in the sense that, by making such statements, it potentially infers or assumes that "anything" one states before and/or after such statements might be inferred to be misleading, *dishonest*, and/ or an outright lie?

While it is an absolute truth that sin is bad and not in accordance with Father God's will for one's life, it seems to me that abiding in one of Father God's stated biblical principles of "**Truth**" through "*Honest*" communications, is and should be an easy biblical principle to adhere to, as "*Honesty*" and "Truth," are two sides of the same spiritual coin. Just think about how refreshing one feels about oneself when one operates from a framework of "*Honesty*," "**Truth**," and "Righteousness"! I would contend that such a higher degree of inner "Peace" is directly proportional to a higher level of "*Honesty*," "**Truth**," and "Righteousness" that one practices and lives out on a daily basis!

As one studies, reviews, meditates, marinates, and lives out the biblical principles of "**_Honesty_**", "**Truth**," and "Righteousness," notice how Father God delights in such virtues, as evidence from the following biblical verses from Proverbs:

- 11:1: "_Dishonest scales are an abomination to the LORD, But a **just** weight is His delight_";
- 12:22: "_Lying lips are an abomination to the LORD, But those who deal '**truthfully**' are His delight_";
- 21:3: "_To do 'righteousness' and justice Is more acceptable to the LORD than sacrifice._"

Notice how even those closest to Jesus Christ had good intentions but failed to practice and/or live out His proclamation of "**_Honesty_**," as Peter stated in John 13:37 and 38: "_Peter said to Him, 'Lord, why can I not follow You now? I will lay down my life for Your sake.' Jesus answered him, 'Will you lay down your life for My sake? Most assuredly, I say to you, the rooster shall not crow till you have 'denied' Me three times._"

Accordingly, one must exhibit "**_Honesty_**" in all of life's personal dealings, interactions, communications, and statements irrespective of the mode of distribution (i.e. orally or in writing). As Father God "_loves a cheerful giver,_" I would contend that Father God also loves an "**_Honest_**" Saint or Child of Father God!

(Wise Sayings of Solomon)

Proverbs 11:1
Dishonest scales are an abomination to the LORD, But a **_just weight_** is His delight.

Proverbs 11:3
The **_integrity of the upright_** will guide them, But the perversity of the unfaithful will destroy them.

Proverbs 14:*8*

The *wisdom of the prudent* is to understand his way, But the folly of fools is deceit.

Proverbs 14:25

A *true witness* delivers souls, But a deceitful witness speaks lies.

Proverbs 15:27*

He who is greedy for gain troubles his own house, But he who *hates bribes* will live.

Proverbs 16:11

Honest weights and scales are the LORD's; All the weights in the bag are His work.

Proverbs 18:5*

It is not good to show partiality to the wicked, *Or to overthrow the righteous in judgment*.

Proverbs *19:*1*

Better is the poor who _walks in his integrity_ Than one who is perverse in his lips, and is a fool.

Proverbs 20:7*

The righteous man **_walks in his integrity_**; His children are blessed after him.

Proverbs 20:30

Blows that hurt cleanse away evil, *As do stripes the inner depths of the heart.*

Proverbs *21:*2*

Every way of a man is right in his own eyes, **_But the LORD weighs the hearts_**.

Proverbs 21:28

A false witness shall perish, But the man who hears him *will speak endlessly.*

Proverbs *22:*6*

Train up a child in the way he should go, And when he is old he will not depart from it.

(Sayings of the Wise)

Proverbs *22:*17*–*21*

(17)* *Incline your ear and hear the words of the wise,* **And apply your heart to my knowledge;**

(18)* For it is a pleasing thing if you keep them within you; Let them all be fixed upon your lips,

(19)* **So that your trust may be in the LORD; I have instructed you today, even you.**

(20)* Have I not written to you excellent things Of counsels and knowledge,

(21)* **That I may make you know the certainty of the** *words of truth* **That you may answer** *words of truth***, To those who send to you?**

Proverbs 22:28

Do not remove the ancient landmark Which your fathers have set.

Proverbs 22:29*

Do you see a man who *excels in his work*? He will stand before kings; He will not stand before unknown men.

Proverbs 23:10–11

Do not remove the ancient landmark, Nor enter the fields of the fatherless; For their Redeemer is mighty; He will *plead their cause* against you.

(Further Sayings of the Wise)

Proverbs *24:*26*
He who gives a *right answer* kisses the lips.

(Further Wise Sayings of Solomon)

Proverbs *26:*16*
The lazy man is *wiser* in his own eyes Than seven men who can answer sensibly.

Proverbs *27:*6*
Faithful are the wounds of a friend, But the kisses of an enemy are deceitful.

Proverbs *27:*17*
As iron sharpens iron, So a man *sharpens* the countenance of his friend.

Proverbs *28:*6*
Better is the poor who *walks in his integrity* Than one perverse in his ways, though he be rich.

Proverbs 28:18*
Whoever walks *blamelessly* will be saved, But he who is perverse in his ways will suddenly fall.

Proverbs 28:20
A *faithful* man will abound with blessings, But he who hastens to be rich will not go unpunished.

Proverbs *28:*23*
He who *rebukes* a man will find more favor afterward Than he who flatters with the tongue.

Proverbs 29:24
Whoever is a partner with a thief hates his own life; He swears to **_tell the truth_,** but reveals nothing.

(The Virtuous Wife)

Proverbs *31:*10*–*12*

(10)* Who can find a *virtuous* wife? For her worth is far above rubies.

(11)* The heart of her husband safely trusts her; So he will have no lack of gain.

(12)* She does him good and not evil, All the days of her life.

CHAPTER 37

HOPE, DESIRE

When one thinks and marinates on these two words that comprise this Chapter Theme's Narrative of "***HOPE/DESIRE***," what resonates with me, from a general biblical perspective, are the concepts of "good vs. evil," "light vs. dark," or "righteousness vs. unrighteousness." With such a diametric difference in my interpretation of these two terms, a point of clarification is needed.

When one examines the biblical definitions for the word ***Hope***, it is generally defined as "confident expectation or confident assurance." ***Hope*** denotes a strong sense of reality without doubt and no element of feelings. With ***Hope***, one has a solid foundation upon which to base this earthly journey by recognizing and believing that Father God's Words are "truths," as well as the fact that Father God always keeps His promises!

In support of the above biblical definitions for the Theme of "***Hope***," one needs only to look to the following biblical scripture verses, namely Romans 8:24 and 25, which states: "*For we were saved in this **hope**, but **hope** that is seen is not **hope**; for why does one still **hope** for what he sees? But if we **hope** for what we do not see, we eagerly wait for it with perseverance.*" As well as the all too familiar faith scriptural verse in Hebrews 11:1, which states: "*Now faith is the substance of things **hoped** for, the evidence of things not seen.*"

One could expound on numerous other biblical reference points surrounding the biblical truth of **_Hope_** through faith, as well as **_Hope_** through Christ Jesus and the Holy Spirit. But suffice it to say that Proverbs 23:18 nicely captures the essential elements of **_Hope_** in stating: "_For surely there is a hereafter, And your **hope** will not be cut off._"

In contrast to the "**_Hope_**" that is found in Jesus Christ, I would contend that "**_Desire_**" is, more likely than not, driven by one's sin nature, or stated another way when one moves from basic needs to wants, then **_Desires_** transitions from being content with Father God supplying all of one's needs (i.e. Philippians 4:19: "_And my God shall supply all your need according to His riches in glory by Jesus Christ._") to a position where one's sin nature presses against one's heart and mind, moving one from the lane of righteousness into the lane of selfishness and/or fleshly **_Desires_**. When such movement and/or transition takes place, one activates one's sin nature, which is generally borne out from the hidden little niches recessed within one's mind, thoughts, and heart from which one's secret and hidden **_Desires_** evolve (Romans 7:17–20).

The one known anecdote to minimizing one's sinful **_Desires_** is to commit to the Lord by trusting in Him, being submissive to His will and purpose for one's life, and allowing the supernatural presence of the Holy Spirit to dwell within, through and upon, each human being, twenty-four hours a day, seven days a week! In essence, an individual's **_Desires_** become His **_Desires_**; one's will must be submissive to do His will and one's rebellious nature transitions into a life of joyous obedience.

(Guidance for the Young)

Proverbs *3:*13*–18

(13)* **Happy is the man who finds wisdom, And the man who gains understanding;**

(14) For her proceeds are better than the profits of silver, And her gain than fine gold.

(15) She is more precious than rubies, And all the things you may *desire* cannot compare with her.

(16) Length of days is in her right hand, In her left hand riches and honor.

(17) Her ways are ways of pleasantness, And all her paths are peace.

(18) She is a tree of life to those who take hold of her, And happy are all who retain her.

(The Excellence of Wisdom)

Proverbs *8:*6*–*11*

(6)* **Listen, for I will speak of excellent things, And from the opening of my lips** *will come right things;*

(7)* **For my mouth will speak truth; Wickedness is an abomination to my lips.**

(8)* **All the words of my mouth are with righteousness; Nothing crooked or perverse is in them.**

(9)* They are plain to him who understands, And right to those who find knowledge.

(10) Receive my instruction, and not silver, And knowledge rather than choice gold;

(11)* **For** *wisdom* **is better than rubies, And all the things one may** *desire* **cannot be compared with her.**

(Wise Sayings of Solomon)

Proverbs 10:3*

The LORD will not allow the righteous soul to famish, But He casts away the *desire* of the wicked.

Proverbs 10:24

The fear of the wicked will come upon him, And the *desire* of the righteous will be granted.

Proverbs 10:28

The ***hope*** of the righteous will be gladness, But the expectations of the wicked will perish.

Proverbs 11:7

When a wicked man dies, his expectation will perish, And the ***hope*** of the unjust perishes.

Proverbs 11:23*

The ***desire*** of the righteous is only good, But the expectations of the wicked is wrath.

Proverbs 13:4*

The soul of a lazy man ***desires***, and has nothing; But the soul of the diligent shall be made rich.

Proverbs *13:*12*

Hope deferred makes the heart sick, But when the *desire* comes, it is a tree of life.

Proverbs 13:19

A ***desire*** accomplished is sweet to the soul, But it is an abomination to fools to depart from evil.

Proverbs 18:1

A man who isolates himself seeks his own ***desire***; He rages against all wise judgment.

Proverbs 19:18

Chasten your son while there is ***hope***, And do not set your heart on his destruction.

Proverbs 19:*22*

What is ***desired*** in a man is kindness, And a poor man is better than a liar.

Proverbs 21:10

The soul of the wicked ***desires*** evil; His neighbor finds no favor in his eyes.

Proverbs 21:*20*

There is **_desirable_** treasure, And oil in the dwelling of the wise, But a foolish man squanders it.

Proverbs *21:25*–*26*

The **_desire_** of the lazy man kills him, For his hands refuse to labor. He covets greedily all day long, **But the righteous gives and does not spare.**

(Sayings of the Wise)

Proverbs 23:1–3

(1) When you sit down to eat with a ruler, Consider carefully what is before you;

(2) And put a knife to your throat If you are a man given to appetite.

(3) Do not **_desire_** his delicacies, For they are deceptive food.

Proverbs 23:6–8

(6) Do not eat the bread of a miser, Nor **_desire_** his delicacies;

(7) For as he thinks in his heart, so is he. "Eat and drink!" he says to you, But his heart is not with you.

(8) The morsel you have eaten, you will vomit up, And waste your pleasant words.

Proverbs 23:17*–18*

Do not let your heart envy sinners, But be zealous for the fear of the LORD all the day; For surely there is a hereafter, And your **_hope_** will not be cut off.

Proverbs 24:1–2

Do not be envious of evil men, Nor **_desire_** to be with them; For their heart devises violence, And their lips talk of troublemaking.

Proverbs *24:13–*14*

My son, eat honey (wisdom) because it is good, And the honeycomb (wisdom) which is sweet to your taste; **So shall the knowledge of wisdom be** to your soul; If you have found it, there is a prospect, And your _hope_ will not be cut off.

Proverbs 24:19–20

Do not fret because of evildoers, Nor be envious of the wicked; For there will be no _prospect_ for the evil man; The lamp of the wicked will be put out.

(Further Wise Sayings of Solomon)

Proverbs *26:*12*

Do you see a man wise in his own eyes? There is more _hope_ for a fool than for him.

Proverbs 29:20*

Do you see a man hasty in his words? There is more **_hope_** for a fool than for him.

CHAPTER 38

HUMILITY

How does one adequately describe this Chapter Theme of "**_Humility_**"? Below, you will find my best definition of this biblical term and how I try to live it out. My most illustrative biblical example highlighting the importance of "**_Humility_**" can be found in John 13:1–17, whereby Jesus, leading by example, undertook the task of "_washing the feet_" (John 13:14) of the disciples, which as we know, occurred in the upper room, minutes prior to the Last Supper, hours before His crucifixion for the sins of all believers in Christ Jesus.

The significance of Jesus "_washing the disciples feet_" (John 13:10) can best be highlighted as follows:

A. For Jesus, it was a crystal clear and demonstrative example of both authentic and true, "**_Humility_**" and Servanthood;

B. For His disciples, the "_washing of their feet_" (John 13:12–17), especially Peter, was in direct contrast to what some have described as their hardness of heart attitudes at that time; and

C. For Christ followers, the "_washing of feet_" (John 13:14) is quite symbolic of the believers' role in the body of Christ, that being "_washing the feet_" (John 13:14) of others, as well as being a "servant" to others, especially to the "_least of these_" (Matthew

25:40) by giving of what I personally coach about of the "**4 T's**", i.e., Time, Talent, Treasury, and Tent (Self)!

Additionally, when one studies and meditates on this Chapter Theme's Proverbs verses, the following four, from my personal perspective, build what I like to call the "House of '*Humility*.'" The four structural pillars are built on the following Proverbs verses:

- 11:2: "*When pride comes, then comes shame; But with the* **humble** *is wisdom*";
- 15:33: "*The fear of the LORD is the instruction of wisdom, And before honor is* **humility**";
- 16:19: "*Better to be of a* **humble** *spirit with the lowly, Than to divide the spoil with the proud*"; and,
- 18:12: "*Before destruction the heart of man is haughty, And before honor is* **humility**."

Now, if the above structural pillars of the "House of '*Humility*'" are solidly in place in one's biblical and spiritual life and walk in Christ Jesus, then the following Proverbs verse will solidify the roof that is placed on the "House of '*Humility*,'" and as Proverbs 25:21–22 clearly states: "*If your enemy is hungry, give him bread to eat; And if he is thirsty, give him water to drink; For so you will heap coals of fire on his head, And the LORD will reward you!*"

Thus, as Jesus Christ "*washed the feet*" of His disciples (John 13:14), the night proceeding His crucifixion on Calvary's Cross for my sins and everyone who believes in the name of Jesus Christ as Lord of one's life, then from my "*Humble*" perspective, the least that one could and should do is to follow Jesus Christ's example and place honor, pride, station in life/wealth accumulation, as well as material possessions to the side, or better yet, behind oneself and graciously and **Humbly,** "*wash and serve the feet of others, especially the 'least of these'*"! And as for me, there is no greater service to the Lord and resulting joy that comes to my heart, as I personally challenge myself and try as best as I can to do and outdo Jesus Christ in **Humility,** by "*washing the feet of others*"! (John 13:14)

(Guidance for the Young)

Proverbs *3:*34*
Surely He scorns the scornful, But gives grace to the *humble.*

(The Excellence of Wisdom)

Proverbs *8:12*–14*
(12)* "I, wisdom, dwell with prudence, And find out knowledge and discretion.
(13)* The fear of the LORD is to hate evil; *Pride and arrogance and the evil way And the perverse mouth I hate.*
(14)* Counsel is mine, and sound wisdom; I am understanding, I have strength.

(Wise Sayings of Solomon)

Proverbs *11:*2*
When pride comes, then comes shame; But with the *humble* **is wisdom.**

Proverbs 13:*7*
There is one who makes himself rich, yet has nothing; *And one who makes himself poor,* yet has great riches.

Proverbs *13:*10*
By pride comes nothing but strife, But with the *well-advised* **is wisdom.**

Proverbs *15:*16*
Better is a little **with the fear of the LORD, Than great treasure with trouble.**

Proverbs *15:*33*

The fear of the LORD is the instruction of wisdom, And before honor is _humility_.

Proverbs *16:*19*

Better to be of a _humble_ spirit with the lowly, Than to divide the spoil with the proud.

Proverbs *18:*12*

Before destruction the heart of man is haughty, And before honor is _humility_.

Proverbs 20:9

Who can say, _"I have made my heart clean, I am pure from my sin"_?

Proverbs *22:*4*

By _humility_ and the fear of the LORD Are riches and honor and life.

Proverbs 22:11

He who loves _purity_ of heart And has grace on his lips, The king will be his friend.

(Sayings of the Wise)

Proverbs 22:29*

Do you see a man who excels in his work? _He will stand before kings;_ He will not stand before unknown men.

Proverbs *24:*17*–*18*

Do not rejoice when your enemy falls, And do not let your heart be glad when he stumbles; Lest the LORD see it and it displease Him, And He turn away His wrath from him.

(Further Wise Sayings of Solomon)

Proverbs 25:6*–7*

Do not exalt yourself in the presence of the king, And *do not stand* in the place of the great; *For it is better that he say to you, "Come up here,"* Than that you should be put lower in the presence of the prince, Whom your eyes have seen.

Proverbs *25:*21*–*22*

If your enemy is hungry, give him bread to eat; And if he is thirsty, give him water to drink; For so you will heap coals of fire on his head, And the LORD will reward you!

Proverbs 25:*27*

It is not good to eat much honey; *So to seek one's own glory is not glory.*

Proverbs 27:1

Do not boast about tomorrow, For you do not know what a day may bring forth.

Proverbs 27:2*

Let another man praise you, and not your own mouth; A stranger, and not your own lips.

Proverbs 27:18

Whoever keeps the fig tree will eat its fruit; *So he who waits on his master will be honored.*

Proverbs 27:21*

The refining pot is for silver and the furnace for gold, *And a man is valued by what others say of him.*

Proverbs 29:23*

A man's pride will bring him low, But the **humble** in spirit will retain honor.

(The Wisdom of Agur)

Proverbs 30:32–33

If you have been foolish in exalting yourself, Of if you have devised evil, put your hand on your mouth. For as the churning of milk produces butter, And wringing the nose produces blood, So the forcing of wrath produces strife.

CHAPTER 39

INSTRUCTION, LEARNING, CORRECTION, DISCIPLINE, REPROOF

A s I was meditating on the combined Chapter Theme Narratives for *Correction*, *Discipline*, *Reproof*, *Instruction*, **and** *Learning*; the difficulty of separating these five Themes into separate and independent Chapters, became more challenging, in that *Correction* and *Discipline* are in essence, one and the same, in that *Correction* has, at its root, *Discipline*. Such that whether one plants the seed of *Correction* followed by the watering of *Discipline*, what spawns from that is the tree of *Instruction* and *Learning*. As *Instruction* takes hold and broadens itself in the DNA of an individual, then hopefully and prayerfully, a more righteous and Christlike attitude and approach to life will (might) emerge.

As one will note in this "teachable moments" Chapter, the verses from Proverbs in these five areas of individual growth and development are, from my perspective, rather specific, directional, as well as instructional. Accordingly, I will only make specific reference to a few Proverbs verses on these combined Themes; While, at the same time, I believe that there is directional and significant value in briefly mentioning both Old and New Testament scriptures, that highlights on these combined Themes, namely:

- Job 5:17 and 18: "*Behold, happy is the man whom God **corrects**; Therefore do not despise the **chastening** of the Almighty. For He bruises, but He binds up; He wounds, but His hands make whole*";
- Psalms 94:12 and 13: "*Blessed is the man whom You **instruct**, O Lord, And **teach** out of Your Law. (13) That You may give him rest from the days of adversity, Until the pit is dug for the wicked*";
- 1 Corinthians 11:32: "*But when we are judged, we are **chastened** by the Lord, that we may not be condemned with the world*";
- Hebrews 12:5–11: (5) "*And you have forgotten the exhortation which speaks to you as to sons: "My son, do not despise the **chastening** of the LORD, Nor be discouraged when you are rebuked by Him. (6) For whom the LORD loves He **chastens**, And scourges every son whom He receives. (7) If you endure **chastening**, God deals with you as with sons; for what son is there whom a father does not **chasten**? (8) But if you are without **chastening**, of which all have become partakers, then you are illegitimate and not sons. (9) Furthermore, we have had human fathers who **corrected** us and we paid them respect. Shall we not much more readily be in subjection to the Father of spirits and live? (10) For they indeed for a few days **chastened** us as seemed best to them, but He for our profit, that we may be partakers of His holiness. (11) Now no **chastening** seems to be joyful for the present, but painful; nevertheless, afterward it yields the peaceful fruit of righteousness to those who have been **trained** by it*";
- Psalms 50:17: "*Seeing you hate **instruction** And cast My words behind you?*";
- Ephesians 6:4: "*And you, fathers, do not provoke your children to wrath, but bring them up in the **training** and admonition of the Lord*";

- 1 Timothy 4:7: "*But reject profane and old wives' fables, and exercise yourself toward godliness*";
- 2 Timothy 1:7: "*For God has not given us a spirit of fear, but of power and of love and of a sound mind*"; and,
- Revelation 3:19: "*As many as I love, I rebuke and **chasten**, Therefore, be zealous and repent....*"
- Needless to say, the specific Proverbs for this Chapter Narrative are much too numerous to highlight, but suffice it to say, here are a few of my favorites:
- Proverbs 3:11: "*My son, do not despise the **chastening** of the LORD*";
- Proverbs 3:12: "*For whom the LORD loves he **corrects**, Just as a father the son in whom he delights*";
- Proverbs 6:23: "*For the commandment is a lamp, And the law a light; **Reproofs** of **instruction** are the way of life*";
- Proverbs 13:1: "*A wise son heeds his father's **instruction**, But a scoffer does not listen to rebuke*";
- Proverbs 15:5: "*A fool despises his father's **instruction**, But he who receives **correction** is prudent*";
- Proverbs 15:32: "*He who disdains **instruction** despises his own soul, But he who heeds rebuke gets understanding*";
- Proverbs 19:18: "***Chasten** your son while there is hope; And do not set your heart on his destruction*";
- Proverbs 19:27: "*Cease listening to **instruction**, my son, And you will stray from the words of knowledge*"; and,
- Proverbs 23:12: "*Apply your heart to **instruction**, And your ears to words of knowledge.*"

I have heard it said that "God's ***Discipline*** moves you away from the ugliness of sin and toward the beauty of Holiness" (Lessin, Meet Me in the Meadow 2015).

Accordingly, at the end of the day, one who embraces and understands the importance of Father God's ***Correction***, ***Discipline***, and ***Instruction*** in one's life, has a much greater appreciation and insight regarding the how and why:

a. Father God uses ***Correction/Discipline/Instruction,*** to encourage us, not to discourage us;

b. Father God uses ***Correction/Discipline/Instruction,*** as a means to show us His love for us;

c. Father God uses ***Correction/Discipline/Instruction,*** to confirm that we are His heir apparent, equal with His Son, Christ Jesus;

d. Father God uses ***Correction/Discipline/Instruction,*** to better reveal His love for us by not allowing anything to neglect or interfere with His glory nor supplant all that is good for us;

e. Father God uses ***Correction/Discipline/Instruction,*** to proactively move us away from the ugliness of sin and toward the beauty of His Holiness and righteousness;

f. Father God uses ***Correction/Discipline/Instruction,*** as tools for His eternal purpose; and,

g. Father God uses ***Correction/Discipline/Instruction,*** as safeguards or guardrails to bring us back to the pathway of righteousness and peace!

Now, the final question is, "Are you ready to embrace ***Correction/Discipline/Instruction,*** as a proactive measure to become more Christ like?" And my answer is a resounding "Yes!"

(The Beginning of Knowledge)

Proverbs *1:1–6*

(1)   The Proverbs of Solomon the son of David, king of Israel:

(2)*   **To know wisdom and *instruction*, To perceive the words of understanding,**

(3)*   **To receive the *instruction* of wisdom, Justice, judgment, and equity;**

(4)* *To give <u>prudence</u> to the simple, To the young man <u>knowledge</u> and <u>discretion</u>—*

(5)* **A wise man will hear and increase *learning*, And a man of understanding will retain wise counsel**.

(6)* To understand a proverb and an enigma, The words of the wise and their riddles.

Proverbs *1:*7*

The fear of the LORD is the beginning of knowledge, But fools despise wisdom and <u>instruction</u>.

(Shun Evil Counsel)

Proverbs *1:8*–*19*

(8)* My son, hear the ***instruction*** of your father, And do not forsake the law of your mother;

(9) For they will be a graceful ornament on your head, And chains about your neck.

(10)* *<u>My son, if sinners entice you, Do not consent</u>.*

(11) If they say, "Come with us, Let us lie in wait to shed blood; Let us lurk secretly for the innocent without cause;

(12) Let us swallow them alive like Sheol, And whole, like those who go down to the Pit;

(13) We shall find all kinds of precious possessions, We shall fill our houses with spoil;

(14) Cast in your lot among us, Let us all have one purse"—

(15)* *<u>My son, do not walk in the way with them, Keep your foot from their path</u>;*

(16) *For their feet run to evil, And they make haste to shed blood.*

(17) Surely, in vain the net is spread In the sight of any bird;

(18) But they lie in wait for their own blood, They lurk secretly for their own lives.

(19)* ***<u>So are the ways of everyone who is greedy for gain; It takes away the life of its owners</u>.***

(Wisdom, INSTRUCTION, and Guidance for ALL Ages)

Proverbs *3:1*–2*, *3*–4*, *5*–*6*, 7*–*10*, *11*–*12*, and 13*–18*

(1)* *My son, do not forget my law, But let your heart keep my commands;*

(2)* *For length of days and long life And peace they will add to you.*

(3)* **Let not mercy and truth forsake you; Bind them around your neck, Write them on the tablet of your heart,**

(4)* *And so find favor and high esteem In the sight of God and man.*

(5)* **Trust in the LORD with all your heart, And lean not on your own understanding;**

(6)* **In all your ways acknowledge Him, And He shall direct your paths!!!**

(7)* *Do not be wise in your own eyes; Fear the LORD and depart from evil.*

(8)* *It will be health to your flesh, And strength to your bones.*

(9)* **Honor the LORD with your possessions, And with the first fruits of all your increase;**

(10)* **So your barns will be filled with plenty, And your vats will overflow with new wine.**

(11)* **My son, do not despise the chastening of the LORD, Nor detest His correction;**

(12)* **For whom the LORD loves He corrects, Just as a father the son in whom he delights.**

(13)* *Happy is the man who finds wisdom, And the man who gains understanding;*

(14)* *For her proceeds are better than the profits of silver, And her gain than find gold.*

(15)* *She is more precious than rubies, And all the things you may desire cannot compare with her.*

(16)* *Length of days is in her right hand, In her left hand riches and honor.*

(17)* *Her ways are ways of pleasantness, And all her paths are peace.*

(18)* *She is a tree of life to those who take hold of her, And happy are all who retain her.*

Proverbs *3:*21*–26*, *27*–30*, and 31*–35*

(21)* ***My son, let them** (**wisdom, understanding & knowledge**) **not depart from your eyes—Keep sound wisdom and discretion;***

(22)* *So they (wisdom and discretion) will be life to your soul And grace to your neck.*

(23)* *Then you will walk safely in your way, And your foot will not stumble.*

(24)* *When you lie down, you will not be afraid; Yes, you will lie down and your sleep will be sweet.*

(25)* *Do not be afraid of sudden terror, Nor of trouble from the wicked when it comes;*

(26)* *For the LORD will be your confidence, And will keep your foot from being caught.*

(27)* ***Do not withhold good from those to whom it is due, When it is in the power of your hand to do so.***

(28)* ***Do not say to your neighbor, "Go, and come back, And tomorrow I will give it," When you have it with you.***

(29)* *Do not devise evil against your neighbor, For he dwells by you for safety's sake.*

(30)* *Do not strive with a man without cause, If he has done you no harm.*

(31)* Do not envy the oppressor, *And choose none of his ways;*

(32)* For the perverse person is an abomination to the LORD, *But His secret counsel is with the upright.*

(33)* The curse of the LORD in on the house of the wicked, *But He blesses the home of the just.*

(34)* *Surely He scorns the scornful, But gives grace to the humble*.

(35)* *The wise shall inherit glory*, But shame shall be the legacy of fools.

(Security in Wisdom)

Proverbs *4:1*–9*, *10*–*13*, *14*–17, *18*–19 and *20*–*27*

(1)* *Hear, my children, the instruction of a father, And give attention to know understanding;*

(2)* *For I give good doctrine; Do not forsake my law.*

(3)   When I was my father's son, Tender and the only one in the sight of my mother,

(4)* He also *taught* me, and said to me: "*Let your heart retain my words; Keep my commands and live.*

(5)* *Get wisdom! Get understanding! Do not forget, nor turn away from the words of my mouth.*

(6)* *Do not forsake her (wisdom & understanding), and she will preserve you; Love her, and she will keep you.*

(7)* *Wisdom is the principal thing; Therefore get wisdom, And in all your getting, get understanding.*

(8)* *Exalt her (wisdom), and she will promote you; She will bring you honor, when you embrace her.*

(9)* *She will place on your head an ornament of grace; A crown of glory she will deliver to you."*

(10)* *Hear, my son, and receive my sayings, And the years of your life will be many*.

(11)* *I have taught you in the way of wisdom; I have led you in the right paths.*

(12)* *When you walk, your steps will not be hindered, And when you run, you will not stumble*.

(13)* *Take firm hold of instruction, do not let go; Keep her, for she is your life.*

(14)* ***Do not enter the path of the wicked, And do not walk in the way of evil.***

(15) *Avoid it, do not travel on it; Turn away from it and pass on.*

(16) For they (wicked people) do not sleep unless they have done evil; And their sleep is taken away unless they make someone fall.

(17) For they eat the bread of wickedness, And drink the wine of violence.

(18)* ***For the path of the just is like the shinning sun, That shines ever brighter unto the perfect day.***

(19) The way of the wicked is like darkness; They do not know what makes them stumble.

(20)* ***My son, give attention to my words; Incline your ear to my sayings.***

(21)* ***Do not let them depart from your eyes; Keep them in the midst of your heart;***

(22)* ***For they are life to those who find them, And health to all their flesh.***

(23)* ***Keep your heart with all diligence, For out of it spring the issues of life.***

(24)* ***Put away from you a deceitful mouth, And put perverse lips far from you.***

(25) *Let your eyes look straight ahead, And your eyelids look right before you.*

(26)* ***Ponder the path of your feet, And let all your ways be established.***

(27)* ***Do not turn to the right or to the left; Remove your foot from evil.***

(The Peril of Adultery)

Proverbs *5:1*–6, 7*–14, *15*–20, and *21*–*23*

(1)* *My son, pay attention to my wisdom; Lend your ear to my understanding.*

(2) *That you may preserve discretion, And your lips may keep knowledge.*

(3) For the lips of an immoral woman drip honey, And her mouth is smoother than oil;

(4)   But in the end she is bitter as wormwood, Sharp as a two-edged sword.

(5)   Her feet go down to death, Her steps lay hold of hell.

(6)   Lest you ponder her path of life—Her ways are unstable; You do not know them.

(7)*   *Therefore <u>hear me now, my children, And do not depart from the words of my mouth.</u>*

(8)   *Remove your way far from her, And do not go near the door of her house,*

(9)   Lest you give your honor to others, And your years to the cruel one;

(10)   Lest aliens be filled with your wealth, And your labors go to the house of a foreigner;

(11)   And you mourn at last, When your flesh and your body are consumed,

(12)   And say: "How I have hated **instruction**, And my heart despised *correction!*

(13)   *I have not obeyed the voice of my teachers, <u>Nor inclined my ear to those who</u>* **instructed** <u>*me!*</u>

(14)   I was on the verge of total ruin, In the midst of the assembly and congregation."

(15)*   **<u>Drink water from your own cistern, And running water from your own well.</u>**

(16)   Should your fountains be dispersed abroad, Streams of water in the streets?

(17)   Let them be only your own, And not for strangers with you.

(18)*   *<u>Let your fountain be blessed, And rejoice with the wife of your youth</u>.*

(19)*   As a loving deer and a graceful doe, *<u>Let her breasts satisfy you at all times; And always be enraptured with</u> her love.*

(20)   For why should you, my son, be enraptured by an immoral woman, And be embraced in the arms of a seductress?

(21)* **For the ways of man are before the eyes of the LORD, And He ponders all his paths.**

(22)* **His own iniquities entrap the wicked man, And he is caught in the cords of his sin.**

(23)* **He shall die for lack of *instruction*, And in the greatness of his folly he shall go astray.**

(The Folly of Suretyship)

Proverbs *6:1*–5*

(1)* *My son*, if you become surety for your friend, If you have shaken hands in pledge for a stranger,

(2)* *You are snared by the words of your mouth; You are taken by the words of your mouth.*

(3)* *So do this, my son, and deliver yourself;* For you have come into the hand of your friend; *Go and humble yourself; Plead with your friend.*

(4)* *Give no sleep to your eyes, Nor slumber to your eyelids.*

(5)* *Deliver yourself like a gazelle from the hand of the hunter, And like a bird from the hand of the fowler.*

(Beware of Adultery)

Proverbs *6:*20*–29* and *32*–35

(20)* ***My son, keep your father's command, And do not forsake the law of your mother.***

(21)* *Bind them continually upon your heart; Tie them around your neck.*

(22)* *When you roam, they will lead you; When you sleep, they will keep you; And when you awake, they will speak with you.*

(23)* **For the *commandment* is a lamp, And *the law* a light; Reproofs of *instruction* are the way of life,**

(24)* *To keep you from the evil woman, From the flattering tongue of a seductress.*

(25)* *Do not lust after her beauty in your heart, Nor let her allure you with her eyelids.*

(26) For by means of a harlot, *A man is reduced to a crust of bread*; And an adulteress will prey upon his precious life.

(27) Can a man take *fire* to his bosom, And his *clothes not be burned*?

(28) Can one *walk on hot coals*, And his *feet not be seared*?

(29)* *So is he who goes in to his neighbor's wife; Whoever touches her shall not be innocent*.

(32)* **Whoever commits adultery with a woman lacks *understanding*; He who does so destroys his own soul.**

(33)* **Wounds and dishonor he will get, And his reproach will not be wiped away.**

(34) For jealousy is a husband's fury; Therefore he will not spare in the day of vengeance.

(35) He will accept no recompense, Nor will he be appeased though you give many gifts.

Proverbs *7:*1*–5*

(1)* ***My son, keep my words And treasure my commands* within you.**

(2)* ***Keep my commands* and live, And *my law* as the apple of your eye.**

(3)* *Bind them on your fingers; Write them on the tablet of your heart*.

(4)* ***Say to wisdom, "You are my sister," And call understanding your nearest kin,***

(5)* That they may keep you from the immoral woman, From the seductress who flatters with her words.

(The Excellence of Wisdom)

Proverbs *8:*1*–*11*

(1)* **Does not *wisdom* cry out, And *understanding* lift up her voice?**

(2) She takes her stand on the top of the high hill, Beside the way, where the paths meet.

(3) *She cries out* by the gates, at the entry of the city, At the entrance of the doors:

(4) *"To you, O men, I call, And my voice is to the sons of men.*

(5) *O you simple ones, understand prudence, And you fools, be of an understanding heart.*

(6) <u>*Listen, for I will speak of excellent things, And from the opening of my lips will come right things*</u>;

(7) *For my mouth will <u>speak truth</u>;* Wickedness is an abomination to my lips.

(8)* **All the words of my mouth are with righteousness; Nothing crooked or perverse is in them.**

(9) They are all *plain* to him who *understands*, And *right* to those who find *knowledge*.

(10)* Receive <u>*wisdom's*</u> <u>**instruction**</u>, and not silver, And *knowledge* rather than choice gold;

(11)* **For *wisdom* is better than rubies, And all the things one may desire cannot be compared with her.**

Proverbs *8:*32*–36*

(32)* **"Now therefore, *listen* to me, my children, For blessed are those who keep my ways.**

(33)* *Hear <u>instruction</u> and be wise*, **And do not disdain it.**

(34)* Blessed is the man who *listens* to me, Watching daily at my gates, Waiting at the posts of my doors.

(35)* **For whoever finds me finds life, And obtains favor from the LORD;**

(36)* But he who sins against me wrongs his own soul; All those who hate me love death."

(The Way of Wisdom)

Proverbs *9:7–12

(7) "He who corrects a scoffer gets shame for himself, And he who rebukes a wicked man only harms himself.

(8)* Do not correct a scoffer, lest he hate you: ***Rebuke* a *wise* man, and he will love you.**

(9)* Give *instruction* to a *wise* man, and he will be still *wiser*; _Teach_ a just man, and he will increase in _learning_.

(10)* **The fear of the LORD is the beginning of** *wisdom*, **And the** *knowledge* **of the Holy One is** *understanding*.

(11) For by *me* your days will be multiplied, And years of life will be added to you.

(12) If you are *wise*, you are *wise* for yourself, And if you scoff, you will bear it alone."

(Wise Sayings of Solomon)

Proverbs 10:*17*

He who keeps **instruction** is in the way of life, But he who refuses *correction* goes astray.

Proverbs *12:*1*

Whoever loves *instruction* **loves** *knowledge*, **But he who hates** *correction* **is stupid**.

Proverbs *13:*1*

A *wise* **son** *heeds* **his father's** *instruction*, **But a scoffer does not** *listen* **to** *rebuke*.

Proverbs 13:13*

He who despises _the word_ will be destroyed, *But he who* _fears the commandment_ *will be rewarded*.

Proverbs 13:14

The law of the *wise* is a fountain of life, *To turn one away* from the snares of death

Proverbs *13:*18*

Poverty and shame will come to him who disdains *correction*, **But he who** *regards a rebuke* **will be honored.**

Proverbs *13:*24*
He who spares his rod hates his son, But he who loves him _disciplines him promptly_.

Proverbs 14:*6*
A scoffer _seeks wisdom_ and does not find it, But _knowledge_ is easy to him who _understands_.

Proverbs *15:*5*
A fool despises his father's _instruction_, But he who receives _correction_ is _prudent_.

Proverbs *15:*31*
The ear that _hears_ the _rebukes of life_ Will abide among the _wise_.

Proverbs *15:*32*
He who disdains _instruction_ despises his own soul, But he who _heeds rebuke_ gets _understanding_.

Proverbs *15:*33*
The _fear of the LORD_ is the _instruction_ of _wisdom_, And before _honor_ is _humility_.

Proverbs 16:21*
The _wise_ in _heart_ will be called _prudent_, And sweetness of the lips increases _learning_

Proverbs 16:22
Understanding is a wellspring of life to him who has it, But the _correction_ of fools is folly.

Proverbs 16:23*
The _heart_ of the _wise **teaches**_ his mouth, And adds _**learning**_ to his lips.

Proverbs *18:*15*
The _heart_ of the _prudent_ acquires _knowledge_, And the _ear_ of the _wise_ seeks _knowledge_.

Proverbs 19:16

He who _keeps the commandments_ keeps his soul, But he who is careless of his ways will die.

Proverbs *19:*20*

Listen to counsel and receive _instruction_, That you may be _wise_ in your **latter days**.

Proverbs *19:*27*

Cease listening to _instruction_, my son, And you will _stray_ from the **words of knowledge**.

Proverbs 21:*11*

When the scoffer is punished, the simple is made _wise_; But when the _wise_ is **_instructed_**, he receives _knowledge_.

Proverbs *22:*6*

Train up a child in the way he should go, And when he is old, he will not depart from it.

(Sayings of the Wise)

Proverbs *22:*17*–*21*

(17)* _Incline your ear and hear the words of the wise, And apply your heart to my knowledge_:

(18)* _For it is a pleasant thing if you keep them (wise sayings) within you; Let them all be fixed upon your lips,_

(19)* **So that your trust may be in the LORD; I have _instructed_ you today, even you.**

(20)* _Have I not written to you excellent things Of counsels and knowledge,_

(21)* **That I may make you know the certainty of the _words of truth_, That you may answer _words of truth_, To those who send to you?**

Proverbs 22:24–25

Make no friendship with an angry man, And with a furious man do not go, Lest you **learn** his ways And set a snare for your soul.

Proverbs *23:*12*

Apply your heart to *instruction*, And your ears to words of *knowledge*.

Proverbs 23:19*

Hear, my son, and be wise; And guide your heart in the way.

Proverbs 23:22

Listen to your father who begot you, And do not despise your mother when she is old.

Proverbs *23:*23*

***Buy the truth,* and do not sell it, Also *wisdom* and *instruction* and understanding.**

Proverbs 23:26–28

(26) *My son, give me your heart, And let your eyes observe my ways.*

(27) For a harlot is a deep pit, And a seductress is a narrow well.

(28) She also lies in wait as for a victim, And increases the unfaithful among men.

Proverbs *24:*5*–*6*

A *wise* man is strong, Yes, a man of *knowledge* increases strength; For by *wise counsel* you will wage your own war, *And in a multitude of counselors* there is safety.

(Further Sayings of the Wise)

Proverbs 24:30–34

(30) I went by the field of the lazy man, And by the vineyard of the man devoid of understanding;

(31) And there it was, all overgrown with thorns; Its surface was covered with nettles; It's stone wall was broken down.

(32)* When I saw it, I considered it well; I looked on it and received _**instruction**_:

(33)   A little sleep, a little slumber, A little folding of the hands to rest;

(34)   So shall your poverty come like a prowler, And your need like an armed man.

(Further Wise Sayings of Solomon)

Proverbs 25:11
A _word fitly spoken_ is like apples of gold In settings of silver.

Proverbs 25:12
Like an earring of gold and an ornament of fine gold Is a _wise rebuker_ to an obedient ear.

Proverbs *27:*6*
**Faithful are the wounds of a friend**, **But the kisses of an enemy are deceitful.**

Proverbs 28:23*
He who _rebukes a man_ will find more favor afterward Than he who flatters with the tongue.

Proverbs 29:1*
He who is often _rebuked_, and hardens his neck, Will suddenly be destroyed, and that without remedy.

Proverbs 29:15*
The _rod_ and _rebuke_ give _wisdom_, But a child left to himself brings shame to his mother.

(The Wisdom of Agur)

Proverbs 30:2–3

Surely I am more stupid than any man, And do not have the understanding of a man. I neither **learned** *wisdom* Nor have *knowledge* of the Holy One.

CHAPTER 40

INTEGRITY

The dictionary defines "*Integrity*" as "a firm adherence to a code of especially moral or artistic values, or incorruptibility; incapable of being bribed or morally corrupted." In the Bible, the Hebrew word translated "*Integrity*" in the Old Testament means "the condition of being without blemish, completeness, perfection, sincerity, soundness, uprightness, wholeness." "*Integrity*" in the New Testament means "honesty and adherence to a pattern of good works."

In undertaking my former Business and Corporate life, I am reminded of how "Executive Jon" Huntsman, Sr., once described the essence of "*Integrity*", by stating that, "There are no moral shortcuts in the game of business or life. There are basically three kinds of people: the unsuccessful, the temporarily successful, and those who become and remain successful; the difference being one's character or "*Integrity*."

In both my Corporate life, as well as in my everyday life, one of the most important personal attributes that I pride myself on is in the area of "*Integrity*." As one of the cornerstone descriptors of who I am, next to my belief and faith in Father God as well as being a follower and believer "in Christ" Jesus, nothing better describes who I am and how I have attempted to walk this earthly life than the personal quality of "*Integrity*." There is no better personal attribute that can be used to describe an individual than one who walks with "*Integrity*." The only other personal attributes that might come close to describing how one should walk and treat other people would be the personal attributes of "**truth and honesty**." And it goes without saying that Father God's Word addresses these personal attributes, and can be broadly stated from the truth statement contained in Matthew 7:12: "*Therefore, whatever you want men to do to you, do also to them, for this is the Law and the Prophets.*"

No one better than Christ Jesus, perfectly exemplifies a man of "*Integrity*." Consider, for example, after Jesus was baptized, Jesus went into the wilderness and fasted for forty days and nights, during which time Satan approached Him at His weakest and most vulnerable state and attempted to break His "*Integrity*" and corrupt Him. Christ Jesus, while being wholly man and wholly Father God, was nevertheless tempted by Satan, just like we are by Satan, yet Jesus never sinned: "*For we do not have a High Priest who cannot sympathize with our weaknesses, but was in all points tempted as we are, yet without sin*" (Hebrews 4:15).

In talking about the definition of "*Integrity*," no human example exists other than that of our Lord and Savior, Jesus Christ! Jesus is the only person who has never sinned; was completely truthful, trustworthy, honest, and always exhibited a pattern of good works. In contrast, sinful human beings, even with our best attempts at "*Integrity*" are generally flawed, while Christ Jesus's "*Integrity*" was and is perfect! "*Therefore, if anyone is In Christ, he is a new creation; old things have passed away; behold, all things have become new*" (2 Corinthians 5:17). Therefore, all those who are "in Christ" are now partakers of His divine nature, having become new creations, and that new creation is one of "*Integrity*" because it is Christ Jesus's nature.

As stated above, one of the parallel personal attributes that the Bible describes and associates with "*Integrity*" is "**truth**." So what is "**truth**"? Jesus is the only **real truth**, and the only way to attain eternal life. As Jesus stated in John 14:6: "*I am the way, the truth, and the life. No one comes to the Father except through Me.*" How many times did Jesus preface His words by saying, "*Truly, truly I say to you,*" which, in essence, means, "I tell you the **truth**." We all know with certainty that Jesus never lied, and His actions always defined "*Integrity*." Once we come to Christ in faith and repentance, He gives one the gift of the Holy Spirit, who assists one in developing one's incorruptible persona of "*Integrity*." It is impossible to have any real sense of "*Integrity*" without Jesus Christ as one's personal Lord and Savior! Thus, one can consistently embody the strong and incorruptible personal attribute of "*Integrity*" from the ever present and indwelling of the Holy Spirit residing within each and every one who walks "in Christ" (Got Questions Ministries 2002-2015).

(The Value of Wisdom)

Proverbs *2:1*–*9*

(1)* My son, if you receive my words, And treasure my commands within you,

(2)* **So that you incline your ear to wisdom, And apply your heart to understanding;**

(3)* Yes, if you cry out for discernment, And lift up your voice for **understanding,**

(4) If you seek her as silver, And search for her as for hidden treasures;

(5)* **Then you will understand the fear of the LORD, And find the knowledge of God.**

(6)* **For the LORD gives wisdom; From His mouth come knowledge and understanding;**

(7)* **He (Wisdom) stores up sound wisdom for the *upright*; He is a shield to those who walk *uprightly*;**

(8)* **He guards the paths of justice, And preserves the way of His saints.**

(9)* **Then you will understand *righteousness* and justice, Equity and every good path.**

Proverbs *2:*20*–22

(20)* **So you may walk in the way of goodness, And keep to the paths of *righteousness*.**

(21)* **For the _upright_ will dwell in the land, And the _blameless_ will remain in it;**

(22) But the wicked will be cut off from the earth, And the unfaithful will be uprooted from it.

(Wise Sayings of Solomon)

Proverbs 10:9*

He who walks with **_integrity_** walks securely, But he who perverts his ways will become known.

Proverbs 11:1

Dishonest scales are an abomination to the LORD, But a *just weight* is His delight.

Proverbs 11:3

The **_integrity_** of the _upright_ will guide them, But the perversity of the unfaithful will destroy them.

Proverbs 11:6*

The *righteousness* of the _upright_ will deliver them, But the unfaithful will be caught by their lust.

Proverbs 12:17*

He who _speaks truth_ declares *righteousness*, But a false witness, deceit.

Proverbs 12:19*

The _truthful lip_ shall be established forever, But a lying tongue is but for a moment.

Proverbs 12:22*

Lying lips are an abomination to the LORD, But *those who deal truthfully are His delight*.

Proverbs 13:5
A *righteous man* hates lying, But a wicked man is loathsome and comes to shame.

Proverbs 13:*6*
Righteousness guards him whose way is *blameless*, But wickedness overthrows the sinner.

Proverbs 13:11*
Wealth gained by dishonesty will be diminished, But he who *gathers by labor* will increase.

Proverbs 14:11*
The house of the wicked will be overthrown, But the tent of the *upright* will flourish.

Proverbs 14:25
A *true witness* delivers souls, But a deceitful witness speaks lies.

Proverbs 15:27*
He who is greedy for gain troubles his own house, But he who *hates bribes* will live.

Proverbs 16:11
Honest weights and scales are the LORD's; All the weights in the bag are His work.

Proverbs *16:*17*
The highway of the *upright* is to depart from evil; He who keeps his way preserves his soul.

Proverbs 17:7
Excellent speech is not becoming to a fool, Much less lying lips to a prince.

Proverbs 17:15*
He who justifies the wicked, and he who condemns *the just*, Both of them alike are an abomination to the LORD.

Proverbs 17:26

Also, to punish the *righteous* is not good, Nor to strike princes for their *uprightness*.

Proverbs 18:17*

The first one to plead his cause seems right, Until his neighbor comes and examines him.

Proverbs *19:*1*

Better is the poor who walks in his *integrity* Than one who is perverse in his lips, and is a fool.

Proverbs 19:9*

A *false witness* will not go unpunished, And he who *speaks lies* shall perish.

Proverbs 20:6

Most men will proclaim each his own *goodness*, But who can find a faithful man?

Proverbs 20:7*

The *righteous* man walks in his ***integrity***; His children are blessed after him.

Proverbs 20:11*

Even a child is known by his deeds, Whether what he does is *pure and right*.

Proverbs 20:25

It is a snare for a man to devote rashly something as holy, And afterward to *reconsider his vows*.

Proverbs *21:*2*

Every way of a man is *right* in his own eyes, *But the LORD weighs the hearts*.

Proverbs 21:8*

The way of a guilty man is perverse; But as for the *pure*, his work is *right*.

Proverbs *21:*21*

He who follows *righteousness* and *mercy* Finds *life, righteousness* and *honor*.

Proverbs 21:29

A wicked man hardens his face, But as for the _upright_, he establishes his way.

Proverbs 22:1*

A _good name_ is to be chosen rather than great riches; _Loving favor_ rather than silver and gold.

(Sayings of the Wise)

Proverbs 22:28

Do not remove the ancient landmark Which your fathers have set.

Proverbs 22:29*

Do you see _a man who excels in his work_? He will stand before kings; He will not stand before unknown men.

Proverbs 23:1–3
(1) When you sit down to eat with a ruler, *Consider carefully what is before you*;
(2) And put a knife to your throat If you are a man given to appetite.
(3) Do not desire his delicacies, For they are deceptive food.

Proverbs 23:6–8
(6) *Do not eat the bread of a miser, Nor desire his delicacies*;
(7) For as he thinks in his heart, so is he. "Eat and drink!" he says to you, But his heart is not with you.
(8) The morsel you have eaten, you will vomit up, And waste your pleasant words.

Proverbs 23:10–11

Do not remove the ancient landmark, Nor enter the fields of the fatherless; For their Redeemer is mighty; He will plead their cause against you.

Proverbs *23:*23*

Buy the truth, and do not sell it, Also wisdom and instruction and understanding.

Proverbs 23:26–28

(26)   *My son, give me your heart, And let your eyes observe my ways.*

(27)   For a harlot is a deep pit, And a seductress is a narrow well.

(28)   She also lies in wait as for a victim, And increases the unfaithful among men.

(Further Sayings of the Wise)

Proverbs *24:*23*–25*

(23)* These things also belong to the wise: *It is not good to show partiality in judgment.*

(24)   He who says to the wicked, "You are righteous," Him the people will curse; Nations will abhor him.

(25)* **But those who rebuke the wicked will have delight, And a good blessing will come upon them.**

Proverbs *24:*26*

He who gives a _right answer_ kisses the lips.

Proverbs *24:*28*–*29*

Do not be a witness against your neighbor without cause, _For would you deceive with your lips?_ Do not say, "I will do to him just as he has done to me; I will render to the man according to his work."

(Further Wise Sayings of Solomon)

Proverbs 25:8–10

(8) Do not go hastily to court; For what will you do in the end, When your neighbor has put you to shame?

(9) Debate your case with your neighbor, *And do not disclose the secret to another;*

(10) *Lest he who hears it expose your shame, And your reputation be ruined.*

Proverbs 25:13

Like the cold of snow in time of harvest Is a *faithful messenger* to those who send him, For he refreshes the soul of his masters.

Proverbs *27:*6*

Faithful are the wounds of a friend, But the kisses of an enemy are deceitful.

Proverbs *27:*19*

As in water face reflects face, *So a man's heart reveals the man*.

Proverbs 27:21*

The refining pot is for silver and the furnace for gold, *And a man is valued by what others say of him.*

Proverbs 28:2

Because of the transgression of a land, many are its princes; *But by a man of understanding and knowledge Right will be prolonged.*

Proverbs 28:4

Those who forsake the law praise the wicked, But such as *keep the law* contend with them.

Proverbs *28:*6*

Better is the poor who walks in his *integrity* Than one perverse in his ways, though he be rich.

Proverbs 28:7

Whoever _keeps the law_ is a discerning son, But a companion of gluttons shames his father.

Proverbs 28:18*

Whoever walks _blamelessly_ will be saved, But he who is perverse in his ways will suddenly fall.

Proverbs *28:*23*

He who rebukes a man will find more favor afterward Than he who flatters with the tongue.

Proverbs 29:4

The king establishes the land by _justice_, But he who receives bribes overthrows it.

Proverbs 29:10*

The bloodthirsty hate the _blameless_, But the _upright_ seek his well-being.

Proverbs 29:14

The king who judges the poor with _truth_, His thrown will be established forever.

Proverbs 29:27*

An unjust man is an abomination to the _righteous_. And he who is _upright in the way_ is an abomination to the wicked.

CHAPTER 41

JUSTICE, JUDGMENT

W hat is *Justice* and why is it an important criterion for the human race, especially for those of us who are "in Christ," and are constantly seeking *Justice* as part of our everyday life and walk "in Christ"? *Justice* is generally defined as a term used to describe what is right or what it should be!

Justice is one of Father God's attributes and positively flows out of his Holiness. Additionally, one finds that *Justice* and **righteousness** are often used interchangeably and/or synonymously in the Bible. Accordingly, and this fact I find very reassuring, and that being that **righteousness** is a quality characteristic of being **right** or *Just*, which is another attribute of Father God, since it incorporates both His *Justice* and Holiness. And this characteristic is more than highlighted in Proverbs 21:3: "*To do righteousness and justice Is more acceptable to the LORD than sacrifice*"; and Proverbs 8:20: "*I (wisdom), traverse the way of righteousness, In the midst of the paths of justice.*"

With the above definitions provided for *Justice*, let me briefly describe two case studies where I made two personal loans to two Christian gentlemen. One was made on September 30, 2009 for a term of six months in the amount of $5,000, which I respectfully reference as the "$5,000 man." The second was made September 19, 2011, also with a term of six months, to a fellow Harvard Business School alumni, in the amount of $3,000, which I respectfully reference as the "$3,000 man." As I draft this Chapter Narrative during Spring 2016, I must point out that both loans unfortunately remain "Outstanding"! While I have been trying incessantly to recover the outstanding principal amounts due from both personal loans, I will share the "teachable moments" that I have learned from the "$5,000 man" loan, and how several Proverbs verses on this Chapter Theme on *Justice* have borne themselves out.

After numerous email exchanges, conversations, as well as soliciting the assistance and advice from several fellow church members, I was advised that I needed to seek a **Judicial** review with the hope and the prayer that a Small-Claims Court and adjudication would be warranted. Thus, on September 27, 2010, my case was heard, and on October 12, 2010, a civil *Judgment* was entered requiring that the "$5,000 man" repay said principle amount, as well as accumulated outstanding interest. Needless to say, I was hopeful and prayerful that such **Judicial** *Judgment* would force or, at a minimum, motivate the debtor to begin the process of loan repayment.

After more than five years of prevailing upon the "$5,000 man" to make some sort of financial restitution, in the Fall of 2015, I received a surprising communication from the County Clerk's office, indicating that the "$5,000 man" had worked out a repayment plan with the County Clerk's office that would require him to begin making periodic principal repayments to the Court; and from such monthly repayments, a process would begin, whereby loan principal repayments would start by late March 2016. Needless to say, I was pleasantly surprised with the initial $100 loan principal repayment that I received from the Court in late March 2016.

Between March 2016 and August 2016, the "$5,000 man" made NO further loan repayments. I heard the Holy Spirit tell me that it was not worth the effort to expect him to pay off the remaining $4,900 due on said loan. But the Holy Spirit did encourage me to share with him that if he would repay $800 between September 2016 and December 2016 for a total of $900, then I would CANCEL the remaining outstanding balance due of $4,100. Accordingly, by Christmas Eve, the "$5,000 man" did, in fact, finish up his final $800 periodic payments, such that in January 2017, I CANCELLED the remaining $4,100 due on said outstanding balance!

As I reflect on the "teachable moments" (i.e. the wisdom and knowledge imparted from this loan experience), and how it relates to this Chapter Theme of "*Justice/Judgment*," the following takeaways are worth mentioning:

a) Proverbs 17:26: "*Also, to punish the **righteous** is not good, Nor to strike princes for their uprightness.*" In good faith, this financial transaction was made to assist a fellow Christian brother, and while there has been numerous test of one's faith and commitment to do the right thing by honoring and fulfilling one's financial obligations, in the end, *Justice* and **righteousness** prevailed;

b) Proverbs 28:5: "*Evil men do not understand justice, But those who seek the LORD understand all.*" Because *Justice* is part of Father God's character, a person who follows Father God treats others *Justly*. The beginning of *Justice* generally has a keen concern for what and how one's actions directly and indirectly affect others.

c) Proverbs 2:8: "*He guards the paths of justice, And preserves the way of His saints*"; and

d) Proverbs 2:9: "*Then you will understand the **righteousness** and justice, Equity and every good path.*" As a result of these two financial transactions that were made to assist two fellow Christian brothers in their time of need (Luke 6:30: "*Give to everyone who ask of you, And from him who takes away your goods do not ask them back.*"), one must determine in advance what amount of financial resources that one feels comfortable in investing in others; and (Luke 6:31: "*And just as you want men to do to you, you also do to them likewise.*"); No matter what the situation and/or circumstance, one must honor all commitments as if those commitments are being made to Father God; and finally,

e) Proverbs 29:26: "*Many seek the ruler's favor, But **justice for man comes from the LORD.***" As much as one may try to utilize appropriate earthly or secular solutions to human problems, in the end, true resolutions of problems and ultimate ***Justice*** and ***Judgment*** will come from the Lord in His timing and in His way!

(The Beginning of Knowledge)

Proverbs *1:1–4*

(1) The Proverbs of Solomon the son of David, king of Israel:

(2)* **To know wisdom and instruction, To perceive the words of understanding,**

(3)* **To receive the instruction of wisdom, *Justice, judgment*, and equity;**

(4)* To give prudence to the simple, To the young man knowledge and discretion.

(The Value of Wisdom)

Proverbs *2:1*–*9*

(1)* My son, if you receive my words, And treasure my commands within you,

(2)* **So that you incline your ear to wisdom, And apply your heart to understanding;**

(3)* Yes, if you cry out for discernment, And lift up your voice for understanding,

(4)* If you seek her as silver, And search for her as for hidden treasures;

(5)* **Then you will understand the fear of the LORD, And find the knowledge of God.**

(6)* **For the LORD gives wisdom; From His mouth come knowledge and understanding;**

(7)* He (wisdom) stores up sound wisdom for the upright; He is a shield to those who walk uprightly:

(8)* He guards the paths of *justice*, And preserves the way of His saints.

(9)* Then you will understand righteousness and *justice*, Equity and every good path.

(Guidance for the Young)

Proverbs *3:*27*–*28*
Do not withhold good from those to whom it is due, When it is in the power of your hand to do so. Do not say to your neighbor, "Go, and come back, And tomorrow I will give it," When you have it with you.

(The Excellence of Wisdom)

Proverbs *8:12*–21

(12)* "I, wisdom, dwell with prudence, And find out knowledge and discretion.

(13)* The fear of the LORD is to hate evil; Pride and arrogance and the evil way And the perverse mouth I hate.

(14) Counsel is mine, and sound wisdom; I am understanding, I have strength.

(15) By me, kings reign, And rulers decree *justice*.

(16) By me (wisdom) princes rule, and nobles, All the judges of the earth.

(17)* **I love those who love me, And those who seek me diligently will find me.**

(18) Riches and honor are with me, Enduring riches and righteousness.

(19) My fruit is better than gold, yes, than fine gold. And my revenue than choice silver.

(20)* I (wisdom) traverse the way of righteousness, In the midst of the paths of *justice*,

(21) That I (wisdom) may cause those who love me to inherit wealth,
That I (wisdom) may fill their treasures.

(Wise Sayings of Solomon)

Proverbs 11:1
Dishonest scales are an abomination to the LORD, *But a **just** weight is His delight.*

Proverbs 11:23
The desire of the righteous is only good, But the expectation on the wicked is wrath.

Proverbs 13:21*
Evil pursues sinners, *But to the righteous, good shall be repaid.*

Proverbs 13:23
Much food is in the fallow ground of the poor, And for lack of ***justice*** there is waste.

Proverbs 14:19
The evil will **bow** before the good, And the wicked **at the gates** of the *righteous.*

Proverbs 15:3*
The eyes of the LORD are in every place, Keeping watch on the evil and the good.

Proverbs 15:11
Hell and Destruction are before the LORD; So how much more the hearts of the sons of men.

Proverbs 16:5
Everyone proud in heart is an abomination to the LORD; Though they join forces, none will go unpunished.

Proverbs *16:*8*
Better is a little with righteousness, Than vast revenues without _justice_.

Proverbs 16:10
Divination is on the lips of the king; _His mouth must not transgress in_ **_judgment_**.

Proverbs 16:11
Honest weights and scales are the LORD's; All the weights in the bag are His work.

Proverbs *16:*18*
Pride goes before destruction, And a haughty spirit before a fall.

Proverbs 17:11
An evil man seeks only rebellion; _Therefore a cruel messenger will be sent against him._

Proverbs 17:15*
He who **_justifies_** the wicked, and he who condemns the **_just_**, _Both of them alike are an abomination to the LORD_

Proverbs 17:23
A wicked man accepts a bribe behind the back To pervert the ways of **_justice_**.

Proverbs 17:26
Also, to punish the righteous is not good, Nor to strike princes for their uprightness.

Proverbs 18:1
A man who isolates himself seeks his own desire; He rages against all wise **_judgment_**.

Proverbs 18:3
When the wicked comes, contempt comes also; _And with dishonor comes reproach._

Proverbs 18:5*
*It is not good to show partiality to the wicked, Or to overthrow the righteous in **judgment**.*

Proverbs 18:13*
He who *answers* a matter before he hears it, *It is folly and shame to him.*

Proverbs 18:17*
The first one to plead his cause seems right, Until his neighbor comes and *examines* him.

Proverbs 19:5*
*A false witness will not go **unpunished**, And he who speaks lies will not escape.*

Proverbs 19:9*
*A false witness will not go **unpunished**, And he who speaks lies shall perish.*

Proverbs 19:19*
A man of great wrath will suffer punishment; For if you rescue him, you will have to do it again.

Proverbs 19:28
A disreputable witness scorns **justice**, And the mouth of the wicked devours iniquity.

Proverbs 19:29
Judgments are prepared for scoffers, And beatings for the backs of fools.

Proverbs 20:8
A king who sits on the throne of **judgment** Scatters all evil with his eyes.

Proverbs 20:10
Diverse weights and diverse measures, *They are both alike*, an abomination to the LORD.

Proverbs 20:22
Do not say, "I will recompense evil"; *Wait for the LORD, and He will save you.*

Proverbs 20:23
Diverse weights are an abomination to the LORD, And dishonest scales *are not good.*

Proverbs 20:26
A wise king sifts out the wicked, And brings the threshing wheel over them.

Proverbs 20:30
Blows that hurt cleanse away evil, As do stripes the inner depths of the heart.

Proverbs 21:*3*
To do *righteousness* and ***justice***, Is more acceptable to the LORD than sacrifice.

Proverbs 21:7
The violence of the wicked will destroy them, Because they refuse to do ***justice***.

Proverbs 21:*11*
When the scoffer is punished, the simple is made wise; But when the wise is instructed, he receives knowledge.

Proverbs 21:12*
The righteous God wisely considers the house of the wicked, *Overthrowing the wicked for their wickedness.*

Proverbs 21:*15*
It is a joy for the ***just*** to do ***justice***, But *destruction* will come to the workers of *iniquity*.

Proverbs 22:3*
A prudent man *foresees* evil and hides himself, But the simple pass on and are *punished*.

Proverbs 22:5

Thorns and snares are in the way of the perverse; He who guards his soul will be far from them.

Proverbs 22:8*

He who sows iniquity will reap sorrow, And the rod of his anger will fail.

(Sayings of the Wise)

Proverbs *22:*22*–*23*

Do not rob the poor because he is poor, Nor oppress the afflicted at the gate; For the LORD will plead their cause, And plunder the soul of those who plunder them.

Proverbs 22:28

Do not remove the ancient landmark Which your fathers have set.

Proverbs 23:10–11

Do not remove the ancient landmark, Nor enter the fields of the fatherless; *For their Redeemer is mighty*; *He will plead their cause against you.*

Proverbs 24:11–12

Deliver those who are drawn toward death, And hold back those stumbling to the slaughter. If you say, "Surely we did not know this," *Does not He who weighs the hearts consider it? He who keeps your soul, does He not know it?* **And will He not render to each man according to his deeds**?

Proverbs *24:*17*–*18*

Do not rejoice when your enemy falls, And do not let your heart be glad when he stumbles; Lest the LORD see it, and it displease Him, And He turn away His wrath from him.

(Further Sayings of the Wise)

Proverbs *24:*23**–25*

(23)* **These things also belong to the wise:** *It is not good to show partiality in judgment.*

(24) He who says to the wicked, "You are righteous," Him the people will curse; Nations will abhor him.

(25)* *But those who rebuke the wicked will have deligh*t, **And a good blessing will come upon them.**

Proverbs *24:*28*–*29*

Do not be a witness against your neighbor without cause; For would you deceive with your lips? *Do not say, "I will do to him just as he has done to me; I will render to the man according to his work."*

(Further Wise Sayings of Solomon)

Proverbs 25:2

It is the glory of God to conceal a matter, *But the glory of kings is to search out a matter.*

Proverbs 25:8–10

(8) *Do not go hastily to court*; For what will you do in the end, When your neighbor has put you to shame?

(9) *Debate your case with your neighbor, And do not disclose the secret to another*;

(10) Lest he who hears it expose your shame, And your reputation be ruined.

Proverbs *25:*21*–*22*

If your enemy is hungry, give him bread to eat; And if he is thirsty, give him water to drink; For so you will heap coals of fire on his head, And the LORD will reward you.

Proverbs 26:27*
Whoever digs a pit will fall into it, And he who rolls a stone will have it roll back on him.

Proverbs 28:2
Because of the transgression of a land, many are its princes: *But by a man of understanding and knowledge Right will be prolonged.*

Proverbs 28:5*
Evil men do not understand **justice**, But those who seek the LORD understand all.

Proverbs 28:10
Whoever causes the upright to go astray in an evil way, He himself will fall into his own pit; But the blameless will inherit good.

Proverbs 28:17
A man burdened with bloodshed will flee into a pit; Let no one help him.

Proverbs 28:18*
Whoever walks blamelessly will be saved, But he who is perverse in his ways will suddenly fall.

Proverbs 28:21
To show partiality is not good, Because for a piece of bread a man will transgress.

Proverbs 29:4
The king establishes the land by **justice**, But he who receives bribes overthrows it.

Proverbs 29:13*
The poor man and the oppressor have this in common: **The LORD gives light to the eyes of both**.

Proverbs 29:14

The king who ***judges the poor with truth***, His throne will be established forever.

Proverbs 29:16

When the wicked are multiplied, transgression increases; <u>But the righteous will see their</u> ***fall***.

Proverbs 29:24

Whoever is a partner with a thief hates his own life; <u>*He swears to tell the truth, but reveals nothing.*</u>

Proverbs 29:26

Many seek the ruler's favor, ***But justice for man comes from the LORD.***

(The Words of King Lemuel's Mother)

Proverbs 31:4–9

(4) It is not for kings, O Lemuel, It is not for kings to drink wine, Nor for princes intoxicating drink;

(5) Lest they drink and forget the *law*, And pervert the ***justice*** of all the afflicted.

(6) Give strong drink to him who is perishing, And wine to those who are bitter of heart.

(7) Let him drink and forget his poverty, And remember his misery no more.

(8) *Open your mouth for the speechless*, <u>*In the cause of all who are appointed to die.*</u>

(9) *Open your mouth,* ***judge*** *righteously*, <u>*And plead the cause of the poor and needy.*</u>

CHAPTER 42

KNOWLEDGE

W hat is *Knowledge* and how does one obtain it? Some would say that *Knowledge* is acquired, gained, obtained, and/or improved upon from hard work, experience, and study. And to a limited degree, there may be some semblance of truth to such a viewpoint. But I would contend that *Knowledge* is one leg of a three-legged stool that also includes *Wisdom* and *Understanding*. As the Godhead is made up of God the Father, God the Son, and God the Holy Spirit, I would contend that *Knowledge*, *Understanding*, and *Wisdom* are the cornerstones, center, and key components that are derived from the Word of God! (Proverbs 2:1–11)

For example, Proverbs 2:4–6 states unequivocally that: "*If you seek her (wisdom) as silver, And search for her as for hidden treasures; Then you will understand the fear of the LORD, And find the* **knowledge** *of God. For the LORD gives wisdom; From His mouth come* **knowledge** *and understanding.*" Thus, the *Knowledge* of God is obtained by the *Wisdom* of God, and the *Wisdom* of God is found in the Word of God! Given that Jesus is the Word, and as one seeks Him, one not only sees and seeks our Savior, Jesus Christ, but one also sees and seeks God the Father, given that Christ Jesus and Father God are One (John 14:9–11).

As one studies the Gospels, one achieves and gains a deeper and richer *understanding* of the **_Knowledge_** of Father God, as exhibited and exemplified by the life, death, and resurrection of our Lord and Savior, Jesus Christ. The more one reads, receives, studies, meditates, and marinates on the Word of God, the more one is transformed by the **_Knowledge_** of Father God (Romans 12:2).

Knowledge, *Understanding*, and *Wisdom* are directly gained from knowing Father God, being obedient and submissive to His will in one's life, as well as by desiring, embracing, and undertaking a deep, one-to-one intimate relationship with God our Father, God the Son, and God the Holy Spirit. As one engages in the Word of God, the Almighty God will become the sovereign ruler over one's life, and He will bless one with unquestioning grace, peace, mercy, forgiveness, love, **_Knowledge_**, *understanding*, and *wisdom*! And to that I say, AMEN!

(The Beginning of Knowledge)

Proverbs *1:1–4*, *5*–*6*, and *7*

(1)   The Proverbs of Solomon the son of David, king of Israel:

(2)*   **To know *wisdom* and *instruction*, To perceive the words of *understanding*,**

(3)*   **To receive the *instruction* of *wisdom*, Justice, judgment, and equity;**

(4)*   To give prudence to the simple, To the young man **_knowledge_** and discretion—

(5)*   **A wise man will hear and increase *learning*, And a man of *understanding* will attain *wise* counsel;**

(6)*   To understand a proverb and an enigma, The words of the *wise* and their riddles.

(7)*   **The fear of the LORD is the beginning of *knowledge*, But fools despise *wisdom* and *instruction*.**

(The Call of Wisdom)

Proverbs *1:*20*–27 and 28–33*

(20)* ***Wisdom* calls aloud outside; She raises her voice in the open squares**.

(21) She cries out in the chief concourses, At the openings of the gates in the city She speaks her words:

(22)* "How long, you simple ones, will you love simplicity? For scorners delight in their scorning, *And fools hate **<u>knowledge</u>**.*

(23) Turn at my rebuke; Surely I will pour out my spirit on you; I will make my words known to you.

(24) Because I have called and you refused, I have stretched out my hand and no one regarded,

(25) Because you disdained all my counsel, And would have none of my rebuke,

(26) I also will laugh at your calamity; I will mock when your terror comes,

(27) When your terror comes like a storm, And your destruction comes like a whirlwind, When distress and anguish come upon you.

(28) "Then they will call on me, but I will not answer; They will seek me diligently, but they will not find me.

(29)* *Because they hated **<u>knowledge</u>*** And did not choose the fear of the LORD,

(30) They would have none of my *counsel* And despised my every *rebuke*.

(31) Therefore they shall eat the fruit of their own way, And be filled to the full with their own fancies.

(32) For the turning away of the simple will slay them, And the complacency of fools will destroy them;

(33)* But whoever listens to me (***<u>knowledge</u>*** and *wisdom*) will dwell safely, And will be secure, without fear of evil."

(The Value of Wisdom)

Proverbs *2:1*–*6* and *10*–13

(1)* *My son, if you receive my words, And treasure my commands within you,*

(2)* **So that you incline your ear to *wisdom*, And apply your heart to *understanding*;**

(3)* Yes, if you cry out for discernment, And lift up your voice for *understanding*,

(4)* If you seek her (***knowledge*** and *wisdom*) as silver, And search for her (***knowledge*** and *wisdom*) as for hidden treasures;

(5)* **Then you will *understand* the fear of the LORD, And find the *knowledge* of God.**

(6)* **For the LORD gives *wisdom*; From His mouth come *knowledge* and *understanding*;**

(10)* **When *wisdom* enters your heart, And *knowledge* is pleasant to your soul,**

(11)* **Discretion will preserve you; *Understanding* will keep you,**

(12) To deliver you from the way of evil, From the man who speaks perverse things,

(13) From those who leave the paths of uprightness To walk in the ways of darkness....

(Guidance for the Young)

Proverbs 3:19–20

The LORD by *wisdom* founded the earth; By *understanding* He established the heavens; By His ***knowledge*** the depths were broken up, And clouds drop down from dew.

(The Peril of Adultery)

Proverbs 5:1–6

(1) My son, pay attention to my *wisdom*; Lend your ear to my *understanding*,

(2) That you may preserve discretion, And your lips may keep **_knowledge_**.

(3) For the lips of an immoral woman drip honey, And her mouth is smoother than oil;

(4) But in the end she is bitter as wormwood, Sharp as a two-edged sword.

(5) Her feet go down to death, Her steps lay hold of hell.

(6) Lest you ponder her path of life—Her ways are unstable; You do not know them.

(The Excellence of Wisdom)

Proverbs *8:*6*–9*, 10*–*11*, 12*–14*, *17*–21, and *32*–36*

(6)* **Listen, for I (*wisdom*) will speak of excellent things, And from the opening of my lips will come right things;**

(7)* **For my mouth will speak truth; Wickedness is an abomination to my lips.**

(8)* **All the words of my mouth are with righteousness; Nothing crooked or perverse is in them.**

(9)* They are all plain to him who *understands*, And right to those who find **_knowledge_**.

(10)* Receive my *instruction*, and not silver, And **_knowledge_** rather than choice gold;

(11)* **For *wisdom* is better than rubies, And all the things one may desire cannot be compared with her.**

(12)* "I, *wisdom*, dwell with prudence, And find out **_knowledge_** and discretion.

443

(13)* The fear of the LORD is to hate evil; Pride and arrogance and the evil way And the perverse mouth I (*wisdom*) hate.

(14)* Counsel is mine, and sound *wisdom*; I (*wisdom*) am *understanding*, I (*wisdom*) have strength.

(17)* **I (*wisdom*) love those who love me (*wisdom*), And those who seek me (wisdom) diligently will find me (*wisdom*).**

(18) Riches and honor are with me (*wisdom*), Enduring riches and righteousness.

(20)* I (*wisdom*) traverse the way of righteousness, In the midst of the paths of justice,

(21) That I (*wisdom*) may cause those who love me (*wisdom*) to inherit wealth, That I (*wisdom*) may fill their treasuries.

(32)* **"Now therefore, *listen* to me, my children, For blessed are those who keep my ways.**

(33)* **Hear *instruction* and be *wise*, And do not disdain it.**

(34)* *Blessed is the man who listens to me*, Watching daily at my gates, Waiting at the posts of my doors.

(35)* **For whoever finds me finds life, And obtains favor from the LORD;**

(36)* But he who sins against me wrongs his own soul; All those who hate me love death."

(*The Way of Wisdom*)

Proverbs *9:7–12

(7) "He who corrects a scoffer gets shame for himself, And he who rebukes a wicked man only harms himself.

(8)* **Do not correct a scoffer, lest he hate you; Rebuke a wise man, and he will love you.**

(9)* **Give *instruction* to a *wise* man, and he will be still *wiser*; Teach a just man, and he will increase in *learning*.**

(10)* "**The fear of the LORD is the beginning of** *wisdom*, **And the** *knowledge* **of the Holy One is** *understanding*.

(11) For by me your days will be multiplied, And years of life will be added to you.

(12) If you are *wise*, you are *wise* for yourself, And if you scoff, you bear it alone."

(Wise Sayings of Solomon)

Proverbs 10:14*
Wise people store up **_knowledge_**, But the mouth of the foolish is near destruction.

Proverbs 11:*9*
The hypocrite with his mouth destroys his neighbor, But through **_knowledge_** the righteous will be delivered.

Proverbs *12:*1*
Whoever loves *instruction* **loves** _knowledge_, **But he who hates correction is stupid.**

Proverbs 12:23*
A prudent man conceals **_knowledge_**, But the heart of fools proclaims foolishness.

Proverbs 13:16*
Every prudent man acts with **_knowledge_**, But a fool lays open his folly.

Proverbs 14:*6*
A scoffer seeks *wisdom* and does not find it, But **_knowledge_** is easy to him who *understands*.

Proverbs 14:7
Go from the presence of a foolish man, When you do not perceive in him the lips of **_knowledge_**.

Proverbs 14:*16*
A *wise* man fears and departs from evil, But a fool rages and is *self-confident*.

Proverbs 14:18*
The simple inherit folly, But the prudent are crowned with **knowledge**.

Proverbs 14:24
The *crown of the wise* is their riches, But the foolishness of fools is folly.

Proverbs 15:*2*
The *tongue of the wise* uses **knowledge** rightly, But the mouth of fools pours forth foolishness.

Proverbs *15:*3*
The eyes of the LORD are in every place, Keeping watch on the evil and the good.

Proverbs 15:*7*
The lips of the *wise* disperse **knowledge**, But the heart of the fool does not do so.

Proverbs *15:*14*
The heart of him who has *understanding* seeks *knowledge*, But the mouth of fools feeds on foolishness.

Proverbs 16:21*
The *wise* in heart will be called prudent, And sweetness of the lips increases *learning*.

Proverbs 16:23
The heart of the *wise* *teaches* his mouth, And adds *learning* to his lips.

Proverbs *17:*27*
He who has *knowledge* spares his words, And a man of *understanding* is of a calm spirit.

Proverbs *18:*15*
The heart of the prudent acquires _knowledge_, **And the ear of the** _wise_
seeks _knowledge_.

Proverbs 19:*2*
Also it is not good for a soul to be without **_knowledge_**, And he sins who
hastens with his feet.

Proverbs *19:*25*
Strike a scoffer, and the simple will become wary; Rebuke one who has
**understanding****, and he will discern** _knowledge_.

Proverbs *19:*27*
Cease listening to instruction, my son, And you will stray from the words
_of_ _knowledge_.

Proverbs 20:*15*
There is gold and a multitude of rubies, But the lips of **_knowledge_** are a
precious jewel.

Proverbs 21:*11*
When the scoffer is punished, the simple is made _wise_; But when the _wise_
is _instructed_, he receives **_knowledge_**.

Proverbs *22:*6*
Train _up a child in the way he should go, And when he is old, he will not_
depart from it.

Proverbs *22:*7*
The rich rules over the poor, And the borrower is servant to the lender.

Proverbs 22:*12*
The eyes of the LORD preserve **_knowledge_**, But He overthrows the words
of the faithless.

(Sayings of the Wise)

Proverbs *22:*17*–*21* and 24–25

(17)* **Incline your ear and hear the words of the *wise*, And apply your heart to my *knowledge*;**

(18)* For it is a pleasant thing if you keep them (*wise sayings*) within you; Let them all be fixed upon your lips,

(19)* **So that your trust may be in the LORD; I have *instructed* you today, even you.**

(20)* Have I not written to you excellent things Of counsels and *knowledge*,

(21)* **That I may make you know the certainty of the *words of truth* That you may answer *words of truth* To those who send to you?**

(24) Make no friendship with an angry man, And with a furious man do not go,

(25) Lest you *learn* his ways And set a snare for your soul.

Proverbs *23:*4*–*5*

Do not overwork to be rich; *Because of your own understanding, cease!* Will you set your eyes on that which is not? For riches certainly make themselves wings; They fly away like an eagle toward heaven.

Proverbs 23:9*

Do not speak in the hearing of a fool, For he will despise the *wisdom of your words*.

Proverbs *23:*12*

Apply your heart to *instruction*, And your ears to *words of knowledge*.

Proverbs 23:22

Listen to your father who begot you, And do not despise our mother when she is old.

Proverbs *23:*23*
Buy the truth and do not sell it. Also wisdom and instruction and understanding.

Proverbs 24:3*–4*
Through *wisdom* a house is built, And by *understanding* it is established; By **knowledge** the rooms are filled With all precious and pleasant riches.

Proverbs *24:*5*–*6*
A *wise* man is strong, Yes, a man of *knowledge* increases strength; For by *wise* counsel you will wage your own war, And in a multitude of counselors there is safety.

Proverbs *24:13–*14*
My son, eat honey (*wisdom*) because it is good, And the honeycomb (*wisdom*) which is sweet to your taste; **So shall the *knowledge* of *wisdom* be to your soul; If you have found it, there is a prospect, And your hope will not be cut off.**

(Further Wise Sayings of Solomon)

Proverbs 25: 2
It is *the glory of God to conceal a matter*, But *the glory of kings is to search out a matter.*

Proverbs 25:11
A *word fitly spoken* is like apples of gold In settings of silver.

Proverbs 25:12
Like an earring of gold and an ornament of fine gold Is a *wise rebuker to an obedient ear.*

Proverbs *27:*17*
As *iron sharpens iron*, So a *man sharpens the countenance of his friend*.

Proverbs 28:2

Because of the transgression of a land, many are its princes; But by a man of *understanding* and **_knowledge_** Right will be prolonged.

Proverbs 28:5*

Evil men do not *understand* justice, *But those who seek the LORD understand all.*

Proverbs 29:7*

The righteous considers the cause of the poor, But the wicked does not *understand* such **_knowledge_**.

(The Wisdom of Agur)

Proverbs 30:2–3

Surely I am more stupid than any man, And do not have the *understanding* of a man. I neither *learned wisdom* Nor have **_knowledge_** of the Holy One.

CHAPTER 43

Laziness, Lazy, Scoffer, Slacker, Sluggard, Frivolity, Idleness

I n reviewing the various Proverbs verses associated with these Chapter
Themes of *Laziness*, *Lazy*, *Scoffers*, *Slacker*, *Sluggard*, *Frivolity*, and
Idleness, I could not find any—and I mean, any—redeeming qualities
associated with any of these Chapter Themes! For illustrative purposes,
take for example the subtheme "*Scoffers*." Proverbs 9:7–9 clearly states
that a *Scoffer* dislikes any form of advice, wise counsel, and/or instruction, while embracing all forms of hatred. Another example, Proverbs
13:1 illustrates how a *Scoffer* hates to listen to parental instruction, while
turning his nose up to being rebuked.

To further highlight the negative and/or evil continence of a *Scoffer*,
Proverbs 15:12 states the following: "*A scoffer does not love one who corrects him, Nor will he go to the wise*"! What kind of fool is this, who resents
any form of correction, while refusing to seek wise counsel and/or advice,
and inherently willing to seek out someone—or should I say, anyone—
who will tell him what he desires or wants to hear? Such a personal policy
pursuit is self-defeating and only confirms in him, his pride, arrogance,

foolishness, sinfulness, and ultimately, his death. Accordingly, a "*Scoffer*" is on my "Do not touch and/or associate with" list!

One of the best biblical truths against *Laziness* is found in Proverbs 6:6–11, which discusses the positive merits of the busy "ant." In these verses, one can easily observe and discern wisdom that can be gained from being proactive, productive, industrious, and focused with a high degree of intentionality, as well as planning for one's future.

As one further reflects on the illustrative nature of these powerful Proverbs verses, I am reminded of "*The Parable of the Man with the Withered Hand*," or the story of how Jesus heals a man's hand on the Sabbath (Mark 3:1–6). In this factual story of Jesus healing on the Sabbath, Jesus gave the man with the withered hand two specific directives: (1) "*Step forward*" (v. 3) and (2) "*Stretch out your hand*" (v. 5). And because of the man's obedience to Jesus's instructions, Scripture also records in verse 5: "*And he stretched it out, and his hand was restored as whole as the other.*" Thus, what is one of the principle takeaways or "teachable moments" from this story? I would contend that had this man not been obedient to Jesus's instructions to him—by standing up *and* stretching out his hand—he might/or would not have received a blessing of a healed hand!

Accordingly, the same principles of obedience to Father God's Word, effective listening to the indwelling instructions of the Holy Spirit, as well as doing what is being asked—in this case, not **sitting on one's hands** and just expecting a miracle/blessing from Father God—verses executing with intentionality what Father God is requesting of one to do, will more likely than not, result in a current and/or deferred blessing!

Sitting around, being *Lazy*, or being a *Slacker*—or worst yet, being a *Scoffer*—are not biblical, God-based principles.

Finally, as many of this Chapter's Proverbs verses mention (i.e. Proverbs 13:4, 14:23, 19:15, and 20:4) as an example, practicing and/or being *Lazy*, *Frivolity*, and/or a *Slacker,* will directly result in poverty, hunger, as well as possessing a sense of nothingness, especially as it relates to one's physical, emotional, and/or financial well-being. Hard work and productivity, can and will be rewarded in this life as well as in eternity!

(The Folly of Indolence)

Proverbs 6:6–11

(6) Go to the ant, you ***sluggard***! Consider her ways and be wise,

(7) Which, having no captain, Overseer or ruler,

(8) Provides her supplies in the summer, And gathers her food in the harvest.

(9) How long will you *slumber*, O ***sluggard***? When will you rise from your *sleep*?

(10) A little *sleep*, a little *slumber*, A little folding of the hands to *sleep*—

(11) So shall your poverty come on you like a prowler, And your need like an armed man.

Proverbs *9:7–12

(7) "He who corrects a ***scoffer*** gets shame for himself, And he who rebukes a wicked man only harms himself.

(8)* **Do not correct a *scoffer*, lest he hate you; Rebuke a wise man, and he will love you.**

(9)* **Give instruction to a wise man, and he will be still wiser; Teach a just man, and he will increase in learning.**

(10)* **The fear of the LORD is the beginning of wisdom, And the knowledge of the Holy One is understanding.**

(11) For by me your days will be multiplied, And years of life will be added to you.

(12) If you are wise, you are wise for yourself, And if you ***scoff***, you will bear it alone."

(Wise Sayings of Solomon)

Proverbs 10:4*

He who has a ***slack*** hand becomes poor, But the hand of the diligent makes rich.

Proverbs 10:5*
He who gathers in summer is a wise son; He who *sleeps* in harvest is a son who causes shame.

Proverbs 10:26
As vinegar to the teeth and smoke to the eyes, So is the ***lazy*** man to those who send him.

Proverbs 12:11
He who tills his land will be satisfied with bread, But he who follows ***frivolity*** is devoid of understanding.

Proverbs 12:24
The hand of the diligent will rule, But the ***lazy*** man will be put to forced labor.

Proverbs 12:27
The ***lazy*** man does not roast what he took in hunting, But diligence is man's precious possession.

Proverbs *13:*1*
A wise son heeds his father's instruction, But a *scoffer* does not listen to rebuke.

Proverbs 13:4*
The soul of a ***lazy*** man desires, and has nothing; But the soul of the diligent shall be made rich.

Proverbs 14:*6*
A ***scoffer*** seeks wisdom and does not find it, But knowledge is easy to him who understands.

Proverbs *14:*23*
In all labor there is profit, But *idle chatter* leads only to poverty.

Proverbs 15:*12*
A ***scoffer*** does not love one who corrects him, Nor will he go to the wise.

Proverbs 15:19*
The way of the *lazy* man is like a hedge of thorns, But the way of the upright is a highway.

Proverbs 17:21
He who begets a *scoffer* does so to his sorrow, And the father of a fool has no joy.

Proverbs 18:9
He who is *slothful* in his work Is a brother to him who is a great destroyer.

Proverbs 19:15*
Laziness casts one into a deep *sleep*, And an *idle person* will suffer hunger.

Proverbs 19:24
A *lazy* man buries his hand in the bowl, And will not so much as bring it to his mouth again.

Proverbs *19:*25*
Strike a *scoffer* and the simple will become wary; Rebuke one who has understanding, and he will discern knowledge.

Proverbs 19:29
Judgments are prepared for *scoffers*, And beatings for the backs of fools.

Proverbs 20:*4*
The *lazy* man will not plow because of winter; He will beg during harvest and have nothing.

Proverbs 20:*13*
Do not love *sleep*, lest you come to poverty; Open your eyes, and you will be satisfied with bread.

Proverbs *21:*5*
The plans of the diligent lead surely to plenty, But those of everyone who is *hasty*, surely to poverty.

Proverbs 21:*11*

When the **_scoffer_** is punished, the simple is made wise; But when the wise is instructed, he receives knowledge.

Proverbs 21:20*

There is desirable treasure, And oil in the dwelling of the wise, But a _foolish_ man squanders it.

Proverbs 21:24

A proud and haughty man—"**_Scoffer_**" is his name; He acts with arrogant pride.

Proverbs *21:25*–*26*

The desire of the **_lazy_** man kills him, For _his hands refuse to labor_. He covets greedily all day long, **But the righteous gives and does not spare**.

Proverbs 22:*10*

Cast out the **_scoffer_**, and contention will leave; Yes, strife and reproach will cease.

Proverbs 22:13

The **_lazy_** man says, "There is a lion outside! I shall be slain in the streets!"

(Sayings of the Wise)

Proverbs 23:20–21*

Do not mix with winebibbers, Or with gluttonous eaters of meat; For the _drunkard_ and the _glutton_ will come to poverty, And _drowsiness_ will clothe a man with rags.

(Use of Wine)

Proverbs 23:29–35

(29) Who has woe? Who has sorrow? Who has contentions? Who has complaints? Who has wounds without cause? Who has redness of eyes?

(30) Those who linger long as the _wine_, Those who go in search of mixed _wine_.

(31) Do not look on the _wine_ when it is red, When it sparkles in the cup, When it swirls around smoothly;

(32) At the last it bites like a serpent, And stings like a viper.

(33) Your eyes will see strange things, And your heart will utter perverse things.

(34) Yes, you will be like _one who lies down_ in the midst of the sea, Or like one who lies at the top of the mast saying:

(35) "They have struck me, but I was not hurt; They have beaten me, but I did not feel it. _When shall I awake, that I may seek another drink?_"

Proverbs 24:8*–9*

He who plots to do evil Will be called a schemer. The devising of foolishness is sin, And the **scoffer** is an abomination to men.

(Further Sayings of the Wise)

Proverbs 24:30–34

(30) I went by the field of the **lazy** man, And by the vineyard of the man devoid of understanding;

(31) And there it was, all overgrown with thorns; Its surface was covered with nettles; Its stone wall was broken down.

(32) When I saw it, I considered it well; I looked on it and received instruction:

(33) A little _sleep_, a little _slumber_, a _little folding of the hands to rest_;

(34) So shall your poverty come like a prowler, And your need like an armed man.

(Further Wise Sayings of Solomon)

Proverbs 26:9

Like a thorn that goes into the hand of a _drunkard_ Is a proverb in the mouth of fools.

Proverbs *26:13–*16*

(13) The *lazy* man says, "There is a lion in the road! A fierce lion in the streets!"

(14) As a door turns on its hinges, So does the *lazy* man on his bed.

(15) The *lazy* man buries his hand in the bowl; It wearies him to bring it back to his mouth.

(16)* **The *lazy* man is wiser in his own eyes Than seven men who can answer sensibly**.

Proverbs 28:19

He who tills his land will have plenty of bread, But he who follows *frivolity* will have poverty enough!

Proverbs 29:8*

Scoffers set a city aflame, But wise men turn away wrath.

(The Virtuous Wife)

Proverbs 31:27*

She watches over the ways of her household, And does not eat the bread of *idleness*.

CHAPTER 44

LIFE, SOUL, LIVES, ETERNAL LIFE (ETERNITY)

As I am sitting in the windowsill of my third-floor suite here in Paris, looking out on the busy street below, I am caught up thinking about the true essence of "*Life*." As I acknowledge and Thank Father God for these sixty-four years of earthly "*Life*" that He has granted to me thus far! And as I ponder and think about, the next potential earthly day, week, month, and/or years that Father God grants me, I cannot begin to think about nor fully grasp in totality, what "*Eternal Life*" might and/or will be like! As a Christian, I am assured of "*Eternal Life*," but I cannot even begin to fully comprehend what such "*Life*" will be like. Suffice it to say, I am eternally Thankful to Father God, for allowing me to accept Christ Jesus as my Lord and Savior! Additionally, having the indwelling presence of the Holy Spirit, residing within me, speaking, shaping, and directing my "*Life*" and my steps, so that they are marching in accordance with Father God's stated purpose and direction for the next season of my earthly "*Life*"!

So, let me ask this question, one that I occasionally but directly ask myself more often than not, given that the runaway of this "*Earthly Life*" in front of me, is much shorter than the runway that is in the rearview mirror of my past "*Earthly Life*," and that is this: Am I doing all that I can to optimize every second, minute, hour, day, week, month, and years that Father God grants me in this season of my "*Earthly Life*"? I don't know about you, but as an extreme optimist by nature who always believes that the glass is at least half full and not, half empty, I challenge myself daily to live this "*Earthly Life*", in such a way that consistently gives praises, glorifies, and honor to Father God!

So, as for me, I am frequently, if not constantly asking myself,—am I doing all that I can to live a God-centered and God-focused "*Earthly Life*"? By giving on a consistent basis of what I have previously mentioned before of the **4 T's** of Time, Talent, Treasury, and Tent (i.e. Self) for Father God? As God's Word states in Romans 3:23, "*for all have sinned and fall short of the glory of God,*" one must not allow this biblical truth from preventing one from giving one's very best on a daily basis to the purpose driven "*Earthly Life*" that Father God has presented to one and all.

As for me, my daily responsibilities are to "*seek first the kingdom of God and His righteousness, and all these things shall be added unto me*" (Matthew 6:33). Additionally, I must also do as Jesus instructed in Matthew 22:37–39, that being: "*You shall love the Lord your God with all your heart, with all your soul, and with all your mind. This is the first and great commandment. And the second is like it: You shall love your neighbor as yourself.*" And finally, I must be willing to be a "***Servant***" and "***wash the feet of others***" as Jesus instructed and demonstrated in John 13:1–20. And if I am able to consistently and objectively live out these inspired Godly principles, then in the **Life** to come—that being "***Eternal Life***"—that I will be privileged and honored to hear Jesus proclaim: "*Well done, good and faithful servant; you were faithful over a few things, I will make you ruler over many things. Enter into the joy of your Lord*" (Matthew 25:21).

To God be the GLORY!

(Shun Evil Counsel)

Proverbs *1:8*–*19*

(8)* My son, hear the instruction of your father, And do not forsake the law of your mother;

(9) For they will be a graceful ornament on your head, And chains about your neck.

(10)* My son, if sinners entice you, Do not consent.

(11) If they say, "Come with us, Let us lie in wait to shed blood; Let us lurk secretly for the innocent without cause;

(12) Let us swallow them alive like Sheol, And whole, like those who go down to the Pit;

(13) We shall find all kinds of precious possessions, We shall fill our houses with spoil;

(14) Cast in your lot among us, Let us all have one purse"—

(15)* My son, do not walk in the way with them, Keep your foot from their path;

(16) For their feet run to evil, And they make haste to shed blood.

(17) Surely, in vain the net is spread In the sight of any bird;

(18) But they lie in wait for their own blood, They lurk secretly for their own *lives*.

(19)* **So are the ways of everyone who is greedy for gain; It takes away the *life* of its owners.**

(The Value of Wisdom)

Proverbs *2:*10*–22*

(10)* **When wisdom enters your heart, And knowledge is pleasant to your *soul*,**

(11)* **Discretion will preserve you; Understanding will keep you,**

(12) To deliver you from the way of evil, From the man who speaks perverse things,

(13) From those who leave the paths of uprightness To walk in the ways of darkness;

(14) Who rejoice in doing evil, And delight in the perversity of the wicked;

(15) Whose ways are crooked, And who are devious in their paths;

(16) To deliver you from the immoral woman, From the seductress who flatters with her words,

(17) Who forsakes the companion of her youth, And forgets the covenant of her God.

(18) For her **_house_** leads down to death, And her paths to the dead;

(19) None who go to her return, Nor do they regain the *paths of **life***—

(20)* **So you may walk in the way of goodness, And keep to the paths of righteousness.**

(21)* **For the upright will _dwell_ in the land, And the blameless will remain in it;**

(22)* But the wicked will be cut off from the earth, And the unfaithful will be uprooted from it.

(Guidance for the Young)

Proverbs 3:1*–2

My son, do not forget my law, But let your hearts keep my commands; For **_length of days_** and **_long life_** And peace they will add to you.

Proverbs *3:*13*–18*

(13)* **Happy is the man who finds wisdom, And the man who gains understanding;**

(14) For her (wisdom) proceeds are better than the profits of silver, And her gain than fine gold.

(15) She (Wisdom) is more precious than rubies, And all the things you may desire cannot compare with her.

(16) **_Length of days_** is in her right hand, In her left hand riches and honor.

(17) Her ways are ways of pleasantness, And all her paths are peace.

(18)* She (Wisdom) is a **_tree of life_** to those who take hold of her, And happy are all who retain her.

Proverbs *3:*21*–26

(21)* **My son, let them not depart from your eyes—Keep sound wisdom and discretion;**

(22) So they will be _life_ to your _soul_ And grace to your neck.

(23) Then you will walk safely in your way, And your foot will not stumble.

(24)* **When you lie down, you will not be afraid; Yes, you will lie down and your sleep will be sweet.**

(25) Do not be afraid of sudden terror, Nor of trouble from the wicked when it comes;

(26) For the LORD will be your confidence, And will keep your foot from being caught.

(Security in Wisdom)

Proverbs *4:1*–9, *10*–*13*, and *20*–*27*

(1)* Hear, my children, the instruction of a father, And give attention to know understanding;

(2)* For I give you good doctrine: Do not forsake my law.

(3) When I was my father's son, Tender and the only one in the sight of my mother,

(4)* **He also taught me, and said to me: "Let your heart retain my words; Keep my commands, and _live_.**

(5)* **Get wisdom! Get understanding! Do not forget, nor turn away from the words of my mouth.**

(6)* **Do not forsake her (wisdom), and she will preserve you; Love her, and she will keep you.**

(7)* **Wisdom is the principal thing; Therefore get wisdom And in all your getting, get understanding.**

(8) Exalt her (wisdom), and she will promote you; She will bring you honor, when you embrace her.

(9) She will place on your head an ornament of grace; A crown of glory she will deliver to you."

(10)* Hear, my son, and receive my sayings, And the _years_ of your _life_ will be _many_.

(11)* I have taught you in the way of wisdom; I have led you in the right paths;

(12)* When you walk, your steps will not be hindered, And when you run, you will not stumble.

(13)* Take firm hold of instruction, do not let go; Keep her, for she is your _life._

(20)* My son, give attention to my words; Incline your ear to my sayings.

(21)* Do not let them depart from your eyes; Keep them in the midst of your heart;

(22)* For they are _life_ to those who find them, And health to all their flesh.

(23)* Keep your heart with all diligence, For out of it spring the issues of _life_.

(24)* Put away from you a deceitful mouth, And put perverse lips far from you.

(25) Let your eyes look straight ahead, And your eyelids look right before you.

(26)* Ponder the path of your feet, And let all your ways be established.

(27)* Do not turn to the right or the left; Remove your foot from evil.

(The Peril of Adultery)

Proverbs 5:1–6

(1) My son, pay attention to my wisdom; Lend your ear to my understanding,

(2) That you may preserve discretion, And your lips may keep knowledge.

(3) For the lips of an immoral woman drip honey, And her mouth is smoother than oil;

(4)   But in the end she is bitter as wormwood, Sharp as a two-edged sword.

(5)   Her feet go down to death, Her steps lay hold of hell.

(6)   Lest you ponder her path of **life**—Her ways are unstable; You do not know them.

(Beware of Adultery)

Proverbs *6:20*–*29* and *32*–35*

(20)* My son, keep your father's command, And do not forsake the law of your mother.

(21)   Bind them continually upon your heart; Tie them around your neck.

(22)   When you roam, they will lead you; When you sleep, they will keep you; And when you awake, they will speak with you.

(23)* **For the commandment is a lamp, And the law a light; Reproofs of instruction are the *way of life*,**

(24)* To keep you from the evil woman, From the flattering tongue of a seductress.

(25)* Do not lust after her beauty in your heart, Nor let her allure you with her eyelids.

(26)   For by means of a harlot, *A man is reduced to a crust of bread*; And an adulteress will *prey* upon his precious **life**.

(27)   Can a man take *fire* to his bosom, And his *clothes not be burned*?

(28)   Can one *walk on hot coals*, And his *feet not be seared*?

(29)* **So is he who goes in to his neighbor's wife; Whoever touches her shall not be innocent.**

(32)* **Whoever commits adultery with a woman lacks understanding; He who does so destroys his own _soul_.**

(33)* **Wounds and dishonor he will get, And his reproach will not be wiped away.**

(34)   For jealousy is a husband's fury; Therefore he will not spare in the day of vengeance.

(35)* He will accept no recompense, Nor will he be appeased though you give many gifts.

Proverbs *7:*1*–5*

(1)* **My son, keep my words And treasure my commands within you**.

(2)* **Keep my commands and *live*, And my law as the apple of your eye**.

(3)* Bind them on your fingers; Write them on the tablet of your heart.

(4)* **Say to wisdom, "You are my sister," And call understanding your nearest kin**,

(5)* That they may keep you from the immortal woman, From the seductress who flatters with her words.

(The Crafty Harlot)

Proverbs 7:21–23

(21) With her enticing speech she caused him to yield, With her flattering lips she seduced him.

(22) Immediately he went after her, as an ox goes to the slaughter, Or as a fool to the correction of the stocks,

(23) Till an arrow struck his liver, As a bird hastens to the snare, He did not know it would cost his *life*.

(The Excellence of Wisdom)

Proverbs *8:*32*–36*

(32)* **"Now therefore, listen to me (wisdom), my children, For blessed are those who keep my ways**.

(33)* **Hear instruction and be wise, And do not disdain it**.

(34)* **Blessed is the man who listens to me (wisdom)**, Watching daily at my gates, Waiting at the posts of my doors.

(35)* **For whoever finds me (wisdom) finds *life*, And obtains favor from the LORD**;

(36)* But he who sins against me (wisdom) wrongs his own *soul*; All those who hate me love death."

(The Way of Wisdom)

Proverbs *9:4–*6* and 7–12

(4) "Whoever is simple, let him turn in here!" As for him who lacks understanding, she (wisdom) says to him,

(5) "Come, eat of my (wisdom) bread And drink of the wine I (wisdom) have mixed.

(6)* **Forsake foolishness and _live_, And go in the way of understanding.**

(7) "He who corrects a scoffer gets shame for himself, And he who rebukes a wicked man only harms himself.

(8)* **Do not correct a scoffer, lest he hate you; Rebuke a wise man, and he will love you.**

(9)* **Give instruction to a wise man, and he will be still wiser; Teach a just man, and he will increase in learning.**

(10)* **The fear of the LORD is the beginning of wisdom, And the knowledge of the Holy One is understanding.**

(11) For by me _your days will be multiplied_, And _years of life_ will be _added to you._

(12) If you are wise, you are wise for yourself, And if you scoff, you will bear it alone."

(Wise Sayings of Solomon)

Proverbs 10:3*

The LORD will not allow the righteous _**soul**_ to famish, But He casts away the desire of the wicked.

Proverbs 10:11*

The mouth of the righteous is a well of _**life**_, But violence covers the mouth of the wicked.

Proverbs 10:16

The labor of the righteous leads to _**life**_, The wages of the wicked to sin.

467

Proverbs 10:*17*

He who keeps instruction is in the *way of life*, But he who refuses correction goes astray.

Proverb 10:27

The fear of the LORD **_prolongs days_**, But the **_years_** of the wicked will be *shortened*.

Proverbs 11:*4*

Riches do not profit in the *day of wrath*, But righteousness delivers from death.

Proverbs 11:17

The merciful man does good for his own **_soul,_** But he who is cruel troubles his own flesh.

Proverbs 11:19*

As righteousness leads to **_life_**, So he who purses evil pursues it to his own death.

Proverbs *11:*24*–*25*

There is one who scatters, yet increases more; And there is one who withholds more than is right, But it leads to poverty. The generous _soul_ will be made rich, And he who waters will also be watered himself.

Proverbs *11:*29*

He who troubles his _own house_ will inherit the wind, And the fool will be servant to the wise of heart.

Proverbs *11:*30*

The fruit of the righteous is a _tree of life_, And he who _wins souls_ is wise.

Proverbs 12:7*

The wicked are overthrown and are no more, But the **_house_** of the righteous *will stand*.

Proverbs 12:10

A righteous man regards the **_life_** of his animal, But the tender mercies of the wicked are cruel.

Proverbs 12:28*

In the way of righteousness is **_life_**, And in its pathway there is _no death._

Proverbs 13:2

A man shall eat well by the fruit of his mouth, But the **_soul_** of the unfaithful feeds on violence.

Proverbs 13:*3*

He who guards his mouth preserves his **_life_**, But he who opens wide his lips shall have destruction.

Proverbs 13:4*

The **_soul_** of a lazy man desires, and has nothing; But the **_soul_** of the diligent shall be made rich.

Proverbs 13:8*

The ransom of a man's **_life_** is his riches, But the poor does not hear rebuke.

Proverbs 13:9

The **_light_** of the righteous rejoices, But the **_lamp_** of the wicked will be put out.

Proverbs *13:*12*

Hope deferred makes the heart sick, But when the desire comes, it is a _tree of life._

Proverbs 13:*13*

He who despises _the word_ will be destroyed, But he who fears the commandment will be _rewarded_.

Proverbs 13:14

The law of the wise is a **_fountain of life_**, To turn one away from the snares of death.

Proverbs 13:19
A desire accomplished is sweet to the **_soul_**, But it is an abomination to fools to depart from evil.

Proverbs 13:25
The righteous eats to the satisfying of his **_soul_**, But the stomach of the wicked shall be in want.

Proverbs 14:11*
The **_house_** of the wicked will be overthrown, But the _tent_ of the upright will flourish.

Proverbs 14:25
A true witness delivers **_souls_**, But a deceitful witness speaks lies.

Proverbs 14:27*
The fear of the LORD is a **_fountain of life_**, To turn one away from the snares of death.

Proverbs 14:30
A sound heart is **_life_** to the _body_, But envy is rottenness to the _bones_.

Proverbs 15:4
A wholesome tongue is a **_tree of life_**, But perverseness in it breaks the spirit.

Proverbs *15:*6*
In the _house_ of the righteous there is much treasure, But in the revenue of the wicked is trouble.

Proverbs 15:24*
The _way of life_ winds upward for the wise, That he may turn away from the hell below.

Proverbs 15:*27*
He who is greedy for gain troubles his own **_house_**, But he who hates bribes will **_live_**.

Proverbs *15:*31*

The ear that hears the rebukes of *life* Will abide among the wise.

Proverbs *15:*32*

He who disdains instruction despises his own *soul*, But he who heeds rebuke gets understanding.

Proverbs 16:15

In the light of the king's face is *life*, And his favor is like a cloud of the latter rain.

Proverbs *16:*17*

The highway of the upright is to depart from evil; He who keeps his way preserves his *soul*.

Proverbs 16:22*

Understanding is a *wellspring of life* to him who has it, But the correction of fools is folly.

Proverbs 16:24

Pleasant words are like a honeycomb, Sweetness to the *soul* and health to the *bones*.

Proverbs *16:*31*

***A silver-haired head is a crown of glory*, If it is found in the way of righteousness.**

Proverbs 17:*13*

Whoever rewards evil for good, Evil will not depart from his *house*.

Proverbs 18:7

A fool's mouth is his destruction, And his lips are the snare of his *soul*.

Proverbs 18:21

Death and *life* are in the power of the tongue, And those who love it will eat its fruit.

Proverbs 19:*2*

Also it is not good for a **_soul_** to be without knowledge, And he sins who hastens with his feet.

Proverbs 19:*8*

He who gets wisdom loves his own **_soul_**; He who keeps understanding will find good.

Proverbs 19:16*

He who keeps the commandment keeps his **_soul_**, But he who is careless of his ways will die.

Proverbs *19:*20*

Listen to counsel and receive instruction, That you may be wise in your _latter days_.

Proverbs *19:*23*

The fear of the LORD leads to _life_, And he who has it will abide in satisfaction; He will not be visited with evil.

Proverbs 20:20

Whoever curses his father or his mother, His **_lamp_** will be put out in deep darkness.

Proverbs 21:10

The **_soul_** of the wicked desires evil; His neighbor finds no favor in his eyes.

Proverbs 21:12*

The righteous God wisely considers the **_house_** of the wicked, Overthrowing the wicked for their wickedness.

Proverbs *21:*21*

He who follows righteousness and mercy Finds _life_, righteousness and honor.

Proverbs 21:*23*

Whoever guards his mouth and tongue Keeps his **_soul_** from troubles.

Proverbs *22:*4*
By humility and the fear of the LORD Are riches and honor and _life_.

Proverbs 22:5
Thorns and snares are in the way of the perverse; He who guards his **_soul_** will be far from them.

(Sayings of the Wise)

Proverbs *22:*22*–*23*
Do not rob the poor because he is poor, Nor oppress the afflicted at the gate; For the LORD will plead their cause, And plunder the _soul_ of those who plunder them.

Proverbs 22:24–25
Make no friendship with an angry man, And with a furious man do not go, Lest you learn his ways And set a snare for your **_soul_**.

Proverbs *23:*13*–*14*
Do not withhold correction from a child, For if you beat him with a rod, he will not die. You shall beat him with a rod, And deliver his _soul_ from hell.

Proverbs 23:17–18
Do not let your heart envy sinners, But be zealous for the fear of the LORD all the day; For surely there is a **_hereafter_**, And your hope will not be cut off.

Proverbs 24:3*–4*
Through wisdom a **_house_** is built, And by understanding it is established; By knowledge the rooms are filled With all precious and pleasant riches.

Proverbs 24:11–12
Deliver those who are drawn toward death, And hold back those stumbling to the slaughter. If you say, "Surely we did not know this," Does not

He who weights the hearts consider it? He who keeps your _**soul**_, does He not know it? And will He not render to each man according to his deeds?

Proverbs *24:13–*14*

My son, eat honey (wisdom) because it is good, And the honeycomb (wisdom) which is sweet to your taste; **So shall the knowledge of wisdom be to your _soul_; If you have found it, there is a prospect, And your hope will not be cut off.**

Proverbs 24:19–20

Do not fret because of evildoers, Nor be envious of the wicked; For there will be no prospect for the evil man; The _**lamp**_ of the wicked will be put out.

(Further Wise Sayings of Solomon)

Proverbs 25:25

As cold water to a weary _**soul**_, So is good news from a far country.

Proverbs 27:8

Like a bird that wanders from its _nest_ Is a man who wanders from his _place_.

Proverbs 28:2

Because of the transgression of a land, many are its princes; But by a man of understanding and knowledge Right will be _prolonged_.

Proverbs 28:16

A ruler who lacks understanding is a great oppressor, But he who hates covetousness will prolong his _**days**_.

Proverbs 28:18*

Whoever walks blamelessly will be _**saved**_, But he who is perverse in his ways will suddenly fall.

Proverbs 29:10
The bloodthirsty hate the blameless, But the upright seek his *well-being*.

Proverbs 29:13*
The poor man and the oppressor have this in common: The LORD gives *light* to the eyes of both.

Proverbs *29:*17*
Correct your son, and he will give you rest; Yes, he will give delight to your *soul*.

Proverbs 29:24
Whoever is a partner with a thief hates his own **life**; He swears to tell the truth, but reveals nothing.

(The Virtuous Wife)

Proverbs *31:*10*–*12*
(10)* **Who can find a virtuous wife? For her worth is far above rubies.**
(11)* **The heart of her husband safely trusts her; So he will have no lack of gain.**
(12)* **She does him good and not evil All the *days* of her *life*.**

CHAPTER 45

LISTEN, LISTENING,
HEAR, HEARING

As I draft this Chapter Theme's Narrative on the topic of "*Listening/ Hearing*," I find myself in Paris on a beautiful August afternoon, sitting to the shaded side of "The Thinker" at the Rodin Museum. Every time that I am blessed by Father God to visit this historic European city, I always find myself parked at the Rodin Museum, admiring, contemplating, and yes, thinking about numerous life issues, as I admire this wonderful statue and what it represents and reflects to me!

As I was walking over to the Rodin Museum, I was "thinking" about the importance and significance of this Chapter Theme—"*Listening/ Hearing*" and reflecting on the anatomy of the human body. Excluding one's legs, toes, arms, lungs, fingers, and liver, Father God's creation of the core human body generally has only one central body part, comparing the human heart, brain, and mouth, as well as eyes and ears. And as I wrap my head around such attention to detail, I cannot help but to ask myself the weight that Father God must place on one's ability to optimize one's vision capabilities as well as one's "*Listening/Hearing*" capabilities.

While I will limit my comments/reflections primarily on the topic of this Chapter Narrative, I cannot help but to recall how the Apostle

James emphasized the importance of "*Hearing*" as one key quality, as one goes through various trials; whereby, James 1:19 and 20 states: "*So then, my beloved brethren, let every man be swift to hear, slow to speak, slow to wrath; for the wrath of man does not produce the righteousness of God.*"

Thus, given Father God's specific instruction regarding being "quick to *Listen,*" it begs the question of how effective mankind is in this area of spiritual knowledge transfer of wisdom, understanding, and instruction, that are generally derived from the simple process of "*Listening*"!

This Chapter Theme's Proverbs verses are quite numerous, as well as instructive and illuminating regarding the importance of "*Listening/ Hearing.*" As such, please allow me to highlight several of my favorite verses:

- 2:2: "*So that you incline your **ear** to wisdom, And apply your heart to understanding*";
- 4:1: "***Hear,** my children, the instruction of a father, And give attention to know understanding*";
- 4:5: "*Get wisdom! Get understanding! Do not forget, **nor turn away from the words of my mouth***";
- 4:20–22: "*My son, **give attention to my words;** Incline your **ear** to my sayings. Do not let them depart from your eyes; Keep them in the midst of your heart; For they are life to those who find them, And health to all their flesh*";
- 8:32: "*Now therefore, **listen** to me, my children, For blessed are those who keep my ways*";
- 16:20: "*He who **heeds the word wisely** will find good, And whoever trusts in the LORD, happy is he*";
- 19:27: "*Cease **listening** to instruction, my son, And you will stray from the words of knowledge*"; and
- 22:17: "*Incline your **ear and hear** the words of the wise, And apply your heart to my knowledge….*"

Thus, as I sit here reflecting on "The Thinker," I cannot help but ask myself these questions:

A. How effective am I currently at "***Listening***" to the indwelling presence of the Holy Spirit speaking into my being?

B. How effective am I currently at "***Listening/Hearing***" Father God speak to me through His Word, as I attempt to do a better job studying, meditating, and marinating on His Word day and night?

C. And finally, how effective am I currently at seeking wise counsel and "***Listening***" to such advice without the human filter of pride and/or arrogance, getting in the way of Father God Speaking to me through the voices of others? But at the end of the day, all of Father God's children can, could, and should elevate one's ***Listening*** effectiveness, such that one sharpens one's ability toward being "***quick to listen***." What say you? Are you ***Listening*** to Father God?

(Shun Evil Counsel)

Proverbs *1:8*–*19*

(8)* My son, ***hear*** the *instruction* of your father, And do not forsake the law of your mother;

(9) For they will be a graceful ornament on your head, And chains about your neck.

(10)* *My son, if sinners entice you, Do not consent.*

(11) If they say, "Come with us, Let us lie in wait to shed blood; Let us lurk secretly for the innocent without cause;

(12) Let us swallow them alive like Sheol, And whole, like those who go down to the Pit;

(13) We shall find all kinds of precious possessions, We shall fill our houses with spoil;

(14) Cast in your lot among us, Let us all have one purse"—

(15)* *My son, do not walk in the way with them, Keep your foot from their path;*

(16) *For their feet run to evil, And they make haste to shed blood.*

(17) Surely, in vain the net is spread In the sight of any bird;

(18) But they lie in wait for their own blood, They lurk secretly for their own lives.

(19)* **So are the ways of everyone who is greedy for gain; It takes away the life of its owners.**

(The Call of Wisdom)

Proverbs *1:*20*–27 and 28–33

(20)* **Wisdom *calls aloud* outside; She raises her *voice* in the open squares.**

(21) She *cries out* in the chief concourses, At the openings of the gates in the city She *speaks* her *words*:

(22) "How long, you simple ones, will you love simplicity? For scorners delight in their scorning, And fools hate knowledge.

(23) Turn at my rebuke; Surely I will pour out my spirit on you; I will make my *words* known to you.

(24) Because I have *called* and you refused, I have stretched out my hand and no one regarded,

(25) Because you *disdained all my counsel, And would have none of my rebuke,*

(26) I also will laugh at your calamity; I will mock when your terror comes,

(27) When your terror comes like a storm, And your destruction comes like a whirlwind, When distress and anguish come upon you.

(28) "Then they will *call on me, but I will not answer*; They will seek me diligently, but they will not find me.

(29)* Because they hated knowledge And did not choose the fear of the LORD,

(30)* *They would have none of my counsel And despised my every rebuke.*

(31) Therefore they shall eat the fruit of their own way, And be filled to the full with their own fancies.

(32) For the turning away of the simple will slay them, And the complacency of fools will destroy them;

(33) But whoever **listens** to me will dwell safely, And will be secure, without fear of evil."

(The Value of Wisdom)

Proverbs *2:1*–*9*

(1)* My son, if you **receive my words**, And *treasure my commands within you,*

(2)* **So that you _incline your ear_ to wisdom, And *apply your heart* to understanding;**

(3)* Yes, if you cry out for discernment, And lift up your voice for understanding,

(4)* If you seek her as silver, And search for her as for hidden treasures;

(5)* **Then you will understand the fear of the LORD, And find the knowledge of God.**

(6)* *For the LORD gives wisdom; From His mouth come knowledge and understanding;*

(7)* *He (wisdom) stores up sound wisdom for the upright;* **He is a shield to those who walk uprightly:**

(8)* **He guards the paths of justice, And preserves the way of His saints.**

(9)* **Then you will understand righteousness and justice, Equity and every good path.**

(Security in Wisdom)

Proverbs *4:1*–9, *10*–*13*, *14*–17, and *20*–*22*

(1)* **_Hear_**, my children, the *instruction* of a father, And give attention to know understanding;

(2)* For I give you good doctrine: Do not forsake my law.

(3) When I was my father's son, Tender and the only one in the sight of my mother,

(4)* *He also taught me, and said to me:* "*Let your heart <u>retain my words</u>; Keep my commands, and live.*

(5)* **Get** *wisdom*! **Get** *understanding*! *<u>Do not forget, nor turn away from the words of my mouth.</u>*

(6)* **Do not forsake** *her* (*wisdom*), **and** *she* **will preserve you; Love** *her*, **and** *she* **will keep you.**

(7)* **Wisdom is the principal thing; Therefore get** *wisdom* **And in all your getting, get understanding.**

(8) Exalt *her* (*wisdom*), and *she* will promote you; *She* will bring you honor, when you embrace *her*.

(9) *She* will place on your head an ornament of grace; A crown of glory *she* will deliver to you."

(10)* *<u>Hear</u>*, **my son, and** *<u>receive my sayings</u>*, **And the years of your life will be many.**

(11)* **I have taught you in the way of** *wisdom*; **I have led you in right paths;**

(12)* **When you walk, your steps will not be hindered, And when you run, you will not stumble.**

(13)* **Take firm hold of instruction, do not let go; Keep** *her* **(wisdom) for** *she* **is your life.**

(14)* **Do not enter the path of the wicked, And do not walk in the way of evil.**

(15) Avoid it, do not travel on it; Turn away from it and pass on.

(16) For they do not sleep unless they have done evil; And their sleep is taken away unless they make someone fall.

(17) For they eat the bread of wickedness, And drink the wine of violence.

(20)* **My son, *give attention to my words*; Incline your *ear* to *my sayings*.**

(21)* *Do not let them depart from your eyes; Keep them in the midst of your heart;*

(22)* **For they are life to those who find them, And health to all their flesh.**

(The Peril of Adultery)

Proverbs 5:7–14

(7) Therefore ***hear*** me now, my children, And do not depart from the ***words of my mouth***.

(8) Remove your way far from her, And do not go near the door of her house,

(9) Lest you give your honor to others, And your years to the cruel one;

(10) Lest aliens be filled with your wealth, And your labors go to the house of a foreigner;

(11) And you mourn at last, When your flesh and your body are consumed,

(12) And say: "*How I have hated instruction, And my heart despised correction!*

(13) *I have not obeyed the **voice** of my teachers, Nor **inclined my ear** to those who instructed me!*

(14) I was on the verge of total ruin, In the midst of the assembly and congregation."

(The Crafty Harlot)

Proverbs 7:21–27

(21) With her ***enticing speech*** *she caused him to yield*, With her ***flattering lips*** *she seduced him.*

(22) Immediately he went after her, as an ox goes to the slaughter, Or as a fool to the correction of the stocks,

(23) Till an arrow struck his liver. As a bird hastens to the snare, He did not know it *would cost his life*.

(24) Now therefore, **_listen_** _to me_, my children; _Pay attention to the_ **_words_** **_of my mouth_**:

(25) Do not let your heart turn aside to her ways, Do not stray into her paths;

(26) For she cast down many wounded, And all who were slain by her were strong men.

(27) Her house is the way to hell, Descending to the chambers of death.

(The Excellence of Wisdom)

Proverbs*8:*1*–*11* and *32*–36*

(1)* ***Does not wisdom cry out, And understanding lift up her voice***?

(2) She (wisdom) takes her stand on the top of the high hill, Beside the way, where the paths meet.

(3) _She (wisdom) cries out by the gates_, _at the entry of the city, At the entrance of the doors:_

(4) "To you, O men, _I call_, And _my voice_ is to the sons of men.

(5) O you simple ones, understand prudence, And you fools, be of an understanding heart.

(6) **_Listen_**, for I will _speak_ of excellent things, _And from_ _the opening of_ _my lips_ _will come right things_;

(7)* ***For my mouth*** _will_ _speak truth_; Wickedness is an abomination to _my lips_.

(8)* **All the words of my mouth are with righteousness; Nothing crooked or perverse is in them.**

(9) _They are all plain to him who understands, And right to those who find knowledge._

(10) **_Receive_** _my instruction_, and not silver, _And knowledge_ rather than choice gold;

(11)* **For wisdom is better than rubies, And all the things one may desire cannot be compared with her.**

(32)* "Now therefore, *listen* to me (wisdom), my children, For blessed are those who keep my ways.

(33)* *Hear* instruction and be wise, And do not disdain it.

(34)* Blessed is the man who *listens* to me, Watching daily at my gates, Waiting at the posts of my doors.

(35)* For whoever finds me (The LORD) finds life, And obtains favor from the LORD;

(36)* But he who sins against me (The LORD) wrongs his own soul; All those who hate me (The LORD) love death."

(Wise Sayings of Solomon)

Proverbs 10:13*

Wisdom is found on the lips of him who has understanding, But a rod is for the back of him who is devoid of understanding.

Proverbs *12:*15*

The way of a fool is right in his own eyes, But he who *heeds* counsel is wise.

Proverbs 12:18*

There is one who *speaks* like the piercings of a sword, But the *tongue of the wise* promotes health.

Proverbs *13:*1*

A wise son *heeds* his father's instruction, But a scoffer does not *listen* to rebuke.

Proverbs 13:8*

The ransom of a man's life is his riches, But the poor does not *hear* rebuke.

Proverbs *13:*10*

By pride comes nothing but strife, *But with the well-advised is wisdom*.

Proverbs *13:*18*

Poverty and shame will come to him who disdains correction, But he who _regards a rebuke_ will be honored

Proverbs 15:*1*

A _soft answer_ turns away wrath, But a _harsh word_ stirs up anger.

Proverbs 15:*2*

The _tongue_ of the _wise_ uses knowledge rightly, But the _mouth_ of _fools pours_ forth foolishness.

Proverbs 15:4

A _wholesome tongue_ is a tree of life, But the perverseness in it breaks the spirit.

Proverbs *15:*5*

A fool despises his father's instruction, But he who _receives correction_ is prudent.

Proverbs 15:*7*

The lips of the wise disperse knowledge, But the heart of the fool does not do so.

Proverbs 15:*12*

A scoffer does not love one who corrects him, _Nor will he go to the wise._

Proverbs *15:*14*

The heart of him who has understanding _seeks_ knowledge, But the _mouth_ of _fools feeds_ on foolishness.

Proverbs *15:*22*

Without counsel, plans go awry, _But in the multitude of counselors they are established_.

Proverbs 15:23*

A man has joy by the _answer_ of his _mouth_, And a _word spoken_ in due season, how good it is!

Proverbs 15:26
The thoughts of the wicked are an abomination to the LORD, *But the words of the pure are pleasant.*

Proverbs *15:*28*
*The heart of the righteous studies how to answer, **But the mouth of the wicked pours forth evil**.*

Proverbs 15:29*
The LORD is far from the wicked, But He *hears* the prayer of the righteous.

Proverbs *15:*31*
The ear that hears **the rebukes of life, Will abide among the wise.**

Proverbs *15:*32*
He who disdains instruction despises his own soul, But he who *heeds* rebuke gets understanding.

Proverbs *16:*20*
He who *heeds* the *word* wisely will find good, And whoever trusts in the LORD, happy is he.

Proverbs 16:23
The heart of the wise teaches his *mouth*, And adds learning to his *lips*.

Proverbs 17:4
An evildoer gives **heed** to *false lips*; A liar **listens** eagerly to a *spiteful tongue*.

Proverbs 17:7
Excellent speech is not becoming of a fool, Much less *lying lips* to a prince.

Proverbs *17:*27*
He who has knowledge *spares his words*, And a man of understanding is of a calm spirit.

Proverbs 17:28

Even a fool is counted wise when he holds his peace; When he *shuts his lips,* he is considered perceptive.

Proverbs 18:8*

The *words* of a talebearer (gossiper) are like tasty trifles, *And they go down into the inmost body.*

Proverbs 18:*13*

He who *answers* a matter before he **hears** it, It is folly and shame to him.

Proverbs *18:*15*

The heart of the prudent acquires knowledge, And the _ear of the wise_ seeks knowledge.

Proverbs 18:17*

The first one to *plead his cause* seems right, Until his neighbor comes and *examines him.*

Proverbs *19:*20*

Listen to counsel and _receive instruction_, That you may be _wise_ in your latter days.

Proverbs *19:*27*

Cease _listening to instruction_, my son, And you will stray from the _words of knowledge_.

Proverbs 20:12

The **_hearing_ ear** and the seeing eye, The LORD has made them both.

Proverbs 20:*15*

There is gold and a multitude of rubies, But the *lips of knowledge are a precious jewel.*

Proverbs 21:*11*

When the scoffer is punished, the simple is made *wise*; But when the *wise is instructed,* he *receives* knowledge.

Proverbs *21:*13*

Whoever *shuts his ears* **to the cry of the poor Will also cry himself and** *not be heard*.

Proverbs 21:28

A false witness shall perish, But the man who **hears** him will *speak* endlessly.

Proverbs 22:14

The mouth of an immoral woman is a deep pit; He who is abhorred by the LORD will fall there.

(Sayings of the Wise)

Proverbs *22:*17*–*21*

(17)* **Incline your** *ear* **and** *hear* **the** *words* **of the** *wise*, **And apply your heart to my knowledge**.

(18)* For it is a pleasant thing if you keep them within you; Let them all be fixed upon your <u>lips</u>,

(19)* **So that your trust may be in the LORD; I have** *instructed* **you today, even you**.

(20)* Have I not written to you excellent things Of counsels and knowledge,

(21)* **That I may make you know the certainty of the** *words* **of** *truth*, **That you may** *answer words* **of** *truth* **To those who send to you?**

Proverbs 23:9*

Do not *speak* in the **hearing** of a fool, For he will despise the *wisdom of your words*.

Proverbs *23:*12*

Apply your heart to instruction, And your *ears* **to** *words* **of knowledge**.

Proverbs 23:19*

Hear, my son, and be *wise*; And guide your heart in the way.

Proverbs 23:22*

Listen to your father who begot you, And do not despise your mother when she is old.

(Further Wise Sayings of Solomon)

Proverbs 25:8–10

(8) Do not go hastily to court; For what will you do in the end, When your neighbor has put you to shame?

(9) *Debate* your case with your neighbor, And do not *disclose* the secret to another;

(10) Lest he who **hears** it expose your shame, And your reputation be ruined.

Proverbs 25:11

A *word fitly spoken* is like apples of gold In settings of silver.

Proverbs 25:12

Like an earring of gold and an ornament of fine gold Is a wise rebuker to an *obedient ear.*

Proverbs 26:22

The *words* of a talebearer (gossiper) are like tasty trifles, *And they go down into the inmost body*.

Proverbs 26:23

Fervent lips with a wicked heart Are like earthenware covered with silver dross.

Proverbs 26:24*–26

(24)* He who hates, *disguises it with his lips*, And lays up deceit within himself;

(25) When he *speaks* kindly, *do not believe him*, For there are seven abominations in his heart;

(26) Though his hatred is covered by deceit, His wickedness will be revealed before the assembly.

Proverbs *27:*17*

As iron sharpens iron, *So a man sharpens the countenance of his friend.*

Proverbs 28:9

One who turns away his **ear** *from* **hearing** *the law*, Even his prayer is an abomination.

Proverbs 29:1*

He who is often rebuked, and hardens his neck, Will suddenly be destroyed, and that without remedy.

CHAPTER 46

THE LORD, GOD'S WORD, COMMANDMENTS/LAW, GOD'S WILL

What a Life tragedy when individuals, especially those who are "in Christ," fail to gain a deep understanding, appreciation, and over-all acquaintance with our *Creator* and our *Sustainer of Life* (i.e. *Father God*). Equally as sad and unfortunate is one's lack of desire to under-stand the mind and likeness of *Jesus Christ*, **our *Lord***. Failure to gain an in-depth relationship with *Father God* and our *Lord* and *Savior, Jesus Christ*, is akin to missing the primary purpose of one's existence, as well as the greatest privilege available to mankind.

From my perspective, one of the easiest, simplest, and foundational ways to draw near to the *Trinity—Father God, Jesus Christ*, and the *Holy Spirit*—is the basic but all-encompassing practice of reading, studying, meditating, or as I enjoy saying, "marinating" on *God's Word*! *God's Word* serves as a "*lamp to one's feet And a light to one's pathways*" (Psalm 109:105), which provides "*the paths of righteousness*" needed in this earthly Life (Psalms 23). As well as serving and being the compass and "*directional force for one's life and path*" (Proverbs 3:5 and 6). In its purest and simplest form, *God's Word* is the only and meaningful directional narrative, that serves as the purest, simplest, and truthful "**GPS of Life**." What better way than relying on the spoken *Words of God*, captured and beaming forth from the pages of *His Book, the Bible*!

Our challenge, from the most elementary form and fashion, is to just pick up **His Words** as contained in the ***Bible***, and have **His Words** resonate throughout our earthly being via our mind, heart, body, soul, and spirit.

Thus, our duty and daily responsibility is to "*read and meditate on God's Word, day and night*" (Psalms 1:2b and Joshua 1:8). By doing so, I personally believe that the truth of Joshua 1:8b and 9 will become a reality in one's Life: "*For then you will make your way prosperous, and then you will have success. Have I not commanded you? Be strong and of good courage; do not be afraid, nor be dismayed, for the LORD your God is with you wherever you go.*"

Finally, if one desires to make good decisions that *brings one* from extended periods of darkness, then *God's Word* is the ultimate light that shines upon one's pathway. Our challenge and opportunity is to just "*do it*," as Psalms 119:105 states so clearly that: "***God's Word*** *is a lamp to my feet, and a light to my path*"! As such:

(1) If one is in need of stability that will keep one from falling, then ***God's Word*** is a rock beneath one's feet (Matthew 7:24);

(2) If one desires to make decisions that will keep one from darkness, then ***God's Word*** is the light that shines upon one's pathway (Psalms 119:105);

(3) If one desires to feed upon food that will satisfy one's hungry heart, then ***God's Word*** is the bread of Life (Jeremiah 15:16);

(4) If one desires to walk on the pathway of Holiness, then ***God's Word*** will keep one from the snares of sin (Psalm 119:11);

(5) If one desires to live a Life that will be a blessing to others, now as well as in eternity, then ***God's Word*** will bring great rewards (Psalm 19:9–11);

(6) If one is standing for righteousness in the midst of spiritual battles, then **God's Word** is the primary, if not most powerful, weapon in the Armor of God (Ephesians 6:17); and

(7) If one needs to speak clearly and boldly for what one believes, then *God's Word* is righteousness and truth (Psalm 119:172)!

God's Word is *Truth*, *Righteousness*, and *Light* that serves as the *compass* and **GPS** of and for one's **LIFE**!

(The Beginning of Knowledge)

Proverbs *1:*7*

The *fear of the LORD* is the beginning of knowledge, But fools despise wisdom and instruction.

(The Value of Wisdom)

Proverbs *2:1*–*9* and 16–22

(1)* My son, if you receive my words, And treasure my **commands** within you,

(2)* **So that you incline your ear to wisdom, And apply your heart to understanding;**

(3)* Yes, if you cry out for discernment, And lift up your voice for understanding,

(4)* If you seek her (*Wisdom*) as silver, And search for her (*Wisdom*) as for hidden treasures;

(5)* **Then you will understand the *fear of the LORD*, And find the *knowledge of God*.**

(6)* **For *the LORD* gives wisdom; From *His* mouth come knowledge and understanding;**

(7)* *He* **stores up sound wisdom for the upright;** *He* **is a shield to those who walk uprightly;**

(8)* *He* **guards the paths of justice, And preserves the way of** *His* **saints.**

(9)* **Then you will understand righteousness and justice, Equity and every good path**.

(16) To deliver you from the immoral woman, From the seductress who flatters with her words,

(17) Who forsakes the companion of her youth, **_And forgets the covenant of her God_**.

(18) For her house leads down to death, And her paths to the dead;

(19) None who go to her return, Nor do they regain the paths of life—

(20)* **So you may walk in the way of goodness, And keep to the paths of righteousness**.

(21)* **For the upright will dwell in the land, And the blameless will remain in it;**

(22) But the wicked will be cut off from the earth, And the unfaithful will be uprooted from it.

(Guidance for the Young)

Proverbs 3:1–2

My son, **_do not forget my law_**, But let your heart **_keep my commands_**; For length of days and long life And peace they will add to you.

Proverbs *3:*3*–4*

Let not mercy and truth forsake you; Bind them around your neck, Write them on the tablet of your heart, And so find favor and high esteem In the sight of **_God_** and man.

Proverbs *3:*5*–*6*

Trust in the **LORD** with all your heart, And lean not on your own understanding; In all your ways acknowledge **Him**, and **He** shall direct your paths.

Proverbs 3:7*–8*

Do not be wise in your own eyes; **_Fear the LORD_** and depart from evil. It will be health to your flesh, And strength to your bones.

Proverbs *3:*9*–*10*
Honor the LORD with your possessions, And with the first fruits of all your increase; So your barns will be filled with plenty, And your vats will overflow with new wine.

Proverbs *3:*11*–*12*
My son, do not despise the chastening of *the LORD*, Nor detest *His* correction; For whom *the LORD* loves *He* corrects, Just as a father the son in whom he delights.

Proverbs 3:19–20
The LORD by wisdom founded the earth; By understanding *He* established the heavens; By *His* knowledge the depths were broken up, And clouds drop down the dew.

Proverbs 3:25–26
Do not be afraid of sudden terror, Nor of trouble from the wicked when it comes; For *the LORD* will be your confidence, And will keep your foot from being caught.

Proverbs 3:31–32*
Do not envy the oppressor, And choose none of his ways; For the perverse person is an abomination to *the LORD*, But *His* secret counsel is with the upright.

Proverbs 3:33
The curse of *the LORD* is on the house of the wicked, But *He* blesses the home of the just.

Proverbs *3:*34*
Surely *He* scorns the scornful, But gives grace to the humble.

(Security in Wisdom)

Proverbs *4 :*4*–*5*
He also taught me, **and said to me:** *"Let your heart retain my words,*

keep my commands, and live. Get wisdom! Get understanding! Do not forget, nor turn away from the words of my mouth.

(The Peril of Adultery)

Proverbs *5:*21*–*23*

(21)* **For the ways of man are before the eyes of _the LORD_, And _He_ ponders all his paths.**

(22)* **His own iniquities entrap the wicked man, And he is caught in the cords of his sin.**

(23)* **He shall die for lack of instruction, And in the greatness of his folly he shall go astray.**

(The Wicked Man)

Proverbs 6:16–19

(16) These six things _the LORD_ hates, Yes, seven are an abomination to _Him_:

(17) A proud look, A lying tongue, Hands that shed innocent blood,

(18) A heart that devises wicked plans, Feet that are swift in running to evil,

(19) A false witness who speaks lies, And one who sows discord among brethren.

(Beware of Adultery)

Proverbs *6:20*– 29*

(20)* **My son, _keep your father's command_, And _do not forsake the law_** of your mother.

(21) *Bind them continually upon your heart; Tie them around your neck.*

(22) When you roam, they will lead you; When you sleep, they will keep you; And when you awake, they will speak with you.

(23)* **For the _commandment is a lamp_, And the _law a light; Reproofs of instruction_ are the way of life,**

(24)* To keep you from the evil woman, From the flattering tongue of a seductress.

(25) Do not lust after her beauty in your heart, Nor let her allure you with her eyelids.

(26) For by means of a harlot A man is reduced to a crust of bread; And an adulteress will prey upon his precious life.

(27) Can a man take fire to his bosom, And his clothes not be burned?

(28) Can one walk on hot coals, And his feet not be seared?

(29)* So is he who goes in to his neighbor's wife; Whoever touches her shall not be innocent.

Proverbs *7:*1*–5*

(1)* **My son, _keep my words_, And _treasure my commands_ within you.**

(2)* _**Keep my commands and live,** And **my law as the apple of your eye**_.

(3)* _**Bind them on your fingers; Write them on the tablet of your heart**_.

(4)* **Say to wisdom, "You are my sister," And call understanding your nearest kin,**

(5)* That they may keep you from the immortal woman, From the seductress who flatters with her words.

(The Excellence of Wisdom)

Proverbs *8:22–31 and *32*–36*

(22) "**_The LORD_** possessed me at the beginning of **_His way_**, Before **_His_** works of old.

(23) I have been established from everlasting, From the beginning, before there was ever an earth.

(24) When there were no depths I was brought forth, When there were no foundations abounding with water.

(25) Before the mountains were settled, Before the hills, I was brought forth;

(26) While as yet **_He_** had not made the earth or the fields, Or the primal dust of the world.

(27) When *He* prepared the heavens, I was there, When *He* drew a circle on the face of the deep,

(28) When *He* established the clouds above, When *He* strengthened the fountains of the deep,

(29) When *He* assigned to the sea its limit, So that the waters would not transgress *His* command, When *He* marked out the foundations of the earth,

(30) Then I was beside *Him* as a master craftsman; And I was daily *His* delight, Rejoicing always before *Him*,

(31) Rejoicing in *His* inhabited world, And my delight was with the sons of men.

(32)* **"Now therefore, listen to me (Wisdom), my children, For blessed are those who keep my ways.**

(33)* **Hear instruction and be wise, And do not disdain it.**

(34)* Blessed is the man who listens to me (Wisdom), Watching daily at my gates, Waiting at the posts of my doors.

(35)* **For whoever finds me (wisdom) finds *life*, And obtains favor from *the LORD*;**

(36)* But he who sins against me (wisdom) wrongs his own *soul*; All those who hate me love death."

(The Way of Wisdom)

Proverbs *9:7–12

(7) "He who corrects a scoffer gets shame for himself, And he who rebukes a wicked man only harms himself.

(8)* **Do not correct a scoffer, lest he hate you; Rebuke a wise man, and he will love you.**

(9)* **Give instruction to a wise man, and he will be still wiser; Teach a just man, and he will increase in learning.**

(10)* **"The *fear of the LORD* is the beginning of wisdom, And the knowledge of the *Holy One* is understanding.**

(11)   For by me your days will be multiplied, And years of life will be added to you.

(12)   If you are wise, you are wise for yourself, And if you scoff, you will bear it alone."

(Wise Sayings of Wisdom)

Proverbs 10:2*–3*

Treasures of wickedness profit nothing, But righteous delivers from death. *The LORD* will not allow the righteous soul to famish, But *He* casts away the desire of the wicked.

Proverbs *10:*22*

The *blessing of the LORD* makes one rich, And *He* adds no sorrow with it.

Proverbs 10:*29*

The *way of the LORD* is strength for the upright, But destruction will come to the workers of iniquity.

Proverbs 11:1

Dishonest scales are an abomination to *the LORD*, But a just weight is *His* delight.

Proverbs 11:20

Those who are of a perverse heart are an abomination to *the LORD*, But the blameless in their ways are *His* delight.

Proverbs 12:2*

A good man obtains favor from *the LORD*, But a man of wicked intentions *He* will condemn.

Proverbs *12:*22*

Lying lips are an abomination to *the LORD*, But those who deal truthfully are *His delight*.

Proverbs 13:*13*

He who despises **_the word_** will be destroyed, But he who fears the **_com-mandment_** will be rewarded.

Proverbs 13:14

The **_law_** of the wise is a fountain of life, To turn one away from the snares of death.

Proverbs 14:2

He who walks in his uprightness **_fears the LORD_**, But he who is perverse in his ways despises **_Him_**.

Proverbs 14:19

The evil will _bow before the good_, And the wicked at _the gates of the righteous._

Proverbs 14:26*

In the **_fear of the LORD_** there is strong confidence, And **_His_** children will have a place of refuge.

Proverbs 14:27

The **_fear of the LORD_** is a fountain of life. To turn one away from the snares of death.

Proverbs *14:*31*

He who oppresses the poor reproaches his _Maker_, But he who _honors_ _Him_ has mercy on the needy.

Proverbs 15:3*

The **_eyes of the LORD_** are in every place, Keeping watch on the evil and the good.

Proverbs 15:8

The sacrifice of the wicked is an abomination to **_the LORD_**, But the prayer of the upright is **_His delight._**

Proverbs 15:9*
The way of the wicked is an abomination to **_the LORD_**, But **_He_** loves him who follows righteousness.

Proverbs 15:11
Hell and Destruction are before **_the LORD_**; So how much more the hearts of the sons of men.

Proverbs 15:25*
The LORD will destroy the house of the proud, But **_He_** will establish the boundary of the widow.

Proverbs 15:29*
The LORD is far from the wicked, But **_He_** hears the prayer of the righteous.

Proverbs *16:*1*
The preparations of the heart belong to man, But the answer of the tongue is from _the LORD_.

Proverbs 16:*2*
All the ways of a man are pure in his own eyes, But **_the LORD_** weighs the spirits.

Proverbs *16:*3*
Commit your works to _the LORD_, And your thoughts will be established.

Proverbs 16:4
The LORD has made all for **_Himself_**, Yes, even the wicked for the day of doom.

Proverbs 16:7
When a man's ways please **_the LORD_**, _He makes even his enemies to be at peace with him._

Proverbs *16:*9*
A man's heart plans his way, _But the LORD directs his steps._

Proverbs 16:11
*Honest weights and scales are **the LORD's**: All the weights in the bag are **His work***.

Proverbs *16:*20*
He who *heeds the word wisely* will find good, And whoever trusts in *the LORD*, happy is he.

Proverbs *16:*25*
There is a *way* that seems right to a man, But in the end is the *way* of death.

Proverbs 16:33
The lot is cast into the lap, But its every decision is from ***the LORD***.

Proverbs 17:*3*
The refining pot is for silver and the furnace for gold, But ***the LORD*** tests the hearts.

Proverbs 17:5*
He who mocks the poor reproaches his ***Maker***; He who is glad at calamity will not go unpunished.

Proverbs *18:*10*
The name of *the LORD* is a strong tower; The righteous run to it and are safe.

Proverbs *18:*22*
He who finds a wife finds a good thing, And obtains favor from *the LORD*.

Proverbs *18:*24*
A man who has friends must himself be friendly, *But there is a friend who sticks closer that a brother*.

Proverbs *19:*14*

Houses and riches are an inheritance from fathers, But a prudent wife is from _the LORD_.

Proverbs 19:16*

He who **_keeps the commandments_** keeps his soul, But he who is careless of his ways will die.

Proverbs *19:*17*

He who has pity on the poor lends to _the LORD_, And _He_ will pay back what he has given.

Proverbs *19:*21*

There are many plans in a man's heart, Nevertheless, _the LORD's_ counsel—that will stand.

Proverbs 20:12

The hearing ear and the seeing eye, _**The LORD** has made them both._

Proverbs 20:22

Do not say, "I will recompense evil"; _Wait for **the LORD**, and **He will save you**._

Proverbs *20:*24*

A man's steps are of **the LORD**; **How then can a man understand his own way?**

Proverbs 20:25

It is a snare for a man to devote rashly something as **_holy_**, And afterward to reconsider his vows.

Proverbs 20:27*

The spirit of a man is a lamp of **_the LORD_**, Searching all the inner depths of his heart.

Proverbs 21:1

The king's heart is in the hand of **the LORD**, Like the rivers of water; **He** turns it wherever **He** wishes.

Proverbs *21*:2*

Every way of a man is right in his own eyes, *But the LORD* weighs the hearts.

Proverbs 21:*3*

To do righteousness and justice Is more acceptable to **the LORD** than sacrifice.

Proverbs 21:12*

The righteous **God** wisely considers the house of the wicked, Overthrowing the wicked for their wickedness.

Proverbs 21:22

A *wise* man *scales* the city of the *mighty*, And brings down the trusted *stronghold*.

Proverbs 21:30*

There is no wisdom or understanding Or counsel against **the LORD**.

Proverbs 21:*31*

The horse is prepared for the day of battle, *But deliverance is of **the LORD***.

Proverbs 22:2*

The rich and the poor have this in common, ***The LORD** is the maker of them all.*

Proverbs 22:*12*

The ***eyes of the LORD*** preserve knowledge, But **He** overthrows the words of the faithless.

Proverbs 22:14

The mouth of an immoral woman is a deep pit; He who is abhorred by **the LORD** will fall there.

(Sayings of the Wise)

Proverbs *22:*17*–*21*

(17)* **Incline your ear and hear the words of the wise, And apply your heart to my knowledge;**

(18)* For it is a pleasant thing if you keep them within you; Let them all be fixed upon your lips,

(19)* **So that your *trust may be in the LORD*; I have instructed you today, even you.**

(20)* Have I not written to you excellent things Of counsels and knowledge,

(21)* **That I may make you know the certainty of the words of truth, That you may answer words of truth To those who send to you.**

Proverbs *22:*22*–*23*

Do not rob the poor because he is poor, Nor oppress the afflicted at the gate; For *the LORD* will plead their cause, And plunder the soul of those who plunder them.

Proverbs 22:28

Do not remove the *ancient landmark* Which your fathers have set.

Proverbs 23:10–11

Do not remove the *ancient landmark*, Nor enter the fields of the fatherless; For their ***Redeemer*** is mighty; ***He*** will plead their cause against you.

Proverbs 23:17–18

Do not let your heart envy sinners, *But be zealous for **the fear of the LORD** all the day; For surely there is a hereafter, And your hope will not be cut off.*

Proverbs 23:19*

Hear, my son, and be wise; And guide your heart in ***the way***.

Proverbs 24:11–12*

Deliver those who are drawn toward death, And hold back those stumbling to the slaughter. If you say, "Surely we did not know this," Does not

He who weighs the hearts consider it? *He* who keeps your soul, does *He* know it? And will *He* not render to each man according to his deeds?

Proverbs *24:*17*–*18*

Do not rejoice when your enemy falls, And do not let your heart be glad when he stumbles; Lest *the LORD* see it, and it displease *Him*, And *He* turn away *His* wrath from him.

(Further Wise Sayings of Solomon)

Proverbs 25:2

It is the ***glory of God*** to conceal a matter, But the glory of kings is to search out a matter.

Proverbs *25:*21*–*22*

If your enemy is hungry, give him bread to eat; And if he is thirsty, give him water to drink: **For so you will heap coals of fire on his head, *And the LORD* will reward you.**

Proverbs 25:25

As cold water to a weary soul, So is *good news* from a far country.

Proverbs 28:4

Those who ***forsake the law*** praise the wicked, But such as ***keep the law*** contend with them.

Proverbs 28:5*

Evil men do not understand justice, But those who ***seek the LORD*** understand all.

Proverbs 28:7*

Whoever ***keeps the law*** is a discerning son, But a companion of gluttons shames his father.

Proverbs 28:9

One who turns away his ear from ***hearing the law***, Even his prayer is an abomination.

Proverbs 28:14*

Happy is the man who is always _reverent_, But he who hardens his heart will fall into calamity.

Proverbs 28:*25*

He who is of a proud heart stirs up strife, But he who ***trusts in the LORD*** will be prospered.

Proverbs 28:26*

He who trusts in his own heart is a fool, _But whoever walks wisely_ will be _delivered._

Proverbs 29:13*

The poor man and the oppressor have this in common: ***The LORD*** gives light to the eyes of both.

Proverbs 29:18*

Where there is no ***revelation***, the people cast off restraint; But happy is he who ***keeps the law***.

Proverbs 29:25*

The fear of man brings a snare, But whoever ***trusts in the LORD*** shall be safe.

Proverbs 29:26

Many seek the ruler's favor, _But the justice for man comes from_ ***the LORD***.

Proverbs 29:27*

An unjust man is an abomination to the righteous, And he who is ***upright in the way*** is an abomination to the wicked.

(The Wisdom of Agur)

Proverbs *30:2–4, *5*–6, and 7*–9*

(2)   Surely I am more stupid than any man, And do not have the understanding of a man.

(3)   I neither learned wisdom Nor have knowledge of **the Holy One**.

(4)   Who has ascended into heaven, or descended? Who has gathered the wind in **His** fists? Who has bound the waters in a garment? Who has established all the ends of the earth? What is **His** name, and what is **His Son's** name, If you know?

(5)*   ***Every word of God is pure***; ***He** is a shield* to those who put *their trust in Him*.

(6)   *Do not add to* **His words**, lest **He** rebuke you, and you be found a liar.

(Prayer of Devotion)

(7)*   Two things I request of You (Deprive me not before I die):

(8)*   Remove falsehood and lies far from me; Give me neither poverty nor riches—Feed me with the food allotted to me;

(9)*   Lest I be full and deny **You**, And say, "Who is **the LORD**?" Or lest I be poor and steal, And profane the name of **my God**.

(The Virtuous Wife)

Proverbs *31:29–31

(29)   "Many daughters have done well, But you excel them all."

(30)*   **Charm is deceitful and beauty is passing, But a woman who *fears the LORD*, she shall be praised.**

(31)   Give her of the fruit of her hands, And let her own works praise her in the gates.

CHAPTER 47

LOVE, LOVING

From my perspective, there is no greater human attribute, expression, or value of greater importance between individuals, as well as between Father God and man, than "***LOVE***"! In fact, I would contend that there is no greater spiritual attribute, value, or Godly quality than "***LOVE***"! One only has to read, meditate, and marinate on God's Word to read, hear, and feel the awesome "***LOVE***" that Father God has for His human creation. From Genesis 1:1 to Revelation 22:21, we read copious truths expressed by Father God and in God's Word regarding how awesome His "***LOVE***" is for us!

When one thinks about the essence of Father God's "***LOVE***," one cannot help but be reminded of Father God's unselfish and sacrificial "***LOVE***" that He has displayed through the ages, as well as through the advent of eternity. For example, just marinate on John 3:16, which states: "*For God so 'loved' the world that He gave His only begotten Son that whoever believes in Him should not perish but have everlasting life*". This truth is <u>underscored</u>, **bolded**, and *italicized* by meditating and marinating on the subsequent Scripture verse (i.e. John 3:17), which states: "*For God did not send His Son into the world to condemn the world,* ***but that the world through Him might be saved***"! Now from my perspective, if that is not "***LOVE***," then I do not know what is!

Thirdly, and from my humble viewpoint, Father God has provided the "best in class or world-class" template and/or operations manual for living out "*LOVE*," and that is the "*LOVE*" blueprint echoed in 1 Corinthians 13! Think about it: "*and though I have all faith, so that I could move mountains…but have not 'LOVE,' I am nothing*" (v. 2). Or what about these novel behavioral truths: "'*LOVE' suffers long and is kind; 'LOVE' does not envy; 'LOVE' does not parade itself, is not puffed up*" (v. 4); and/or: "*does not behave rudely, does not seek its own, is not provoked, thinks no evil*" (v. 5). And of course, one needs to add some additional seasonings to marinate on the concept of "*LOVE*" as richly stated in verses 6 to 8—by adding a little pepper, as stated in verse 6: "*does not rejoice in iniquity, but rejoices in the truth*"; and some salt, as stated in verse 7: "*bears all things, believes all things, hopes all things, endures all things*"; and of course, one cannot forget the special ingredient or secret sauce that is contained in verse 8: "'*LOVE' never fails…*"! Then as one brings this unique and special blessing out of the oven, we hear, feel, and experience the aroma that our Heavenly Father has provided, whereby He states so eloquently in verse 13: "*And now abide faith, hope, 'LOVE,' these three; but the greatest of these is 'LOVE'*"! Now, how awesome is this!

Fourthly, as one studies 1 John 3:10–23, one gains an outstanding manifesto in which to practice the primer of "*LOVE*." In studying these biblical truths regarding "*LOVE*," one is taught that "*LOVE*" of one's brothers and sisters is a divine obligation. "*LOVE*" used in these biblical truths is not so much used in the sense of friendliness or mere human affection, but it is what one would call "**divine '*LOVE*.'**" One might say it is trying to emulate how Christ "*LOVED*" us. If one attempts to analyze such "*LOVE*" in its simplest form, one comes away with a greater understanding and appreciation that **Christlike** "*LOVE*" cannot be achieved in one's own personal strength, but only accomplished through the empowerment of the Holy Spirit.

As an example, below are listed applicable verses from 1 John 3:10–23 that support the foundational principles of both an imperative and outworking of "*LOVE*":

- (v. 10): "*In this the children of God and the children of the devil are manifest: 'Whoever does not practice righteousness is not of God, nor is he who does not **love** his brother'*";
- (v. 11): "*For this is the message that you heard from the beginning, 'that we should **love** one another'*";
- (vv. 13 and 14): "*Do not marvel, my brethren, if the world hates you. 'We know that we have passed from death to life, because we **love** the brethren. He who does not **love** his brother abides in death'*";
- (v. 16): "*By this we know **love**, because He laid down His life for us. And we also ought to lay down our lives for the brethren*";
- (v. 17): "*But whoever has this world's goods, and sees his brother in need, and shuts up his heart from him, how does the **love** of God abide in him?*"
- (v. 18): "*My little children, 'let us not **love** in word or in tongue, but in deed and in truth'*";
- (vv. 22 and 23): "*And whatever we ask we receive from Him, because we keep His commandments and do those things that are pleasing in His sight. And this is His commandment: 'that we should believe on the name of His Son Jesus Christ and **love** one another, as He gave us commandment'*"!

This last biblical verse, principle, and truth clearly summarizes all of the New Testament commandments, as it uniquely states what one's responsibilities and duties to Father God, as well as to one's fellow Christians. In summary, one's primary duty and responsibility is to trust in the Lord Jesus Christ, followed by one's secondary act of true faith and right conduct, and that is to "***LOVE***" one another! Father God does not make it any clearer than that!

Finally, 1 John 4, especially verses 7–21, specifically highlights God's truth in "***LOVE***," as well as one's responsibility to have "***LOVE***" for one's brother and sister! As one studies, meditates, and marinates on these scriptures, one cannot help but to come to a fuller, deeper, and richer understanding that "*LOVE*" is the primary characteristic of Father God; as well as to recognize the depth of "*LOVE*" that Father God has for all mankind, especially for those who are "in Christ." Accordingly, as one studies the following biblical verses, try to better understand the full nature of Father God, as one recognizes that God is "*LOVE*":

- (v. 7): "*Beloved, let us **love** one another, for **love** is of God; and everyone who **loves** is born of God and knows God*";
- (v. 8): "*He who does not **love** does not know God, for God is **love***";
- (v. 9): "*In this the **love** of God was manifested toward us, that God has sent His only begotten Son into the world, that we might live through Him*";
- (v. 10): "*In this is **love**, not that we **loved** God, but that He **loved** us and sent His Son to be the propitiation for our sins*";
- (v. 11): "***Beloved**, if God so **loved** us, we also ought to **love** one another.*"

Additionally, as one studies, meditates, and marinates specifically on verses 12–16, one can better understand that when one "*LOVES*" one another, the invisible Father God reveals Himself to others through us, as well as shows others the completeness of Father God's "*LOVE*." Accordingly, one's righteous responsibility is to faithfully "*LOVE*" the people that Father God has given to us to *LOVE*. God's Word states:

- (v. 12): "*No one has seen God at any time. 'If we **love** one another, God abides in us, and His **love** has been perfected in us*";
- (v. 13): "*By this we know that we abide in Him, and He in us, because He has given us of His Spirit*";
- (v. 14): "*And we have seen and testify that the Father has sent the Son as Savior of the world*";
- (v. 15): "*Whoever confesses that Jesus is the Son of God, God abides in him, and he in God*";
- (v. 16): "*And we have known and believed the **love** that God has*

*for us. God is **LOVE**, and he who abides in **love** abides in God, and God in him."*

And in conclusion, what better way to summarize the consummation of "___**LOVE**___" than with studying, meditating, and marinating on verses 17–21, which admonish one in this specific truth—"*There is no fear in love*"! as summarized as follows:

- (v. 17): "___**Love** has been perfected among us in this: that we may have boldness in the day of judgment; because as He is, so are we in this world___";
- (v. 18): "*There is no fear in **love**; but perfect **love** casts out fear, because fear involves torment. But he who fears has not been made perfect in **love***";
- (v. 19): "*We **love** Him because He first **loved** us*";
- (v. 20): "*If someone says, 'I **love** God,' and hates his brother, he is a liar; for he who does not **love** his brother whom he has seen, how can he **love** God whom he has not seen?*"; finally,
- (v. 21): "*And this commandment we have from Him: 'that he who **loves** God must **love** his brother also.*"

May one never separate, Wisdom from ___**LOVE**___!

(The Call of Wisdom)

Proverbs *1:*20*–27

(20)* **Wisdom calls aloud outside; She raises her voice in the open squares**.

(21) She cries out in the chief concourses, At the openings of the gates in the city She speaks her words:

(22) "How long, you simple ones, will you ___*love*___ simplicity? For scorners delight in their scorning, And fools hate knowledge.

(23) Turn at my rebuke; Surely I will pour out my spirit on you; I will make my words known to you.

(24) Because I have called and you refused, I have stretched out my hand and no one regarded,

(25) Because you disdained all my counsel, And would have none of my rebuke,

(26) I also will laugh at your calamity; I will mock when your terror comes,

(27) When your terror comes like a storm, And your destruction comes like a whirlwind, When distress and anguish come upon you.

(Guidance for the Young)

Proverbs *3:*3*– 4*

Let not mercy and truth forsake you: **Bind them around your neck, Write them on the tablet of your heart**, *And so find favor and high esteem* In the sight of God and man.

Proverbs *3:*11*–*12*

My son, do not despise the chastening of the LORD, Nor detest His correction; For whom the LORD *loves* **He corrects, Just as a father the son in whom he** *delights*.

(Security in Wisdom)

Proverbs *4:1*–9

(1)* Hear, my children, the *instruction* of a father, And give attention to know understanding;

(2)* For I give you good doctrine: Do not forsake my law.

(3) When I was my father's son, Tender and the only one in the sight of my mother,

(4)* **He also taught me, and said to me: "Let your heart retain my words; Keep my commands, and live.**

(5)* **Get *wisdom*! Get understanding! Do not forget, nor turn away from the words of my mouth.**

(6)* **Do not forsake *her* (*wisdom*), and *she* will preserve you; <u>Love</u> *her*, and *she* will keep you.**

(7)* ***Wisdom* is the principal thing; Therefore, get *wisdom*, And in all your getting, get understanding.**

(8) Exalt *her* (*wisdom*), and *she* will promote you; *She* will bring you honor, when you embrace *her*.

(9) *She* will place on your head an ornament of grace; A crown of glory *she* will deliver to you."

(The Peril of Adultery)

Proverbs *5:*15*–20

(15)* **Drink water from your own cistern, And running water from your own well.**

(16) Should your fountains be dispersed abroad, Streams of water in the streets?

(17) Let them be only your own, And not for strangers with you.

(18) Let your fountain be blessed, And rejoice with the wife of your youth.

(19)* As a ***loving*** deer and a grateful doe, Let her breasts satisfy you at all times; And always be enraptured with her ***love***.

(20) For why should you, my son, be enraptured by an immoral woman, And be embraced in the arms of a seductress?

(The Crafty Harlot)

Proverbs 7:10–20

(10) And there a woman met him, With the attire of a harlot, and a crafty heart.

(11) She was loud and rebellious, Her feet would not stay at home.

(12) At times she was outside, at times in the open square, Lurking at every corner.

(13) So she caught him and kissed him; With an impudent face she said to him:

(14) "I have peace offerings with me; Today I have paid my vows.

(15) So I came out to meet you, Diligently to seek your face. And I have found you.

(16) I have spread my bed with tapestry, Colored coverings of Egyptian linen.

(17) I have perfumed my bed With myrrh, aloes, and cinnamon.

(18) Come, let us take our fill of **_love_** until morning; Let us _delight_ ourselves with **_love_**.

(19) For my husband is not at home; He has gone on a long journey;

(20) He has taken a bag of money with him, And will come home on the appointed day."

(The Excellence of Wisdom)

<u>Proverbs *8:*17*–21* and *32*–36*</u>

(17)* _I (wisdom)_ <u>**love**</u> **those who** <u>_love me_</u>**, And those who seek** _me_ **diligently will find** _me_**.**

(18) Riches and honor are with _me_, Enduring riches and righteousness.

(19)* _My_ fruit is better than gold, yes, than fine gold, Any _my_ revenue than choice silver.

(20)* _I (wisdom)_ traverse the way of righteousness, In the midst of the paths of justice,

(21)* That _I (wisdom)_ may cause those who <u>**_love_**</u> me _(wisdom)_ to inherit wealth, That _I (wisdom)_ may fill their treasuries.

(32)* **"Now therefore, listen to me _(wisdom)_, my children, For blessed are those who keep my ways.**

(33)* **Here instruction and be** _wise_**, And do not disdain it.**

(34)* **Blessed is the man who listens to me, Watching daily at my gates, Waiting at the posts of my doors.**

(35)* **For whoever finds me (*wisdom*) finds life, And obtains favor from the LORD;**

(36)* But he who sins against me (*wisdom/the Lord*) wrongs his own soul; All those who hate me ___love___ death."

(The Way of Wisdom)

Proverbs *9:7–12

(7) "He who corrects a scoffer gets shame for himself, And he who rebukes a wicked man only harms himself.

(8)* Do not correct a scoffer, lest he hate you; **Rebuke a *wise* man, and he will ___love___ you.**

(9)* **Give instruction to a *wise* man, and he will be still wiser; Teach a just man, and he will increase in learning.**

(10)* **"The fear of the LORD is the beginning of *wisdom*, And the knowledge of the Holy One is understanding.**

(11) For by me your days will be multiplied, And years of life will be added to you.

(12) If you are *wise*, you are *wise* for yourself, And if you scoff, you bear it alone."

(Wise Sayings of Solomon)

Proverbs *10:*12*
Hatred stirs up strife, But ___love___ covers all sins.

Proverbs 11:22
As a ring of gold in a swine's snout, So is a ___lovely___ woman who lacks discretion.

Proverbs *12:*1*
Whoever ___loves___ instruction ___loves___ knowledge, But he who hates correction is stupid.

Proverbs 12:4*

An excellent wife is the crown of her husband, But she who causes shame is like rottenness in his bones.

Proverbs 12:14

A man will be satisfied with good by the *fruit of his mouth*, And the recompense of a man's hands will be rendered to him.

Proverbs *13:*22*

A good man leaves an inheritance to his children's children, But the wealth of the sinner is stored up for the righteous.

Proverbs *13:*24*

He who spares his rod hates his son, But he who _loves_ him disciplines him promptly.

Proverbs 15:*9*

The way of the wicked is an abomination to the LORD, But He **_loves_** him who follows righteousness.

Proverbs 15:*12*

A scoffer does not **_love_** one who corrects him, Nor will he go to the wise.

Proverbs 15:17

Better is a dinner of herbs where **_love_** is, Than a fatted calf with hatred.

Proverbs 15:*20*

A wise son makes a father glad, But a foolish man despises his mother.

Proverbs 16:13*

Righteous lips are the *delight* of kings, And they **_love_** him who speaks what is right.

Proverbs 17:6*

Children's children are the crown of old men, And the glory of children is their father.

Proverbs *17:*9*
He who covers a transgression seeks _love_, But he who repeats a matter separates friends.

Proverbs *17:*17*
A friend _loves_ at all times, And a brother is born for adversity.

Proverbs 17:19*
He who **_loves_** transgression **_loves_** strife, And he who exalts his gate seeks destruction.

Proverbs 17:*25*
A foolish son is a grief to his father, And bitterness to her who bore him.

Proverbs 18:21
Death and life are in the power of the tongue, And those who **_love_** it will eat its fruit.

Proverbs *18:*22*
He who finds a wife finds a good thing, **And obtains favor from the LORD.**

Proverbs *18:*24*
A man who has friends must himself be friendly, _But there is a friend who sticks closer than a brother_.

Proverbs 19:*8*
He who gets wisdom **_loves_** his own soul; He who keeps understanding will find good.

Proverbs 19:*13*
A foolish son is the ruin of his father, And the contentions of a wife are a continual dripping.

Proverbs *19:*14*
Houses and riches are an inheritance from fathers, _But a prudent wife is from the LORD_.

Proverbs 19:18
Chasten your son while there is hope, And do not set your heart on his destruction.

Proverbs 19:26
He who mistreats his father and chases away his mother Is a son who causes shame and brings reproach.

Proverbs 20:*13*
Do not **_love_** sleep, lest you come to poverty; Open your eyes, and you will be satisfied with bread.

Proverbs 20:20
Whoever curses his father or his mother, His lamp will be put out in deep darkness.

Proverbs 20:28
Mercy and truth preserve the king, And by **_loving kindness_** he upholds his throne.

Proverbs *21:*9*
Better to dwell in a corner of a housetop, *Than in a house shared with a contentious woman.*

Proverbs 21:17*
He who **_loves_** pleasure will be a poor man; He who **_loves_** wine and oil will not be rich.

Proverbs *21:*19*
Better to dwell in the wilderness, *Than with a contentious and angry woman.*

Proverbs 22:*1*
A good name is to be chosen rather than great riches, **_Loving_** favor rather than silver and gold.

Proverbs *22:*6*
Train up a child in the way he should go, **And when he is old he will not depart from it.**

Proverbs 22:11
He who **_loves_** purity of heart And has grace on his lips, The king will be his friend.

(Biblical Truths of Parental Love)

Proverbs *22:*15*
Foolishness is bound up in the heart of a child; The rod of correction will drive it far from him.

(Sayings of the Wise)

Proverbs *23:*13*–14*, *15*–*16*, 19*–21, 22*, 24–25, and 26*–28

(13)* **_Do not withhold correction from a child, For if you beat him with a rod, he will not die._**

(14)* *You shall beat him with a rod, And deliver his soul from hell.*

(15)* **_My son, if your heart is wise, My heart will rejoice—indeed, I myself;_**

(16)* **_Yes, my inmost being will rejoice When your lips speak right things_**.

(19)* *Hear, my son, and be wise; And guide your heart in the way.*

(20) Do not mix with winebibbers, Or with gluttonous eaters of meat;

(21) For the drunkard and the glutton will come to poverty, And drowsiness will clothe a man with rags.

(22)* *Listen to your father who begot you, And do not despise your mother when she is old.*

(24)   *The father of the righteous will greatly rejoice, And he who begets a wise child will delight in him.*

(25)   *Let your father and your mother be glad, And let her who bore you rejoice.*

(26)*   *My son, give me your heart, And let your eyes observe my ways.*

(27)   For a harlot is a deep pit, And a seductress is a narrow well.

(28)   She also lies in wait as for a victim, And increases the unfaithful among men.

(Further Sayings of Solomon)

Proverbs *25:*21*–*22*

If your enemy is hungry, give him bread to eat, And if he is thirsty, give him water to drink; For so you will heap coals of fire on his head, And the LORD will reward you.

Proverbs *25:*24*

It is better to dwell in a corner of a housetop, *Than in a house shared with a contentious woman*.

Proverbs 27:5*

Open rebuke is better Than ***love*** carefully concealed.

Proverbs *27:*6*

***Faithful are the wounds of a friend*, But the kisses of an enemy are deceitful.**

Proverbs 27:*9*

Ointment and perfume *delight* the heart, *And the sweetness of a man's friend gives delight by hearty counsel.*

Proverbs 27:10

Do not forsake your own friend or your father's friend, Nor go to your brother's house in the day of your calamity; *Better is a neighbor nearby than a brother far away.*

Proverbs 27:11
My son, be wise, and make my heart glad, That I may answer him who reproaches me.

Proverbs *28:*23*
He who rebukes a man will find more favor afterward Than he who flatters with the tongue.

Proverbs *29:*3*
Whoever *loves* wisdom makes his father rejoice, **But a companion of harlots wastes his wealth.**

Proverbs 29:13*
The poor man and the oppressor have this in common: *The LORD gives light to the eyes of both.*

Proverbs *29:*15*
The rod and rebuke are wisdom, But a child left to himself brings shame to his mother.

Proverbs *29:*17*
Correct your son, and he will give you rest; Yes, he will give delight to your soul.

(The Virtuous Wife)

Proverbs *31:*10*–*12*, *28*–*30*
(10)* **Who can find a *virtuous wife*? For her worth is far above rubies.**
(11)* *The heart of her husband safely trusts her;* **So he will have no lack of gain.**
(12)* *She does him good and not evil All the days of her life.*

(28)* *Her children rise up and call her blessed; Her husband also, and he praises her*:
(29) *"Many daughters have done well, But you excel them all."*
(30)* **Charm is deceitful and beauty is passing,** *But a woman who fears the LORD, she shall be praised.*

CHAPTER 48

MARRIAGE: HUSBAND (MAN) AND WIFE (WOMAN)

I n reviewing the appendix section of my version of the NKJV Bible, there are listed at least fifty-three different biblical verses and associated topics on the subject, "*Marriage*." In looking back at my life, I found one key area, whereby I have gotten completely ahead of Father God, and that is in this central area of life (i.e. "*Marriage*"). Unfortunately for me, I failed to "*wait on the Lord*" as I jumped into my first "*Marriage*" at age twenty-two, and only six weeks after graduating from the University of Southern California. Over the years, I have come to realize that my primary reasons for getting "*Married*" so young, as well as right after college, was because everyone in my "circle of friends" had been or where in the processes of getting "*Married*." Accordingly, I felt this great sense of urgency to "follow the crowd," so to speak, by venturing into one of the most sacred aspects of life (i.e. "*Marriage*") at a time when I was emotionally, financially, and spiritually unprepared to "tie the knot" from a Christian perspective of "*Marriage*."

One of the central aspects of my first failed "*Marriage*" centered on the fact that I was "hungry for love," as well as "starved for sexual intimacy;" Whereby I thought and naively believed that "*Marriage*" would address. Additionally, given the fact that I lost my virginity in the summer of my twenty-first year of life, I naively thought that by getting "*Married*" to the woman whom I lost my virginity to, that somehow and someway this "*Marriage*" would smooth over with Father God, the fact that I had "sinned against God" from my fornications, lust, and sexual immoralities, that I had committed prior to getting "*Married*" the first time!

How naive and off-centered I was back then as it relates to the spiritual concept of "*Marriage*." As those who have known me before, as well as now, might argue this position or fact, and that being that I still did not learn the "teachable moment" of "*Marriage*" from my initial foray into the concept of "*Marriage*"! Given the fact that I have been divorced twice, and I am still working on my third and final "*Marriage*," I have—more recently than not, during periodic phases of time in these past fifteen years of "*Marriage*,"—attempted to better understand Father God's concept of "*Marriage*" from His biblical perspective. Accordingly, I have been studying Father God's Word with a greater sense of purpose, by meditating, marinating, and trying as best as I humanly can, to gain a better understanding of the central and key life application principles and truths, that are needed for a successful biblical "*Marriage*." And from my studies and life experiences, I keep coming back to several central and foundational biblical principles, that are conceptually easy to understand, but from my experience and perspective, can sometimes be challenging to implement!

These biblical principles and associated Scripture verses, effectively serve as criteria for: *Marriage*, and include the following:

1. **ONENESS** (Genesis 2:18–24);
2. **COMMITMENT** (Genesis 24:58–60);
3. **ROMANCE** (Song of Solomon 4:9 and 10);
4. **JOY** (Jeremiah 33:10–11);
5. **PROCREATION** (Malachi 2:14–15);
6. **BONDS OF TRUST**, DOES NOT EQUAL UNFAITHFULNESS (Matthew 5:32);

7. **PERMANENCY**, as DIVORCE is not an OPTIONALITY (Matthew 19:6);

8. **DEATH** is the **ONLY AGENT** of **DISSOLUTION** (Romans 7:2 and 3);

9. LOVE (1 Corinthians 13 and Ephesians 5:21–33);

10. Serves as a living precursor and symbol of Christ and His Church, i.e. the **Bride of Christ** (Ephesians 5:23 and 32); and

11. **GOOD, HOLY, and HONORABLE in the SIGHT of GOD** (Hebrews 13:4).

From my perspective, in attempting to gain a better, fuller, and richer understanding of Father God's ideals for "*Marriage*," one can reflect on these three basic aspects and/or tenets:

1. That a *man* leaves his parents and, in a public act, promises and commits himself to his *wife* (*MARRIAGE ONENESS*);

2. That a *man* and *woman* are joined together by taking responsibility for each other's welfare, as well as by loving one's *mate/spouse* above all others (*MARRIAGE COMMITMENT*); and

3. That a *man* and *woman* become "*ONE FLESH*" in multiple forms of and stages of life, including but not limited to intimacy, commitment, and submission to one another; and always—and I repeat, always—forsaking the allure of others, while committing, engaging, and remembering that one's sexual union, is only reserved, with and for, the confines of "*Marriage*" (**MARRIAGE ONENESS, MARRIAGE INTIMACY, AND MARRIAGE SUBMISSION TO EACH OTHER**)!

Additionally, when those "in Christ" think about the Body of Christ's upcoming "*Marriage*" to the Son of God, one cannot help but to think about all the preparatory steps we must take as the "*Bride of Christ*," including but not limited to the following:

1. *SUBMISSION*: As one steps away from one's sinful nature and unrighteous past, one can then elect to become "*washed in the blood of Christ,*" by one's acceptance of Jesus Christ as one's Lord and Savior of one's life;

2. *OBEDIENCE*: As an active, engaged, and participative member of the Body of Christ, one has become a representative known as the "*Bride of Christ,*" whereby one becomes at One with Him by living, working, and serving mankind in a manner that is reflective of the "*Christ in me*";

3. *LOVE*: As the "*Bride of Christ,*" one understands the importance of operating from within and under Father God's umbrella of Love, that He has bestowed on ALL who are the "*Bride of Christ,*" as such, one must Love others like God Loves Us; and

4. *PEACE*: As one's **ultimate** *Husband* when Jesus Christ ascended into Heaven, He stated that in Him, one may have Peace; even as one might have trials and tribulations, but to be of good cheer, since He has overcome the world (John 16:33).

How exciting it is to know that one's ultimate "*Marriage*" has already been ordained, as Jesus has preceded those who are "in Christ" and who represent the "*Bride of Christ,*" as He will return, so that all members who represent the "*Bride of Christ,*" will reign with Him on the new earth! What an awesome gift and blessing for any nuptial pair!

Finally, I returned to my former home church on April 28, 2019 at First AME Church in Los Angeles, California, and those "*Married*" in the month of April were recognized. What an **AWESOME** blessing to witness one married couple who were recognized and celebrating **sixty-four years of "*Marriage*"**! As I sat in my pew seat, I silently mentioned to Father God, *What a blessing to witness such an* **AMAZING** *testimony to Father God's principles of '***MARRIAGE***!'* Hallelujah and *to God be the GLORY!*

(The Peril of Adultery)

Proverbs *5:*15*– 20 and *21–*23*

(15)* *__Drink water from your own cistern, And running water from your own well__*.

(16) Should your fountains be dispersed abroad, Streams of water in the streets?

(17) Let them be only your own, And not for strangers with you.

(18)* *__Let your fountain be blessed__, And rejoice with the wife of your youth.*

(19)* **As a loving deer and a graceful doe,** *__Let her breasts satisfy you at all times; And always be enraptured__ with her love*.

(20) For why should you, my son, be enraptured by an i*mmoral* __**woman**__, And be embraced in the arms of a seductress?

(21)* **For the ways of __man__ are before the eyes of the LORD, And *He* ponders all *his* paths.**

(22)* **__His__ own iniquities entrap the wicked __man__, And __he__ is caught in the cords of __his__ sin.**

(23)* **__He__ shall die for lack of instruction, And in the greatness of __his__ folly __he__ shall go astray.**

(Beware of Adultery)

Proverbs *6:*32*–35

(32)* **Whoever commits adultery with a __woman__ lacks understanding; __He__ who does so destroys __his__ own soul.**

(33)* **Wounds and dishonor __he__ will get, And __his__ reproach will not be wiped away.**

(34) For jealousy is a __**husband's**__ fury; Therefore __he__ will not spare in the day of vengeance.

(35) __He__ will accept no recompense, Nor will __he__ be appeased though __you__ give many gifts.

(Wise Sayings of Solomon)

Proverbs 11:16
A gracious **_woman_** retains honor, But ruthless **_men_** retain riches.

Proverbs 11:17
The merciful **_man_** does good for _his_ own soul, But _he_ who is cruel troubles _his_ own flesh.

Proverbs 11:18
The wicked **_man_** does deceptive work, But _he_ who sows righteousness will have a sure reward.

Proverbs 11:22
As a ring of gold in a swine's snout, So is a lovely **_woman_** who lacks discretion.

Proverbs *11:*29*
He who troubles his own house will inherit the wind, And the fool will be servant to the wise of heart.

Proverbs 12:4*
An _excellent_ **_wife_** is the crown of _her_ **_husband_**, But _she_ who causes shame is like rottenness in _his_ bones.

Proverbs *13:*22*
A _good man_ leaves an _inheritance_ to his _children's children_, But the _wealth_ of the sinner is stored up for the righteous.

Proverbs 14:1
The _wise_ **_woman_** builds _her house_, But the foolish pulls it down with _her_ hands.

Proverbs 15:17*
Better is a dinner of herbs where love is, Than a fatted calf with hatred.

Proverbs 15:27*

He who is greedy for gain troubles *his own house*, But *he* who hates bribes will live.

Proverbs 17:1

Better is a dry morsel with quietness, Than a *house* full of feasting with strife.

Proverbs 17:*13*

Whoever rewards evil for good, *Evil will not depart from his house.*

Proverbs *18:*22*

He who finds a **wife** finds a good thing, And obtains favor from the LORD.

Proverbs 19:*13*

A foolish *son* is the ruin of *his **father***, And the contentions of a ***wife*** are a continual dripping.

Proverbs *19:*14*

Houses and riches are an inheritance from *fathers*, But a prudent *wife* is from the LORD.

Proverbs *21:*9*

Better to dwell in a corner of a housetop, Than in a house shared with a contentious *woman*.

Proverbs *21:*19*

Better to dwell in the wilderness, Than with a contentious and angry *woman*.

(Sayings of the Wise)

Proverbs 23:26–28

(26) *My son, give me your heart, And let your eyes observe my ways.*

(27) For a harlot is a deep pit, And a seductress is a narrow well.

(28) She also lies in wait as for a victim, And increases the unfaithful among *men*.

Proverbs 24:3*–4*

Through *wisdom* a *house* is built, And by understanding it is established; By knowledge the rooms are filled With all precious and pleasant riches.

(Further Sayings of the Wise)

Proverbs *24:*27*

Prepare *your* outside work, Make it fit for *yourself* in the field; *And afterward build your house*.

(Further Wise Sayings of Solomon)

Proverbs *25:*24*

It is better to dwell in a corner of a housetop, Than in a house shared with a contentious *woman*.

Proverbs 26:21

As charcoal is to burning coals, and wood to fire, So is a contentious *man* to kindle strife.

Proverbs 27:8

Like a bird that wanders from its nest Is a *man* who wanders from *his* place.

Proverbs 27:15*–16

A continual dripping on a very rainy day And a contentious *woman* are alike; Whoever restrains *her* restrains the wind, And grasps oil with his right hand.

(The Wisdom of Agur)

Proverbs 30:18–19

There are three things which are too wonderful for me, Yes, four which

I do not understand: The way of an eagle in the air, The way of a serpent on rock, The way of a ship in the midst of the sea, And the way of a **_man_** with a _virgin_.

Proverbs 30:20
This is the way of an adulterous **_woman_**: _She_ eats and wipes _her_ mouth, And says, "_I have done no wickedness._"

Proverbs 30:21–23
(21) For three things the earth is perturbed, Yes, for four it cannot bear up:

(22) For a servant when he reigns, A fool when he is filled with food,

(23) A hateful **_woman_** when _she_ is **_married_**, And a maidservant who succeeds her mistress.

(The Virtuous Wife)

Proverbs *31:*10*–*12* and 13–*31*
(10)* **Who can find a virtuous _wife_? For _her_ worth is far above rubies.**

(11)* **The heart of _her husband_ safely trust _her_; So _he_ will have no lack of gain.**

(12)* **_She_ does _him_ good and not evil All the days of _her_ life.**

(13) **_She_** seeks wool and flax, And willingly works with **_her_** hands.

(14) **_She_** is like the merchant ships, **_She_** brings **_her_** food from afar.

(15) **_She_** also rises while it is yet night, And provides food for **_her_** household, And a portion for **_her_** maidservants.

(16)* **_She_ considers a field and buys it; From _her_ profits _she_ plants a vineyard.**

(17)* **_She_ girds _herself_ with strength, And strengthens _her_ arms.**

(18)* **_She_ perceives that _her_ merchandise is good, And _her_ lamp does not go out by night.**

(19) **_She_** stretches out **_her_** hands to the distaff, And **_her_** hand holds the spindle.

(20)* *She* extends *her* hand to the poor, Yes, *she* reaches out *her* hands to the needy.

(21) *She* is not afraid of snow for *her* household, For all *her* household is clothed with scarlet.

(22) *She* makes tapestry for *herself*; *Her* clothing is fine linen and purple.

(23) *Her husband* is known in the gates, When *he* sits among the elders of the land.

(24) *She* makes linen garments and sells them, And supplies sashes for the merchants.

(25)* Strength and honor are *her* clothing; *She* shall rejoice in time to come.

(26)* *She* opens *her* mouth with wisdom, And on *her* tongue is the law of kindness.

(27)* *She* watches over the ways of *her* household, And does not eat the bread of idleness.

(28)* *Her* children rise up and call *her* blessed; *Her husband* also, and *he* praises *her*:

(29) "Many daughters have done well, But you excel them all."

(30)* Charm is deceitful and beauty is passing, But a *woman* who fears the LORD, *she* shall be praised.

(31)* Give *her* of the fruit of *her* hands, And let *her* own works praise *her* in the gates.

CHAPTER 49

MERCY, COMPASSION

When I think of the biblical principle of *Mercy*, I cannot help but think of the Godhead (i.e. God the Father, God the Son, and God the Holy Spirit). This same trifecta, when I think of *Mercy*, I am also mindful of **Kindness/Goodness** as well as **Forgiveness**. It seems to me that you cannot have one without the other. In other words, one cannot appropriately exhibit *Mercy* without also exhibiting, **Kindness/Goodness** and **Forgiveness**. But for the purpose of this Chapter Narrative, the primary focus will center on *Mercy*, with secondary discussions on **Kindness/ Goodness**.

Contained within Father God's Word are numerous scriptural verses commanding one to operate from a central platform of *Mercy*, especially when one is holistically interacting with people from all walks of life, believers as well as nonbelievers. To mention a few, they would include the following biblical passages: Psalms 119:156, Proverbs 3:3, Proverbs 14:31, Isaiah 63:9, Daniel 4:27, Matthew 5:7, Luke 6:36, Romans 9:15, Romans 12:1, Romans 12:20–21, and Ephesians 2:4.

Let me peel back Proverbs 14:31 as I share my reflections regarding the Godly principle of *Mercy*. Proverbs 14:31, which states: "*He who oppresses the poor reproaches his Maker, But he who honors Him has **mercy** on the needy*"! As one marinates on the biblical principle of *Mercy*, one, first and foremost, cannot fully comprehend on the _**Mercy**_ that Father God has given and provided to each and every human being, especially to those who are Father God's children, as believers, by accepting and believing in Jesus Christ as our Lord and Savior, and marinating on all that Father God's Grace and _**Mercy**_ connote to all who represent the Church by being members of the Body of Christ. Just think about it, to receive the gift of Salvation and Eternal Life, it doesn't get any better than that!

Therefore, how can I, as a child of Father God, not do my part in the life application of being an heir to Father God's Kingdom, being a coheir with Jesus Christ; not exhibit, on a real-time basis, Father God's _**Mercy**_ to other people—rich and poor, friend or foe, black or white, Christian or Muslim. As we all are aware, one can <u>never</u> repay Father God for His Everlasting _**Mercy**_ and Grace, by saving a sinner turned saint, like myself; But the very, very least that I/one can do is apply the Godly principle of _**Mercy**_ to all that I/one come into contact with. For me, this requires a high degree of intentionality, so that the more opportunities that Father God presents to me to live out and exhibit _**Mercy**_ on a daily basis, then the more opportunities, that I have to let the light of Father God be exhibited throughout my daily walk, thereby allowing Father God's Glory, Praise, and Honor to be displayed for all the world to see, as Father God receives His righteous glory before His creation! (Matthew 5:16)

To God be the GLORY!

(Guidance for the Young)

Proverbs *3:*3*– 4*

Let not _mercy_ and truth forsake you; Bind them around your neck, Write them on the tablet of your heart, And so find favor and high esteem In the sight of God and man.

Proverbs *3:*27*–28*

**Do not withhold good from those to whom it is due, When it is in the power of your hand to do so.** **Do not say to your neighbor, "Go, and come back, And tomorrow I will give it,"** _**When you have it with you.**_

(Wise Sayings of Solomon)

Proverbs *10:*12*
Hatred stirs up strife, *But love covers all sins.*

Proverbs 11:17
The ***merciful*** man does good for his own soul, But he who is cruel troubles his own flesh.

Proverbs *11:*24*
There is one who scatters, yet increases more; **And there is one who withholds more than is right, But it leads to poverty.**

Proverbs *11:*25*
The generous soul will be made rich, And he who waters will also be watered himself.

Proverbs 12:10
A righteous man regards the life of his animal, But the tender ***mercies*** of the wicked are cruel.

Proverbs *13:*7*
There is one who makes himself rich, yet has nothing; *And one who makes himself poor, yet has great riches.*

Proverbs 14:*21*
He who despises his neighbor sins; But he who has ***mercy*** on the poor, happy is he.

Proverbs 14:*22*
Do they not go astray who devise evil? But ***mercy*** and truth belong to those who devise good.

Proverbs *14:*31*
He who oppresses the poor reproaches his Maker, But he who honors Him has *mercy* on the needy.

Proverbs 15:17
Better is a dinner of herbs where love is, Than a fatted calf with hatred.

Proverbs *16:*6*
In _mercy_ and truth Atonement is provided for iniquity; And by the fear of the LORD one departs from evil.

Proverbs *17:*9*
He who covers a transgression seeks love, But he who repeats a matter separates friends.

Proverbs *17:*17*
A friend loves at all times, And a brother is born for adversity.

Proverbs 18:10*
The name of the LORD is a strong tower; The righteous run to it and are safe.

Proverbs 19:*11*
The discretion of a man makes him slow to anger, _And his glory is to overlook a transgression_.

Proverbs *19:*17*
He who has pity on the poor lends to the LORD, And He will pay back what he has given.

Proverbs 19:*22*
What is desired in a man is kindness, And a poor man is better than a liar.

Proverbs 20:28
Mercy and truth preserve the king, And by loving kindness he upholds his throne.

Proverbs *21:*13*
Whoever shuts his ears to the cry of the poor Will also cry himself and not be heard.

Proverbs *21:*21*

He who follows righteousness and _mercy_ Finds life, righteousness and honor.

Proverbs 21:25–*26*

The desire of the lazy man kills him, For his hands refuse to labor. **He covets greedily all day long, _But the righteous gives and does not spare._**

(Sayings of the Wise)

Proverbs 24:11–12

Deliver those who are drawn toward death, And hold back those stumbling to the slaughter. If you say, "Surely we did not know this." Does not he who weighs the hearts consider it? He who keeps the soul, does He not know it? And will He not render to each man according to his deeds?

Proverbs *24:*17*–*18*

Do not rejoice when your enemy falls, And do not let your heart be glad when he stumbles. **Lest the LORD see it, and it displease Him, And He turn away His wrath from him.**

(Further Sayings of the Wise)

Proverbs *24:*28*–*29*

Do not be a witness against your neighbor without cause, **For would you deceive with your lips?** _Do not say, "I will do to him just as he has done to me;_ **I will render to the man according to his work."**

(Further Wise Sayings of Solomon)

Proverbs 25:8–10

(8) _Do not go hastily to court;_ For what will you do in the end, When your neighbor has put you to shame?

(9) _Debate your case with your neighbor, And do not disclose the secret to another;_

(10) Lest he who hears it exposes your shame, And your reputation be ruined.

Proverbs *25:*21*–22*

If your enemy is hungry, give him bread to eat; And if he is thirsty, give him water to drink; **For so you will heap coals of fire on his head, And the LORD will reward you.**

Proverbs 28:8

One who increases his possessions by usury and extortion *Gathers it for him who will pity the poor.*

Proverbs *28:*13*

He who covers his sins will not prosper, *But whoever confesses and forsakes them, will have* mercy.

Proverbs 28:27*

He who gives to the poor will not lack, But he who hides his eyes will have many curses.

Proverbs 29:7*

The righteous considers the cause of the poor, But the wicked does not understand such knowledge.

Proverbs 29:13*

The poor man and the oppressor have this in common: *The LORD gives light to the eyes of both.*

(The Words of King Lemuel's Mother)

Proverbs 31:8–9

Open your mouth for the speechless, In the cause of all who are appointed to die. Open your mouth, judge righteously, And plead the cause of the poor and needy.

(The Virtuous Wife)

Proverbs *31:*20*

She extends her hand to the poor, Yes, she reaches her hands to the needy.

CHAPTER 50

PATIENCE

The title of this Chapter Theme, "*Patience*," is more likely than not one area within every person, especially those who are believers, which can be very problematic, because, speaking from my own life experiences, it is one of great challenge to accomplish, yet provides great blessings,\ if one is able to operate from a platform of *Patience*.

Father God's Word speaks directly regarding this Christian virtue in numerous passages in both the Old and New Testaments. Two of my favorites regarding the Christian virtue of *Patience* are contained in Isaiah 40:31: "*But those who **wait** on the LORD Shall renew their strength; They shall mount up with wings like eagles, They shall run and not be weary, They shall walk and not faint.*" And James 1:2-6: "*My brethren, count it all joy when you fall into various trials, knowing that the testing of your faith produces **patience**. But let **patience** have its perfect work, that you may be perfect and complete, lacking nothing. If any of you lacks wisdom, let him ask of God, who gives to all liberally and without reproach, and it will be given to him. But let him ask in faith, with no doubting....*"

Had I adequately mastered or at least better learned and/or understood the Christian virtue of "*Patience*," then maybe I would not have rushed into marriage—not once, not twice, but three foolish times—when the timing as well as my bride/wife was not my God-inspired "soul mate."

Or how about the fact that my longest tenure with the numerous Fortune 500 companies that I worked for was only for a tenure of seven and a half years, and that being Hercules, Inc. And speaking of Hercules, the best "Head Coach" that I ever worked with and for when I was initially hired for the VP- Finance position, was the CFO by the name of Mr. Keith Elliott. During one of my annual performance reviews, Keith made mention of a "two-edged" asset or strength that I possessed, which was also a corresponding weakness, that being "***Patience***"! Keith stated, from a strategic strength/asset perspective, he applauded me for taking immediate action when the situation presented itself, which from a core competency perspective, was one of my stronger character traits as I was keenly looking and working to identify, address, and solve a particular issue and/or problem. On the flip side of this same coin, there were times when my desire to immediately "solve the issue or problem of the day," might have closed off or limited my vision and/or listening abilities, to better or world-class solutions, vs. immediate or best in class solutions for that particular issue of the day!

Thus, as I or anyone for that matter reads, studies, and meditates on the various biblical passages on the biblical principle of "***Patience***," I am reminded of the following two Proverbs verses that speak to the importance of ***Patience***, namely Proverbs 16:32, which states: "*He who is **slow to anger** is better than the mighty, And he who rules his spirit than he who takes a city.*" Additionally, Proverbs 21:5, which states: "*The plans of the diligent lead surely to plenty, But those of everyone who is **hasty**, surely to poverty.*"

I don't know about you, but I need to better emulate the Christian virtue of "***Patience***" such that I will stop drinking and wading in the emotional stream of poverty! What say you?

(Wise Sayings of Solomon)

Proverbs *14:*29*
He who is _slow to wrath_ has great understanding, But he who is impulsive exalts folly.

Proverbs 15:18
A wrathful man stirs up strife, But he who is **_slow_** *to anger* allays contention.

Proverbs 16:*32*
He who is **_slow_** to anger is better than the mighty, And he who rules his spirit than he who takes a city.

Proverbs 19:*11*
The discretion of a man makes him **_slow_** to anger, And his glory is to *overlook a transgression.*

Proverbs *20:*21*
An inheritance gained hastily at the beginning *Will not be blessed at the end.*

Proverbs 20:22
Do not say, "I will recompense evil"; **_Wait for the LORD_**, *and He will save you.*

Proverbs *21:*5*
The plans of the diligent lead surely to plenty, But those of everyone who is hasty, surely to poverty.

(Sayings of the Wise)

Proverbs 22:29*
Do you see a man who excels in his work? He will stand before kings; He will not stand before unknown men.

(Further Wise Sayings of Solomon)

Proverbs 25:15

By long forbearance a ruler is persuaded, And a *gentle* tongue breaks a bone.

Proverbs 27:18

Whoever keeps the fig tree will eat its fruit; *So he who **waits** on his master will be honored.*

Proverbs 28:28

When the wicked arise, *men hide themselves*; But when they perish, *the righteous increase.*

CHAPTER 51

PEACE, SPIRIT

For me, when I think about meditating and marinating on the biblical principle of **_PEACE_**, I, more often than not, reflect and recite Philippians 4:6 and 7, which states: "_Be anxious for nothing, but in everything by prayer and supplication, with thanksgiving, let your requests be made known to God, and the 'peace' of God, which surpasses all understanding, will guard your hearts and minds through Christ Jesus_"! What a wonderful and outstanding biblical passage of Scripture that, at least for me, gives great comfort, contentment, and tranquility in the face of any and all challenges, trials, and tribulations, that one might face or have faced, and I have had my share of each.

But as I recite and meditate on Father God's promise that His **_Peace_**, not might or sometimes, but will <u>always</u> surpass all earthly and human understanding, it begs the question, as well as reminds me of Jesus's Words in John 14:27, which states: "**_Peace I leave with you, My Peace I give to you; not as the world gives do I give to you. Let not your heart be troubled, neither let it be afraid._**" Accordingly, when my knees become a little shaky, or my inner faith might not be as strong in the Lord as it should be, the Holy Spirit will successfully bring to mind two additional foundational biblical principles of truth regarding **_Peace_**, namely Romans 5:1, which states: "_Therefore, having been justified by faith, we have **peace**_ *with God through our Lord Jesus Christ.*" And Father God's equally companion biblical words of encouragement can be found in Colossians 3:15, which states: "*And let the **peace** of God rule in your hearts, to which also you were called in one body; and be thankful.*"

So, how and/or what do these biblical scriptures regarding the spiritual truth of **PEACE,** do to motivate me to become and/or strive for? Namely, as it relates to this topic, to achieve and/or inherit Godly wisdom, which can be defined as the capacity to see things the way the Lord sees them and respond according to His principles and biblical truths. And just as Jesus professed that in this life, one would encounter, challenges, trials, tribulations, and sufferings; and through it all, I/one must stay focused on God's **Peace** in each and every life situation. Given that as one strives for Godly wisdom and God's **Peace** as exhibited in a life lived under the Heavenly halo of **PEACE**, one must always remember to rest in the Lord, knowing that He is always with us, in us, and through us, through the indwelling of the Holy Spirit, as He directs one's mind, body, heart, spirit and soul, to rest in the **PEACE** of our Lord Jesus Christ!

(The Call of Wisdom)

Proverbs *1:*20*–27 and 28–33*

(20)* **Wisdom calls aloud outside; She raises her voice in the open squares.**

(21) She cries out in the chief concourses, At the openings of the gates in the city She speaks her words:

(22)* "How long, you simple ones, will you love simplicity? For scorners delight in their scorning, And fools hate knowledge.

(23)* Turn at my rebuke; *Surely I will pour out my spirit on you;* I will make my words known to you.

(24) Because I have called and you refused, I have stretched out my hand and no one regarded,

(25) Because you disdained all my counsel, And would have none of my rebuke,

(26) I also will laugh at your calamity; I will mock when your terror comes,

(27) When your terror comes like a storm, And your destruction comes like a whirlwind, When distress and anguish come upon you.

(28) "Then they will call on me, but I will not answer; They will seek me diligently, but they will not find me.

(29) Because they hated knowledge And did not choose the fear of the LORD,

(30) They would have none of my counsel And despised my every rebuke.

(31) Therefore they shall eat the fruit of their own way, And be filled to the full with their own fancies.

(32) For the turning away of the simple will slay them, And the complacency of fools will destroy them;

(33)* But whoever listens to me will dwell safely, And will be secure, without fear of evil."

(Guidance for the Young)

Proverbs 3:1–2

My son, do not forget my law, But let your heart keep my commands; For length of days and long life And **_peace_** they will add to you.

Proverbs *3:*5*–*6*

*Trust in the LORD with all your heart, And lean not on your own understanding; In all your ways acknowledge Him, **And He shall direct your paths**!*

Proverbs *3:*13*–18

(13)* ***Happy* is the man who finds wisdom, And the man who gains understanding;**

(14) For her proceeds are better than profits of silver, And her gain than fine gold.

(15)   She (*wisdom*) is more precious than rubies, And all the things you may desire cannot compare with her.

(16)   Length of days is in her right hand, In her left hand riches and honor.

(17)* Her ways are ways of *pleasantness*, And all her paths are ***peace****.*

(18)   She is a tree of life to those who take hold of her, And *happy* are all who retain her.

(The Crafty Harlot)

Proverbs 7:10–20

(10)   And there a woman met him, With the attire of a harlot, and a crafty heart.

(11)   She was loud and rebellious, Her feet would not stay at home.

(12)   At times she was outside, at times in the open square, Lurking at every corner.

(13)   So she caught him and kissed him; With an impudent face she said to him:

(14)   "I have ***peace*** offerings with me; Today I have paid my vows.

(15)   So I came out to meet you, Diligently to seek your face. And I have found you.

(16)   I have spread my bed with tapestry, Colored coverings of Egyptian linen.

(17)   I have perfumed my bed With myrrh, aloes, and cinnamon.

(18)   Come, let us take our fill of love until morning; Let us delight ourselves with love.

(19)   For my husband is not at home; He has gone on a long journey;

(20)   He has taken a bag of money with him, And will come home on the appointed day."

(Wise Sayings of Solomon)

Proverbs *11:*12*

He who is devoid of wisdom despises his neighbor, But a man of understanding holds his _peace_.

Proverbs 11:13

A talebearer reveals secrets, But he who is of a faithful **_spirit_** conceals a matter.

Proverbs 12:20*

Deceit is in the heart of those who devise evil, But counselors of **_peace_** have joy.

Proverbs 14:30

A *sound heart* is life to the body, But envy is rottenness to the bones.

Proverbs 15:4

A *wholesome* tongue is a tree of life, But perverseness in it breaks the **_spirit_**.

Proverbs 15:13

A *merry* heart makes a *cheerful* countenance, But by sorrow of the heart the **_spirit_** is broken.

Proverbs 15:15*

All the days of the afflicted are evil, But he who is of a *merry* heart *has a continual feast.*

Proverbs 15:26

The thoughts of the wicked are an abomination to the LORD, *But the words of the pure are pleasant.*

Proverbs 16:*2*

All the ways of a man are pure in his own eyes, But the LORD weighs the **_spirits_**.

Proverbs 16:7*

When a man's ways please the LORD, He makes even his enemies to be at *peace* with him.

Proverbs *16:*18*

Pride goes before destruction, And a haughty *spirit* before a fall.

Proverbs *16:*19*

Better to be of a humble *spirit* with the lowly, Than to divide the spoil with the proud.

Proverbs 16:*32*

He who is *slow to anger* is better than the mighty, And he who rules his *spirit* than he who takes a city.

Proverbs 17:1

Better is a dry morsel with quietness, Than a house full of feasting with strife.

Proverbs 17:*22*

A *merry* heart does good, like medicine, But a broken *spirit* dries the bones.

Proverbs *17:*27*

He who has knowledge spares his words, And a man of understanding is of a calm *spirit*.

Proverbs 17:28

Even a fool is counted wise when he holds his *peace*; When he *shuts his lips*, he is considered perceptive.

Proverbs 18:14

The *spirit* of a man will sustain him in sickness, But who can bear a broken *spirit*?

Proverbs 18:18

Casting lots causes contentions to *cease*, And keeps the mighty apart.

Proverbs 20:3
It is honorable for a man to stop striving, Since any fool can start a quarrel.

Proverbs 20:27*
The ***spirit*** of a man is the lamp of the LORD, Searching all the inner depths of his heart.

Proverbs *21:*9*
Better to dwell in a corner of a housetop, Than in a house shared with a contentious woman.

Proverbs 21:14
A gift in secret pacifies anger, And a bribe behind the back, strong wrath.

Proverbs *21:*19*
Better to dwell in the wilderness, Than with a contentious and angry woman.

Proverbs *21:*21*
He who follows righteousness and mercy Finds life, righteousness and honor.

Proverbs 21:*23*
Whoever guards his mouth and tongue <u>Keeps his soul from troubles</u>.

Proverbs *22:*4*
By humility and the fear of the LORD Are riches and honor and life.

(Sayings of the Wise)

Proverbs *24:*5*–*6*
A wise man is strong, Yes, a man of knowledge increases strength; For by wise counsel you will wage your own war, And in a multitude of counselors there is _safety_.

(Further Wise Sayings of Solomon)

Proverbs 25:8–10

(8)   Do not go hastily to court; For what will you do in the end, When your neighbor has put you to shame?

(9)   *Debate your case with your neighbor,* And do not disclose the secret to another;

(10) Lest he who hears it expose your shame, And your reputation be ruined.

Proverbs *25:*21*–*22*

If your *enemy* is hungry, *give him bread to eat*; And *if he is thirsty, give him water to drink*; For so you will heap coals of fire on his head, *And the LORD will reward you*.

Proverbs *25:*24*

It is better to dwell in a corner of a housetop, **Than in a house shared with a contentious woman**.

Proverbs 25:25

As cold water to a weary soul, *So is good news* from a far country.

Proverbs 25:28*

Whoever has no rule over his own ***spirit*** Is like a city broken down, without walls.

Proverbs 27:15*–16

A continual dripping on a very rainy day And a contentious woman are alike; *Whoever restrains her restrains the wind*, And grasps oil with his right hand.

Proverbs 28:*25*

He who is of a proud heart stirs up strife, *But he who trusts in the LORD will be prospered.*

Proverbs 28:26

He who trust in his own heart is a fool, *But whoever walks wisely will be delivered.*

Proverbs 29:8*

Scoffers set a city aflame, *But wise men turn away wrath.*

Proverbs 29:9*

If a wise man contends with a foolish man, Whether the fool rages or laughs, there is no _**peace**_.

Proverbs 29:13*

The poor man and the oppressor have this in common: *The LORD gives light to the eyes of both.*

Proverbs *29:*17*

Correct your son, and _**he will give you rest**_**; Yes,** _**he will give delight to your soul**_.

Proverbs 29:23*

A man's pride will bring him low, But the humble in _**spirit**_ will retain honor.

Proverbs 29:25*

The fear of man brings a snare, _But whoever trusts in the LORD shall be safe._

CHAPTER 52

PLANNING, PREPARATION, FORESIGHT, DEVISE, TEACHING

As I personally look back on my life's journey, the central Chapter Themes of *__Planning__*, *__Foresight__*, *__Teaching__* and *training*, have been central foundational principles and pillars of my life. In most areas of my life, with the exception of marriage, *__Planning__* has been an integral part of my life journey. In fact, one of my fundamental tenets in coaching is grounded in the following life principle: "He/She who fails to __Plan__, __Plans__ to fail"!

From my perspective, God's Word in the Gospels, as well as within the body of Proverbs, speaks unequivocally to the importance of these Chapter Themes, and the interplay that is required in *__Planning__* from a human, biblical, and spiritual perspective.

For example, Matthew 6:33 and 34 states that one is to: "*__But seek first the kingdom of God and His righteousness, and all these things shall be added to you. Therefore do not worry about tomorrow, for tomorrow will worry about its own things. Sufficient for the day is its own trouble.__*"

When one overlays the above two biblical truths, of seeking *Father God first in all one does*—and by all means, *not worrying*—these from my perspective, serve as both, the foundational platform, as well as the structural roof of one's life. This is then supported by multiple biblical principles and truths, which serve as structural pillars within one's life, for example:

- Proverbs 15:22: "*Without counsel, **plans** go awry, But in the multitude of counselors they are established*";
- Proverbs 16:9: "*A man's heart **plans** his way, But the LORD **directs his steps**"*;
- Proverbs 21:5: "*The **plans** of the diligent lead surely to plenty, But those of everyone who is hasty, surely to poverty*";

And of course, one of my most favorite Proverbs verses that indirectly have application to this Chapter Theme on ***Planning*** are the following:

- Proverbs 3:5: "*Trust in the LORD with all your heart, And lean not on your own understanding*";
- Proverbs 3:6: "*In all your ways acknowledge Him, And He shall **direct your paths**"*!

Accordingly, at the end of the day, the Lord has established a foundational ***Planning*** principle and covenant that states the overall importance, one must have, by placing Father God first and foremost in all phases of one's ***Plans***, life, and lifestyle choices. Thus, He will provide the appropriate *guidance* as well as *instructional* guide ***Plan,*** for any and all areas, phases, challenges and trials, that this life may throw one's way!

(Guidance for the Young)

Proverbs *3:*27*–30

(27)* **Do not withhold good from those to whom it is due, When it is in the power of your *hand* to do so.**

(28)* **Do not say to your neighbor, "Go, and come back, And tomorrow I will give it," When you have it with you.**

(29) Do not **_devise_** evil against your neighbor, For he dwells by you for safety's sake.

(30) Do not strive with a man without cause, If he has done you no harm.

(The Wicked Man)

Proverbs 6:12–15 and 16–19

(12) A worthless person, a wicked man, Walks with a perverse mouth;

(13) He winks with his eyes, He shuffles his feet, He points with his fingers;

(14) Perversity is in his heart, He **_devises_** evil continually, He sows discord.

(15) Therefore his calamity shall come suddenly; Suddenly he shall be broken without remedy.

(16) These six things the LORD hates, Yes, seven are an abomination to Him:

(17) A proud look, A lying tongue, Hands that shed innocent blood,

(18) A heart that **_devises_** wicked **_plans_**, Feet that are swift in running to evil,

(19) A false witness who speaks lies, And one who sows discord among brethren.

(Wise Sayings of Solomon)

Proverbs 12:20*

Deceit is in the heart of those who **_devise_** evil, But counselors of peace have joy.

Proverbs 14:*22*

Do they not go astray who **_devise_** evil? But mercy and truth belong to those who **_devise_** good.

Proverbs *15:*22*
Without counsel, _plans_ go awry, But in the multitude of counselors, they are established.

Proverbs *16:*1*
The _preparations_ of the heart belong to man, But the answer of the tongue is from the LORD.

Proverbs *16:*9*
A man's heart _plans_ his way, But the LORD directs his steps.

Proverbs 16:27–30*
(27) An ungodly man digs up evil, And it is on his lips like a burning fire.
(28) A perverse man sows strife, And a whisperer separates the best of friends.
(29) A violent man _entices_ his neighbor, And leads him in a way that is not good.
(30)* He winks his eye to _**devise**_ perverse things; He _purses_ his lips and brings about evil.

Proverbs 18:18
Casting lots causes contentions to cease, And keeps the mighty apart.

Proverbs *19:*21*
There are many _plans_ in a man's heart, Nevertheless the LORD's counsel—that will stand.

Proverbs 20:*4*
The lazy man _will not plow because of winter;_ He will beg during harvest and have nothing.

Proverbs 20:18*
**Plans** are established by counsel; By wise counsel wage war.

Proverbs *20:*24*
A man's steps are of the LORD; How then can a man understand his own way?

Proverbs *21:*5*
The *plans* of the diligent lead surely to plenty, But those of everyone who is hasty, surely to poverty.

Proverbs 21:*20*
There is desirable pleasure, And oil in the dwelling of the wise, But a foolish man squanders it.

Proverbs 21:*31*
The horse is **_prepared_** for the day of battle, *But deliverance is of the LORD.*

Proverbs 22:*3*
A prudent man **_foresees_** evil and hides himself, But the simple pass on and are punished.

Proverbs *22:*7*
The rich rules over the poor, And the borrower is servant to the lender.

(Sayings of the Wise)

Proverbs 22:26*–27
Do not be one of those who shakes hands in a pledge, One of those who is surety for debts; If you have nothing with which to pay, Why should he take away your bed from under you?

Proverbs 22:29*
Do you see a man who excels in his work? He will stand before kings; He will not stand before unknown men.

Proverbs 24:1-2
Do not be envious of evil men, Nor desire to be with them; For their heart **_devises_** violence, And their lips talk of troublemaking.

Proverbs *24:*5*–*6*
A wise man is strong, Yes, *a man of knowledge increases strength; For by wise counsel you will wage your own war, And in a multitude of counselors there is safety*.

Proverbs 24:8*–9*
He who *plots* to do evil, Will be called a schemer. The ***devising*** of foolishness is sin, And the scoffer is an abomination to men.

(Further Sayings of the Wise)

Proverbs *24:*27*
Prepare **your outside work,** *Make it fit* **for yourself in the field;** *And afterward build your house*.

Proverbs 24:30–34
(30) I went by the field of the lazy man, And by the vineyard of the man devoid of understanding;

(31) And there it was, all overgrown with thorns; Its surface was covered with nettles; Its stone wall was broken down.

(32) When I saw it, I considered it well; *I looked on it and received instruction:*

(33) A little sleep, a little slumber, A little folding of the hands to rest;

(34) So shall your poverty come like a prowler, And your need like an armed man.

(Further Wise Sayings of Solomon)

Proverbs 27:1*
Do not boast about tomorrow, For you do not know what a day may bring forth.

Proverbs 27:12*
A prudent man ***foresees*** evil and hides himself; The simple pass on and are punished.

Proverbs 27:23–27

(23) *Be diligent* to know the *state of your flocks*, And <u>attend</u> to your herds;

(24) For riches are not forever, Nor does a crown endure to all generations,

(25) When the hay is removed, and the tender grass shows itself, And the herbs of the mountains are gathered in,

(26) The lambs *will provide* your clothing, And *the goats the price of a field;*

(27) <u>*You shall have enough*</u> goats' milk for your food, For the food of your household, And the nourishment of your maidservants.

(The Wisdom of Agur)

Proverbs 30:24*–28*

(24)* There are four things which are little on the earth, But they are exceedingly *wise*:

(25)* The ants are a people not strong, Yet they ***prepare*** their food in the summer;

(26)* The rock badgers are a feeble folk, Yet they <u>make</u> their homes in the crags;

(27)* The locusts have no king, Yet they all *advance in ranks*;

(28)* *The spider skillfully grasps with its hands*, And it is in kings' palaces.

Proverbs 30:32–33

If you have been foolish in exalting yourself, Or if you have ***devised*** evil, put your hand on your mouth. For as the churning of milk produces butter, And wringing the nose produces blood, So the forcing of wrath produces strife.

CHAPTER 53

POOR, POVERTY, NEEDY
LIMITED RESOURCES

W hy is it—both in Old Testament times as well as New Testament times, especially for those of us, living in the twenty-first century—that we are challenged by our attitudes, viewpoints, and societal norms regarding the ***Poor***, **Disadvantaged**, ***Needy,*** and those of ***Limited Resources*** as to what to do, how to become engaged, and to a great degree, where best to provide assistance, whether that is sharing and giving of financial resources or just giving of one's Time, Talent, Treasury, or Tent (i.e. the **4 T's**, as I like to reference it).

From my life experiences and observations, especially among Christians, forsaking of one's responsibilities for assisting the ***Poor*** and/or ***Poverty*** **stricken**—partly due to inertia, partly due to generally expecting someone else to pick up on such "call to arms," or just total indifference, since it's not someone I know or care about—seems to be the standard order of the day response, even among Christians. However, in both Old and New Testament scriptures, one can see the hand of Father God at work and desiring for His children to show compassion to the ***Poor*** and ***Needy***. Jesus stated unequivocally in Matthew 26:11 and Mark 14:7: "*For you have the **poor** with you always*." He also states that those who show mercy to the *Poor*, **the sick, the** *Needy*, and the "*least of these*" are, in effect, ministering to Him personally (Matthew 25:35–40) and will be rewarded accordingly.

Nevertheless, it is an absolute truth that *Poverty's* reach is devastatingly widespread and growing. God's people cannot bury one's head in the sand by refusing to look away from one's smartphones, nor be somewhat and/or totally indifferent toward the needs of the *Poor* given Father God's stipulated mandate and expectations for His people to take care of His *Poor* and the "*least of these*" in today's societies, locally as well as globally, are woven throughout the entirety of the Scripture. Take, for example, how Father God honored King Josiah's goodness and support of the *Needy* in Jeremiah 22:16: "*He judged the cause of the **poor** and **needy**; Then it was well. Was not this knowing Me"? says the LORD.*" Or another Old Testament reference of truth regarding one's responsibilities to assist the *Poor* and *Needy* are contained in Deuteronomy 15:10 and 11, whereby Moses instructed the people on how to treat the *Poor* and *Needy*: "*You shall surely give to him, and your heart should not be grieved when you give to him, because for this thing the LORD your God will bless you in all your works and in all to which you put your hand, For the **poor** will never cease from the land; therefore I command you, saying, 'You shall open your hand wide to your brother, to your **poor** and your **needy**, in your land.'*" And of course, this sentiment is captured perfectly in Proverbs 14:31(b): "*But he who honors Him has mercy on the **needy**.*"

Conversely, the first part of Proverbs 14:31(a) states: "*He who oppresses the **poor** reproaches his Maker.*" Proverbs, like this one, clearly and succinctly delineates in the Scripture that Father God loves the *Poor* and is offended when His children neglect them and their needs, as evidenced in the following verses: (Proverbs 11:4; 17:5; 19:17; 22:2, 9, 16, 22–23; 28:8; 29:7; and 31:8–9), to name a few. Additionally, the consequences of ignoring the plight and conditions of the *Poor* are also made clear in the following Proverbs verses. For example, Proverbs 21:13 states: "*Whoever shuts his ears to the cry of the **poor** Will also cry himself and not be heard.*"

And note the stern language in Proverbs 28:27: "*He who gives to the **poor** will not lack, But he who hides his eyes will have many curses*"!

Not to be outdone, the New Testament is equally transparent regarding how one is to respond to the needs of the ***Poor***. Take, for example, 1 John 3:17–18, which clearly states the importance of exhibiting love through actionable and intentional giving and sharing to the ***Poor*** and ***Needy***: "*But whoever has this world's goods, and sees his **brother in need**, and shuts up his heart from him, how does the love of God abide in him?*" "*My little children, let us not love in word or in tongue, but in deed and in truth.*" And has been previously mentioned in paragraph two, Matthew 25:34–40 states that those who have exhibited righteousness and shown mercy and care to the "***least of these***," they have equally shown such mercy and care to Father God.

As one acknowledges the biblical principle that one's salvation is a gift from Father God, one must also understand and fully embrace the biblical principle that we were created in God's image to do good works. The biblical principle of good works is clearly defined in James 2:14–26, and concludes in James 2:26 with these inspiring words of truth: "*For as the body without the spirit is dead, so faith without works is dead also.*"

Given that Jesus has commanded that we "*love one another*" (John 13:34–35), as well as commanded that "*If you love Me, keep My commandments*" (John 14:15), then what better way to demonstrate the love, kindness, compassion and mercy of Jesus Christ, than by intentionally reaching out, serving, and "***washing the feet***" of the "***least of these***" who reside among us! Let's make Father God proud and honor Him by assisting the ***Poor*** and the ***Needy*** in our neighborhoods and communities, in our state, in our nation, and throughout the world, as the need to serve and assist the ***Poor*** and the ***Needy*** is waiting for you to lift a hand—God's hand! Can you feel His touch?

(The Folly of Indolence)

<u>Proverbs 6:6–11*</u>
(6)   Go to the ant, you *sluggard*! Consider her ways and be *wise*,

(7)   Which, having no captain, Overseer or ruler,

(8)   Provides her supplies in the summer, And gathers her food in the harvest.

(9)   How long will you *slumber*, O *sluggard*? When will you rise from your *sleep*?

(10) A little *sleep*, a little *slumber*, A little folding of the hands to sleep—

(11)* So shall your **_poverty_** come on you like a prowler, And your need like an armed man.

(Beware of Adultery)

<u>Proverbs 6:30–31</u>
(30) People do not despise a thief *If he steals to satisfy himself when he is starving*.

(31) Yet when he is found, he must restore sevenfold; He may have to give up all the substance of his house.

(Wise Sayings of Solomon)

<u>Proverbs 10:4*</u>
He who has a slack hand becomes **_poor_**, But the hand of the diligent makes rich.

<u>Proverbs 10:15</u>
The rich man's wealth is his strong city; The destruction of the **_poor_** is their **_poverty_**.

<u>Proverbs *11:*24*–*25*</u>
There is one who scatters, yet increases more; And there is one who withholds more than is right, But it leads to _poverty_. The generous soul will be made rich, And he who waters will also be watered himself.

Proverbs 12:9
Better is the one who is slighted but has a servant, Than he who honors himself but _**lacks bread**_.

Proverbs 13:4*
The soul of a lazy man desires, and has **nothing**; But the soul of the diligent shall be made rich.

Proverbs *13:*7*
There is one who makes himself rich, yet has _nothing_; And one who makes himself _poor_, yet has great riches.

Proverbs 13:8*
The ransom of a man's life is his riches, But the _**poor**_ does not hear rebuke.

Proverbs *13:*18*
**Poverty** **and shame will come to him who disdains correction, But he who regards a rebuke will be honored.**

Proverbs 13:23
Much food is in the fallow ground of the _**poor**_, And for lack of justice there is _waste_.

Proverbs 14:4*
Where no oxen are, the trough is clean; But much increase comes by the strength of an ox.

Proverbs 14:20
The _**poor**_ man is hated even by his own neighbor, But the rich has many friends.

Proverbs 14:*21*
He who despises his neighbor sins; But he who has mercy on the _**poor**_, happy is he.

Proverbs *14:*23*
In all labor there is profit, But idle chatter leads only to _poverty_.

Proverbs *14:*31*

He who oppresses the _poor_ reproaches his Maker, But he who honors Him has mercy on the _needy_.

Proverbs *15:*16*

Better is a little with the fear of the LORD, **Than great treasure with trouble.**

Proverbs 15:17

Better is a dinner of herbs where love is, Than a fatted calf with hatred.

Proverbs 15:25*

The LORD will destroy the house of the proud, _But He will establish the boundary of the widow._

Proverbs *16:*8*

Better is a little with righteousness, Than vast resources without justice.

Proverbs *16:*19*

Better to be of a humble spirit with the lowly, Than to divide the spoil with the proud.

Proverbs 17:5*

He who mocks the **_poor_** reproaches his Maker; He who is glad at calamity will not go unpunished.

Proverbs 18:23

The **_poor_** man uses entreaties, But the rich answers roughly.

Proverbs *19:*1*

Better is the poor who walks in his integrity **Than one who is perverse in his lips, and is a fool.**

Proverbs 19:4

Wealth makes many friends, But the **_poor_** is separated from his friend.

Proverbs 19:7

All the brothers of the ***poor*** hate him; How much more do his friends go far from him! He may pursue them with words, yet they abandon him.

Proverbs 19:15*

Laziness casts one into a deep sleep, *And an idle person will suffer hunger.*

Proverbs *19:*17*

He who has pity on the *poor* lends to the LORD, And He will pay back what he has given.

Proverbs 19:*22*

What is desired in a man is kindness, And a ***poor*** man is better than a liar.

Proverbs 20:*13*

Do not love sleep, lest you come to ***poverty***; Open your eyes, and you will be satisfied with *bread.*

Proverbs *21:*5*

The plans of the diligent lead surely to plenty, But those of everyone who is hasty, surely to *poverty*.

Proverbs *21:*13*

Whoever shuts his ears to the cry of the *poor* Will also cry himself and not be heard.

Proverbs 21:17*

He who loves pleasure will be a ***poor*** man; He who loves wine and oil will not be rich.

Proverbs 22:2*

The rich and the ***poor*** have this in common, The LORD is the maker of them all.

Proverbs *22:*7*

The rich rules over the poor, And the borrower is servant to the lender.

Proverbs *22:*9*

He who has a generous eye will be blessed, For he gives of his *bread* to the *poor*.

Proverbs 22:16*

He who oppresses the ***poor*** to increase his riches, And he who gives to the rich, will surely come to ***poverty***.

(Sayings of the Wise)

Proverbs *22:*22*–*23*

Do not rob the *poor* because he is *poor*, Nor oppress the afflicted at the gate; For the LORD will plead their cause, And plunder the soul of those who plunder them.

Proverbs 22:28

Do not remove the ancient landmark Which your fathers have set.

Proverbs 23:10–11

Do not remove the ancient landmark, Nor enter the fields of the *fatherless*; For their Redeemer is mighty; He will plead their cause against you.

Proverbs 23:19*–21*

(19)* Hear, my son, and be *wise*: And guide your heart in the way.

(20) Do not mix with winebibbers, Or with gluttonous eaters of meat;

(21)* For the drunkard and the glutton will come to ***poverty***, And drowsiness will clothe a man with *rags*.

(Further Sayings of the Wise)

Proverbs 24:30–34

(30) I went by the field of the *lazy* man, And by the vineyard of the man devoid of understanding;

(31) And there it was, all overgrown with thorns; Its surface was covered with nettles; It's stone wall was broken down.

(32) When I saw it, I considered it well; I looked on it and received instruction:

(33) A little *sleep*, a little *slumber*, a *little folding of the hands to rest*;

(34) So shall your **_poverty_** come like a prowler, And your **_need_** like an armed man.

(Further Wise Sayings of Solomon)

Proverbs *25:*21*–*22*

If your enemy is <u>hungry</u>, give him bread to eat; And if he is <u>thirsty</u>, give him water to drink; For so you will heap coals of fire on his head, And the LORD will reward you.

Proverbs 27:7

A satisfied soul loathes the honeycomb, But to a **_hungry soul_** every bitter thing is sweet.

Proverbs 28:3

A **_poor_** man who oppresses the **_poor_** *Is like a driving rain which <u>leaves no food</u>.*

Proverbs *28:*6*

Better is the _poor_ who walks in his integrity Than one perverse in his ways, though he be rich.

Proverbs 28:8

One who increases his possessions by usury and extortion Gathers it for him who will pity the **_poor_**.

Proverbs 28:11*

The rich man is wise in his own eyes, But the **_poor_** who has understanding searches him out.

Proverbs 28:15

Like a roaring lion and a charging bear Is a wicked ruler over **_poor_** people.

Proverbs 28:19

He who tills his land will have plenty of bread, But he who follows frivolity will have **_poverty_** enough!

Proverbs 28:22

A man with an evil eye hastens after riches, And does not consider that **_poverty_** will come upon him.

Proverbs *28:*27*

He who gives to the _poor_ will not lack, But he who hides his eyes will have many curses.

Proverbs 29:7*

The righteous considers the cause of the **_poor_**, But the wicked does not understand such knowledge.

Proverbs 29:13*

The **_poor_** man and the oppressor have this in common: The LORD gives light to the eyes of both.

Proverbs 29:14

The king who judges the **_poor_** with truth, His throne will be established forever.

(Prayer of Devotion)

Proverbs 30:7*–9*

(7)* Two things I request of You (Deprive me not before I die):

(8)* Remove falsehood and lies far from me; Give me neither **_poverty_** nor riches—*Feed me with the food allotted to me*;

(9)* Lest I be full and deny You, And say, "Who is the LORD?" Or lest I be **_poor_** and steal, And profane the name of my God.

Proverbs 30:11–14

(11) There is a generation that curses its father, And does not bless its mother.

(12)   There is a generation that is pure in its own eyes, Yet is not washed from its filthiness.

(13)   There is a generation—oh, how lofty are their eyes! And their eyelids are lifted up.

(14)   There is a generation whose teeth are like swords, And whose fangs are like knives, To devour the **_poor_** from off the earth, And the **_needy_** from among men.

(The Words of King Lemuel's Mother)

Proverbs 31:4–9*

(4)   It is not for kings, O Lemuel, It is not for kings to drink wine, Nor for princes intoxicating drink;

(5)   Lest they drink and forget the law, And pervert the justice of all the afflicted.

(6)   Give strong drink to him who is perishing, And wine to those who are bitter of heart.

(7)   Let him drink and forget his **_poverty_**, And remember his misery no more.

(8)   Open your mouth for the speechless, In the cause of all who are appointed to die.

(9)*   Open your mouth, judge righteously, And plead the cause of the **_poor_** and **_needy_**.

(The Virtuous Wife)

Proverbs *31:19–*20*

(19)   She stretches out her hands to the _distaff_, And her hand holds the spindle.

(20)* **She extends her hand to the _poor_, Yes, she reaches out her hands to the _needy_.**

CHAPTER 54

PRIDE, PROUD, HAUGHTY, SELF-ESTEEM, CONCEITED, ARROGANCE

W hat is **_Pride_** or being **_Proud_** or **_Prideful_**? Some might define it as being *"puffed up,"* having a big head, or possessing a selfish nature and not a selfless or humble nature. In the Chapter Narrative on HUMILITY, I mentioned the visual image of Jesus Christ, as my depiction of HUMILITY (i.e. one who is selfless in nature, as one who puts the interest of others before themselves). In contrast, a **_Prideful_** or **_Proud_** persona, is generally characterized as one who puts or places themselves (oneself) above the interest of others (i.e. being in a state of selfishness, one who operates from the position of me, myself, and I).

In essence, being **_Prideful_**, **_Self-Esteeming_**, and/or **_Arrogant_** are the sinful sides of this two-sided coin; Whereby one side has Humility as its face, which, from my perspective, reflects a Christlike attitude of righteousness and love. While on the flipside of this same coin, one will find the image of Satan, who's reflecting image is one of selfishness, unrighteousness, and where a "me only" attitude is ever present.

Additionally, one can safely state that Humility/Love and **_Pride_** are anathema to each other. Therefore, when one operates from a righteous state of Humility, one innately is operating from a position of Love for others; Whereby when one operates from the sinful state of **Pride**, one pursues the lifestyle of selfishness and love of self. Thus, as illustrated in "*The Parable of the 'Good Samaritan'*" (Luke 10:25–37), the **Prideful** nature is an enigma *of* the Jewish priest and Jewish lawyer, who were only concerned about themselves and their self-image. This is contrasted with the caring, sharing, loving, and giving attitude and nature of the "*Good Samaritan*", who interrupted his journey to assist and provide support to the injured Samaritan.

Thus, the question du jour, is which side of this two-headed coin dominates one's nature: (1) Humility, love and righteousness; or (2) **Pride**, selfishness, and the "me only" mindset? I would contend that all of us—those "in Christ," as well as nonbelievers—operate from one side of this "two-headed" coin or the other on a daily basis. The real or key question that one must ask oneself is which side of the coin am I? Which side of this two-headed coin is one's dominate attribute or state of mind?

Pride is a sin, no way around it, as biblical scripture calls out the ill effects of one's **Pride** and/or **Prideful** nature, as evident from the following selected Scripture verses:

- Proverbs 3:34: "*Surely He scorns the scornful, But gives grace to the humble*";
- Proverbs 16:18: "***Pride** goes before destruction, And a **haughty** spirit before a fall*";
- Proverbs 16:19: "*Better to be of a humble spirit with the lowly, Than to divide the spoil with the **proud***";
- Proverbs 29:23: "*A man's **pride** will bring him low, But the humble in spirit will retain honor.*"

And the unequivocal nature of **Pride** being sinful is unambiguously stated in the following Scripture verses:

- James 4:6: "*But He gives more grace. Therefore He says: 'God resists the **proud**, But gives grace to the humble*";
- 1 John 2:16: "*For all that is in the world—the lust of the flesh, the lust of the eyes, and the **pride** of life—is not of the Father but is of the world*"; and last, but definitely not least,
- Proverbs 8:13: "*The fear of the LORD is to hate evil; **Pride** and **arrogance** and the evil way And the perverse mouth I hate*"!

Given that "*all have sinned and fall short of the glory of God*" (Romans 3:23), the question that each person must ask themselves is this: "Which side of this 'two-sided coin' will one intentionally spend—the spiritual face side of *HUMILITY* and *LOVE*, or the sinful worldly side of being **Proud**, **Selfish**, and **Prideful**? For me, the choice is easy—*HUMILITY* and *LOVE*, are the order of the day!

To God be the GLORY!

(Guidance for the Young)

Proverbs *3:*3*–4*
Let not mercy and truth forsake you; Bind them around your neck, Write them on the tablet of your heart, And so find favor and <u>high esteem</u> In the sight of God and man.

(The Wicked Man)

Proverbs 6:16–19
(16) These six things the LORD hates, Yes, seven are an abomination to Him;
(17) A ***proud*** look, A lying tongue, Hands that shed innocent blood,
(18) A heart that devises wicked plans, Feet that are swift in running to evil,
(19) A false witness who speaks lies, And one who sows discord among brethren.

(The Excellence of Wisdom)

Proverbs *8:12–16

(12) "I, wisdom, dwell with prudence, And find out knowledge and discretion.

(13) The fear of the LORD is to hate evil; **_Pride_** and **_arrogance_** and the evil way And the perverse mouth I hate.

(14) Counsel is mine, and sound wisdom; I am understanding, I have strength.

(15) By me kings reign, And rulers decree justice.

(16) By me princes rule, and nobles, All the judges of the earth.

(Wise Sayings of Solomon)

Proverbs *11:*2*

When _pride_ comes, then comes shame; But with the humble is wisdom.

Proverbs *12:*1*

Whoever loves instruction loves knowledge, **_But he who hates correction is stupid_.**

Proverbs 12: 9

Better is the one who is slighted but has a servant, _Than he who honors himself_ but lacks bread.

Proverbs *13:*10*

By _pride_ comes nothing but strife, But with the well-advised is wisdom.

Proverbs 14:3

In the mouth of a fool is a rod of **_pride_,** But the lips of the wise will preserve them.

Proverbs 14:16

A wise man fears and departs from evil, But a fool rages and is **_self-confident_**.

Proverbs 15:25*

The LORD will destroy the house of the **_proud_**, But He will establish the boundary of the widow.

Proverbs 16:5

Everyone **_proud_** in heart is an abomination to the LORD; Though they join forces, none will go unpunished.

Proverbs *16:*18*

**Pride** goes before destruction, And a **haughty** spirit before a fall.

Proverbs *16:*19*

Better to be of a humble spirit with the lowly, _Than to divide the spoil with the **proud**._

Proverbs 17:19*

He who loves transgression loves strife, And he who **_exalts his gate_** seeks destruction.

Proverbs 18:1

A man who isolates himself seeks his own desire; He rages against all wise judgment.

Proverbs 18:11

The rich man's wealth is his strong city, And like a high wall in **_his own esteem_**.

Proverbs *18:*12*

Before destruction the heart of a man is **haughty**, **And before honor is humility.**

Proverbs 20:6*

Most men will _proclaim each his own goodness_, But who can find a faithful man?

Proverbs 20:14*

"It is good for nothing", cries the buyer; But when he has gone his way, *then he boasts*.

Proverbs *21:*2*

Every way of a man is right in his own eyes, **But the LORD weighs the hearts.**

Proverbs 21:4

A ***haughty*** look, a ***proud*** heart, And the plowing of the wicked are sin.

Proverbs *21:*13*

Whoever shuts his ears to the cry of the poor *Will also cry himself and not be heard*.

Proverbs 21:24*

A ***proud*** and ***haughty*** man—"Scoffer" is his name; He acts with ***arrogant pride***.

Proverbs *22:*7*

The rich rules over the poor, **And the borrower is servant to the lender.**

(Sayings of the Wise)

Proverbs *23:*4*–5

Do not overwork to be rich; Because of your own understanding, cease! ***Will you set your eyes on that which is not?*** **For riches certainly make themselves wings; They fly away like an eagle toward heaven.**

Proverbs *24:*17*–*18*

Do not rejoice when your enemy falls, And do not let your heart be glad when he stumbles. **Lest the LORD see it, and it displease Him, And He turn away His wrath from him.**

(Further Wise Sayings of Solomon)

Proverbs 25:6*–7*

*Do not **exalt** yourself in the presence of the king, And do not <u>stand in the</u> <u>place of the great</u>;* For it is better that he says to you, "Come up here," Than that you should be put lower in the presence of the prince, Whom your eyes have seen.

Proverbs 25:14

<u>*Whoever falsely boasts of giving*</u> *Is like clouds and wind without rain.*

Proverbs 25:*27*

It is not good to eat much honey; <u>*So to seek one's own glory is not glory*</u>.

Proverbs 26:5*

Answer a fool according to his folly, <u>*Lest he be wise in his own eyes*</u>.

Proverbs 26:12*

<u>*Do you see a man wise in his own eyes*</u>*? There is more hope for a fool than for him.*

Proverbs *26:*16*

<u>The lazy man is wiser in his own eyes</u> Than seven men who can answer sensibly.

Proverbs 27:1

Do not boast about tomorrow, For you do not know what a day may bring forth.

Proverbs 27:2*

*Let another man <u>praise</u> you, **<u>and not your own mouth</u>**; A stranger, **<u>and not your own lips</u>**.*

Proverbs 27:21*

The refining pot is for silver and the furnace for gold, *And a man is <u>valued</u> by what others say of him.*

Proverbs 28:3

A poor man who oppresses the poor Is like a driving rain which leaves no food.

Proverbs 28:11

The rich man is wise in his own eyes, But the poor who has understanding searches him out.

Proverbs 28:14*

Happy is the man who is always reverent, *But he who hardens his heart will fall into calamity.*

Proverbs 28:*25*

He who is of a ***proud*** heart stirs up strife, But he who trusts in the LORD will be prospered.

Proverbs 29:1*

He who is often rebuked, and hardens his neck, Will suddenly be destroyed, and that without remedy.

Proverbs 29:5

A man who flatters his neighbor Spreads a net for his feet.

Proverbs 29:23*

A man's ***pride*** will bring him low, But the humble in spirit will retain honor.

(The Wisdom of Agur)

Proverbs 30:11–14

(11) *There is a generation that curses its father, And does not bless its mother.*

(12) *There is a generation that is pure in its own eyes, Yet is not washed from its filthiness.*

(13) *There is a generation - oh, how lofty are their eyes! And their eyelids are lifted up.*

(14) *There is a generation <u>whose teeth are like swords, And whose fangs are like knives, To devour the poor from off the earth, And the needy from among men</u>.*

Proverbs 30:32–33

If you have been foolish in ***exalting yourself***, Or if you have devised evil, put your hand on your mouth. For as the churning of milk produces butter, And wringing the nose produces blood, So the forcing of wrath produces strife.

CHAPTER 55

PRUDENT, PRUDENCE

As I was pondering how best to position this Chapter Narrative on the Theme "***Prudent/ Prudence***," the Holy Spirit led me to consider a slightly different approach for this Chapter Narrative. So, instead of the standard experiential Narrative, I decided to highlight and summarize approximately fourteen Proverbs verses and what one might glean from a deeper dive into that particular Proverbs verse's meaning. As I reviewed, studied, and meditated on this Chapter's Proverbs verses, one central observation became crystal clear—Wisdom spawns numerous offspring, namely: Knowledge, Understanding, Instruction, and ***Prudence***, to name a few direct relatives!

1) Proverbs 1:4: "*To give **prudence** to the simple, To the young man knowledge and discretion*"! By listening to and reading Proverbs verses, one will develop/acquire ***Prudence*** or savvy.

2) Proverbs 8:5: "*O you simple ones, understand **prudence**, And you fools, be of an understanding heart*"! Irrespective of one's social/economic status, wisdom via ***Prudence*** can be obtained by all.

3) Proverbs 8:12: "*I, wisdom, dwell with **prudence**, And find out knowledge and discretion*"! Wisdom lives in the same house with

**Prudence**, as they go hand-in-hand; Thus, if one has wisdom, then by definition, one also has insight.

4) Proverbs 12:16: "_A fool's wrath is known at once, But a **prudent man covers shame**._" It's been said that a foolish person does not restrain themselves; as such, their wrath becomes immediately evident; While a _**Prudent**_ person is experienced enough to ignore another's insult while mastering the art of self-control.

5) Proverbs 12:23: "_A **prudent** man conceals knowledge, But the heart of fools proclaims foolishness_"! It goes without saying that, a _**Prudent**_ and wise person does not have to overtly display their knowledge or wisdom; Whereas foolishness can be seen in the presence of fools, before they totally reveal for all to see, their foolish character.

6) Proverbs 13:16: "_Every **prudent** man acts with knowledge, But a fool lays open his folly_"! It's been said that a person's conduct reveals one's character; Accordingly, a _**Prudent**_ person acts in a responsible way.

7) Proverbs 14:8: "_The wisdom of the **prudent** is to understand his way, But the folly of fools is deceit._" It goes without saying, that a _**Prudent**_ person's wisdom, results in understanding as well as knowing how to behave honestly, conscientiously, and obediently; Whereas a foolish person does not recognize wisdom, while embracing deceit and careless choices and lifestyles.

8) Proverbs 14:15: "_The simple believes every word, But the **prudent** considers well his steps._" A _**Prudent**_ individual employs the force field of faith and the Word of God, to direct one's step and way for living out a purpose driven life; While the naïve and gullible person is susceptible to simple and foolish ideas, fads, and/or words.

9) Proverbs 14:18: "_The simple inherit folly, But the **prudent** are crowned with knowledge_"! It's abundantly clear that the simple inherits folly, since they refuse to listen and/or abide by

wise council and knowledge; While the **_Prudent_** is honored and rewarded for acquiring knowledge and applying it on a consistent basis.

10) Proverbs 15:5: "_A fool despises his father's instruction, But he who receives correction is **prudent**_"! It goes without saying, that a foolish son or daughter, who fails to heed one's parental guidance and/or instructions, clearly lacks wisdom; Whereas, the son or daughter who accepts parental correction, while not necessarily pleasant, generally benefits from such correction and becomes wiser because of it.

11) Proverbs 16:21: "_The wise in heart will be called **prudent**, And sweetness of the lips increases learning_"! It goes without saying, that a wise individual, will be acknowledged and recognized for their discernment and insight; While at the same time, one's pleasant and conversational manner, will enhance others to listen and learn.

12) Proverbs 18:15: "_The heart of the **prudent** acquires knowledge, And the ear of the wise seeks knowledge_"! It goes without saying, that the heart of the **_Prudent_** person never ceases to learn and acquire knowledge, as their mind is generally and frequently receptive to gaining knowledge, wisdom, and understanding.

13) Proverbs 19:14: "_Houses and riches are an inheritance from fathers, But a **prudent** wife is from the LORD_"! While any inheritance of money and/or real estate/material/property, may on the surface, appear invaluable; A much greater gift and/or blessing is one that is received from Father God, that being a **_Prudent_** and wise wife! As one who has been divorced twice, this Proverbs verse resonates firmly within me!

14) Proverbs 22:3: "_A **prudent** man foresees evil and hides himself, But the simple pass on and are punished_"! It goes without saying, that a person looks ahead, plans ahead, and/or anticipates uncertainty or evil ahead; While the simple or foolish person refuses to anticipate, visualize, and/or acknowledge evil, folly,

and/or foolishness, and as a result, suffers and/or is punished for such failures. The net result of a lack of **_Prudence,_** in the pathway of life, could result in bumpy conditions, as well as casualties in this earthly life!

(The Beginning of Knowledge)

Proverbs *1:1–4* and *5*–6*

(1)   The Proverbs of Solomon the son of David, king of Israel:

(2)*   **To know wisdom and instruction, To perceive the words of understanding,**

(3)*   **To receive the instruction of wisdom, Justice, judgment, and equity;**

(4)*   To give **_prudence_** to the simple, To the young man knowledge and discretion—

(5)*   **A wise man will hear and increase learning, And a man of understanding will attain wise counsel;**

(6)*   To understand a proverb and an enigma, The words of the wise and their riddles.

(Balance Generosity with Good Stewardship)

Proverbs 6:1–5

(1)   My son, if you become *surety* for your friend, If you have shaken hands in *pledge* for a stranger,

(2)   You are *snared* by the words of your mouth; You are taken by the words of your mouth.

(3)   So do this, my son, and deliver yourself; For you have come into the hand of your friend: Go and humble yourself; Plead with your friend.

(4)   *Give* no sleep to your eyes, Nor *slumber* to your eyelids.

(5)   *Deliver* yourself like a gazelle from the hand of the hunter, And like a bird from the hand of the fowler.

(The Excellence of Wisdom)

Proverbs *8:*1*–11* and *12*–14*

(1)* **Does not *wisdom* cry out, And understanding lift up her voice?**

(2) **She (wisdom)** takes her stand on the top of the high hill, Beside the way, where the paths meet.

(3) **She (wisdom)** cries out by the gates, at the entry of the city, At the entrance of the doors:

(4) "To you, O men, I call, And my voice is to the sons of men.

(5)* O you simple ones, understand **_prudence_**, And you fools, be of an understanding heart.

(6) Listen, for I will speak of excellent things, And from the opening of my lips will come right things;

(7)* **For my mouth will speak truth; Wickedness is an abomination to my lips.**

(8)* **All the words of my mouth are with righteousness; Nothing crooked or perverse is in them.**

(9) They are all plain to him who understands, And right to those who find knowledge.

(10)* Receive my instruction, and not silver, And knowledge rather than choice gold;

(11)* **For wisdom is better than rubies, And all the things one may desire cannot be compared with her.**

(12)* "I, **wisdom**, dwell with **_prudence_**, And find out knowledge and discretion.

(13) The fear of the LORD is to hate evil; Pride and arrogance and the evil way And the perverse mouth, I hate.

(14)* Counsel is mine, and sound **wisdom**; I am understanding, I have strength.

(Wise Sayings of Solomon)

Proverbs 12:16

A fool's wrath is known at once, But a ***prudent*** man covers shame.

Proverbs 12:23*

A ***prudent*** man conceals knowledge, But the heart of fools proclaims foolishness.

Proverbs *13:*7*

There is one who makes himself rich, yet has nothing; *And one who makes himself poor, yet has great riches.*

Proverbs 13:16*

Every ***prudent*** man acts with knowledge, But a fool lays open his folly.

Proverbs *13:*22*

***A good man leaves an inheritance to his children's children,* But the wealth of the sinner is stored up for the righteous.**

Proverbs 14:*8*

The wisdom of the ***prudent*** is to understand his way, But the folly of fools is deceit.

Proverbs 14:*15*

The simple believes every word, But the ***prudent*** considers well his steps.

Proverbs 14:18*

The simple inherit folly, But the ***prudent*** are crowned with knowledge.

Proverbs 15:4

A wholesome tongue is a tree of life, But perverseness in it breaks the spirit.

Proverbs *15:*5*

A fool despises his father's instruction, But he who receives correction is *prudent*.

Proverbs 16:21*

The wise in heart will be called _**prudent**_, And sweetness of the lips increases learning.

Proverbs *18:*15*

The heart of the _prudent_ acquires knowledge, And the ear of the wise seeks knowledge.

Proverbs *19:*14*

Houses and riches are an inheritance from fathers, But a _prudent_ wife is from the LORD.

Proverbs 20:*13*

Do not love sleep, lest you come to poverty; Open your eyes, and you will be satisfied with bread.

Proverbs 21:20*

There is desirable treasure, And oil in the dwelling of the wise, But a foolish man squanders it.

Proverbs 22:*3*

A _**prudent**_ man foresees evil and hides himself, But the simple pass on and are punished.

Proverbs *22:*7*

The rich rules over the poor, _And the borrower is servant to the lender._

(Sayings of the Wise)

Proverbs 22:29*

Do you see a man who excels in his work? He will stand before kings; He will not stand before unknown men.

Proverbs 23:24–25

The father of the righteous will greatly rejoice, And he who begets a wise *child will delight in him. Let your father and your mother be glad, And let her who bore you rejoice.*

Proverbs *24:*5*–*6*

A wise man is strong, Yes, a man of knowledge increases strength; *For by wise counsel you will wage your own war, And in a multitude of counselors there is safety.*

Proverbs 24:21–22

My son, fear the LORD and the king; *Do not associate with those given to change;* For their calamity will rise suddenly, And who knows the ruin those two can bring?

(Further Wise Sayings of Solomon)

Proverbs 25:8–10

(8) *Do not go hastily to court; For what will you do in the end, When your neighbor has put you to shame?*

(9) *Debate your case with your neighbor, And do not disclose the secret to another;*

(10) *Lest he who hears it exposes your shame, And your reputation be ruined.*

Proverbs 25:26*

A righteous man who falters before the wicked Is like a murky spring and a polluted well.

Proverbs 25:*27*

It is not good to eat much honey; *So to seek one's own glory is not glory.*

Proverbs 25:28*

Whoever has no rule over his own spirit Is like a city broken down, without walls.

Proverbs 27:12*

A **_prudent_** man foresees evil and hides himself; The simple pass on and are punished.

Proverbs 27:23–27

(23) *Be diligent to know the state of your flocks, And attend to your herds;*

(24) *For riches are not forever, Nor does a crown endure to all generations,*

(25) When the hay is removed, and the tender grass shows itself, And the herbs of the mountains are gathered in,

(26) The lambs will provide your clothing, And the goats the price of a field;

(27) You shall have enough goats' milk for your food, For the food of your household, And the nourishment of your maidservants.

Proverbs 28:10

Whoever causes the upright to go astray in an evil way, He himself will fall into his own pit; But the _blameless_ will inherit good.

Proverbs 28:19

He who tills his land will have plenty of bread, But he who follows frivolity will have poverty enough!

Proverbs 29:11*

A fool vents all his feelings, *But a wise man holds them back.*

Proverbs 29:*18*

Where there is no revelation, the people cast off restrain; *But happy is he who keeps the law.*

(The Wisdom of Agur)

Proverbs 30:32–33

If you have been foolish in exalting yourself, Or if you have devised evil, put your hand on your mouth. For as the churning of milk produces butter, And wringing the nose produces blood, So the forcing of wrath produces strife.

CHAPTER 56

REBUKE, REPROACH,
PUNISHMENT, UNPUNISHED

One of my core life coaching principles is a concept/principle that I affectionately call *"Teachable Moments."* The core principle of this life coaching concept rests in the firm belief that everything in life that happens to an individual—whether good, bad, and/or indifferent—results in positive or negative consequences, which are, by definition, life's *"Teachable Moments."* And by *"Teachable Moments,"* one gains wisdom, knowledge, and experiences that can position one for future success or failure the next time an individual faces the exact or a similar set of circumstances. For example, if one has hit a home run or scored a touchdown or secured an important new client, the ongoing challenge becomes in looking back at such success, how does one then build sustainability, into one's DNA or core operating principles as a result of the before mentioned life experiences. And quite naturally, the opposite is true: If one has failed at a project, task, assignment, and/or has stubbed one's toe on something, then the challenge becomes in how effective one is, in analyzing one's mistakes and/or failed opportunities, and not wallowing in defeat, but using any setback, as a setup for future learning opportunities for future success. Thus, the concept of *"Teachable Moments."*

This same concept of "*Teachable Moments*," especially in the area or areas where things did not come off as planned, is quite naturally analogous to the biblical principle of "**_Rebuke_**." I enjoy reading the numerous Proverbs verses, that speak quite firmly and directly, on the positive attributes that can and do emerge from being "**_Rebuked_**." For example, note the following Proverbs verses:

- Proverbs 9:8: "*Do not correct a scoffer, lest he hate you;* **Rebuke** *a wise man, and he will love you*";
- Proverbs 13:18: "*Poverty and shame will come to him who disdains correction, But he who regards a* **rebuke** *will be honored*";
- Proverbs 15:31 and 32: "*The ear that hears the* **rebukes** *of life Will abide among the wise. He who disdains instruction despises his own soul, But he who heeds* **rebuke** *gets understanding*";
- Proverbs 17:10: "**Rebuke** *is more effective for a wise man Than a hundred blows on a fool*";
- Proverbs 25:11 and 12: "*A word fitly spoken is like apples of gold In settings of silver. Like an earring of gold and an ornament of fine gold Is a wise* **rebuker** *to an obedient ear*";
- Proverbs 27:5: "*Open* **rebuke** *is better Than love carefully concealed*";
- Proverbs 27:6: "**_Faithful are the wounds of a friend, But the kisses of an enemy are deceitful_**"; and,
- Proverbs 28:23: "*He who* **rebukes** *a man will find more favor afterward Than he who flatters with the tongue.*"

Essentially, the way in which a person receives a **_Rebuke_** and/or a **_Reproach,_** is an indicator of a person's character. Ask yourself the question regarding how one responds or reacts when a parent, teacher, employer, or friend *corrects*, **_Rebukes_**, or **_Reproaches_** you? Instead of resenting any form of criticism, which in essence, is a form of a "*Teachable Moments*;" A wise person will savor such "*Teachable Moments*," take them to heart, and thus become a wiser individual, benefiting by increasing one's stored knowledge of useful, constructive criticism, insights, experiences, and learnings, i.e. a net positive, "*Teachable Moments*" experience!

(The Call of Wisdom)

Proverbs *1:*20*–27 and 28–33*

(20)* **Wisdom calls aloud outside; She raises her voice in the open squares.**

(21) She cries out in the chief concourses, At the openings of the gates in the city She speaks her words:

(22) "How long, you simple ones, will you love simplicity? For scorners delight in their scorning, And fools hate knowledge.

(23) Turn at my *rebuke*; Surely I will pour out my spirit on you; I will make my words know to you.

(24) Because I have called and you refused, I have stretched out my hand and no one regarded,

(25) Because you disdained all my counsel, And would have none of my *rebuke*,

(26) I also will laugh at your calamity; I will mock when your terror comes,

(27) When your terror comes like a storm, And your destruction comes like a whirlwind, When distress and anguish come upon you.

(28) "Then they will call on me, but I will not answer; They will seek me diligently, but they will not find me.

(29)* Because they hated knowledge And did not choose the fear of the LORD,

(30) They would have none of my counsel And despised my every *rebuke*.

(31) Therefore they shall eat the fruit of their own way, And be filled to the full with their own fancies.

(32) For the turning away of the simple will slay them, And the complacency of fools will destroy them;

(33)* But whoever listens to me will dwell safely, And will be secure, without fear of evil."

(Guidance for the Young)

Proverbs *3:*11*–*12*

My son, do not despise the *chastening* of the LORD, Nor detest His *correction;* For whom the LORD loves He *corrects,* Just as a father the son in whom he delights.

(Beware of Adultery)

Proverbs *6:20*–29* and *32*–35*

(20)* My son, keep your father's command, And do not forsake the law of your mother.

(21) Bind them continually upon your heart; Tie them around your neck.

(22) When you roam, they will lead you; When you sleep, they will keep you; And when you awake, they will speak with you.

(23)* **For the commandment is a lamp, And the law a light; *Reproofs* of *instruction* are the way of life,**

(24)* To keep you from the evil woman, From the flattering tongue of a seductress.

(25) Do not lust after her beauty in your heart, Nor let her allure you with her eyelids.

(26) For by means of a harlot, A man is reduced to a crust of bread; And an adulteress will prey upon his precious life.

(27) Can a man take fire to his bosom, And his clothes not be burned?

(28) Can one walk on hot coals, And his feet not be seared?

(29)* So is he who goes in to his neighbor's wife; Whoever touches her shall not be innocent.

(32)* **Whoever commits adultery with a woman lacks understanding; He who does so destroys his own soul.**

(33)* **Wounds and dishonor he will get, And his _reproach_ will not be wiped away.**

(34) For jealousy is a husband's fury; Therefore he will not spare in the day of vengeance.

(35)* He will accept no recompense, Nor will he be appeased though you give many gifts.

(The Way of Wisdom)

Proverbs *9:7–12

(7) "He who _corrects_ a scoffer gets shame for himself, And he who _rebukes_ a wicked man only harms himself.

(8)* **Do not _correct_ a scoffer, lest he hate you; _Rebuke_ a wise man, and he will love you.**

(9)* **Give instruction to a wise man, and he will be still wiser; Teach a just man, and he will increase in learning.**

(10)* **The fear of the LORD is the beginning of wisdom, And the knowledge of the Holy One is understanding.**

(11) For by me your days will be multiplied, And years of life will be added to you.

(12) If you are wise, you are wise for yourself, And if you scoff, you will bear it alone."

(Wise Sayings of Solomon)

Proverbs 10:*17*

He who keeps instruction is in the way of life, But he who refuses _correction_ goes astray.

Proverbs 11:21*

Though they join forces, the wicked will not go _**unpunished**_; But the posterity of the righteous will be delivered.

Proverbs *12:*1*

Whoever loves instruction loves knowledge, But he who hates *correction* is stupid.

Proverbs *13:*1*

A wise son heeds his father's instruction, But a scoffer does not listen to *rebuke*.

Proverbs 13:8*

The ransom of a man's life is his riches, But the poor does not hear *rebuke*.

Proverbs *13:*18*

Poverty and shame will come to him who disdains *correction*, But he who regards a *rebuke* will be honored.

Proverbs *13:*24*

He who *spares his rod* hates his son, But he who loves him *disciplines* him promptly.

Proverbs *14:*31*

He who oppresses the poor *reproaches* his Maker, But he who honors Him has mercy on the needy.

Proverbs 14:34

Righteousness exalts a nation, But sin is a ***reproach*** to any people.

Proverbs 15:10*

Harsh *discipline* is for him who forsakes the way, And he who hates *correction* will die.

Proverbs *15:*31*

The ear that hears the *rebukes* of life Will abide among the wise.

Proverbs *15:*32*

He who disdains instruction despises his own soul, But he who heeds *rebuke* gets understanding.

Proverbs 16:5

Everyone proud in heart is an abomination to the LORD; Though they join forces, none will go **_unpunished_**.

Proverbs 17:5*

He who mocks the poor **_reproaches_** his Maker; He who is glad at calamity will not go **_unpunished_**.

Proverbs 17:*10*

Rebuke is more effective for a wise man Than a hundred blows on a fool.

Proverbs 17:26

Also, to **_punish_** the righteous is not good, Nor to strike princes for their uprightness.

Proverbs 18:3

When the wicked comes, contempt comes also; And with dishonor comes **_reproach_**.

Proverbs 19:5*

A false witness will not go **_unpunished_**, And he who speaks lies will not escape.

Proverbs 19:*9*

A false witness will not go **_unpunished_**, And he who speaks lies shall perish.

Proverbs 19:18

Chasten your son while there is hope, And do not set your heart on his destruction.

Proverbs 19:19*

A man of great wrath will suffer **_punishment_**; For if you rescue him, you will have to do it again.

Proverbs *19:*25*
Strike a scoffer, and the simple will become wary; _Rebuke_ one who has understanding, and he will discern knowledge.

Proverbs 19:26
He who mistreats his father and chases away his mother Is a son who causes shame and brings _reproach_.

Proverbs 20:26
A wise king sifts out the wicked, _And brings the threshing wheel over them_.

Proverbs 20:30
Blows that _hurt_ cleanse away evil, As do _stripes_ the inner depths of the heart.

Proverbs 21:*11*
When the scoffer is _**punished**_, the simple is made wise; But when the wise is instructed, he receives knowledge.

Proverbs 21:12*
The righteous God wisely considers the house of the wicked; _Overthrowing_ the wicked for their wickedness.

Proverbs 22:*3*
A prudent man foresees evil and hides himself, But the simple pass on and are _**punished**_.

Proverbs 22:8*
He who sows iniquity will reap _sorrow_, And the _rod_ of his anger will fail.

Proverbs 22:*10*
Cast out the scoffer, and contention will leave; Yes, strife and _**reproach**_ will cease.

Proverbs 22:*12*
The eyes of the LORD preserve knowledge, But He _overthrows_ the words of the faithless.

Proverbs 22:14
The mouth of an immoral woman is a deep pit; He who is *abhorred by the LORD* will *fall* there.

Proverbs 22:16*
He who *oppresses* the poor to increase his riches, And he who gives to the rich, will surely come to poverty.

(Sayings of the Wise)

Proverbs *22:*22*–*23*
Do not rob the poor because he is poor, Nor *oppress* the afflicted at the gate; For the LORD will plead their cause, And _plunder_ the soul of those who _plunder_ them.

Proverbs *23:*13*–*14*
Do not withhold *correction* from a child, For if you _beat_ him with a _rod_, he will not die. You shall _beat_ him with a _rod_, And deliver his soul from hell.

Proverbs 24:19–20
Do not fret because of evildoers, Nor be envious of the wicked; For there will be no prospect for the evil man; The lamp of the wicked *will be put out.*

(Further Sayings of the Wise)

Proverbs *24:*23*–*25*
(23)* *These things also belong to the wise*: **It is not good to show partiality in judgment.**
(24) He who says to the wicked, "You are righteous," Him the people will curse; Nations will abhor him.
(25)* **But those who _rebuke_ the wicked will have delight, And a good blessing will come upon them.**

(Further Wise Sayings of Solomon)

Proverbs 25:11–12

A word fitly spoken is like apples of gold In settings of silver. Like an earring of gold and an ornament of fine gold Is a wise **rebuker** to an obedient ear.

Proverbs 26:4*–5*

Do not answer a fool according to his folly, Lest you also be like him. *Answer a fool according to his folly*, Lest he be wise in his own eyes.

Proverbs 27:5*

Open **rebuke** is better Than love carefully concealed.

Proverbs *27:*6*

Faithful are the **wounds** *of a friend*, **But the kisses of an enemy are deceitful.**

Proverbs 27:11

My son, be wise, and make my heart glad, That I may answer him who **reproaches** me.

Proverbs 27:12*

A prudent man foresees evil and hides himself; The simple pass on and are **punished**.

Proverbs *27:*17*

As iron sharpens iron, *So a man sharpens the countenance of his friend.*

Proverbs 28:10

Whoever causes the upright to go astray in an evil way, He himself will *fall into his own pit*; But the blameless will inherit good.

Proverbs 28:17

A man burdened with bloodshed will flee into a pit; Let no one help him.

Proverbs 28:20
A faithful man will abound with blessings, But he who hastens to be rich will not go ***unpunished***.

Proverbs *28:*23*
He who _rebukes_ a man will find more favor afterward Than he who flatters with the tongue.

Proverbs *28:*27*
He who gives to the poor will not lack, *But he who hides his eyes will have many curses.*

Proverbs 29:1*
He who is often ***rebuked***, and hardens his neck, Will suddenly be *destroyed*, and that without remedy.

Proverbs *29:*15*
The _rod_ and _rebuke_ give wisdom, But a child left to himself brings shame to his mother.

Proverbs *29:*17*
Correct your son, and he will give you rest; Yes, he will give delight to your soul.

(The Wisdom of Agur)

Proverbs *30:*5*–6
Every word of God is pure; He is a shield to those who put their trust in Him. Do not add to His words, Lest He _rebuke_ you, and you be found a liar.

CHAPTER 57

RELATIONSHIPS: FAMILY

As one reads the Proverbs verses found in this Chapter Theme, one notices words and phrases such as the following: "***instructions of your father***"; "***receive my words***"; "***treasure my commands***"; "***incline your ear to wisdom***"; "***apply your heart to understanding***" (Proverbs 2 verses). "***Do not forget my law***"; "***let your heart keep my commands***" (Proverbs 3 verses). "***Hear instruction of a father***"; "***let your heart retain my words***"; "***Keep my commands and give attention to my words***"; "***Incline your ear to my sayings***" (Proverbs 4 verses). From such biblical Proverbs phrases, I personally have summarized this Chapter Theme regarding ***Relationships—Family***, with the central focus being the ***Relationships between a Parent(s) and a Child***, down to this foundational key and principle Proverbs verse exemplified as such by Proverbs 22:6: "***Train up a child in the way he should go, And when he is old he will not depart from it.***"

Not that I am, by any stretch of the imagination, an expert on the tools, skills, techniques, and/or critical words needed to adequately "***train up a child in the way he(she) should go.***" One comes away with the importance of "***Discipline***," and what I like to coach and teach about, that being the disciplinary principle and expression of "***Tough Love***";

Whereby someone is treated rather sternly with the intention of helping such person in the long run.

I will briefly discuss such principles in the following paragraphs:

Christian Discipline: It's probably safe and fair to say that everyone has his or her definition of appropriate *Discipline* **for** *Children*. The Bible does, in fact, provide biblical principles and guidelines through its verses on this topic. For example, Proverbs 23:13–14 states: "*Do not withhold correction from a **child**, For, if **you** beat **him** with a rod, **he** will not die. **You** shall beat **him** with a rod, And deliver **his soul** from hell.*" Other Proverbs verses that support *Discipline* include the following verses—22:15, 20:30, and 13:24, which states: "***He who spares his** rod hates **his son**, But **he who** loves him disciplines him** promptly.*"

As one can read in these few Proverbs verses (and there are others), the Bible strongly encourages the importance of *Discipline*. Needless to say, one must have in one's individual life, *Discipline*; Thereby allowing one to become productive individuals in society. And it goes without saying that *Discipline* is much better learned when we are *Young* and easier to train, mold, and influence. It's been said that *Children* who are not *Disciplined* while growing up, often become rebellious, have no respect for authority, which often leads to difficult challenges in following and obeying Father God. The Book of Proverbs contains outstanding verses of wisdom on the topic of *Discipline*. The key then becomes how to appropriately apply *Discipline* correctly and in accordance with biblical principles. Thus, *Parents* must take ownership and become familiar with the scriptural advice regarding *Discipline,* offered in this Chapter Theme.

Tough Love: As stated previously, *Tough Love* generally has an element of *Sternness* associated with it, which sometimes adversely impacts the *Giver* as well as the *Receiver*. How often does one sometimes feel when a *Parent* has to exhibit "*Tough/Stern*" *Love* to an *Offspring* in order to break an evil prone behavioral pattern that we as *Parents* know, that unless such behavior is broken early on, the downside consequences could be long lasting and extremely detrimental to such *Offspring's* overall personal characteristics and life journey. While teaching and coaching quality life behaviors and patterns can result in a more productive and fruitful life for **One's Children**. Quite naturally, dispensing firm **Disciplinary** measures and tactics, can sometimes be as unpleasant to the **Parent** as well as **One's Offspring**. Nevertheless, it does require a high degree of courage, understanding, firmness, and wisdom; Otherwise, **One** stymies **One's Offspring**. Additionally, **One** can stymie **Their** opportunity to eradicate **Their** problematic behavior altogether. Accordingly, **One** potentially reduces the opportunity and incentive for **One's Offspring** to change **Themselves**; Whereby, such opportunities for change can be eliminated and/or reduced due to age, stubbornness, and/or overall hardness of the heart.

As **Parents** proactively take on the importance of **Tough Love** and **Discipline**, the higher the probability that Proverbs 22:6 can become not probable but consequential: "***Train up a child in the way he should go, And when he is old he will not depart from it***"; Then the greater chance that **Tough Love** will better mold a child for the future!

(Shun Evil Counsel)

Proverbs *1:8–*19*

(8) **My son**, hear the instruction of **your father**, And do not forsake the law of **your mother**;

(9) For they will be a graceful ornament on **your** head, And chains about **your** neck.

(10) **My son**, if sinners entice **you**, Do not consent.

(11) If they say, "Come with us, Let us lie in wait to shed blood; Let us lurk secretly for the innocent without cause;

(12) Let us swallow them alive like Sheol, And whole, like those who go down to the Pit;

(13) We shall find all kinds of precious possessions, We shall fill our houses with spoil;

(14) Cast in **your** lot among us, Let us all have one purse"—

(15) **My son**, do not walk in the way with them, Keep **your** foot from their path;

(16)   For their feet run to evil, And they make haste to shed blood.

(17)   Surely, in vain the net is spread In the sight of any bird;

(18)   But they lie in wait for their own blood, They lurk secretly for their own lives.

(19)* **So are the ways of everyone who is greedy for gain; It takes away the life of its owners.**

(The Value of Wisdom)

Proverbs *2:1*–*9* and *10*–22*

(1)*   *My* *son*, if *you* receive *my* words, And treasure *my* commands with *you*,

(2)*   **So that *you* will incline *your* ear to wisdom, And apply *your* heart to understanding;**

(3)*   Yes, if *you* cry out for discernment, And lift up *your* *voice* for understanding,

(4)*   If *you* seek her as silver, And search for her as for hidden treasures;

(5)*   **Then *you* will understand the fear of the LORD, And find the knowledge of God.**

(6)*   **For the LORD gives wisdom; From His mouth come knowledge and understanding;**

(7)*   **He stores up sound wisdom for the upright; He is a shield to those who walk uprightly;**

(8)*   **He guards the paths of justice, And preserves the way of His saints.**

(9)*   **Then *you* will understand righteousness and justice, Equity and every good path.**

(10)* **When wisdom enters *your* heart, And knowledge is pleasant to *your* soul,**

(11)* **Discretion will preserve *you*; Understanding will keep *you*,**

(12)   To deliver *you* from the way of evil, From the man who speaks perverse things,

(13) From those who leave the paths of uprightness To walk in the ways of darkness;

(14) Who rejoice in doing evil, And delight in the perversity of the wicked;

(15) Whose ways are crooked, And who are devious in their paths;

(16) To deliver *you* from the immoral woman, From the seductress who flatters with her words,

(17) Who forsakes the companion of her youth, And forgets the covenant of her God.

(18) For her house leads down to death, And her paths to the dead;

(19) None who go to her return, Nor do they regain the paths of life—

(20)* **So *you* may walk in the way of goodness, And keep to the paths of righteousness.**

(21)* **For the upright will dwell in the land, And the blameless will remain in it;**

(22)* But the wicked will be cut off from the earth, And the unfaithful will be uprooted from it.

(Guidance for the Young)

Proverbs *3:1*–2*, *3*–4, *5*–*6*, 7*–8*, *9*–*10*, *11*–*12*, *21*–26, and *27*–30*

(1)* ***My son***, do not forget ***my*** law, But let ***your*** heart keep ***my*** commands;

(2)* For length of days and long life And peace they will add to ***you***.

(3)* **Let not mercy and truth forsake *you*; Bind them around your neck, Write them on the tablet of *your* heart,**

(4) And so find favor and high esteem In the sight of God and man.

(5)* *Trust in the LORD with all *your* heart, And lean not on *your* understanding;*

(6)* *In all *your* ways acknowledge Him, And He shall direct *your* paths.*

(7)* Do not be wise in *your* own eyes; Fear the LORD and depart from evil.

(8)* It will be health to *your* flesh, And strength to *your* bones.

(9)* **Honor the LORD with *your possessions*, And with the first fruits of all *your* increase;**

(10)* **So *your barns* will be filled with plenty, And *your vats* will overflow with new wine.**

(11)* ***My son*, do not despise the chastening of the LORD, Nor detest His correction;**

(12)* **For whom the LORD loves, He corrects, Just as a *father, the son*, in who *he* delights.**

(21)* ***My son*, let them not depart from *your eyes*—Keep sound wisdom and discretion;**

(22) So they will be life to *your* soul And grace to *your* neck.

(23) Then *you* will walk safely in *your* way, And *your* foot will not stumble.

(24)* When *you* lie down, *you* will not be afraid; Yes, *you* will lie down and *your* sleep will be sweet.

(25) Do not be afraid of sudden terror, Nor of trouble from the wicked when it comes;

(26) For the LORD will be *your* confidence, And will keep *your* foot from being caught.

(27)* **Do not withhold good from those to whom it is due, When it is in the power of *your* hand to do so.**

(28)* **Do not say to *your* neighbor, "Go, and come back, And tomorrow *I* will give it," When *you* have it with *you*.**

(29) Do not devise evil against *your* neighbor, For he dwells by *you* for safety's sake.

(30) Do not strive with a man without cause, If he has done *you* no harm.

(Security in Wisdom)

Proverbs *4:1*–9, *10*–*13*, *14*–17, *18*–19, and *20*–*27*

(1)* Hear, *my children*, the instruction of a *father*, And give attention to know understanding;

(2) For *I* give *you* good doctrine: Do not forsake *my* law.

(3) When *I* was *my father's son*, Tender and the only one in the sight of *my mother*,

(4)* *He* also taught *me*, and said to *me*: "**Let** *your* **heart retain** *my* **words; Keep** *my* **commands, and live.**

(5)* **Get wisdom! Get understanding! Do not forget, nor turn away from the words of** *my* **mouth.**

(6) **Do not forsake her (wisdom), and she will preserve** *you*: **Love her, and she will keep** *you*.

(7)* **Wisdom is the principal thing; Therefore get wisdom, And in all** *your* **getting, get understanding.**

(8) Exalt her, and she will promote *you*; She will bring *you* honor, when *you* embrace her.

(9) She will place on *your* head an ornament of grace; A crown of glory she will deliver to *you*."

(10)* **Hear,** *my son*, **and receive** *my* **sayings, And the years of** *your life* **will be many.**

(11)* *I* **have taught** *you* **in the way of wisdom;** *I* **have led** *you* **in right paths.**

(12)* **When** *you* **walk,** *your* **steps will not be hindered, And when** *you* **run,** *you* **will not stumble.**

(13)* **Take firm hold of instruction, do not let go; Keep her, for she is** *your* **life.**

(14)* **Do not enter the path of the wicked, And do not walk in the way of evil.**

(15) Avoid it, do not travel on it; Turn away from it and pass on.

(16) For they do not sleep unless they have done evil; And their sleep is taken away unless they make someone fall.

(17) For they eat the bread of wickedness, And drink the wine of violence.

(18)* **But the path of the just is like the shining sun, That shines ever brighter unto the perfect day**.

(19) The way of the wicked is like darkness; They do not know what makes them stumble.

(20)* _My son_, give attention to _my_ words; Incline _your_ ear to _my_ sayings.

(21)* **Do not let them depart from _your_ eyes; Keep them in the midst of _your_ heart**;

(22)* **For they are life to those who find them, And health to all their flesh**.

(23)* **Keep _your heart_ with all diligence, For out of it spring the issues of life**.

(24)* **Put away from _you_ a deceitful mouth, And put perverse lips far from _you_.**

(25) Let _your_ eyes look straight ahead, And _your_ eyelids look right before _you_.

(26)* **Ponder the path of _your feet_, And let all _your_ ways be established.**

(27)* **Do not turn to the right or the left; Remove _your foot_ from evil.**

(The Peril of Adultery)

Proverbs *5:1*–6, 7–14, *15*–20, and *21*–*23*

(1)* _My **son**_, pay attention to _my_ wisdom; Lend _your_ ear to _my_ understanding,

(2)* That _**you**_ may preserve discretion, And _your_ lips may keep knowledge.

(3) For the lips of an immoral woman drip honey, And her mouth is smoother than oil;

(4) But in the end she is bitter as wormwood, Sharp as a two-edged sword.

(5) Her feet go down to death, Her steps lay hold of hell.

(6) Lest **_you_** ponder her path of life—Her ways are unstable; **_You_** do not know them.

(7) Therefore hear **_me_** now, **_my children_**, And do not depart from the words of **_my_** mouth.

(8) Remove **_your_** way far from her, And do not go near the door of her house,

(9) Lest **_you_** give **_your_** honor to others, And **_your_** years to the cruel one;

(10) Lest aliens be filled with **_your_** wealth, And **_your_** labors go to the house of a foreigner;

(11) And **_you_** mourn at last, When **_your_** flesh and **_your_** body are consumed.

(12) And say: "How **_I_** hated instruction, And **_my_** heart despised correction!

(13) **_I_** have not obeyed the voice of **_my_** teachers, Nor inclined **_my_** ear to those who instructed **_me_**!

(14) **_I_** was on the verge of total ruin, In the midst of the assembly and congregation."

(15)* **_Drink water from your own cistern, And running water from your own well._**

(16) Should **_your_** fountains be dispersed abroad, Streams of water in the streets?

(17) Let them be only **_your_** own, And not for strangers with **_you_**.

(18)* **_Let your fountain be blessed, And rejoice with the wife of your youth._**

(19)* **_As a loving deer and a graceful doe, Let her breasts satisfy you at all times; And always be enraptured with her love._**

(20) For why should **_you_**, **_my son_**, be enraptured by an immoral woman, And be embraced in the arms of a seductress?

(21)* **For the ways of _man_ are before the eyes of the LORD, And _He_ ponders all _his_ paths.**

(22)* **_His_ own iniquities entrap the wicked _man_, And _he_ is caught in the cords of _his_ sin.**

(23)* **_He_ shall die for lack of instruction, And in the greatness of his folly _he_ shall go astray.**

(Balance Generosity with Good Stewardship)

Proverbs *6:1–5

(1) **_My son_**, if **_you_** become surety for **_your_** friend, if **_you_** have shaken hands in pledge for a stranger,

(2) **_You_** are snared by the words of **_your_** mouth; **_You_** are taken by the words of **_your_** mouth.

(3) So do this, **_my son_**, and deliver **_yourself_**; For **_you_** have come into the hand of **_your_** friend; Go and humble **_yourself_**; Plead with **_your_** friend.

(4) Give no sleep to **_your_** eyes, nor slumber to **_your_** eyelids.

(5) Deliver **_yourself_** like a gazelle from the hand of the hunter, And like a bird from the hand of the fowler.

(Beware of Adultery)

Proverbs *6:20–29 and *32*–35*

(20) **_My son_**, keep **_your father's_** command, And do not forsake the law of **_your mother_**.

(21) Bind them continually upon **_your_** heart; Tie them around **_your_** neck.

(22) When **_you_** roam, they will lead **_you_**; When **_you_** sleep, they will keep **_you_**; And when **_you_** awake, they will speak with **_you_**.

(23)* **For the commandment is a lamp, And the law a light; Reproofs of instruction are the way of life,**

(24) To keep **_you_** from the evil woman, From the flattering tongue of a seductress.

(25) Do not lust after her beauty in **_your_** heart, Nor let her allure **_you_** with her eyelids.

(26) For by means of a harlot A **_man_** is reduced to a crust of bread; And an adulteress will prey upon **_his_** precious life.

(27) Can a **_man_** take fire to **_his_** bosom, And **_his_** clothes not be burned?

(28) Can **_one_** walk on hot coals, And **_his_** feet not be seared?

(29) So is **_he_** who goes in to **_his_** neighbor's wife; Whoever touches her shall not be innocent.

(32)* **Whoever commits adultery with a woman lacks understanding; _He_ who does so destroys _his_ own soul.**

(33)* **Wounds and dishonor _he_ will get, And _his_ reproach will not be wiped away.**

(34) For jealousy is a **_husband's_** fury; Therefore **_he_** will not spare in the day of vengeance.

(35)* **_He_ will accept no recompense, Nor will _he_ be appeased though _you_** give many gifts.

Proverbs *7:*1*–5*

(1)*   **_My son_, keep _my_ words And treasure _my_ commands within _you_.**

(2)*   **Keep _my_ commands and live, And _my_ law as the apple of _your_ eye.**

(3)*   Bind them on **_your_** fingers; Write them on the tablet of **_your_** heart.

(4)*   **Say to wisdom, "You are _my sister_," And call understanding _your_ nearest _kin_,**

(5)*   That they may keep **_you_** from the immortal woman, From the seductress who flatters with her words.

(The Crafty Harlot)

Proverbs 7:24–27

(24) Now therefore, listen to **_me_, _my children_**; Pay attention to the words of **_my_** mouth:

(25) Do not let **_your_** heart turn aside to her ways, Do not stray into her paths;

(26) For she has cast down many wounded, And all who were slain by her were strong men.

(27) Her house is the way to hell, Descending to the chambers of death.

(Wise Sayings of Solomon)

Proverbs 10:1

A wise **son** makes a glad **father**, But a foolish **son** is the grief of **his mother**.

Proverbs 10:5*

He who gathers in summer is a wise **son**; **He** who sleeps in harvest is a **son** who causes shame.

Proverbs *11:*29*

He who troubles *his own house* will inherit the wind, And the fool will be servant to the wise of heart.

Proverbs *13:*1*

A wise *son* heeds *his father's* instruction, But a scoffer does not listen to rebuke.

Proverbs *13:*22*

A *good man* leaves an inheritance to *his children's children*, But the wealth of the sinner is stored up for the righteous.

Proverbs *13:*24*

He who spares *his* rod hates *his son*, But *he* who loves *him disciplines him* promptly.

Proverbs 14:26*

In the fear of the LORD there is strong confidence, And **His children** will have a place of refuge.

Proverbs *15:*5*

A fool despises *his father's* instruction, But *he* who receives correction is prudent.

Proverbs *15:*6*

In the _house_ of the _righteous_ there is much treasure, But in the revenue of the wicked is trouble.

Proverbs 15:*20*

A wise **_son_** makes a **_father_** glad, But a foolish **_man_** despises **_his mother_**.

Proverbs 17:1

Better is a dry morsel with quietness, Than a _house_ full of feasting with strife.

Proverbs 17:2

A wise servant will rule over a **_son_** who causes shame, And will share an inheritance among the **_brothers_**.

Proverbs 17:6*

Children's children are the crown of _old men_, And the glory of **_children_** is **_their father_**.

Proverbs *17:*17*

_A friend loves at all times, And a _brother_ is born for adversity_.

Proverbs 17:21

_He_ who begets a _scoffer_ does so to **_his_** sorrow, And the **_father_** of a _fool_ has no joy.

Proverbs 17:*25*

A _foolish_ **_son_** is a grief to **_his father_**, And bitterness to **_her_** who bore **_him_**.

Proverbs 18:19

A **_brother_** offended is harder to win than a strong city, And contentions are like the bars of a castle.

Proverbs *18:*24*

A _man_ who has _friends_ must _himself_ be friendly, But there is a _friend_ who sticks closer than a _brother_.

Proverbs 19:7

All the **_brothers_** of the poor hate **_him_**; How much more do **_his_** _friends_ go far from **_him_**! **_He_** may pursue them with words, yet they abandon **_him_**.

Proverbs 19:*13*

A _foolish_ **_son_** is the ruin of **_his father_**, And the contentions of a **_wife_** are a continual dripping.

Proverbs *19:*14*

Houses and riches are an inheritance from _fathers_, But a prudent _wife_ is from the LORD.

Proverbs 19:18

Chasten **_your son_** while there is hope, And do not set **_your_** heart on **_his_** destruction.

Proverbs 19:26

_He_ who mistreats **_his father_** and chases away **_his mother_** Is a **_son_** who causes shame and brings reproach.

Proverbs *19:*27*

_Cease listening to instruction, _my son_, And _you_ will stray from the words of knowledge_.

Proverbs 20:7*

The righteous **_man_** walks in **_his_** integrity; **_His children_** are blessed after **_him_**.

Proverbs 20:11*

Even a **_child_** is known by **_his_** deeds, Whether what **_he_** does is pure and right.

Proverbs 20:20

Whoever curses **_his father_** or **_his mother_**, **_His_** lamp will be put out in deep darkness.

Proverbs *22:*6*

Train up a __child__ in the way __he__ should go, And when __he__ is old __he__ will not depart from it.

Proverbs *22:*15*

Foolishness is bound up in the heart of a __child__, The rod of correction will drive it far from __him__.

(Sayings of the Wise)

Proverbs 22:28

Do not remove the ancient landmark Which your **_fathers_** have set.

Proverbs 23:10–11

Do not remove the ancient landmark Nor enter the fields of the **_father-less_**; For **_their_** *Redeemer* is mighty; **_He_** will plead **_their_** cause against **_you_**.

Proverbs *23:*13*–*14*

Do not withhold correction from a __child__, For if __you__ beat __him__ with a rod, __he__ will not die. __You__ shall beat __him__ with a rod, And deliver __his__ soul from hell.

Proverbs *23:*15*–*16*

__My son__, if __your__ heart is wise, __My__ heart will rejoice—indeed, __I myself__; Yes, __my__ inmost being will rejoice When __your__ lips speak right things.

Proverbs 23:19*

Hear, **_my son,_** and be wise; And guide **_your_** heart in the way.

Proverbs 23:22*

Listen to **_your father_** who begot **_you_**, And do not despise **_your mother_** when **_she_** is old.

Proverbs 23:24–25

The **_father_** of the righteous will greatly rejoice, And **_he_** who begets a wise *child* will delight in *him*. Let *your father* and *your mother* be glad, And let *her* who bore *you* rejoice.

Proverbs 23:26–28

(26) *My son*, give *me your* heart, And let *your* eyes observe *my* ways.

(27) For a harlot is a deep pit, And a seductress is a narrow well.

(28) She also lies in wait as for a victim, And increases the unfaithful among men.

Proverbs *24:13–*14*

My son, eat honey (wisdom) because it is good, And the honeycomb which is sweet to *your* taste; **So shall the knowledge of wisdom be to *your* soul; If *you* have found it, there is a prospect, And *your* hope will not be cut off.**

Proverbs 24:21–22

My son, fear the LORD and the king; Do not associate with those given to change; For their calamity will rise suddenly, And who knows the ruin those two can bring?

(Further Sayings of the Wise)

Proverbs 24:27*

Prepare *your* outside work, Make it fit for *yourself* in the field; And afterward build *your* house.

(Further Sayings of Solomon)

Proverbs 27:8

Like a bird that wanders from the nest Is a *man* who wanders from *his* place.

Proverbs 27:10

Do not forsake *your* own *friend* or *your father's* friend, Nor go to *your*

brother's house in the day of **your** calamity; Better is a *neighbor* nearby than a **brother** far away.

Proverbs 27:11

My son, be wise, and make **my** heart glad, That **I** may answer him who reproaches **me**.

Proverbs 28:7

Whoever keeps the law is a discerning **son**, But a companion of gluttons shames **his father**.

Proverbs 28:24

Whoever robs **his father** or **his mother**, And says, "It is not transgression," The *same* is companion to a destroyer.

Proverbs *29:*3*

Whoever loves wisdom makes *his father* rejoice, But a companion of harlots wastes *his* wealth.

Proverbs *29:*15*

The rod and rebuke give wisdom, But a *child* left to *himself* brings shame to *his mother*.

Proverbs *29:*17*

Correct *your son*, and *he* will give *you* rest; Yes, *he* will give delight to *your* soul.

Proverbs 29:21

He who pampers **his** servant from childhood Will have him as a **son** in the end.

(The Wisdom of Agur)

Proverbs 30:11

There is a *generation* that curses its **father**, And does not bless its **mother**.

Proverbs 30:17

The eye that mocks *his father*, And scorns obedience to *his mother*, The ravens of the valley will pick it out, And the young eagles will eat it.

(The Words of King Lemuel's Mother)

Proverbs 31:1–3

(1)　The words of King Lemuel, the utterance which *his mother* taught *him*:

(2)　What, *my son*? And what, *son* of *my* womb? And what, *son* of *my* vows?

(3)　Do not give *your* strength to women, Nor *your* ways to that which destroys kings.

CHAPTER 58

RELATIONSHIPS:
FRIENDSHIPS, NEIGHBORS

As I approached this Chapter Narrative regarding "***Relationships:
Friendships/Neighbors***," I heard the Holy Spirit speak into my
heart regarding three primary biblical principles on this subject matter, namely Matthew 22:39, which states: "*And the second is like it:* '***You
shall love your neighbor as yourself***"; Luke 10:25–37 ("*The Parable of the
Good Samaritan*"), and 1 Corinthians 13 ("*The Love Doctrine*"). Matthew
22:37–40 states: "*You shall love the Lord your God with all your heart, with
all your soul, and with all your mind. This is the first and great commandment. And the second is like it:* '***You shall love your neighbor as yourself!***
On these two commandments hang all the Law and the Prophets." When
one closely examines verse 39 again, which states: "**You shall love your
neighbor as yourself**," one cannot help but ask these two questions: (1)
Who is my ***Neighbor***? And, (2) Love of self and love of ***Neighbor***—what
does that really mean?

In answering the question of who is my ***Neighbor***, one only needs to
read, study, and meditate on "*The Parable of the Good Samaritan*" (Luke
10:25–37). Most of us know and can recall, the elements of this biblical principled story. But how many of us have actually peeled back the

"onion," so to speak, and asked ourselves: Which of these three persons do I most identify with in my interactions with friends and foe? (1) Am I the priest, who, noticed the injured man, and when he saw him, he passed by on the other side of the street/pathway? (2) Am I the Levite, who, when he arrived at the site, he came, he looked, and then passed by on the other side? (3) Or am I more like the Samaritan, who, saw a person in dire need of assistance, and assisted the injured man, above and beyond the everyday call of duty?

Would it be safe to say, that most of us, will vacillate between all three principal characters, during one's normal and daily Christian walk? But the key question for all to answer is: Which characteristic or personality would Christ Jesus desire for one to emulate? Needless to say, the unqualified answer is "*The Good Samaritan*"! But I would challenge, one and all, to evaluate truthfully, how often we actually operate from the mindset of "*The Good Samaritan.*"

Thus, the question du jour remains: Who is my **_Neighbor_**? From my perspective, it is **_Anyone_**, regardless of race, ethnicity, station in life, friend or foe, kind or cruel, righteous or unbeliever. For as we all know, all of mankind has been created in the image of Christ Jesus. And Christ Jesus came to save the lost, for which I was, but now, I am saved, by the grace of Father God through faith, which is a gift of Father God, and "*not by my works, least I should boast*" (Ephesians 2:8–10). Thus, one **must** emulate Christ Jesus and **befriend <u>any</u> and <u>all</u> that need the love of Christ**, whether for a moment, a day, a week, a month, a year, or a lifetime. We are **all** called to be a **_Friend_ to one another**; as such you, **my _Friend_, are my _Neighbor_**!

So how does one "***love thy neighbor as you love yourself***"? To answer this question, one needs to look no further than 1 Corinthians 13, which is generally known as the "*Love Doctrine.*" Restating the core biblical principles contained in verses 4–8, which state: "*Love suffers long and is kind; love does not envy; love does not parade itself, is not puffed up; does not behave rudely, does not seek its own, is not provoked, thinks no evil;*

*does not rejoice in iniquity, but rejoices in the truth; bears all things, believes all things, hopes all things, endures all things. **Love never fails**"*!

Love is the greatest of all human attributes, as it is one of the key attributes of Father God Himself. It's been said that love makes one's actions and gifts useful. From Father God's outward displays of **love**, He provides a platform for our salvation, through His grace, mercy, forgiveness, and faith. As such, **one must also exhibit such love to one's *Neighbor*, expecting nothing in return.** Accordingly, **the more one exhibits Christlikeness, the more love that one extends to others, whether *Friend*, foe, or *Neighbor*.** At the end of the day, **loving one's *Neighbor* as oneself involves unselfish caring, sharing, and service to others**. And in summary, **as Father God loves, we must love:** "*And now abide faith, hope, love, these three; but the greatest of these is love*"! (1 Corinthians 13:13)

(Guidance for the Young)

Proverbs *3:*27*–*28*
Do not withhold good from *those to whom it is due*, When it is in the power of *your* hand to do so. Do not say to *your neighbor*, "Go, and come back, And tomorrow *I* will give it," When *you* have it with *you*.

Proverbs 3:29
Do not devise evil against ***your neighbor***, For he dwells by *you* for safety's sake.

Proverbs 3:30
Do not strive with a *man* without cause, If *he* has done *you* no harm.

(Balance Generosity with Good Stewardship)

Proverbs *6:1–5
(1)   My *son*, if *you* become surety for ***your friend***, if *you* have shaken hands in pledge for a stranger,

(2)   *You* are snared by the words of *your* mouth; *You* are taken by the words of *your* mouth.

(3)   So do this, my *son*, and deliver *yourself*; For *you* have come into the hand of *your friend*; Go and humble *yourself*; Plead with *your friend*.

(4)   Give no sleep to *your* eyes, Nor slumber to *your* eyelids.

(5)   Deliver *yourself* like a gazelle from the hand of the hunter, And like a bird from the hand of the fowler.

(Beware of Adultery)

Proverbs *6:20*–29*

(20)* My *son*, keep your father's command, And do not forsake the law of your mother.

(21)   Bind them continually upon your heart; Tie them around your neck.

(22)   When you roam, they will lead you; When you sleep, they will keep you; And when you awake, they will speak with you.

(23)* **For the commandment is a lamp, And the law a light; Reproofs of instruction are the way of life**,

(24)* To keep you from the *evil woman*, From the flattering tongue of a *seductress*.

(25)   Do not *lust* after *her* beauty in your heart, Nor let *her allure* you with *her* eyelids.

(26)   For by means of a *harlot*, A man is reduced to a crust of bread; And an *adulteress* will *prey* upon *his* precious life.

(27)   Can a man take fire to *his* bosom, And *his* clothes not be burned?

(28)   Can one walk on hot coals, And *his* feet not be seared?

(29)* So is *he* who goes in to *his **neighbor's wife***; Whoever *touches her* shall not be innocent.

(Wise Saying of Solomon)

Proverbs 11:*9*

The hypocrite with *his* mouth destroys *his **neighbor***, But through knowledge the righteous will be delivered.

Proverbs *11:*12*

He who is devoid of wisdom despises *his neighbor*, But a *man* of understanding holds *his* peace.

Proverbs 11:13

A talebearer reveals secrets, *But he who is of a faithful spirit conceals a matter.*

Proverbs 12:2*

A good man obtains favor from the LORD, But a *man* of wicked intentions He will condemn.

Proverbs 12:*26*

The righteous should choose *his **friends*** carefully, For the way of the wicked leads them astray.

Proverbs 13:17

A wicked messenger falls into trouble, But a *faithful ambassador* brings health.

Proverbs *13:*20*

He who walks with *wise men* will be *wise*, But the *companion* of fools will be destroyed.

Proverbs 14:20

The *poor man* is hated even by *his own **neighbor***, But the rich has many *friends*.

Proverbs 14:*21*

He who despises *his **neighbor*** sins; But *he* who has *mercy on the poor*, *happy is he*.

Proverbs 16:28
A *perverse man* sows strife, And a whisperer separates the best of **_friends_**.

Proverbs 16:29
A *violent man* entices *his **neighbor***, And leads *him* in a way that is not good.

Proverbs *17:*9*
He who covers a transgression seeks love, But _he_ who _repeats a matter_ separates _friends_.

Proverbs *17:*17*
A _friend_ loves at all times, And a _brother_ is born for adversity.

Proverbs 17:18
A *man* devoid of understanding shakes hands in a pledge, And becomes surety for his ***friend***.

Proverbs 18:1
A *man* who *isolates himself* seeks *his* own desire; *He* rags against all wise judgment.

Proverbs 18:17*
The first one to plead *his* cause seems right, Until *his **neighbor*** comes and examines *him*.

Proverbs 18:19
A *brother* offended is harder to win than a strong city, And contentions are like the bars of a castle.

Proverbs *18:*24*
A _man_ who has _friends_ must _himself_ be _friendly_, But there is a friend who sticks closer than a brother.

Proverbs 19:4
*Wealth makes many **friends**, But the poor is separated from his **friend**.*

Proverbs 19:6

Many entreat the favor of the nobility, And every *man* is a **_friend_** *to one* **_who_** *gives gifts.*

Proverbs 19:7

All the *brothers of the poor* hate *him*; How much more do *his* **friends** go far from *him*! *He* may pursue *them* with words, yet *they* abandon *him*.

Proverbs 20:19

He who goes about as a talebearer reveals secrets: Therefore do not **_associate_** with *one who flatters* with *his* lips.

Proverbs 21:10

The soul of the wicked desires evil; *His* **neighbor** finds no favor in *his* eyes.

Proverbs 22:11

He who loves purity of heart And has grace on *his* lips, The king will be *his* **_friend_**.

(Sayings of the Wise)

Proverbs 22:24–25

Make no **_friendship_** with an *angry man*, And with a *furious man* do not go, Lest **_you_** learn *his* ways And set a snare for **_your_** soul.

Proverbs 22:28

Do not remove the ancient landmark Which your *fathers* have set.

Proverbs 23:6–8

(6)   Do not eat the bread of a *miser*, Nor desire *his* delicacies;

(7)   For as *he* thinks in *his* heart, so is *he*. "Eat and drink!" *he* says to **_you_**, But *his* heart is not with **_you_**.

(8)   The morsel **_you_** have eaten, **_you_** will vomit up, And waste **_your_** pleasant words.

Proverbs 23:10–11

Do not remove the ancient landmark, Nor enter the fields of the *fatherless*; *For their Redeemer is mighty*; *He will plead their cause against* **_you_**.

Proverbs 23:20–21

(20) *Do not mix with winebibbers*, Or *with gluttonous eaters of meat*;

(21) For the *drunkard* and the *glutton* will come to poverty, And drowsiness will clothe a man with rags.

Proverbs 24:17*–18*

Do not rejoice when **_your_** enemy falls, And do not let **_your_** heart be glad when *he* stumbles; Lest the LORD see it, and it displease Him, And He turn away His wrath from *him*.

(Further Sayings of the Wise)

Proverbs 24:28–29*

Do not be a witness against **_your neighbor_** without cause, For would **_you_** deceive with **_your_** lips? Do not say, "**_I_** will do to *him* just as *he* has done to *me*; **_I_** will render to the *man* according to *his* work."

(Further Wise Sayings of Solomon)

Proverbs 25:8–10

(8) Do not go hastily to court; For what will **_you_** do in the end, When **_your neighbor_** has put **_you_** to shame?

(9) Debate **_your_** case with **_your neighbor_**, And do not disclose the secret to *another*;

(10) Lest *he* who hears it expose **_your_** shame, And **_your_** reputation be ruined.

Proverbs 25:17

Seldom set foot in **_your neighbor's_** house, Lest **_he_** become weary of **_you_** and hate **_you_**.

Proverbs 25:*18*

A **_man_** who bears false witness against **_his neighbor_** Is like a club, a sword, and a sharp arrow.

Proverbs 25:19

Confidence in an _unfaithful man_ in time of trouble Is like a bad tooth and a foot out of joint.

Proverbs *25:*21*–*22*

If _your_ enemy is hungry, give _him_ bread to eat; And if _he_ is thirsty, give _him_ water to drink; For so _you_ will heap coals of fire on _his_ head, And the LORD will reward _you_.

Proverbs 26:18–19

Like a madman who throws firebrands, arrows, and death, Is the _man_ who deceives _his **neighbor**_, And says, "_I_ was only joking!

Proverbs 27:2

Let another _man_ praise **_you_**, and not **_your_** own mouth; A stranger, and not **_your_** own lips.

Proverbs 27:5*

Open rebuke is better Than love carefully concealed.

Proverbs *27:*6*

Faithful are the wounds of a friend, But the kisses of an _enemy_ are deceitful.

Proverbs 27:*9*

Ointment and perfume delight the heart, And the sweetness of a _man's_ _friend_ gives delight by hearty counsel.

Proverbs 27:10

Do not forsake **_your_** own **_friend_** or **_your_** father's **_friend_**, Nor go to **_your_** _brother's_ house in the day of **_your_** calamity; Better is a **_neighbor_** nearby than a _brother_ far away.

Proverbs 27:14

He who blesses *his **friend*** with a loud voice, rising early in the morning, It will be counted a curse to *him*.

Proverbs *27:*17*

*As iron sharpens iron, **So a man sharpens the countenance of his friend.***

Proverbs 27:18

Whoever keeps the fig tree will eat its fruit; So *he* who waits on *his master* will be honored.

Proverbs *27:*19*

As in water face reflects face, So a *man's* heart reveals the *man*.

Proverbs 28:3

*A poor **man** who oppresses the poor* Is like a driving rain which leaves no food.

Proverbs 28:7*

Whoever keeps the law is a discerning ***son***, But a ***companion*** of gluttons shames his ***father***.

Proverbs *28:*23*

He who rebukes a *man* will find more favor afterward Than *he* who flatters with the tongue.

Proverbs 28:*25*

He who is of a proud heart stirs up strife, *But he who trusts in the LORD will be prospered.*

Proverbs *29:*3*

Whoever loves wisdom makes *his father* rejoice, But a *companion* of harlots wastes *his* wealth.

Proverbs 29:5

*A **man** who flatters **his neighbor*** Spreads a net for *his feet*.

Proverbs 29:13*

The poor man and the oppressor have this in common: *The LORD gives light to the eyes of both.*

Proverbs 29:24

Whoever is a *partner* with a thief hates *his* own life; *He* swears to tell the truth, but reveals nothing.

Proverbs 29:25

The fear of *man* brings a snare, *But whoever trusts in the LORD shall be.*

CHAPTER 59

RESPECT, REVERENCE

DISCLAIMER: With all due respect, regarding the Chapter Theme Narrative, "***Respect/Reverence***," it was a challenge for me in trying to specifically identify Proverbs verses that spoke specifically to these two Chapter Themes. Instead, most Proverbs verses contained indirect references to these two Chapter Themes of "***Respect/Reverence***." Additionally, it goes without saying, that almost every Proverbs verse mentioned in the respective Themes of (a)*Fear of the Lord*, (b) *Honor*, and/or (c) *Trust* could rightly be listed under this Chapter Theme of "***Respect/Reverence***." Thus, as one reviews these direct and indirect Proverbs verse selections captured under this Chapter Theme of "***Respect/Reverence***," the reader is strongly encouraged to review and reference in parallel, these three Chapter Themes also—(a) *Fear of the Lord*, (b) *Honor*, and (c) *Trust*—for additional spiritual Proverbs verses and insight, regarding this Chapter Theme of "***Respect/Reverence***"!

Given the above stated disclaimer, I would highlight one indirect, as well as direct Proverbs verse, that speaks specifically to this Chapter Theme of "***Respect/Reverence***," namely, Proverbs 1:7, which states: "***The fear of the LORD is the beginning of knowledge, But fools despise wisdom and instruction***"! It is my belief, that should a person desire to be wise, then the first place to begin gaining wisdom is by ***Reverencing*** Father

God and trusting and obeying Him. It goes without saying, that the created human being should and must _honor_, **_Respect_**, **_Reverence_**, _trust_, and _worship_ the Creator, that being our Heavenly Father!

Secondly, Proverbs 28:14 states: "_Happy is the man who is always reverent, But he who hardens his heart will fall into calamity._" One element of true and genuine happiness is to have a tender heart before the Lord, that exhibits **_Respect_** and **_Reverence_**, on a consistent and ongoing basis. For it's been said that Father God can resist the proud and haughty, but He cannot resist a broken and contrite heart that exhibits remorse, repentance, **_Respect_**, and Godly **_Reverence_**.

Finally, when one reflects on the concept of **_Respect_**, I cannot underestimate the fact that human **_Respect_** is generally achieved and earned, from one's actions, sacrifices, as well as the proactive, tough, and unselfish choices that one makes that benefits others. But in the end, the greatest acknowledgement of _honor_, _glory_, **_Respect_**, and **_Reverence_**, can be found and displayed daily, from one's **_Respect_** and **_Reverence_** to our Heavenly Father who created us, our Savior and Lord Jesus Christ, who died and paid our sin debt in full; that allowed one and all, to move from a life status of sinner, to a life status of Christian saint; From a life of eternal damnation to one of eternal life; to honoring Father God; and being blessed in having the indwelling Holy Spirit, that rest within us, upon us, and through us, guiding and directing one's pathways toward light, righteousness, **_Respect_**, and **_Reverence_** to Father God!

To God be the GLORY, Forever and Forever. Amen!

(The Beginning of Knowledge)

Proverbs *1:*7*
The _fear of the LORD_ is the beginning of knowledge, But fools despise wisdom and instruction.

(Security in Wisdom)

Proverbs *4:1*–9

(1)*   Hear, my children, the instruction of a father, And give attention to know understanding;

(2)*   For I give you good doctrine: Do not forsake my law.

(3)   When I was my father's son, Tender and the only one in the sight of my mother,

(4)*   **He also taught me, and said to me: "Let your heart retain my words; Keep my commands, and live.**

(5)*   **Get *wisdom*! Get understanding! Do not forget, nor turn away from the words of my mouth.**

(6)*   **Do not forsake her, and she will preserve you; Love her, and she will keep you.**

(7)*   ***Wisdom* is the principal thing: Therefore get wisdom. And in all your getting, get understanding.**

(8)   *Exalt* her, and she will promote you; She will bring you honor, when you embrace her.

(9)   She will place on your head an ornament of grace; A crown of glory she will deliver to you.

(Wise Sayings of Solomon)

Proverbs 11:16

A gracious woman retains honor, But ruthless men retain riches.

Proverbs *16:*31*

***A silver-haired head is a crown of glory,* If it is found in the way of righteousness.**

(Sayings of the Wise)

Proverbs 23:22*

Listen to your father who begot you, And do not despise your mother when she is old.

Proverbs 24:21–22

My son, **fear the LORD** *and the king*; Do not associate with those given to change; For their calamity will rise suddenly, And who knows the ruin those two can bring?

(Further Sayings of Solomon)

Proverbs 25:2

It is the **glory of God** to conceal a matter, But the *glory of kings* is to search out a matter.

Proverbs 26:1

As snow in summer and rain in harvest, So *honor* is not fitting for a fool.

Proverbs 27:18

Whoever keeps the fig tree will eat its fruit; *So he who waits on his master will be honored.*

Proverbs 28:14*

Happy is the man who is always **reverent**, But he who hardens his heart will fall into calamity.

Proverbs 29:18*

Where there is no revelation, the people cast off restraint; But happy is he who *keeps the law*.

Proverbs 29:23*

A man's pride will bring him low, *But the humble in spirit will retain honor.*

Proverbs 29:25*

The fear of man brings a snare, But whoever **_trusts in the LORD_** shall be safe.

(The Virtuous Wife)

Proverbs *31:*30*–31*

Charm is deceitful and beauty is passing, But a woman who _fears the LORD_, she shall be _praised_. Give her of the fruit of her hands, And let her own works _praise_ her in the gates.

CHAPTER 60

RICH, RICHES, WEALTH, INHERITANCE, TREASURE

This Chapter Theme entitled "***Rich***, ***Riches***, ***Wealth***, ***Inheritance***, ***Treasure***" provides numerous "on-ramps," from which one can build a Chapter Narrative on. For example, on the two subtheme topics of ***Riches*** and ***Wealth***, one could quite naturally detail and highlight, the numerous Bible verses and principles that are mentioned regarding these two subthemes. Take, for example, the following verses from 1 Timothy 6:6–10: "*Now godliness with contentment is great **gain**. For we brought nothing into this world, and it is certain we can carry nothing out. And having food and clothing, with these we shall be content. But those who desire to be **rich** fall into temptation and a snare, and into many foolish and harmful lusts which drown men in destruction and perdition. For the love of **money** is a root of all kinds of evil, for which some have strayed from the faith in their greediness, and pierced themselves through with many sorrows.*"

One would think that it would be fair to say that most of us, at some point in time during one's life, have struggled with one and/or all five of the above biblical verses/principles, at some point in time during one's Christian walk or walk in life, in general.

As an example, take verse 6, which, on the surface, seems easy for most of us to say, that *contentment* is not a major issue in one's life. But examine the verse carefully: "*Now godliness with contentment is great gain*." Now, how many of us can truthfully say that one's Christian life is fully immersed in "*godliness*," which results in "*contentment*," which results in "***Great Gain***"? I cannot speak for you, but for me, as much as I try each and every day, to walk in "*godliness*," I can objectively and frankly state, that I have not been successful in walking in "*godliness,*" twenty-four seven! It's not for lack of trying, but something as easy as a bad or sinful thought; or don't have someone say or do something negative toward me, which can throw one off the narrow lanes of "*godliness*" and righteousness!

Or how often is one truly satisfied with "*contentment*"? On this one spiritual principle, I can objectively state that I would give myself a grade of B+ or so, given the fact that I strive to consciously live "below one's means." Take, for example, my mode of basic transportation. Upon returning from Brussels, Belgium in March 1999, I purchased a brand new 1999 Jeep Grand Cherokee. Today, some twenty-plus years and 195,000 miles later, I am blessed, favored, forgiven, and mightily Loved by Father God, to still be driving this same vehicle for basic transportation! I generally share with the residents from the Durham Rescue Mission, when I am facilitating the Dave Ramsey's Financial Peace University course that if "a donkey was good enough for Christ Jesus to ride into Jerusalem on Palm Sunday," then a twenty-plus-year-old Jeep donkey, is good enough for me! To God be the Glory!

Time and Chapter Narrative space does not allow me to "peel back the onion" on these other four verses of biblical scriptures from 1 Timothy 6:6–10, especially verse 10, which states the principle: "*For the love of **money** is a root of all kinds of evil…*"! So, ask oneself this question and/or questions: What is your challenging "Idol or Idols," that rob one from enjoying a richer walk "in Christ Jesus"? I believe that "All of Us" have at least one "Idol" that maybe wrestling with one's walk "in Christ Jesus;" Thereby limiting the way He would really like us to be walking and following in His Word!

So, in conclusion, one needs to ask oneself, "What is one's true '*Treasure*'?" Jesus Christ stated unequivocally in Matthew 6:33: "*But seek first the kingdom of God and His righteousness, and all these things shall be added to you.*" And within God's Kingdom, one can obtain the "***Treasures***" of wisdom and understanding, as captured from these Proverbs verses, 2:1–9, from the initial verses in the section "*The Value of Wisdom*":

(1) *"My son, if you receive my words, And **treasure** my commands within you,*

(2) *So that you will incline your ear to wisdom, And apply your heart to understanding;*

(3) *Yes, if you cry out for discernment, And lift up your voice for understanding,*

(4) *If you seek her as **silver**, And search for her as for hidden **treasures**;*

(5) *Then you will understand the fear of the LORD, And find the knowledge of God.*

(6) *For the LORD gives wisdom; From His mouth come knowledge and understanding;*

(7) ***He stores up sound wisdom for the upright**; He is a shield to those who walk uprightly;*

(8) *He guards the paths of justice, And preserves the way of His saints.*

(9) *Then you will understand righteousness and justice, Equity and every good path*"!

Accordingly, at the end of the day, what is one's true ***Riches***, ***Wealth***, and ***Treasure***! I would content that one's greatest ***Treasure***, is being a child of the Most High God!

To God be the GLORY!

(Shun Evil Counsel)

Proverbs *1:*19*

So are the ways of ever one who is <u>greedy for *gain*</u>; It takes away the life of its owners.

(The Value of Wisdom)

Proverbs *2:*1*–*9*

(1)* **My son, if you receive my words, And *treasure* my commands within you,**

(2)* **So that you will incline your ear to wisdom, And apply your heart to understanding:**

(3)* Yes, if you cry out for discernment, And lift up your voice for understanding,

(4) If you seek her as *silver*, And search for her as for hidden ***treasures*:**

(5)* **Then you will understand the fear of the LORD, And find the knowledge of God.**

(6)* **For the LORD gives wisdom; From His mouth come knowledge and understanding;**

(7)* **He *stores* up sound wisdom for the upright; He is a shield to those who walk uprightly;**

(8)* **He guards the paths of justice, And preserves the way of His saints.**

(9)* **Then you will understand righteousness and justice, *Equity* and every good path.**

(Guidance for the Young)

Proverbs *3:*9*–*10*

Honor the LORD with your *possessions*, And the *first fruits of all your increase*; So your *barns will be filled with plenty*, And your *vats will overflow with new wine*.

Proverbs *3:*13*–18

(13)* **Happy is the man who finds wisdom, And the man who gains understanding;**

(14) For her _proceeds_ are _better_ than the _profits of silver_, And her _gain_ than _fine gold_.

(15) She is _more precious than rubies_, And all the things you may desire cannot compare with her.

(16) Length of days is in her right hand, In her left hand **riches** and honor.

(17) Her ways are ways of pleasantness, And all her paths are peace.

(18) She is a tree of life to those who take hold of her, And happy are all who retain her.

Proverbs 3:35*

The wise shall **inherit** glory, But shame shall be the _legacy_ of fools.

(The Peril of Adultery)

Proverbs 5:7–14

(7) Therefore hear me now, my children, And no not depart from the words of my mouth.

(8) Remove your way far from her, And do not go near the door of her house,

(9) Lest you give your honor to others, And your years to the cruel one;

(10) Lest aliens be filled with your **wealth**, And your labors go to the house of a foreigner;

(11) And you mourn at last, When your flesh and your body are consumed.

(12) And say: "How I have hated instruction, And my heart despised correction!

(13) I have not obeyed the voice of my teachers, Nor inclined my ear to those who instructed me!

(14) I was on the verge of total ruin, In the midst of the assembly and congregation."

(Beware of Adultery)

Proverbs *7:*1*–5*

(1)* **My son, keep my words, And _treasure_ my commands within you.**

(2)* **Keep my commands and live, And my law as the apple of your eye.**

(3)* Bind them on your fingers, Write them on the tablet of your heart.

(4)* **Say to wisdom, "You are my sister," And call understanding your nearest kin,**

(5)* That they may keep you from the immoral woman, From the seductress who flatters with her words.

(The Excellence of Wisdom)

Proverbs *8:*17*–21

(17)* **I love those who love me (wisdom), And those who seek me diligently will find me.**

(18) **_Riches_** and honor are with me, Enduring **_riches_** and righteousness.

(19) My fruit (wisdom) is better than _gold_, yes, than fine _gold_, And my _revenue_ than choice _silver_.

(20) I traverse the way of righteousness, In the midst of the paths of justice,

(21) That I may cause those who love me to **_inherit wealth_**, That I may fill their **_treasuries_**.

(Wise Sayings of Solomon)

Proverbs 10:2*

Treasures of wickedness profit nothing, But righteousness delivers from death.

Proverbs 10:4*

He who has a slack hand becomes poor, But the hand of the diligent makes **_rich_**.

Proverbs 10:5*
He who *gathers in summer* is a wise son; He who sleeps in harvest is a son who causes shame.

Proverbs 10:15
The **rich man's wealth** is his strong city; The destruction of the poor is their poverty.

Proverbs *10:*22*
The *blessing of the LORD* makes one *rich*, And He adds no sorrow with it.

Proverbs 11:*4*
Riches do not *profit* in the day of wrath, But righteousness delivers from death.

Proverbs 11:16
A gracious woman retains honor, But ruthless men retain **riches**.

Proverbs *11:*24*
There is one who scatters, yet increases more; And there is one who withholds more than is right, **But it leads to poverty.**

Proverbs *11:*25*
The generous soul will be made *rich*, And he who waters will also be watered himself.

Proverbs 11:28*
He who trusts in his **riches** will fall, But the righteous will flourish like foliage.

Proverbs *11:*29*
He who troubles his own house will *inherit* the wind, But the fool will be servant to the wise of heart.

Proverbs 12:9
Better is the one who is slighted but has a servant, Than he who honors himself but *lacks bread*.

Proverbs 13:4*
The soul of a lazy man desires, and has nothing; But the soul of the diligent shall be made *rich*.

Proverbs *13:*7*
There is one who makes himself *rich*, yet has *nothing*; And one who makes himself poor, yet has *great riches*.

Proverbs 13:8*
The ransom of a man's life is his *riches*, But the poor does not hear rebuke.

Proverbs 13:*11*
Wealth gained by dishonesty will be diminished, *But he who gathers by labor will increase.*

Proverbs *13:*22*
A good man leaves an *inheritance* to his children's children, But the *wealth* of the sinner is *stored* up for the righteous.

Proverbs 14:18*
The simple *inherit* folly, But the prudent are crowned with knowledge.

Proverbs 14:20
The poor man is hated even by his own neighbor, But the *rich* has many friends.

Proverbs *14:*23*
In all labor there is profit, **But idle chatter leads only to poverty**.

Proverbs 14:24
The crown of the wise is their *riches*, But the foolishness of fools is folly.

Proverbs *15:*6*
In the house of the righteous there is much *treasure*, But in the *revenue* of the wicked is trouble.

Proverbs *15:*16*
Better is a little with the fear of the LORD, Than great *treasure* with trouble.

Proverbs 15:17
Better is a dinner of herbs where love is, Than *a fatted calf* with hatred.

Proverbs 15:*27*
He who is *greedy for gain* troubles his own house, But he who hates bribes will live.

Proverbs *16:*8*
Better is a *little* with righteousness, Than *vast revenues* without justice.

Proverbs 16:16*
How much better to get wisdom than *gold*! And to get understanding is to be chosen rather than *silver*.

Proverbs *16:*19*
Better to be of a humble spirit with the lowly, *Than to divide the spoil with the proud*.

Proverbs 17:2
A wise servant will rule over a son who causes shame, And will share an *inheritance* among the brothers.

Proverbs 18:11
The ***rich man's wealth*** is his *strong city*, And like a high wall in his own esteem.

Proverbs 18:23
The poor man uses entreaties, But the ***rich*** answers roughly.

Proverbs *19:*1*
Better is the poor who walks in his integrity, *Than one who is perverse in his lips, and is a fool*.

Proverbs 19:4
Wealth makes many friends, But the poor is separated from his friend.

Proverbs 19:6*
Many entreat the favor of the *nobility*, And every man is a friend to one who gives gifts.

Proverbs 19:10
Luxury is not fitting for a fool, Much less for a servant to rule over princes.

Proverbs *19:*14*
***Houses and riches are an inheritance from fathers*, But a *prudent wife* is from *the LORD*.**

Proverbs 20:15*
There is *gold* and a multitude of *rubies, But the lips of knowledge are a precious jewel.*

Proverbs 20:17
Bread gained by deceit is sweet to a man, But afterward his mouth will be filled with gravel.

Proverbs *20:*21*
An *inheritance gained* hastily at the beginning Will not be blessed at the end.

Proverbs 21:4
A haughty look, a proud heart, And the *plowing* of the wicked are sin.

Proverbs *21:*5*
The plans of the diligent lead surely to *plenty*, But those of everyone who is hasty, surely to poverty.

Proverbs 21:6
*Getting **treasures** by a lying tongue Is the fleeting fantasy of those who seek death.*

Proverbs *21:*13*
Whoever shuts his ears to the cry of the poor Will also cry himself and not be heard.

Proverbs 21:17*
He who loves *pleasure* will be a poor man; He who loves *wine and oil* will not be **_rich_**.

Proverbs 21:*20*
There is *desirable **treasure**,* And *oil* in the *dwelling* of the *wise,* But a foolish man squanders it.

Proverbs *21:25–*26*
The *desire* of the lazy man kills him, For his hands refuse to labor. He *covets greedily* all day long, **But the righteous gives and does not *spare*.**

Proverbs 22:*1*
A good name is to be chosen rather than *great **riches**, Loving favor* rather than *silver and gold.*

Proverbs 22:2*
The **_rich_** and the poor have this in common, *The LORD is the maker of them all.*

Proverbs *22:*4*
By humility and the fear of the LORD Are _riches_ and honor and life.

Proverbs *22:*7*
The _rich_ rules over the poor, And the borrower is servant to the lender.

Proverbs *22:*9*
He who has a *generous eye* will be *blessed*, For he *gives* of his *bread* to the poor.

Proverbs 22:16*

He who oppresses the poor to *increase* his **riches**, And he who *gives* to the **rich**, will surely come to poverty.

(Sayings of the Wise)

Proverbs *22:*22*–*23*

Do not *rob* the poor because he is poor, Nor *oppress* the afflicted at the gate; For the LORD will plead their cause, And plunder the soul of those who plunder them.

Proverbs *23:*4*–*5*

*Do not overwork to be **rich**; Because of your own understanding, cease! Will you set your eyes on that which is not? For **riches** certainly make themselves wings; They fly away like an eagle toward heaven.*

Proverbs 23:6–8

(6) Do not eat the *bread* of a ***miser***, Nor desire his *delicacies*;

(7) For as he thinks in his heart, so is he. "Eat and drink!" he says to you, But his heart is not with you.

(8) The morsel you have eaten, you will vomit up, And waste your pleasant words.

Proverbs 23:19*–21*

(19)* Hear, my son, and be wise: And guide your heart in the way.

(20) Do not mix with winebibbers, Or with gluttonous eaters of *meat*;

(21)* For the drunkard and the glutton will come to poverty, *And drowsiness will clothe a man with rags.*

Proverbs 24:3*–4*

Through wisdom a house is built, And by understanding it is established; By knowledge the rooms are filled With all precious and pleasant **riches**.

(Further Wise Sayings of Solomon)

Proverbs 27:20*

Hell and Destruction are never full; *So the eyes of man are never satisfied.*

Proverbs 27:23–27

(23) Be diligent to know the *state of your flocks*, And *attend to your herds*;

(24) For **riches** are not forever, Nor does a *crown* endure to all generations.

(25) When the *hay* is removed, and the *tender grass* shows itself, And the *herbs of the mountains* are gathered in,

(26) The *lambs* will provide your *clothing*, And the *goats* the *price of a field*;

(27) *You shall have enough goats' milk for your food, For the food of your household*, And the nourishment of your maidservants.

Proverbs *28:*6*

Better is the poor who walks in his integrity Than one perverse in his ways, though he be _rich_.

Proverbs 28:8*

One who *increases* his *possessions* by usury and extortion Gathers it for him who will pity the poor.

Proverbs 28:10

Whoever causes the upright to go astray in an evil way, He himself will fall into his own pit; But the *blameless* will **inherit** good.

Proverbs 28:11*

The **rich** man is wise in his own eyes, But the poor who has understanding searches him out.

Proverbs *28:*13*

He who covers his sins will not _prosper_, But whoever confesses and forsakes them will have mercy.

Proverbs 28:19
He who tills his land will have plenty of bread, But he who follows frivolity will have poverty enough!

Proverbs 28:20
A faithful man will *abound with blessings*, But he who hastens to be **rich** will not go unpunished.

Proverbs 28:22
A man with an evil eye *hastens after **riches***, And does not consider that poverty will come upon him.

Proverbs *29:*3*
Whoever loves wisdom makes his father rejoice, But a companion of harlots wastes his *wealth*.

(The Wisdom of Agur) (Prayer of Devotion)

Proverbs 30:7*–9*
(7)* Two things I request of You (Deprive me not before I die):
(8)* Remove falsehood and lies far from me; Give me neither poverty nor **riches**—*Feed me with the food allotted to me*;
(9)* Lest I be full and deny You, And say, "Who is the LORD?" Or lest I be poor and steal, And profane the name of my God.

(The Virtuous Wife)

Proverbs *31:*10*–*12* and *16*–*18*
(10)* **Who can find a virtuous wife? For her *worth* is far above *rubies*.**
(11)* **The heart of her husband safely trusts her; So he will have *no lack of gain*.**
(12)* **She does him good and not evil, All the days of her life.**

(16)* **She considers a *field* and *buys it*; *From her profits she plants a vineyard*.**
(17)* **She girds herself with strength, And strengthens her arms.**
(18)* **She perceives that her *merchandise* is good, And her lamp does not go out by night.**

CHAPTER 61

RIGHTEOUSNESS,
UPRIGHT, RIGHT, JUST

A s I reflect on this Chapter's primary Theme of "***Righteousness***," I am enamored with the number of Proverbs verses, directly and indirectly, dealing with addressing and/or referencing the primary Theme of ***Righteousness***. In fact, no other Chapter in this "*Book of Proverbs*" devotes as much spiritual insight, teachings, and knowledge sharing as the Proverbs verses contained in this Chapter Theme.

With that said and as I think through my personal experiences, reflections, and thoughts on "***Righteousness***," it is always a good idea to at least attempt to broadly define this spiritual doctrine and principle. Various dictionaries define "***Righteousness***" as "behavior that is morally justifiable or ***Right***," and/or "justice, ***Justness***, or divine holiness," and/or "the condition of being acceptable to God as made possible by God," and/or "conduct in relationship with others."

With the above broad definitions of "***Righteousness***," I believe it goes without saying that we all know and recognize sin, evilness, and/or wickedness when we see it, hear it, being made aware of it, and/or individually partake in it. For God's Word states unequivocally in Romans 3:23: "*for all have sinned and fall short of the glory of God.*" But more importantly, we find in Galatians 5:22 and 23: "*But the fruit of the Spirit is love, joy, peace, patience, kindness, goodness, faithfulness, gentleness, and self-control. Against such there is no law.*"

Thus, my contention or thesis is as follows: That here is a natural tug-of-war that exist, between man's sinful nature and the spontaneous work of the Holy Spirit, producing in those who are believers, opportunities to operate from and within the characteristics that are found in the nature of our Lord Jesus Christ. Take, for example the following three Proverbs verses (Proverbs 10:30–32), which, from my perspective, highlight the ever-present daily battles one faces in the areas of good/goodness vs. evil/evil desires, and/or doing **Right**/being **Righteous** vs. wickedness/being wicked:

- Proverbs 10:30: "*The **righteous** will never be removed, But the wicked will not inhabit the earth*";
- Proverbs 10:31: "*The mouth of the **righteous** brings worth wisdom, But the perverse tongue will be cut out*"; and
- Proverbs 10:32: "*The lips of the **righteous** know what is acceptable, But the mouth of the wicked what is perverse.*"

Which of the following two biblical principles/truth is easier to observe? (1) "*Therefore submit to God. Resist the devil and he will flee from you*" (James 4:7). Or acknowledge the factual truth that one can and should, "*Draw near to God and He will draw near to you*" (James 4:8). Needless to say, both of the above verses are God's stated truths; However, the challenge or the question du jour is sometimes this: Why, as a general principle—at least from my life experiences and observations—is exhibiting **Righteous**, Christlike behaviors, while operating and exhibiting the "**Fruit of the Spirit**," sometimes harder to operate from and sustain on a consistent basis, than the random, periodic, and/or episodic tendencies we sometimes operate from via one's sinful, evil, and sometimes wicked ways?

From my perspective and life experiences, achieving and operating from a *wholesome,* if not perfect state of **_Righteousness,_** is nearly impossible for mankind, as well as believers to achieve on their own, especially given the fact that this Christlike attribute or character trait, is generally too high a standard to achieve in this earthly life. But with that said, the "*good news*" is that **_Righteousness_** can only be obtained by mankind through the cleansing of sin by Christ Jesus, and the indwelling presence of the Holy Spirit!

Left to our own ways and methods of operations, we have very limited abilities to achieve **_Righteousness_**. But Christians do indeed possess the **_Righteousness_** of Christ because: "*God made Him, who knew no sin to be sin for us, that we might become the **righteousness** of God in Him*" (2 Corinthians 5:21)! What an amazing and awesome biblical truth that on Calvary's Cross, Christ Jesus paid our sin debt in full, such that His life of perfect **_Righteousness_** would be exchanged, whereby: "*For we must all appear before the judgment seat of Christ, that each one may receive the things done in the body, according to what he has done, whether good or bad*" (2 Corinthians 5:10). Accordingly, Father God will not see our sin, but the **Holy _Righteousness_** of the Lord Jesus Christ!

Thus, my personal challenge—and I would assume as well, of all Christians—is to put on what I will call "The **Armor of _Righteousness,_**" and operate from this most important state of Christlike behavior now, in all that one does, says, acts, and behaves; So that, at the end of this journey, we will all hear the Lord God say: "*Well done good and faithful servant; you were faithful over a few things, I will make you ruler over many things. Enter into the joy of your Lord*" (Matthew 25:21). "Amazing Grace, how sweet the sound, that saved a wretched like me; I once was lost, but now I'm found...." How sweet is the sound of Father God's **_Righteousness_**!

(The Value of Wisdom)

Proverbs *2:1–*9* and *10*–22*

(1)   My son, if you receive my words, And treasure my commands within you,

(2)* **So that you incline your ear to *wisdom*, And apply your heart to understanding;**

(3)* Yes, if you cry out for discernment, And lift up your voice for understanding,

(4)* If you seek *her* as silver, And search *for **her*** as for hidden treasures;

(5)* **Then you will understand the fear of the LORD, And find the knowledge of God.**

(6)* **For the LORD gives *wisdom*; From His mouth come knowledge and understanding;**

(7)* **He stores up sound *wisdom* for the _upright_; He is a shield to those who walk _uprightly_;**

(8)* **He guards the paths of *justice*, *And preserves the way of His saints*.**

(9)* **Then you will understand _righteousness_ and *justice*, Equity and every good path.**

(10)* **When *wisdom* enters your heart, And knowledge is pleasant to your soul,**

(11)* **Discretion will preserve you; Understanding will keep you,**

(12)* To deliver you from the way of evil, From the man who speaks perverse things,

(13)* From those who leave the paths of **_uprightness_** To walk in the ways of darkness;

(14) Who rejoice in doing evil, And delight in the perversity of the wicked;

(15) Whose ways are crooked, And who are devious in their paths;

(16) To deliver you from the immoral woman, From the seductress who flatters with her words,

(17) Who forsakes the companion of her youth, And forgets the covenant of her God.

(18) For her house leads down to death, And her paths to the dead;

(19) None who go to her return, Nor do they regain the paths of life—

(20)* **So you may walk in the way of goodness, And keep to the paths of _righteousness_.**

(21)* **For the _upright_ will dwell in the land, And the _blameless_ will remain in it;**

(22)* But the wicked will be cut off from the earth, And the unfaithful will be uprooted from it.

(Guidance for the Young)

Proverbs *3:*11*–*12*

My son, do not despise the chastening of the LORD, Nor detest His correction; For whom the LORD loves He corrects, _Just_ as a father the son in whom he delights.

Proverbs *3:*27*–*28*

Do not withhold good from those to whom it is due, When it is in the power of your hand to do so. **Do not say to your neighbor, "Go, and come back, And tomorrow I will give it,"** _When you have it with you._

Proverbs *3:29–30 and 31–*34*

(29) Do not devise evil against your neighbor, For he dwells by you for safety's sake.

(30) Do not strive with a man without cause, _If he has done you no harm._

(31) Do not envy the oppressor, And choose none of his ways;

(32)* For the perverse person is an abomination to the LORD, But His secret counsel is with the _upright_.

(33)* The curse of the LORD is on the house of the wicked, But He blesses the home of the _just_.

(34)* **Surely He _scorns_ the _scornful_, But gives grace to the humble.**

(Security in Wisdom)

Proverbs *4:*10*–*13*

(10)* **Hear, my son, and receive my sayings, And the years of your life will be many.**

(11)* **I have taught you in the way of wisdom; I have led you in _right_ paths.**

(12)* **When you walk, your steps will not be hindered, And when you run, you will not stumble.**

(13)* **Take firm hold of instruction, do not let go; Keep her, for she is your life.**

Proverbs *4:*18*–19

(18)* **But the path of the _just_ is like the shinning sun, That shines ever brighter unto the perfect day.**

(19) The way of the wicked is like darkness; They do not know what makes them stumble.

Proverbs *4:*26*–*27*

(26)* **Ponder the path of your feet, And let all your ways be established.**

(27)* **Do not turn to the _right_ or to the left; Remove your foot from evil.**

(The Excellence in Wisdom)

Proverbs *8:*6*–9*

(6)* **Listen, for I will speak of excellent things, And from the opening of my lips will come _right_ things;**

(7)* **For my mouth will speak truth; Wickedness is an abomination to my lips.**

(8)* **All the words of wisdom's mouth are with _righteousness_; Nothing crooked or perverse is in them.**

(9)* They are all plain to him who understands, And **_right_** to those who find knowledge.

Proverbs *8:*17*-21*

(17)* **I, (Wisdom), love those who love me, And those who seek me diligently will find me.**

(18)* Riches and honor are with me, Enduring riches and **_righteousness_**.

(19)* My fruit is better than gold, yes, than fine gold, And my revenue than choice silver.

(20)* I, (Wisdom), traverse the way of **_righteousness_**, In the midst of the paths of _justice_.

(21)* That I, (Wisdom), may cause those who love me to inherit wealth,
That I, (Wisdom), may fill their treasures.

(The Way of Wisdom)

Proverbs *9:7–12

(7) "He who corrects a scoffer gets shame for himself, And he who rebukes a wicked man only harms himself.

(8)* **Do not correct a scoffer. Lest he hate you; Rebuke a wise man, and he will love you.**

(9)* **Give instruction to a wise man, and he will be still wiser; Teach a _just_ man, and he will increase in learning.**

(10)* **The fear of the LORD is the beginning of wisdom, And the knowledge of the Holy One is understanding.**

(11) For by me your days will be multiplied, And years of life will be added to you.

(12) If you are wise, you are wise for yourself, And if you scoff, you will bear it alone."

(Wise Sayings of Solomon)

Proverbs 10:2*

Treasures of wickedness profit nothing, But _**righteousness**_ delivers from death.

Proverbs 10:3

The LORD will not allow the _**righteous**_ soul to famish, But He casts away the desire of the wicked.

Proverbs 10:*6*

Blessings are on the head of the _**righteous**_, But violence covers the mouth of the wicked.

Proverbs 10:7
The memory of the *righteous* is blessed, But the name of the wicked will rot.

Proverbs 10:9*
He who walks with integrity walks *securely*, But he who perverts his ways will become known.

Proverbs 10:11*
The mouth of the *righteous* is a well of life, But violence covers the mouth of the wicked.

Proverbs 10:16
The labor of the *righteous* leads to life, The wages of the wicked to sin.

Proverbs *10:*20*
The tongue of the *righteous* is choice silver; The heart of the wicked is worth little.

Proverbs *10:*21*
The lips of the *righteous* feed many, But fools die for lack of wisdom.

Proverbs 10:24
The fear of the wicked will come upon him, And the desire of the *righteous* will be granted.

Proverbs 10:25
When the whirlwind passes by, the wicked is no more, But the *righteous* has an everlasting foundation.

Proverbs 10:28
The hope of the *righteous* will be gladness, But the expectation of the wicked will perish.

Proverbs *10:*29*
The way of the LORD is strength for the *upright*, But destruction will come to the workers of iniquity.

Proverbs 10:30
The *righteous* will never be removed, But the wicked will not inhabit the earth.

Proverbs 10:*31*
The mouth of the *righteous* brings forth wisdom, But the perverse tongue will be cut out.

Proverbs 10:32*
The lips of the *righteous* know what is *acceptable*, But the mouth of the wicked what is perverse.

Proverbs 11:1
Dishonest scales are an abomination to the LORD, But a *just* weight is His delight.

Proverbs 11:3
The integrity of the *upright* will guide them, But the perversity of the unfaithful will destroy them.

Proverbs 11:*4*
Riches do not profit in the day of wrath, But *righteousness* delivers from death.

Proverbs 11:5
The *righteousness* of the *blameless* will direct his way *aright*, But the wicked will fall by his own wickedness.

Proverbs 11:6*
The *righteousness* of the *upright* will deliver them, But the unfaithful will be caught in their lust.

Proverbs 11:8
The *righteous* is delivered from trouble, And it comes to the wicked instead.

Proverbs 11:*9*

The hypocrite with his mouth destroys his neighbor, But through knowledge the **_righteous_** will be delivered.

Proverbs 11:10–11

When it goes well with the **_righteous_**, the city rejoices; And when the wicked perish, there is jubilation. By the blessing of the **_upright_** the city is exalted, But it is overthrown by the mouth of the wicked.

Proverbs 11:18*

The wicked man does deceptive work, But he who sows **_righteousness_** will have a sure reward.

Proverbs 11:19*

As **_righteousness_** leads to life, So he who pursues evil pursues it to his own death.

Proverbs 11:20

Those who are of a perverse heart are an abomination to the LORD, But the _blameless_ in their ways are His delight.

Proverbs 11:21*

Though they join forces, the wicked will not go unpunished; But the posterity of the **_righteous_** will be delivered.

Proverbs 11:23

The desire of the **_righteous_** is only good, But the expectation of the wicked is wrath.

Proverbs *11:*24*–*25*

There is one who scatters, yet increases more; And there is one who withholds more than is _right_, But it leads to poverty. The generous soul will be made rich, And he who waters will also be watered himself.

Proverbs 11:27*

He who earnestly seeks _good_ finds favor, But trouble will come to him who seeks evil.

Proverbs 11:28*

He who trusts in his riches will fall, But the _righteous_ will flourish like foliage.

Proverbs *11:*30*

The fruit of the _righteous_ is a tree of life, And he who wins souls is wise.

Proverbs 11:31

If the _righteous_ will be recompensed on the earth, How much more the ungodly and the sinner.

Proverbs 12:2

A _good_ man obtains favor from the LORD, But a man of wicked intentions He will condemn.

Proverbs 12:3

A man is not established by wickedness, But the root of the _righteous_ cannot be moved.

Proverbs 12:5*

The thoughts of the _righteous_ are _right_, But the counsels of the wicked are deceitful.

Proverbs 12:6

The words of the wicked are, "Lie in wait for blood," But the mouth of the _upright_ will deliver them.

Proverbs 12:7*

The wicked are overthrown and are no more, But the house of the _righteous_ will stand.

Proverbs 12:10

A *righteous* man regards the life of his animal, But the tender mercies of the wicked are cruel.

Proverbs 12:12*

The wicked covet the catch of evil men, But the root of the *righteous* yields fruit.

Proverbs 12:13*

The wicked is ensnared by the transgression of his lips, But the *righteous* will come through trouble.

Proverbs *12:*15*

The way of a fool is *right* in his own eyes, But he who heeds counsel is wise.

Proverbs 12:*17*

He who speaks truth declares *righteousness*, But a false witness, deceit.

Proverbs 12:21*

No grave trouble will overtake the *righteous*, But the wicked shall be filled with evil.

Proverbs 12:*26*

The *righteous* should choose his friends carefully, For the way of the wicked leads them astray.

Proverbs 12:28*

In the way of *righteousness* is life, And in its pathway there is no death.

Proverbs 13:5

A *righteous* man hates lying, But a wicked man is loathsome and comes to shame.

Proverbs 13:*6*

Righteousness guards him whose way is *blameless*, But wickedness overthrows the sinner.

Proverbs 13:9
The light of the ***righteous*** rejoices, But the lamp of the wicked will be put out.

Proverbs 13:21*
Evil pursues sinners, But to the ***righteous***, good shall be repaid.

Proverbs *13:*22*
A good man leaves an inheritance to his children's children, But the wealth of the sinner is stored up for the *righteous*.

Proverbs 13:25
The ***righteous*** eats to the satisfying of his soul, But the stomach of the wicked shall be in want.

Proverbs 14:2
He who walks in his ***uprightness*** fears the LORD, But he who is perverse in his ways despises Him.

Proverbs 14:*9*
Fools mock at sin, But among the ***upright*** there is favor.

Proverbs 14:11*
The house of the wicked will be overthrown, But the tent of the ***upright*** will flourish.

Proverbs *14:*12*
There is a way that seems *right* to a man, But its end is the way of death.

Proverbs 14:19
The evil will bow before the *good*, And the wicked at the gates of the ***righteous***.

Proverbs 14:32
The wicked is banished in his wickedness, But the ***righteous*** has a refuge in his death.

Proverbs 14:34
Righteousness exalts a nation, But sin is a reproach to any people.

Proverbs 15:*2*
The tongue of the wise uses knowledge *rightly*, But the mouth of fools pours forth foolishness.

Proverbs *15:*6*
In the house of the *righteous* there is much treasure, But in the revenue of the wicked is trouble.

Proverbs 15:8
The sacrifice of the wicked is an abomination to the LORD, But the prayer of the *upright* is His delight.

Proverbs 15:*9*
The way of the wicked is an abomination to the LORD, But He loves him who follows *righteousness*.

Proverbs *15:*16*
Better is a little with the fear of the LORD, **Than great treasure with trouble.**

Proverbs 15:19*
The way of the lazy man is like a hedge of thorns, But the way of the *upright* is a highway.

Proverbs 15:21*
Folly is joy to him who is destitute of discernment, But a man of understanding walks *uprightly*.

Proverbs *15:*28*
The heart of the *righteous* studies how to answer, But the mouth of the wicked pours forth evil.

Proverbs 15:29*
The LORD is far from the wicked, But He hears the prayer of the *righteous*.

Proverbs *16:*8*
Better is a little with _righteousness_, Than vast revenues without _justice_.

Proverbs 16:12
It is an abomination for kings to commit wickedness, For a throne is established by _righteousness_.

Proverbs 16:13*
Righteous lips are the delight of kings, And they love him who speaks what is _right_.

Proverbs *16:*17*
The highway of the _upright_ is to depart from evil; He who keeps his way preserves his soul.

Proverbs *16:*25*
There is a way that seems _right_ to a man, But its end is the way of death.

Proverbs *16:*31*
The silver-haired head is a crown of glory, If it is found in the way of _righteousness_.

Proverbs 17:*15*
He who justifies the wicked, and he who condemns the _just_, Both of them alike are an abomination to the LORD.

Proverbs 17:26
Also, to punish the _righteous_ is not good, Nor to strike princes for their _uprightness_.

Proverbs 18:5*
It is not good to show partiality to the wicked, Or to overthrow the _righteous_ in judgment.

Proverbs *18:*10*
The name of the LORD is a strong tower; The _righteous_ run to it and are safe.

Proverbs 18:17*

The first one to plead his cause seems *right*, Until his neighbor comes and examines him.

Proverbs *19:*17*

He who has pity on the poor lends to the LORD, And He will pay back what he has given.

Proverbs 19:22*

What is desired in a man is *kindness, And a poor man is better than a liar.*

Proverbs 20:6

Most men will proclaim each his own *goodness,* But who can find a *faithful* man.

Proverbs 20:7*

The *righteous* man walks in his integrity; His children are blessed after him.

Proverbs 20:8

A king who sits on the throne of judgment *Scatters all evil with his eyes.*

Proverbs 20:11*

Even a child is known by his deeds, Whether what he does is pure and **right**.

Proverbs *21:*2*

Every way of a man is *right* in his own eyes, But the LORD weighs the hearts.

Proverbs 21:*3*

To do *righteousness* and *justice* Is more acceptable to the LORD than sacrifice.

Proverbs 21:7

The violence of the wicked will destroy them, Because they refuse to do *justice.*

Proverbs 21:8*

The way of a guilty man is perverse; But as for the pure, his work is **_right_**.

Proverbs 21:12*

The **_righteous_** God wisely considers the house of the wicked, Overthrowing the wicked for their wickedness.

Proverbs 21:*15*

It is a joy for the **_just_** to do _justice_, But destruction will come to the workers of iniquity.

Proverbs 21:18

The wicked shall be a ransom for the **_righteous_**, And the unfaithful for the **_upright_**.

Proverbs *21:*21*

He who follows _righteousness_ and mercy Finds life, _righteousness_, and honor.

Proverbs *21:25*–*26*

The desire of the lazy man kills him, For his hands refuse to labor. He covets greedily all day long, **But the _righteous_ gives and does not spare.**

Proverbs 21:29

A wicked man hardens his face; But as for the **_upright_**, he establishes his way.

Proverbs *22:*6*

**Train up a child in the way he should go, And when he is old, he will not depart from it.**

(Sayings of the Wise)

Proverbs *22:*22*–*23*

**Do not rob the poor because he is poor, Nor oppress the afflicted at the** *gate; For the LORD will plead their cause,* **And plunder the soul of those who plunder them.**

Proverbs 22:29*

Do you see a man who excels in his work? He will stand before kings; He will not stand before unknown men.

Proverbs *23:*15*–*16*

My son, if your heart is wise, My heart will rejoice—indeed, I myself; Yes, my inmost being will rejoice When your lips speak *right* things.

Proverbs 23:24–25

The father of the ***righteous*** will greatly rejoice, And he who begets a wise child will delight in him. Let your father and your mother be glad, And let her who bore you rejoice.

Proverbs *24:15–*16*

Do not lie in wait, O wicked man, against the dwelling of the ***righteous***; Do not plunder his resting place; **For a *righteous* man may fall seven times And rise again, But the wicked shall fall by calamity.**

(Further Sayings of the Wise)

Proverbs *24:*23*–25*, 26*, 27*, and 28*–*29*

(23)* **These things also belong to the *wise*: It is not good to show partiality in judgment.**

(24)* **He who says to the wicked, "You are *righteous*," Him the people will curse; Nations will abhor him.**

(25)* **But those who rebuke the wicked will have delight, And a good blessing will come upon them.**

(26)* **He who gives a *right* answer kisses the lips.**

(27)* **Prepare your outside work, Make it fit for yourself in the field; And afterward build your house.**

(28)* **Do not be a witness against your neighbor without cause, For would you deceive with your lips?**

(29)* **Do not say, "I will do to him _just_ as he has done to me; I will render to the man according to his work."**

(Further Wise Sayings of Solomon)

Proverbs 25:4–5

Take away the dross from silver, And it will go to the silversmith for jewelry. Take away the wicked from before the king, And his throne will be established in **_righteousness_**.

Proverbs *25:*21*–*22*

If your enemy is hungry, give him bread to eat; And if he is thirsty, give him water to drink; For so you will heap coals of fire on his head, And the LORD will reward you!

Proverbs 25:26*

A **_righteous_** man who falters before the wicked Is like a murky spring and a polluted well.

Proverbs *27:*6*

Faithful are the wounds of a friend, **But the kisses of an enemy are deceitful.**

Proverbs 27:18

Whoever keeps the fig tree will eat its fruit; _So he who waits on his master will be honored._

Proverbs 28:1*

The wicked flee when no one pursues, But the **_righteous_** are bold as a lion.

Proverbs 28:2

Because of the transgression of a land, many are its princes; But by a man of understanding and knowledge **_Right_** will be prolonged.

Proverbs 28:4

Those who forsake the law praise the wicked, But such as *keep the law* contend with them.

Proverbs 28:5*

Evil men do not understand *justice*, But those who *seek the LORD* understand all.

Proverbs 28:10

Whoever causes the **_upright_** to go astray in an evil way, He himself will fall into his own pit; But the *blameless* will inherit good.

Proverbs 28:12

When the **_righteous_** rejoice, there is great glory; But when the wicked arise, men hide themselves.

Proverbs 28:18*

Whoever walks *blamelessly* will be saved, But he who is perverse in his ways will suddenly fall.

Proverbs 28:20

A *faithful* man will abound with blessings, But he who hastens to be rich will not go unpunished.

Proverbs *28:*23*

He who rebukes a man will find more favor afterward Than he who flatters with the tongue.

Proverbs 28:28

When the wicked arise, men hide themselves; But when they perish, the **_righteous_** increase.

Proverbs 29:2

When the **_righteous_** are in authority, the people rejoice; But when a wicked man rules, the people groan.

Proverbs 29:6

By transgression an evil man is snared, But the **_righteous_** sings and rejoices.

Proverbs 29:7*

The **_righteous_** considers the cause of the poor, But the wicked does not understand such knowledge.

Proverbs 29:10

The bloodthirsty hate the _blameless_, But the **_upright_** seek his well-being.

Proverbs 29:13*

The poor man and the oppressor have this in common: The LORD gives light to the eyes of both.

Proverbs 29:14

The king who judges the poor with truth, His throne will be established forever.

Proverbs 29:16

When the wicked are multiplied, transgression increases; But the **_righteous_** will see their fall.

Proverbs 29:25

The fear of man brings a snare, _But whoever trusts in the LORD shall be safe._

Proverbs 29:26

Many seek the ruler's favor, _But justice for man comes from the LORD._

Proverbs 29:27*

An unjust man is an abomination to the **_righteous_**, And he who is **_upright_** in the way is an abomination to the wicked.

(The Wisdom of Agur)

Proverbs 30:11–14

(11) There is a generation that curses its father, And does not bless its mother.

(12) There is a generation that is *pure* in its own eyes, Yet is not washed from its filthiness.

(13) There is a generation-oh, how lofty are their eyes! And their eyelids are lifted up.

(14) There is a generation whose teeth are like swords, And whose fangs are like knives, To devour the poor from off the earth, And the needy from among men.

(The Words of King Lemuel's Mother)

Proverbs 31:4–9*

(4) It is not for kings, O Lemuel, It is not for kings to drink wine, Nor for princes intoxicating drink;

(5) Lest they drink and forget the law, And pervert the *justice* of all the afflicted.

(6) Give strong drink to him who is perishing, And wine to those who are bitter of heart.

(7) Let him drink and forget his poverty, And remember his misery no more.

(8) Open your mouth for the speechless, In the cause of all who are appointed to die.

(9)* Open your mouth, judge **_righteously_**, And plead the cause of the poor and needy.

CHAPTER 62

SACRIFICE

As one reads, reflects, and marinates on the Proverbs verses under this Chapter Theme, one may rightly note, that many of these verses are "kissing cousins" to Chapter 28—the Chapter Theme on "*GIVING*"; And from my perspective, that would be an accurate assessment. For example, here are several noteworthy Chapter 62 Proverbs verses on the Chapter Theme of "***Sacrifice***":

a) 11:24: "*There is one who scatters, yet increases more; And there is one who withholds more than is right, But it leads to poverty*";

b) 11:25: "*The generous soul will be made rich, And he who waters will also be watered himself*";

c) 13:7: "*There is one who makes himself rich, yet has nothing; And one who makes himself poor, yet has great riches*";

d) 21:3: "*To do righteousness and justice Is more acceptable to the LORD than **sacrifice**";* and

e) 28:27: "*He who gives to the poor will not lack, But he who hides his eyes will have many curses.*"

As I marinated on this Chapter Theme, I personally took stock of Proverbs 28:27, not so much regarding any potential "curses" that might have been the consequences from me "*hiding my eyes*," but for me, I am always challenging myself by asking the question, "Am I doing enough?" I personally struggle with this concern as I personally reflect on how Father God has and continues to Bless me in numerous ways. I, more frequently than not, question whether or not I need to "up my game" in making "*Sacrifices*," not only for the poor and needy, but also for others—friends and foe alike!

(Wise Sayings of Solomon)

Proverbs *11:*24*
There is one who scatters, yet increases more; And there is one who withholds more than is right, But it leads to poverty.

Proverbs *11:*25*
The *generous soul* will be made rich, *And he who waters will also be watered himself.*

Proverbs *13:*7*
There is one who makes himself rich, yet has nothing; *And one who makes himself poor, yet has great riches*.

Proverbs 15:8
The *sacrifice* of the wicked is an abomination to the LORD, But the prayer of the upright is His delight.

Proverbs 21:*3*
To do righteousness and justice Is more acceptable to the LORD than *sacrifice*.

Proverbs 21:27*
The *sacrifice* of the wicked is an abomination; How much more when he brings it with wicked intent!

(Sayings of the Wise)

Proverbs 22:28

Do not remove the ancient landmark Which your fathers have set.

Proverbs 23:1–3

(1) When you sit down to eat with a ruler, *Consider carefully what is before you;*

(2) *And put a knife to your throat If you are a man given to appetite.*

(3) *Do not desire his delicacies, For they are deceptive food.*

Proverbs *23:*4*–*5*

Do not overwork to be rich; Because of your own understand, cease! Will you set your eyes on that which is not? For riches certainly make themselves wings; They fly away like an eagle toward heaven.

Proverbs 23:10–11

Do not remove the ancient landmark, Nor enter the fields of the fatherless; For their Redeemer is mighty; He will plead their cause against you.

(Further Wise Sayings of Solomon)

Proverbs *25:*21*–*22*

If your enemy is hungry, give him bread to eat; And if he is thirsty, give him water to drink; For so you will heap coals of fire on his head, And the LORD will reward you!

Proverbs 27:18

Whoever keeps the fig tree will eat its fruit; So he who *waits on his master* will be honored.

Proverbs 27:23–27

(23) *Be diligent to know the state of your flocks, And attend to your herds;*

(24) For riches are not forever, Nor does a crown endure to all generations.

(25) When the hay is removed, and the tender grass shows itself, And the herbs of the mountains are gathered in,

(26) *The lambs will provide your clothing, And the goats the price of a field;*

(27) *You shall have enough goats' milk for your food, For the food of your household, And the nourishment of your maidservants.*

Proverbs *28:*27*

He who gives to the poor will not lack, But he who hides his eyes will have many curses.

(The Virtuous Wife)

Proverbs *31:19–*20*

(19) *She stretches out her hands to the distaff, And her hands hold the spindle.*

(20)* **She extends her hand to the poor, Yes, she reaches out her hands to the needy.**

CHAPTER 63

SELF-CONTROL, RESTRAINT, GUARDS/SLOW ACTIONS

Would it be safe to say, that all individuals have had or are currently struggling with varying degrees of **_Self-Control_**? I know I have and I continue to struggle today with **_Self-Control_** in various facets of my life. For example, "*anger*" continues to be a challenging, persistent and "teachable moment," negative characteristic that I frequently struggle with. The Scripture is loaded with God's Word on the topic of "*anger*" as a negative characteristic for all people, especially those who are "in Christ."

For example, Proverbs 16:32 states: "*He who is **slow to anger** is better than the mighty, And he who rules his spirit than he who takes a city.*" Or reference another example in Proverbs 19:11, which states: "*The discretion of a man makes him **slow to anger**, And his glory is to overlook a transgression.*" And of course, there are numerous other Scripture verses on the topic of "*anger*," and one of my favorite verses is found in James 1:19 and 20, which states: "*So then, my beloved brethren, let every man be swift to hear, **slow to speak, slow to wrath**; for the **wrath** of man does not produce the righteousness of God.*"

So, have I conquered the "*anger*" phase that still dwells within me? No, not yet; but as I continue to meditate and marinate on God's Word in all areas of "**Self-Control**," I am constantly reminded and fervently striving to totally embrace and apply the ninth "**Fruit of the Spirit**," that being <u>**Self-Control**</u> (Galatians 5:22 and 23).

(Security in Wisdom)

<u>Proverbs *4:*23*–*27*</u>

(23)* *Keep your heart with all diligence,* **For out of it spring the issues of life.**

(24)* *Put away from you a deceitful mouth, And put perverse lips far from you.*

(25) Let *your eyes* look *straight ahead, And your eyelids look right before you.*

(26)* *Ponder the path of your feet, And let all your ways be established.*

(27)* *Do not turn to the right or the left; Remove your foot from evil.*

(Beware of Adultery)

<u>Proverbs *6:20–29</u>

(20) My son, keep your father's command, And do not forsake the law of your mother.

(21) Bind them continually upon your heart; Tie them around your neck.

(22) When you roam, they will lead you; When you sleep, they will keep you; And when you awake, they will speak with you.

(23)* *For the commandment is a lamp, And the law a light;* <u>*Reproofs of instruction*</u> *are the way of life,*

(24) To keep you from the evil woman, From the flattering tongue of a seductress.

(25) Do not lust after her beauty in your heart, Nor let her allure you with her eyelids.

(26) For by means of a harlot A man is reduced to a crust of bread; And an adulteress will prey upon his precious life.

(27) Can a man take fire to his bosom, And his clothes not be burned?

(28) Can one walk on hot coals, And his feet not be seared?

(29) So is he who goes in to his neighbor's wife; Whoever touches her shall not be innocent.

(Wise Sayings of Solomon)

Proverbs 10:19*
In the multitude of words sin is not lacking, But he who **restrains** his lips is *wise*.

Proverbs 11:22
As a ring of gold in a swine's snout, *So is a lovely woman who lacks* **discretion**.

Proverbs 12:16
A **fool's wrath** is known at once, But a prudent man covers shame.

Proverbs 13:3*
He who **guards his mouth** preserves his life, *But he who opens wide his lips shall have destruction.*

Proverbs 13:*13*
He who despises the word will be destroyed, *But he who **fears the commandment** will be rewarded.*

Proverbs 13:14
*The **law of the wise** is a fountain of life*, To turn one away from the snares of death.

Proverbs *14:*29*
He who is ***slow to wrath*** has great understanding, But he who is ***impulsive*** exalts folly.

Proverbs 15:*1*
A **soft answer** turns away wrath, But a harsh word stirs up **anger**.

Proverbs 15:18
A wrathful man stirs up strife, But he who is **_slow to anger_** allays contention.

Proverbs 15:27*
He who is greedy for gain troubles his own house, _But he who_ <u>hates bribes</u> _will live._

Proverbs 16:24
Pleasant words _are like a honeycomb,_ Sweetness to the soul and health to the bones.

Proverbs 16:*32*
He who is **_slow to anger_** is better than the mighty, And he who _rules his_ <u>spirit</u> than he who takes a city.

Proverbs 19:*11*
The discretion of a man makes him **_slow to anger_**, _And his glory is to_ <u>overlook</u> _a transgression._

Proverbs 19:16
He who <u>keeps the commandment</u> keeps his soul, But he who is careless of his ways will die.

Proverbs 20:1
Wine is a mocker, Strong drink is a brawler, _And whoever is led astray by it is not wise._

Proverbs 20:11*
Even a child is known by his deeds, Whether what he does is pure and right.

Proverbs 21:20*
There is desirable treasure, And oil in the dwelling of the wise, But a foolish man squanders it.

Proverbs 21:23*
Whoever _**guards his mouth and tongue**_ Keeps his soul from troubles.

Proverbs 22:5
Thorns and snares are in the way of the perverse; He who _**guards his soul**_ will be far from them.

Proverbs *22:*6*
**Train up a child in the way he should go,** And when he is old he will not depart from it.

Proverbs *22:*7*
The rich rules over the poor, _And the borrower is servant to the lender._

(Sayings of the Wise)

Proverbs 22:29*
Do you see a man who excels in his work? He will stand before kings; He will not stand before unknown men.

Proverbs 23:1–3
(1)   When you sit down to eat with a ruler, _Consider carefully what is before you;_
(2)   _And put a knife to your throat If you are a man given to appetite._
(3)   _Do not desire his delicacies,_ For they are deceptive food.

Proverbs 23:6–8
(6)   _Do not eat the bread of a miser, Nor desire his delicacies;_
(7)   For as he thinks in his heart, so is he. "Eat and drink!" he says to you, But his heart is not with you.
(8)   The morsel you have eaten, you will vomit up, And waste your pleasant words.

Proverbs 23:19*–21
(19)*   _Hear,_ my son, _and be wise, And guide your heart in the way._
(20)   _Do not mix_ with winebibbers, Or with gluttonous eaters of meat;

(21) For the drunkard and the glutton will come to poverty, And drowsiness will clothe a man with rags.

Proverbs 23:26–28

(26) My son, *give me your heart, And let your eyes observe my ways.*

(27) For a harlot is a deep pit, And a seductress is a narrow well.

(28) She also lies in wait as for a victim, And increases the unfaithful among men.

(Use of Wine)

Proverbs 23:29–35

(29) Who has woe? Who has sorrow? Who has contentions? Who has complaints? Who has wounds without cause? Who has redness of eyes?

(30) Those who linger long at the wine, Those who go in search of mixed wine,

(31) *Do not look on the wine when it is red, When it sparkles in the cup, When it swirls around smoothly;*

(32) At the last it bites like a serpent, And stings like a viper.

(33) Your eyes will see strange things, And your heart will utter perverse things.

(34) Yes, you will be like one who lies down in the midst of the sea, Or like one who lies at the top of the mast saying:

(35) "They have struck me, but I was not hurt; They have beaten me, but I did not feel it. When shall I awake, that I may seek another drink?"

(Further Sayings of the Wise)

Proverbs 24:28*–29

Do not be a witness against your neighbor without cause, For would you deceive with your lips? Do not say, "I will do to him just as he has done to me; I will render to the man according to his work."

(Further Wise Sayings of Solomon)

Proverbs 25:15
By long forbearance a ruler is persuaded, And a ***gentle tongue*** breaks a bone.

Proverbs 25:16
Have you found honey? *Eat only as much as you need*, Lest you be filled with it and vomit.

Proverbs 25:17
Seldom set foot in your neighbor's house, Lest he become weary of you and hate you.

Proverbs *25:*21*–*22*
If your enemy is hungry, *give him bread to eat*; And if he is thirsty, *give him water to drink*; For so you will heap coals of fire on his head, And the LORD will reward you.

Proverbs 25:26
A righteous man *who falters before the wicked* Is like a murky spring and a polluted well.

Proverbs 25:*27*
It is not good to eat much honey; So to seek one's own glory is not glory.

Proverbs 25:28*
Whoever has *no rule over his own spirit* Is like a city broken down, without walls.

Proverbs 26:4*–5*
Do not answer a fool *according to his folly*, Lest you also be like him. *Answer a fool according to his folly*, Lest he be wise in his own eyes.

Proverbs 27:15*–16
A continual dripping on a very rainy day And a contentious woman are

alike; *Whoever* **restrains** *her* **restrains** *the wind*, And grasps oil with his right hand.

Proverbs 28:7
Whoever <u>keeps the law</u> is a discerning son, But a companion of gluttons shames his father.

Proverbs 29:11*
A fool vents all his feelings, But a wise man <u>holds</u> *them back.*

Proverbs 29:18*
Where there is no revelation, the people cast off **restraint**; But happy is he who <u>keeps the law</u>.

(The Wisdom of Agur)

Proverbs 30:32–33
If you have been foolish in exalting yourself, Or if you have devised evil, *put your hand on your mouth.* For as the churning of milk produces butter, And wringing of the nose produces blood, *So the forcing of wrath produces strife.*

CHAPTER 64

SHAME, DISGRACE, DISHONOR, REGRET

I would affirmatively state that everyone who has ever lived, has experienced some degree of **_Shame_**, **_Dishonor_**, **_Disgrace_**, and/or **_Regret_**, especially regarding sins committed in one's past. As we all know, that except for Christ Jesus: "*for all have sinned and fall short of the glory of God*" (Romans 3:23).

Accordingly, the primary Theme of this Chapter Narrative (i.e. **_Shame_**) has befallen all mankind, whether they be God's first family of Adam and Eve, who had to live with the **_Shame_**, **_Dishonor_**, **_Disgrace_**, and **_Regret_,** for committing mankind's first sin against God, by eating the forbidden fruit from "*the tree of the knowledge of good and evil*" in the Garden of Eden (Genesis 2:17).

Or how about the Apostle Peter who experienced **_Shame_**, **_Dishonor_**, **_Disgrace_**, and **_Regret_**, whereby on the night before Jesus Christ was crucified, during the Passover meal, when Peter emphatically stated that he would never betray Christ Jesus; yet, as we all know, Peter subsequently denied Christ Jesus on three separate occasions (Matthew 26:31–35, 69–75; Mark 14:27–31; and John 18:15–27). Can you imagine how the Apostle Peter must have felt, knowing that, within a few hours of Christ

Jesus's declaration that Peter would indeed deny knowing Him, what **_Shame_**, **_Dishonor_**, **_Disgrace_**, and **_Regret_** Peter must have felt and experienced, as "_Peter went out and wept bitterly_" (Luke 22:62).

When I examine my own life, and remember the numerous times that I have knowingly sinned and/or allowed my sinful nature to dominate my human desire to be obedient to God's Word, His stated purpose and will for my life, has indeed resulted in a sense of personal **_Shame_**, **_Disgrace,_** and/or **_Regret_**. But I also must remember and believe what the Bible teaches that: "_If we confess our sins, He is faithful and just to forgive us our sins and to cleanse us from all unrighteousness_" (1 John 1:9). And while one has sincere **_Regrets_** from one's past mistakes and/or sins, **_Shame_**, **_Dishonor_**, **_Disgrace_**, and/or **_Regret,_** should not and must not define who we are, given the fact that: "_But as many as received Him, to them He gave the right to become children of God, to those who believe in His name; who were born, not of blood, nor of the will of the flesh, nor of the will of man, but of God_" (John 1:12 and 13).

Accordingly, one must acknowledge and recognize that we all have a **_Shameful_** past, but we also a have much brighter future, recognizing that while we once walked in foolishness and rebellion to Father God, but we now can claim Father God's blessings, by walking in the newness and hope of eternal life (Titus 3:3–7). Thus, one can walk today, not with **_Shame_**, **_Dishonor_**, **_Disgrace_**, or **_Regret_** over one's past sins and mistakes, but with the blessed assurance, that Father God has forgiven, forgotten, and "_washed under the blood of Christ Jesus_" one's past missteps (Hebrew 10:16–18), especially knowing and believing in this simple biblical principle and truth that: "_I have been crucified with Christ; it is no longer I who live, but Christ lives in me; and the life which I now live in the flesh I live by faith in the Son of God, who loved me and gave Himself for me_" (Galatians 2:20).

(Guidance for the Young)

Proverbs 3:35*

The wise shall inherit glory, But **_shame_** shall be the legacy of fools.

(Beware of Adultery)

Proverbs *6:*32*–35

(32)* **Whoever commits adultery with a woman lacks understanding; He who does so _destroys his own soul_.**

(33)* **Wounds and _dishonor_ he will get, _And his reproach will not be wiped away_.**

(34) For jealousy is a husband's fury; Therefore he will not spare in the day of vengeance.

(35) He will accept no recompense, Nor will he be appeased though you give many gifts.

(The Way of Wisdom)

Proverbs *9:7–12

(7) "He who corrects a scoffer gets **_shame_** for himself, And he who rebukes a wicked man only harms himself.

(8)* **Do not correct a scoffer. lest he hate you; Rebuke a wise man, and he will love you.**

(9)* **Give instruction to a wise man, and he will be still wiser; Teach a just man, and he will increase in learning.**

(10)* **"The fear of the LORD is the beginning of wisdom, And the knowledge of the Holy One is understanding**.

(11) For by me your days will be multiplied, And years of life will be added to you.

(12) If you are wise, you are wise for yourself, And if you scoff, you bear it alone."

(Wise Sayings of Solomon)

Proverbs 10:5*
He who gathers in summer is a wise son; He who sleeps in harvest is a son who causes ***shame.***

Proverbs *11:*2*
When pride comes, then comes _shame_; But with the humble is wisdom.

Proverbs *11:*12*
He who is devoid of wisdom *despises* his neighbor, But a man of under-standing holds his peace.

Proverbs 12:4*
An excellent wife is the crown of her husband, But she who causes ***shame*** is like rottenness in his bones.

Proverbs *12:*15*
***The way of a fool is right in his own eyes*, But he who heeds counsel is wise.**

Proverbs 12:16
A fool's wrath is known at once, But a prudent man covers ***shame***.

Proverbs 13:5
A righteous man hates lying, But a wicked man is loathsome and comes to ***shame***.

Proverbs *13:*18*
Poverty and _shame_ will come to him who disdains correction, But he who regards a rebuke will be honored.

Proverbs 14:35
The king's favor is toward a wise servant, But his wrath is against him who causes ***shame.***

Proverbs 17:2
A wise servant will rule over a son who causes *shame*, And will share an inheritance among the brothers.

Proverbs 18:3
When the wicked comes, contempt comes also; And with ***dishonor*** comes *reproach*.

Proverbs 18:*13*
He who answers a matter before he hears it, It is folly and *shame* to him.

Proverbs 19:26
He who mistreats his father and chases away his mother Is a son who causes *shame* and brings *reproach*.

Proverbs 19:28
A *disreputable* witness scorns justice, And the mouth of the wicked devours iniquity.

(Further Sayings of the Wise)

Proverbs *24:*28*–*29*
Do not be a witness against your neighbor without cause, For would you deceive with your lips? Do not say, "I will do to him just as he has done to me; I will render to the man according to his work."

(Further Wise Sayings of Solomon)

Proverbs 25:8–10
(8)   Do not go hastily to court; For what will you do in the end, When your neighbor has put you to *shame*?
(9)   Debate your case with your neighbor, And do not disclose the secret to another;
(10) Lest he who hears it expose your *shame*, *And your reputation be ruined.*

Proverbs 25:14
Whoever falsely boasts of giving Is like clouds and wind without rain.

Proverbs 25:17
Seldom set foot in your neighbor's house, Lest he become *weary* of you and hate you.

Proverbs 28:7
Whoever keeps the law is a discerning son, But a companion of gluttons **shames** his father.

Proverbs *29:*15*
The rod and rebuke give wisdom, But a child left to himself brings shame to his mother.

CHAPTER 65

SIN, SINNER, SINFUL, TRANSGRESSION, UNFAITHFUL

As I draft this Chapter Theme Narrative on the topic, "***Sin/Sinner***," I am extremely reflective of this Theme, especially given the fact that we celebrated Easter Sunday just this past week. As I reflect on "the Cross," and I envision Christ Jesus being nailed on Calvary's Cross, hanging there between two thieves and Christ Jesus, our Lord and Savior, an innocent man, bearing the ***Sins*** of the world—past, present, and future—on His shoulders. I cringe just thinking about the agony and pain of what He must have endured; my ***Sins***, your ***Sins***, as well as **ALL** **_SINS_** of every person who has lived, is living now, and yet to be born. Just the weight of **ALL** of mankind's **_SINS_** is enough to bring me to my knees, weeping for my failure to live a more righteous life, while being eternally grateful and blessed that our Heavenly Father provided a way out from the penalty of eternal death, caused by my ***Sinful*** nature, by planning and allowing for our Lord and Savior, Christ Jesus, to pay mankind's substantial penalty of death, by His substitutionary death, for mine and your ***Sins***, especially for all those who have accepted Christ Jesus as their Lord and Savior!

It's been said, that ***Sin*** does not play favorites; As such, it is an equal opportunity tempter and employer! ***Sin***, because of our ***Sinful*** and flesh

701

nature, works its ugly way into everyone's life, without regard for age, race, or economic status: "*for all have **sinned** and fall short of the glory of God*" (Romans 3:23). Irrespective of the form factor that **Sin** takes, **Sin** always tempts one to choose our own way rather than Father God's way. Jesus said in John 10:10: "*The thief* (i.e. Satan) *does not come except to steal, and to kill and to destroy,*" resulting in rebellious behavior that can be harmful and addictive, and more times than not, can result in repetitive **Sinful** behavior, Thereby making such **Sin** and/or **Sinful** behavior engrained into one's **Sinful** nature, and/or one's personal DNA, so to speak.

So, what is **Sin** and why is it so bad? Most would agree that **Sin** can generally be defined as "any action, and/or attitude of thought, that falls short of Father God's Holiness." **Sin** is **Sin**, yet many of us, myself included, attempt to put varying layers or degrees of variation on **Sin**. For example, all would agree that the physical actions of murder, adultery, and theft are categorically **Sins**. But the *desire* to commit murder, adultery, and/or theft, are **Sins** as well, whether or not one lives such thoughts out (Matthew 5:21 and 28).

It goes without saying that **Sin** is **Sin**, since there are no "shades of gray" as it relates to **Sin**. Ever since Adam and Eve first **Sinned** in the Garden of Eden (Genesis 2:17, 3:17–19), every person born since Adam and Eve, has inherited a **Sinful** nature (Psalm 51:5; Romans 3:23 and 5:12).

Sin by its very nature is cunning, deceptive, and ultimately destructive, such that Satan uses any and all means to get one off track toward being obedient to God's Word, will, and purpose for one's life. One's descent into a pattern of disobedience which arises from one's inherited **Sinful** nature, generally begins in one's mind. Once one's thinking becomes engaged, it generally extends itself toward one's behavior, and from there, one's behavior morphs into a full-fledged action-oriented beast of unrighteous behaviors and deeds. And while it's not uncommon for such **Sin/ Sinful** actions to increase, but the associated benefits from such actions are generally of a short duration, that one eventually experiences a sense of bitterness, emptiness, guilt, pain, loss, shame, and/or sorrow.

Another example or element of man's **_Sin/Sinful_** nature is how one deals with, handles, and/or addresses, the ever-present element of temptation, which, unfortunately, is inevitable in one's human walk. For example, here's what God's Word states regarding the subject of temptation, as contained in James 1:13–15: "_Let no one say when he is tempted, 'I am tempted by God'; for God cannot be tempted by evil, nor does He Himself tempt anyone. But each one is tempted when he is drawn away by his own desires and enticed. Then, when desire has conceived, it gives birth to **sin**; and **sin**, when it is full-grown, brings forth death._"

But, even as one is frequently tempted by Satan, one can girdle oneself with the "**full armor of God**" (Ephesians 6:10–18) and find rest and comfort with the only offensive weapon that one has, that being God's Word. For example, James 4:7 and 8 states: "_Therefore submit to God. Resist the devil and he will flee from you. Draw near to God and He will draw near to you. Cleanse your hands, you **sinners**; and purify your hearts, you double-minded._" And 1 Corinthians 10:13, which states: "_No temptation has overtaken you except such as is common to man; but God is faithful, who will not allow you to be tempted beyond what you are able, but with the temptation will also make the way of escape, that you may be able to bear it._"

Accordingly, as stated in James 1:12: "_Blessed is the man who endures temptation; for when he has been approved, he will receive the crown of life which the Lord has promised to those who love Him._"

Finally, and in summary, one's faith in Christ Jesus, sets one free from the domination of **_Sin_** in one's life, since: "_There is therefore now no condemnation to those who are In Christ Jesus, who do not walk according to the flesh, but according to the Spirit_" (Romans 8:1). To be free from **_Sin_** means that all who have made Christ Jesus the Lord of their lives, are no longer enslaved by **_Sin_**. One has the power through the Holy Spirit, to live victoriously over **_Sin_** (1 Corinthians 15:56–58 and Romans 8:37).

Even though we once allowed our fleshy desires and **_Sinful_** nature to dominate us, those who are "in Christ Jesus," have the indwelling presence of the Holy Spirit to guide us, protect us, and shower us with the Father's love! While we still live in a fallen world, unfortunately we, who are still fleshly creatures, may still occasionally **Sin** (1 John 1:9, 2:1; Romans 7:21 and 22), we can rest in the assurance that we have been born again (John 3:3). "*Therefore, if anyone is In Christ, he is a new creation; old things have passed away; behold, all things have become new*" (2 Corinthians 5:17). And from my perspective, having gone from **Sinner** to Saint, thanks to the blood that was shed, by our Lord and Savior, Christ Jesus, on Calvary at "the Cross," then I must say unequivocally: "Amen, Amen, and Amen. Thank You, Christ Jesus!"

(Shun Evil Counsel)

Proverbs *1:10–*19*

(10) My son, if ***sinners*** entice you, Do not consent.

(11) If *they* say, "Come with *us*, Let *us* lie in wait to shed blood; Let *us* lurk secretly for the innocent without cause;

(12) Let *us* swallow them alive like Sheol, And whole, like those who go down to the Pit;

(13) *We* shall find all kinds of precious possessions, *We* shall fill *our* houses with spoil;

(14) Cast in your lot among *us*, Let *us all* have one purse"—

(15) My son, do not walk in the way with *them*, Keep your foot from *their* path;

(16) For *their* feet run to evil, And *they* make haste to *shed blood*.

(17) Surely, in vain *the net* is spread In the sight of any bird;

(18) But *they* lie in wait for *their* own blood, *They* lurk secretly for *their* own lives.

(19)* **So are the ways of *everyone* who is greedy for gain; It takes away the life of its *owners*.**

(The Value of Wisdom)

Proverbs *2:*20*–22

(20)* **So you may walk in the way of goodness, And keep to the paths of righteousness.**

(21)* **For the upright will dwell in the land, And the blameless will remain in it;**

(22) But the _wicked_ will be cut off from the earth, And the **_unfaithful_** will be uprooted from it.

(The Peril of Adultery)

Proverbs *5:*21*–*23*

(21)* **For the ways of man are before the eyes of the LORD, And He ponders all his paths.**

(22)* **His own _iniquities_ entrap the wicked man, And he is caught in the cords of his _sin_.**

(23)* **He shall die for lack of instruction, And in the greatness of his folly he shall go astray.**

(The Wicked Man)

Proverbs 6:16–19

(16) These six things the LORD hates, Yes, seven are an abomination to Him;

(17) _A proud look, A lying tongue, Hands that shed innocent blood,_

(18) _A heart that devises wicked plans, Feet that are swift in running to evil,_

(19) _A false witness who speaks lies, And one who sows discord among brethren._

(Beware of Adultery)

Proverbs *6:30–35

(30) People do not despise a *thief* If he *steals* to satisfy himself when he is starving.

(31) Yet when he is found, he must restore sevenfold; He may have to give up all the substance of his house.

(32)* *Whoever **commits adultery** with a woman lacks understanding; He who does so destroys his own soul*.

(33)* **Wounds and dishonor he will get, And his *reproach* will not be wiped away.**

(34)* For jealousy is a husband's fury; Therefore he will not spare in the day of vengeance.

(35) He will accept no recompense, Nor will he be appeased though you give many gifts.

(Excellence of Wisdom)

Proverbs *8:27–31

(27) When He prepared the heavens, I (*wisdom*) was there, When He drew a circle on the face of the deep,

(28) When He established the clouds above, When He strengthened the foundations of the deep,

(29) When He assigned to the sea its limit, So that the waters would not **transgress** His command, When He marked out the foundations of the earth,

(30) Then I was beside Him as a master craftsman; And I was daily His delight, Rejoicing always before Him,

(31) Rejoicing in His inhabited world, And my delight was the with the sons of men.

Proverbs *8:*32*–36*

(32)* **"Now therefore, listen to me, my children, For blessed are those who keep my (*wisdom*) ways.**

(33)* **Hear instruction and be *wise*, And do not disdain it.**

(34)* **Blessed is the man who listens to me, Watching daily at my gates. Waiting at the posts of my doors.**

(35)* **For whoever finds me finds life, And obtains favor from the LORD;**

(36)* But he who ***sins*** against me wrongs his own soul; All those who hate me love death."

(The Way of Folly)

Proverbs 9:13–18

(13) A foolish woman is clamorous; She is simple, and knows nothing.

(14) For she sits at the door of her house, On a seat by the highest places of the city,

(15) *To call to those who pass by,* Who go straight on their way:

(16) *"Whoever is simple, let him turn in here"; And as for him who lacks understanding, she says to him,*

(17) *"Stolen water is sweet, And bread eaten in secret is pleasant."*

(18) *But he does not know that the dead are there, That her guests are in the depths of hell.*

(Wise Sayings of Solomon)

Proverbs *10:*12*
Hatred stirs up strife, But love covers all *sins*.

Proverbs 10:16
The labor of the righteous leads to life, The wages of the *wicked* to ***sin***.

Proverbs 10:19*
In the multitude of words ***sin*** is not lacking, But he who restrains his lips is *wise*.

Proverbs 11:1
Dishonest scales are an *abomination to the LORD*, But a just weight is His delight.

Proverbs 11:3
The integrity of the upright will guide them, But the *perversity* of the **unfaithful** will destroy them.

Proverbs 11:6*
The righteousness of the upright will deliver them, But the **unfaithful** will be caught by their **_lust_**.

Proverbs 11:16
A gracious woman retains honor, But *ruthless* men retain riches.

Proverbs 11:31
If the righteous will be recompensed on the earth, How much more the *ungodly* and the **_sinner_**.

Proverbs 12:13*
The *wicked* is ensnared by the **_transgression_** of his lips, But the righteous will come through trouble.

Proverbs 13:2
A man shall eat well by the fruit of his mouth, But the soul of the **_unfaithful_** feeds on *violence*.

Proverbs 13:*6*
Righteousness guards him whose way is blameless, But *wickedness* overthrows the **_sinner_**.

Proverbs 13:15
Good understanding gains favor, But the way of the **_unfaithful_** is hard.

Proverbs 13:21*
Evil pursues **_sinners_**, But to the righteous, good shall be repaid.

Proverbs *13:*22*

A good man leaves an inheritance to his children's children, But the wealth of the _sinner_ is stored up for the righteous.

Proverbs 14:*9*

Fools mock at **_sin_**, But among the upright there is favor.

Proverbs 14:*21*

He who _despises_ his neighbor **_sins_**; But he who has mercy on the poor, happy is he.

Proverbs 14:34

Righteousness exalts a nation, But **_sin_** is a reproach to any people.

Proverbs 15:26

The _thoughts_ of the _wicked_ are an _abomination to the LORD_, But the words of the pure are pleasant.

Proverbs 16:5

Everyone _proud in heart_ is an _abomination to the LORD_; Though they join forces, none will go unpunished.

Proverbs 16:10

Divination is on the lips of the king; His mouth must not **_transgress_** in judgment.

Proverbs 16:12

It is an _abomination for kings_ to commit _wickedness_, For a throne is established by righteousness.

Proverbs 16:27

An _ungodly man_ digs up _evil_, And it is on his lips like a burning fire.

Proverbs 17:4

An _evildoer_ gives heed to _false lips_; A liar listens eagerly to a spiteful tongue.

Proverbs *17:*9*
He who covers a *transgression* seeks love, But he who repeats a matter separates friends.

Proverbs 17:15*
He who justifies the <u>wicked</u>, and he who *condemns* the just, Both of them alike are an *abomination to the LORD.*

Proverbs 17:19*
He who loves ***transgression*** loves strife, And he who exalts his gate seeks destruction.

Proverbs 19:*2*
Also it is not good for a soul to be without knowledge, And he **<u>sins</u>** who hastens with his feet.

Proverbs 19:*11*
The discretion of a man makes him slow to anger, And is glory is to overlook a ***transgression***.

Proverbs 20:2
The wrath of a king is like the roaring of a lion; Whoever provokes him to anger **<u>sins</u>** against his own life.

Proverbs 20:9
Who can say, "I have made my heart clean, I am pure from **<u>sin</u>**"?

Proverbs 20:10
Diverse weights and diverse measures, They are both alike, an *abomination to the LORD.*

Proverbs 20:23
Diverse weights are an *abomination to the LORD,* And *dishonest scales* are not good.

Proverbs 21:4
A haughty look, *a proud heart*, And the *plowing of the wicked* are **<u>sin</u>**.

Proverbs 21:7

The <u>violence</u> of the <u>wicked</u> will destroy them, Because they refuse to do justice.

Proverbs 21:8*

The way of a *guilty man is <u>perverse</u>;* But as for the pure, his work is right.

Proverbs 21:14

A gift in secret pacifies anger, And a bribe behind the back, strong wrath.

Proverbs 21:*15*

It is a joy for the just to do justice, *But destruction will come to the workers of **<u>iniquity</u>**.*

Proverbs 21:18

The <u>*wicked*</u> shall be a ransom for the righteous, And the ***<u>unfaithful</u>*** for the upright.

Proverbs 22:*12*

The eyes of the LORD preserve knowledge, But He overthrows the words of the *faithless.*

Proverbs 22:14

The mouth of an *<u>immoral woman</u>* is a deep pit; He who is abhorred by the LORD will fall there.

(Sayings of the Wise)

Proverbs *22:*22*–*23*

Do not <u>rob</u> the poor because he is poor, Nor <u>oppress</u> the afflicted at the gate; For the LORD will plead their cause, *And plunder the soul of those who plunder them.*

Proverbs 22:28

Do not remove the ancient landmark Which your fathers have set.

Proverbs 23:10–11

Do not remove the ancient landmark, Nor enter the fields of the fatherless; For their Redeemer is mighty; He will plead their cause against you.

Proverbs 23:17*–18*

Do not let your heart *envy* **sinners**, But be zealous for the fear of the LORD all the day; For surely there is a hereafter, And your hope will not be cut-off.

Proverbs 23:26–28

(26)   My son, give me your heart, And let your eyes observe my ways.

(27)   *For a harlot is a deep pit, And a seductress is a narrow well.*

(28)   She also lies in wait as for a victim, And increases the **unfaithful** among men.

Proverbs 24:8*–9*

He who plots to do *evil* Will be called a *schemer*. The devising of foolishness is **sin**, And the scoffer is an *abomination to men*.

Proverbs 24:19–20

Do not fret because of *evildoers*, Nor be envious of the *wicked*; For there will be no prospect for the *evil* man; The lamp of the *wicked* will be put out.

(Further Wise Sayings of Solomon)

Proverbs 25:19

Confidence in an **unfaithful** man in time of trouble Is like a bad tooth and a foot out of joint.

Proverbs 26:27*

Whoever digs a pit will fall into it, And he who rolls a stone will have it roll back on him.

Proverbs 28:2

Because of the **transgression** of a land, many are its princes; But by a man of understanding and knowledge Right will be prolonged.

Proverbs 28:10

Whoever *causes* the upright to *go astray* in an *evil way, He himself will fall into his own pit*; But the blameless will inherit good.

Proverbs *28:*13*

He who covers his <u>sins</u> will not prosper, But whoever confesses and forsakes them will have mercy.

Proverbs 28:17

A man burdened with bloodshed will flee into a pit; Let no one help him.

Proverbs 28:18*

Whoever walks blamelessly will be saved, But he who is <u>*perverse*</u> in his ways *will suddenly fall*.

Proverbs 28:21

To show partiality is not good, Because for a piece of bread a man will ***transgress***.

Proverbs 28:24

Whoever <u>*robs*</u> his father or his mother, And says, "<u>*It is no **transgression**,*</u>" *The same is companion to a destroyer.*

Proverbs 29:1*

He who is often rebuked, and hardens his neck, Will suddenly be destroyed, and that without remedy.

Proverbs 29:6*

By ***transgression*** an *evil* man is snared, But the righteous sings and rejoices.

Proverbs 29:10

The <u>*bloodthirsty*</u> hate the blameless, But the upright seek his well-being.

Proverbs 29:16

When the <u>*wicked*</u> are multiplied, ***transgression*** increases; But the righteous will see their fall.

Proverbs 29:22

An angry man stirs up strife, And a furious man abounds in **_transgression._**

Proverbs 29:24

Whoever is a partner with a **_thief_** hates his own life; He swears to tell the truth, but reveals nothing.

Proverbs 29:27*

An _unjust_ man is an _abomination_ to the righteous, And he who is upright in the way is an _abomination_ to the _wicked._

(The Wisdom of Agur)

Proverbs 30:32–33

If you have been foolish in exalting yourself, _Or if you have devised evil_, put your hand on your mouth. For as the churning of milk produces butter, And wringing the nose produces blood, _So the forcing of wrath produces strife._

CHAPTER 66

SPEECH (LIPS, MOUTH, SPEAKING, TONGUE, VOICE, WORDS)

"Father God, please ***Speak*** to my heart! As I recognize that I have eyes to see and ears to hear, but my prayer request is such that I desire to align my will with your will, such that I can most appropriately and most adequately receive your ***Spoken Word*** and receive it with a most willing heart! Thank You, Father God, as I yield myself to your ***Spoken Word***.'"

As one meditates and marinates on the various Proverbs verses that comprise this Chapter Theme on ***Speech***, personally, I am both blown away, while at the same time, extremely grateful, that Father God is more than willing to ***Speak*** to me through His written Word, even when my heart is slow to hear, listen, and/or apply His ***Spoken Word*** to my faith, and sometimes less than faithful walk!

For example, hear how the following Proverbs verses can ***Speak*** volumes to a willing and receptive heart:

- 1:2: "*To know wisdom and instruction, To perceive the **words** of understanding*";
- 1:20 and 21: "*Wisdom **calls** aloud outside; She raises her **voice** in the open squares. She **cries out** in the chief concourses, At the openings of the gates in the city She **speaks** her **words**";
- 8:1: "*Does not wisdom **cry out**, And understanding lift up her **voice***"?;
- 8:6: "*Listen, for I will **speak** of excellent things, And from the opening of my **lips** will come right things*";
- 8:7: "*For my **mouth** will **speak** truth; Wickedness is an abomination to my **lips**"*; and
- 8:8: "*All the **words** of my **mouth** are with righteousness; Nothing crooked or perverse is in them.*"

So, the question du jour, to myself as well as to all believers "in Jesus Christ," is to accept and acknowledge, that as Father God willingly and freely *Speaks* volumes of truth, wisdom, righteousness, and understanding through His *Word*, how willing am I, to appropriately and adequately, receive the *Spoken Word* of God in my heart, and apply it to my daily Christian walk? Thus, my daily challenge is to be "*swift to hear*" the *Spoken* Word of God and allow it to "transform" my heart and walk "in Christ" on a daily basis!

And to that I rejoice and *Proclaim*, "To God be the GLORY!"

(The Beginning of Knowledge)

Proverbs *1:1–6*
(1) The Proverbs of Solomon the son of David, king of Israel:
(2)* **To know *wisdom* and *instruction*, To perceive the <u>words</u> of understanding,**
(3)* **To receive the *instruction* of *wisdom*, Justice, judgment, and equity;**

(4)* To give prudence to the simple, To the young man knowledge and discretion—

(5)* **A *wise* man will hear and increase learning, And a man of understanding will attain *wise* counsel,**

(6)* To understand a proverb and an enigma, The ***words*** of the *wise* and their riddles.

(The Call of Wisdom)

Proverbs *1:*20*–27 and 28–33*

(20)* *Wisdom **calls aloud** outside; She raises her **voice** in the open squares.*

(21) She ***cries out*** in the chief concourses, At the openings of the gates in the city She ***speaks*** her ***words***:

(22) "How long, you simple ones, will you love simplicity? For scorners delight in their scorning, And fools hate knowledge.

(23) Turn at my *rebuke*; Surely I will pour out my spirit on you; I will make my ***words*** known to you.

(24) Because I have ***called*** and you refused, I have stretched out my hand and no one regarded,

(25) Because you disdained all my counsel, And would have none of my *rebuke,*

(26) I also will laugh at your calamity; I will mock when your terror comes,

(27) When your terror comes like a storm, And your destruction comes like a whirlwind, When distress and anguish come upon you.

(28) "Then they will ***call*** on me, but I will not ***answer***; They will seek me diligently, but they will not find me.

(29) Because they hated knowledge And did not choose the fear of the LORD,

(30) They would have none of my counsel And despised my every *rebuke.*

(31) Therefore they shall eat the fruit of their own way, And be filled to the full with their own fancies.

(32) For the turning away of the simple will slay them, And the complacency of fools will destroy them;

(33)* But whoever listens to me will dwell safely, And will be secure, without fear of evil."

(The Value of Wisdom)

Proverbs *2:1*–*6*

(1)* My son, if you receive my **_words_**, And treasure my commands within you,

(2)* **So that you incline your ear to *wisdom*, And apply your heart to understanding;**

(3)* Yes, if you **_cry out_** for discernment, And *lift up* your **_voice_** for understanding,

(4)* If you seek her (*Wisdom*) as silver, And search for her as for hidden treasures;

(5)* **Then you will understand the fear of the LORD, And find the knowledge of God.**

(6)* **For the LORD gives *wisdom*; From His **_mouth_** come knowledge and understanding.**

Proverbs *2:*10*–12*

(10)* **When *wisdom* enters your heart, And knowledge is pleasant to your soul,**

(11)* **Discretion will preserve you; Understanding will keep you,**

(12)* To deliver you from the way of evil, From the man who **_speaks_** perverse things.

Proverbs *2:16*–22*

(16)* To deliver you from the immoral woman, From the seductress who *flatters* with her **_words_**,

(17)   Who forsakes the companion of her youth, And forgets the covenant of her God.

(18)   For her house leads down to death, And her paths to the dead;

(19)   None who go to her return, Nor do they regain the paths of life—

(20)* **So you may walk in the way of goodness, And keep to the paths of righteousness.**

(21)* **For the upright will dwell in the land, And the blameless will remain in it;**

(22)* But the wicked will be cut off from the earth, And the unfaithful will be uprooted from it.

(Security in Wisdom)

Proverbs *4:1*–9

(1)*   Hear, my children, the *instruction* of a father, And give attention to know understanding;

(2)*   For I give you good doctrine: Do not forsake my law.

(3)   When I was my father's son, Tender and the only one in the sight of my mother,

(4)*   He also taught me, and <u>**said**</u> to me: "**Let your heart retain my <u>words</u>; Keep my commands, and live.**

(5)*   **Get *wisdom*! Get understanding! Do not forget, nor turn away from the <u>words</u> of my <u>mouth</u>.**

(6)*   **Do not forsake her, and she will preserve you; Love her, and she will keep you.**

(7)*   ***Wisdom* is the principle thing: Therefore get *wisdom*. And in all your getting, get understanding.**

(8)   Exalt her, and she will promote you; She will bring you honor, when you embrace her.

(9)   She will place on your head an ornament of grace; A crown of glory she will deliver to you."

Proverbs *4:*10*–*13*

(10)* **Hear, my son, and receive my _sayings_, And the years of your life will be many.**

(11)* **I have taught you in the way of _wisdom_; I have led you in the right paths.**

(12)* **When you walk, your steps will not be hindered, And when you run, you will not stumble.**

(13)* **Take firm hold of _instruction_, do not let go; Keep her, for she is your life.**

Proverbs *4:*20*–*27*

(20)* **My son, give attention to my _words_: Incline your ear to my _sayings_.**

(21)* **Do not let them depart from your eyes; Keep them in the midst of your heart:**

(22)* **For they are life to those who find them, And health to all their flesh.**

(23)* **Keep your heart with all diligence, For out of it spring the issues of life.**

(24)* **Put away from you a deceitful _mouth_, And put perverse _lips_ far from you.**

(25) Let your eyes look straight ahead, And your eyelids look right before you.

(26)* **Ponder the path of your feet, And let all your ways be established.**

(27)* **Do not turn to the right or the left; Remove your foot from evil.**

(The Peril of Adultery)

Proverbs 5:1–6

(1) My son, pay attention to my _wisdom_; Lend your ear to my understanding.

(2) That you may preserve discretion, And your _lips_ may keep knowledge.

(3) For the **_lips_** of an immoral woman drip honey, And her **_mouth_** is smoother than oil;

(4) But in the end she is bitter as wormwood, Sharp as a two-edged sword.

(5) Her feet go down to death, Her steps lay hold of hell.

(6) Lest you ponder her path of life—her ways are unstable; You do not know them.

Proverbs 5:7–14

(7) Therefore hear me now, my children, And do not depart from the **_words_** of my **_mouth_**.

(8) Remove your way far from her, And do not go near the door of her house,

(9) Lest you give your honor to others, And your years to the cruel one;

(10) Lest aliens be filled with your wealth, And your labors go to the house of a foreigner;

(11) And you mourn at last, When your flesh and your body are consumed,

(12) And say: "How I have hated _instruction_, And my heart despised correction!

(13) I have not obeyed the **_voice_** of my teachers, Nor inclined my ear to those who _instructed_ me!

(14) I was on the verge of total ruin, In the midst of the assembly and congregation."

(The Folly of Suretyship)

Proverbs *6:1–5

(1) My son, if you become surety for your friend, If you have shaken hands in pledge for a stranger,

(2) You are snared by the **_words_** of your **_mouth_**; You are taken by the **_words_** of your **_mouth_**.

(3) So do this, my son, and deliver yourself; For you have come into

the hand of your friend; Go and humble yourself; Plead with your friend.

(4) Give no sleep to your eyes, Nor slumber to your eyelids.

(5) Deliver yourself like a gazelle from the hand of the hunter, And like a bird from the hand of the fowler.

(The Wicked Man)

Proverbs *6:12–15

(12) A worthless person, a wicked man, Walks with a perverse **_mouth_**;

(13) He winks with his eyes, He shuffles his feet, He points with his fingers;

(14) Perversity is in his heart, He devises evil continually, He sows discord.

(15) Therefore his calamity shall come suddenly; Suddenly he shall be broken without remedy.

Proverbs *6:16–19

(16) These six things the LORD hates, Yes, seven are an abomination to Him:

(17) A proud look, A _lying_ **_tongue_**, Hands that shed innocent blood,

(18) A heart that devises wicked plans, Feet that are swift in running to evil,

(19) A false witness who **_speaks_** lies, And one who sows discord among brethren.

(Beware of Adultery)

Proverbs *6:20–29*

(20) My son, keep your father's _command_, And do not forsake the law of your mother.

(21) Bind them continually upon your heart; Tie them around your neck.

(22) When you roam, they will lead you; When you sleep, they will keep you; And when you awake, they will **_speak_** with you.

(23)* **For the commandment is a lamp, And the law a light; Reproofs of** *instruction* **are the way of life,**

(24) To keep you from the evil woman, From the *flattering* **tongue** of a seductress.

(25) Do not lust after her beauty in your heart, Nor let her allure you with her eyelids.

(26) For by means of a harlot, A man is reduced to a crust of bread; And an adulteress will prey upon his precious life.

(27) Can a man take fire to his bosom, And his clothes not be burned?

(28) Can one walk on hot coals, And his feet not be seared?

(29)* So is he who goes in to his neighbor's wife; Whoever touches her shall not be innocent.

Proverbs *7:*1*–5*

(1)* **My son, keep my _words,_ And treasure my *commands* within you.**

(2)* **Keep my *commands* and live, And my law as the apple of your eye.**

(3)* Bind them on your fingers; Write them on the tablet of your heart.

(4)* **_Say_ to wisdom, "You are my sister," And _call_ understanding your nearest kin,**

(5)* That they may keep you from the immortal woman, From the seductress who *flatters* with her **words**.

(The Crafty Harlot)

Proverbs *7:21–27

(21) With her *enticing* **speech** she caused him to yield, With her *flattering* **lips** she seduced him.

(22) Immediately he went after her, as an ox goes to the slaughter, Or as a fool to the correction of the stocks,

(23) Till an arrow struck his liver. As a bird hastens to the snare, He did not know it would cost his life.

(24) Now therefore, listen to me, my children; Pay attention to the **words** of my **mouth**:

(25) Do not let your heart turn aside to her ways, Do not stray into her paths;

(26) For she has cast down many wounded, And all who were slain by her were strong men.

(27) Her house is the way to hell, Descending to the chambers of death.

(The Excellence of Wisdom)

Proverbs *8:*1*–11*

(1)* **Does not *wisdom cry out*, And understanding lift up her *voice*?**

(2) She takes her stand on the top of the high hill, Beside the way, where the paths meet.

(3) She ***cries out*** by the gates, at the entry of the city, At the entrance of the doors:

(4) "To you, O men, I ***call***, And my *voice* is to the sons of men.

(5) O you simple ones, understand prudence, And you fools, be of an understanding heart.

(6)* **Listen, for I will *speak* of excellent things, And from the opening of my *lips* will come right things;**

(7)* **For my *mouth* will *speak* truth; Wickedness is an abomination to my *lips*.**

(8)* **All the *words* of my *mouth* are with righteousness; Nothing crooked or perverse is in them.**

(9)* **They are plain to him who understands, And right to those who find knowledge.**

(10) Receive my *instruction*, and not silver, And knowledge rather than choice gold;

(11)* **For *wisdom* is better than rubies, And all the things one may desire cannot be compared with her.**

Proverbs *8:12–14

(12) "I, *wisdom*, dwell with prudence, And find out knowledge and discretion.

(13)* The fear of the LORD is to hate evil; Pride and arrogance and the evil way And the perverse **_mouth_** I hate.

(14) Counsel is mine, and sound _wisdom_; I am understanding, I have strength.

(Wise Sayings of Solomon)

Proverbs 10:*6*

Blessings are on the head of the righteous, But violence covers the **_mouth_** of the wicked.

Proverbs 10:11*

The **_mouth_** of the righteous is a well of life, But violence covers the **_mouth_** of the wicked.

Proverbs 10:13*

Wisdom is found on the **_lips_** of him who has understanding, But a rod is for the back of him who is devoid of understanding.

Proverbs 10:14*

Wise people store up knowledge, But the **_mouth_** of the foolish is near destruction.

Proverbs 10:18

Whoever hides hatred has _lying **lips**_, And whoever **_spreads_** slander is a fool.

Proverbs 10:19*

In the multitude of **_words_** sin is not lacking, _But he who restrains his **lips** is wise._

Proverbs *10:*20*

The _tongue_ of the righteous is choice silver; The heart of the wicked is worth little.

Proverbs *10:*21*
The _lips_ of the righteous feed many, But fools die for lack of wisdom.

Proverbs 10:*31*
The **_mouth_** of the righteous brings forth _wisdom_, But the perverse **_tongue_** will be cut out.

Proverbs 10:32*
The **_lips_** of the righteous know what is acceptable, But the **_mouth_** of the wicked what is perverse.

Proverbs 11:*9*
The hypocrite with his **_mouth_** destroys his neighbor, But through knowledge the righteous will be delivered.

Proverbs 11:11
By the blessing of the upright the city is exalted, But it is overthrown by the **_mouth_** of the wicked.

Proverbs 11:26
The people will **_curse_** him who withholds grain, But blessing will be on the head of him who sells it.

Proverbs 12:6
The **_words_** of the wicked are, "Lie in wait for blood," But the **_mouth_** of the upright will deliver them.

Proverbs 12:13*
The wicked is ensnared by the transgression of his **_lips_**, But the righteous will come through trouble.

Proverbs 12:14
A man will be satisfied with good by the fruit of his **_mouth_**, And the recompense of a man's hands will be rendered to him.

Proverbs 12:*17*
He who **_speaks_** truth declares righteousness, But a false witness, deceit.

Proverbs 12:18*

There is one who **_speaks_** like the piercings of a sword, But the **_tongue_** of the _wise_ promotes health.

Proverbs 12:*19*

The _truthful_ **_lip_** shall be established forever, But a _lying_ **_tongue_** is but for a moment.

Proverbs *12:*22*

Lying lips are an abomination to the LORD, But those who deal truthfully are His delight.

Proverbs 12:25*

Anxiety in the heart of man causes depression, But a _good_ **_word_** makes it glad.

Proverbs 13:2

A man shall eat well by the fruit of his **_mouth_**, But the soul of the unfaithful feeds on violence.

Proverbs 13:*3*

He who guards his **_mouth_** preserves his life, But he who opens wide his **_lips_** shall have destruction.

Proverbs 13:*13*

He who despises the **_word_** will be destroyed, But he who fears the _commandment_ will be rewarded.

Proverbs 14:3

In the **_mouth_** of a fool is a rod of pride, But the **_lips_** of the _wise_ will preserve them.

Proverbs 14:7

Go from the presence of a foolish man, When you do not perceive in him the **_lips_** of knowledge.

Proverbs *14:*23*
In all labor there is profit, But *idle chatter* leads only to poverty.

Proverbs 14:25
A true witness delivers souls, But a deceitful witness **speaks** lies.

Proverbs 15:*1*
A **soft answer** turns away wrath, But a *harsh* **word** stirs up anger.

Proverbs 15:*2*
The **tongue** of the wise uses knowledge rightly, But the **mouth** of fools *pours forth* foolishness.

Proverbs 15:4
A *wholesome* **tongue** is a tree of life, But perverseness in it breaks the spirit.

Proverbs 15:*7*
The **lips** of the *wise* **disperse** knowledge, But the heart of the fool does not do so.

Proverbs *15:*14*
The heart of him who has understanding seeks knowledge, But the mouth of fools feeds on foolishness.

Proverbs 15:23*
A man has joy by the **answer** of his **mouth**, And a **word spoken** in due season, how good it is!

Proverbs 15:26
The thoughts of the wicked are an abomination to the LORD, But the **words** of the pure are pleasant.

Proverbs *15:*28*
The heart of the righteous studies how to *answer*, But the *mouth* of the wicked *pours forth* evil.

Proverbs *15:*31*

The ear that hears the *rebukes* of life Will abide among the *wise*.

Proverbs *15:*32*

He who disdains *instruction* despises his own soul, But he who heeds *rebuke* gets understanding.

Proverbs *16:*1*

The preparations of the heart belong to man, But the *answer* of the *tongue* is from the LORD.

Proverbs 16:10

Divination is on the *lips* of the king; His *mouth* must not transgress in judgment.

Proverbs 16:13*

Righteous *lips* are the delight of kings, And they love him who *speaks* what is right.

Proverbs *16:*20*

He who heeds the *word* wisely will find good, And whoever trusts in the LORD, happy is he.

Proverbs 16:21*

The *wise* in heart will be called prudent, And *sweetness of the lips* increases learning.

Proverbs 16:23

The heart of the *wise* teaches his *mouth*, And adds learning to his *lips*.

Proverbs 16:24

Pleasant words are like a honeycomb, Sweetness to the soul and health to the bones.

Proverbs 16:26

The person who labors, labors for himself, For his hungry *mouth* drives him on.

Proverbs 16:27–30

(27)　An ungodly man digs up evil, And it is on his *__lips__* like a burning fire.

(28)　A perverse man sows strife, And a *__whisperer__* separates the best of friends.

(29)　A violent man entices his neighbor, And leads him in a way that is not good.

(30)　He winds his eye to devise perverse things; He purses his *__lips__* and brings about evil.

Proverbs 17:4

An evildoer gives heed to false *__lips__*; A liar listens eagerly to a spiteful *__tongue__*.

Proverbs 17:7

Excellent *__speech__* is not becoming to a fool, Much less *lying* *__lips__* to a prince.

Proverbs 17:20

He who has a deceitful heart finds no good, And he who has a perverse *__tongue__* falls into evil.

Proverbs *17:*27*

He who has knowledge spares his __words__, And a man of understanding is of a calm spirit.

Proverbs 17:28

Even a fool is counted *wise* when he holds his peace; When he *__shouts his lips__*, he is considered perceptive.

Proverbs 18:4*

The *__words__* of a man's *__mouth__* are deep waters; The wellspring of *wisdom* is a flowing brook.

Proverbs 18:6

A fool's *__lips__* enter into contention, And his *__mouth__* calls for blows.

Proverbs 18:7

A fool's **_mouth_** is his destruction, And his **_lips_** are the snare of his soul.

Proverbs 18:8*

The **_words_** of a _talebearer (gossiper)_ are like tasty trifles, And they go down into the inmost body.

Proverbs 18:*13*

He who **_answers_** a matter before he hears it, It is folly and shame to him.

Proverbs 18:20*

A man's stomach shall be satisfied from the fruit of his **_mouth_**; From the produce of his **_lips_** he shall be filled.

Proverbs 18:21

Death and life are in the power of the **_tongue_**, And those who love it will eat its fruit.

Proverbs *19:*1*

Better is the poor who walks in his integrity, Than one who is perverse in his _lips_, and is a fool.

Proverbs 19:5*

A false witness will not go unpunished, And he who **_speaks_** lies will not escape.

Proverbs 19:7

All the brothers of the poor hate him; How much more do his friends go far from him! He may pursue them with **_words_**, yet they abandon him.

Proverbs 19:*9*

A false witness will not go unpunished, And he who **_speaks_** lies shall perish.

Proverbs 19:24

A lazy man buries his hand in the bowl, And will not so much as bring it to his **_mouth_** again.

Proverbs *19:*27*
Cease listening to instruction, my son, And you will stray from the <u>words</u> of knowledge.

Proverbs 19:28
A disreputable witness scorns justice, And the **<u>mouth</u>** of the wicked devours iniquity.

Proverbs 20:9
Who can **<u>say</u>**, "I have made my heart clean, I am pure from my sin"?

Proverbs 20:14
"It is good for nothing," **<u>cries</u>** the buyer; But when he has gone his way, then he **boasts**.

Proverbs 20:*15*
There is gold and a multitude of rubies, But the **<u>lips</u>** of knowledge are a precious jewel.

Proverbs 20:17
Bread gained by deceit is sweet to a man, But afterward his **<u>mouth</u>** will be filled with gravel.

Proverbs 20:19
He who goes about as a *talebearer (gossiper)* **reveals** secrets; Therefore do not associate with one who **<u>flatters</u>** with his **<u>lips</u>**.

Proverbs 20:20
Whoever **<u>curses</u>** his father or his mother, His lamp will be put out in deep darkness.

Proverbs 20:22
Do not **<u>say</u>**, "I will recompense evil"; Wait on the LORD, and He will save you.

Proverbs 21:6

Getting treasures by a *lying **tongue*** Is the fleeting fantasy of those who seek death.

Proverbs *21:*13*

Whoever shuts his ears to the _cry_ of the poor Will also _cry_ himself and not be heard.

Proverbs 21:*23*

Whoever guards his ***mouth*** and ***tongue*** Keeps his soul from troubles.

Proverbs 21:28

A false witness shall perish, But the man who hears him will ***speak*** endlessly.

Proverbs 22:11

He who loves purity of heart And has grace on his ***lips***, The King will be his friend.

Proverbs 22:*12*

The eyes of the LORD preserve knowledge, But He overthrows the ***words*** of the faithless.

Proverbs 22:13

The lazy man ***says***, "There is a lion outside! I shall be slain in the streets!"

Proverbs 22:14

The ***mouth*** of an immoral woman is a deep pit; He who is abhorred by the LORD will fall there.

(Sayings of the Wise)

Proverbs *22:*17*–*21*

(17)* **Incline your ear and hear the _words_ of the _wise_, And apply your**
    heart to my knowledge:

(18)* For it is a pleasant thing if we keep them within you; Let them all be fixed upon your _lips_.

(19)* **So that your trust may be in the LORD; I have _instructed_ you today, even you**.

(20)* Have I not written to you of excellent things Of counsels and knowledge,

(21)* **That I may make you know the certainty of the _words_ of truth, That you may _answer words_ of truth To those who send to you?**

Proverbs *22:*22*–*23*

Do not rob the poor because he is poor, _Nor oppress the afflicted at the gate_; For the LORD will _plead_ their cause, And plunder the soul of those who plunder them.

Proverbs 23:6–8

(6)   Do not eat the bread of a miser, Nor desire his delicacies;

(7)   For as he thinks in his heart, so is he. "Eat and drink!" he _says_ to you, But his heart is not with you.

(8)   The morsel you have eaten, you will vomit up, And waste your pleasant _words_.

Proverbs 23:9*

Do not _speak_ in the hearing of a fool, For he will despise the wisdom of your _words_.

Proverbs *23:*12*

Apply your heart to _instruction_, And your eyes to _words_ of knowledge.

Proverbs *23:*15*–*16*

My son, if your heart is _wise_, My heart will rejoice—indeed, I myself; Yes, my inmost being will rejoice When your _lips speak_ right things.

Proverbs 24:1–2

Do not be envious of evil men, Nor desire to be with them; For their heart devises violence, And their _lips talk_ of troublemaking.

Proverbs 24:7

Wisdom is too lofty for a fool; He does not open his **_mouth_** in the gate.

(Further Sayings of the Wise)

Proverbs *24:*26*

He who gives a right _answer_ kisses the _lips_.

Proverbs *24:*28*–*29*

Do not be a witness against your neighbor without cause, For would you deceive with your _lips_? Do not _say_, "I will do to him just as he has done to me; I will render to the man according to his work."

(Further Wise Sayings of Solomon)

Proverbs 25:8–10

(8) Do not go hastily to court; For what will you do in the end, When your neighbor has put you to shame?

(9) **_Debate_** your case with your neighbor, And do not **_disclose_** the secret to another;

(10) Lest he who hears it expose your shame, And your reputation be ruined.

Proverbs 25:11

A **_word_** fitly **_spoken_** is like apples of gold In settings of silver.

Proverbs 25:12

Like an earring of gold and an ornament of fine gold *Is a wise rebuker to an obedient ear.*

Proverbs 25:14

Whoever falsely **_boasts_** of giving, Is like clouds and wind without rain.

Proverbs 25:15

By long forbearance a ruler is persuaded, And a gentle **_tongue_** breaks a bone.

Proverbs 25:23*

The north wind brings forth rain, And a backbiting **_tongue_** an angry countenance.

Proverbs 26:4*–5*

Do not **_answer_** a fool according to his folly, Lest you also be like him. **_Answer_** a fool according to his folly, Lest he be _wise_ in his own eyes.

Proverbs 26:*7*

Like the legs of the lame that hang limp Is a proverb in the **_mouth_** of fools.

Proverbs 26:*9*

Like a thorn that goes into the hand of a drunkard Is a proverb in the **_mouth_** of fools.

Proverbs *26:*16*

The lazy man is _wiser_ in his own eyes, Than seven men who can _answer_ sensibly.

Proverbs 26:18–19

Like a madman who throws firebrands, arrows, and death, _Is the man who deceives his neighbor_, And **_says_**, _"I was only joking!"_

Proverbs 26:20*

Where there is no wood, the fire goes out, And where there is no talebearer (gossiper), strife ceases.

Proverbs 26:22

The **_words_** of a _talebearer (gossiper)_ are like tasty trifles, And they go down into the inmost body.

Proverbs 26:23

Fervent **_lips_** with a wicked heart Are like earthenware covered with silver dross.

Proverbs 26:24*–26

(24)* He who hates, disguises it with his **_lips_**, And lays up deceit within himself;

(25) When he **_speaks_** kindly, do not believe him, For there are seven abominations in his heart;

(26) Though his hatred is covered by deceit, His wickedness will be revealed before the assembly.

Proverbs 26:28*

A *lying* **_tongue_** hates those who are crushed by it, And a *flattering* **_mouth_** works ruin.

Proverbs 27:1

Do not **_boast_** about tomorrow, For you do not know what a day may bring forth.

Proverbs 27:2*

Let another man **_praise_** you, and not your own **_mouth_**; A stranger, and not your own **_lips_**.

Proverbs 27:14

He who blesses his friend with a *loud* **_voice_**, rising early in the morning, It will be counted a curse to him.

Proverbs 27:15*–16

A *continual* *dripping* on a very rainy day And a *contentious* woman are *alike*; Whoever restrains her restrains the wind, And grasps oil with his right hand.

Proverbs *27:*17*

As iron sharpens iron, **_So a man sharpens the countenance of his friend_**.

Proverbs 27:21*

The refining pot is for silver and the furnace for gold, And a man is valued by what others **_say_** of him.

Proverbs *28:*23*

He who rebukes a man will find more favor afterward Than he who _flatters_ with the _tongue_.

Proverbs 28:24

Whoever robs his father or his mother, And **_says_**, "It is no transgression," The same is companion to a destroyer.

Proverbs 29:5

A man who **_flatters_** his neighbor Spreads a net for his feet.

Proverbs 29:6

By transgression an evil man is snared, But the righteous **_sings_** and **_rejoices_**.

Proverbs 29:11*

A fool **_vents_** all his feelings, But a _wise_ man holds them back.

Proverbs 29:19

A servant will not be corrected by mere **_words_**; For though he understands, he will not **_respond_**.

Proverbs 29:20*

Do you see a man hasty in his **_words_**? There is more hope for a fool than for him.

Proverbs 29:24

Whoever is a partner with a thief hates his own life; He swears _to **tell**_ the truth, but reveals nothing.

(The Wisdom of Agur)

Proverbs *30:*5*–6

Every _word_ of God is pure; He is a shield to those who put their trust in Him. Do not add to His **_words_**, Lest He _rebuke_ you, and you be found a liar.

Proverbs 30:20

This is the way of an adulterous woman: She eats and wipes her **_mouth_**, And **_says_**, "I have done no wickedness."

Proverbs 30:32–33

If you have been foolish in **_exalting_** yourself, Or if you have devised evil, put your hand on your **_mouth_**. For as the churning of milk produces butter, And wringing the nose produces blood, So the forcing of wrath produces strife.

(The Words of King Lemuel's Mother)

Proverbs 31:8

Open your **_mouth_** for the **_speechless_**, In the cause of all who are appointed to die.

Proverbs 31:9

Open your **_mouth_**, judge righteously, And plead the cause of the poor and needy.

(The Virtuous Wife)

Proverbs *31:25*–31*

(25)* Strength and honor are her clothing; She shall **_rejoice_** in time to come.

(26)* **She opens her _mouth_ with wisdom, And on her _tongue_ is the law of kindness.**

(27)* She watches over the ways of her household, And does not eat the bread of idleness.

(28)* **Her children rise up and _call_ her blessed; Her husband also, and he _praises_ her:**

(29) "Many daughters have done well, But you excel them all."

(30)* **Charm is deceitful and beauty is passing, But a woman who fears the LORD, she shall be _praised_.**

(31)* Give her of the fruit of her hands, And let her own works **_praise_** her in the gates.

CHAPTER 67

TRUTH, TRUST, TRUSTWORTHY

John 3:20 and 21 states the following: "*For everyone practicing evil hates the light and does not come to the light, lest his deeds should be exposed. But he who does the 'truth' comes to the light, that his deeds may be clearly seen, that they have been done in God.*"

As followers "in Christ," when one is asked what one thinks about a subject and/or topic, it is not uncommon for a believer not to share one's opinion, but instead to state and confirm what one believes. As one who is "in Christ," one's faith is not based upon one's opinion on a topic, but instead, it should be based on the simple "***Truth***" of God.

Truth is dramatically different from the concept of one's opinion, in that "***Truth,***" is generally grounded and founded in the nature, the character, and the will of Father God. ***Truth*** is differentiated from opinion, given the fact that "***Truth***" is eternal. ***Truth*** is an absolute, given the fact that national interests, personal interests, societal interests, and/or cultural interests do not influence "***Truth***." Nations may rise and fall, cultures come and go, societal interests ebb and flow, and personal interest can differ, from day to day, or from one life experience to another.

Truth is the central or main artery of every form of life, nation, society, and/or culture, that must have and/or be practiced, in order to sustain itself. ***Truth*** is an anchor for the soul of every human life, nation, society, and/or culture that desires to maintain a steady foothold or foundation, against the head and/or crosswinds of adversity.

Truth is the guiding light that *always* directs and illuminates, the path of every life, nation, society, and culture that desires to walk (journey) free, from the deceptions that lead one into darkness.

Truth is the power source, that excites and ignites, a life, nation, society, and culture into righteousness and godliness, thereby preventing and/or minimizing the direct and/or indirect attacks from the "prince of darkness."

Truth tends to stick to one's soul, when one understands the "why" behind what one needs to do. For example, everyone knows that one should always be grateful to those who extend a hand, provide a favor, or just practice, "Love;" but does one really gain an understanding as to why one needs to be grateful? Gratitude can reduce and/or eliminate, self-pity and the harmful effects of pride; While a daily measure of "*Truth,*" can provide joy to one's overall well-being, as one gains contentment for one's soul. It's been said that gratefulness keeps one focused on Father God's goodness, while a stronghold of "*Truth,*" can stabilize one's soul. Understanding the why behind "*Truth,*" can lead to a richer and deeper sense of "*Truth*" in one's heart.

Let the words of "*Truth*" be the cornerstone of one's love songs; Let the knowledge of "*Truth*" always be in and a part of one's daily prayer and devotional life; Let the daily practice of "*Truth,*" always reside in one's lifelong display of kindness; Let the beauty of "*Truth,*" always be in one's praise and worship; Let the words and utterances of "*Truth,*" always be in one's proclamations; Let the elements of "*Truth,*" always guide one's choices, one's character, and one's values; Let the celebration of "*Truth*" always be made, lived out, and exhibited, as a praise and/or shout out, in the name of our Lord Jesus Christ!

(Lessin, Meet Me in the Meadow 2015) (Partial Reference Source)

Finally, And inclusion, Let's always remember , What Jesus said to His believers in John 8:31 and 32: "... *If you abide in my Word, You are my disciples indeed. And you shall know the "**truth**", And the "**truth**" shall make you free.*"

(Guidance for the Young)

Proverbs*3:1*–2*, *3*–4*, *5*–*6*, 7*–8*, *9*–*10*, *11*–*12*, *27*–30*, and 31–35*

(1)* *My son, do not forget my law, But let your heart keep my commands;*

(2)* *For length of days and long life And peace they will add to you.*

(3)* **Let not mercy and *truth* forsake you; Bind them around your neck, Write them on the tablet of your heart,**

(4)* *And so find favor and high esteem In the sight of God and man.*

(5)* ***Trust* in the LORD with all your heart, And lean not on your own understanding;**

(6)* **In all your ways acknowledge Him, And He shall direct your paths!**

(7)* *Do not be wise in your own eyes; Fear the LORD and depart from evil.*

(8)* *It will be health to your flesh, And strength to your bones.*

(9)* **Honor the LORD with your possessions, And with the first fruits of all your increase;**

(10)* **So your barns will be filled with plenty, And your vats will overflow with new wine.**

(11)* **My son, do not despise the chastening of the LORD, Nor detest His correction;**

(12)* **For whom the LORD loves he corrects, Just as a father the son in whom he delights.**

(27)* *Do not withhold good from those to whom it is due, When it is in the power of your hand to do so.*

(28)* *Do not say to your neighbor, "Go, and come back, And tomorrow I will give it," When you have it with you.*

(29)* *Do not devise evil against your neighbor, For he dwells by you for safety's sake.*

(30)* *Do not strive with a man without cause, If he has done you no harm.*

(31) *Do not envy the oppressor, And choose none of his ways;*

(32)* *For the perverse person is an abomination to the LORD, But His secret counsel is with the upright.*

(33) The curse of the LORD is on the house of the wicked, *But He blesses the home of the just.*

(34)* Surely He scorns the scornful, *But gives grace to the humble.*

(35)* *The wise shall inherit glory*, But shame shall be the legacy of fools.

(The Excellence of Wisdom)

Proverbs *8:*6*–*11*

(6)* **Listen, for I (*wisdom*) will speak of excellent things, And from the opening of *my* lips will come right things;**

(7)* **For the mouth of wisdom will speak _truth_; Wickedness is an abomination to wisdom's lips.**

(8)* **All the words of my (*wisdom's*) mouth are with righteousness; Nothing crooked or perverse is in them.**

(9)   They are all plain to him who understands, And right to those who find knowledge.

(10)* Receive my (*wisdom's*) instruction, and not silver, And knowledge rather than choice gold.

(11)* **For *wisdom* is better than rubies, And all the things one may desire cannot be compared with her (*wisdom*).**

Proverbs *8:*17*–21*

(17)* **I (*wisdom*) love those who love me, And those who seek me diligently will find me.**

(18)* *Riches and honor are with me, Enduring riches and righteousness.*

(19)* *My fruit is better than gold, yes, than fine gold, And my revenue than choice silver.*

(20)* I traverse the way of righteousness, In the midst of the path of
justice,

(21)* That I (*Wisdom*) may cause those who love me to inherit wealth,
That I (*wisdom*) may fill their treasures.

(Wise Sayings of Solomon)

Proverbs 11:1
Dishonest scales are an abomination to the LORD, *But a just weight is his
delight.*

Proverbs 11:28*
He who **trusts** in his riches will fall, But the righteous will flourish like
foliage.

Proverbs 12:*17*
He who speaks **truth** declares righteousness, But a false witness, deceit.

Proverbs 12:*19*
The **truthful** lip shall be established forever, But a lying tongue is but for
a moment.

Proverbs *12:*22*
**Lying lips are an abomination to the LORD, But those who deal truth-
fully are His delight.**

Proverbs 13:*11*
Wealth gained by dishonesty will be diminished, *But he who gathers by
labor will increase.*

Proverbs 13:*13*
*He who despises the word will be destroyed, But he who fears the command-
ment will be rewarded.*

Proverbs 14:*22*

Do they not go astray who devise evil? But mercy and **_truth_** belong to those who devise good.

Proverbs 14:25

A **_true_** witness delivers souls, But a deceitful witness speaks lies.

Proverbs 15:4

A _wholesome_ tongue is a tree of life, But perverseness in it breaks the spirit.

Proverbs 16:*2*

All the ways of a man are pure in his own eyes, _But the LORD weighs the spirits._

Proverbs *16:*6*

In mercy and _truth_ Atonement is provided for iniquity; And by the fear of the LORD one departs from evil.

Proverbs 16:16*

How much better to get wisdom than gold! And to get understanding is to be chosen rather than silver.

Proverbs *16:*20*

He who heeds the word wisely will find good, And whoever _trusts_ in the LORD, happy is he.

Proverbs 17:4

An evildoer gives heed to false lips; A liar listens eagerly to a spiteful tongue.

Proverbs 17:7

Excellent speech is not becoming to a fool, Much less lying lips to a prince.

Proverbs 18:5*

It is not good to show partiality to the wicked, Or to overthrow the righteous in judgment.

Proverbs 18:8*
The words of a talebearer (gossiper) are like tasty trifles, And they go down into the inmost body.

Proverbs *18:*10*
The name of the LORD is a strong tower; The righteous run to it and are safe.

Proverbs 18:*13*
He who answers a matter before he hears it, It is folly and shame to him.

Proverbs *18*15*
The heart of the prudent acquires knowledge, And the ear of the wise seeks knowledge.

Proverbs 18:17*
The first one to plead his cause seems right, Until his neighbor comes and examines him.

Proverbs *19:*1*
Better is the poor who walks in his integrity, Than one who is perverse in his lips, and is a fool.

Proverbs 19:*9*
A false witness will not go unpunished, And he who speaks lies shall perish.

Proverbs *19:*21*
There are many plans in a man's heart, Nevertheless, the LORD's counsel—that will stand.

Proverbs 19:28
A disreputable witness scorns justice, And the mouth of the wicked devours iniquity.

Proverbs 20:10
Diverse weights and diverse measures, They are both alike, an abomination to the LORD.

Proverbs 20:17
Bread gained by deceit is sweet to a man, But afterward his mouth will be filled with gravel.

Proverbs 20:19
He who goes about as a talebearer reveals secrets, Therefore do not associate with one who flatters with his lips.

Proverbs 20:23
Diverse weights are an abomination to the LORD, And dishonest scales are not good.

Proverbs 20:25
It is a snare for a man to devote rashly something as holy, And afterward to reconsider his vows.

Proverbs 20:28
Mercy and ***truth*** preserve the king, And by lovingkindness he upholds his throne.

Proverbs 20:30
Blows that hurt cleanse away evil, As do stripes the inner depths of the heart.

Proverbs 21:6
Getting treasures by a lying tongue Is the fleeting fantasy of those who seek death.

Proverbs 21:14
A gift in secret pacifies anger, And a bribe behind the back, strong wrath.

Proverbs 21:28
A false witness shall perish, But the man who hears him will speak endlessly.

Proverbs *22:*6*
Train up a child in the way he should go, And when he is old, he will not depart from it.

Proverbs 22:*12*

The eyes of the LORD preserve knowledge, But He overthrows the words of the faithless.

(Sayings of the Wise)

Proverbs *22:*17*–*21*

(17)* **Incline your ear and hear the words of the *wise*, And apply your heart to my knowledge;**

(18)* For it is a pleasant thing if you keep them (*wise sayings*) within you; Let them all be fixed upon your lips,

(19)* **So that your *trust* may be in the LORD; I have instructed you today, even you.**

(20)* Have I not written to you excellent things Of counsels and knowledge,

(21)* **That I may make you know the certainty of the *words of truth*, That you may answer *words of truth* To those who send to you?**

Proverbs 22:29*

Do you see a man who excels in his work? He will stand before kings; He will not stand before unknown men.

Proverbs *23:*4*–*5*

Do not overwork to be rich; Because of your own understanding, cease! Will you set your eyes on that which is not? For riches certainly make themselves wings; They fly away like an eagle toward heaven.

Proverbs 23:22

Listen to your father who begot you, And do not despise your mother when she is old.

Proverbs *23:*23*

Buy the *truth*, and do not sell it, Also wisdom and instruction and understanding.

(Further Sayings of the Wise)

Proverbs *24:*23*–*25*

(23)* _These things also belong to the wise_: It is not good to show partiality in judgment.

(24)* He who says to the wicked, "You are righteous," Him the people will curse; Nations will abhor him.

(25)* But those who rebuke the wicked will have delight, And a good blessing will come upon them.

Proverbs *24:*26*

He who gives a right answer kisses the lips.

Proverbs *24:*28*–29

Do not be a witness against your neighbor without cause, For would you deceive with your lips? Do not say, "I will do to him just as he has done to me; I will render to the man according to his work."

(Further Wise Sayings of Solomon)

Proverbs 25:2

It is the glory of God to conceal a matter, But the glory of kings is to search out a matter.

Proverbs 25:13

Like the cold of snow in time of harvest _Is a faithful messenger to those who send him, For he refreshes the soul of his masters._

Proverbs 25:14

Whoever falsely boasts of giving Is like clouds and wind without rain.

Proverbs 25:*18*

A man who bears false witness against his neighbor Is like a club, a sword, and a sharp arrow.

Proverbs 25:19
Confidence in an unfaithful man in time of trouble Is like a bad tooth and a foot out of joint.

Proverbs *25:*21*–*22*
If your enemy is hungry, give him bread to eat; And if he is thirsty, give him water to drink; For so you will heap coals of fire on his head, And the LORD will reward you!

Proverbs 26:18–19
Like a madman who throws firebrands, arrows, and death, Is the man who deceives his neighbor, And says, "I was only joking!"

Proverbs 26:20*–21
Where there is no wood, the fire goes out; And where there is no talebearer, strife ceases. As charcoal is to burning coals, and wood to fire, So is a contentious man to kindle strife.

Proverbs 26:22
The words of a talebearer (gossiper) are like tasty trifles, And they go down into the inmost body.

Proverbs 26:24*–26
(24)* He who hates, disguises it with his lips, And lays up deceit within himself;
(25) When he speaks kindly, *do not believe him*, For there are seven abominations in his heart;
(26) Though his hatred is covered by deceit, His wickedness will be revealed before the assembly.

Proverbs 26:28*
A lying tongue hates those who are crushed by it, And a flattering mouth works ruin.

Proverbs 27:5*
Open rebuke is better Than love carefully concealed.

Proverbs *27:*6*
Faithful are the wounds of a friend, But the kisses of an enemy are deceitful.

Proverbs 27:*9*
Ointment and perfume delight the heart, And the sweetness of a man's friend gives delight by hearty counsel.

Proverbs 27:10
Do not forsake your own friend or your father's friend, Nor go to your brother's house in the day of your calamity; Better is a neighbor nearby than a brother far away.

Proverbs *27:*19*
As in water face reflects face, So a man's heart reveals the man.

Proverbs *28:*13*
He who covers his sins will not prosper, But whoever confesses and forsakes them will have mercy.

Proverbs *28:*23*
He who rebukes a man will find more favor afterward Than he who flatters with the tongue.

Proverbs 28:*25*
He who is of a proud heart stirs up strife, But he who **trusts** in the LORD will be prospered.

Proverbs 28:26*
He who **trusts** in his own heart is a fool, But whoever walks wisely will be delivered.

Proverbs 29:4
The king establishes the land by justice, But he who receives bribes overthrows it.

Proverbs 29:5

A man who flatters his neighbor Spreads a net for his feet.

Proverbs 29:12

If a ruler pays attention to lies, All his servants become wicked.

Proverbs 29:14

The king who judges the poor with **_truth_**, His throne will be established forever.

Proverbs 29:24

Whoever is a partner with a thief hates his own life; He swears to tell the **_truth_**, but reveals nothing.

Proverbs 29:25*

The fear of man brings a snare, But whoever **_trusts_** in the LORD shall be safe.

Proverbs 29:26

Many seek the ruler's favor, *But justice for man comes from the LORD.*

(The Wisdom of Agur)

Proverbs *30:*5*–6

Every word of God is pure; He is a shield to those who put their _trust_ in Him. Do not add to His words, Lest He rebuke you, and you be found a liar.

(The Virtuous Wife)

Proverbs *31:*10*–*12*

(10)* **Who can find a virtuous wife? For her worth is far above rubies.**

(11)* **The heart of her husband safely _trusts_ her; So he will have no lack of gain.**

(12)* **She does him good and not evil All the days of her life.**

CHAPTER 68

UNDERSTAND, UNDERSTANDING

Have you ever asked yourself what is the meaning of the word or phrase "*Understanding*"? Or better yet, what does this Chapter Theme topic of "*Understanding*" mean in the context of God's Word?

First, let me peel back the onion and provide several definitions that I obtained from *Roget's II: The New Thesaurus* for this Chapter Theme's central topic of "*Understanding*." The **verb**: "to perceive and recognize the meaning of." The **adjective**: "Cognizant of and comprehending the needs, feelings, problems, and views of others." And the **noun**: "the faculty of thinking, reasoning, acquiring and applying knowledge"! As one studies these three definitions, it's not uncommon for one to rank, the "**noun**" and the "**verb**" definitions, a little higher than the **adjective** definition, as more relative in one's walk "in Christ," given that, to some, they relate more fully to the term and Chapter Theme topic of "*Understanding*."

As one studies the Proverbs verses for this Chapter Theme of "*Understanding*," one of my bedrock and foundational Proverbs is contained in **Proverbs *3:*5*and*6***, which states: "***Trust in the Lord with all your heart, And lean not on your own understanding; In all your ways acknowledge Him, And He shall direct your paths***"! When one peels back the onion on verse 5, one finds a pair of somewhat contradictory biblical directives! One states positively to "*trust in the LORD,*" and

755

in the next breath, **not** to "*lean (trust) on your own* **understanding**." It appears that these two biblical phrases are mutually exclusive—one must "*Trust in the LORD with all one's heart,*" but at the same time, one should not depend upon one's own ability to **Understand** everything Father God is doing in one's life, one's family, one's country, and even one's world!

One could conjecture that most of us, if not all of us, desperately desire to fully **Understand** what Father God is doing and/or what Father God's plans are for one's life. But I would contend, that in many, if not most, of the areas of an individual's life, that one must accept and acknowledge, that one cannot fully **Understand,** the ways and plans of Father God on one's life. Isaiah 55:8–9 clearly states and reminds all believers as to why one doesn't fully **Understand** the ways of Father God: "***For My thoughts are not your thoughts, Nor are your ways My ways," says the LORD. "For as the heavens are higher than the earth, So are My ways higher than your ways, And My thoughts than your thoughts.***"

So as one looks to gain a better understanding of Father God's Word and His ways, one must first and foremost: "*Trust in the LORD with all your heart*"; and at the same time remember and recognize that: "*Wisdom is in the sight of him who has* **understanding**..." (Proverbs 17:24); And equally recognize that: "*Wisdom rests in the heart of him who has* **understanding**" (Proverbs 14:33); And: "*The heart of him who has* **understanding** *seeks knowledge*" (Proverbs 15:14).

Thus, to summarize, every believer must make a free choice, to either live one's life according to personal preferences, or to the unchanging and unflappable Word of God. Accordingly, one should: "*Buy the truth, and do not sell it, Also wisdom and instruction and* **understanding**" (Proverbs 23:23). For in the end, a believer might not fully **Understand** how Father God causes: "***all things to work together for good to those who love God, to those who are the called according to His purpose***" (Romans 8:28). However, when a believer trusts Father God with all one's heart, one is assured that: "***God will never leave you nor forsake you***" (Joshua 1:5 and Hebrews 13:5)! Now, that's a promise that one can both trust and **Understand**!

(The Beginning of Knowledge)

Proverbs *1:1–6*

(1) The Proverbs of Solomon the son of David, king of Israel:

(2)* **To know wisdom and instruction, To perceive the words of** *understanding,*

(3)* **To receive the instruction of wisdom, Justice, judgment and equity;**

(4)* To give prudence to the simple, To the young man knowledge and discretion—

(5)* **A wise man will hear and increase learning, And a man of** *understanding* **will attain wise counsel.**

(6)* To *understand* a proverb and an enigma, The words of the wise and their riddles.

(The Value of Wisdom)

Proverbs *2:1*–*9* and *10*–*11*

(1)* My son, if you receive my words, And treasure my commands within you,

(2)* **So that you incline your ear to wisdom, And apply your heart to** *understanding;*

(3)* Yes, if you cry out for discernment, And lift up your voice for *understanding,*

(4) If you seek her as silver, And search for her as for hidden treasures;

(5)* **Then you will** *understand* **the fear of the LORD, And find the knowledge of God.**

(6)* **For the LORD gives wisdom; From His mouth come knowledge and** *understanding;*

(7)* **He stores up sound wisdom for the upright; He is a shield to those who walk uprightly;**

(8)* **He guards the paths of justice, And preserves the way of His saints.**

(9)* Then you will _understand_ righteousness and justice, Equity and every good path.

(10)* When wisdom enters your heart, And knowledge is pleasant to your soul,

(11)* Discretion will preserve you; _Understanding_ will keep you.

(Guidance for the Young)

Proverbs *3:*5*–*6*
Trust in the LORD with all your heart, And lean not on your own under-standing; In all your ways acknowledge Him, And He shall direct your paths!

Proverbs *3:*13*–18

(13)* Happy is the man who finds wisdom, And the man who gains _understanding_;

(14) For **her** proceeds are better than the profits of silver, And **her** gain than fine gold.

(15) **She** is more precious than rubies, And all the things you may desire cannot compare with **her**.

(16) Length of days is in **her** right hand, In **her** left hand riches and honor.

(17)* **Her** ways are ways of pleasantness, And all **her** paths are peace.

(18) **She** is a tree of life to those who take hold of **her**, And happy are all who retain **her**.

Proverbs 3:19–20
The LORD by wisdom founded the earth; By _understanding_ He estab-lished the heavens; By His knowledge the depths were broken up, And clouds drop down the dew.

(Security in Wisdom)

Proverbs *4:1*–9*

(1)* Here, my children, the instruction of a father, And give attention to know **_understanding_**;

(2) For I give you good doctrine: Do not forsake my law.

(3) When I was my father's son, Tender and the only one in the sight of my mother,

(4)* **He also taught me, and said to me: "Let your heart retain my words; Keep the commands, and live.**

(5)* **Get wisdom! Get _understanding_! Do not forget, nor turn away from the words of my mouth.**

(6) **Do not forsake her, and she will preserve you; Love her, and she will keep you.**

(7)* **Wisdom is the principal thing; Therefore get wisdom, And in all your getting, get _understanding_.**

(8)* Exalt her, and she will promote you; She will bring you honor, when you embrace her.

(9)* She will place on your head an ornament of grace; A crown of glory she will deliver to you."

(The Peril of Adultery)

Proverbs 5:1–6

(1) My son, pay attention to my wisdom; Lend your ear to my **_understanding_**.

(2) That you may preserve discretion, And your lips may keep knowledge.

(3) For the lips of an immoral woman drip honey, And her mouth is smoother than oil;

(4) But in the end she is bitter as wormwood, Sharp as a two-edged sword.

(5) Her feet go down to death, Her steps lay hold of hell.

(6)   Lest you ponder her path of life—her ways are unstable; You do not know them.

(Beware of Adultery)

Proverbs *6:*32*–35*

(32)* **Whoever commits adultery with a woman lacks *understanding*; He who does so destroys his own soul.**

(33)* **Wounds and dishonor he will get, And his reproach will not be wiped away.**

(34)   For jealousy is a husband's fury; Therefore he will not spare in the day of vengeance.

(35)* He will accept no recompense, Nor will he be appeased though you give many gifts.

Proverbs *7:*1*–5*

(1)* **My son, keep my words, And treasure my commands within you**

(2)* **Keep my commands and live, And my law as the apple of your eye.**

(3)* Bind them on your fingers; Write them on the tablet of your heart.

(4)* **Say to wisdom, "You are my sister," And call *understanding* your nearest kin,**

(5)* That they may keep you from the immortal woman, From the seductress who flatters with her words.

(The Crafty Harlot)

Proverbs 7:6–9

(6)   For at the window of my house I looked through my lattice,

(7)   And saw among the simple, I perceived among the youths, A young man devoid of *understanding*,

(8)   Passing along the street near her corner; And he took the path to her house

(9)   In the twilight, in the evening, In the black and dark night.

(The Excellence of Wisdom)

Proverbs *8:*1*–*11*

(1)* **Does not wisdom cry out, And *understanding* lift up her voice?**

(2) She takes her stand on the top of the high hill, Beside the way, where the paths meet.

(3) She cries out by the gates, at the entry of the city, At the entrance of the doors:

(4) "To you, O men, I call, And my voice is the sons of men.

(5)* O you simple ones, ***understand*** prudence, And you fools, be of an ***understanding*** heart.

(6)* **Listen, for I will speak of excellent things, And from the opening of my lips will come right things;**

(7)* **For my mouth will speak truth; Wickedness is an abomination to my lips.**

(8)* **All the words of my mouth are with righteousness; Nothing crooked or preserve is in them.**

(9)* They are all plain to him who ***understands***, And right to those who find knowledge.

(10)* Receive my instruction, and not silver, And knowledge rather than choice gold;

(11)* **For wisdom is better than rubies, And all the things one may desire cannot compare with her.**

Proverbs *8:12–14*

(12) "I, wisdom, dwell with prudence, And find out knowledge and discretion.

(13)* The fear of the LORD is to hate evil; Pride and arrogance and the evil way And the perverse mouth I hate.

(14)* Counsel is mine, and sound wisdom; I am ***understanding***, I have strength.

(The Way of Wisdom)

Proverbs *9:1–*6*

(1)   Wisdom has built her house, She has hewn out her seven pillars;

(2)   She has slaughtered her meat, She has mixed her wine, She has also furnished her table.

(3)   She has sent out her maidens, She cries out from the highest places of the city,

(4)   "Whoever is simple, let him turn in here!" As for him who lacks *understanding*, she says to him,

(5)   "Come, eat of my bread And drink of the wine I have mixed.

(6)*   **Forsake foolishness and live, And go in the way of *understanding*.**

Proverbs *9:7–12

(7)   "He who corrects a scoffer gets shame for himself, And he who rebukes a wicked man only harms himself.

(8)*   **Do not correct a scoffer. Lest he hate you; Rebuke a wise man, and he will love you.**

(9)*   **Give instruction to a wise man, and he will be still wiser; Teach a just man, and he will increase in learning.**

(10)* **"The fear of the LORD is the beginning of wisdom, And the knowledge of the Holy One is *understanding*.**

(11) For by me your days will be multiplied, And years of life will be added to you.

(12) If you are wise, you are wise for yourself, And if you scoff, you bear it alone."

(The Way of Folly)

Proverbs 9:13–18

(13) A foolish woman is clamorous; She is simple, and knows nothing.

(14) For she sits at the door of her house, On a seat by the highest places of the city,

(15) To call to those who pass by, Who go straight on their way:

(16) "Whoever is simple, let him turn in here"; And as for him who lacks **_understanding_**, she says to him,

(17) "Stolen water is sweet, And bread eaten in secret is pleasant."

(18) But he does not know that the dead are there, That her guests are in the depths of hell.

(Wise Sayings of Solomon)

Proverbs 10:13*
Wisdom is found on the lips of him who has **_understanding_**, But a rod is for the back of him who is devoid of **_understanding_**.

Proverbs 10:23*
To do evil is like sport to a fool, But a man of **_understanding_** has wisdom.

Proverbs *11:*12*
He who is devoid of wisdom despises his neighbor, But a man of _understanding_ holds his peace.

Proverbs 12:11
He who tills his land will be satisfied with bread, But he who follows frivolity is devoid of **_understanding_**.

Proverbs 13:15*
Good **_understanding_** gains favor, But the way of the unfaithful is hard.

Proverbs 14:*6*
A scoffer seeks wisdom and does not find it, But knowledge is easy to him who **_understands_**.

Proverbs 14:*8*
The wisdom of the prudent is to **_understand_** his way, But the folly of fools is deceit.

Proverbs *14:*29*
He who is slow to wrath has great *understanding*, But he who is impulsive exalts folly.

Proverbs *14:*33*
Wisdom rests in the heart of him who has *understanding*, But what is in the heart of fools is made known.

Proverbs *15:*14*
The heart of him who has *understanding* seeks knowledge, But the mouth of fools feeds on foolishness.

Proverbs 15:21*
Folly is joy to him who is destitute of discernment, But a man of *understanding* walks uprightly.

Proverbs *15:*32*
He who disdains instruction despises his own soul, But he who heeds rebuke gets *understanding*.

Proverbs 16:16*
How much better to get wisdom than gold! And to get *understanding* is to be chosen rather than silver.

Proverbs 16:22*
Understanding is a wellspring of life to him who has it; But the correction of fools is folly.

Proverbs 17:18
A man devoid of *understanding* shakes hands in a pledge, And becomes surety for his friend.

Proverbs *17:*24*
Wisdom is in the sight of him who has *understanding*, But the eyes of a fool are on the ends of the earth.

Proverbs *17:*27*
**He who has knowledge spares his words, And a man of _understanding_
is of a calm spirit.**

Proverbs 18:2
A fool has no delight in **_understanding_**, But in expressing his own heart.

Proverbs 19:*8*
He who gets wisdom loves his own soul; He who keeps **_understanding_**
will find good.

Proverbs *19:*25*
**Strike a scoffer, and the simple will become wary; Rebuke one who has
understanding, and he will discern knowledge.**

Proverbs 20:5
Counsel in the heart of man is like deep water, But a man of **_understanding_** will draw it out.

Proverbs *20:*24*
**A man's steps are of the LORD; How then can a man _understand_ his
own way?**

Proverbs 21:*16*
A man who wanders from the way of **_understanding_** Will rest in the
assembly of the dead.

Proverbs 21:30*
There is no wisdom or **_understanding_** Or counsel against the LORD.

(Sayings of the Wise)

Proverbs *22:*17*–*21*
(17)* **Incline your ear and hear the words of the wise, And apply your
heart to my knowledge:**

(18)* For it is a pleasant thing if we keep them within you; Let them all be fixed upon your lips.

(19)* **So that your trust may be in the LORD; I have instructed you today, even you**.

(20)* Have I not written to you of excellent things Of counsels and knowledge,

(21)* **That I may make you *know* the certainty of the words of truth, That you may answer words of truth To those who send to you?**

Proverbs *23:*4*–*5*

Do not overwork to be rich; Because of your own *understanding*, cease! Will you set your eyes on that which is not? For riches certainly make themselves wings; *They fly away like an eagle toward heaven*.

Proverbs *23:*23*

Buy the truth, and do not sell it, Also wisdom and instruction and *understanding*.

Proverbs 24:3*–4*

Through wisdom a house is built, And by ***understanding*** it is established; By knowledge the rooms are filled With all precious and pleasant riches.

(Further Sayings of the Wise)

Proverbs 24:30–34

(30) I went by the field of the lazy man, And by the vineyard of the man devoid of ***understanding***;

(31) And there it was, all overgrown with thorns; Its surface was covered with nettles; Its stone wall was broken down.

(32) When I saw it, I considered it well; I looked on it and received instruction:

(33) A little sleep, a little slumber, A little folding of the hands to rest;

(34) So shall your poverty come like a prowler, And your need like an armed man.

(Further Wise Sayings of Solomon)

Proverbs *25:*21*–*22*
If your enemy is hungry, give him bread to eat; And if he is thirsty, give him water to drink; For so you will heap coals of fire on his head, And the LORD will reward you!

Proverbs 28:2
Because of the transgression of a land, many are its princes; But by a man of **understanding** and knowledge Right will be prolonged.

Proverbs 28:5*
Evil men do not **understand** justice, But those who seek the LORD **understand** all.

Proverbs 28:11*
The rich man is wise in his own eyes, But the poor who has **understanding** searches him out.

Proverbs 28:16
A ruler who lacks **understanding** is a great oppressor, But he who hates covetousness will prolong his days.

Proverbs 29:7*
The righteous considers the cause of the poor, But the wicked does not **understand** such knowledge.

Proverbs 29:19
A servant will not be corrected by mere words; For though he **understands**, he will not respond.

(The Wisdom of Agur)

Proverbs 30:2–3

Surely I am more stupid than any man, And do not have the **_understanding_** of a man. I neither learned wisdom Nor have knowledge of the Holy One.

Proverbs 30:18–19

There are three things which are too wonderful for me, Yes, four which I do not **_understand_**: The way of an eagle in the air, The way of a serpent on a rock, The way of a ship in the midst of the sea, And the way of a man with a virgin.

CHAPTER 69

WICKED, WICKEDNESS

*A*LL SIN IS **WICKEDNESS**!
As I began thinking about what I was going to share regarding this second to last Chapter Theme Narrative, i.e. "*Wickedness,*" the Holy Spirit finally convicted me on the realization that *All Sin is* **WICKEDNESS**!

So, let me attempt to unpack the above statement of truth! All sin is not of God, and everything that is not of God is *Wicked*. As you read earlier in the Chapter Theme Narrative on Adultery (Chapter 4), I have had my challenges in this area, which as we all know, is specifically called out in the Ten Commandments listed in Exodus 20:3–17. And as I thought about my adulterous and lustful past, I said to myself with prideful thinking that, at least, I have not killed/murdered anyone, which in my naïve and immature moment of random thinking, I was stack ranking adultery/lust, while sinful in their true nature, does not belong in the same sin or sinful bucket as murder! In that fleeting and prideful moment, I was putting the sin of murder in the bucket labeled "*Wickedness*" and neglecting to include in that same "*Wickedness*" bucket, my sin of adultery/lust. How *stupid* was that!

Then, my mind and thoughts pivoted to Romans 3:23, which states: "*For all have sinned and fall short of the glory of God.*" And yes, all believers know that we all have sinned, yesterday, today, and/or tomorrow, and from the original sin in the Garden of Eden by Adam and Eve, to today's modern-day Christian, the sinful nature of mankind, continues to challenge, even the most righteous believer, as one does, his or her best, in walking the narrow road of righteousness.

So, I would contend that everything that is not of God is **_Wicked_**; And given that sin and **_Wickedness_** are an abomination to Father God; Let's do all that one can, to rise above one's sinful and **_Wicked_** nature, and commit to: "Therefore _submit to God. Resist the devil and he will flee from you_" (James 4:7); Such that one can walk more purposefully, given the Holy Spirit's directions, on the pathway of righteousness, which leads to Christlikeness!

(The Value of Wisdom)

Proverbs *2:*10*–15

(10)* **When wisdom enters your heart, And knowledge is pleasant to your soul,**

(11)* **Discretion will preserve you; Understanding will keep you,**

(12) To deliver you from the way of _evil_, From the man who speaks _perverse_ things,

(13) From those who leave the paths of uprightness To walk in the ways of darkness;

(14) Who rejoice in doing _evil_, And delight in the _perversity_ of the _wicked_;

(15) Whose ways are _crooked_, And who are _devious_ in their paths....

Proverbs *2:*20*–22*

(20)* **So you may walk in the way of goodness, And keep to the paths of righteousness.**

(21)* **For the upright will dwell in the land, And the blameless will remain in it;**

(22)* But the **_wicked_** will be cut off from the earth, And the _unfaithful_ will be uprooted from it.

(Guidance for the Young)

Proverbs 3:25–26

Do not be afraid of sudden terror; Nor of trouble from the *wicked* when it comes; For the LORD will be your confidence, And will keep your foot from being caught.

Proverbs *3:29–30 and 31–35*

(29) Do not devise *evil* against your neighbor, For he dwells by you for safety's sake.

(30) Do not strive with a man without cause, If he has done you no harm.

(31) Do not envy the *oppressor*, And choose none of his ways;

(32)* For the *perverse* person is an abomination to the LORD, But His secret counsel is with the upright.

(33) The curse of the LORD is on the house of the *wicked*, But He blesses the home of the just.

(34)* **Surely He *scorns* the *scornful*, But gives grace to the humble.**

(35)* The wise shall inherit glory, But shame shall be the legacy of fools.

(Security in Wisdom)

Proverbs *4:*10*–*13*, *14*–17, and *18*–19

(10)* **Hear, my son, and receive my sayings, And the years of your life will be many.**

(11)* **I have taught you in the way of wisdom; I have led you in the right paths;**

(12)* **When you walk, your steps will not be hindered, And when you run, you will not stumble.**

(13)* **Take firm hold of instruction, do not let go; Keep her (wisdom) for she is your life.**

(14)* **Do not enter the path of the *wicked*, And do not walk in the way of evil.**

(15) Avoid it, do not travel on it; Turn away from it and pass on.

(16) For they do not sleep unless they have done *evil*; And their sleep is taken away unless they make someone fall.

(17) For they eat the bread of **_wickedness_**, And drink the wine of violence.

(18)* **But the path of the just is like the shining sun, That shines ever brighter unto the perfect day.**

(19) The way of the *wicked* is like darkness; They do not know what makes them stumble.

(The Peril of Adultery)

Proverbs *5:*21*–*23*

(21)* **For the ways of man are before the eyes of the LORD, And He ponders all his paths.**

(22)* **His own _iniquities_ entrap the _wicked_ man, And he is caught in the cords of his _sin_.**

(23)* **He shall die for lack of instruction, And in the greatness of his folly he shall go astray.**

(The Wicked Man)

Proverbs *6:12–15 and 16–19

(12) A worthless person, a **_wicked_** man, Walks with a *perverse* mouth;

(13) He winks with his eyes, He shuffles his feet, He points with his fingers;

(14) *Perversity* is in his heart, He *devises evil* continually, He sows *discord*.

(15) Therefore his calamity shall come suddenly; Suddenly he shall be broken without remedy.

(16) These six things the LORD hates, Yes, seven are an abomination to Him;

(17) A proud look, A lying tongue, Hands that shed innocent blood,

(18) A heart that *devises* **wicked** plans, Feet that are swift in running to *evil*,

(19) A false witness who speaks lies, And one who sows *discord* among brethren.

(Beware of Adultery)

Proverbs *6:*23*–25

(23)* **For the commandment is a lamp, And the law a light; Reproofs of instruction are the way of life,**

(24) To keep you from the *evil* woman, From the flattering tongue of a seductress.

(25) Do not lust after her beauty in your heart, Nor let her allure you with her eyelids.

(The Excellence of Wisdom)

Proverbs *8:*1*–*11*

(1)* **Does not wisdom cry out, And understanding lift up her voice?**

(2) She takes her stand on the top of the high hill, Beside the way, where the paths meet.

(3) She cries out by the gates, at the entry of the city, At the entrance of the doors:

(4) "To you, O men, I call, And my voice is the sons of men.

(5)* O you simple ones, understand prudence, And you fools, be of an understanding heart.

(6)* **Listen, for I will speak of excellent things, And from the opening of my lips will come right things;**

(7)* **For my mouth will speak truth;** *Wickedness* **is an abomination to my lips.**

(8)* **All the words of my mouth are with righteousness; Nothing** *crooked* **or** *preserve* **is in them.**

(9)* They are all plain to him who understands, And right to those who find knowledge.

(10)* Receive my instruction, and not silver, And knowledge rather than choice gold;

(11)* **For wisdom is better than rubies, And all the things one may desire cannot compare with her**.

(The Way of Wisdom)

Proverbs *9:7–12

(7) "He who corrects a scoffer gets shame for himself, And he who rebukes a _wicked_ man only harms himself.

(8)* **Do not correct a scoffer, lest he hate you; Rebuke a wise man, and he will love you**.

(9)* **Give instruction to a wise man, and he will be still wiser; Teach a just man, and he will increase in learning**.

(10)* **The fear of the LORD is the beginning of wisdom, And the knowledge of the Holy One is understanding**.

(11) For by me your days will be multiplied, And years of life will be added to you.

(12) If you are wise, you are wise for yourself, And if you scoff, you will bear it alone."

(Wise Sayings of Solomon)

Proverbs 10:2*–3*

Treasures of _wickedness_ profit nothing, But righteousness delivers from death. The LORD will not allow the righteous soul to famish, But He casts away the desire of the _wicked_.

Proverbs 10:*6*

Blessings are on the head of the righteous, But _violence_ covers the mouth of the _wicked_

Proverbs 10:7

The memory of the righteous is blessed, But the name of the _wicked_ will rot.

Proverbs 10:11*
The mouth of the righteous is a well of life, But *violence* covers the mouth of the *wicked*.

Proverbs 10:16
The labor of the righteous leads to life, The wages of the *wicked* to sin.

Proverbs *10:*20*
The tongue of the righteous is choice silver; The heart of the *wicked* is worth little.

Proverbs 10:24
The fear of the *wicked* will come upon him, And the desire of the righteous will be granted.

Proverbs 10:25
When the whirlwind passes by, the *wicked* is no more, But the righteous has an everlasting foundation.

Proverbs 10:27
The fear of the LORD prolongs days, But the years of the *wicked* will be shortened.

Proverbs 10:28
The hope of the righteous will be gladness, But the expectation of the *wicked* will perish.

Proverbs 10:30
The righteous will never be removed, But the *wicked* will not inhabit the earth.

Proverbs 10:*31*
The mouth of the righteous brings forth wisdom, But the *perverse* tongue will be cut out.

Proverbs 10:32*

The lips of the righteous know what is acceptable, But the mouth of the **_wicked_** what is _perverse_.

Proverbs 11:5

The righteousness of the blameless will direct his way aright, But the **_wicked_** will fall by his own **_wickedness_**.

Proverbs 11:7

When a **_wicked_** man dies, his expectation will perish, And the hope of the unjust perishes.

Proverbs 11:8

The righteous is delivered from trouble, And it comes to the **_wicked_** instead.

Proverbs 11:10

When it goes well with the righteous, the city rejoices; And when the **_wicked_** perish, there is jubilation.

Proverbs 11:11

By the blessing of the upright the city is exalted, But it is overthrown by the mouth of the **_wicked_**.

Proverbs 11:16

A gracious woman retains honor, But _ruthless_ men retain riches.

Proverbs 11:18*

The **_wicked_** man does deceptive work, But he who sows righteousness will have a sure reward.

Proverbs 11:21*

Though they join forces, the **_wicked_** will not go unpunished; But the posterity of the righteous will be delivered.

Proverbs 11:23*

The desire of the righteous is only good, But the expectation of the **_wicked_** is _wrath_.

Proverbs 11:31

If the righteous will be recompensed on the earth, How much more the _ungodly_ and the _sinner_?

Proverbs 12:2*

A good man obtains favor from the LORD, But a man of **_wicked_** intentions He will condemn.

Proverbs 12:3

A man is not established by **_wickedness_**, But the root of the righteous cannot be moved.

Proverbs 12:5*

The thoughts of the righteous are right, But the counsels of the **_wicked_** are deceitful.

Proverbs 12:6

The words of the **_wicked_** are, "Lie in wait for blood," But the mouth of the upright will deliver them.

Proverbs 12:7*

The **_wicked_** are overthrown and are no more, But the house of the righteous will stand.

Proverbs 12:10

A righteous man regards the life of his animal, But the tender mercies of the **_wicked_** are cruel.

Proverbs 12:12*

The **_wicked_** covet the catch of _evil_ men, But the root of the righteous yields fruit.

Proverbs 12:13*
The **_wicked_** is ensnared by the _transgression_ of his lips, But the righteous will come through trouble.

Proverbs 12:21*
No grave trouble will overtake the righteous, But the **_wicked_** shall be filled with _evil_.

Proverbs 12:*26*
The righteous should choose his friends carefully, For the way of the **_wicked_** leads them astray.

Proverbs 13:5
A righteous man hates lying, But a **_wicked_** man is loathsome and comes to shame.

Proverbs 13:*6*
Righteousness guards him whose way is blameless, But **_wickedness_** overthrows the _sinner_.

Proverbs 13:9
The light of the righteous rejoices, But the lamp of the **_wicked_** will be put out.

Proverbs 13:17
A **_wicked_** messenger falls into trouble, But a faithful ambassador brings health.

Proverbs 13:25
The righteous eats to the satisfying of his soul, But the stomach of the **_wicked_** shall be in want.

Proverbs 14:11*
The house of the **_wicked_** will be overthrown, But the tent of the upright will flourish.

Proverbs 14:17
A quick-tempered man acts foolishly, And a man of _wicked_ intentions is hated.

Proverbs 14:19
The _evil_ will bow before the good, And the _wicked_ at the gates of the righteous.

Proverbs 14:32
The _wicked_ is banished in his _wickedness_, But the righteous has a refuge in his death.

Proverbs *15:*6*
In the house of the righteous there is much treasure, But in the revenue of the _wicked_ is trouble.

Proverbs 15:8
The sacrifice of the _wicked_ is an abomination to the LORD, But the prayer of the upright is His delight.

Proverbs 15:*9*
The way of the _wicked_ is an abomination to the LORD, But He loves him who follows righteousness.

Proverbs 15:26
The thoughts of the _wicked_ are an abomination to the LORD, But the words of the pure are pleasant.

Proverbs *15:*28*
The heart of the righteous studies how to answer, But the mouth of the _wicked_ pours forth _evil_.

Proverbs 15:29*
The LORD is far from the _wicked_, But He hears the prayer of the righteous.

Proverbs 16:4

The LORD has made all for Himself, Yes, even the **_wicked_** for the day of doom.

Proverbs 16:12

It is an abomination for kings to commit **_wickedness_**, For a throne is established by righteousness.

Proverbs 17:*15*

He who justifies the **_wicked_**, and he who condemns the just, Both of them alike are an abomination to the LORD.

Proverbs 17:23

A **_wicked_** man accepts a bribe behind the back To _pervert_ the ways of justice.

Proverbs 18:3

When the **_wicked_** comes, contempt comes also; And with dishonor comes reproach.

Proverbs 18:5*

It is not good to show partiality to the **_wicked_**, Or to overthrow the righteous in judgment.

Proverbs 19:28

A disreputable witness scorns justice, And the mouth of the **_wicked_** devours _iniquity_.

Proverbs 20:26

A wise king sifts out the **_wicked_**, And brings the threshing wheel over them.

Proverbs 21:4

A haughty look, a proud heart, And the plowing of the **_wicked_** are sin.

Proverbs 21:7

The violence of the **_wicked_** will destroy them, Because they refuse to do justice.

Proverbs 21:10
The soul of the *wicked* desires *evil*; His neighbor finds no favor in his eyes.

Proverbs 21:12*
The righteous God wisely considers the house of the *wicked*, Overthrowing the *wicked* for their *wickedness*.

Proverbs 21:18
The *wicked* shall be a ransom for the righteous, And the *unfaithful* for the upright.

Proverbs 21:27*
The sacrifice of the *wicked* is an abomination; How much more when he brings it with *wicked* intent!

Proverbs 21:29
A *wicked* man hardens his face, But as for the upright, he establishes his way.

(Sayings of the Wise)

Proverbs *24:15–*16*
Do not lie in wait, O *wicked* man, against the dwelling of the righteous; Do not plunder his resting place; **For a righteous man may fall seven times And rise again, But the *wicked* shall fall by calamity.**

Proverbs 24:19–20
Do not fret because of *evildoers*, Nor be envious of the *wicked*; For there will be no prospect for the *evil* man; The lamp of the *wicked* will be put out.

(Further Sayings of the Wise)

Proverbs *24:*23*–*25*
(23)* **These things also belong to the *wise*: It is not good to show partiality in judgment.**

(24)* **He who says to the _wicked_, "You are righteous," Him the people will curse; Nations will abhor him.**

(25)* **But those who rebuke the _wicked_ will have delight, And a good blessing will come upon them.**

(Further Wise Sayings of Solomon)

Proverbs 25:4–5

Take away the dross from silver, And it will go to the silversmith for jewelry. Take away the **_wicked_** from before the king, And his throne will be established in righteousness.

Proverbs 25:26*

A righteous man who falters before the **_wicked_** Is like a murky spring and a polluted well.

Proverbs 26:23

Fervent lips with a **_wicked_** heart Are like earthenware covered with silver dross.

Proverbs 26:24*–26

(24)* He who hates, disguises it with his lips; And lays up *deceit* within himself;

(25) When he speaks kindly, do not believe him; For there are seven *abominations* in his heart;

(26) Though his hatred is covered by deceit, His **_wickedness_** will be revealed before the assembly.

Proverbs 26:27*

Whoever digs a pit will fall into it, And he who rolls a stone will have it roll back on him.

Proverbs 28:1*

The **_wicked_** flee when no one pursues, But the righteous are bold as a lion.

Proverbs 28:4
Those who forsake the law praise the **_wicked_**, But such as keep the law contend with them.

Proverbs 28:12
When the righteous rejoice, there is great glory; But when the **_wicked_** arise, men hide themselves.

Proverbs 28:15
Like the roaring lion and a charging bear Is the **_wicked_** ruler over poor people.

Proverbs 28:17
A man burdened with _bloodshed_ will flee into a pit; Let no one help him.

Proverbs 28:28
When the **_wicked_** arise, men hide themselves; But when they perish, the righteous increase.

Proverbs 29:2
When the righteous are in authority, the people rejoice; But when a **_wicked_** man rules, the people groan.

Proverbs 29:7*
The righteous considers the cause of the poor, But the **_wicked_** does not understand such knowledge.

Proverbs 29:10
The _bloodthirsty_ hate the blameless, But the upright seek his well-being.

Proverbs 29:12
If a ruler pays attention to lies, All his servants become **_wicked_**.

Proverbs 29:13
The poor man and the _oppressor_ have this in common: The LORD gives light to the eyes of both.

Proverbs 29:16

When the **wicked** are multiplied, *transgression* increases; But the righteous will see their fall.

Proverbs 29:22

An angry man stirs up strife, And a furious man abounds in *transgression*.

Proverbs 29:27*

An *unjust* man is an *abomination* to the righteous, And he who is upright in the way is an *abomination* to the **wicked**.

(The Wisdom of Agur)

Proverbs 30:11–14

(11) There is a generation that curses its father, And does not bless its mother.
(12) There is a generation that is pure in its own eyes, Yet is not washed from its *filthiness*.
(13) There is a generation—oh, how lofty are their eyes! And their eyelids are lifted up.
(14) There is a generation whose teeth are like swords, And whose fangs are like knives, To devour the poor from off the earth, And the needy from among men.

Proverbs 30:20

This is the way of an adulterous woman: She eats and wipes her mouth, And says, "I have done no **wickedness**."

CHAPTER 70

WISDOM, WISE

This has been such a wonderful journey for me, to have been given this opportunity by Father God, through the indwelling Holy Spirit, to have been called to take the most *Wisdom*-filled book in the Bible, (i.e. "*The Book of Proverbs*"), and to capture, reflect, and summarize each individual verse into seventy Chapter Themes, that comprise this **Book of Proverbs and Wisdom: A Reference Manual**! And what a wonderful blessing to conclude this journey with the final Chapter Theme entitled "***Wisdom***"!

In the next several paragraphs, I will attempt to answer and address the question, "*What is Wisdom?*" From my perspective and personal life experiences, **Wisdom** can best be described as "***the ability to stay in and operate from the lane of righteousness and truth, while managing and dealing with the ever-present trade winds and cross currents of life.***" I am also a firm believer that the Bible, is the "**GPS of Life**" (Psalms 25:4–12); Whereby every issue, problem, direction, and/or purpose for one's life, is more than adequately addressed, answered, explained, provided, and/or enlightened by Father God's Word. The key to unlocking Father God's **Wisdom** for one's life and/or life circumstance, is by reading, studying, and *marinating/"meditating on Father God's Word day and night"* (Psalm 1:2b and Joshua 1:8).

As one thinks about the *Wisdom* contained in Father God's Word, I am reminded of Jesus's teaching about the vine and branches in John 15:1–17, specifically verses 4, 5, and 7, which state: (4) "***Abide in Me, and I in you. As the branch cannot bear fruit of itself, unless it abides in the vine, neither can you, unless you abide in Me***. (5) *'I am the vine, you are the branches. He who abides in Me, and I in him, bears much fruit; for without Me you can do nothing*. (7) *If you abide in Me, and My words abide in you, you will ask what you desire, and it shall be done for you*."

Accordingly, from my perspective, the theme of *Wisdom* and its necessity in one's life, finds its fulfillment "in Christ Jesus"! And specifically, as one reads, studies, and marinates on "*The Book of Proverbs*," one cannot help but to gain, seek, obtain, and understand *Wisdom*. Take, for example, one of my most beloved and foundational Proverbs verses, that being Proverbs *1:*7*: "*The fear of the LORD is the beginning of knowledge, But fools despise wisdom and instruction.*" And a corresponding bookend Proverbs verse is contained in Proverbs *9:*10*: "*The fear of the LORD is the beginning of wisdom, And the knowledge of the Holy One is understanding.*" Therefore, what one can take away from these two Proverbs verses is the spiritual truth that: "*the fear of the LORD is the beginning of* **wisdom**." As such, the more one seeks to know Christ Jesus, and know Him better, the more *Wisdom* one gains from *abiding in the vine of Christ*. While the world around us can be crazy, foolish, and unpredictable, one can and does gain *Wisdom* that is found only "in Christ Jesus" and Father God's Word!

Finally, as one learns to gain *Wisdom* from Father God's Word, as well as from one's walk with Jesus Christ, one has the ultimate safety net or lifeline for obtaining *Wisdom* and that is to just ask Father God! His Word is crystal clear in James 1:5, which states: "*If any of you lacks wisdom, let him ask of God, who gives to all liberally and without reproach, and it will be given to him.*" In conclusion, *Wisdom* is available to one and all, from multiple touch points; Thus, let's claim it, gain it, study it, worship it, and walk in the *Wisdom* that is "in Christ Jesus"; Therefore, the lordship of Christ Jesus, and the resulting *Wisdom* gained therefrom, should dominate every area of one's LIFE!

TO GOD BE THE GLORY!
(The Beginning of Knowledge)

Proverbs *1:1–4*

(1)   The Proverbs of Solomon the son of David, king of Israel:

(2)*   **To know *wisdom* and instruction, To perceive the words of understanding,**

(3)*   **To receive the instruction of *wisdom*, Justice, judgment, and equity;**

(4)*   To give prudence to the simple, To the young man knowledge and discretion—

Proverbs *1:*5*–6

(5)*   **A *wise* man will hear and increase learning, And a man of *understanding* will attain *wise* counsel.**

(6)*   To *understand* a proverb and an enigma, The words of the *wise* and their riddles.

Proverbs *1:*7*

The fear of the LORD is the beginning of knowledge, But fools despise wisdom and instruction.

(The Call of Wisdom)

Proverbs *1:*20*–27 and 28–33

(20)* *Wisdom* **calls aloud outside; *She* raises her voice in the open squares.**

(21)   *She* cries out in the chief concourses, At the openings of the gates in the city *She* speaks her words:

(22)   "How long, you simple ones, will you love simplicity? For scorners delight in their scorning, And fools hate knowledge.

(23)   Turn at *my* rebuke; Surely *I* will pour out *my* spirit on you; *I* will make *my* words known to you.

(24)   Because *I* have called and you refused, *I* have stretched out *my* hand and no one regarded,

(25) Because you disdained all _my_ counsel, And would have none of _my_ rebuke,

(26) _I_ also will laugh at your calamity; _I_ will mock when your terror comes,

(27) When your terror comes like a storm, And your destruction comes like a whirlwind, When distress and anguish come upon you.

(28) "Then they will call on _me_, but _I_ will not answer; They will seek _me_ diligently, but they will not find _me_.

(29) Because they hated knowledge And did not choose the fear of the LORD,

(30) They would have none of _my_ counsel And despised _my_ every rebuke.

(31) Therefore they shall eat the fruit of their own way, And be filled to the full with their own fancies.

(32) For the turning away of the simple will slay them, And the complacency of fools will destroy them;

(33) But whoever _listens to me_ will dwell safely, And will be secure, without fear of evil."

(The Value of Wisdom)

Proverbs *2:1*–*9* and *10*–22*

(1)* My son, if you receive my words, And treasure my commands within you,

(2)* **So that you incline your ear to _wisdom_, And apply your heart to _understanding_;**

(3)* Yes, if you cry out for discernment, And lift up your voice for _understanding_,

(4)* If you seek _her_ as silver, And search _for her_ as for hidden treasures;

(5)* **Then you will _understand_ the fear of the LORD, And find the knowledge of God.**

(6)* **For the LORD gives _wisdom_; From His mouth come knowledge and _understanding_;**

(7)* **He stores up sound _wisdom_ for the upright; He is a shield to those who walk uprightly;**

(8)* **He guards the paths of justice, And preserves the way of His saints.**

(9)* **Then you will _understand_ righteousness and justice, Equity and every good path.**

(10)* **When _wisdom_ enters your heart, And knowledge is pleasant to your soul,**

(11)* **Discretion will preserve you; _Understanding_ will keep you,**

(12)* To deliver you from the way of evil, From the man who speaks perverse things,

(13) From those who leave the paths of uprightness To walk in the ways of darkness;

(14) Who rejoice in doing evil, And delight in the perversity of the wicked;

(15) Whose ways are crooked, And who are devious in their paths;

(16) To deliver you from the immoral woman, From the seductress who flatters with her words,

(17) Who forsakes the companion of her youth, And forgets the covenant of her God.

(18) For her house leads down to death, And her paths to the dead;

(19) None who go to her return, Nor do they regain the paths of life—

(20)* **So you may walk in the way of goodness, And keep to the paths of righteousness.**

(21)* **For the upright will dwell in the land, And the blameless will remain in it;**

(22)* But the wicked will be cut off from the earth, And the unfaithful will be uprooted from it.

(Guidance for the Young)

Proverbs *3:1*–2*, *3*–*4*, *5*–*6*, 7*–8*, *9*–*10*, *11*–*12*,
13–18, 19–20, 21*–26*, *27*–30, and 31–35*

(1)* *My son, do not forget my law, But let your heart keep my commands;*

(2)* *For length of days and long life And peace they will add to you.*

(3)* **Let not *mercy* and *truth* forsake you; Bind them around your neck, Write them on the tablet of your heart,**

(4)* **And so find *favor* and *high esteem* In the sight of God and man.**

(5)* <u>**Trust in the LORD with all your heart, And lean not on your own *understanding*;**</u>

(6)* <u>**In all your ways acknowledge Him, And He shall direct your paths.**</u>

(7)* Do not be <u>*wise*</u> in your own eyes; Fear the LORD and depart from evil.

(8)* It will be health to your flesh, And strength to your bones.

(9)* <u>**Honor the LORD with your possessions, And with the first fruits of all your increase;**</u>

(10)* <u>**So your barns will be filled with plenty, And your vats will overflow with new wine.**</u>

(11)* <u>**My son, do not despise the chastening of the LORD, Nor detest His correction;**</u>

(12)* <u>**For whom the LORD loves He corrects, Just as a father the son in whom he delights.**</u>

(13)* **Happy is the man who finds <u>*wisdom*</u>, And the man who gains *understanding*;**

(14) For *her* (*wisdom*) proceeds are better than the profits of silver, And *her* gain than fine gold.

(15) *She* is more precious than rubies, And all the things you may desire cannot compare with *her*.

(16) Length of days is in *her* right hand, In *her* left hand riches and honor.

(17)* *Her* ways are ways of pleasantness, And all *her* paths are peace.

(18) *She* is a tree of life to those who take hold of *her*, And happy are all who retain *her*.

(19) The LORD by *wisdom* founded the earth; By *understanding* He established the heavens;

(20) By His knowledge the depths were broken up, And clouds drop down the dew.

(21)* My son, let them (*wisdom*, *understanding*, and *knowledge*) not depart from your eyes—**Keep sound *wisdom* and discretion;**

(22) So they (*wisdom* and *discretion*) will be life to your soul And grace to your neck.

(23)* Then you will walk safely in your way, And your foot will not stumble.

(24)* When you lie down, you will not be afraid; Yes, you will lie down and your sleep will be sweet.

(25) Do not be afraid of sudden terror, Nor of trouble from the wicked when it comes;

(26)* For the LORD will be your confidence, And will keep your foot from being caught.

(27)* **Do not withhold good from those to whom it is due, When it is in the power of your hand to do so.**

(28)* **Do not say to your neighbor, "Go, and come back, And tomorrow I will give it." When you have it with you.**

(29) *Do not devise evil against your neighbor, For he dwells by you for safety's sake.*

(30) *Do not strive with a man without cause, If he has done you no harm.*

(31) *Do not envy the oppressor, And choose none of his ways;*

(32)* *For the perverse person is an <u>abomination to the LORD</u>, But His <u>secret counsel is with the upright</u>.*

(33) *The curse of the LORD is on the house of the wicked, <u>But He blesses the home of the just</u>.*

(34)* **Surely He scorns the scornful, But gives grace to the humble.**

(35)* The <u>**wise**</u> shall inherit glory, But shame shall be the legacy of fools.

(Security in Wisdom)

Proverbs *4:1*–9, *10*–*13*, *14*–17, *18*–19, and *20*–*27*

(1)* Hear, my children, the instruction of a father, And give attention to know *understanding*;

(2)* For I give you good doctrine: Do not forsake my law.

(3) When I was my father's son, Tender and the only one in the sight of my mother,

(4)* He also taught me, and said to me: "Let your heart retain my words; Keep my commands, and live.

(5)* **Get <u>*wisdom*</u>! Get *understanding*! Do not forget, nor turn away from the words of my mouth.**

(6)* **Do not forsake <u>*her*</u> (<u>*wisdom*</u>), and <u>*she*</u> will preserve you; Love <u>*her*</u>, and <u>*she*</u> will keep you.**

(7)* **<u>*Wisdom*</u> is the principal thing; Therefore get <u>*wisdom*</u> And in all your getting, get *understanding*.**

(8) Exalt <u>*her*</u> (<u>*wisdom*</u>), and <u>*she*</u> will promote you; <u>*She*</u> will bring you honor, when you embrace <u>*her*</u>.

(9) <u>*She*</u> will place on your head an ornament of grace; A crown of glory <u>*she*</u> will deliver to you."

(10)* **Hear, my son, and receive my sayings, And the years of your life will be many.**

(11)* **I have taught you in the way of _wisdom_; I have led you in the right paths;**

(12)* **When you walk, your steps will not be hindered, And when you run, you will not stumble.**

(13)* **Take firm hold of instruction, do not let go; Keep _her (wisdom)_ for _she_ is your life.**

(14)* **Do not enter the path of the wicked, And do not walk in the way of evil.**

(15) Avoid it, do not travel on it; Turn away from it and pass on.

(16) For they do not sleep unless they have done evil; And their sleep is taken away unless they make someone fall.

(17) For they eat the bread of wickedness, And drink the wine of violence.

(18)* **But the path of the just is like the shining sun, That shines ever brighter unto the perfect day.**

(19) The way of the wicked is like darkness; They do not know what makes them stumble.

(20)* **My son, give attention to _my_ words; Incline your ear to _my_ sayings.**

(21)* **Do not let them depart from your eyes; Keep them in the midst of your heart;**

(22)* **For they are life to those who find them, And health to all their flesh.**

(23)* **Keep your heart with all diligence, For out of it spring the issues of life.**

(24)* **Put away from you a deceitful mouth, And put perverse lips far from you.**

(25) Let your eyes look straight ahead, And your eyelids look right before you.

(26)* **Ponder the path of your feet, And let all your ways be established.**

(27)* **Do not turn to the right or the left; Remove your foot from evil.**

(The Peril of Adultery)

Proverbs *5:1*–2*

My son, pay attention to my ***wisdom***; Lend your ear to my *understanding*, That you may preserve discretion, And your lips may keep knowledge.

Proverbs *5:*21*–*23*

(21)* **For the ways of man are before the eyes of the LORD, And He ponders all his paths.**

(22)* **His own iniquities entrap the wicked man, And he is caught in the cords of his sin.**

(23)* **He shall die for lack of instruction, And in the greatness of his folly he shall go astray.**

(The Folly of Indolence)

Proverbs *6:6–11

(6)   Go to the ant, you sluggard! Consider her ways and be ***wise***.

(7)   Which, having no captain, Overseer or ruler,

(8)   Provides her supplies in the summer, And gathers her food in the harvest.

(9)   How long will you slumber, O sluggard? When will you rise from your sleep?

(10) A little sleep, a little slumber, A little folding of the hands to sleep—

(11) So shall your poverty come to you like a prowler, And your need like an armed man.

Proverbs *7:*1*–5*

(1)*   **My son, keep my words, And treasure my commands within you.**

(2)*   **Keep my commands and live, And my law as the apple of your eye.**

(3)   Bind them on your fingers; Write them on the tablet of your heart.

(4)* Say to _wisdom_, "You are my sister," And call _understanding_ your nearest kin,

(5)* That they may keep you from the immoral woman, From the seductress who flatters with her words.

(The Excellence of Wisdom)

Proverbs *8:*1*–*11*, 12*–21, 22–31, and *32*–36*

(1)* **Does not _wisdom_ cry out, And _understanding_ lift up her voice?**

(2) _She_ (_wisdom_) takes _her_ stand on the top of the high hill, Beside the way, where the paths meet.

(3) _She_ (_wisdom_) cries out by the gates, at the entry of the city, At the entrance of the doors:

(4) "To you, O men, _I_ call, And _my_ voice is to the sons of men.

(5)* O you simple ones, _understand_ prudence, And you fools, be of an _understanding_ heart.

(6) **Listen, for _I_ (_wisdom_) will speak of excellent things, And from the opening of _my_ lips will come right things;**

(7)* **For _my_ mouth will speak truth; Wickedness is an abomination to _my_ (_wisdom's_) lips.**

(8)* **All the words of _my_ (_wisdom's_) mouth are with righteousness; Nothing crooked or perverse is in them.**

(9) They are all plain to him who _understands_, And right to those who find knowledge.

(10)* Receive _my_ (_wisdom's_) instruction, and not silver, And knowledge rather than choice gold.

(11)* **For _wisdom_ is better than rubies, And all the things one may desire cannot be compared with _her_ (_wisdom_).**

(12)* "_I, wisdom_, dwell with prudence, And find out knowledge and discretion.

(13) The fear of the LORD is to hate evil; Pride and arrogance and the evil way And the perverse mouth, _I_ (_wisdom_) hate.

(14)* Counsel is ***mine***, and sound ***wisdom; I (wisdom)*** am *understanding,* ***I (wisdom)*** have strength.

(15) By ***me (wisdom)*** kings reign, And rulers decree justice.

(16) By ***me (wisdom)*** princes rule, and nobles, All the judges of the earth.

(17)* **I (*wisdom*) love those who love *me* (*wisdom*), And those who seek *me* (*wisdom*) diligently will find *me* (*wisdom*).**

(18) Riches and honor are with ***me (wisdom)***, Enduring riches and righteousness.

(19)* ***My (wisdom)*** fruit is better than gold, yes, than fine gold, Any ***my (wisdom)*** revenue than choice silver.

(20) ***I (wisdom)*** traverse the way of righteousness, In the midst of the path of justice,

(21) That ***I (wisdom)*** may cause those who love ***me (wisdom)*** to inherit wealth, That ***I (wisdom)*** may fill their treasures.

(22) "The LORD possessed ***me (wisdom)*** at the beginning of His way, Before His works of old.

(23) ***I (wisdom)*** have been established from everlasting, From the beginning, before there was ever an earth.

(24) When there were no depths ***I (wisdom)*** was brought forth, When there were no fountains abounding with water.

(25) Before the mountains were settled, Before the hills, ***I (wisdom)*** was brought forth;

(26) While as yet He had not made the earth or the fields, Or the primal dust of the world.

(27) When He prepared the heavens, ***I (wisdom)*** was there, When He drew a circle on the face of the deep,

(28) When He established the clouds above, When He strengthened the fountains of the deep,

(29) When He assigned to the sea its limit, So that the waters would not transgress His command, When He marked out the foundations of the earth,

(30) Then **I (*wisdom*)** was beside Him as a master craftsman; And **I (*wisdom*)** was daily His delight, Rejoicing always before Him.

(31) Rejoicing in His inhabited world, And **_my_ (*wisdom*)** delight was the sons of men.

(32)* **"Now therefore, listen to _me_ (*wisdom*), my children, For blessed are those who keep _my_ (*wisdom*) ways,**

(33)* **Hear instruction and be _wise_, And do not distain it.**

(34)* **Blessed is the man who listens to _me_ (*wisdom*), Watching daily at _my_ (*wisdom*) gates, Waiting at the posts of _my_ (*wisdom*) doors.**

(35)* **For whoever finds _me_ (*wisdom*) finds life, And obtains favor from the LORD;**

(36)* But he who sins against _me_ (*wisdom*) wrongs his own soul; All those who hate _me_ (*wisdom*) love death."

(The Way of Wisdom)

Proverbs *9:1*–* 6* and 7–12*

(1)* ___Wisdom___ has built _**her**_ house, _**She**_ has hewn out _**her**_ seven pillars;

(2) _**She**_ has slaughtered _**her**_ meat, _**She**_ has mixed _**her**_ wine, _**She**_ has also furnished _**her**_ table.

(3) _**She**_ has sent out _**her**_ maidens, _**She**_ cries out from the highest places of the city,

(4) "Whoever is simple, let him turn in here!" As for him who lacks *understanding*, **_she_ (*wisdom*)** says to him,

(5) "Come, eat of **_my_ (*wisdom*)** bread And drink of the wine **_I_ (*wisdom*)** have mixed.

(6)* **Forsake foolishness and live, And go in the way of *understanding*.**

(7) "He who corrects a scoffer gets shame for himself, And he who rebukes a wicked man only harms himself.

(8)* Do not correct a scoffer, lest he hate you; **Rebuke a _wise_ man, and he will love you.**

(9)* **Give instruction to a _wise_ man, and he will be still _wiser_; Teach a just man, and he will increase in learning.**

(10)* **"The fear of the LORD is the beginning of _wisdom_, And the knowledge of the Holy One is _understanding_.**

(11)* For by _me (wisdom)_ your days will be multiplied, And years of life will be added to you.

(12)* If you are _wise_, you are _wise_ for yourself, And if you scoff, you will bear it alone."

(Wise Sayings of Solomon)

Proverbs 10:1*

The Proverbs of Solomon:

A _wise_ son makes a glad father, But a foolish son is the grief of his mother.

Proverbs 10:5*

He who gathers in summer is a _wise_ son; He who sleeps in harvest is a son who causes shame.

Proverbs 10:8

The _wise_ in heart will receive commands, But a prating fool will fall.

Proverbs 10:13*

Wisdom is found on the lips of him who has _understanding_, But a rod is for the back of him who is devoid of _understanding_.

Proverbs 10:14*

Wise people store up knowledge, But the mouth of the foolish is near destruction.

Proverbs 10:19*

In the multitude of words sin is not lacking, But he who restrains his lips is _wise_.

Proverbs *10:*21*

The lips of the righteous feed many, But fools die for lack of _wisdom_.

Proverbs *10:*22*
The blessing of the LORD makes one rich, And He adds no sorrow with it.

Proverbs 10:23*
To do evil is like sport to a fool, But a man of understanding has **_wisdom_**.

Proverbs 10:*31*
The mouth of the righteous brings forth **_wisdom_**, But the perverse tongue will be cut out.

Proverbs *11:*2*
When pride comes, then comes shame; But with the humble is _wisdom_.

Proverbs *11:*12*
He who is devoid of _wisdom_ despises his neighbor, But a man of _understanding_ holds his peace.

Proverbs *11:*24*
There is one who scatters, yet increases more; And there is one who withholds more than is right, But it leads to poverty.

Proverbs *11:*25*
The generous soul will be made rich, And he who waters will also be watered himself.

Proverbs *11:*29*
He who troubles his own house will inherit the wind, And the fool will be servant to the _wise_ of heart.

Proverbs *11:*30*
The fruit of the righteous is a tree of life, And he who wins souls is _wise_.

Proverbs *12:*1*
Whoever loves instruction loves knowledge, But he who hates correction is stupid.

Proverbs 12:8*

A man will be commended according to his **_wisdom_**, But he who is of a perverse heart will be despised.

Proverbs *12:*15*

The way of a fool is right in his own eyes, But he who heeds counsel is _wise_.

Proverbs 12:18*

There is one who speaks like the piercings of a sword, But the tongue of the **_wise_** promotes health.

Proverbs *13:*1*

A _wise_ son heeds his father's instruction, But a scoffer does not listen to rebuke.

Proverbs *13:*10*

By pride comes nothing but strife, But with the well-advised is _wisdom_.

Proverbs 13:14

The law of the **_wise_** is a fountain of life, To turn one away from the snares of death.

Proverbs *13:*20*

He who walks with _wise_ men will be _wise_, But the companion of fools, will be destroyed.

Proverbs *13:*22*

A good man leaves an inheritance to his children's children, But the wealth of the sinner is stored up for the righteous.

Proverbs *13:*24*

He who spares his rod hates his son, But he who loves him disciplines him promptly.

Proverbs 14:1
The _**wise**_ woman builds her house, But the foolish pulls it down with her hands.

Proverbs 14:3
In the mouth of a fool is a rod of pride, But the lips of the _**wise**_ will preserve them.

Proverbs 14:*6*
A scoffer seeks _**wisdom**_ and does not find it, But knowledge is easy to him who _understands_.

Proverbs 14:*8*
The _**wisdom**_ of the prudent is to _understand_ his way, But the folly of fools is deceit.

Proverbs *14:*12*
**There is a way that seems right to a man, But its end is the way of death**.

Proverbs 14:*16*
A _**wise**_ man fears and departs from evil, But a fool rages and is self-confident.

Proverbs 14:24
The crown of the _**wise**_ is their riches, But the foolishness of fools is folly.

Proverbs *14:*33*
Wisdom rests in the heart of him who has _understanding_, But what is in the heart of fools is made known.

Proverbs 14:35
The king's favor is toward a _**wise**_ servant, But his wrath is against him who causes shame.

Proverbs 15:*2*
The tongue of the _**wise**_ uses knowledge rightly, But the mouth of fools pours forth foolishness.

Proverbs 15:*7*
The lips of the _wise_ disperse knowledge, But the heart of the fool does not do so.

Proverbs 15:*12*
A scoffer does not love one who corrects him, Nor will he go to the _wise_.

Proverbs *15:*16*
Better is a little with the fear of the LORD, Than great treasure with trouble.

Proverbs 15:*20*
A _wise_ son makes a father glad, But a foolish man despises his mother.

Proverbs *15:*22*
Without counsel, plans go awry, But in the multitude of counselors, they are established.

Proverbs 15:24*
The way of life winds upward for the _wise_, That he may turn away from hell below.

Proverbs *15:*31*
The ear that hears the rebukes of life Will abide among the _wise_.

Proverbs *15:*32*
He who disdains instruction despises his own soul, But he who heeds rebuke gets understanding.

Proverbs *15:*33*
The fear of the LORD is the instruction of _wisdom_, And before honor is humility.

Proverbs *16:*3*
Commit your works to the LORD, And your thoughts will be established.

Proverbs *16:*8*
Better is a little with righteousness, Than vast revenues without justice.

Proverbs *16:*9*
A man's heart plans his way, But the LORD directs his steps.

Proverbs 16:14
As messengers of death is the king's wrath, But a *wise* man will appease it.

Proverbs 16:16*
How much better to get *wisdom* than gold! And to get *understanding* is to be chosen rather than silver.

Proverbs *16:*17*
The highway of the upright is to depart from evil; He who keeps his way preserves his soul.

Proverbs *16:*18*
Pride goes before destruction, And a haughty spirit before a fall.

Proverbs *16:*19*
Better to be of a humble spirit with the lowly, Than to divide the spoil with the proud.

Proverbs *16:*20*
He who heeds the word *wisely* will find good, And whoever trusts in the LORD, happy is he.

Proverbs 16:21*
The *wise* in heart will be called prudent, And sweetness of the lips increases learning.

Proverbs 16:*22*
Understanding is a wellspring of life to him who has it; But the correction of fools is folly.

Proverbs 16:23

The heart of the *wise* teaches his mouth, And adds learning to his lips.

Proverbs *16:*31*

A silver-haired head is a crown of glory, If it is found in the way of righteousness.

Proverbs 17:2

A *wise* servant will rule over a son who causes shame, And will share an inheritance among the brothers.

Proverbs 17:*10*

Rebuke is more effective for a *wise* man Than a hundred blows on a fool.

Proverbs 17:16*

Why is there in the hand of a fool the purchase price of *wisdom*, Since he has no heart for it?

Proverbs *17:*17*

A friend loves at all times, And a brother is born for adversity.

Proverbs *17:*24*

Wisdom is in the sight of him who has *understanding*, But the eyes of a fool are on the ends of the earth.

Proverbs 17:28

Even a fool is counted *wise* when he holds his peace; When he shuts his lips, he is considered perceptive.

Proverbs 18:1

A man who isolates himself seeks his own desire; He rages against all *wise* judgment.

Proverbs 18:4*

The words of a man's mouth are deep waters; The wellspring of *wisdom* is a flowing brook.

Proverbs *18:*15*
The heart of the prudent acquires knowledge, And the ear of the <u>wise</u> seeks knowledge.

Proverbs *18:*22*
<u>He who finds a wife finds a good thing, And obtains favor from the LORD.</u>

Proverbs *18:*24*
<u>A man who has friends must himself be friendly, But there is a friend who sticks closer than a brother.</u>

Proverbs *19:*1*
<u>Better is the poor who walks in his integrity Than one who is perverse in his lips, and is a fool.</u>

Proverbs 19:*8*
He who gets **<u>wisdom</u>** loves his own soul; He who keeps *understanding* will find good.

Proverbs *19:*20*
Listen to counsel and receive instruction; That you may be <u>wise</u> in your latter days.

Proverbs *19:*21*
There are many plans in a man's heart, *<u>Nevertheless the LORD's counsel—that will stand.</u>*

Proverbs 20:1
Wine is a mocker, Strong drink is a brawler, And whoever is led astray by it is not **<u>wise</u>**.

Proverbs 20:15*
There is gold and a multitude of rubies, But the lips of **<u>knowledge (wisdom)</u>** are a precious jewel.

Proverbs 20:18
Plans are established by counsel; By **<u>wise</u>** counsel wage war.

Proverbs 20:26
A *wise* king sifts out the wicked, And brings the threshing wheel over them.

Proverbs 20:29*
The glory of young men is their strength, *And the splendor of old men is their gray head*.

Proverbs *21:*2*
Every way of a man is right in his own eyes, But the LORD weighs the hearts.

Proverbs *21:*5*
The plans of the diligent lead surely to plenty, But those of everyone who is hasty, surely to poverty.

Proverbs 21:*11*
When the scoffer is punished, the simple is made *wise*; But when the *wise* is instructed, he receives knowledge.

Proverbs 21:12*
The righteous God *wisely* considers the house of the wicked, Overthrowing the wicked for their wickedness.

Proverbs *21:*13*
Whoever shuts his ears to the cry of the poor Will also cry himself and not be heard.

Proverbs 21:*20*
There is desirable treasure, And oil in the dwelling of the *wise*, But a foolish man squanders it.

Proverbs *21:*21*
He who follows righteousness and mercy Finds life, righteousness and honor.

Proverbs 21:22
A *wise* man scales the city of the mighty, And brings down the trusted stronghold.

Proverbs 21:30*
There is no **wisdom** or *understanding* Or counsel against the LORD.

Proverbs *22:*6*
Train up a child in the way he should go, And when he is old he will not depart from it.

Proverbs *22:*7*
The rich rules over the poor, And the borrower is servant to the lender.

Proverbs *22:*9*
He who has a generous eye will be blessed, For he gives of his bread to the poor.

(Sayings of the Wise)

Proverbs *22:*17*–*21*
(17)* **Incline your ear and hear the words of the *wise*, And apply your heart to my knowledge.**
(18)* For it is a pleasant thing if you keep *them* (**wisdom**/*knowledge*) within you; Let *them* (**wisdom**/*knowledge*) all be fixed upon your lips.
(19)* **So that your trust may be in the LORD; *I* (*wisdom*) have instructed you today, even you.**
(20)* Have *I* (**wisdom**) not written to you excellent things Of counsels and knowledge.
(21)* **That *I* (*wisdom*) may make you know the certainty of the words of truth, That you may answer words of truth To those who send to you?**

Proverbs *23:*4*–*5*
Do not over work to be rich; Because of your own *understanding*, cease!

Will you set your eyes on that which is not? For riches certainly make themselves wings; They fly away like an eagle toward heaven.

Proverbs 23:9*

Do not speak in the hearing of a fool, For he will despise the *wisdom* of your words.

Proverbs *23:*12*

Apply your heart to instruction, And your ears to words of knowledge.

Proverbs *23:*15*–*16*

My son, if your heart is *wise*, My heart will rejoice—indeed, I myself; Yes, my inmost being will rejoice When your lips speak right things.

Proverbs 23:19*

Hear, my son, and be *wise*; And guide your heart in the way.

Proverbs *23:*23*

Buy the truth, and do not sell it, Also *wisdom* and instruction and understanding.

Proverbs 23:24–25

The father of the righteous will greatly rejoice, And he who begets a *wise* child will delight in him. Let your father and your mother be glad, And let her who bore you rejoice.

Proverbs 24:3*–4*

Through *wisdom* a house is built, And by *understanding* it is established; By knowledge the rooms are filled With all precious and pleasant riches.

Proverbs *24:*5*–*6*

A *wise* man is strong, Yes, a man of knowledge increases strength; For by *wise* counsel you will wage your own war, And in a multitude of counselors there is safety.

Proverbs 24:7

Wisdom is too lofty for a fool; He does not open his mouth in the gate.

Proverbs *24:*10*
If you faint in the day of adversity, Your strength is small.

Proverbs *24:13*–*14*
My son, eat honey (*wisdom*) because it is good, And the honeycomb which is sweet to your taste; **So shall the knowledge of *wisdom* be to your soul; If you have found it, there is a prospect, And your hope will not be cut off.**

Proverbs *24:*17*–*18*
Do not rejoice when your enemy falls, And do not let your heart be glad when he stumbles; Lest the LORD see it, and it displease Him, And He turn away His wrath from him.

(Further Sayings of the Wise)

Proverbs *24:*23*–*25*, *26*, *27*, and *28*–*29*

(23)* *These things also belong to the <u>wise</u>: It is not good to show partiality in judgment.*

(24)   He who says to the wicked, "You are righteous," Him the people will curse; Nations will abhor him.

(25)* *But those who rebuke the wicked will have delight, And a good blessing will come upon them.*

(26)* *He who gives a right answer kisses the lips.*

(27)* *Prepare your outside work, Make it fit for yourself in the field; And afterward build your house.*

(28)* *Do not be a witness against your neighbor without cause, For would you deceive with your lips?*

(29)* *Do not say, "I will do to him just as he has done to me; I will render to the man according to his work."*

(Further Wise Sayings of Solomon)

Proverbs 25:12
Like an earring of gold and an ornament of fine gold Is a *wise* rebuker to an obedient ear.

Proverbs *25:*21*–*22*
If your enemy is hungry, give him bread to eat; And if he is thirsty, give him water to drink: For so you will heap coals of fire on his head, And the LORD will reward you.

Proverbs 26:4–5*
Do not answer a fool according to his folly, Lest you also be like him. Answer a fool according to his folly, Lest he be *wise* in his own eyes.

Proverbs *26:*11*
As a dog returns to his own vomit, So a fool repeats his folly.

Proverbs *26:*12*
Do you see a man *wise* in his own eyes? There is more hope for a fool than for him.

Proverbs *26:13–*16*
(13) The lazy man says, "There is a lion in the road! A fierce lion is in the streets!"
(14) As a door turns on its hinges, So does the lazy man on his bed.
(15) The lazy man buries his hand in the bowl; It wearies him to bring it back to his mouth.
(16)* **The lazy man is *wiser* in his own eyes Than seven men who can answer sensibly.**

Proverbs *27:*6*
Faithful are the wounds of a friend, But the kisses of an enemy are deceitful.

Proverbs 27:11

My son, be _wise_, and make my heart glad, That I may answer him who reproaches me.

Proverbs *27:*17*

As iron sharpens iron, So a man sharpens the countenance of his friend.

Proverbs 28:11*

The rich man is _wise_ in his own eyes, But the poor who has _understanding_ searches him out.

Proverbs *28:*13*

He who covers his sins will not prosper, But whoever confesses and forsakes them will have mercy.

Proverbs *28:*23*

He who rebukes a man will find more favor afterward Than he who flatters with the tongue.

Proverbs 28:26*

He who trusts in his own heart is a fool, But whoever walks _wisely_ will be delivered.

Proverbs *29:*3*

Whoever loves _wisdom_ makes his father rejoice, But a companion of harlots wastes his wealth.

Proverbs 29:8*

Scoffers set a city aflame, But _wise_ men turn away wrath.

Proverbs 29:9*

If a _wise_ man contends with a foolish man, Whether the fool rages or laughs, there is no peace.

Proverbs 29:11*

A fool vents all his feelings, But a _wise_ man holds them back.

Proverbs *29:*15*

The rod and rebuke give _wisdom_, But a child left to himself brings shame to his mother.

(The Wisdom of Agur)

Proverbs 30:1–3

(1) The words of Agur the son of Jakeh, his utterance. This man declared to Ithiel to Ithiel and Ucal:

(2) Surely I am more stupid than any man, And do not have the _understanding_ of a man.

(3) I neither learned **_wisdom_** Nor have knowledge of the Holy One.

Proverbs 30:24–28

(24) There are four things which are little on the earth, But they are exceedingly **_wise_**;

(25) The ants are a people not strong, Yet they prepare their food in the summer;

(26) The rock badgers are a feeble folk, Yet they make their homes in the crags;

(27) The locusts have no king, Yet they all advance in ranks;

(28) The spider skillfully grasps with its hands, And it is in kings' palaces.

(The Virtuous Wife)

Proverbs *31:24–27*

(24) She makes linen garments and sells them, And supplies sashes for the merchants.

(25)* Strength and honor are her clothing; She shall rejoice in time to come.

(26)* **She opens her mouth with _wisdom_, And on her tongue is the law of kindness**.

(27)* She watches over the ways of her household, And does not eat the bread of idleness.

Author's Bio

My inspiration for *The Book of Proverbs and Wisdom: A Reference Manual* began with a significant career advancement that propelled both a geographical change and a life-altering change in Father God's plan for me. In 1996, I held the position of Vice President (VP) Finance for the Food and Functional Products division of Hercules, Inc. a Specialty

Chemical Company based in Wilmington, Delaware. At the time, I was forty-three years old and was thankfully progressing in my previously set goal of becoming a Global Chief Financial Officer (CFO) of a Fortune 100 company on or before my fifty-fifth birthday.

In the early summer of 1996, Hercules's Global Chief Financial Officer, Mr. Keith Elliott, promoted me to the Chief Financial Officer (CFO) position for the Europe region of Hercules, Inc. This promotion signaled an international opportunity for my family and I, to be based in the European headquarters of Brussels, Belgium. So, naturally, I looked upon this opportunity with great anticipation and excitement to continue to build out my international experience and travel, especially in Europe, then the second largest global international business center in the world. I was elated that my then spouse, Victoria, my second daughter, Sydney, and I could each experience the world from a different geographical and cultural viewpoint.

By mid-July 1996, my family and I had finalized our decision to accept this European international expatriate assignment. We were off to see the world! I always have appreciated this three-year period of living overseas in Belgium for the cultural and linguistic exposure, the experience of traveling and viewing historical places and landmarks, and the importance of diversity and inclusion in business and everyday life. All of this would not have come true if not for Father God's everlasting grace, provisions, and will for my life.

It just so happened that, less than a year after moving to Belgium, on my forty-fourth birthday on January 17, 1997, I felt the Holy Spirit speak to me during my daily morning devotional period. As clearly as one of my best friends sitting right next to me speaking with me, I heard the Holy Spirit speak the following directive: "By your mid-fifties, I, the Holy Spirit, want you working for me!"

I looked up to Father God with the biggest doubt that one might muster up, and said, "Okay, right!" and went on about my business.

And over the next decade or so, leading up to my fifty-fifth year on earth, I continued to work on my personal pursuit of becoming a Global CFO of a Fortune 100 company in Corporate America. After relocating back to the East Coast in 1999, with a home base in Chapel Hill, North Carolina, I held various positions in the field of Corporate Finance with Fortune 100 companies, including VP- Auditing Services for Pharmacia & Upjohn, Divisional VP and Corporate Controller of Pharmacia Monsanto Division, and VP and Corporate Controller of Bristol-Myers Squibb in New York City.

I then transitioned out of the pharmaceutical space to the technology domain with an opportunity at Microsoft in the mid-2000s. While serving as General Manager and Division Controller of Microsoft's Platform Services Group in Redmond, Washington, the Word of the Lord again came to me loud and clear. Exactly on my fifty-fifth birthday, the Holy Spirit spoke so strongly and reminded me of His goal that He wanted me to work for the Lord. After reevaluating my lifelong business and professional goal, I knew that the Lord's work outweighed any personal, business, and/or professional goal and/or goals of mine in Corporate

America. After making the formal decision to retire early from the business world on February 1, 2008, I relocated back to Chapel Hill, North Carolina to start this new season of my life, working FULL-TIME for the LORD!

That summer, I began the processes of giving back to various faith-based, nonprofit, charitable, and community-based organizations on an as needed basis. For example, I partnered with North Carolina A&T University, a historically Black college, to create and launch a Corporate Speaker's Bureau/Network. From 2008 to 2013, on a monthly basis, senior executives from Fortune 100 companies were invited to share their successful career journeys with NC A&T business major students. I leveraged my network of the Executive Leadership Council (ELC), the premier African-American Corporate networking organization of which I have been a professional member since 1993, to add to this exciting chance for African-American and other people of color business majors, to hear the leadership philosophies and experiences of Corporate (ELC) executives.

During this same time period, I became a financial coach and mentor to individuals in the Triangle communities in North Carolina (Chapel Hill, Durham, and Raleigh). In 2010, I joined New Hope Church in Durham, where I facilitated a financial coaching class entitled "Jesus on Money." That class officially launched my financial facilitation programs with several churches, facilitating, for example, Dave Ramsey's Financial Peace University (FPU), which also included me developing and authoring a biblical devotional FPU study guide. And from such affiliations, I expanded to group financial coaching sessions, in addition to individual coaching sessions.

At the same time, I felt the need to expand my daily walk with Father God, by communing with Him from a wider, personal perspective. By studying His Word more and going much deeper with my personal prayer sessions, I was especially drawn to the *Book of Proverbs*. By 2011, I began an in-depth study of the Book, which has always been one of my favorite Books of the Bible. I greatly appreciated the wisdom and deep spiritual insights gained by reading, studying, meditating, and praying over the Book's thirty-one meaningful chapters.

During the 2012 Christmas holiday season, after visiting Joel Osteen's Lakewood Church in Houston, Texas with my eldest daughter, Crystal, I once again received loud and clear instructions, this time, to develop, draft, and eventually publish, a modern version of a biblical reference manual that contained every verse of Scripture in the *Book of Proverbs*. Father God wanted me to craft a rich, in-depth reference manual, in which any individual might be able to easily find, locate, and study each and every Proverbs verse in the format of a reference manual.

And so, after nearly six years of intense writing, rewriting, editing, and reediting, I am extremely blessed to bring forward ***The Book of Proverbs and Wisdom: A Reference Manual*** for your spiritual insight, edification, and knowledge transfer of Father God's truths and spiritual wisdom. "**The Book**" contains seventy chapters of "Chapter Themes." Each Chapter Theme is preceded by a "Chapter Narrative" preface, which provides you, the reader, with an illuminating Narrative of my personal experiences that relates to each Chapter Theme. In each Chapter Narrative, you'll also find a brief summary of my thoughts regarding said Chapter Theme.

Please enjoy this work and may Father God's Blessings, enrich your individual or group study of the insightful wisdom, knowledge, understanding, and truths that are contained in Father God's Word, especially as one studies the Bible's *Book of Proverbs*.

Blessings, ***PEACE***, ***JOY***, and ***LOVE***,
Curt "CT" Tomlin
May 3, 2019

REFERENCES

Got Questions Ministries. 2002-2015. *Got Questions.* Accessed July 27, 2019. https://www.gotquestions.org/.

Harris, R. Laird. 1980. *Theological Wordbook of the Old Testament.* Edited by R. Laird Harris, Gleason Jr. Archer and Bruce Waltke. 2 vols. Chicago, Illinois: Moody Press.

Lessin, Roy. 2015. *Meet Me in the Meadow.* March 11. Accessed July 27, 2019. meetmeinthemeadow.com.

—. 2015. *Meet Me in the Meadow.* May 1. Accessed July 27, 2019. meetmeinthmeadow.com.

—. 2010. *Meet Me in the Meadow: Moments with God Series.* Bloomingdale, Illinois: Christian Art Gifts Incorporated.

Ronald Rolheiser, O.M.I. 1999. *The Holy Longing: The Search for a Christian Spirituality.* New York, New York: Doubleday.

CPSIA information can be obtained
at www.ICGtesting.com
Printed in the USA
LVHW010113270820
664360LV00001BA/2